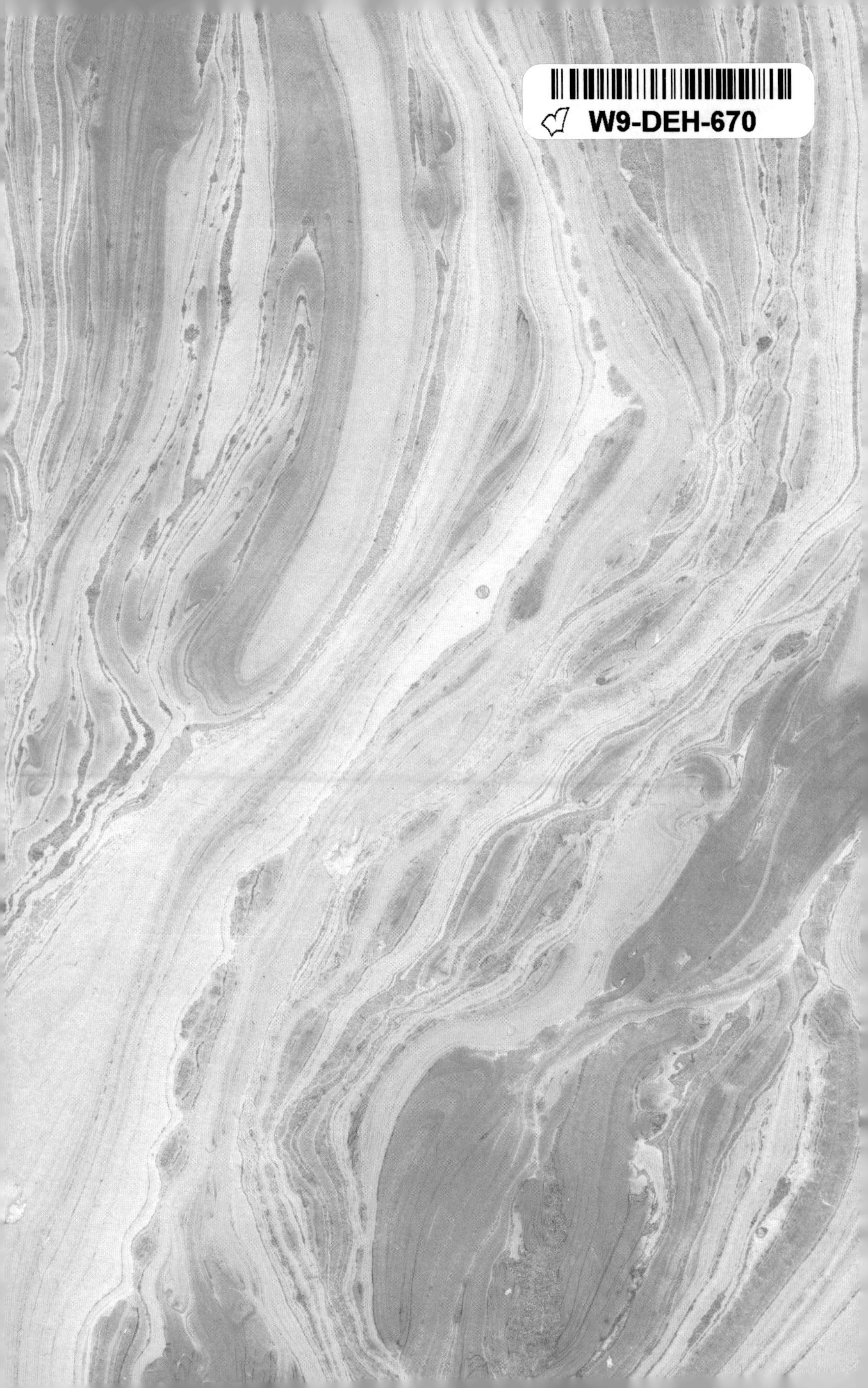

A Code of Jewish Ethics

VOLUME 2

Love Your Neighbor as Yourself

Also by Rabbi Joseph Telushkin

NONFICTION

The Nine Questions People Ask About Judaism
(with Dennis Prager)

Why the Jews? The Reason for Antisemitism
(with Dennis Prager)

Jewish Literacy: The Most Important Things to Know About the Jewish Religion, Its People, and Its History

Jewish Humor: What the Best Jewish Jokes Say About the Jews

Jewish Wisdom: Ethical, Spiritual, and Historical Lessons from the Great Works and Thinkers

Words That Hurt, Words That Heal: How to Use Words Wisely and Well

Biblical Literacy: The Most Important People, Events, and Ideas of the Hebrew Bible

The Book of Jewish Values: A Day-by-Day Guide to Ethical Living

The Golden Land: The Story of Jewish Immigration to America

The Ten Commandments of Character: Essential Advice for Living an Honorable, Ethical, Honest Life

A Code of Jewish Ethics, Volume 1: You Shall Be Holy

FICTION

The Unorthodox Murder of Rabbi Wahl

The Final Analysis of Dr. Stark

An Eye for an Eye

Heaven's Witness
(with Allen Estrin)

A Code of Jewish Ethics

VOLUME 2

Love Your Neighbor as Yourself

RABBI

JOSEPH TELUSHKIN

BELL TOWER / NEW YORK

Published in the United States by Bell Tower, an imprint of the Crown Publishing Group, a division of Random House, Inc., New York.
www.crownpublishing.com

Library of Congress Cataloging-in-Publication Data
Telushkin, Joseph
A code of Jewish ethics / Joseph Telushkin.—1st ed.
Includes bibliographical references and index.
Contents: 1. Love Your Neighbor as Yourself.
1. Jewish ethics. 2. Jewish ethics—Anecdotes. 3. Judaism—
Essence, genius, nature. I. Title.
BJ1285.2.T45 2009
296.3'6—dc22 2005014556

ISBN: 978-1-4000-4836-6

Printed in the United States of America

Marbleized paper on endpapers and section openers by
Savitri's Recycled Hand-made Paper & Stationery / www.savitris.com

DESIGN BY BARBARA STURMAN

2 4 6 8 10 9 7 5 3 1

First Edition

For Zalman C. Bernstein,

who arranged his blessed life so that his good deeds,
his many kindnesses, and his support of Jewish learning and living
would continue even now that he is no longer with us.

ACKNOWLEDGMENTS

As I have noted before, one of the great pleasures of completing a book is having the opportunity to publicly thank those who have helped me. In the writing of *A Code of Jewish Ethics, Volume 2: Love Your Neighbor as Yourself,* I was once again blessed by generous and wise friends, many of whom read and critiqued the manuscript in its entirety (or almost), and offered me much helpful advice. Having had the opportunity to thank many of these people in the first volume of this code, I wish to acknowledge them yet again.

Dr. Isaac Herschkopf, a psychiatrist, faculty member of the NYU School of Medicine, author of *Hello Darkness, My Old Friend,* an important study of anger, and a beloved friend, read through the entire manuscript twice, repeatedly offering me insights, illustrative anecdotes, and periodic challenges that forced me to refine my own thinking. Just how significant Ike's influence on this book has been can be confirmed by consulting his name in the index.

As he has done now for two preceding books, Rabbi Israel Stein (or Izzy, as he is universally known) checked every biblical, talmudic, and post-talmudic reference in this book, about a thousand references in total. He corrected a number of errors that crept in, noted some other sources that I overlooked, and offered other suggestions as well (see, for example, page 223). Rabbi Stein's effort was extraordinary, and his friendship a gift. I cannot overstate my gratitude.

My dear friend Rabbi Irwin Kula read through the entire manuscript in a three-week period, a remarkable effort given his own exceedingly busy schedule as president of CLAL (along with Rabbi Brad Hirschfeld), and the recent publication of his widely hailed *Yearnings: Embracing the Sacred Messiness of Life.* A person dominated by equal doses of intelligence and passion, Irwin marked up my pages with long, well-argued, and often alternative understandings of Jewish teachings (see, for example, pages 157–158). I am deeply grateful for his effort.

As is the case with Irwin, Daniel Taub has read almost everything I have written. A friend now for more than twenty-five years, Daniel is a man with enormous reservoirs of both Jewish and secular knowledge, and along with that, a wonderful stylist. I am grateful that under great time constraints, he read so much of the manuscript and, as always, many of his suggestions have been incorporated into the text (see, for example, page 428).

My friend Rabbi Dr. Michael Berger of Emory University has helped me for more than fifteen years with careful readings of my books-in-progress. A scholar of wide-ranging knowledge, particularly of the Bible, and of rabbinic and medieval Jewish literature and thought, he has made many important suggestions that have been incorporated into the text, while conveying instances in which he thought my analyses of certain sources were overstated.

This is the tenth book that David Szonyi has worked on with me. His editing makes my style clearer, his Jewish knowledge is broad, and I am very thankful for David's help. As I have often said in the past, any writer is blessed to have David Szonyi as a freelance editor.

A particularly special thanks goes to Toinette Lippe, my editor at Bell Tower, and a woman who has worked closely with me on this code (and on three other books as well) since the idea for it first evolved. Toinette's belief in this project has been profoundly moving to me, and her editing superb. I actually look forward to getting marked-up manuscripts back from her, and how many writers can say that?

Richard Pine of InkWell Management has represented me as a literary agent for more than twenty-five years. One of the most decent and insightful people I know, Richard is, in addition, a man of extraordinary loyalty. He also has the ability to encourage a writer when he needs encouragement, a talent that has often blessed me.

More than in any of my previous books, I consulted a variety of friends on individual chapters and in areas in which they have expertise, both intellectual and personal. On the subject of charity, Beverly Woznica, who holds a major position with the UJC (United Jewish Communities), offered me wonderful insights, particularly on the ethics of fund-raising, and on why solicitors for charitable organizations should feel no self-consciousness when seeking contributions (see, for example, page 222). One of the chapter's early readers, Robert Mass, a passionate student of Jewish texts and ethics, a former law review editor, and a highly accomplished lawyer, greatly helped organize what turned out to be the book's longest, and in some ways, most complicated chapter in a manner that made Judaism's manifold teachings on this subject very accessible. I am grateful as well to my friend Sam Sutton, who has among the most generous hearts of anyone I know (see pages 181–

182). Sam, the former president of Sephardic Bikur Holim, also offered me good guidance on the subject of visiting the sick.

On that same subject, I profited greatly from suggestions by Jonathan and Barbara Greenwald (see, for example, pages 81–82) and Donna Gilbert (see page 79), whose experiences either with illness themselves or with helping the ill repeatedly enriched the chapter's content. Rabbi David Woznica shared with me insights on this subject, as well as on comforting mourners and on loving one's neighbor, help for which I am profoundly grateful (see, for example, pages 68*n* and 312).

Terry Wohlberg, who helped found the Chevra Kadisha (see chapter 8) at Sinai Temple in Los Angeles, is the one who first suggested—and I am embarrassed to say that I might not have thought to do so on my own—that I include the section "Final Kindness," which delineates Judaism's teachings on how to prepare the dead for burial. The section also profited from her careful reading (see page 106). David Zinner of Kavod v'Nichum, a man of comprehensive knowledge on this subject, offered me many suggestions (see, for example, page 109) on a subject I had never before adequately studied or properly appreciated.

On the issue of Jews and non-Jews, my longtime friend Rabbi Robert Hirt of Yeshiva University was one of my earliest readers. A man who has enriched my life repeatedly with his trademark warmth and common sense, Bob offered me important advice on the chapter's direction. In addition to reading this section, Rabbi Saul Berman, a talmudist and scholar of Jewish law, reviewed it with me for hours at his home. Saul challenged my understanding of certain texts, and gave me much wise advice. The experience of studying and discussing some of these texts with him was one of the highlights of my years working on this book.

On the subject of tolerance, my thinking was deeply affected by a man whom I have never met (I still hope to), but whom I regard with extraordinary respect and appreciation, Sir Jonathan Sacks, the British chief rabbi. Rabbi Sacks's *The Dignity of Difference* is a genuine contribution that establishes, as I understand his argument, why differences between believers as to how they approach God (as long as they don't lead to contempt, violence, and cruelty) should not just be tolerated, but should be regarded as, quite possibly, pleasing to the Lord.

On the subject of issues of life and death, I am very grateful to my friend Rabbi Leonid Feldman, who pushed me to formulate some very sensitive issues with greater precision, and who saved me on several occasions from some confusing ambiguities (for a different example of his insights, see page 449). I cannot overstate my gratitude to Dr. Kenneth Prager, who offered me insights on the sensitive subject of end-of-life issues, along with the benefit of his experience as the director of Clinical Ethics at Columbia University Medical Center. When it was clear that I was not fully grasping all aspects of some of the medical issues he was discussing, Kenneth wrote out his conclusions and sent them to me (see pages 393–394). His ideas, based on years of study and of experience, are important, and I am honored to present them in this book.

Much essential work has been done on the subject of how we treat and mistreat animals. Among those who have most influenced my thinking on this matter are Dr. Richard Schwartz, author of *Judaism and Global Survival,* and Matthew Scully, author of *Dominion,* both of whom I have met only through their writings. The two months that I spent researching this aspect of the book, and what I learned about factory farming in America, influenced this lifelong carnivore to stop eating meat and chicken, a change that continues to surprise those who know me to no end (see pages 342–343).

My wife, Dvorah, herself a wonderful writer, has been the chief cheerleader for this project—to systematically gather and present Judaism's ethical teachings—since its inception. Her suggestions about the manuscript and her support mean everything to me. As I wrote years ago in the dedication to an earlier book, "For Dvorah, with whom I look forward to growing old, while remaining young." I am so grateful to my daughter Naomi, a careful reader and a wonderful stylist, and my son Benjamin, who expressed several suggestions as to how to augment my presentation (see his observation as to why someone's treatment of animals is an important indicator of the person's character; page 309). To be read and commented on by my daughter Shira, a passionate, insightful, and increasingly knowledgeable student of the Talmud, was particularly helpful. My daughter Rebecca has been studying in India during the writing of much of this book, but our discussions of issues of ethics, both over the phone and in person, have greatly benefited me.

I am happy to have this opportunity to thank my beloved brother-in-law, Stephen Friedgood, an extraordinarily talented graphic artist, for setting up and maintaining my websites, josephtelushkin.com and acodeofjewishethics.com. Stephen's creative mind, commitment to excellence, and wonderful aesthetic sensibilities bless any project with which he is associated.

I wish to acknowledge again my friend of more than forty years, Dennis Prager, whose effect on my life has been incalculable. The understanding of Judaism that Dennis and I evolved in our twenties, although modified and refined, has guided us both ever since our first literary effort, *Eight Questions People Ask About Judaism.*

While working on this book, I spent many days in the library of the Jewish Theological Seminary of America, one of the great research centers in Jewish life. I would like to thank Professor David Kraemer, a Talmud scholar and head of the library, for the warmth and hospitality he and the library staff have always extended me.

I acknowledge with thanks Rabbi Abraham Twerski, M.D., Dennis Prager, Yitta Halberstam Mandelbaum, Howard Jonas, Rabbi Jack Riemer, and Rabbi Hanoch Teller for granting me permission to quote from their books, works that I hope will affect you as they have affected me.

I am pleased to acknowledge once again three people involved in my professional life. Ruth Wheat of the B'nai B'rith Lecture Bureau has arranged my lectures throughout North America for almost twenty-five years. She is a warm friend, and my work with her has been a blessing. Donna Rosenthal, the highly talented executive vice chairman of CLAL, and a woman of great warmth and kindness, has made my relationship with CLAL a constantly fruitful and pleasant one. Carolyn Starman Hessel, the director of the Jewish Book Council, has done more than anyone I know to promote and popularize the buying and reading of Jewish books. I am honored to serve on the board of the Jewish Book Council, to work with the council on the Sami Rohr Prize, and most of all, to have Carolyn as a friend.

I would like to publicly acknowledge and thank Michael Jesselson, who arranged to have a thousand copies of Volume 1 of the code sent upon publication to many hundreds of rabbis of all denominations and to other leading and influential figures within the American-Jewish community. He has now graciously offered to send out 2,500 copies of this volume. Michael's commitment to Jewish ethics is profound, and his action was done in honor of the beloved memory of his father, Ludwig Jesselson, one of the great philanthropists of the past generation, and a man who throughout his life was guided, both in his business and personal affairs, by Judaism's ethical teachings.

I would like to thank again my two beloved friends, Terry and David Wohlberg, whose belief in this project and whose encouragement and support for it—and with whom I have spent many hours in intense study and discussion—have blessed me since the project's inception.

This publication was made possible by the support of Keren Keshet, and it is to Zalman C. Bernstein, the man whose legacy established this wonderful foundation, that I have dedicated this book.

CONTENTS

Tzedaka: The Jewish Laws of Charity

II

Jews and Non-Jews

Non-Jews and Jewish Law

III

The Animal World

Judaism's Attitude to Animals

IV

When Life Is at Stake

Matters of Life and Death

V

Justice and Tolerance

Two Cardinal Virtues

A Code of Jewish Ethics

VOLUME 2

Love Your Neighbor as Yourself

INTRODUCTION

"Love your neighbor as yourself" is the best-known commandment in the Bible. While we are all familiar with these words (they are perhaps the most famous words ever written, in the Bible or anywhere else), we rarely hear anyone talk about how to apply them in daily life. When was the last time you heard someone say that they were going to do something because of the commandment "Love your neighbor as yourself"?

And yet Jewish tradition regards this verse as the Torah's preeminent command (Jerusalem Talmud, *Nedarim* 9:4). Therefore, it seems important—I can think of no subject more important—to bring together in one volume a comprehensive summation of what Jewish tradition teaches about fulfilling this commandment. Many people are unaware of just how many Jewish ethical teachings are rooted in this law. Thus, although there is no commandment among the Torah's 613 laws requiring us to visit the sick, practice hospitality, and comfort mourners, all of which are cornerstones of Jewish morality, they are regarded as emanating from the commandment "Love your neighbor as yourself" (Maimonides, "Laws of Mourning" 14:1; see chapters 3–7 and 9 in this book).

Charity, a subject to which a full fifth of this volume is devoted (chapters 12–20), is based upon Torah laws, but what most powerfully motivates us to be charitable and help others is love, and the empathy and concern that grow out of loving others in the way we love ourselves.

Loving, compassionate behavior extends to all humanity, and grows out of the biblical teaching that every human being, both Jew and Gentile, is created in God's image (Genesis 1:27; see also Leviticus 19:34). As the biblical prophet teaches: "Have we not all one Father? Did not one God create us?"*

---

*Even in the talmudic era, a time of generally poor Jewish-Gentile relations, the Rabbis ordained that charity be given even to idolaters (see pages 200–201).

(Malachi 2:10; see chapters 21–22). Justice and tolerance, the virtues that demand from us fairness and respect, are also based on the love we should feel for those, like ourselves, created in the image of God (see chapters 29 and 30).

Judaism does not ordain love for animals, but it does preach compassion, and the Talmud promises God's blessings on those who act toward all of God's creatures with kindness: "Whoever has compassion for [God's] creatures is shown compassion from Heaven" (*Shabbat* 151b). It seemed therefore appropriate to include Judaism's extensive teachings on the proper treatment of animals (there are more laws in the Torah on this subject than there are concerning the Sabbath).

The specific language of the biblical verse reads, "Love your neighbor as yourself." The explicit command is to love our neighbor; the implicit command is to love ourselves. Jewish law upholds the right of self-defense (chapter 25) and requires us to violate Judaism's most basic ritual laws (such as observing the Sabbath and Yom Kippur) when human life, ours or someone else's, is at stake (chapter 27). And love for others is behind commandments such as intervening when another's life is at risk (see chapter 26).

God's particular esteem for the commandment to love is reflected in an old Jewish folktale that speculates on how God decided on the location of the Beit HaMikdash, the Holy Temple in Jerusalem.

Many thousands of years ago, even before Jerusalem was a city, two brothers lived there in neighboring farms. One brother was married. Every year, he found that his farm did not produce enough food to satisfy his family's needs, and they all lived in poverty. The other brother lived alone, and his needs were easily provided for by his farm. One year, both brothers had bumper crops. When the harvest was completed, the richer brother said to himself: "I have so much more than I need, I will take some of my harvest and leave it in my brother's barn." He decided to do so in the dead of night, so that his brother would not realize what he had done, and would assume that the extra food was part of his own harvest. That same evening, the poorer brother thought to himself: "This year, I finally have more than enough for my family. But for my brother, that which he harvests is all that he has. He has no family, only his possessions." And out of love for his brother he decided that that very evening, he would take some of his harvest to his brother's barn, so that his brother could rejoice at the bounty of his crop. During the night, each of the brothers set out in a cart and left part of their harvest in the other's barn. When they awoke in the morning, they saw that their harvest was in no way diminished, and each thought that he had only dreamed about helping the other, but had not actually done so. And so, that night each brother brought food to his brother's barn once more. In the morning, once again, each store of food was undiminished.

On the third night, each made sure to stay up and set out in the middle of the night. This time, they encountered each other on the road, and both realized what the other had done. They ran toward each other and embraced.

Of the spot where they kissed, God said, "This is where I want My Temple built."

A stylistic note: *Love Your Neighbor as Yourself* is written in the format in which Jewish legal codes have been written since the Mishnah (circa 200 C.E.): chapters and numbered paragraphs. This style was followed a millennium later in Maimonides' *Mishneh Torah,* and in Rabbi Joseph Karo's sixteenth-century *Shulchan Arukh.* Each chapter of this book covers one portion of a large area of Jewish ethics. For example, the section on charity *(tzedaka)* contains nine chapters detailing, among other things, "Priorities in Giving" (chapter 14), "Soliciting and Motivating Others to Give" (chapter 17), and "On Giving to Beggars and Other Poor People" (chapter 18). Within the chapters, each of the numbered paragraphs deals with a separate and discrete point. In the chapter on beggars, paragraph 3 explains why giving to beggars is a particularly high form of charitable giving, and paragraph 4 explains the circumstances in which we should respond immediately to a beggar's plea without investigating whether he is telling the truth.

The distilling of the book into separate paragraphs keeps the code's teachings focused and enables readers to consult the book more easily when looking for ethical guidance from Jewish teachings.

The first volume in this code, *You Shall Be Holy,* dealt primarily with issues of character development (such as judging others fairly, cultivating gratitude, and distinguishing when forgiveness is obligatory, when optional, and when forbidden). But, ultimately, the goal of refining our characters is to affect and transform how we treat others, the subject of this book.

As I had occasion to note in the introduction to Volume 1: Over three thousand years ago, when God revealed Himself to Abraham, the first Jew, He told him, "And you shall be a blessing" [in the lives of those with whom you come in contact]; (Genesis 12:2). I think it fair to say that if we undertake to incorporate into our behavior the age-old Jewish teachings in this book, we, too, will become a blessing in the lives of all those with whom we come in contact, and a blessing in our own lives as well.

I

Loving Your Neighbor

Love Your Neighbor as Yourself

You shall not take revenge or bear a
grudge against a member of your people.
Love your neighbor as yourself;
I am God.

Leviticus 19:18

1

THE MAJOR PRINCIPLE OF THE TORAH

The central commandment

1. Even though the Torah ascribes no special significance to the verse "Love your neighbor as yourself," Jewish sources have long understood this commandment as having special—and in some ways preeminent—significance. Rabbi Akiva (second century) declared that the injunction to love your neighbor "is the major principle of the Torah" (Jerusalem Talmud, *Nedarim* 9:4).

2. More than a century before Akiva, Hillel presented a negative formulation of this law, "What is hateful to you, do not do to your neighbor." He also declared this to be Judaism's central teaching: "This is the whole Torah! All the rest is commentary" (*Shabbat* 31a).* Occasionally, I have heard people describe Hillel's formulation of the Golden Rule as representing a lower, more pragmatic ethic than the positive but vaguely phrased "Love your neighbor." But, in fact, Hillel was concerned with offering people practical guidance on how to make this law part of their daily behavior, and he understood that it is first necessary to teach people what not to do.

In defining Judaism initially by what one shouldn't do, Hillel may have been emulating God's articulation of the Ten Commandments. Thus, my friend Dr. Isaac Herschkopf notes that "God did not command us to be honest, truthful, and faithful. Rather, He commanded us, 'Don't steal,' 'Don't bear false witness,' 'Don't commit adultery.' It might be less positive, but it is undeniably more effective."

*For more on the significance of moral behavior within Judaism, see *A Code of Jewish Ethics, Volume 1: You Shall Be Holy,* pages 10–25.

A 1980s experiment conducted with American sixth-graders addressed young people's differing responses to positive and negative formulations of the Golden Rule ("Do unto others as you would have others do unto you"). Educator Ron Rembert asked the students to compose two lists, one consisting of actions they would want others to do for them, the others of actions they would not want done. Their list of "Do's" was short, focusing primarily on "love," "respect," and "help." Their list of "Don'ts" was longer, and included "Don't hit . . . steal . . . laugh at . . . snub . . . cheat." Rembert pointed out that "the list of 'Don'ts' . . . included specific behaviors which are relatively easy to identify [while] the list of 'Do's' . . . focused upon general attitudes and behaviors which are more difficult to define." Professor Jeffrey Wattles cited this study in his book The Golden Rule, *and noted that "The students concluded that the negative version of the Golden Rule would be easier to follow than the positive version."*[1]

---

3. The centrality of love in Jewish teachings also characterizes many post-talmudic texts. To cite but one example: The medieval *Tanna D'Bei Eliyahu* attributes to God one crucial request from the Jewish people: "This is what the Holy One said to Israel: 'My children, what do I want from you? I want no more than that you love one another and treat one another with dignity.' "

4. In the Torah, the commandment to love is immediately preceded by prohibitions against taking revenge and bearing a grudge. At some point, we all hurt other people—intentionally or not—and then hope fervently that our victims not take revenge or bear us a grudge. To love our neighbor as ourself means, therefore, to act toward others as we would like them to act toward us. If we want those we have provoked to let go of vengeful feelings, then we must act the same way when others hurt us.

Holding on to grudges is self-destructive as well as destructive. Rabbi Abraham Twerski, M.D., a psychiatrist who has devoted most of his professional career to working with people with addictions, notes that recovering alcoholics often relapse because of their inability to suppress anger and grudges against people who have hurt them. One man—who understood how vital it was for his own well-being not to bear grudges—told Twerski: "Carrying resentments is like letting someone whom you don't like live inside your head rent-free."

This insight applies to everyone, not just recovering alcoholics, for many of us spend hours, days, even months, preoccupied with thoughts of the person or people we most dislike. Rabbi Twerski asks wisely: "Why would anyone allow that?"[2]

—

5. The commandment to love is followed by the words "I am God." What is the connection between these two statements? Jewish tradition understands the commandment to love our neighbor as rooted in the belief that *all* human beings are created by God and thus are part of one extended family. As the prophet Malachi asks: "Have we not all one Father? Did not one God create us?" (Malachi 2:10). From this perspective, the command to love other people is similar to the expectation that we love our siblings; we and they share a parent or parents in common. In addition, the failure to show love and kindness to others reveals not only an emotionally stingy nature, but also a denial of the biblical teaching that the people we encounter are, like us, created by God in His image and should be treated as such.

—

On purely logical grounds, if there is no God commanding us to love our neighbor, then there is no rational *reason why we should feel obligated to do so. John Locke wrote in* An Essay Concerning Human Understanding *(1690): "Should that most unshaken rule of morality and foundation of all social virtues, 'that one should do [unto others] as he would be done unto,' be proposed to one who had never heard of it before . . . might he not without any absurdity ask a reason why?" Since Locke posed this question over three centuries ago, no one has offered a* logically *compelling reason why we should love our neighbor as ourself (on the relationship between God and ethics, see* A Code of Jewish Ethics, Volume 1: You Shall Be Holy, *pages 480–486).*

—

6. While the command to "love your neighbor as yourself" is explicitly stated, a moment's reflection reveals that this verse suggests an implicit command as well: to love ourselves. A person who has low regard for himself is unlikely to consistently carry out the injunction "as yourself" in a loving way. Indeed, one wonders whether there has ever been an abusive parent with a decent self-image. This is why even if self-love does not come naturally or easily, we are obligated—for the sake of others as well as ourselves—to cultivate a sense of self-esteem and liking.

Think about your own behavior. Are you more likely to be patient, forgiving, and generous to others when you are feeling good about yourself or when you are feeling low and self-critical? A sense of personal well-being and accomplishment tend to translate into a more joyful and accepting attitude toward others, including family members. However, when we are feeling unsure of ourselves and self-critical, we often become more disapproving and less forgiving of others.

———

A healthier attitude toward ourselves is one I saw cited in a newspaper article and attributed to an anonymous third-grade boy: "I can't make people like me, but if I wasn't me, I would like me."

———

What does it mean to love your neighbor as yourself?

7. The wording of the Torah's commandment—with its emphasis on "neighbor,"* implying a person whom we see often—suggests that this mitzvah relates to tangible behavior and not simply to abstract love, as would be the case had the Torah instructed us to "Love humanity."† That is why Jewish legal texts generally focus on the actions this commandment entails. Thus, Maimonides emphasizes loving *behavior* far more than the emotion of love:

- In "Laws of Mourning," he describes as outgrowths of this command a series of additional Jewish laws, including the commandments to visit the sick (see chapters 5–7), to make sure that the dead are properly attended to and buried (see chapter 8), to comfort mourners (see chapter 9), and to act hospitably (see chapter 3). Maimonides also notes our

---

*The precise meaning of the Hebrew word *re-acha* is "your fellow," which, like neighbor, suggests someone with whom we routinely have contact (of course, we are also obligated to act in a loving and helpful way even toward those with whom we have more casual interactions or perhaps none, such as victims of a natural catastrophe). I have followed the translation of "Love your neighbor as yourself" since it is so widely known.

†The character Linus, in Charles Schultz's comic strip *Peanuts,* was famed for his comment "I love humanity! It's people I can't stand." A scene from Dostoevsky's *The Brothers Karamazov* expresses this more fully. Zosma describes to a visitor to his monk's cell a conversation he had years earlier with a doctor: "He spoke just as frankly as you have done, but with humor, bitter humor. 'I love mankind,' he said, 'but I'm surprised at myself: the more I love mankind in general, the less I love men in particular, that is, separately as individuals.' " The longer the doctor spoke, the sadder and more tragic his confession became: " 'In my thoughts,' he said to me, 'I've often had a passionate desire to serve humanity, and would perhaps have actually gone to the cross for mankind if I had ever been required to do so, and yet at the same time, as I well know from my personal experience, I'm incapable of enduring two days in the same room with any other person. . . . Within one day, I can end up hating the very best of men, some because they've taken too long over their dinner, others because they've caught a cold and keep blowing their noses. I become a misanthrope,' he said, 'the minute I come into contact with people.' "

obligation to provide for the needs of a bride, and to bring the bride and groom joy at their wedding (see pages 27–28). Maimonides understands the law of love of neighbor as meaning that whatever you want others to do for you, you should do for them ("Laws of Mourning" 14:1).

• In "Laws of Character Development" *(De'ot),* he offers additional examples of how to practice this commandment. For example: "One should speak in praise of another, and be careful about another's money [and possessions] just as he is careful about his own money, and wants his own dignity preserved" (6:3).[3] These examples express two important components of loving behavior: emotional support for others (praising them), and material support (helping safeguard their money).[4]

• In "Laws of Gifts to the Poor," Maimonides notes that among the commandments violated by someone who does not actively involve himself in redeeming captives is "Love your neighbor as yourself" (8:10).

• In Maimonides' enumeration of the 613 commandments, he describes how this law should be translated into action: "Whatever I wish for myself, I should wish the same for that person. And whatever I do not wish for myself or for my friends, I should not wish for that person. That is the meaning of the verse, 'Love your neighbor as yourself' " (*Book of the Commandments,* positive commandment # 206).

A contemporary Jewish writer comments on what it means in concrete terms to fulfill Maimonides' words, "Whatever I do not wish for myself or for my friends, I should not wish for that person": "As I would not want to suffer hunger, homelessness, joblessness, ill health, and disease, and personal tragedies of every kind, so too I would not wish that on others. And I would have to act to prevent these misfortunes happening to them." Regarding Maimonides' words, "Whatever I wish for myself, I should wish the same for that person," he continues: "If I wish to have peace of mind, security, a decent living, friends, family, good health for myself, I am to wish that for others also, and to act in such a way as to allow others to have those blessings" (Danny Siegel).[5]

Nachmanides (thirteenth century) questioned the literal meaning of "Love your neighbor as yourself," reasoning that the Torah would not issue such a command because "man cannot be expected to love his neighbor as his own soul." Rather, the Torah meant that "we should wish our neighbor to enjoy the same well-being as we enjoy ourselves," and to have this wish with "no reservations" (that is, without the desire to feel superior to our neighbor).

Building on this insight, Naftali Hertz Wessely (eighteenth century), author of a commentary on Leviticus (part of Moses Mendelssohn's Biur *commentary on the Torah) offers an example that illustrates why feeling the same level of love for all others as for ourselves is impossible: "To fulfill such a command to the letter, man would have to grieve for his fellow's sorrows just as he grieves for his own. This would be intolerable since scarcely a moment passes without hearing of someone's misfortunes."*[6] *If people consistently react to the sufferings of others with the same intensity with which they react to their own (for example, grieving over the death of someone else's child as they would grieve if their own child died), we would soon find ourselves, and all humanity, in a permanent state of depression.**

Another reason why it is important to define the commandment to love in terms of behavior rather than emotions: Emotions are vague and can be difficult, sometimes even impossible, to delineate. Even people who are emotionally or physically brutal to others—for example, some spouses to each other, some parents to children—often insist that they love those whom they mistreat. And they mean it, or at least think they do. Thus, I have often heard it said of a parent known to be abusive that, at some level, he actually loves his children. If, indeed, that is true, then it underscores why defining love in terms of emotions, instead of deeds, is pointless since the word "love" could then be used to encompass behavior ranging from the greatest kindness and consideration to outright cruelty. It is only when love is defined in terms of behavior that people can be offered practical guidance in how to treat others.

---

8. Deuteronomy 10:18–19 provides yet another indication that love in the Torah is defined primarily through actions. Verse 19 commands the Israelites "to love the stranger, for you were strangers in the land of Egypt," while verse 18 teaches that God "loves the stranger, giving him food and clothing." The Torah's instruction to the Israelites to follow in God's ways (Deuteronomy 28:9), means that their *love* for the stranger should be

*This would be bad not only for the person experiencing the depression, but also for the recipient of the depressed person's love. The late rabbi Louis Jacobs made the point that he would not want his doctor to take his case too personally because, overcome with emotion, he would not be able to think or operate rationally.

expressed, as is God's, by providing them with food and clothing and taking care of their other needs.

Also, the rationale for loving the stranger, "for you were strangers in the land of Egypt," makes no sense if it refers to emotions. Why should the fact that the Israelites were "strangers" in Egypt, in and of itself, cause them to *feel* love for other strangers? But it makes perfect sense if what is being commanded is loving behavior, so that Jews are instructed to treat the stranger "in the way Jews would have liked to have been treated when they were strangers in Egypt" (Professor Steven Harvey).[7]

Professor Harvey points out that while it is impossible to expect masses of people to feel the same "sincere and unbounded desire and concern for the well-being of others [as they have for themselves], what can be commanded is the performance of acts of love, treating others as one would if one truly cared about their well-being."[8]

---

9. There is perhaps yet another reason the Torah commanded us to love our neighbor rather than humanity in general. It is often harder to love our neighbors, the flesh-and-blood people who live near us and whose faults and annoying characteristics we are well aware of, than to love mankind, consisting of people whom we have never met and never will meet.* It is wise to be guided by the words of Israel Ba'al Shem Tov (1698–1760), the founder of Chasidism: "Just as we love ourselves despite the faults we know we have, so we should love our fellows despite the faults we see in them." Acting lovingly and helpfully, therefore, should not depend on idealizing those whom we love, nor should we show them love only because we judge them to be saintly. After all, if other people withheld love from us because of our imperfections, we would never be loved. And just as we want others to love us despite our faults, so, too, should we love others.

As yourself

10. The words "as yourself" mandate that it is not enough to simply act in a kind way to others; we must go further and ask ourselves: "Am I acting

*Many people are moved to tears by unhappy events that happen to *fictional* characters in movies, yet do not react with anywhere near the same intensity when equally unhappy events befall actual people they know. The same is true with happy events; we cry when the hero and heroine fall in love, but not when our neighbors do.

toward the other person in the way that I would want myself and others dear to me to be treated?" For example, when the issue is raised before the U.S. Congress of increasing the minimum wage (particularly in the case of adults),* the congressmen, all of whom earn well in excess of the minimum wage, should ask themselves: "If I needed to work at a low-level unskilled job, would I find it possible to live on the current minimum wage, or would it need to be raised in order to have my basic needs met?"

By posing these sorts of questions, and answering them honestly, we may well be pushed to behavior in which we would not otherwise engage.

The early twentieth-century American businessman Arthur Nash, a deeply religious Christian, described in his autobiography an incident that helped define him. A factory owner who had rented floor space from Nash ran a sweatshop. Nash had not known much about the man's business, but when it started to founder and the man couldn't pay his bills, including his rent, Nash took it over. When payroll time came, Nash was shocked to learn that some workers in the sweatshop were earning as little as $4 a week (a very low sum even in 1918, when this incident happened). Nash was in a quandary. His own clothing company, which paid much more generous wages, was in a shaky financial situation and had lost money the previous year. When Nash told his son that he felt morally compelled to raise the sweatshop workers' salaries, his son objected, arguing that their own finances were in peril. Despite that, Nash concluded that even though he would probably have to soon close the sweatshop, until such time as he did, he would pay the workers a fair wage. He called together a group of employees, and told them: "First, I want you to know that brotherhood is a reality with me. You are all my brothers and sisters, children of the same great Father that I am, and entitled to all the justice and fair treatment that I want for myself. And so long as we run this shop . . . I am going to treat you as my brothers and sisters, and the Golden Rule is going to be our only governing law. Which means that whatever I would like to have you do to me were I in your place, I am going to do to you." At that point, Nash, who did not know the workers by name, asked each employee to raise his or her hand as their name was called: "I read the first name. Under it was written: 'Sewing on buttons, $4.00 per week.' I looked straight [in front of me] at the little group, but saw no hand. Then I looked to my right, and there saw [an] old lady . . . holding up her trembling hand. At first I could not speak because, almost instantly, the face of my

---

*A lower minimum wage in the case of teenagers under eighteen might be necessary in order to encourage employers to hire them.

own mother came between that of the old lady and myself. I thought of my mother being in such a situation, and of what, in the circumstances, I would want someone to do for her. . . . As I looked at that old lady, and saw only my mother, I finally blurted out: 'I don't know what it's worth to sew on buttons; I never sewed a button on. But your wages to begin with will be $12.00 a week.'"

Nash continued going down the list, tripling the salaries of the lowest-paid workers, and raising the highest-paid workers (who were also underpaid) some 50 percent. His behavior, though fulfilling the command to "Love your neighbor as yourself," should have been financially ruinous, as his son had predicted, but it didn't work out that way. Within months, the shop was producing three times the quantity of goods it had produced a year earlier. Nash learned that after his presentation, one worker had told the others that after a speech like that, they should all "work like hell." Indeed, that is what the workers did. Starting with this event, "Nash turned his business into a laboratory for the application of the Golden Rule, and the business prospered greatly" (Jeffrey Wattles).[9]

Almost eighty years later, Aaron Feuerstein, a Jewish businessman, went one step further than Nash. In December 1995, Feuerstein had just returned home from his seventieth birthday party when he learned that his Malden Mills textile factory in Lawrence, Massachusetts, had burned down. Over twenty employees had been injured, some seriously.

Some three thousand employees worked at Malden Mills, and when they saw the destruction wrought by the fire, they assumed, as one worker put it, "The fire's out of control. Our jobs are gone."

*But Feuerstein had a different response. An observant Jew who studies both the Talmud and Shakespeare daily, he likes to recall a Mishnaic aphorism of which his father was particularly fond: "In a place where there are no men, try to be a man" (*Ethics of the Fathers *2:5). In the immediate aftermath of the fire, Feuerstein met with a thousand employees and assured them, "We're going to stay—and rebuild."*

Two days later, when wages were due, all the employees were paid on time; Feuerstein even added an extra check with a Christmas bonus and a note: "Do not despair. God bless each of you."

The following day he convened a meeting of all the employees and told them: "For the next thirty days, it might be longer, all employees will be paid full salaries." Feuerstein ended up spending millions of dollars of his own money keeping all the employees on salary and full benefits for three months.

American law certainly did not require Feuerstein to act as he did and, for that matter, Jewish business law did not require him to do so either. But the principle of "Love your neighbor as yourself" guided Feuerstein's behavior. As he explained at the time: "I have a responsibility to the workers, both blue-collar and white-collar. . . . It would have been unconscionable to put 3,000 people on the streets and deliver a death blow to the cities of Lawrence and Methuen."

Unfortunately, the economic recovery of Malden Mills did not proceed as smoothly as that of the sweatshop transformed by Arthur Nash, and five years later, Feuerstein had to file for bankruptcy protection (the company, which produces polar fleece fabric, has continued to stay in business). Yet when the CBS television program 60 Minutes *asked Feuerstein if, knowing how things would play out, he would have acted as he did, and would do so again in the future, he responded, "Yes, it was the right thing to do. We are charged with acting not for the moment but rather for the larger goal."*

Does "love your neighbor" mandate loving evil people as much as you love yourself?

11. While many of the sayings attributed to Jesus in the New Testament parallel Jewish teachings (not surprisingly, given that Jesus was raised as a Jew, and is cited in the New Testament as advocating observance of Jewish law),* a number of statements attributed to him in the Sermon on the Mount are innovative and not found in Jewish sources. Among them is "Love your enemies and pray for those who persecute you" (Matthew 5:44). Although no teaching in the Hebrew Bible mandates loving one's enemy, the Bible makes it clear that a person must treat his adversary justly: Thus, "If you see your enemy's donkey lying down under its burden and would refrain from raising it, you must nevertheless raise it with him" (Exodus 23:5). The book of Proverbs, while not requiring love of our enemies, does mandate a measure of compassion and a standard of behavior that can diminish hatred: "If your enemy is hungry, give him bread to eat. And if he is thirsty, give him water to drink" (Proverbs 25:21).†

---

*"Do not imagine that I have come to abolish the Law [the Torah] or the prophets. . . . I tell you solemnly, till heaven and earth disappear, not one dot, not one little stroke, shall disappear from the Law until its purpose is achieved." The law's "purpose" is, of course, the universal recognition of God and His moral law, a goal that neither Christianity nor Judaism believes was realized in Jesus' lifetime, or since. Jesus concluded his message with a stern warning: "Therefore, the man who infringes even the least of these commandments and teaches others to do the same will be considered the least in the kingdom of heaven, but the man who keeps them and teaches them will be considered great in the kingdom of heaven" (Matthew 5:17–19).

†A secular formulation of the obligation to treat our enemies with justice is reflected in a wry and witty aphorism of the American journalist Edgar Watson Howe (1853–1937): "You needn't love your enemy, but if you refrain from telling lies about him, you are doing well enough." On another occasion, he wrote: "Instead of loving your enemy, treat your friends a little better."

---

*What is unclear in Jesus' admonition to "love your enemy" is why the person is an enemy. If it is because some personal rivalry has created hostility between the two of you, then Jesus' insistence that you love him as a fellow human being is not a radical demand (it is more like telling players on a football team who have been incited to hate their opponents not to do so, but to love them instead). If, however, Jesus intended such love to apply even when your enemy is an evil oppressor, then what form does Jesus expect such love to take? Are you really expected to help such a person or a government comprised of evil leaders? If so, how?**

Two verses after issuing this command, Jesus suggests that if you wish to be morally worthy, your love for those who wish you harm should be as strong as, if not stronger than, your love even for your friends: "for if you [only] love those who love you, what right have you to claim any credit?" (Matthew 5:46). The implication is that loving your friends does not deserve approbation since they love you. What shows you to be worthy and idealistic is loving those who hate you and wish you harm (in the context in which Jesus made this demand, he might well have been instructing his fellow Jews to love the Romans who ruled over Judaea and who, among other things, crucified tens of thousands of Jews, imposed excessively burdensome and sometimes confiscatory taxes, and periodically desecrated the Jerusalem Temple).

To my mind, a more nuanced approach to evil and unjust people was taught by Confucius (551–479 B.C.E.*): On one occasion when he was asked, "What do you think of repaying evil with kindness?" Confucius replied: "Then what are you going to repay kindness with? Repay kindness with kindness but repay evil with justice"* (Analects).†

Saul Bellow, the Nobel Prize–winning writer, expressed concern about love that makes no moral demands of its object: "A man is only as good as what he loves," is how Bellow put it (Seize the Day). *These words should be kept in mind when we hear, for example, of "good" people who are friends of vicious people. A reader of biographies of Adolf Hitler, for instance, might form the impression*

---

*For a discussion of how the evangelist Billy Graham understood this and other New Testament teachings (Romans 13) as mandating that Christian workers in the Soviet Union—a government that was totalitarian, atheistic, and anti-Christian—"obey the authorities" and be "better workers," see *A Code of Jewish Ethics, Volume 1: You Shall Be Holy,* pages 137–138.

†Another time, Confucius was asked: "What would you say if all the people in a village like a person?" "That is not enough," he replied. "And what would you say if all the people in a village dislike a person?" "That is not enough," Confucius said. "It is better when the good people of a village like him, and the bad people of a village dislike him. When you are disliked by the bad persons, you are a good person" (Lin Yutang, *The Wisdom of Confucius*).

that the woman who loved and lived with him, Eva Braun, was an essentially sweet, though politically naïve, woman. But the single most important thing we know about her is that she loved Adolf Hitler.

The medieval biblical exegete Rashbam commented on the words "Love your neighbor" that "if your neighbor is good [love him], but if he is evil, 'the fear of the Lord is to hate evil'" (Proverbs 8:13). Nechama Leibowitz, perhaps the greatest Bible teacher of the twentieth century (see also pages 21–23) has argued that although Rashbam is famed for his "strict adherence to the plain sense of the text," in this instance he has violated his own principle since "the text itself affords no hint of any such distinction between a good and evil man. On the contrary, it employs a neutral comprehensive term, 'neighbor.'"[*10]

In this instance, it could be argued that Leibowitz herself is being overly literal. "Love your neighbor" is given as a general command without restrictions, in the same way as "Honor your father and mother." However, does Leibowitz assume that this law enjoins a child to act lovingly and respectfully toward a parent who, for example, sexually abused her?

Sixteen verses after "love your neighbor," the Torah similarly places no limitations on the command to love "as yourself" the stranger who resides with you (Leviticus 19:34). This implies, for example, that Israeli Jews have a biblical obligation to love Arabs who live among them in peace. But I suspect that Leibowitz does not believe that this command also applies to those Arabs who engage in acts of terror or who support groups or countries that seek to destroy Israel.

To insist that a child is obligated to love and respect a father who sexually abused her or that an Israeli must love a "stranger" who commits acts of terror is to turn a beautiful and generally applicable Torah law into a self-destructive statute. In short, as Rashbam teaches, we are commanded to love our neighbor as ourself in the large majority of instances, but not all.

---

*Although I prefer Rashbam's understanding of the text to that of Leibowitz's, the fact that he does not define what he means by "evil" is problematic. Thus, on occasion, I have heard some observant Jews refer to Jews who don't observe Judaism's ritual laws as *resha'im,* evil people, and who seem to believe, in consequence, that the law commanding love of neighbor does not apply to them. This is very unfortunate and morally wrong. The word "evil" should apply in the general sense in which people use this term, as referring to people who engage in cruel and harmful behavior to others. In modern times, the ultra-Orthodox sage, the Chazon Ish, ruled that since God is not as evident in the world today as He was, for example, during the revelation at Mount Sinai, observant Jews should not regard nonobservant Jews as *apikorsim,* heretics, people who knew God and rejected Him. The late rabbi Joseph Lookstein often said that he loved all Jews except for Jews who didn't love other Jews.

Moral imagination

12. Over the past century, society has witnessed extraordinary advances in medicine, science, and technology. These came about because an individual, or many individuals, used the full resources of his or her intellectual imagination to solve problems that had previously been thought to be insoluble. However, during the same period, there has been no comparable worldwide advance in ethical behavior.* That is, in part, because human beings rarely use the full resources of their intellect to solve moral problems. Exercising moral imagination means using our intelligence to devise creative and innovative ways to help others. Concerning charity, for example, it means not only providing immediate assistance to the impoverished, but also helping the poor in ways that will enable them to support themselves and no longer need help (see pages 187–189). Therefore, in any situation in which help is required, we should use our intelligence to discover the most effective and loving way to help those in need.

Amos Oz, the Israeli novelist and essayist, describes an incident that happened when he was eight years old. His father, Yehudah Klausner (Oz's family name was Klausner), had published his first book, a literary study entitled The Novella in Hebrew Literature. *Excited at the book's publication, Oz's father would go each day to the local bookstore to see if any of the three copies on display had been sold. For many days, no copies sold, and his father's sorrow "filled the apartment like a smell." On the same block on which his family lived, Oz's father had a dear friend, Israel Zarchi, a novelist whose books sold quite well. Oz remembers how his father complained to Zarchi that while many readers snapped up the sort of popular novels Zarchi wrote, scholarly books, such as he produced, were ignored. But then, one day, Oz's father came home in a wonderful mood: "They're sold. They've all been sold." Even better, the bookstore had already ordered more copies.*

The following night, Oz's parents went out to celebrate and left Amos at the Zarchi house. Oz spent the evening in Zarchi's study, where he suddenly noticed

*In some nations, and for certain types of disadvantaged people, the moral climate has certainly improved. There is more acceptance and services for mentally challenged people in many countries today than in the past, and much greater accommodations are made for the physically handicapped than used to be the case. In the United States, there has been an enormous decline in racism and sexism, which has led to much greater opportunities for African-Americans and women. On the other hand, the mass murders of the twentieth century—among them the Holocaust, the tens of millions of people murdered by Stalin in Russia and by Mao in China, and the terrible killings in Cambodia and Rwanda—exceed by far the killings that took place in previous centuries.

on the little coffee table by the sofa four copies of his father's book. Oz knew that one copy had been given by his father to Zarchi. He quickly surmised who had purchased the other three: "I felt a rush of gratitude inside me that almost brought tears to my eyes." Zarchi, realizing that Oz had seen the books, picked up the three copies and hid them in a drawer; he did not want anyone else to realize what he had done.

More than fifty years later, writing his memoir, A Tale of Love and Darkness, *Oz still could not get over the depth of Zarchi's kindness: "I count two or three writers among my best friends, friends who have been close to me and dear to me for decades, yet I am not certain that I could do for one of them what Israel Zarchi did for my father. Who can say if such a generous ruse would have even occurred to me? After all, he, like everyone else in those days, lived a hand-to-mouth existence, and the three copies of* The Novella in Hebrew Literature *must have cost him at least the price of some much-needed clothes."*[11]

---

13. Before you take action in a situation in which someone has done something wrong, consider how you would like someone to respond if you were the one in the wrong. Unless what has happened poses an immediate threat, try to act in a way that will lead the other person back to good behavior. Thus, the late rabbi Avrohom Pam was once proctoring a test when he noticed a student copying from another. Instead of tearing up the student's test, failing him for the course, or arranging for him to be suspended or expelled, Rabbi Pam went over to the young man and whispered: "If you don't understand the question, please come up to my desk and I'll explain it to you." Years later, the student confided to Rabbi Pam that many of the things he learned from the rabbi "I have long forgotten, but what happened that day I will never forget."*[12]

Nechama Leibowitz, the Bible scholar, was once invited to appear on an Israeli radio program in which participants spoke about the most interesting person they had met. Most guests related incidents that occurred between them and well-known figures in political and intellectual life, or in the arts. But Nechama (who was known throughout Israel by her first name) described a policeman

*Obviously, behavior like Rabbi Pam's depends upon circumstances. Thus, if many other students had witnessed the student cheating, Rabbi Pam might have had to react more forcefully, lest they conclude that cheating was regarded by the school as a minor matter. He was obviously making a judgment as to what would be the best remedy in the case of this particular student. Based on the student's subsequent comment, it is clear that he chose wisely.

whom she had met many years earlier. At the time, shortly after Israel was founded (1948), Nechama was teaching at a teachers' college in Jerusalem where there was a close-knit relationship between the students and faculty. But one day, some money was taken out of a student's purse. A few days later, a valuable pen disappeared; and then a student's watch was gone. The school was in an upheaval; clearly, there was a thief among them.

While Leibowitz was conducting a class with the school's fifty students, the principal came in with an elderly police officer. When Nechama asked if she should leave, the policeman said: "No, no. What I am going to say is no secret." He then turned to the students: "I'm a very experienced policeman. I started my career in the days of the British Mandate. I've already investigated hundreds of cases like this one. It is clear to me that this is an inside job—someone among you is a thief and he knows it." The officer continued: "Now I want to talk to the thief who's sitting here in this room. Only you know who has stolen things from your fellow students three times—only you and God Almighty. No one else in this room, including me, has any idea who you are. You have succeeded three times; for all I know, maybe you've succeeded in getting away with it more than three times. Let me tell you from experience, once you've succeeded in getting away with stealing, you will continue—and probably won't get caught."

The policeman's eyes scanned the room, but his words continued to be directed only to the thief. "You'll see that it is not so difficult to steal and so you will continue. You'll be rich; you'll have money and jewelry and watches and other nice things that other people don't have. And you won't get caught, because we in the police force know that very few robberies get solved. You might become respected, wealthy, and a person of prominence, but . . . you'll be a thief all your life. *You'll never be able to clear yourself of that fact.*

"Now, I'm going to make a suggestion. It's now 12:30. We're all going to go home soon because it's Erev Shabbat *[and it will soon be the Sabbath]. Between one and two o'clock at the latest, [and don't tell anybody what you've done],* put the things you stole in some open place where they can be found—and you'll be absolved, you'll no longer be a thief."*

The police officer picked up his briefcase, said Shabbat Shalom, *and left the room.*

That afternoon, Nechama was at home preparing for the Sabbath when the

---

*I am following the version of the story recorded in Leah Abramowitz, *Tales of Nehama,* pages 120–121, along with Abramowitz's comments. I have added on these words which I recall Nechama Leibowitz saying when I heard her tell the story in a class in Jerusalem twenty-five years ago. Memory is tricky, but from my recollection the policeman emphasized that the culprit should not tell anyone what he had done. Thus, once he returned the items, he would no longer be a thief and no one need ever know about it.

phone rang. It was the principal. With great excitement, he told her that the missing money, pen, and watch were all sitting on the table in the school's main corridor. Someone had quietly placed them there for all to see.

Leibowitz's relating of this story on the radio a decade later did far more than arouse people's interest in this clever policeman. Over the years, people who heard her tell this story, or heard about it from others, used this same technique with equal success. On one occasion, Nechama received a letter from the principal of a youth village near Beersheba: "I want to meet with you as soon as possible; please let me know when you can give me an appointment." Nechama invited the man to come over as soon as it was convenient for him.

He told her that over a period of approximately two months, eight ballpoint pens had disappeared (this was at a time when ballpoint pens were new and somewhat costly). "I remembered your radio program several years ago, and I called an assembly in the dining room. More or less like that policeman you described, I told all the children: 'There's one person in this room who knows he's a thief—that he's taken eight pens, and maybe we'll never discover who he is. But one bad deed leads to another; he might be successful, and he might never be caught, but he'll be a thief all his life, no matter what else happens to him.'"

The director then told the class that the teachers' room would be left open so that the thief could return what he had stolen when no one was around. But unlike what happened in Nechama's story, the pens were not returned that day. A full three weeks went by and still they had not been returned. Then, one day, while he was alone in the teachers' room, a boy came in with the eight pens in his hand. His head lowered, he put the pens on the desk.

The director asked him: "Tell me, what took you so long? Why did you wait three weeks to return these things?"

The boy explained that for many days after the director's speech, he had wanted to return the pens, but there were always children around, waiting to see if the thief would show up. Finally, with the passage of time, the other students had given up, so that now he could return the pens without their seeing him.

The director knew, however, that something more was going on. Why, after all, had the boy come in while he was sitting there, instead of just dropping off the pens when no one would see? He remained silent, waiting for the boy to speak. Finally, the boy said: "Perhaps you can tell me some way in which I can do teshuva *(penitence) for what I did?"*

The director reassured the boy, "The fact that you have returned the pens is proof you have done teshuva."

"No, no," the boy insisted. "I have to do something more. I did something bad, so now I have to do something good in its place."

"Like what?" asked the director.

"Well," said the boy, "like going to the blind institute across the street after school twice a week to read to the children there."

Clearly, the behavior of both this police officer and school principal were acts of moral imagination, using their intelligence, not to catch a thief, but to stop someone from becoming one.*†

2

HOW TO FULFILL THIS COMMANDMENT

1. A paradox: if we love our neighbor only because we are commanded to do so, we have not fulfilled the commandment properly. After all, the Torah commanded us to love our neighbor as ourself, and just as we don't love ourselves because we are commanded to do so, so, too, we should not love our neighbor *only* because we are required to.

But what if love of others does not come naturally or easily to us? The answer: Start by performing acts of kindness for others. "If you wish to be joined in a loving relationship with your friend, do business [that is, provide] for his good" (*Derekh Eretz Zuta,* 2).‡[1]

Rabbi Avrohom Pam used to quote this rabbinic teaching to explain why parents usually love their children even more than their children love them. Adults deepen and develop parental love, Rabbi Pam noted, as an outgrowth of constantly giving to their children.[2] A father whose son was having trouble learning to read told me that he spent four months working with his son for over an hour a day. By the end of the period, the son's reading abilities

---

*The student, too, showed moral imagination.

†In truth, what these two men did was far greater than merely stopping someone from becoming a thief. They took someone who had already committed a few thefts, and they reversed it. Bringing a person to *teshuva,* repentance and transformation, might well be an even greater achievement than mere prevention.

‡Dr. Isaac Herschkopf notes that "it is a consistent psychiatric truism that if we act in a healthy fashion—even if it involves doing things we don't feel like doing—we can't help but become healthy. For example, if we behave as if we are not phobic and don't avoid the feared stimulus, we inevitably cure our phobia. It makes sense that the same would be true of altruism." The contemporary American novelist, Louis Auchincloss has a character comment in *The Rector of Justin,* "Keep doing good deeds and you will become a good person. In spite of yourself."

had been raised three grade levels. But, the father confided, "What was even more remarkable was how the bond created through this study made me feel so much closer to my son. I had loved him dearly even before I had invested this time. But there is no question that the experience of working with him daily made my love deeper." When we devote time and effort to a person or a cause, that person or cause becomes dearer to us. And although we generally assume that what motivates us is love, we don't always realize that the giving itself intensifies, and sometimes even creates, the love.

In Strive for Truth *(an English translation of the modern* Mussar *work* Michtav Me-Eliyahu*), *Rabbi Eliyahu Dessler (1892–1953) asks: "Is giving a consequence of love or is love a result of giving?" He offers a provocative explanation for why we love those to whom we give: "We usually think that it is love which causes giving because we observe that a person showers gifts and favors on the one he loves. But there is another side to the argument. Giving may bring about love for the same reason that a person loves what he himself has created or nurtured: he recognizes in it part of himself. Whether it is a child he has brought into the world, an animal he has raised, a plant he has tended, or even a thing he has made or a house he has built, a person is bound in love to the work of his hands, for in it he finds himself."[3] Rabbi Dessler concludes: "If one were only to reflect that a person comes to love the one to whom he gives, he would realize that the only reason the other person seems a stranger to him is because he has not yet given to him. . . . If I give to someone, I feel close to him; I have a share in his being. It follows that if I were to start bestowing good upon everyone I come in contact with, I would soon feel that they are all . . . my loved ones. . . . Someone who has been granted the merit to reach this sublime level can understand the commandment to 'Love your neighbor as yourself' in its literal sense. . . . By giving . . . of yourself you will find in your soul that you and he are indeed one. You will feel in the clearest manner possible that he really is to you 'as yourself.' "[4]*

Rabbi Aryeh Carmell, perhaps the leading disciple of Rabbi Dessler and his English translator, has embodied his mentor's teaching in a powerful story, "The Midnight Rescue":

"It was past midnight. I was walking through the deserted city to my hotel on the other side of the river. The night was dark and foggy and I couldn't get a taxi. As I approached the bridge, I noticed a shabby figure leaning over the parapet. A 'down and out' I thought. Then he disappeared. I heard a splash. My God, *I thought,* he's done it. Suicide.

**Michtav Me-Eliyahu* literally means "A letter from Eliyahu."

"I ran back under the bridge, onto the embankment, and waded into the river, grabbing him as he came past, borne by the current. I dragged him up onto the embankment. He was quite a young guy. He was still breathing. A couple of people noticed and I shouted to them to get an ambulance. They managed to stop a taxi and between us we half-dragged, half-carried the man into the taxi. . . . I got in and told [the driver] to drive to the nearest hospital emergency room. I waited until the man was admitted, gave my report, and got a taxi back to my hotel at last.

"I had ruined a good suit, and knew I would have a terrible cold in the morning. I could feel it coming on. But anyway I had saved a life. I had a hot bath and got into bed but it sill worried me. Such a young man. Why had he done it?

"The next morning, as soon as I was free, I bought a large bunch of grapes and set off for the hospital. I was determined to find out what was behind this matter. Maybe I could help.

"Why was I so interested in the guy? In this great city there were at least a half a dozen would-be suicides every night. Their plight did not touch me. Then it dawned on me. Of course. First you give, *then you* care. *I had given quite a lot. I had risked my life and gotten a bad cold in the bargain. I had invested something of myself in that man. Now my love and care were aroused. That's how it goes. First we* give, *then we come to love."*[5]

---

2. Make acting with love something you think about every day. Because the command to love is a general injunction that doesn't always impose clear-cut and immediate responsibilities,* it is easy to go for hours, days, even weeks, without once thinking: "Have I been fulfilling the command to love my neighbor as myself?" To counteract this tendency, the great kabbalist Rabbi Isaac Luria (died 1572) taught that each morning, before praying, we should resolve: "Behold, I accept the positive command of the Creator to 'Love your neighbor as yourself.' "

If we do this every day, we increase the likelihood that it will happen. Indeed, as Rabbi Zelig Pliskin teaches, love of neighbor is the most omnipresent of commandments: "In every encounter with other people, you have an opportunity to either fulfill or violate this commandment."[6]

3. Help others to fulfill their potential. Since loving our neighbor involves wishing for others what we wish for ourselves (see pages 12–13), we

---

*As opposed, for example, to the laws of kashrut, which an observant Jew is compelled to think about every time he or she sits down to eat.

need to do what we can to help others achieve their goals. Sometimes we hold back out of fear that our peers' achievements will come at our own expense. We all know, or have heard, of instances in which managers have refrained from promoting subordinates because they feared the subordinates might outperform them. Compare this behavior with an incident in the Torah. During the Israelites' sojourn in the desert, an unnamed man comes to tell Moses that two men, Eldad and Medad, are prophesying. Although there is no implication that they are speaking falsely in God's name, or saying untrue or irresponsible things, nonetheless, Joshua, Moses' top aide, says to Moses: "My lord Moses, restrain them." Apparently, he is concerned that the two men might become Moses' competitors. Unlike Joshua, Moses is not bothered, and he responds: "Are you jealous for my sake? Would that all the Lord's people were prophets, and the Lord put his spirit upon them!" (Numbers 11:26–29). Moses' trust in God and his generous love of neighbor free him from the ego concerns that cause many of us to act unlovingly to others, and to refuse to encourage their accomplishments.

4. Rejoice in your neighbor's success. The German word *Schadenfreude* describes a common, but ignoble, human tendency: the feeling of some satisfaction, even pleasure, at a neighbor's, even a friend's, misfortune. Dr. Joshua Halberstam, a philosophy professor at New York University, notes that gossip, for example, "thrives on *Schadenfreude.* You're on the phone describing the marital troubles of a mutual friend. Both you and your phone mate are sympathetic and want to help, but both of you also love the crisis. Neither emotion is faked: the sympathy is real, and so is the secret satisfaction."*

Though *Schadenfreude* may be common, an important aspect of loving our neighbor is rejoicing in her achievements and happiness. I once heard a rabbinic colleague describe why he liked someone: "He's really happy at his friends' successes." In order to achieve such happiness, we need to be emotionally healthy. It is impossible for a person who is jealous to properly fulfill the command to "Love your neighbor as yourself."

5. Rejoice in your neighbor's joy. Jewish sources cite helping a bride and groom to rejoice as an example of how to fulfill this commandment. So seriously does Jewish law take this responsibility that the Chaffetz Chayyim's

---

*Halberstam defines *Schadenfreude* as the opposite of envy: "Envy is your private dejection at seeing another succeed; *Schadenfreude* is your private joy at seeing another fail" (*Everyday Ethics,* page 6; for Jewish perspectives on envy and jealousy and how to combat them, see *A Code of Jewish Ethics, Volume 1: You Shall Be Holy,* pages 300–311).

son recorded that his father told him that someone who attends a wedding and makes no effort to bring joy to the newly married couple—for example, through singing, dancing, and speaking warm words to them—is guilty of a form of stealing. The family making the wedding celebration spends a great deal of money and expects the guests to do what they can to make the bride and groom happy. Therefore, to attend a wedding feast and not try to bring joy is a transgression.[7]

6. Speak well of others. As noted, Maimonides rules that one way to fulfill the commandment of love is "to speak in praise of the other" ("Laws of Character Development" 6:3). Many of us don't do this often enough. When two people speak about a third person they know, the conversation, particularly if it lasts for more than a few minutes, often focuses on some flaw that person has. While many Jews realize that this violates the law against *lashon hara,** few realize that it also breaks the commandment to love our neighbor as ourselves; surely, we would be hurt, and feel betrayed, if we knew that others were engaging in such discussions about us.

The unknown mitzvah of lashon hatov

The Hebrew term *lashon hara* refers to negative, critical speech about others. Maimonides proposes, in effect, the precise opposite, *lashon hatov,* good speech, in which we praise others and relate anecdotes that show them in a good light. A friend relates that when "I meet someone I know with their offspring, I compliment the parent to their child. I try to relate something specific that the parent once did, rather than a generic compliment." We often think in terms of complimenting children to their parents, but it is equally important for parents that their children realize that others hold them in high regard.

The Jerusalem writer Sara Rigler offers additional practical suggestions on how to make lashon hatov *a part of daily behavior: "Every night at dinnertime or bedtime, tell your spouse one positive thing about each of your children: 'When Rachel spoke on the phone with her grandmother today, she showed her a lot of love and respect.'" We should also note our spouse's good points to our children [unfortunately, some couples do the opposite and complain about their mate to their children]: "Daddy was very tired tonight, but even so, he helped you with*

*See *A Code of Jewish Ethics, Volume 1: You Shall Be Holy,* pages 332–378.

your homework." Similarly, we should mention our friends' good traits to one another: "Debbie is reliable. She promised to do something for me, and even though it was inconvenient, she followed through." We should speak lashon hatov *about those who work for us as well (many people harp on the flaws of their employees): "My secretary is sick, but she came in today because she knew it was important and I really needed her."*

Concludes Rigler: "With each of these simple statements, you fulfill the most glorious of all mitzvot: *'Love your neighbor as yourself.'* "[8]

---

7. Be generous with time, particularly when the consequences to the other person are significant. I remember reading a comment of Simone Weil (a philosopher and member of the French resistance)* that during the Nazi occupation of France, she knew many people who would willingly have stood on line for hours to procure rationed eggs, but who would not have done so to save the life of someone unrelated to them. In contrast, Yitta Halberstam Mandelbaum relates an incident about the late rabbi Shlomo Carlebach, the great Jewish spiritual teacher, songwriter, and performer, told to her by a woman who was waiting to board a plane from Toronto to New York. The rabbi's flight was fully booked and about to be boarded when an airline representative made an announcement: "There are two people who have medical emergencies and desperately need to get back to New York. We're asking for two volunteers to give up their seats for the sake of these people. The next flight to New York is in three hours. We know it's a great sacrifice and we're sorry to put you in this position. Is there anybody here willing to extend themselves to help these people?" One hand in the crowd immediately shot up. "I'm ready," shouted Rabbi Shlomo Carlebach. A man known to be extraordinarily busy, Carlebach was constantly traveling from concert to concert, and then meeting with and counseling people late into the night. The woman who was present at the airport that morning told Yitta: "Of all of us gathered there that morning, it was Shlomo who probably had the most compelling need to get back fast. He had the least time to spare. But miraculously, he also had the most time to give."[9]

8. Offer justifiable criticism to another. A Midrash teaches: "Love unaccompanied by criticism is not love" (*Genesis Rabbah* 54:3). If two people in a relationship never criticize each other, and never question the other's

*Though of Jewish background, Weil did not identify as a Jew and, unfortunately, expressed, on occasion, hostile anti-Jewish views.

behavior, neither will grow morally. This applies both to relationships between peers and to those between parents and children. King David had an arrogant son, Adonijah, who went about announcing that he would soon be king, even while his frail father still reigned. The Bible points out that David bore some responsibility for the young man's obnoxious behavior since throughout Adonijah's life, he had never challenged him about his bad deeds and asked, "Why did you do that?" (I Kings 1:6). We all need someone who loves us enough to ask us when we have acted inappropriately, "Why did you do that?"*

The question the Bible raises, "Why did you do that?" is precisely the right question to ask when someone has acted in a way that seems to us inappropriate. It is preferable for several reasons to pose such a question, rather than to immediately criticize or condemn the behavior:

- *Maybe the other person has a good reason for his behavior which we have no way of knowing.*
- *By asking this question, the person may on her own reach the conclusion that she erred. If so, she will learn the lesson far more effectively than if we criticize her.*
- *By asking a question, rather than offering criticism—as many of us are apt to do—we are showing respect for the other, a respect that will make it easier for the person to assess his own behavior without becoming defensive.*†[10]

It would seem, therefore, that the problem with King David's behavior was not that he indulged his children, but that he didn't hold them accountable.‡

---

*When we ask this question, what is critical is our tone of voice. The parent should speak in an inquisitive (not inquisitorial) style, the implication being "Explain to me why you did that," rather than suggesting by his voice that what he is really feeling is anger and contempt ("How could you do that!").

†Rabbi Irwin Kula made the point that asking this question of another forces us to step outside of our comfort zone; few of us are comfortable confronting others. So, first, we need to ask ourselves: Is what the other person did really hurtful, or am I overreacting? Is there a benefit of the doubt I should be giving? Did I perhaps contribute to this situation? Am I judging too harshly and too quickly?

‡In a far worse instance, Amnon, David's firstborn son and presumed successor, raped his half sister Tamar. The Bible records that when David heard what happened, "he was very angry." But there is no indication that he expressed that anger to Amnon or punished him in any way. Indeed, the ancient Septuagint translation of the Bible into Greek records that David, though angry, "did not rebuke his son Amnon" (see II Samuel 13).

If someone has hurt you—particularly if it has happened often—you must make your feelings known to the person. If you don't, the other will have no reason to know how painful her behavior is, and your anger, in turn, will grow and may lead to a rupture in the relationship. A wise woman I know told a number of people about unkind comments they had made to her, comments that had deeply hurt and infuriated her. To her shock, these people had not realized how wounding their words were. One woman even cried when she realized how much she had hurt my friend. Witnessing these responses, my friend's anger and bitterness ended and she was able to resume feeling close to, and loving, these people. So, part of the command to love your neighbor is to offer even those with whom we are angry the opportunity to apologize and change and to reenter our circle of love.

---

9. The *Chaffetz Chayyim* teaches that we fulfill the command to love our neighbor when we point out to someone that something he is doing will expose him to disapproval and ridicule (see *Ahavat Chesed [Love of Kindness]* 3:7).[11] To cite a minor, but not trivial, example: Point out to somebody if he is going to an event inappropriately dressed. Though it might be uncomfortable to speak up, if you say nothing, the person may well be embarrassed. In a comparable situation, you would want someone to say something to you.

10. When you give a gift to a friend, don't do so anonymously. The Talmud teaches in the name of Rav: "If one gives a gift to a friend, he must inform him" (*Shabbat* 10b).* Apparently, the Rabbis believed that a person should know who it is that cares about him enough to give him a gift (this would not necessarily apply to a charitable gift, in which case it might be preferable to let the gift remain anonymous and spare the recipient embarrassment). The model for making known one's gift is God Himself. *The Ethics of the Fathers* teaches that when God created man He not only made man in His image, but also that "it was a special [additional] act of love that He informed man that he was created in God's image" (3:14). Feeling loved by God is among the greatest gifts a human being can receive, and that is likely why God makes His love known. So, too, should we make our love known to our friends, through our gifts, our deeds, and our words.

---

*On the same page, the Talmud offers the view of Rabbi Chamma bar Chanina that the giver need not inform the recipient that he is the one who gave the gift, but the Talmud quickly clarifies that the giver need not inform only in an instance when his identity will become known in any case.

It is also important to include a note when we send a gift. By expressing our reasons for offering the gift, even if it is only to say, "I love you," we are, in effect, giving two gifts instead of one.

11. Other people's emotional needs may be very real, and should be satisfied. The sober-minded Rabbi Israel Salanter was once seen standing for an extended period in the middle of the street speaking in a lighthearted and joking manner to an acquaintance. A devotee of the rabbi, surprised by such behavior, questioned him about it. Rabbi Salanter answered: "The man was feeling extremely bitter and depressed, and it was a great act of kindness to cheer him and to make him forget his troubles and his worries. Could I have done this by lecturing him about fear of God or the need for moral improvement? Surely, this could only be done by cheerful speech about down-to-earth matters."

Rabbi Beroka (dates unknown, but in the early centuries of the Common Era) used to go to the marketplace in the city of Bei Lefet (in today's Iran), where the prophet Elijah sometimes appeared to him. Once, Rabbi Beroka asked Elijah: "Is there anyone in this marketplace who has a place in the World-to-Come?" Soon, a man walked by, and Elijah informed him that this man was destined for the World-to-Come. Rabbi Beroka ran after the man and learned that he had risked his life to protect endangered Jews and to alert the Jewish community to antisemitic decrees about to be enacted. A short time later, two other men walked by, and Elijah told him: "These two also have a share in the World-to-Come."

Rabbi Beroka asked them: "What is your occupation?" The men replied: "We are comedians, and we go to cheer up those who are depressed. Also, when we see two people quarreling, we work hard to make peace between them" (Ta'anit *22a). In comparison with the heroic behavior of the first man, the actions of the two comedians seems much less significant. Yet that is not how the Talmud views it. There is much unhappiness in the world, and lightening the burden of those who are sad is of vital importance.*

This same thought is reflected in a teaching of Rabbi Nachman of Bratslav: "With happiness you can give a person life. Thus, a person might be in terrible agony and not be able to express what is in his heart. There is no one to whom he can unburden his heart, so he remains deeply pained and worried. If you come to such a person with a happy face, you can cheer him up and literally give him life. This is a great thing and by no means a minor matter."[12]

---

12. Pray for others. In addition to reciting the prayers in the siddur, the Jewish prayer book, many people offer private prayers to God. Usually, these prayers focus on issues of health, romantic happiness, family welfare (issues involving one's spouse and children), and *parnassah* (financial success and employment). Indeed, I suspect that if an analysis was done of the contents of the tens of thousands of notes tucked into the crevices of the Western Wall in Jerusalem each year,* these themes would predominate. But if we are instructed to want good things for others much as we want them for ourselves (see chapter 1, paragraph 7), then we should express this in our prayers. Therefore, before praying for ourselves and our family's welfare, it is appropriate to offer prayers on behalf of others.

Think of people whom you know are in need. For example:

- Those who are lonely and looking for a partner
- A couple whose child is in crisis
- Someone undergoing professional and/or financial hardship
- Someone who is ill

Offering such prayers will also ensure that we keep other people's needs in mind. Most of us, if we hear of a friend who has lost her job, feel bad at hearing the news, but, unless it's a particularly close friend, we soon stop thinking about it. However, if we pray each morning that she find work, her situation will remain in our consciousness, and we will be far more likely not only to pray on her behalf, but perhaps do something tangible to help her (such as searching out job leads or speaking to others who might be able to assist her).

---

*A friend confided to me that when his daughter became sick with a protracted, serious illness, "Nothing meant more to me personally than when my rabbi [Haskel Lookstein] told me, several times, that for over a year he had been praying daily for my daughter's complete recovery" (*refu'ah shleimah*).*

See pages 72–73 for a prayer that may be offered when we hear a siren, such as that of a passing ambulance.

*These notes are periodically collected and buried, unread.

The highest level of love: When love of neighbor moves us to take risks and make difficult sacrifices

13. The only person whom the Bible describes as literally fulfilling this Torah command is Jonathan, the oldest son of King Saul, who befriended David "and loved him as himself" (I Samuel 18:3). Jonathan gave David his cloak, sword, bow, and belt (I Samuel 18:4). Jonathan's loyalty to his friend forced him into a terrible conflict with his father, Saul, who perceived David as the major threat to his kingship. On occasion, Saul even urged Jonathan to kill David (I Samuel 19:1). Instead, Jonathan did all that he could to dissuade Saul from carrying out his campaign against David,* and warned David of his father's intentions (see I Samuel 20:9–23). Jonathan's relationship with Saul soon deteriorated and, on one occasion—infuriated by Jonathan's continuing friendship with David—Saul threw his spear at him (I Samuel 20:33).

Though Jonathan, as Saul's firstborn son, was heir to the throne, he recognized that his friend was more fit for the position than he, and said to David, "You are going to be king over Israel, and I shall be second to you" (I Samuel 23:17).

Unfortunately, this did not happen, as Jonathan, more loyal to his father than his father was to him, battled alongside Saul against the Philistines, and both men were killed (along with two of Jonathan's three brothers; I Samuel 31:2–6).†[13]

In the past century, among the greatest practitioners of love of neighbor were those Christians and other non-Jews in Europe who, during the Holocaust, risked their lives to save Jews. To cite just two examples:

- In 1940, Bert and Annie Bochove were living above a drugstore they owned outside of Amsterdam. When the Nazis occupied Holland and started deporting Jews, the couple took in Annie's close friend, Henny, and shortly thereafter Henny's husband and sister. Bert Bochove soon constructed a large hiding place between his house and the house next door. He also built a balcony, where he and his wife would air out blankets; that way, those in hiding could crawl onto the balcony, hide behind the blankets, and get some fresh air. In recounting his wartime experiences, Bochove told an interviewer: "And that was the way it went till

---

*Occasionally, during Saul's increasingly rare rational moments, Jonathan's arguments made an impact; see I Samuel 19:6.

†The Rabbis cite the relationship of David and Jonathan as representing a perfect and pure love, one that did not depend on any extraneous causes (*The Ethics of the Fathers* 5:16).

there were thirty-seven people [we were hiding]. . . . We didn't ever talk about [our decision to hide Jews]. It was something you had to do, and it was easy to do because it was your duty."*[14] (Obviously, only a person of extraordinary courage and commitment to love of neighbor would say that "*it was easy to do* because it was your duty.")

• Rabbi Lawrence Kushner tells the story of how a relative of one of his students was saved: "A light snow was falling and the streets were crowded with people. It was Munich in Nazi Germany. One of my rabbinic students, Shifra Penzias, told me her great-aunt, Sussie, had been riding a city bus home from work when SS storm troopers suddenly stopped the coach and began examining the identification papers of the passengers. Most were annoyed, but a few were terrified. Jews were being told to leave the bus and get into a truck around the corner. My student's great-aunt watched from her seat in the rear as the soldiers systematically worked their way down the aisle. She began to tremble, tears streaming down her face. When the man next to her noticed she was crying, he politely asked her why.

" 'I don't have the papers you have. I am a Jew. They're going to take me.'

"The man exploded with disgust. He began to curse and scream at her. 'You stupid bitch,' he roared. 'I can't stand being near you.'

"The SS men asked what all the shouting was about.

" 'Damn her,' the man shouted angrily. 'My wife has forgotten her papers again! I'm so fed up. She always does this.'

"The soldiers laughed and moved on.

"My student said that her great-aunt never saw the man again. She never even knew his name."[15]

And more recent examples:

• In April 1994, the president of Rwanda, a member of the Hutu tribe, was assassinated. This event triggered a Nazi-like campaign by the Hutus

---

*In 1956, Bochove emigrated to the United States. After he died in 1991, his widow Betty (his first wife, Annie, had died in 1949) told an interviewer: "Bert always wanted to be buried in a pine box. So we went to pick out a casket and we saw the fancy ones with velvet lining. We said, 'No, he just wanted the pine box.' The man there said, 'But you don't want that. Those are the Jewish ones.' Then we saw the pine box and that's what we chose. At the cemetery, when the casket was lowered a little, we saw that there was a Jewish star on top. And we thought, 'That's just the way it should be' " (see Gay Block and Malka Drucker, *Rescuers: Portraits of Moral Courage During the Holocaust,* page 47).

against the Tutsi tribe, whom they blamed for the murder, and whom they claimed had earlier oppressed them. In little more than a month, an estimated 800,000 Tutsis were murdered by machete-wielding Hutus. One man, Paul Rusesabagina, a hotel manager and himself a Hutu, repeatedly risked his life, and saved 1,268 Tutsis from certain death by sequestering them at his hotel.*

• In New York City, in January 2007, Wesley Autrey, a fifty-year-old African-American construction worker, saw a stranger, a young man named Cameron Hollopeter, collapse on a New York subway platform, his body convulsing. Hollopeter managed to get up, but then stumbled and fell onto the tracks. At that very second, the headlights of an oncoming train appeared. "I had to make a split-second decision," Autrey said. He leaped onto the tracks and lay on top of Hollopeter, holding him down as five cars passed over them, just inches above Autrey's head. In a manner reminiscent of Bert Bochove, Autrey, who was uninjured, said: "I don't feel like I did something spectacular. I just saw someone who needed help. I did what I felt was right."

• In April 2007, a severely disturbed student named Seung-Hui Cho shot and murdered thirty-two people at Virginia Tech, the worst such attack ever to occur at an American university. A great hero on that tragic day was Dr. Liviu Librescu, a Romanian-born Israeli-American scientist. Though seventy-six years old, Librescu was still actively teaching at Virginia Tech. At one point, Cho, who was firing into classrooms, tried to enter Dr. Librescu's class. Librescu held the door shut, as he urged his students to escape through the windows. Ho kept firing through the door, and Dr. Librescu was struck by five bullets; finally, a shot to the head ended his life. But in the interim, all except one of the students escaped. Caroline Merrey described how she and twenty other students made it to safety, as Librescu kept shouting at them to hurry. Another student, Asael Arad, said that he and the other students "lived because of him."

Librescu was murdered on Yom HaShoah (the Holocaust Remembrance Day). Two days later (April 18, 2007), in a speech at the U.S. Holocaust Memorial Museum, President George W. Bush said: "That day [referring to the slaughter at Virginia Tech] we saw horror, but we also saw quiet acts of courage. We saw the courage in a teacher named

---

*The story of Rusesabagina's remarkable act of heroism is portrayed in the film *Hotel Rwanda*.

Liviu Librescu. With the gunman set to enter his class, this brave professor blocked the door with his body while his students fled to safety. On the Day of Remembrance, this Holocaust survivor gave his own life so that others may live. And this morning, we honor his memory, and we take strength from his example."

These episodes remind us not only how difficult it is to fully carry out the commandment "Love your neighbor as yourself," but how few people fulfill it in the most trying circumstances.

The contemporary Jewish philosopher Professor David Shatz has persuasively argued that while we rightfully regard these people as heroes, Jewish law does not obligate *a person to put his or her life at risk. Although Jewish law forbids killing an innocent person to save one's own life (see page 352), it does not insist that a bystander intervene at risk of his life as, for example, Paul Rusesabagina repeatedly did, as Wesley Autrey did, and as Liviu Librescu did (at the cost of his life).*[16] *And yet, thank God, there are people who go beyond the demands of the law, and model for us the greatness of which human beings are capable.**

The neighbor's responsibility

14. While the biblical law imposes upon us the responsibility to act in a loving way toward our neighbor, the neighbor, too—and we are all neighbors to others—has a responsibility to allow other people to love him or her. Someone who rebuffs friendly overtures or frequently responds with annoyance or coldness—and I recognize this is often done unconsciously—makes it difficult for those endeavoring to fulfill this commandment.

Similarly, there are people who expect others to know what their precise needs are, and who respond with annoyance and in anger when their needs, even if unexpressed, are not met. This makes it hard for even the most sincere practitioners of love of neighbor to fulfill the commandment.

Martin Buber related a tale about the Chasidic rebbe, Moshe Leib of Sassov (1745–1807), who claimed to have learned the meaning of love from a peasant who was sitting near him in a tavern:† *"He was sitting in an inn along with*

---

*For two additional instances in which people risked their lives to save others, see pages 366–367.

†Right away Buber makes us aware that we're dealing with an unusual sort of rabbi.

other peasants, drinking. For a long time he was as silent as all the rest, but when he was moved by the wine, he asked one of the men seated beside him, 'Tell me, do you love me or don't you love me?' The other replied, 'I love you very much.' But the first peasant replied, 'You say that you love me, but you do not know what I need. If you really loved me, you would know.' The other had not a word to say to this, and the peasant who had put the question fell silent again. But I understood. To know the needs of men and to bear the burden of their sorrow, that is the true love of men."[17]

I first came across this story about thirty-five years ago, and was deeply affected by it, for it states that it is our obligation to know the needs and sorrows of others, and seek to help them even without being asked.

One day, though, it occurred to me that the second peasant might truly have loved his friend, but just didn't know what was bothering him or precisely what he needed. Indeed, how many people who know you—and who may well love you—might not be aware of all the things that cause you to be upset or sad? Rather than accuse his friend of not loving him, perhaps the first peasant should have told his friend what he needed or what was troubling him and thereby offered him the chance to be helpful and empathetic.

*This is particularly important for those people who want their spouses or partners to know what it is they need without their having to spell it out (the implicit statement seems to be "If I have to tell you what I need, then even if you do it, that's not enough"). This attitude leads to people, like the first peasant in the story, feeling unloved, and to the partner—who might have large reservoirs of love and goodwill—being made to feel unjustifiably guilty for supposedly being insensitive and unloving.**

While it is our neighbor's responsibility to show us love, it is not his responsibility to be a mind reader. The fact that someone might not be intuitive does not make him a bad or unloving neighbor. So, make sure you give your neighbor, your friends, and your spouse, a chance to love you.

---

15. To be a good neighbor, you must be willing to accept help, not just offer it. Rabbi Abraham Twerski, the psychiatrist who founded the Gateway Rehabilitation Center, a program in Pittsburgh that helps recovering addicts, writes of Bonnie, a woman who had remained sober for almost a year. During an extended cold spell, the furnace in her apartment broke down; for

*In addition, telling people what we need once or twice is usually insufficient. People often have to be reminded of the specific needs of others, just as we ourselves often have to be reminded of others' needs.

three nights, until a repairman was able to fix it, she slept in an unheated apartment.

When a mutual friend of both Bonnie and Rabbi Twerski learned what had happened, she said to Bonnie: "How silly of you. You could have called me or any of your friends and stayed with us." Bonnie responded: "I don't like to impose."

When the friend related what had happened to Rabbi Twerski, he called Bonnie and told her that he was disappointed because he had hoped to be able to ask her to help newcomers to the twelve-step program adjust to their struggle. Bonnie was taken aback: "You can call on me anytime, Doctor. I'll be glad to help."

"No, I cannot," Twerski responded. "If you cannot accept help, you cannot give it either."[18]

At first reading, Rabbi Twerski's words sound almost harsh and punitive, but he recognized that a person who cannot accept help implies that asking for, or accepting, assistance is shameful* (in other words, if you cannot bring yourself to ask others for help, how can you expect others to ask you for help). That is why such people are not the best at offering help since even when they extend assistance they may unconsciously convey the attitude that those who need help should be embarrassed.

In addition, by accepting help, we enable another person to fulfill the command to "Love your neighbor," while when we refuse help, we limit someone else's ability to observe this commandment.

Erving Goffman's book Stigma, *a study of how people with disabilities cope, cited the comment of a person with a handicap who had learned through experience the wisdom of sometimes accepting even unnecessary offers of help: "If [a person with a handicap] wants the ice to be broken, he must admit the value of help and allow people to give it to him. Innumerable times I have seen the fear or bewilderment in people's eyes vanish as I have stretched out my hand for help, and I have felt life and warmth stream from the helping hands I have taken. We are not always aware of the help we may give by accepting aid, that in this way we may establish a foothold for contact."*[19]

A tale related by Rabbi Aaron Levine reminds us of the great, but sometimes overlooked, benefit in being able to solicit help: "A little boy was struggling to lift

---

*Alternatively, Bonnie might have just suffered from low self-esteem and felt that she didn't deserve to impose on others because she wasn't worth it, while other people were.

a heavy stone but could not budge it. The boy's father, who happened to be watching, said to his son, "Are you using all your strength?"

"Yes, I am," the boy said with irritation.

"No, you're not," the father answered. "You have not asked me to help you."[20]

Convicts, wives, and the commandment of love: Two teachings from the Talmud

16. To most people's surprise, even shock, the Talmud teaches that the law of love of neighbor applies even to a prisoner sentenced to be executed. According to the Rabbis, this law dictates that the sentence be carried out as quickly as possible; what society owes the prisoner is a *mitah yaffa,* "a good death," which Jewish law understands as meaning a quick one (*Ketubot* 37b).*

Perhaps no rabbinic teaching on the love of neighbor so highlights the notion that this commandment is concerned more with appropriate actions than with feelings. It is difficult to imagine that the Torah expects us to *feel* as deep a sense of love, for example, for a premeditated murderer as we feel for ourselves. But what this law does demand is that we treat the individual as we would want to be treated if we were the one sentenced to die. The law requires therefore that we never torture a convict by prolonging his death (the Romans practiced crucifixion, which Jewish law forbade, specifically to extend and intensify the person's suffering).†

One can think of few human beings more deserving of a painful death than Adolf Eichmann, the main administrator of the Nazis' Final Solution. When he was executed in Israel in 1962, there were many tens of thousands of Israelis who

---

*Also, as my friend Professor Michael Berger notes, "an unmessy one." Thus, decapitation is quick, but because it leaves the body disfigured and open to disgrace and ridicule it is not regarded as "a good death," and was not permitted in Jewish law.

†The Talmud also cites the law of love of neighbor to justify permitting a child to perform a bloodletting procedure upon a parent. Jewish law, based on Exodus 21:15, ruled that a child who intentionally wounded a parent and drew blood was subject to a death sentence (*Sanhedrin* 84b; one senses that this law was meant to underscore the seriousness of striking a parent; there is no record of such a punishment ever being carried out). Because bloodletting was a medical procedure (for most of recorded history, it was believed that drawing out supposedly sick blood from an ill person improved the person's health) the Rabbis ruled that in this case the Torah law didn't apply; they reasoned that while parents would not want to be struck by a child, they would want the child to perform such a procedure since it could prolong the parent's life or perhaps even effect a cure. The Rabbis based their ruling on the law of "Love your neighbor as yourself," and reasoned: Treat your "neighbor"—in this instance, your parent—as you would want to be treated.

were survivors of the Holocaust and victims of Eichmann's behavior. Yet, in line with Jewish law, he was given a quick death by hanging.

---

17. Love of neighbor and of one's wife. The Talmud also applies the verse concerning love of neighbor to one's wife (*Kiddushin* 41a).* Reuven Kimelman, a professor of Talmud at Brandeis University, expands on this rabbinic law, explaining why it is important to specifically apply this verse to one's spouse: "I have been at social events where I have heard men say things about their wives that they wouldn't say about their business partners if they intended to stay in business with them. Yet, if you ask them why they speak like that about their wives, they answer, 'Oh, my wife knows that I love her.' The proof of whether you have fulfilled 'Love your neighbor as yourself' toward your wife is not that you think you fulfilled it, but that she does."†

Kimelman's insight offers us important guidance on how to fulfill this command toward everyone, not just one's wife. Most of us, when acting kindly, treat others as we would like to be treated, which is indeed what Maimonides insisted upon. But sometimes even this behavior, though laudable, may not be enough since what the other person *needs* from us might not be the same as what we need from them. Thus, it is not enough for a man to feel that he treats his wife in what he considers a loving manner; the question is, does he give her what she needs to feel that he loves her?

In the more egalitarian world in which we now live, this application of love of neighbor cuts in both directions: Does your wife feel that you love her as you love yourself? Does your husband feel that you love him as you love yourself?

Rabbi Zelig Pliskin emphasizes that although it might seem self-evident that we are obliged to love our spouse and other close relatives, "it is still necessary to mention since some people are careful to do chesed *(acts of kindness) for strangers, but forget that they have a similar, and even greater, obligation toward their relatives."[21] That is because people often take their loved ones for granted. Consequently, for example, they feel safe in criticizing their spouses, children, or*

*The Talmud makes this point to underscore the importance of a man meeting a woman before he marries her (sometimes, when a marriage was arranged, the couple would meet only at the time of the ceremony), lest he find himself unattracted and even repulsed, and come to violate the command to love one's neighbor as oneself.

†I am paraphrasing this comment, which I heard orally from Dr. Kimelman over twenty years ago, so these are not his precise words.

siblings, whether facetiously or seriously, in the presence of others. They would not do this with other people because they know it would jeopardize the relationship. "With a loved one, however, they feel that the relationship is so secure they can get away with this behavior. Often, they discover too late that such is not the case" (Dr. Isaac Herschkopf).

Hospitality

Let all who are hungry come in and eat,
let all who are needy come in and
make Passover.

Passover Haggadah

3

BEING A GOOD HOST

1. The Hebrew term for "hospitality" is *hachnasat orchim,* literally "bringing in guests." This Hebrew usage implies that we should actively recruit ("bring in") guests, and look for opportunities to invite people to our home.

My life was deeply and permanently enriched by an act of hospitality I experienced more than thirty years ago. A friend and I found ourselves in central Louisiana with the Sabbath approaching. We had with us the Jewish Travel Guide, *and found in it an invitation: "Anyone visiting Alexandria, Louisiana, who wishes kosher food should contact Dr. Bernard Kaplan," whose phone number was listed. We called and were invited to spend Shabbat with him, his wife, Jean, and their family of six, and shortly thereafter seven, children. We have remained close with them (unfortunately, Dr. Kaplan has since died) ever since. Their behavior exemplifies the meaning of* hachnasat orchim; *their notice in the* Jewish Travel Guide *actively recruited and welcomed guests.*

Guidelines from the Bible

2. The Torah describes in detail a hot afternoon when the patriarch Abraham saw three men* passing near his tent. "As soon as [Abraham] saw them, he ran from the entrance of the tent to greet them and . . . said: 'My Lords, if I find favor in your eyes, do not go on past your servant. Let a little water be brought; bathe your feet and recline under the tree. And let me fetch a morsel of bread that you may refresh yourselves. . . . They replied, 'Do as you have said.' " Abraham rushed to inform Sarah about the guests. The couple immediately started to prepare a lavish meal, which Abraham personally served to the guests. Later, when the men continued on their journey, Abraham walked alongside them to see them off (Genesis 18:1–16).

*Only later, after he had entertained them, did Abraham realize that the three men were angels disguised as human beings.

Jewish tradition derives several still-binding principles of hospitality and good manners from Abraham's behavior:

• *Receive your guests warmly and enthusiastically.* When Abraham first saw the three men walking in the desert, he ran to greet them. Then, in extending his invitation, he emphasized that the travelers would be honoring him if they accepted his hospitality ("... if I find favor in your eyes, do not go past your servant"), thereby making it more comfortable for them to do so. By displaying such enthusiasm, Abraham made his guests feel wanted.

• *Think first of what your guests most need.* Knowing that the men had been walking in the desert for hours, Abraham brought them water to drink and in which to bathe their feet. He also offered them a shady tree—a valuable commodity in the desert—under which to rest. Knowing that they were probably hungry, he immediately prepared food.

• *Deliver more than you promise.* At first, all Abraham told the men is that he would "fetch a morsel of bread that you may refresh yourselves." But he soon served them an elaborate meal, complete with lamb and cakes. The Talmud infers from Abraham's behavior that one of the "distinguishing characteristic of righteous people" is that "they say little but do a lot" (*Bava Mezia* 87a).*

Promising people less rather than more is also prudent behavior. People who arrive with limited expectations are apt to be appreciative of all that they are given, while those who arrive with great, and possibly exaggerated, expectations are likely to focus on all that they expected to receive and didn't.

• *Personally attend to your guests' needs.* Abraham had a large staff (see Genesis 14:14), but he waited on his guests himself (Genesis 18:8). We learn from this that even if you have maids and other employees, make sure to do some of the work for your guests with your own hands.

Rabbi Gamliel, the president of the Sanhedrin, personally waited upon guests at his son's wedding. Rabbi Eliezer thought it inappropriate to be served by so distinguished a host (as if a guest at the White House was waited

*In addition, by telling guests that you are preparing only a little, they'll feel less self-conscious about accepting the invitation.

*upon by the resident), and reproved Rabbi Joshua for permitting Gamliel to serve him. Joshua answered: "We find that someone even greater than Gamliel served his guests: Abraham . . ." (*Kiddushin *32b).*

The Chaffetz Chayyim's family once saw him making the bed for an expected guest, and asked him not to bother; they would do it. The Chaffetz Chayyim continued making the bed, and said to them: "When it comes to the mitzvah of putting on tefillin *would you also like to fulfill it for me to save me the bother?"*[1]

• *Accompany your guests on their way.* When Abraham's guests concluded their visit, he walked with them for a distance. By this gesture, he made it clear that he had enjoyed their company so much that he wished to remain with them a little longer. Like Abraham, we should do more than see our guests to the door; at the very least, we should escort them into the street or to their car.

When guests leave our house, my wife, Dvorah, insists on our waiting until the guests drive away, and we all stand and wave.

---

3. When Abraham dispatches his trusted servant Eliezer to the far-off city of Nahor to find a wife for Isaac, Abraham's son, the patriarch offers Eliezer no specific guidelines other than that the woman should come from the area of Nahor in which Abraham was raised. En route to the city, Eliezer decides that the most important characteristic he should seek in a spouse for Isaac is kindness and hospitality. As he enters the town, he offers the following prayer: "O Lord, God . . . Here I stand by the spring as the daughters of the townsmen come out to draw water. Let the maiden to whom I say, 'Please, lower your jar so that I may drink,' and who replies, 'Drink, and I will also water your camels,' let her be the one whom you have decreed for Your servant Isaac' " (Genesis 24:12–14). A few minutes later, he sees Rebecca coming to the well with a jug on her shoulder. Eliezer asks her for a small sip, and she offers him water, and then offers to bring water for his camels.* When he asks her if there is room in her father's house to spend the night, she immediately invites him to lodge there, and Eliezer understands that his

---

*Not a small undertaking, given that Eliezer had ten camels with him, and each camel can consume as much as twenty gallons of water.

prayers have been answered. Rebecca soon becomes Isaac's wife and Judaism's second matriarch. But her worthiness to have such a role is first revealed through her kindness and warm hospitality.

4. After Moses kills an Egyptian taskmaster who is mercilessly beating an Israelite slave, he learns that the matter has become known and he is forced to flee Egypt. Almost immediately, he finds himself in a new confrontation when he sees the male shepherds of Midian preventing the seven daughters of Jethro from using the local well. He stands up on their behalf and enables them to draw water. The women return home and tell their father that "an Egyptian rescued us from the shepherds; he even drew water for us and watered the flock" (Exodus 2:19). Jethro immediately dispatches his daughters back to the well: "Why did you leave the man? Ask him in to break bread." Moses accepts Jethro's hospitality, and shortly thereafter takes one of the daughters, Zipporah, as his wife (Exodus 2:21).

This episode reminds us of what should be self-evident, but often isn't: Take special care to be kind and hospitable to those who have helped you. Also, bear in mind, as Jethro did but his daughters did not, that all people, even those who appear to be self-sufficient, might be in need of hospitality.

5. The Bible and runaway slaves. The Torah commands nations as well as individuals to be hospitable. Three thousand years before the American Supreme Court ruled that slaves who fled to freedom in the North should be forcibly returned to slavery (*Dred Scott* decision, 1857), the Torah commanded precisely the opposite: "You shall not turn over to his master a slave who seeks refuge with you from his master. He shall live with you in any place he may choose among the settlements in your midst, wherever he pleases; you must not ill-treat him" (Deuteronomy 23:16–17). In modern times, this ancient biblical law would seem to mandate granting political asylum (the ultimate act of hospitality) to those fleeing dictatorial and totalitarian regimes.*

---

*In context, Maimonides understands this law as applying to a non-Hebrew slave belonging to a Hebrew master who wishes to move to Israel (see "Laws of Slavery" 8:9–10). In Onkelos's translation of the Torah, he interprets the verse as referring to a non-Hebrew slave of a Gentile master who flees to Israel. While the Torah, written many thousands of years ago, obviously did not offer specific legislation for a society such as the United States, it would seem that the ethical upshot of this verse, "You shall not turn over to his master a slave who seeks refuge with you from his master," would apply to a society such as ours, and certainly to the Jewish community in Israel.

While in his twenties, Rabbi Bradley Artson, the dean of the Ziegler School of Rabbinic Studies at the American Jewish University in Los Angeles, worked as a legislative aide to the speaker of the California state assembly. Artson recalls that one of his duties was to respond to constituents' letters: "At the height of the [1970s] influx of Indochinese refugees (the so-called boat people), we were inundated with letters opposing their admission to California. That same week, the San Francisco Chronicle *reported the case of a woman whose will stipulated that her pet dog be put to sleep after her death. We received hundreds of letters from people who offered to take the dog into their own homes while simultaneously protesting the rescue of the drowning refugees."**[2]

---

6. The book of Proverbs teaches: "Better a meal of vegetables where there is love than a fattened ox where there is hate" (Proverbs 15:17). In other words, we would all like to be guests where we sense our presence is wanted and appreciated. As the Talmud puts it: "One who shows his white teeth to his friend [in a smile] is better than one who gives him milk to drink" (*Ketubot* 111b).

Other biblical verses extol hospitality as well. Most notably, Job, defending himself against accusations that his sufferings must have come as punishment for his sins, reminds his accusers that, among his other virtues, "the stranger did not lodge in the street, but I opened my door to the traveler" (Job 31:32).

The sin of inhospitality: Sodom, Moab, and Ammon

7. Several biblical episodes focus on inhospitality as indicative of terrible character. Most notorious in this regard are the citizens of Sodom. In the chapter following the Bible's depiction of Abraham's gracious reception of his three guests, two of the guests proceed to the city of Sodom, where Abraham's nephew, Lot, resides. Like his uncle, Lot provides the men with extensive hospitality, including a lavish meal. However, the Sodomites were extremely antagonistic to visitors, and the men of the town surrounded Lot's house, and demanded that he expel the visitors so that they could rape them. God quickly proceeds to destroy Sodom, presumably for this, as well as

---

*See page 289 regarding Menachem Begin's first act as Israel's prime minister.

other offenses, though this sin, their desire to attack Lot's guests, is the only one specified (Genesis 19).

---

*The Rabbis of the Talmud tell the following story about Sodom. When a poor man came to the city, each citizen would give him a dinar, a coin of some value, with the owner's name inscribed on it. However, the citizens would conspire not to sell the man any food, not even a morsel of bread. Eventually, the poor man would die of starvation, and the Sodomites would come and each one would take back his coin (*Sanhedrin *109b).*

---

8. The Torah expresses great condemnation of the citizens of Moab and Ammon, "because they did not meet you [the Israelites] with food and water on your journey after you left Egypt . . ." (Deuteronomy 23:5).

---

*In the talmudic discussion of this verse, Rabbi Yochanan comments on the capacity of inhospitality to "repulse those who would otherwise be near, while [timely hospitality] draws near those who would otherwise be distant" (*Sanhedrin *103b).*

Guidelines from the Talmud and medieval codes

9. "Hospitality is even greater than receiving the divine presence" (*Shabbat* 127a). Rabbi Judah, the author of this teaching, derived this conclusion from the behavior of Abraham, who was visited by God, but who immediately broke away when he saw needy travelers in the distance (Genesis 18:1–2).

10. The Talmud records that Rabbi Huna, when making a meal, would open the door of his home and announce, "Let whoever is in need come in and eat" (*Ta'anit* 20b). This behavior might not be feasible for most of us today, but what we *can* do is volunteer at a soup kitchen where all who are hungry are invited to a meal.

11. A well-known talmudic comment about hospitality initially comes across as disparaging to women: "A woman looks with a more grudging eye upon guests than a man" (*Bava Mezia* 87a). Although it seems from this statement that the Talmud regards women as more reluctant than men to extend themselves, Rabbi Berel Wein offers a more nuanced explanation.[3]

Some women might be less happy about having guests than men, Wein concedes, but it has nothing to do with being selfish; rather, they know that the work involved will overwhelmingly fall on them. The husband might be happy to sit at the table and converse with the visitors, but the cooking, serving, cleaning, and other chores will fall primarily on the wife. Hence, hospitality must be understood as a project for the whole family, and one in which every family member participates. "Otherwise," as the late rabbi Richard Israel, a longtime and enthusiastic practitioner of *hachnasat orchim,* wrote, "the burden will fall on too few members of the family, who may not only be too busy to enjoy guests, but may even come to resent them."[4]

As regards the importance of acknowledging the family members who work hardest on the Sabbath preparations, Rabbi Reuven Bulka tells of a woman who complained to her rabbi about her spouse's insensitivity: "I work most of the week, but take off on Friday to create a special ambience on the Sabbath. I bake the challah, make fresh gefilte fish, prepare special chicken soup, and prepare other foods that we particularly like, like potato kugel. I even make his favorite desserts. I also clean the house and make sure that everything looks wonderful and is ready."

"That all sounds good to me," the rabbi said. "So what's the problem?"

"The problem is that after I do all this, what does my husband do? He thanks God for the delicious meal."

The woman was, of course, referring to the Birkat HaMazon, *the Grace after Meals, and while such thanks to God is appropriate, there is something very "wrong if that is the only thanks offered. The after meal gratitude must . . . acknowledge everyone who helped prepare the meal."*[5]

---

12. Hosts should maintain a pleasant expression on their face. If a host looks anxious or displeased, even if it is because of something unrelated, the guest will feel that something she is doing is upsetting the host.[6]

13. In a similar vein, Maimonides teaches that "one should not look at the face of a person who is eating, or at the portion [he has taken] lest he become embarrassed" ("Laws of Blessings" 7:6). Such scrutiny will make the guest feel that his table manners are being observed or that you are begrudging him the food he is eating. In either case, the guest will become self-conscious and eat less than he would like.

14. Don't refrain from offering hospitality out of fear that you are not sufficiently affluent to host your guests lavishly: "One is not obligated to feed his guests meat and wine," the *Sefer Chasidim* (# 56) reminds us: just serve what you can afford. When people become overly concerned about the impression they are making, they will either refrain from extending hospitality because of the expense and effort, or will spend more than they can afford. Neither alternative is good. The main requirement in fulfilling the mitzvah of hospitality is being hospitable.

On the other hand, it is always wise to prepare some extra food, instead of the precise amount you think you'll need. A Midrash tells of a man named Bar Yochani who was preparing a banquet for some Roman notables. When he spoke about the event with Rabbi Eliezer ben Yossi, the rabbi advised him, "If you intend to invite twenty, prepare enough for twenty-five, and if you intend to invite twenty-five, prepare enough for thirty."

Instead, Bar Yochani prepared one portion less than he needed, undoubtedly assuming that of the twenty-five guests he invited, at least one would cancel. None did, and he found himself short a dish. That guest, in turn, was furious at him.

Later, Bar Yochani asked Rabbi Eliezer how he could be so knowledgeable about the etiquette of entertaining: "Has God revealed to you scholars the secrets of entertaining as well?" The rabbi answered that he had learned this lesson from the Bible. The text teaches, "When Abner came to David in Hebron accompanied by twenty men, David made a feast for Abner and for the men with him" (II Samuel 3:20). It doesn't simply say, "David made a feast," but it adds, "and for the men with him" (in other words, David prepared more than enough since he had no way of knowing precisely how many people would accompany Abner; see Esther Rabbah *2:4).*

While such advice would apply, I believe, to guests at one's house, or at a celebratory kiddush *in synagogue (in which a larger crowd than expected might show up), I don't think it need apply to a formal celebration in which guests are asked to send back response cards noting whether or not they are attending. While it is possible that a very small number of people who don't respond might show up, it is even more likely that, from a large crowd, a few will cancel at the last minute. I mention this, because in the case of formal catered events, preparing for an additional 20 percent—or even 10 percent—of guests (as Rabbi Eliezer ben Yossi suggested) can be prohibitively expensive.*

---

15. When hosting, try to ensure that nothing is said that embarrasses a guest. For example, don't ask a visitor a question about the Torah—or any subject—unless you have reason to believe that he is knowledgeable in the area about which you are speaking (*Sefer Chasidim* 684).* In short, avoid a situation that will leave a guest feeling ignorant or looked down upon. For example, if you have occasion to explain a basic Jewish ritual (perhaps the lighting of Shabbat candles or the kiddush over the wine), make sure not to do so in a condescending manner. Similarly, if you have wealth, make sure that you don't flaunt it in a manner that may make a guest feel poor (even if just in comparison to you).

At the Passover Seder, many Jews read aloud from the Haggadah both in Hebrew and in English. A dear friend who is fluent in Hebrew makes sure to be the first at his Seder to read a paragraph in English. That way, when he later asks a guest who cannot read Hebrew to read a passage, the person does not feel that he is being looked upon condescendingly or as an ignoramus if he reads in English.

---

16. At all costs, avoid inhospitality. The Talmud attributes the destruction of the Second Temple—perhaps the greatest catastrophe in Jewish life prior to the Holocaust—to an act of extreme inhospitality. An unnamed host sent out his servant to invite guests to a reception he was throwing. Among the invitees he named were many distinguished rabbis, along with a man named Kamtza. The servant, however, accidentally invited a man with a similar name, Bar Kamtza, who, unbeknownst to the servant, his master despised. When the host saw Bar Kamtza at the party, he told him to leave. Bar Kamtza pleaded with the host not to eject him, and even offered to pay half the party's expenses, and later all the expenses, just so that he not be humiliated in front of the other guests. The host ignored Bar Kamtza's pleas, pulled him out of his chair, and threw him out. Bar Kamtza grew enraged not only at the host, but at the rabbis who were present and who had not intervened on his behalf. He went to the Roman officials who ruled over Judaea and convinced them that the Jews were plotting a revolt, an act which set in motion a whole series of unhappy events and which culminated in the siege of Jerusalem and the Temple's destruction (*Gittin* 55b–56a).

The upshot for us of this sad story? Once a person is in your home, even

---

*See *A Code of Jewish Ethics, Volume 1: You Shall Be Holy,* page 218, which cites a midrashic tale in which Rabbi Yannai, in a moment of anger, embarrassed an unlearned guest at his table, an act for which he soon repented.

if you dislike him, treat him politely. Bar Kamtza's subsequent behavior reveals him to have been a person of the lowest-possible character (this is probably the reason the host didn't want him present, and the rabbis stood by and said nothing when he was ejected). But even so, it would have been far better had the host and the rabbis acted differently.

A friend who read this section commented that the term "inhospitality" was being used too broadly. He argued that inhospitality is generally an act of omission, that is, a lack of hospitality. But what was done to Bar Kamtza was far worse. It was an act of humiliation, exacerbated by his begging the host not to eject him. Bar Kamtza's not being invited in the first place might have been inhospitable, but unlikely to provoke such rage.

Additional guidelines

17. Feed guests immediately, particularly those who are poor or who have come from a distance. The Chaffetz Chayyim, when entertaining Shabbat guests who he had reason to believe were painfully hungry, would delay singing the *Shalom Aleichem*—a song that precedes the Friday night meal—so that the meal could be served more quickly. Only after the guests had eaten would the *Shalom Aleichem* be sung.*

18. Be hospitable both to the "hungry" and the "needy." A prayer recited near the beginning of the Passover Seder enjoins us: "Let all who are *hungry* come in and eat, let all who are *needy* come in and make Passover." Most participants in the Seder understand "needy" as simply a synonym for "hungry," and the prayer as a reminder to care for the destitute. Shmuel Yosef Agnon, the Israeli Nobel laureate in literature, wrote a story, "The Passover Celebrants," to highlight the difference between "hungry" and "needy." In a small eastern European town lived a *shammes,* a synagogue attendant, who was so poor that he didn't have enough money to buy food for his Passover Seder. He walked around the town alone, too embarrassed to confide to others the depth of his poverty. In the same town lived a wealthy widow, whose husband had recently died. Out of habit, she prepared a beautiful Seder, but

---

*My friend, Professor Michael Berger, rightly notes that such behavior is appropriate only in an instance when the guests' hunger is very great; however, this behavior of the Chaffetz Chayyim should not serve as a precedent for people eating before *Shalom Aleichem* simply because they are hungry.

because she had no one to share it with, she, too, was in distress. In the street, she met the *shammes,* and invited him to celebrate the Seder with her. By the end of the evening, the two forged a powerful connection, and there was reason to hope that soon he would no longer be "hungry," and she would no longer be "needy."

In today's relatively affluent Jewish community, there might be more lonely Jews than impoverished ones (though impoverished Jews do exist). Think, therefore, of the elderly, the widowed, the divorced, the socially awkward, and those who might have little societal status. When you make your guest list, think of those who, if not invited, will dine alone.

During the years following my father's death, several of my mother's neighbors extended her repeated and continued hospitality whenever she was in Brooklyn. One couple in particular, Rabbi David and Chani Schertzer, invited my mother to both Friday evening dinners and Shabbat lunches every Shabbat for fifteen years, an outstanding—I would say staggering—act of hospitality and generosity.

Many Jews call up their synagogue in advance of Passover to ask for names of people who would appreciate hospitality for the Seder. This is a very worthy tradition.

---

*Chaim Weizmann, Israel's first president and a longtime Zionist leader, once said: "The only people invited to lunch are people who have a place to eat even if they are not invited." The Talmud, therefore, urged Jews to "Let your house be open wide, and let the poor be members of your household" (*The Ethics of the Fathers *1:5).*

---

19. When an accident happens,* and something is spilled or broken, minimize your expressions of distress so that the guest is not made to feel ashamed. Rabbi Akiva Eger (1761–1837), a German-Jewish scholar, was hosting a holiday meal when a guest tipped over his wine cup and stained the beautiful tablecloth. Within seconds, Rabbi Eger nudged the table, thereby toppling his own cup as well, and remarked, "The table must be somewhat unbalanced."

*I originally wrote, "If an accident happens," but changed it to "When . . ." because accidents invariably occur, and we should not feel shocked or particularly unlucky when a routine accident, such as a spill or the breaking of a glass or dish, occurs.

This story highlights Rabbi Eger's sensitivity, but it also reminds us that it takes intelligence and creativity to be a truly thoughtful person. Within the briefest period after the guest spilled the wine, Rabbi Eger perceived what was needed to ease the man's embarrassment.

---

*A modern-day version of this story, related to me by Dr. Isaac Herschkopf: "I was dining with Lord Attenborough, the renowned British director [*Gandhi*] and actor [*The Great Escape*], at a restaurant. Just as he reached the punch line of a hilarious story, our teenage busboy accidentally spilled some water. The table erupted in laughter. I, and apparently Attenborough, noticed the busboy wincing in horror, thinking that we were all laughing at him. Attenborough immediately stifled the laughter, grabbed the young man by the arm, and pulled him over. He patiently and lovingly explained that the table was laughing at a funny story he had told, and not, of course, at the busboy's mishap. The young man went from about to cry to a beaming smile in less than a minute. . . . As funny as the anecdote must have been," my friend recalled, "I have no recollection of it. I will always remember, however, the extraordinary kindness and hospitality shown by Attenborough, the most prominent person in that room, to that busboy."*

A final thought: On the great merit of being a host

20. In an essay titled "Hospitality Should Be Practiced Religiously," Rabbi Richard Israel reflects on the role that *hachnasat orchim* played in his own life, going back to his first experience of a deeply needed act of hospitality many decades earlier: "Forty years ago in Safed [Israel], a friend and I were desperately looking for a hotel room late one Friday afternoon. There were none to be found. A young schoolteacher, whom I remember today only as Judah, witnessed our consternation as we vainly sought accommodations. He approached us and said, 'It is unthinkable that Jews should be without a place to stay on Shabbat. You will come home with me.' . . . Since that time, my life was saved by a Jewish doctor who took me into his home in southern India when I was very ill with boils; I was invited home for lunch by a lady in Rome because she heard me speaking Hebrew; as a student, I schnorred my way across the country never paying for lodging because there was always the home of a friend of a friend of a friend with whom I could stay. I could multiply the stories endlessly. I will never be able to reciprocate these people's hospitality. All that I can do is to give to guests what some other hosts have given to me and hope that they will do the same for others."[7]

In the same essay, Rabbi Israel offers commonsense advice that will help make entertaining more satisfying and pleasant for hosts and guests alike: Let your guests help you clear away food, clean the dishes, and restore the house to order. Doing so will not only make your life easier and help you avoid the feeling of dread at what you will be stuck with when the guests leave, it actually makes guests (at least the considerate ones) feel more relaxed about accepting your hospitality,[8] and feel more included in your family. In an odd way, I've always felt complimented when my hosts feel comfortable enough to let me share in the process of cleaning up.

4

THE DUTIES OF A GUEST

1. Be grateful to your hosts. This is the criterion the Talmud uses to distinguish good guests from bad ones: "What does a good guest say? 'How much trouble has my host gone to for me. How much meat he set before me. How much wine he brought me. How many cakes he served me. And all this trouble he has gone to for my sake!' But what does a bad guest say? 'What kind of effort did the host make for me? I have eaten only one piece of meat and I have drunk only one cup of wine! Whatever trouble the host went to was done only for the sake of his wife and children' " (*Berachot* 58a).

Think about the effort your hosts have made on your behalf. If they have been generous to you in providing hospitality, then be generous to them in assessing their behavior and expressing gratitude.

2. In the *Birkat HaMazon* (Grace after Meals), a special prayer is inserted for guests to recite on their hosts' behalf: "May the Merciful One bless the master of this house, the lady of this house, both them, their home, their family, and all that is theirs."

—

The Talmud offers a more specifically phrased version of the blessing for hosts: "May it be God's will that my host not be shamed in this world or humiliated in the World-to-Come" (Berachot *46a*). *Rabbi Judah would add on to this: "And may he be very successful in all his financial undertakings" [literally, "with all his possessions"]. Maimonides notes that a guest may add on additional personal blessings for his hosts ("Laws of Blessings" 2:7). In recent years, the various Art-Scroll prayer books, noting that the special elongated blessing for the host has fallen into disuse for no discernible reason, have reinserted it as part of the* Birkat HaMazon.

---

3. Never use information you learn about your hosts to damage their good name. Often, while spending an evening in a couple's house, guests glean insights into the couple's marriage, aesthetic sensibilities, their children's personalities, their relationship with their children, and even their financial status. Sometimes this information is both highly personal and negative, and many people engage in unkind gossip and "character analysis" after leaving a dinner party. Few things seem more unjust than accepting other people's hospitality, thanking them, and then, like a spy, utilizing information we have acquired in their home to criticize them or disseminate embarrassing information about them. If you think that the comments you make about your host or hostess are rarely unkind, then ask yourself if you would be willing to make the same remarks directly to them. If the answer is no, then why communicate them to others?

I know that when my wife and I invite people over for dinner or a party, we work hard for many hours, sometimes even several days, to make the evening as pleasant as possible for our guests. The thought that they might leave and pass on critical observations to each other and to others about us is painful. I don't think I am being paranoid in fearing that this is what many of them do; regretfully, I realize how often I have done so myself.

---

4. In a counterintuitive ruling, the Talmud instructs us not to speak too highly of our hosts. For example, if your hosts were very generous and caring, limit the number of people to whom you tell this, lest people come to exploit their generosity (see *Bava Mezia* 24a). Obviously, all depends on the character of the people to whom you are speaking. Good people will not use this information to exploit others. If you are uncertain about the character of the people to whom you are speaking, limit your complimentary remarks about your hosts.

5. The Talmud permits a departure from truthfulness when the food is not to your liking. Thus, when Rabbi Joshua ben Chananiah was served a meal that he didn't care for, and the hostess, noticing that he left most of his food on the plate, asked him, "Why did you not eat?" He answered, "I have already eaten earlier" (*Eruvin* 53b).*

6. Don't exploit your host's hospitality by bringing another guest, certainly not without permission (*Bava Bathra* 98b). If you wish to bring another guest, check with your host and don't make her feel pressured to accommodate extra visitors: Your guest is your responsibility, not your host's.

Similarly, when invited to a wedding or a Bar or Bat Mitzvah, it is not appropriate to ask whether you can bring your children when they were not invited (unless you have good reason to believe it was an oversight). Celebrations are expensive, and many people hosting such events operate on limited budgets; pressuring them to invite additional guests is unfair.

7. When asked if you are hungry, answer honestly. Many guests think it impolite to acknowledge their hunger, fearing that it might appear as if they came only for the food. But such exaggerated sensitivity, which can lead to lying, is condemned as wrong in Jewish sources (*Kallah Rabbati* 9).

8. Even if you are reserved by nature, make an effort to be sociable. Just as guests are uncomfortable when the host makes no effort to engage them in conversation, so, too, hosts feel bad when their guests are overly quiet and seem withdrawn. Therefore, when your host speaks, interact, and don't offer one-word responses. Rabbi Simcha Zissel Ziv (1824–1898; one of the foremost students of Rabbi Israel Salanter, and a primary figure in the *Mussar* movement) and a friend were invited to lunch at an inn owned by a widow. Throughout the meal, Rabbi Ziv engaged in a long conversation with the rather talkative woman, while his friend, when not eating, turned his attention to a holy book he was studying (obviously inappropriate behavior). After they left, Rabbi Ziv said to his friend, "It seems to me that you are guilty of stealing a meal from that woman." "She invited us," the shocked friend said, "and she certainly didn't expect us to pay." Rabbi Ziv was not assuaged: "She didn't expect us to pay money. The payment she wanted was that we listen and talk to her. And this, you didn't do."[1]

---

*For more on the subject of when it is permissible to lie to one's host, see *A Code of Jewish Ethics, Volume 1: You Shall Be Holy,* pages 440–441.

9. A guaranteed way to bring joy to your hosts is to show interest in their children (*Pele Yoetz,* "Guests") and to find things about them to compliment.

10. Don't give food to your host's children without first asking the parents' permission (*Chullin* 94a). Many parents have different standards as to which foods they want their children to eat and which they don't, and these wishes should be respected, particularly when you are a guest in their home.

A woman I know brought muffins and candies to some young children, who quickly started devouring them. A few minutes later, a panicked nanny rushed into the room and started gathering up the sweets, explaining that the children were allergic to sugar.

Common sense suggests that this talmudic ruling would apply as well in today's world to not giving food to other people's pets, some of whom, like humans, have allergies or are on restricted diets. In addition, you might, for example, be undoing years of training by the host to ensure that the dog or cat doesn't beg for food at the table.

---

11. When visiting someone's home, don't stay too long. The Midrash speaks of guests who are greeted the first day with fattened chickens, the second day with ordinary meat, and less and less on each succeeding day, until they are served only vegetables.[2]

Repaying hospitality: Two instances from the Bible

12. The Bible describes a tense period when King David's son Absalom led a revolt against him, and David, along with his greatly outnumbered troops, was forced to flee Jerusalem. Upon reaching the town of Machana'im, several men, among them a man named Barzillai, presented David and his forces with couches, basins, earthenware, and much food, "for they knew that the troops must have grown hungry, faint, and thirsty in the wilderness" (II Samuel 17:7–29). Strengthened by the help extended him in his hour of need, David was soon able to rouse his troops and put down the rebellion. Though Barzillai wished no reward for his behavior, many years later, when David was near death, he asked his son and successor, Solomon, to make sure that Barzillai's sons "be among those who eat at your table," for "they [along with their father] befriended me when I fled from your brother Absalom" (I Kings 2:7).

13. Another exemplar of hospitality is an unnamed woman in the city of Shunem. The prophet Elisha came to her town often, and she arranged with her husband to have a fully furnished room, with a bed, a table, a chair, and a lampstand, always available for him. Elisha so appreciated the hospitality—the Bible does not record other instances of people concerned about his needs—that he asked his servant Gechazi to find out what he, in turn, could do for this woman. Like Barzillai, the woman wanted nothing, but when Gechazi informed the prophet that she was childless, Elisha summoned her, and said: "At this season next year, you will be embracing a son" (II Kings 4:8–16). Years later, Elisha saved this boy's life (4:17:37).*

If you have been shown warm hospitality, you should ask yourself after you leave: What can I do for my hosts?

A few suggestions: Write your hosts a letter or e-mail, or call. When you express gratitude, do so in a specific way: Note, for example, a food you particularly liked or something in the conversation that was important to you. If, at the table, a discussion touched on a book that sounded interesting, buy it for your hosts.

---

*The Talmud, citing this episode, concludes that women are often more insightful in discerning character than men. Thus, though both this woman and her husband repeatedly met Elisha when he traveled to Shunem, it was she, not her husband, who recognized his sanctity (*Berachot* 10b).

Visiting the Sick

Whoever visits the sick person causes the sick person to live.

Nedarim 40a

5

PROVIDING MORE THAN JUST COMPANY

1. There is no specific verse in the Torah commanding us to visit the sick. Maimonides cites the obligation to do so, along with obligations such as extending hospitality and comforting mourners, as logical outgrowths of the commandment "Love your neighbor as yourself" (Leviticus 19:18): "[These words imply that] whatever you would like other people to do for you [such as visiting you when you are sick], you should do for your fellow . . . ("Laws of Mourning" 14:1).[1]

2. The talmudic rabbis understood another biblical verse, "You shall follow after the Lord your God" (Deuteronomy 13:5), as mandating that, to the extent possible, we emulate God's actions and attributes (*Sotah* 14a). The example offered in relation to visiting the sick is God's appearance to Abraham shortly after he was circumcised (see Genesis 17:23–18:5). Jewish sources cite this as the first example of *bikur cholim* (visiting the sick), and those who fulfill this commandment are regarded as engaging in an act of *imitatio dei* (imitating God).

When Rabbi Aryeh Levine was in his final years and frail, a son was born to his beloved student Yaakov David Perlin. Reb Aryeh not only attended the circumcision, but also came to visit the baby a few days later. When Rabbi Perlin expressed astonishment that Reb Aryeh had come on such a sweltering day, he smiled and exclaimed, "This is the third day since the child's circumcision. And the Torah tells us that the Almighty Himself came to visit Abraham our father on the third day after his circumcision. We have to follow in His ways."*[2]

---

*Although the Torah doesn't specify when God appeared to Abraham, the Talmud teaches that this visit occurred on the third day after the circumcision (*Bava Mezia* 86b). The rabbinic belief is that this is when the patient suffers the most. This is probably based on Genesis 34:25, which

3. The seminal talmudic passage on visiting the sick occurs in the tractate *Nedarim* (40a): "One of Rabbi Akiva's students became sick, and none of the sages came to visit him. Rabbi Akiva, however, went to visit him and, because he swept and cleaned the floor for him, the student became better. The student said to Rabbi Akiva, 'My teacher, you have brought me back to life.' Rabbi Akiva went out and taught: 'Whoever does not visit the sick, it is as if he spilled blood.' "

The student may well have been too poor to hire someone to nurse him or even to clean his room. Rabbi Akiva understood that a lack of care, along with a lack of clean surroundings, could lead to the young man's becoming sicker and even dying. Indeed, given the conditions of the time (second century), the student may well have been lying on a dirt floor.

A friend suggests that no less helpful to the student than Rabbi Akiva's cleaning (given that sweeping dirt off a dirt floor still leaves dirt) was the attention he bestowed on this neglected patient. From this perspective, the student's comment to Akiva might also mean "My teacher, you have given me a reason to live."

---

4. The Talmud relates the story of Rabbi Akiva and his student within the context of another story: "Rabbi Chelbo became ill. Rabbi Kahana went out and announced in public, 'Rabbi Chelbo is very ill.' Nonetheless, no one came to visit him" (*Nedarim* 39b–40a). In the Akiva story, no one went to visit the sick student, either. How might we account for this?

The Talmud itself offers no explanation for this seemingly indifferent behavior. One possible reason is that because visiting the sick is both time-consuming and often emotionally taxing (particularly when the patient is very ill), many people prefer to assume, without investigating, that somebody else is taking care of the patient, at the very least, family members. Therefore, they don't bother to visit themselves (the expression "out of sight, out of mind" aptly describes the attitude many of us have toward the sick).

To counter this tendency, Rabbi Zelig Pliskin suggests that we challenge ourselves with the following question: "When I hear that someone is ill, do I just forget about it, or do I go and visit?"[3]

---

describes Jacob's sons, Shimon and Levi, as attacking the men of Shechem "on the third day [after their circumcision] when they were in pain." Dr. Isaac Herschkopf explains: "It is not likely that the pain and/or weakness would be greater three days post-operation than immediately after. It is more likely that in the days prior to antibiotics, by the third day an infection had arisen, leading to increased pain, fever, and weakness." On the other hand, a friend with five sons told me that they all experienced increased pain on the third day.

We can learn from Rabbi Kahana that we should let others know when someone is sick and in need of visitors, and we should keep on announcing it even if we have little or no success at first. Many synagogues announce at the end of services the names of people who would like visitors. Of course, such announcements should be made only after consulting with the patient since not everyone wants the fact or nature of their illness known. For example, there are physicians and therapists who don't mention that they are sick because they fear that patients might leave them, or that prospective patients might avoid them. The same applies to many other professionals as well.

---

5. The Talmud cites a teaching that Rabbi Dimi heard from the sages in Israel: "Whoever visits the sick causes the sick person to live, and whoever does not visit the sick causes the sick person to die" (*Nedarim* 40a). When stated so starkly, the words sound hyperbolic,* but the Chaffetz Chayyim offers a more nuanced explanation of the life-and-death effects that either visiting or ignoring a patient may have: "The visitors who attend to the needs of the sick may know of some remedy or medical attention [i.e., an appropriate physician] which might hasten his cure. . . . If a poor man is not visited, his very life may be jeopardized. Usually he cannot afford the food he needs in his illness. He has no one to consult with concerning his condition. Sometimes he cannot even afford to call a doctor or to buy medicine. His worries increase when he realizes that he has lain in bed for several days and no one has opened the door to care for him or to revive him. All these factors weaken his resistance and reinforce his illness, and this might cause his death" (*Ahavat Chesed* 3:3).

Many of these factors apply to all those who are ill, not just the poor. Any patient living alone might not properly care for herself and certainly might not eat properly. And most sick people, poor or affluent, who do not receive visitors, are likely to become depressed. Therefore, for example, it is particularly important to visit a person who is hospitalized in a city in which he/she does not live, since such people are frequently ignored (*Ahavat Chesed* 3:3).

6. We are not required to visit a patient with a contagious disease since we are not obligated to put ourselves at risk to fulfill this commandment. However, we should perhaps not be too quick to avail ourselves of this

*We all know of ill people who have visitors and die, and others who have no visitors and survive. Furthermore, there are some people for whom it is very difficult for psychological reasons to pay sick visits, and this talmudic teaching should not be understood as applying to them.

leniency since, as Dr. Fred Rosner, a physician and a medical ethicist, notes: "Today, one can protect oneself from contracting a contagious disease by avoiding direct contact with the patient and by taking other precautionary steps as dictated by the medical circumstances."[4]

7. The Talmud rules, "Even an eminent person should visit one of lesser eminence" (*Nedarim* 39b). This ruling is cited both by Maimonides ("Laws of Mourning" 14:4) and the *Shulchan Arukh* (*Yoreh Deah* 335:2).* We should never stand on ceremony and think that it is beneath our dignity or unnecessary for us to visit someone in need.

However, there is an additional benefit in a well-known person visiting a lesser-known one; the visitor's prominence will draw attention to the patient and his needs. When the Chazon Ish heard that a yeshiva student in B'nai Brak (the neighborhood in which the rabbi lived) had a painful throat ailment and wasn't receiving proper attention, he bought a jar of honey and visited the student. As he intended, in addition to providing the sick student with help and emotional support, the visit prompted more concern and attention for the young man's plight.[5]

The Sadviner Rav, the leader of a small synagogue in Brooklyn, used to go to a nearby hospital to ask after the health of an elderly member of his congregation who was confined there. Although the patient was not permitted visitors, the rabbi would daily seek out his physicians and nurses to ask about the man's condition. When a nurse asked him, "Why are you coming here every day? You know you can't go in to see him," the rabbi replied: "I come for two reasons. You know, the man has no family. I want him to know that I care about him, and that I'm thinking about him. Secondly, I want the doctors and nurses to know that there is someone who cares about him and is thinking about him."[6]

As a general rule, if the doctors and nurses see that a patient is important to others (many visitors coming, flowers being sent), that is likely to make the patient more important to them (see the postscript on the next page).

---

8. The *Sefer Chasidim* instructs us to focus on those people who are most in need of a visit and of material assistance. For example: "If a poor man and a rich man become ill at the same time, and many people go to the

*These words can also be translated as "Even an adult should visit a minor," a statement that underscores the importance of visiting sick children.

rich man, you should go the poor man first, even if the rich man is a scholar, because many are visiting the rich man, but no one is going to the poor" (paragraph 361).

9. Rabbi Fishel Schachter suggests that we expand the range of people whom we visit beyond family members and close friends: "I will try to extend myself to those in my community who are sick, even if they are not within my immediate social circle."[7]

Divine rewards for fulfilling this commandment

10. Not only do the Rabbis assure us that visiting the sick will save us from punishment in the next world (*Nedarim* 40a),* but also that we will be rewarded both during this lifetime and in the World-to-Come (*Shabbat* 127a).

A new category of those who should be visited

11. While modern medicine has made it possible for many people to live longer lives, many of the very elderly have lost friends, are physically incapable of getting around, and often lead lonely, isolated lives. Visiting shut-ins and "taking them shopping, or simply breaking up the monotony of a long day for them certainly falls into the category of *bikur cholim.*"[8]

Postscript: The power of goodness

12. In *Do Unto Others,* Rabbi Abraham Twerski, M.D., offers a powerful story about *bikur cholim,* which explains how fulfilling the mitzvah of visiting the sick can transform and elevate the lives of both the ill person and those who visit him.

Yossi was born with a defective heart. His parents were advised that he would need an operation when he turned seven, and that the operation was best done in America.

Yossi's parents, both Israelis, knew no one in America, so when the time came, a mutual friend put them in touch with me, and I found a medical center in Pittsburgh, where I live, where the surgery could be performed. Several months later, Yossi and his parents arrived.

---

*The same passage also promises that one who visits the sick will have control over his evil inclination *(yetzer hara)* and will acquire good and reliable friends.

Neither Yossi nor his parents understood a single word of English, so I put out the word in the Pittsburgh community for anyone who spoke Hebrew to contact me. Twenty-nine people volunteered, and I contacted all of them for an emergency meeting.

At this meeting, I explained the predicament. Yossi would be hospitalized for at least two weeks, and it was absolutely essential that an interpreter be available at all times. There was no way he could make himself understood by the staff. I asked people to volunteer several hours of their time to be in attendance, and we arranged a schedule that covered twenty-four hours a day for two weeks. Each person had an assigned time, and we agreed that one person would not leave until the next arrived. The plan operated like clockwork. Yossi and his parents were never left alone, and not only was there effective interpretation, but the family also received the support of interested people. The postoperative period was not without many anxious moments, and Yossi's parents swear that without the moral support of so many friends, they could never have survived it.

The entire hospital was impressed by this community cooperation and devotion, and when Yossi was discharged, the surgeon waived his bill! The family had no insurance coverage, and the hospital wrote off whatever they could and gave them the lowest rate. This was paid through donations made by friends of the small community that had sprung up around Yossi. Before Yossi left for home, a gala party was held, attended by the volunteers, contributors, surgeon, and other members of the hospital staff. Tearful good-byes were said, there was much embracing, lots of people gave of themselves and got back this: they had helped to save a little boy. Along the way, each one discovered qualities inside them that might never have been tapped if not for Yossi. On top of this, many friendships had been formed during this period, and these people, who had not known each other, became close friends, having worked for a common cause.

Six years later, on a visit to Israel, I made a surprise visit to Yossi, but he wasn't home: he was playing basketball! I went to the playground and could not stop my tears of joy when I saw the robust little boy who had once been so hampered by illness playing a game of hoops. On my return to Pittsburgh, I contacted the participants in Yossi's operation for a reunion, and we all bonded as we shared the news. One man originally had been reluctant to help because he was so terrified of hospitals. Now he related that he no longer hesitated to visit friends when they were ill; he had gotten over a phobia that controlled him.

It's twenty years later. Yossi is happily married and has a child. He sends cards twice a year, which we circulate. In this way the group stays in touch, and when a member needs help or wants to share happiness, we are there. What we *did for Yossi pales in comparison to what Yossi did for us. Each of us is stronger as a result of this event. That is the power of goodness.* *[9]

6

THREE OBLIGATIONS

1. Nachmanides specifies that those who visit the sick should strive to

- provide tangible assistance;
- pray for the ill person;
- cheer and comfort the patient (Nachmanides, *Torat ha-Adam*).

The seventeenth-century mystical and legal work Shnei Luchot Ha-Berit† *teaches that the commandment to visit the sick involves three aspects of ourselves:*

- *Our body—to rush to meet the patient's needs, such as by bringing medicine, or cleaning their house*
- *Our soul—to pour out our heart and soul in prayer for the patient's well-being*
- *Our money—to make sure that the patient has enough to cover his costs*[1]

Dr. Isaac Herschkopf suggests a fourth aspect: our mind—to think of creative ways to cheer the patient.

Providing tangible assistance

2. The word *bikur* ("visit," as in *bikur cholim*) derives from the Hebrew word for examination (*b-k-r*): "It is our religious obligation not only to visit

---

*My friend Rabbi David Woznica notes that this moving story also demonstrates the power of being involved in a community. Rabbi Twerski was able to marshal twenty-nine volunteers in large part both because of his and their involvement in the Jewish community.

†Written by Isaiah Horowitz, the book is usually referred to by the abbreviation *Sh'la,* as in "The *Sh'la* teaches that . . ."

the sick in hospitals and nursing homes, and the homebound, but to determine in what other ways we may be of help" (Rabbi Isaac Trainin).[2]

—

Try to ascertain the various, and often overlooked, needs of the patient, even those that may not seem to bear directly on her health: Does her family require meals? What about child care? Also, particularly in cases of serious and extended illness, consider the needs of the whole family. As Rabbi Aaron Glatt, a physician and the author of* Visiting the Sick, *notes, "[The] patient is sick, but the whole family is affected."[3] Thus, when my sister Shalva was six weeks old, she caught the whooping cough, which, at that time, was a life-threatening ailment for a patient so young. My parents took turns staying up with her night after night, and their nerves and health were affected. Decades later, my mother still recounted with appreciation her gratitude to her sister-in-law, my aunt Nunya Bialik, who came over on several nights to tend to my sister and provide my parents with some relief.*

—

My friend Rabbi David Woznica told me the following: "When my grandmother was hospitalized in what would be the last days of her life, I noticed that her fingernail polish had worn off. Though she was not one to complain about such things, I knew that having her nails look nice would mean a lot to her. So, I polished her nails, something I had never done before. . . . I later learned from other visitors that she told many of them that I had applied the nail polish. It was a source of pride for her and remains a beautiful memory for me to this day."

—

3. As already noted, practical assistance, particularly to the poor, can mean the difference between life and death, and certainly between a highly painful or a less painful convalescence. A friend of mine knew a woman who was suffering from intractable back pain. At first, he assumed that there was no treatment for the pain. But then he learned that there was a medicine available for $60, which the sick woman had not purchased because of the cost. He gave the woman a thousand dollars, obviously far more than she needed to buy the medicine, explaining later: "If she was suffering such immense pain and not buying the medication, I could only imagine what

---

*For example, if an elderly person is sick, does his or her equally elderly spouse need help getting around?

other things she needed which she felt too poor to purchase." The first obligation, therefore, is to provide the sick person with whatever is needed to cure the illness or to relieve the pain.

4. As we learn from the episode in which Rabbi Akiva scrubbed his sick student's floor (see page 63), it is important to help clean and freshen the patient's room to provide a healing environment.

5. Make sure that the sick person has nourishing food. If you don't have the skill—or time—to cook yourself, then purchase and bring over tasty and healthy food. Many sick people lose their appetites, and providing delicious food can encourage them to eat and build up their strength. One man told me: "When my mother was sick, she would rarely eat, claiming she had no appetite. I would go out to stores to buy the foods that I knew were her favorites and she would eat them. Later, when she became very ill, even those foods wouldn't tempt her. That's one of the reasons I knew the end was near."

There are organizations that provide meals to sick people and to shut-ins unable to leave their homes, a phenomenon common among the very old. Contact these organizations and find out how you and/or they can be of assistance.

6. Make known, when necessary and appropriate, the names of doctors who could be consulted by the patient. Use a personal connection to a physician if this will enable a sick person to see the doctor more quickly.

When speaking to a patient about the medical treatment he or she is receiving, choose your words carefully. Rabbi Aaron Glatt cautions visitors to "resist the temptation to criticize the care/physician/hospital/medication that the patient is receiving. Unless you are truthfully a health care expert in the particular field of that patient's illness, you are in all probability not knowledgeable enough about the care with which the patient is being provided. All you will realistically accomplish is to undermine his faith in the caregivers. . . . I have seen many patients shaken and bewildered by well-intentioned visitors who confused them and undermined their trust in their institution or physician."[4] *Therefore, if you have important information to convey about alternative treatment options, make sure to do so in a careful, constructive, and unalarming manner.*

---

7. People often don't think clearly when they are sick. Sometimes, they make rash decisions; at other times, they do nothing, even when taking action is urgent. By providing a calm and nurturing presence, you can help guide a patient to the right choices—and you need not be a doctor or a great scholar to do so.

The Bible (II Kings 5) relates that the Syrian general Na'aman was a leper. When Syria's king became convinced that the Israelite prophet Elisha could cure Na'aman's ailment, he dispatched the general to the king of Israel, along with a note asking that the king arrange for Na'aman to be cured. In response, the Israelite king panicked. Because leprosy was incurable, he feared that the Syrian king, by making a seemingly impossible demand, was looking for a pretext to invade Israel. But Elisha was not alarmed; he instructed the king to send Na'aman to him. When he arrived, Elisha sent out a messenger who told him to "bathe seven times in the Jordan, and your flesh shall be restored and you shall be clean" (II Kings 5:10). His instruction angered Na'aman; he had expected something more dramatic, even miraculous, to occur—for example, that the Israelite prophet would stand alongside him, invoke Israel's God by name, then wave his hand over the infected areas, and he would be cured. But to be sent to bathe in the shallow and decidedly unimpressive Jordan River . . . what was the sense of that? "Are not the Amanah and the Pharpar, the rivers of Damascus, better than all the waters of Israel? I could bathe in them and be clean" (II Kings 5:12).

The enraged Na'aman was prepared to dismiss the prophet's advice and return home when one of his servants confronted him with just the sort of commonsense reasoning that frantic, agitated people often lack: "Sir, if the prophet told you to do something difficult, would you not do it? How much more so when he has only said to you, 'Bathe and be clean' " (II Kings 5:13). Allowing himself to be convinced, Na'aman bathed in the Jordan and was healed.

Obviously, we might not have the power that God granted Elisha to bestow miraculous cures, but all his powers would have been insufficient if not for the wise and calming words of Na'aman's servant. And the power to listen carefully, give our full attention, and offer good advice is one that many of us have.

On the etiquette for speaking to the sick, see chapter 7.

Praying for the ill person

8. "He who visits and does not pray [literally "ask for mercy"] on behalf of the patient has not fulfilled the commandment to visit the sick" (Ramah, *Shulchan Arukh, Yoreh Deah* 335:4; see also Maimonides, "Laws of Mourning" 14:6).

---

*Prayers may be said both when visiting the sick and also at other times (for example, during the Torah reading; see paragraph 11). In addition, many people offer private prayers to God during their morning prayers (or at any time).**

---

9. The concept of seeking God's blessing for the sick is rooted in the Torah. When God strikes Miriam with illness for having spoken unfairly of her brother, Moses, it is he who prays to God on her behalf: *El na, refah na lah* ("O God, please heal her"; Numbers 12:13).

Some years ago, I mentioned to Rabbi Zalman Schachter-Shalomi that living in the bustling environment of Manhattan, my conversations were frequently interrupted by the piercing wail of a siren. My first response would often be annoyance, which I knew was inappropriate. Reb Zalman suggested that the moment I heard a siren, signifying an ambulance, a fire truck, or a police car,

*It is good to encourage children to pray as well; Judaism has a strong belief in the efficacy of young children's prayers. Doing so also enables the children (some of whom might not be able to pay a hospital visit) to feel involved in the process of caring for the sick. In *The Healing Visit,* Chana Shofnos and Bat Tova Zwebner write of a father whose young child was scheduled for elective surgery. The father told his older son, a boy who was himself not yet four, about the upcoming operation, but being highly anxious himself, the father feared that he had just provoked nervousness in his son. When the boy went to preschool that day, the father sent along a note explaining to the teacher about the surgery, so that he would be aware of any possible changes in the boy's demeanor. After his son came home, the father noticed that he was much calmer than he had been in the morning. When he asked his son about his day, the boy described how, when the other children went outside to play, the teacher asked him to remain and to sit down next to him. He told the boy that he knew his brother was in the hospital and that, with God's help, the doctors would make him well. Then, the teacher started to recite *Tehillim* (Psalms; a traditional Jewish activity when praying on behalf of the sick). "My son didn't know how to say *Tehillim.* His whole face lit up as he told me what he'd done instead. 'My *rebbe* (teacher) said I could say *Alef-beit* (recite the alphabet) for my brother, and I did! I helped my brother! Then the rebbe gave me pretzels and we went outside.'" As Shofnos and Zwebner note: "By letting the child [pray] for his baby brother, he was given the feeling of being an active participant in his brother's recovery" (*The Healing Visit,* pages 107–108). A well-known Chasidic story tells of a young man who was illiterate and couldn't read the prayers. Instead, he recited the alphabet, and asked God to arrange the letters into prayers.

I should stop whatever I was doing and pray that help would arrive in time. Ever since then, when I hear a siren, I say Moses' five-word prayer.

Offering such a prayer is good for our own character as well. A person who listened to this suggestion told me that about two weeks later, he was on the highway when suddenly the traffic ground to a halt. In the distance, he could see an ambulance. He said that in these circumstances he would normally think, "My bad luck." Many of us act like that, which is, of course, ironic. Somebody else has had an accident, and we think, "My bad luck." Instead, the man decided to pray for the next twenty minutes for those who were hurt. "I hope it helped the injured people," he told me, "but I don't know if it did. What I do know is that it helped me."

—

10. The Talmud records a prayer to be offered in the presence of a sick person: *Hamakom yerachem aleicha b'tokh she'ar cholei yis'ra'el* ("May God have compassion on you, along with the other sick of Israel" (*Shabbat* 12b).*[5] It seems appropriate that in societies such as the United States, where Jews are granted full equality, we should end the prayer for the sick with the words *ve-cholei teivel* ("sick of the world"), so that the prayer would read, "May God have compassion on you, along with the other sick of Israel, and of the whole world."

Indeed, as both the Talmud and the *Shulchan Arukh* make clear, Jews should visit both Jews and non-Jews who are ill (*Gittin* 61a, and *Yoreh Deah* 335:9).

11. When praying for sick people (such prayers are recited, for example, during the Torah reading in the synagogue and are offered by many people privately), the tradition is to refer to the person by his or her Hebrew name, followed by the Hebrew name of the person's mother. Thus, if a man named Jacob (in Hebrew, Yaakov), son of Rebecca Hannah (in Hebrew, Rivka Chana), is ill, we offer a prayer on behalf of "Yaakov ben Rivka Chana."

—

In most contexts, the Jewish tradition refers to a person by the father's name, but in prayers beseeching God's mercy for the sick, we mention the mother's. Why? Jewish sources offer no definitive explanation, but Hebrew etymology suggests a possible reason. The word for "compassion" in Hebrew is rachamim, *which*

*The standard prayer recited today for the sick starts with the word *Mi-sheh-beirakh* ("May He Who blessed") and is found in the prayer book.

derives from the word rechem, *womb. We associate the womb with the mother, and mother love is commonly thought of as more compassionate and unconditional than father love (even in extreme old age, suffering people often call out, "Mama"). In short, when what the sick person is most in need of is mother love, this is the love we beseech God to bestow on him or her.*

---

12. While Jewish tradition strongly prefers that people pray in Hebrew, Jewish law rules that we may pray in the presence of a sick person in whatever language he or she understands (*Shulchan Arukh, Yoreh Deah* 335:5). However, in my experience, at least some of the prayers offered in the presence of a sick person should be recited in Hebrew, since hearing the words in *lashon kodesh* (the holy language) is moving to almost everyone.* Rabbi Bradley Artson writes of a hospital visit he paid to a woman who spoke with him "in almost scientific objectivity about her illness until I took her hand and started to recite a *mi-sheh-beirakh* [the prayer for the ill]. . . . Tears welled in her eyes, and by the end of the short prayer she was sobbing beyond control. Moved beyond words by the power of prayer, she was finally open to feel and to share, a process more healing than all the analysis and discussion that had come before."[6]

A friend comments: "Was she moved only by the prayer, or also because he took her hand? Physical contact is so important, particularly when we are sick and isolated."†

A suggestion from Rabbi Tsvi Schur, a chaplain: "When a patient asks me to pray for him or her, I always agree to do so, but request that he or she offer a prayer on behalf of my family as well."[7]

---

13. Pray for whatever the sick person most needs you to pray for. Some years ago, a beloved friend of mine, a strong believer in natural healing and

*I had occasion to pray at the bedside of a very sick elderly Catholic gentleman who was near death and who was surrounded by his children and grandchildren. I started to pray in Hebrew, and also recited a chapter of Psalms in Hebrew, and this caused great excitement among the people gathered; I heard them whispering to each other that I was praying in the language spoken by Jesus (who knew both Hebrew and Aramaic).

†In the Orthodox world, many men will not grasp the hand of a female patient to whom they are not closely related. But female visitors can recite the prayer and express physical affection and support.

alternative medicine, realized that his best, perhaps only, chance for survival was to submit to an arduous regimen of chemotherapy. After struggling with the decision, he decided to undergo it, but asked that a rabbi initiate each session with a prayer over the drugs that were to be pumped into him. That prayer gave him the peace of mind to continue with the treatment, which proved successful.

14. Encourage the patient to pray for himself, for such prayers may well be the most efficacious of all. As the Psalmist writes: "Hear my prayer, O Lord, give ear to my cry, do not disregard my tears . . ." (Psalm 39:13). The Bible records that King Hezekiah (ca. 700 B.C.E.), one of Judah's most righteous kings, fell desperately ill, and the prophet Isaiah instructed him to put his affairs in orders, "for you are going to die; you will not get well" (II Kings 20:1). As soon as the prophet departed, Hezekiah turned to the wall, cried profusely, and prayed to God: "Please, O Lord, remember how I have walked before you sincerely and wholeheartedly and have done what is pleasing to you" (II Kings 20:3).

Isaiah was still inside the court when God's word came to him again and told him to tell the king that God had heard his request and seen his tears, "and I [that is, God] will add fifteen years to your life" (II Kings 20:6). And so it was.

With this biblical precedent in mind, patients should be encouraged to pour out their hearts to God.*

Many readers are shocked by the bluntness of Isaiah's words, delivered at God's behest, telling King Hezekiah that he is going to die and offering him no hope at all. Indeed, Jewish law forbids offering a sick person so discouraging a prognosis; most Jewish scholars permit one to offer a somewhat more optimistic assessment than is medically warranted (see A Code of Jewish Ethics, Volume 1: You Shall Be Holy, *pages 441–444). Perhaps when speaking to a nation's leader, one must sometimes speak bluntly, so that the leader will provide for his successor, something he might not do if he thought that he was going to recover.*

Patients who do recover from their illness or from an accident are instructed to offer a prayer of thanksgiving to God in the form of a blessing recited in

*This might well apply even to patients who are not conventionally religious. Rabbi Norman Lamm, the former president and now chancellor of Yeshiva University, writes: "During World War II, it was said that 'There are no atheists in foxholes.' I believe the same can be said of hospital beds, especially in the intensive care units" (*Seventy Faces: Articles of Faith,* Volume 2, page 36).

synagogue, and known as Birkat HaGomel (Berachot *54b*).* *This blessing, recited between sections of the Torah reading, reads: "Blessed are You, our God, King of the Universe, Who bestows [*HaGomel*] goodness upon the guilty, Who has bestowed every goodness upon me." The congregation then responds: "May He who has bestowed goodness upon you, bestow every goodness upon you forever."*

---

15. A patient who is very ill should be encouraged to recite the *vidui* (pronounced "vee-do-ee") prayer, a confession of sins, which a Jew is supposed to recite shortly before dying. Because this is a sensitive topic to raise with an ill person, the *Shulchan Arukh* instructs visitors to reassure the patient that it is only being recited as a precaution, which it is: "Many have said the *vidui* and not died, and many have not said the *vidui* and have died." If the patient is unable to recite it aloud, he should confess it in his heart. And if he is unable to recite it by himself, others may recite it with him or for him. (*Yoreh Deah* 338:1).†

My friend Rabbi Irwin Kula notes that when he meets with a seriously ill person who may be aware that his time is likely limited, he holds the person's hand and poses—when appropriate—a number of questions: Have you been thinking about any people in particular? Is there anybody you want me to call? Is there someone to whom you have something important to say? Is there someone to whom you wish to apologize? Is there anything you are frightened about? Is there anything you regret, and perhaps would like to try to undo? Kula understands the vidui *as a spiritual practice that assumes that everything that happens to us can be an invitation toward a* cheshbon ha-nefesh, *a spiritual self-accounting and an act of inner repair.*

Cheer and comfort the patient

16. The Rabbis declared that each visitor to a sick person has the capacity to take away a sixtieth of the patient's illness (*Nedarim* 39b).‡ A stream of

*Those who have returned from a dangerous trip and those who have been released from captivity are also to recite this prayer.

†The text of the *vidui,* which concludes with the recitation of the *Sh'ma,* is found in *A Code of Jewish Ethics, Volume 1: You Shall Be Holy,* page 172.

‡Rashi explains that this teaching applies particularly when the visitor is of the same age *(ben gilo)* as the patient. People often feel more at ease with their peers; and it is reassuring for older

visitors underscores to the patient that people care about him, which is itself an important factor in motivating someone to get better. In instances where a person is unable to visit, a phone call or a note can also be comforting (for more on telephoning a patient, see page 87).

An elderly member of the congregation that Rabbi Avrohom Pam, the renowned head of Brooklyn's Yeshiva Torah Vodaath, attended, became ill and was hospitalized. Rabbi Pam was not able to go to the hospital, but wrote the man a letter saying how much he missed seeing him at the synagogue, how he prayed every day for his recovery, and how he wished he could visit him. The elderly patient was very pleased at receiving a letter from so prominent a figure and even happier at learning that Rabbi Pam was praying for him daily. He showed the letter to all who came to visit him and his physical condition improved greatly, so that he was soon released from the hospital. When Rabbi Pam learned of the impact made by his letter, he said, "What did it take to write that letter? A pen and a piece of paper." As Rabbi Fishel Schachter concludes: "With that quick gesture, [Rabbi Pam] restored a person to life. That is the power of a moment of thoughtfulness, a ten-minute phone call, a half-hour visit, a get-well card, a small gift . . . Even if one can make that day—or just that hour—more bearable, one has accomplished a deed of heroic proportions."*[8]

Rabbi Joseph Ozarowski, a hospital chaplain, recalls: "I once walked into the Intensive Care Unit and saw a male patient wearing a kippah. *I had barely introduced myself before this gentleman, through his oxygen mask, began spouting wonderful comments on the weekly Torah portion. Behind me, the patient's wife exclaimed: 'I don't believe this! I don't believe this!' When I explored this further, I learned that the man had been confused and dazed for forty-eight hours before my visit. My presence, it seems, brought this man back to reality, and I was literally able to remove a fraction of his illness."*[9]

---

patients in particular to see friends their own age who are still alive and healthy. Maimonides, perhaps concerned that people not take the statement about removing a sixtieth of the illness literally, wrote: "One who visits the sick person is considered to have taken away a portion of his illness, making his disease less severe" ("Laws of Mourning" 14:4).

*Because of the biblical law ordaining that priests *(Kohanim)* have no contact with dead bodies (see Leviticus 21:1 and Ezekiel 44:25), observant Jews of priestly descent, such as Rabbi Pam, will not normally go into cemeteries except to attend the burial of an immediate relative and will not enter hospitals (where it often happens that a dead body is present) except to visit very close relatives. *Kohanim* are, of course, permitted to visit sick people at their homes.

17. We should encourage the patient by our demeanor; our facial expression conveys as much as our words. Rabbi Eliezer ben Isaac of Worms (eleventh century) noted that sick people often study their visitors' faces. If the visitors look shocked or disheartened, the patient will assume that he is very sick, and this fear alone might cause his health to deteriorate. "[Therefore], enter cheerfully, for the heart and eyes [of the patient] are on those who come in" *(Orchot Chayyim)*.[10]

If you believe that you will not be able to control your expression when you see the patient, who might be frail or disfigured (for example, if you are visiting someone who has suffered severe burns), then it is better not to visit, but to call. (Of course, the better response would be to try to train yourself to control your reactions.) Similarly, if you have a pessimistic disposition, it is preferable that you stay at home and write a letter. Make sure that a more cheerful person checks the wording of your letter before you send it.

A friend comments: "When I visit a friend or loved one who has been disfigured, I focus on their eyes. Soon their disfigurement disappears from my field of vision."

Always watch your words when speaking to the patient or to members of his family. Rabbi Mordechai Kamenetzky tells of an episode related to him by the mother of a sick child. An acquaintance called and told her: "I heard your son was diagnosed with [such-and-such]."

The mother answered, "Yes."

"Oh, I know all about it. My nephew had it."

The woman then went on to speak in a very helpful and informative way, discussing different treatments and medicines, and referring to many of the top specialists in the field.

Finally, the mother asked, "So how's your nephew?"

*The woman answered matter-of-factly, "Oh, he died a few months ago."**[11]

A nineteenth-century Jewish work edited by Zvi Hirsch Edelman, The Path

---

*My daughter Shira, after reading this section, asked me: "If the person had died, but the woman really had helpful information to transmit, what should she have done?" It seems to me that the best thing would have been to be more up front in her original comment, saying, for example, "Unfortunately, my nephew had the same illness—his case was, I believe, much more severe than your son's—and things did not work out. But I learned a few things that might be helpful to you." On the other hand, if the woman really could offer no reason to the mother to be optimistic, then there would be no point in calling, since she would have nothing helpful to say. Why tell someone about a great specialist in the field, for example, if the specialist can't help the boy in any case?

of Good Men, *records a similar tale, although in this case the sick man provided an understandably sharp retort to the tactless visitor:*

"A visitor came to see a sick man and asked him what ailed him. After the sick man told him, the visitor said: 'Oh, my father died of the same disease.'

"The sick man became extremely distressed, but the visitor said, 'Don't worry, I'll pray to God to heal you.'

"To which the sick man answered: 'And when you pray, add that I may be spared visits from any more stupid people.' "[12]

---

18. The patient's physical surroundings need to be cheerful. When Donna Gilbert's late husband, Dr. Spencer Gilbert, was hospitalized with what proved to be a fatal condition, she made sure to have pictures of their children and grandchildren all over the room's walls. Every day, the Gilberts' children would visit and/or call to tell their father of good things going on in their lives, and of cute things his grandchildren had said or done. Because of the risk of infection, visitors had to wear a mask when visiting the room. Realizing that it could be demoralizing to constantly look at masks and not faces, Mrs. Gilbert, before entering the room, would knock on the door's window, so that her husband could see her face and her smile before she put on a mask. All of these things are what kept up Dr. Gilbert's spirits in the face of a highly debilitating, and ultimately fatal, illness.*

19. Make a special effort to visit people who receive few or no visitors. If no one comes to see them, they may conclude that no one cares whether they

*Her husband, Spencer (I have been dear friends with the Gilberts for thirty years), was, in turn, a model of how a sick person should behave. Though in considerable pain and facing a discouraging prognosis (from a form of rapidly progressing leukemia), he remained focused on his love and concern for his family and friends, and on his desire that he always remain a part of their lives. Thus, knowing that he probably had little time left, he asked the family to use his *tallit* at all happy occasions (for example, that at future family weddings, the bride and groom stand under it). He also assured his wife and children that if he were to die, he would die satisfied, having done what he wanted in life (there was therefore no reason for anyone to feel any guilt, for they had brought such joy into his life); he requested only that his grandchildren know who he was. During the last weeks of his life, I was privileged to call him daily, to count down together the days until his immune system (which had been compromised by his treatments) was supposed to return. However, when in the middle of this period we celebrated our son's Bar Mitzvah, Spencer told me several times not to call for a few days, so that I could focus on the joy of the occasion. I still tried to make sure to call, but I was profoundly moved that at so difficult a time in his life he was still worrying about me. He also remained a man of faith until the end. When his wife, Donna, said to him in those last days, "There is so much joy in our family, more grandchildren to be born, *simchas* to celebrate. You must be right here with me to see it," he said, "I will see it, but from up above."

live or die. Conversely, their spirits will be particularly raised by your thoughtfulness and concern. Returning from the synagogue on Shabbat morning, Rabbi Moshe Feinstein would make a detour to visit a chronically ill man. He used to note that this was a particularly important mitzvah, because people who are ill for a long time tend to become forgotten as time passes.[13]

—

A man I know spent a great deal of time in a hospital when his mother was ill. When she dozed off, he would ask nurses if there were any patients who hadn't been receiving visitors, and he would spend time with them.

—

*Rabbi Aryeh Levine was an expert at making patients feel at ease. On one occasion, when he greeted a bedridden patient with great warmth, the startled patient said to him, "From where do you know me?" The rabbi answered, "We met at the foot of Mount Sinai when the Torah was given."**[14]

—

7

ETIQUETTE FOR VISITING THE SICK

1. As a general rule, only close relatives and friends come during the first days of a person's illness. If nonintimate friends and more distant relatives start to visit, the patient may become alarmed and assume that he must be very sick, and that people are trying to see him before he dies. However, when serious illness occurs suddenly, all may visit (Jerusalem Talmud, *Peah* 3:7; *Shulchan Arukh*, *Yoreh Deah* 335:1).

—

I once read that the singer Frank Sinatra was known to visit friends who were sick and near death, and sing to them. Once, while in a hospital making one of

*An old Jewish tradition teaches that when the Torah was given at Sinai, the souls of Jews from all future generations were present as well.

these visits, he learned that another friend of his was also a patient there and had been scheduled for a minor procedure. When he stopped off at the second man's bedside, the man was shocked. "Oh my God! I didn't know I was that sick."

—

2. Be sure to knock and ask permission before entering. Hospital patients constantly have their privacy invaded; doctors, nurses, and social workers often walk in unannounced. Therefore, it is empowering to patients to control access to their hospital room; after all, in most homes, it is only very young children (infants and toddlers) whose rooms are entered without knocking. In addition, by entering the room suddenly, you may embarrass the person if he or she is dressing or attending to intimate bodily needs.*[1]

—

Rabbi Bradley Artson suggests that we phone ahead to let the patient know that we are coming. Doing so creates anticipation and heightens the pleasure for the ill person. In addition, because many decisions are made for sick persons by others, "when you phone and ask if it is all right to visit, the patient is able to exercise some control" and can indicate if she is not in the mood for a visit.[2]

Calling ahead also can be helpful to the patient's primary caregiver. Many caregivers, such as a spouse, a child, or a parent, stay with a patient for many hours at a time, unwilling to leave unless someone else is present. Knowing that you will be visiting enables them to plan some time during which they can get away.

My friend Toinette Lippe also notes that if you don't call ahead and find out when is the best time, your visit may coincide with that of another person, and this can be overwhelming for a patient, or you may arrive to find the patient having a procedure performed.

On the other hand, you have to know the character of the ill person. There are some self-effacing individuals who will discourage you from coming and tell you not to bother when they would, in fact, greatly enjoy a visit. Also, particularly if you are close to the sick person, she may respond well to a surprise, unexpected visit.

—

My friend Jonathan Greenwald, who once experienced an extended illness that often left him depleted, told me: "I found it valuable when there were two visitors

---

*"No one would ever dream of entering someone's house, and certainly not their bedroom, without permission, yet [many] visitors neglect this most basic courtesy in a hospital or nursing home setting" (Rabbi Aaron Glatt, M.D., *Visiting the Sick*, page 33).

who would talk with each other. I found it comforting to listen and it was nice not to have to talk myself. I would comment when I cared to, and there was no awkwardness this way if I fell silent."

---

3. If the patient welcomes it, and you are prepared to do so, visit frequently: "One should visit many times . . . and those who do the mitzvah even more often are praiseworthy, as long as they do not bother or disturb the sick person" (Maimonides, "Laws of Mourning" 14:4).

4. Sit down when you enter the room. Standing implies that you're only staying briefly and preparing to leave; this can make the patient feel anxious, with the impression that your time together will be very limited.* In addition, "being on the same level as the ill person indicates empathy, eliminating a feeling of hierarchy that might separate visitors and sufferer . . ." (Rabbi Joseph Ozarowski, a hospital chaplain).[3] Also, look the person in the eye; such contact is always reassuring. Stand or sit near the patient and, when appropriate, hold and massage his hand. We speak of being "touched" when we mean being emotionally moved. Touching a sick person, whether he is physically or emotionally ill, can be profoundly moving and reassuring for the patient.

5. If the patient is asleep when you come to visit, and it is inappropriate to awaken her, leave a note. As Rabbenu Asher (ca. 1250–1328) noted, it will be pleasing to the patient to learn that so-and-so visited. Before leaving, sit for a little while and offer a prayer.

6. Even if a patient is seriously ill, try to engage him in discussion about issues other than his illness. This might seem obvious, but people often treat the sick as if their lives were about illness and nothing else. Such an attitude can demoralize a sick person and make him feel that his life is, in effect, over. When Rabbi Shlomo Zalman Auerbach visited Rabbi Moshe Landau, who was near death, Rabbi Landau apologized to Rabbi Auerbach for having criticized a position he had taken in something he had written. Rabbi Auerbach assured him that there was no need to seek forgiveness—it was not a personal attack, but "a dispute for the sake of heaven." But he then went on to tell Rabbi Landau why he still thought he was wrong. Weak as he was, Rabbi Landau was roused by Rabbi Auerbach's critique and argued back with a

*For the same reason, take off your coat and hang it up, or fold it and put it on the side.

vigor no one would have thought he still possessed. As Rabbi Hanoch Teller, Rabbi Auerbach's biographer, wrote: "Reb Shlomo Zalman perceived that under the tubes and intravenous lines was a Jew who craved . . . to engage in the rigorous debate of halachic issues that had been the very essence of his life. All of the resuscitation devices in the hospital could not provide the give-and-take of learning—the very oxygen of life—of which he was currently denied."[4]

—

In June 1986, my father, Shlomo Telushkin, the accountant for the Lubavitcher Rebbe, suffered a serious stroke, one from which he never fully recovered. For several days, my father lay in a hospital bed in a coma, and I was with him when he came out of it. During those days, we received calls twice daily from the Rebbe's office, asking about my father's condition. Then, a few days later, I received a call from Rabbi Krinsky, one of the Rebbe's closest aides: an accounting issue had come up, and the Rebbe had said, "Ask Shlomo."

"But you know how sick and disoriented my father is?" I protested. Indeed, my father was still in intensive care.

"We reminded the Rebbe of that," Rabbi Krinsky answered. "He, of course, remembered, but he insisted that we ask your father."

I immediately went back to my father's room and posed the question to him. He looked at me, puzzled, then said the answer was obvious and told it to me. At that moment, I experienced a powerful sense of the Rebbe's deep humanity. He had made a calculation and asked my father a question that he knew my father would be able to answer, and by doing so reminded my father that he was still needed and could be of service.

—

David Techner, a funeral director for the Jewish community in Detroit, relates: "I recently talked with a teenager who had been diagnosed with terminal cancer. People had been visiting with him just a few days after the diagnosis and finding it very difficult. He said to me, 'I'm not even [feeling] sick yet, and they're sitting shiva!' We have to be very careful to keep in mind that terminally ill people are still sensitive, living human beings."[5]

—

7. Encourage the patient with an optimistic attitude. Often, this can be expressed more effectively through deeds than words. Rabbi Aaron Levine tells of an incident related to him by the late rabbi Shimon Schwab, the long-time leader of the Orthodox German-Jewish community in New York City's Washington Heights: "A lady bought a new raincoat as a present for a sick

woman. Usually, one brings flowers, a nightgown, or a similar present. When the sick woman inquired about the unusual present, the visitor responded in surprise, 'What do you mean? The weather is bad outside; soon you'll need the raincoat.' The patient's countenance lit up, and it was obvious that she was greatly encouraged and heartened by these words, and the very thoughtful gesture."[6]

An author I know had a friend with young children who was being treated for cancer. There was reason for optimism, but obviously the friend felt great anxiety. The author gave his friend one of his books and inscribed inside: "I look forward to dancing with you at your children's weddings." Later, the patient, who responded well to chemotherapy, told the author that this inscription had meant a great deal to him.

While an optimistic attitude is indeed crucial, avoid facile optimism. A friend with cancer—fortunately, he is now better—told me how irritating it was when people who knew little about his illness would say to him, "Don't worry, everything is going to be fine." My friend confided that what he was really hearing was "Blah, blah, blah," and, as he put it, "it was not a comfort."

His experience reminded me of an old joke. A patient is telling his doctor of various pains and problems he is having and the doctor keeps saying, "I wouldn't worry." Finally, the patient, exasperated by the physician's nonchalance, says, "Doctor, if you were the one who had these aches, I wouldn't worry either."

*In short, my friend, who had good reason to be nervous about his condition, felt that these visitors' words were empty, and how could empty words fill the void he was feeling? For optimism to be comforting, the speaker has to believe what he is saying.**

---

*During World War II, a family close to Rabbi Abraham Twerski's family received the shocking news that their son was missing in action. Twerski's father, Rabbi Jacob Twerski, a Chasidic rebbe, would visit the family and try to keep up their hopes. He continually emphasized that "missing in action" did not mean that their son had been killed; he might well have been captured and was now a prisoner of war, an unpleasant fate, but better than death. Rabbi Twerski recalls how his father would enter the grieving family's home exuding confidence and assuring them that they would see their son again. Indeed, when the war ended, they were blessed with the news that their son had been a POW, was well, and would soon be on his way home. When the soldier returned first to his army base, he found a large stack of letters that had accumulated in his absence. It turned out that Rabbi Twerski had written the young soldier a letter each week during the two years he was in captivity: "I know when my father wrote these letters. He did so each week just before he made his visit to the family. Writing the letters reinforced his own

8. Make the patient laugh. Recall old times and funny anecdotes. Dr. Iṣaac Herschkopf claims that this is the "single most therapeutic thing a visitor can do. So many hospitalized people later remark that the visits they remembered most vividly and fondly were the ones that left them in tears, either joy at the expression of love by a dear visitor, or laughter at remembrance of good times past, and expectation of similar laughs in the future."

Norman Cousins, the well-known essayist and long-term editor of the periodical Saturday Review, *was diagnosed with heart disease and other serious ailments, and told by his physicians that his days were numbered. In his remarkable book* Anatomy of an Illness as Perceived by the Patient, *Cousins describes how he developed a recovery program involving large doses of Vitamin C and megadoses of laughter induced, for example, by watching comic films: "I made the joyous discovery that ten minutes of genuine belly laughter had an anesthetic effect and would give me at least two hours of pain-free sleep. When the pain-killing effect of the laughter wore off, we would switch on the motion picture projector again and not infrequently, it would lead to another pain-free interval." At the time of Cousins's death in 1990, twenty-six years had passed since his heart disease had first manifested itself.*

---

9. Send the patient a get-well card or note (even if you have visited, and certainly if you haven't): "Almost every hospital room I've visited has the cards taped proudly to a wall, in a place where the sick person can easily see them; they are a constant reminder that people do care" (Rabbi Bradley Artson).[7] In addition, receiving mail is one of the highlights of the day for people facing long hospital stays or who are homebound.[8]

10. Jewish law prohibits sharing bad news with a patient who is very sick and even mandates withholding news of the death of a close relative; the Rabbis feared that such news might cause a further decline in the patient's health (*Mo'ed Kattan* 26b).

In October 1959, an assassin threw an explosive device in the Israeli Knesset at Prime Minister David Ben-Gurion, who was wounded in his arm and foot.

---

belief and strengthened his hope that the young man was indeed alive. . . . Of course my father feared the worst, but fear is destructive, and so he combated it with the hope inherent in the writing of these letters. He continued to combat fear by communicating his confidence to the family. It was by the virtue of these acts that the family survived the ordeal" (Rabbi Abraham Twerski, *Do Unto Others,* pages 156–157).

While Ben Gurion was hospitalized, Nehemiah Argov, his military secretary and perhaps his closest aide, committed suicide. On the advice of Ben-Gurion's doctors, who feared the effect such news would have on the prime minister's recovery, the Voice of Israel (the country's main radio station; at the time, Israel had no television) was instructed not to broadcast news of Argov's death; it was also arranged that the newspapers Ben-Gurion regularly read would print a few special copies with no mention of the death. A messenger picked up these copies and brought them to the prime minister.*[9]

---

11. If you are on bad terms with the patient, the traditional Jewish attitude is that you should refrain from visiting (Ramah, *Shulchan Arukh, Yoreh Deah* 335:2). Rabbi Avraham Danzig's (1748–1820) code of Jewish law, *Chochmat Adam,* explains: "An enemy should not visit a sick person nor should he go to comfort a mourner, for the sick man or the mourner may think that his enemy is rejoicing at his misfortune" (15:1). However, one does find in other, somewhat later sources a softening in Jewish law's attitude toward a visit paid by an adversary: "If one who hates a person sends a message that he would like to visit either the sick or the mourners toward whom he has enmity, and these individuals allow him to visit, not only is it permitted, more than that, it is a good thing because it will generate peace between them. Therefore, there are those who write that today we have the custom to permit one who hates another to visit him, since hopefully this will lead to peace between them" (*Arukh Ha-Shulchan, Yoreh Deah* 335:6).[10] Thus, if you are confident that you are not feeling pleasure in the patient's sufferings, then visiting during this vulnerable time may lead to a reconciliation. However, call before you come and apprise the patient's family of your intention to visit. The family members will check with the patient and make sure that your visit will not upset her.

12. Try to visit sick people before Jewish holidays. Bring the patient *challot* and wine (if permitted): "In particular, provision should be made for the kindling of Sabbath candles and the Chanukah menorah. The psychological significance of being able to fulfill these mitzvot and the trauma to the observant patient engendered by their omission is of therapeutic significance" (Rabbi J. David Bleich).[11]

---

*Argov had struck a cyclist with his car, and the man was knocked unconscious. Argov drove the man to the hospital. Later that night, fearing that the cyclist would die (he didn't), Argov wrote a note bequeathing all his money to the cyclist's family and then shot himself.

13. If you can't visit in person, you may fulfill the command of *bikur cholim* by telephoning the patient (although this is regarded as an incomplete fulfillment of the mitzvah). Rabbi Moshe Feinstein emphasizes that a personal visit is much better than a phone call for several reasons:

- A visit brings the sick person a sense of comfort that cannot be duplicated in any other way.
- Seeing the patient with your own eyes will stimulate you to pray more intensely on the person's behalf (*Igrot Moshe, Yoreh Deah,* 1:223).[12]

Nonetheless, when a visit will not or cannot be made (e.g., the person is in another city or country), a phone call can be immensely moving to the patient. Also, in contrast to ancient and medieval times, when those who lived at a great distance would have no chance to be in touch (a letter could take weeks or months to arrive), the telephone enables many people to call the patient and to express concern personally.

———

A point of etiquette: When you telephone, ask the patient if visitors are present. Given that visitors made the effort to be there, it can sometimes be discourteous and unfair for the patient's attention to be focused on a telephone conversation (except if the visitor is an immediate family relative who comes often and stays for an extended period). Therefore, in such a case, keep the conversation brief (except in the rare circumstance when you cannot call again), and call again, ideally at a time when there are no visitors present.

In addition, when you know that the patient is monitoring his computer, a get-well e-mail can boost the person's morale.

———

Two Special Circumstances

When the illness is serious

14. The legal code, *Chochmat Adam,* teaches: "The custom among many holy congregations, especially in the holy congregation of Berlin, was that when an individual was sick, the person in charge of the *Bikur Cholim* Society, or some other person, would visit him on the third day of his illness and tell him, 'It is our custom to visit all sick people at this time, so do not let our visit cause you any concern. We advise you to prepare a directive delineating your wishes, and including any outstanding obligations you have toward others or that others have toward you' " (in other words, instruct the patient to make sure that all his or her financial affairs are in order; chapter 151, paragraph 11).

Rabbi J. David Bleich believes that the policy of the nineteenth-century Berlin Jewish community should serve as a model for present-day physicians when counseling seriously ill patients. The doctor should make it clear that he or she offers identical advice about taking care of their affairs to all patients, and not only when the doctor fears the worst. "In this way, the patient will neither be lulled with a false sense of security, nor will he perceive a cause for undue alarm."[13]

When the patient is in a coma

15. Usually, visits to comatose patients are done more for the sake of family members who might be at the patient's bedside, rather than for the sake of the patient. In such situations, people sometimes speak very bluntly about the patient's condition and say things they would never say if they thought the patient could hear them. Yet, from the experience of patients who have later been restored to full consciousness, we now know that some seemingly unconscious people hear and comprehend what is being said around them.

A woman I know, who was in a coma, heard her doctor discuss her prognosis in the most discouraging terms ("she has very little time to live"). Later, after regaining consciousness, the woman said to the startled and discomfited physician, "Was it nice of you to say that I had little time to live with me there in the same room with you?"

Here are two guidelines for speaking in the presence of comatose patients:

- Don't say anything you would not say in the presence of a fully conscious person. If necessary, go outside to speak.

- Don't regard a visit to the bedside of a comatose patient as only a visit to the patient's family. Speak loving, encouraging words to the patient, maybe even into his ear and, if appropriate, sing to the patient and hold his hand.

When you are the sick person

16. The biblical law to judge people fairly (see *A Code of Jewish Ethics, Volume 1: You Shall Be Holy,* pages 70–94) applies to those who are sick no less than healthy people. If someone does not come to visit you during your ailment, don't assume that the person is a fair-weather friend, or is irresponsible or uncaring. For one thing, the person may not have heard about your illness. I know of a rabbi whom a congregant regarded with great bitterness after he had been hospitalized and did not receive a rabbinic visit or call. Unfortunately, although a message had been left for the rabbi, he never received it. Yet the ill person and his family harbored animosity toward the rabbi: "I'm not important enough in his eyes to be visited," the patient told others. What should have been regarded as a simple mistake—the patient's family was too proud to make a second call to the rabbi's office—turned into an unfortunate falling-out.

In addition, it sometimes happens that although people have heard that you are sick, they don't stay in touch because of difficulties they themselves are enduring. During my father's prolonged final illness, two friends did not contact my mother, much to her surprise and chagrin. We subsequently learned that during this same period, both had been going through severe and extended cases of illness and death in their own families; they cared about my father, but just weren't able to stay in touch.

17. Just as Jewish law rules that those in need of charity should not see themselves solely as recipients, but should also give charity (see page 245), so, too, are sick people expected, when possible, to visit others who are as sick or even sicker. A visit by a sick person, particularly one who strives to bear his suffering with a certain level of equanimity and faith, can be very encouraging to another patient. It can inspire the other ill person to not just see himself as a sufferer and victim, but as someone from whom things are still expected. In addition, it can sometimes be easier for an ill person to open up and express all that he is feeling to someone who is, like himself, in diminished health and feeling weak.

When Rabbi Moshe Feinstein was very ill and hospitalized, he learned that New York's longtime senator, Jacob Javits, had been admitted to the same hospital and was suffering from Lou Gehrig's disease. Over the protest of his nurse, Reb Moshe climbed down from his hospital bed and into his wheelchair, and set off to see the senator. To her dismayed question, "Where are you going?" Reb Moshe answered, "When a Jew such as Senator Javits, who has done so much for the Jewish community, is in the hospital, I must be mevaker choleh *(visit the sick)."*[14]

Similarly, when Rabbi Aryeh Levine was hospitalized, as soon as his condition eased, he started visiting patients in nearby rooms. Rabbi Levine's manner was so consoling that patients beseeched him for blessings. Yet he was not fully satisfied with his own behavior, confiding to Rabbi Yaakov Rakovsky, the chaplain at Jerusalem's Hadassah Hospital: "These ailing people come to me and ask that I should pray for them. . . . Yet at times there sneaks into my heart what the Rabbis taught in the Talmud: 'Whoever pleads for Heaven's compassion for someone else and he needs the same thing himself, he is answered first' [Bava Kamma *92a*]. *The result," Reb Aryeh confessed, "is that I do not do my task honestly, faithfully, because probably in my unconscious mind, when I pray for others to get well, my intention is that I should be cured first. My heart is sorely troubled by this. So I implore the Holy, Blessed One, that He should really answer first the prayers of all the sick people who come to see me."*[15]

A psychiatrist told me: "I was once taken to my hospital's emergency room because I had fainted; it turned out to be nothing serious. As I was lying on a gurney waiting for a test, one of the emergency room doctors, a former student of mine, came over to mention they were having trouble with another patient who was hysterical. They didn't know what to do with her. With my permission, they moved my gurney next to hers so I could make an evaluation and diagnosis and suggest some remediation. After that, they moved me adjacent to another agitated patient for the same reason. It sounds like a funny story, but in truth it was the best thing they could do for me; it made me feel needed, rather than helpless" (Dr. Isaac Herschkopf).

A final thought: Establishing a Bikur Cholim *Society*

18. Many communities and congregations have *bikur cholim* societies, organizations that can be contacted by those who are ill or by their families, and which arrange for hospital visits and other assistance on their behalf. Check on the Internet to learn if your community has such a service or contact your synagogue. If one exists, consider joining it. If no such group exists, call up friends who you feel may share an interest in establishing one and convene a meeting. A *bikur cholim* society can be started with even just a few people and, as time passes, others will undoubtedly join your effort. Rabbi Aaron Levine, author of *How to Perform the Great Mitzvah of Bikur Cholim,** includes in his book a discussion of how such a society was started in Baltimore. While people primarily associate *bikur cholim* with visits paid to

---

*For more information on how such a group functions, see Levine's book, pages 77–84.

hospital patients, the Baltimore organizers quickly identified several other needs, among them:

- visiting shut-ins;
- transporting people to and from medical appointments;
- delivering meals to homes where someone is temporarily incapacitated;
- providing home hospitality for family members of out-of-town hospital patients or for out-of-town patients seeing doctors on an outpatient basis.

Final Kindness

Death appears to be the ultimate state of being cut off and isolated. But love responds by stepping forward in solidarity with the deceased.

Rabbi Irving (Yitz) Greenberg

8

OBLIGATIONS TO THE DEAD

1. In Jewish law, there is a rich vocabulary of terms for our obligations to the dead.* Unfortunately, these words are largely unknown today, even among many otherwise committed Jews. A number of the most significant terms will be elaborated upon in this chapter.

- *Chesed shel emet* (true kindness). The Rabbis regard deeds done on behalf of the dead (such as preparing a body for burial) as the most selfless acts of kindness. When we perform a compassionate act for another, our motives are often not entirely pure. For example, a part of us might be hoping that the other person will one day be in a position to help us in return (that is why many people are particularly happy to be able to do a favor for an influential or wealthy person). However, when caring for the dead, we obviously do not expect any payback. Hence, such kindness is defined as "true [i.e. disinterested] kindness."†

- *K'vod ha-meit* (respect for the dead). The respect that Jewish law expects us to show in the presence of the dead (for example, one should not eat or drink near a dead body) and the respect that we must show the dead body itself (thus, Jewish law opposes cremation; see paragraph 7).

---

*I wish to record two debts of gratitude. The first is to David Zinner, executive director of Kavod v'Nichum, a nonprofit resource group that educates and advocates for *Chevra Kadisha* societies throughout North America. David shared with me his wide-ranging expertise in Jewish laws and traditions concerning treatment of the dead, and offered many important suggestions. The second is to Rochel Berman's *Dignity Beyond Death: The Jewish Preparation for Burial,* a pathbreaking, comprehensive, and inspiring work on this subject. Anyone wishing to know all the rituals involved in a *tahara,* and precisely how to carry them out, would do well to consult, in addition to Berman's book, Abner Weiss, *Death and Bereavement,* and Mosha Epstein, *Tahara Manual of Practices.*

†The origin of the term is biblical. Shortly before Jacob dies, he summons Joseph to discuss burial arrangements and asks Joseph to treat him with "kindness [*chesed*] and truth [*emet*]" (Genesis 47:29–31; for more on Jacob's requests of Joseph, see page 99).

• *Shomer* (guard; plural, *shomrim*). The person or persons who stay with the body from death until the funeral.

• *Chevra Kadisha* (the Holy Society). Groups responsible for attending to the dead (and sometimes to the dying) have existed in Jewish communities for at least two thousand years. *Chevra Kadisha* societies are composed of both men and women (male corpses are handled by men, female corpses by women), and it is they who prepare the body for burial.

• *Tahara* (purification). The pouring of water over the dead body after it has first been cleansed, and the name for the entire ceremony in which the body is prepared for burial (see paragraphs 9–12, 14).

• *Tachrichim.* The simple white garments in which the body is dressed (see paragraph 15).

• *Aron.* The word *aron* is familiar to many Jews from the synagogue, where the *Aron Kodesh* ("the holy ark") houses the Torah scrolls. The word *aron* also refers to the casket in which the body is buried; Jewish tradition strongly favors interring the dead in a simple wooden casket (see paragraph 18), although in Israel, burial in the ground in *tachrichim,* but without a casket, is common.

When death occurs

2. From the moment of death, the body should not be left unattended, and a *shomer* is called in to stay with the deceased until the funeral. The *shomer* sits in the same room with the body (at a distance of no less than four *amot,* about seven feet), and recites psalms, thus helping to escort the deceased from this world to the next. As regards Judaism's commitment to not leaving the body alone, Rabbi Yitz Greenberg observes: "Death appears to be the ultimate state of being cut off and isolated. But love responds by stepping forward in solidarity with the deceased."[1]

Jewish law regards this task as so important that it exempts the *shomer* from other religious commandments. Thus, during the time a male *shomer* is attending the dead body, he is exempt from the obligations of prayer and tefillin, while all *shomrim,* both men and women, are exempt "from all other [positive] commandments stated in the Torah" (*Berachot* 18a).

"If the body of the deceased is preserved in a refrigerator unit . . . , the shomer *should be in the same room as the unit, or at least be able to see the door of the unit from outside the room. Otherwise, the* shomer *should be in the same room as the body, or at least be able to see the body" (Rabbi Abner Weiss).*[2]

After the terrorist attack on New York City's Twin Towers on September 11, 2001, religious Jews came to recite psalms on behalf of the victims. At first, this went on near the site, and then continued in a trailer set up as a chapel outside the office of the medical examiner, where remains of the dead were delivered. Some two hundred Jews, many of them affiliated with Manhattan's Congregation Ohab Zedek, were involved in the effort, which continued around the clock for seven and a half months. On Shabbat, when observant Jews don't travel, students from Yeshiva University's Stern College for Women, near the medical examiner's office, recited psalms in four-hour shifts. Armin Osgood, who organized the volunteers throughout the whole period, recalls an incident when a police officer approached one of the students and said, "'I know you are saying Psalms. I have a favorite. Would you mind reciting it?' The student agreed. As the young woman recited the psalm, the policewoman wept for her colleagues who had perished in the disaster." Rabbi Dr. Norman Lamm, Yeshiva University's president at the time, commented: "The idea that you can have companionship even in death is a very consoling thought, whether you are Jewish or not."*[3]

In the past, when conditions were less hygienic, the most important reason the shomer *was excused from commandments such as prayer and tefillin is that the Rabbis did not want his attention to be distracted from protecting the deceased's body from mice (see* Berachot *18a). The desire to protect the body from rodents applied not only in ancient times, but even—among poorer Jews—in the last century. A poignant chapter in* In My Father's Court, *Isaac Bashevis Singer's memoir of his childhood in early twentieth-century Poland, concerns "a gruesome question" posed to his rabbinical father one Saturday night. A man entered the Singer house, and asked his father, "May a man sleep with his dead wife?"*

---

*Among Orthodox Jews, women traditionally sit as *shomrim* for women, and men for members of either sex, but this tradition was waived during the unprecedented months-long period following 9/11.

To his father's shocked response that he could not understand such a question, the man answered. "Rabbi, I am not insane. My wife died on Friday. I live in a cellar where there are rats. The funeral will take place on Sunday. I cannot leave the corpse on the floor because the rats would, God forbid, gnaw it to bits. I have only one bed. She must lie in that bed. And I, Rabbi, cannot sleep on the floor either. The rats would get me, too. I have already sat up one night, but my strength is gone. So I want to know, Rabbi, may I lie in bed with this corpse?" Singer's parents, in cooperation with his father's congregants, immediately took up a collection (of goods, not just money) and found a mattress which they brought over to the poor man's apartment.[4] *Interestingly, Singer does not explain (the incident happened when he was a child, so perhaps he did not recall) why the body was not removed from the apartment and taken to a room where a* shomer *could watch over it and recite Psalms.**

Communal responsibility

3. "Rabbi Judah said in the name of Rav, 'If there is a dead person in the town, all the residents of the town are forbidden to engage in work' " (until the deceased is buried; *Mo'ed Kattan* 27b). Residents are expected to stop work and attend to the needs of the dead, a restriction lifted only if the town has a *Chevra Kadisha.*

In Jewish tradition, God is credited as the first one to perform the function of a Chevra Kadisha. *When Moses died, he was alone on Mount Nebo, and the Torah records that God Himself buried him (Deuteronomy 34:6).*†

*A talmudic text (*Megillah *13b) records that Moses was born and died on the same date, the seventh of the month of Adar. In honor of Moses, Judaism's first and most distinguished recipient of the services of a* Chevra Kadisha, *this has long been the date on which many* Chevra Kadisha *societies hold annual dinners celebrating their work.*

---

*In light of the higher standards of cleanliness now prevalent, Rabbi Moshe Feinstein argues the function of the *shomer* has changed from the guarding of the body against mutilation by animals and other types of physical damage to one of "honoring the dead" (*Igrot Moshe, Yoreh Deah,* 1:225).

†In consequence, "no one knows [Moses'] burial place to this day" (Deuteronomy 34:6).

Showing respect to the dead

4. *K'vod ha-meit,* the honor due to the dead, dictates a variety of activities (and some prohibitions), among them that the following procedures be performed for all deceased Jews: washing, *tahara* (purification), dressing the body in appropriate garments (*tachrichim;* for more on how these procedures are carried out, see paragraphs 14–15), and burial. As a general guideline, Jacob Stromer (cited in Rabbi Mosha Epstein's *Tahara Manual of Practices*) suggests reliance on the Torah's most famous commandment, "Love your neighbor as yourself:" "I believe that each member of the *Chevra* should treat the *niftar* (the deceased) as if the situation was reversed. A sort of postmortem [golden rule should apply. Treat] the *meit* (the dead person) as you would want [your dead body] to be treated."[5]

5. *K'vod ha-meit* also dictates that burial occur as quickly as possible, ideally within a day of the death. To leave a body unburied and exposed for longer than that is regarded as an affront both to God (in whose image human beings are created) and to the dignity of the deceased. This ruling is based on the biblical law that even a person executed because of a capital offense must be buried on the day of his death (Deuteronomy 21:23). If the Torah regards it as an affront to leave the body of a person who has committed a capital crime unburied, how much more so, Jewish law reasons, should one not allow the body of a regular person to remain unburied.

Rabbinic law is so concerned with the prompt burial of the dead that even though Torah law forbids a *kohen* (priest) from having contact with dead bodies except those of his closest relatives (see Leviticus 21:1–4), if the High Priest himself* encounters a dead body on the road and there is no one else who can attend to its burial, then he must do so (*Mishnah Nazir* 7:1; see also, *Shulchan Arukh, Yoreh Deah,* 374:1–3; contact with a dead body invalidates a priest from carrying out his priestly responsibilities for a full week).

Although burial within a day (or at least on the day following death; a person might die at 8 a.m and the funeral take place the following morning at eleven) is generally adhered to, Jewish law permits a delay in certain circumstances, these also dictated by *k'vod ha-meit.* The most common reason is to allow for the arrival of close relatives coming from a distance. Since it is assumed that the dead person would have wanted these people present, delay-

*Unlike other *kohanim,* the High Priest is forbidden contact with any dead bodies, including those of his own parents (Leviticus 21:11).

ing the funeral in effect honors his or her wishes. Such a situation happens, for example, when relatives must fly in from another country.*

There are other reasons for delaying a funeral. For example, funerals are not generally conducted on mid-to-late Friday afternoons, since this can lead to extreme time pressure or even to desecration of the Sabbath. Therefore, if somebody dies on Friday, the funeral usually takes place on Sunday.

Funerals may also be delayed when there is a need for an autopsy, such as when a person has died under suspicious circumstances (for more on autopsies, see paragraph 8).

Another increasingly common reason for delaying a burial is to enable the body to be buried in Israel. Although flying has made burial there an increasingly popular option, particularly for religiously observant Jews, the precedent for arranging for burial in the Holy Land is Genesis, in which Joseph arranges, at his father's request, to have Jacob's body transported from Egypt back to Israel (then known as Canaan), so that Jacob can be buried in the cave in which his father, mother, and grandparents were interred (50:2–14).†

My father, Shlomo Telushkin, of blessed memory, died in New York on a Thursday morning, December 24. It is difficult to arrange a burial on December 25, Christmas, which that year fell on a Friday. Some friends of my father, fearing that his burial would be delayed until Sunday (a full three days after his death) pressured our family to have the funeral and burial that very day, within just a few hours of his death. We resisted, knowing that if we did so, there would be no time to gather many of the people dearest to my father. "I'm not going to have a service for my father with only ten or fifteen people," I insisted. "My father deserves more than that." Fortunately, by paying the cemetery workers five times the normal rate, we were able to arrange to have my father's funeral and burial the following morning.‡

---

6. Embalming. The principle of *k'vod ha-meit* dictates that a body not be tampered with, and nothing done to speed or slow down the body's natural

*The reason, though, has to be substantial. David Zinner notes that families will sometimes ask to delay a funeral for inappropriate reasons, such as to allow a grandchild time to finish a research paper for school.

†So important to Jacob is burial in his parents' plot that even after Joseph assures him that he will take care of it, Jacob insists that he take an oath that he will do so (Genesis 47:29–31).

‡Members of the Chabad (Lubavitch) community expressed their willingness to come and dig the grave, but it was not permitted for nonunion workers to do so.

decomposition. Thus, Jewish law opposes embalming. Yet the Torah does speak of the embalming of Jacob (Genesis 50:2–3) and Joseph (Genesis 50:26). Embalming was widely practiced in Egypt* and was, in any case, necessary in the case of Jacob since the process of mourning for him in Egypt, followed by his burial in Canaan, occupied about four months (see Genesis 50:3–10). Leaving a body unburied for so long a period would lead to terrible decay and odors.

Nonetheless, the process of embalming, which involves puncturing organs, an incision in a major artery and vein, and the pumping of formaldehyde into the artery, is regarded as abhorrent to the Jewish notion of respect for the dead. Thus, when a body is shipped to Israel, in lieu of embalming, the Israeli government sanctions using a lightweight wooden casket lined with aluminum and sometimes preserved with ice packs.[6]

7. Cremation. Jewish law opposes cremation, and regards it as an extreme lack of respect for the dead body.† Although no explicit biblical law prohibits cremation, the prophet Amos, writing over 2,700 years ago, speaks of the punishment of the nation of Moab for its many sins, specifying that it had "burned the bones of the king of Edom into lime" (Amos 2:1).

The Torah takes burial and the gradual decomposition of the dead body for granted: "For dust you are, and to dust you shall return" (Genesis 3:19). Genesis 23 details the great lengths to which Abraham went to purchase a large burial plot for his wife, Sarah, which later served as the burial plot for him and many of his descendants.‡ Obviously, Abraham would have saved time and money if he had arranged for Sarah's body to be cremated, but he didn't. Also, God's burial of Moses serves as an important precedent for Jews, since Torah law instructs its adherents to imitate God (Deuteronomy 28:9).

The Jews' long-standing opposition to cremation was familiar to their non-Jewish neighbors. Roman historian Tacitus (ca. 56–ca. 120) notes that the Jews "bury rather than burn their dead" (*The Histories* 5:5).

---

*The Egyptian practice of body preservation seems to have been different from modern-day embalming. Thus, when Joseph's remains were later taken to be buried in Canaan, all that remained were bones (Exodus 13:19 and Joshua 24:32).

†If a person, while alive, made arrangements to be cremated, no *tahara* is performed. If, however, the children of the deceased arrange for cremation, and the deceased was not aware that they were going to do so, a *tahara* may be performed (see Rabbi Mosha Epstein, *Tahara Manual of Practices*, page 43).

‡To this day, that site, known as the *Me'arat He-Machpela* (in English it is referred to as the "Cave of the Matriarchs and Patriarchs"), remains one of Judaism's holiest sites.

It is rarely noted that King Saul was partially cremated (I Samuel 31:12), though in an unusual circumstance. Saul had committed suicide to avoid capture by the Philistines, whom, he feared, would torture him and then desecrate his body. While Saul's suicide enabled him to avoid torture, the Philistines did, as he feared, make a mockery of his corpse, cutting off his head and impaling his body, along with those of three of his sons, in a public square. The residents of Yavesh Gil'ad, whom Saul had saved from torture and humiliation many years earlier,* rescued his body from the Philistines and then burned it, apparently to avoid the possibility of having further indignities inflicted upon it. However, they seem to have only partially burned the body (perhaps just the decaying flesh), for the following verse records that they buried the bones of Saul and his sons. This incident constitutes a rare instance in which cremation was done for the sake of *k'vod ha-meit* and is therefore not seen as dishonoring the deceased's body.

Maimonides rules that if, prior to death, a person expresses an explicit wish not to be buried (but presumably to be cremated instead), this wish should be ignored ("Laws of Mourning" 12:1). Nonetheless, if a person is cremated, there is no explicit prohibition against burying the ashes† in a Jewish cemetery,[7] although many Jewish cemeteries do not allow cremated remains to be buried on their grounds.

The intensity of Judaism's opposition to cremation is fueled by several factors. Most significantly, because the body, though now dead, once housed the soul, it is believed to retain a certain sanctity. To draw an analogy: the Aron Kodesh *in which the Torah scrolls are kept is simply a wooden ark. However, once Torah scrolls have been placed inside it, it acquires a certain sanctity, some of which adheres even after it stops being used to house Torah scrolls. Thus, most Jews, particularly religious ones, would find it incongruous, to say the least, to stoke a fireplace with the wood of a no-longer-functioning* Aron Kodesh. *Similarly, and even more so than in the case of an* Aron Kodesh, *a certain sanctity adheres to a body even after death, so that it must be treated with respect.*

A second reason is an emotional one, rooted in recent Jewish historical experience. Burning bodies is what the Nazis did to the Jews after they gassed them,

---

*An Ammonite leader, Nachash, had threatened to blind the residents of Yavesh Gil'ad in their right eyes; "I will make this a humiliation for all Israel" (I Samuel 11:2). Learning of their plight, Saul had gathered an enormous army, destroyed the Ammonite attackers, and saved the people of Yavesh Gil'ad.

†In actuality, what is left after a body is burned is not ashes, but bone fragments, teeth, and dental fillings; these are often pulverized before being given to the family.

and cremation, fairly or unfairly, remains associated in the psyche of many Jews with the Nazis' behavior. What the Nazis did to Jewish bodies, many feel, Jews must not do to themselves or to each other.

Rabbi Elie Spitz articulates an additional reason not to cremate, which he terms "concern for the welfare of the mourner." In Spitz's words: "Burial helps the mourner by providing a sense of closure. When the mourner sees the coffin being lowered into the earth and when he hears the sound of pebbles and soil hitting the coffin, it hurts terribly, but from that moment on, he knows that death is real. . . . Cremation always takes place out of sight of the family, for it is a violent act. And so, for the mourner, there is no act that marks closure. A grave is an address to which a family can come ever afterward in order to commune with its memories."[8]

There is a widespread belief (one that I have heard many Jews articulate) that Judaism opposes cremation because it will be impossible for cremated bodies to be resurrected at the end of days. But God, whom the Torah teaches created the world out of nothing (creatio ex nihilo), *would have as little trouble, if He so wished, resurrecting a dead body from cremated remains as He would resurrecting any other dead body. Also, given that most of the 6 million Jews murdered in the Holocaust were cremated by the Nazis, it is absurd, and cruel, to believe that they would be denied resurrection because their bodies were burned.**

---

8. Autopsies. As a general, but not absolute, rule, Jewish law opposes autopsies and regards the cutting up of a dead body as *nivul ha-meit,* a humiliation of the dead. However, there are a number of exceptions in which autopsies are permitted. Most obviously are cases in which a death occurs under suspicious circumstances, and police authorities insist upon it. In such instances, autopsies may be able to determine if death was due to

*Perhaps such people believe that the punishment of not being resurrected will be inflicted only on those who intentionally cremate themselves. Thus, in a related but altogether different circumstance, when corneal transplants started to be performed, Rabbi Eliezer Waldenberg opposed them (*Tzitz Eliezer,* Volume 13, *Yoreh Deah,* # 91), and went so far as to argue that a person who donated his eyes would, at the time of resurrection, be restored to life without eyes. Rabbi Reuven Frank has noted that Rabbi Waldenberg did not base this teaching on any Jewish source; "rather, it is his own intuitive feeling" ("Halachic Aspects of Organ Transplantation," *Journal of Halacha and Contemporary Society,* number 5, Spring 1983, pages 55–56); Rabbi Waldenberg's fear was also that doctors, in their haste to retrieve the eyes while they were still "warm and fresh," might remove the eyes before the patient was actually dead. Happily, in a later ruling, Rabbi Waldenberg reversed himself and permitted the transplanting of corneas (*Tzitz Eliezer,* Volume 14, *Yoreh Deah,* # 84), and his view is now, and has long been, the accepted view of rabbinic scholars.

homicide, suicide, or accidental injury. Such knowledge, which may help convict a guilty person and exonerate an innocent one, override objections to autopsies.

Related to this are instances in which determining the cause of death may have implications for public safety. I remember an incident in New York some years ago when a previously healthy person died suddenly and unexpectedly and an autopsy revealed food poisoning. It was quickly determined that the cause of death was a container of contaminated fish. Because the fish had been widely sold, the autopsy probably saved other lives as it caused health officials to withdraw this product from the market immediately, so that people who had already bought it were warned to discard it.

Autopsies are also permitted when someone has died from a hereditary illness and doctors need to discern if the death has any implications for surviving relatives.

Autopsies may also be allowed when the deceased was receiving an experimental treatment and the doctors need to see whether the treatment was effective (for example, "when a new chemotherapeutic drug is being evaluated for toxicity and efficacy"; Rabbi Moshe Dovid Tendler).[9] Thus, a dear friend of mine was being given an experimental course of treatment for cancer. When he died, the doctors asked the widow—both she and her husband were religiously observant Jews who would, under normal circumstances, never have permitted an autopsy—if they could perform an autopsy to check on the status of the treatment. Permission was granted, and it was determined that the treatment had, in fact, effectively treated the cancer; unfortunately, the body's immune system had been temporarily compromised and the patient had died of pneumonia. Here, too, the information yielded by the autopsy was effective in helping others.*

Rabbi Maurice Lamm notes that "even in cases where the rabbis have permitted the post-mortem, they have always insisted that any part of the body that is removed must thereafter be buried with the body, and that it be returned to the *Chevra Kadisha* for this purpose as soon as possible. [Also], the medical dissection must be performed with utmost respect for the deceased, and not handled lightly by insensitive personnel."[10]

---

*Another increasingly common reason to cut open a body after death is for organ transplantation. Where the organ or organs can save other lives, it is regarded as an honor for the dead to make such a donation; few mitzvot are as highly esteemed in Judaism as saving a life. As for Judaism's insistence that all organs be interred, such interment will occur when the recipient of the transplanted organ dies. Of course, this might not always be the case—for example, if the recipient chooses to be cremated.

---

*Part of the Jewish concern with autopsies is that medical students and other medical personnel—perhaps in an effort to desensitize their discomfort in dealing with a dead body—*sometimes *treat it disrespectfully.* Dr. Isaac Herschkopf recalls a medical school classmate playing jump rope with a cadaver's dissected small intestine. While no one else in the laboratory acted in so disrespectful a manner, Herschkopf also recalls that no one reprimanded the student or stopped him. Reports of "jokes" played with body parts of corpses, although perhaps urban legends, have long been part of medical school lore. Herschkopf recalls hearing of a medical student who gave a toll collector the coins in his cadaver's hand, and drove off, leaving the hand in the booth. There is good reason to believe that respect for, and treatment of, cadavers at medical schools has increased in recent years (for an example, see the footnote below), yet when an autopsy must be performed, the last thing in the world Jewish law would want is to have it handled by someone who is not conscious that this dead body was someone's mother or father or child and, equally important, a human being created in God's image. A dear friend, who has participated in many* taharot, *commented on how often mourners thank her for her work and note how comforting it is for them to know that their parent's body was treated with gentleness and reverence by members of their own community.*

Tahara

9. The three primary tasks of the *Chevra Kadisha* are

- washing the deceased's body;
- performing the ritual of purification *(tahara)*;
- dressing the body, and placing it in the casket.

---

*I am obviously not accusing all students or medical personnel of doing so, but generally bodies are treated in a secular setting with less reverence than that shown by the *Chevra Kadisha.* (On the other hand, I read a beautiful article by Ranit Mishori, a Jewish medical student at the Georgetown University School of Medicine, in which he wrote of the exquisite care and respect he and his lab partners demonstrated toward the elderly woman whose body they dissected and studied; see "The Past Life of My Cadaver, *Washington Post,* December 11, 1999.) Instances in which disrespect is shown are not confined to irreverent medical personnel. The late rabbi Richard Israel, himself a member of a *Chevra Kadisha,* wrote of an "attorney general of one of the mid-Atlantic states [who] gave permission to use unclaimed bodies to test automobile bumpers, not to test damage to the bodies, mind you, but damage to the bumpers. I don't know if these bodies really cared, but the line between an offense to the living and an offense to the dead is so thin that the Jewish tradition has chosen not to acknowledge it" (*The Kosher Pig and Other Curiosities of Modern Jewish Life,* pages 97–98).

Ideally, the *tahara* should be performed within three hours prior to the funeral, but when this is difficult to arrange, the *tahara* may be performed on the night preceding the funeral.

10. Washing. Before cleansing the body, the members of the *Chevra Kadisha* formally request forgiveness from the dead person. This request is a remarkable assertion of Judaism's belief that the soul retains cognizance even after the body has died. A member of the *Chevra Kadisha* recites as follows (in presenting this prayer, I am using names, since the alternative, referring to a person as "So-and-so," sounds soulless): "Sarah, daughter of Jacob:* We beg your forgiveness for any distress we may cause you. We will do everything possible not to cause you any discomfort by an act of disrespect or by omitting any element of the *tahara.* Everything we do is for the sake of your honor." The members also offer a prayer to God: "Master of the Universe! Have compassion for Reuven, son of Isaac, this deceased, for he is a descendant of Abraham, Isaac, and Jacob your servants. . . . Through mercy, hide and disregard the transgressions of this departed. May he tread with righteous feet into the Garden of Eden, for that is the place of the pious, and God protects the pious."

The *Chevra Kadisha* then cleans the dead body with great care. Fingernails and toenails are cleaned with toothpicks, and the hair is combed. The body is washed from head to foot, starting with the head, followed by the neck, the right upper arm, arm, and hand, the right upper half of the body, the private parts, the right thigh, leg, and foot, the left upper arm, arm, and hand, the left upper half of the body, the left thigh, leg, and foot.† Each body part is first washed with lukewarm water and then cleansed with a piece of cloth. Intimate parts of the body are kept covered until such time as they are being cleaned, and then are covered again.‡ As noted, because of issues of modesty, men of the *Chevra Kadisha* tend to male dead and women to female dead.

Once the front of the body is washed, it is rolled onto its left side, thereby enabling the *Chevra Kadisha* to wash the person's right side, starting from the shoulder to the foot. Then, the body is rolled onto its right side, so

---

*Traditionally, the father's name is mentioned, though, of course, one may mention both parents' names; for example, Sarah, daughter of Jacob and Rebecca.

†See the discussion of the cleaning in Abner Weiss, *Death and Bereavement,* pages 57–58.

‡The nakedness of the body during the cleaning is in accordance with a verse in Job: "Naked came I out of my mother's womb, and naked I shall return there" (1:21). While the body must be unclothed to be washed, it would be considered disrespectful to leave the body uncovered at other times; hence *tachrichim.*

that the left side of the back may be washed. The body is never placed face-down.

While the washing and *tahara* are taking place, objects are never passed or handed over the dead body. It is also forbidden to engage in activities that the dead cannot do (except for those germane to preparing the body for burial), such as eating, drinking, smoking, and unnecessary talking.*

Concerning not passing items over the deceased's body, my friend Terry Wohlberg, a member of a Chevra Kadisha *which she helped organize at Sinai Temple in Los Angeles, likens "this respect to the way that we wouldn't pass an item in front of someone at the dinner table without saying, 'Excuse me.'" Similarly, "refraining from passing an item over the body emphasizes that we are to treat the deceased in the same way that we would if they were alive. When I do these things in practice, and not just think about or read about them, I am more able to relate to the deceased as once living. Thus, throughout the washing, we never turn our back on the deceased when getting supplies, and later, when leaving the room. In Jewish tradition, you don't turn your back when the* Aron Kodesh, *the ark containing the Torah scrolls, is open. In secular society, you show respect by not turning your back on a president or a queen. The dead too are entitled to this type of respect." Wohlberg emphasizes that the carrying out of these rituals enables her to feel "a sense of the deceased's 'aware soul' that is hovering." This is in consonance with an old Jewish teaching that the spirit of the dead hovers on earth for seven days after death (see* Shabbat *152b).*

---

11. Because of their close contact with dead bodies, members of a *Chevra Kadisha* should receive inoculations against tetanus, as well as hepatitis B, and should wear gloves at all times when dealing with a dead body.

12. As noted, part of respect for the dead involves ensuring that all body parts, even those that have been disconnected from the body (such as might happen in the case of an accident or autopsy), are buried with the body. This includes "blood which flows at the time of death [and which] may not be washed away. It is considered part of the body and must be buried with the

*Religious males who are accustomed to wearing the fringes of their tzitzit over their garments are instructed to tuck them into their pants. This is reminiscent of a teaching in the Talmud: "A person may not walk in a cemetery with *tefillin* on his head, or while reading from a Torah scroll in his arm. And if he does, he transgresses [the biblical verse], 'One who mocks a pauper blasphemes his Maker'" (Proverbs 17:5; *Berachot* 18a). This passage is understood as meaning that it is a mockery of the dead, who cannot perform commandments, to do so in their presence.

deceased. Blood spots on sheets are cut out and placed at the foot of the casket. Open wounds are treated with a coagulant, and the cloth used for this is likewise placed at the foot of the casket."[11] If there is a great deal of blood, then the body is not washed, and the *tahara,* which involves pouring water over the body, is not performed. Rather, the body is placed in the casket along with the clothes it is wearing (the clothing is not removed as it is likely soaked with blood as well, and the blood must also be buried).

Rochel Berman, author of Dignity Beyond Death, *tells of an instance in which a woman visiting the United States from Australia drowned, and the legal authorities insisted on an autopsy: "The family requested that the blood lost during the [autopsy] be preserved in several containers and placed in the casket, thereby enabling a proper Jewish burial."*[12]

When murder has occurred

13. "If a Jew is found murdered, let him be buried as he was found, without a shroud [but in the clothes he was wearing], and without even his shoes being removed" (*Shulchan Arukh, Yoreh Deah* 364:4). One reason is to ensure that the blood is buried along with the body. However, since this law is followed even when there is no blood (for instance, when the person is strangled), there must be another rationale as well. Two seventeenth-century commentaries on the *Shulchan Arukh,* known as the *Shakh* and the *Taz,* along with the nineteenth-century *Kitzur* [Shortened] *Shulchan Arukh,* explain that we bury the victim as we found him "in order to provoke in people the desire to avenge [the crime]" (see *Kitzur Shulchan Arukh* 197:12).

Regarding Jews who are killed by terrorists (such as "suicide bombers"), Nossen Friedman, a member of the Chevra Kadisha *of Boro Park (Brooklyn) explains: "Those that die dressed in the bloody garments of a soldier or a terrorist victim died* al Kiddush Hashem, *to sanctify God's name,* which constitutes man's ultimate purpose. This is viewed as a badge of honor."*[13]

In Israel, the organization ZAKA, founded in 1989, goes to the scene of every terrorist attack to identify victims (approximately 1,100 Israelis were killed in

---

*The reason being that they were targeted because they were Jews.

terrorist bombings and attacks between 2000–2006). Its members collect every drop of blood and the smallest body parts, and arrange to have them buried.

Sometimes they are also called upon to relax the general Jewish restriction against relatives viewing or touching a body after death. A member of ZAKA's Chevra Kadisha *explains: "Often the shock is so great that the family does not believe what happened unless they view the body for themselves. According to tradition, we allow them to do it because just as we believe in* k'vod ha-meit, *respect for the dead, we also believe in* k'vod ha-chaim, *respect for the living." Dr. Yehuda Hiss, a pathologist at Israel's National Center of Forensic Medicine, notes that while psychologists at one time were inclined to reject family members' requests to view bodies or the remains of victims, the current policy is to accommodate such requests: "The families want to touch the body one last time to prepare for separation." Hiss explains that sometimes all that remains of a person is a foot, yet family members will want to touch or hug it since that constitutes their sole remaining concrete connection with their loved one.**[14]

---

14. *Tahara.* "I will pour upon you pure water, and you will be purified of all your defilements" (Ezekiel 36:25). Already in the time of the Mishnah (early third century C.E.), we learn that corpses should be washed (*Shabbat* 23:5).

Just before the *tahara* is performed, the body is raised to a vertical position, or as upright as possible. Water† is then poured over the head so that it flows over the entire body. A total of nine *kavim* of water (assumed to be twenty-four quarts; some authorities believe that eighteen quarts are sufficient) is used in the *tahara,* divided into three buckets. The water is poured in a continuous flow over the body; thus, as the first bucket is about to fin-

*It is not an uncommon phenomenon for survivors to wear or sleep with the dead person's clothing, specifically because it still smells of their loved one. Thus, Benazir Bhutto, the assassinated former prime minister of Pakistan, was in her twenties when her father, Zulfihar Ali Bhutto, was deposed and later executed. Hours after he was killed, her father's jailer handed over to Bhutto her father's few remaining possessions, including his *shalwar,* a long shirt: "The scent of his cologne was still on his clothes, the scent of Shalimar. I hugged his *shalwar* to me. . . . That night and for many others, I [continued to try] to keep my father near me by sleeping with his shirt under my pillow." Bhutto recalled how years earlier she had been a student at Harvard University a few years after Senator Robert Kennedy had been assassinated. One of Kennedy's daughters, Kathleen, was a student there as well: "I remember [she] had at the time a blue parka jacket that belonged to her father, and she would wear it often and keep it very close to her."

A rabbinic friend told me of a widow who confided in him that when she wore her late husband's sweater, she still felt his hugs.

†Tap water is fine.

ish, another member of the *Chevra Kadisha* starts pouring from the second bucket (if there is an interruption in the pouring of the water, the process begins again). After (or during the time) the water is poured, the members of the *Chevra Kadisha* make the following declaration in Hebrew: *"Tahor hu! Tahor hu! Tahor hu!"* (He is pure! He is pure! He is pure!), or *"Tehora hee! Tehora hee! Tehora hee"* (She is pure! She is pure! She is pure!). The body is then placed back on the table on which it has been lying and wiped until it is dry.

15. Dressing. Once the body is dry, it is dressed, the final act prior to placement in the casket. *Tachrichim,* simple white garments, are used. There is a strong preference for the garments to be made of linen, but cotton, if necessary (for example, to save money), is acceptable. An old tradition (in the realm of custom, not law) dictates that the garments be sewn by pious older women.* The shrouds are prepared without pockets, symbolizing that we carry nothing, including material wealth, with us when we die.[15] In the case of a man, it is also common to wrap a *tallit,* a prayer shawl, around the burial shroud.† One of its fringes *(tzitziyot)* is cut, thereby rendering the *tallit* ritually unusable, for it is considered inappropriate to bury a *tallit* that is valid for use. It is also common to put over the garments a *kittel,* the simple white linen or cotton garment that many religious Jewish men wear over their regular clothing on the High Holidays.‡ Some earth from the Land of Israel is sprinkled in the areas of the heart and the private parts of the deceased. Also, small pieces of broken earthenware are put over the eyes and mouth. David Zinner, of Kavod v'Nichum, an advocacy group for *Chevra Kadisha* societies, speculates that this is symbolic of the belief that our task in this life is to reassemble or repair the broken shards of the world and make them whole.

The very simplicity of the garments used as tachrichim *is intentional and was introduced two millennia ago to spare the poor embarrassment and expense. As the Talmud teaches: "Formerly, the expense of burying the dead was harder for [many] a family to bear than the death itself, so that sometimes family members*

---

*For the exact composition of each garment, see Rabbi Abner Weiss, *Death and Bereavement,* pages 59–62. Today, ready-made garments are also considered acceptable (see Rabbi Mosha Epstein, *Tahara Manual Practices,* page 9).

†Most women do not wear *tallitot,* but if the dead woman had done so, it is appropriate to bury her in a *tallit* as well.

‡The *kittel* is also worn by some men at the Passover Seder, and by some grooms under the chuppah (wedding canopy).

fled to escape the expense. This was so until Rabban Gamliel . . . ordered that he be buried in a plain linen shroud [instead of in expensive garments]. Since then, people have buried their dead in simple linen garments" (Mo'ed Kattan *27b*).

—

Rabbi Jack Riemer has noted that there are many lessons for daily life to be learned from the kittel. *The first is the essential equality of all human beings. On Yom Kippur, for example, if all the men in a synagogue are dressed in a* kittel *(there is no reason women can't wear one as well), one cannot distinguish between rich and poor, between a banker wearing a custom-made suit, and a physical laborer wearing an ill-fitting jacket bought off the rack. All stand equal before God. In Riemer's words, "The* kittel *covers for at least three days a year all of the class differences between men."*

Also, in the ancient Roman world the color of a man's garments was a sign of his status. The nobility wore purple, slaves were dressed in unbleached clothing (basically, whatever clothes their masters gave them), and free men wore simple white togas. By putting on a white robe, a Jew wished to show that he was not a member of the often-decadent nobility, nor a slave. Rather, he was a free person. Perhaps that is why the kittel *also became the garment of choice for the Passover Seder.*

Finally, the kittel, *because it is a burial garment, reminds the wearer, as he stands in synagogue on Yom Kippur, that he is mortal. As he looks at the other congregants, dressed like himself in their burial shrouds, it also reminds him that everyone else is also mortal. If he is going to make peace with those with whom he has feuded, he had better do so now. Who, other than God, knows if he or they will be around the following year?*[16] *By spending the High Holidays in one's burial shroud, one in effect is always confronting the question posed by Hillel: "If not now, when?"*

—

The highly regarded American-Jewish writer Philip Roth, by no means a traditional Jew, recalls how he, nonetheless, arranged for his father to be buried in a tallit. *When Herman Roth died, Roth's brother found a shallow box containing two neatly folded prayer shawls in their father's bedroom. Later, "When the mortician, at the house, asked us to pick out a suit for him, I said to my brother, 'A suit? He's not going to the office! No, no suit—it's senseless. He should be buried in a shroud,' I said, thinking that was how Jews were buried traditionally. . . . I thought how bizarrely out of character an urban earthling like my insurance-man father, a sturdy man rooted all his life in everydayness, would look in a shroud even while I understood that that was the idea."*[17]

Rochel Berman relates a story told her by a man who was advising a be-

reaved family on the funeral: "The daughter . . . told me that her father was an impeccable dresser. She said that he was always perfectly attired for every occasion. She therefore wanted her father buried in his finest tuxedo. I told her that I'm sure that her father had the greatest outfit when he played golf and just the right set of tennis clothes, and that when he went to a wedding he had the best looking tux. So, it only follows that for this occasion, he would also want to have the proper attire. I then described the process of tahara *and the significance of* tachrichim. *The daughter listened carefully, and then said, '. . . I never thought of it that way.' She then convinced her mother that* tachrichim *would be the most appropriate clothing for this occasion."*[18]

While the tachrichim, kittel, *and* tallit *are the standard garments in which to bury the dead, I know of one instance in which, for a singularly compelling reason, a different garment was used. When Abraham Bachner, a Holocaust survivor who was a member of Young Israel of Kew Gardens Hills in Queens, New York died, his rabbi, Fabian Schonfeld, recounted at the funeral a conversation he had a short time earlier with Mr. Bachner: "'Rabbi,' he said to me, 'I have been a member of your congregation for the past thirty years. I tried to be an honest, observant Jew. I attended services regularly on Saturdays and weekdays, no matter what the weather. I know that my time is up and I will soon be summoned before the heavenly court. I want to be buried not in* tachrichim, *as required by Jewish law, but rather in my concentration-camp uniform, the one I wore in Auschwitz, the one in which I was liberated.'*

"I could not understand his strange request and asked for an explanation. Abe said to me, 'You see, Rabbi, when I reach the seat of justice on high, the heavenly prosecutors probably have a list of grievances against me upon which they will base my guilty verdict. When they place my transgressions on one side of the scales of the heavenly court, I will place on the other side my concentration-camp uniform. The hunger, the fear, the humiliation I suffered each minute while I was a katzetnik *(inmate) will surely tip the scales of justice in my favor. I hope, Rabbi, that you understand. I must be buried in my uniform. It is my defense case . . . '" And, indeed, the rabbi explained, he had carried out Mr. Bachner's wish.*[19]

---

16. After the body is dressed, it is lifted by the members of the *Chevra Kadisha* and gently lowered into the casket. Before closing it, the *Chevra Kadisha* offers a request for forgiveness: "Leah, daughter of Isaac, we ask forgiveness of you if we did not treat you respectfully, but we acted in accordance with our custom. May you be an advocate for all of Israel. Go in peace, rest in peace, and arise in your turn at the End of Days."

The power of the Chevra Kadisha *to help bring healing to a bereaved family is reflected in a recollection of Professor Jacob Neusner, the talmudic scholar, shortly after the death of his beloved father-in-law, Max Richter: "These men [the members of the* Chevra Kadisha*] showed me more of what it means to be a Jew, of what Torah stands for, than all the books I ever read. They tended to the corpse gently and reverently, yet did not pretend it was other than a corpse. At the end of the process, the head of the [*Chevra Kadisha*] said in a loud voice, that the dead should hear, and the living: 'Mordechai ben Menachem, all we have done is for your honor. And if we have not done our task properly, we beg your forgiveness.'"*

---

17. Once the casket is closed, it is not opened again before being placed into the ground. An exception may be made when a formal identification of the deceased is required by law, though ideally, even in such a case, this should take place before the *tahara.*

The choice of casket

18. Just as Jewish tradition prescribes that the body be dressed in the simplest and plainest garments, so, too, it wants the casket to be simple, ideally a plain wooden box.* The basis for this is the talmudic text cited earlier that indicates Judaism's preference for simple shrouds: "Formerly, when they would bring out the deceased for burial, the rich would be on a tall bed ornamented with rich covers, the poor on a plain bier [the body was covered], and the poor felt ashamed. Therefore, a law was passed that all should be brought out on a plain bier, out of concern for the honor of the poor" (*Mo'ed Kattan* 27a–b).

A final thought

19. The most well-known responsibility to the dead is performed not by the *Chevra Kadisha* but rather by the deceased's children and/or other family members: the recitation of the Kaddish. Well-known as this prayer is, many Jews are surprised to learn that it contains no allusion to death. Rather, the

*In Israel, as noted, the body is commonly dressed in shrouds and put directly into the ground.

Kaddish proclaims the greatness of God (its opening words, starting with *Yitgadal ve-Yitkadash Shmei Rabbah,* mean "Magnified and sanctified be His great name throughout the world which He has created according to His will"). Presumably, the Kaddish was chosen as the memorial prayer for the dead because the greatest testament to the deceased is that he or she has left behind descendants who intend to lead lives committed to Judaism, and who attend synagogue services and pledge to work toward perfecting the world under the rule of God.*

—

Until recent times, recitation of the Kaddish among traditional Jews was generally restricted to males. This was, in my view, very unfortunate, for as I know from my own experience of reciting Kaddish for both of my parents, Helen and Shlomo Telushkin, of blessed memory, the recitation of the Kaddish greatly consoles the mourner. During the eleven months I said Kaddish for each of my parents, I constantly felt the zechut *(privilege) that I was doing something on their behalf. I also felt connected to them every day, and this enabled me to gradually adjust to their loss. The healing and consoling effects of reciting the Kaddish are so well known and commented upon that it seems at the very least unjust to deny its recitation to women. In addition, throughout Jewish history, the fact that a woman didn't say the Kaddish had the effect of diminishing the significance of girl children. Thus, in eastern Europe, when a first son was born, even if the parents already had several female children, the baby boy would often be referred to lovingly as a* kaddishel; *only with the birth of this child could the parents be assured that they would have a descendant who could recite the memorial prayer for them after they died.*

In recent years, there has been a large increase in the number of women saying Kaddish, and one hopes that the number of women doing so continues to grow. It should be noted that even in the past there were women who said Kaddish.† *A gem of modern Jewish literature is a letter written by Henrietta Szold, the founder of Hadassah. In 1916, Szold's mother died, and because Szold came from a family with eight daughters and no sons, a friend named Haym Peretz offered to say the Kaddish on her mother's behalf. "It is impossible for me to find words with which to tell you how deeply I was touched," Szold wrote Peretz. "It is*

*My friend Rabbi Israel Stein likes to say: "By reciting the Kaddish, the mourners are affirming that though they have lost a loved one, they have not lost their faith in God."

†Rabbi Joseph Soloveitchik shared a recollection with a student of having been at a service in Vilna at what had been the Vilna Gaon's synagogue, and of a woman attending the evening *Ma'ariv* service there at which she recited the Kaddish (Aaron Rakeffet-Rothkoff, *The Rav,* Volume 2, page 36).

beautiful what you have offered to do—I shall never forget it." Yet she went on to *explain why she could not accept his offer:*

"I cannot ask you to say Kaddish after my mother. The Kaddish means to me that the survivor publicly and markedly manifests his wish and intention to assume the relation of the Jewish community which his parents had, and that so the chain of tradition remains unbroken from generation to generation. . . . You can do that for the generations of your family, I must do that for the generations of my family.

"I believe that the elimination of women from such duties was never intended by our law and custom—women were freed from positive duties when they could not perform them, but not when they could. It was never intended that, if they could perform them, their performance of them would not be considered as valuable and valid as when one of the male sex performed them. And of the Kaddish I feel sure this is particularly true.

"My mother had eight daughters and no sons; and yet never did I hear a word of regret pass the lips of either my mother or my father that one of us was not a son. When my father died, my mother would not permit others to take her daughters' place in saying the Kaddish, and so I am sure I am acting in her spirit when I am moved to decline your offer. But beautiful your offer remains nevertheless, and, I repeat, I know full well that it is much more in consonance with the generally accepted Jewish tradition than is my family's tradition."[20]

Comforting Mourners

When they saw him [Job] from a distance . . . they broke into loud weeping; each one tore his robe and threw dust into the air onto his head. They sat with him on the ground seven days and seven nights. None spoke a word to him, for they saw how very great was his suffering.

Job 2:11–13

9

CARING FOR THE BEREAVED

When death occurs

1. In addition to attending to the dead (see preceding chapter), the first obligation of friends and neighbors is to offer help to the immediate family members who have suffered the loss. This could entail assistance in making funeral arrangements (the mourners might not be thinking clearly), calling people to tell them when and where the funeral will take place, or organizing the meal for the mourners upon their return from the cemetery (see paragraph 6).

2. What one should *not do* immediately after the death is to offer consolation: "Do not comfort your friend at a time when his deceased lies before him" (*The Ethics of the Fathers* 4:18). At such a time, the mourner is not yet ready for this.

Shiva

3. According to Jewish law, seven days of intense mourning, *shiva,** are observed by the deceased's seven closest relatives:

- father and mother
- brother and sister
- son and daughter

**Shiva* is the Hebrew word for seven. Following shiva, there is a less-intense period known as *shloshim* (thirty), which concludes on the thirtieth day of mourning. Finally, in the case of parents (but not other relatives), the laws of mourning continue for an entire year; the Kaddish prayer, however, is recited for only eleven months. The reason for this practice is an unusual one. According to Jewish tradition, even the wicked are punished in the afterworld for no more than twelve months. Since Kaddish is recited in part to help elevate the soul of the dead, reciting it for the full twelve months would imply that one's parent was among the wicked.

- spouse (other relatives, such as a grandchild, may choose to observe shiva, but these seven relatives are obligated to do so)

During the week of shiva, mourners are expected to remain in the house of mourning* (usually the house of the deceased or of one or more of the mourners) and to receive those who come to be *menachem avel* (comfort the mourners). The mourners sit on low stools. In English, we speak of "feeling low" as a synonym for depression; in Jewish law, the depression is acted out literally.

Throughout the week, prayer services are conducted in the mourners' house.

During shiva, mourners may not shave, bathe, wear leather shoes (which Jewish tradition regards as particularly comfortable), engage in sexual relations, or launder their clothes.

4. The *Shulchan Arukh* teaches: "During the first three days [the mourner] should neither greet anyone [by saying 'Shalom'] and if others don't know that he is in mourning and greet him, he should not respond to the greeting, but should inform them that he is a mourner." From the third to the seventh day, a mourner should not offer a greeting, but may respond to another's greeting. From then on, he may both accept and initiate greetings (*Yoreh Deah* 385:1, based on *Mo'ed Kattan* 21b). Dr. Ron Wolfson comments: "The great wisdom in this insight lies in allowing the mourner to focus on his or her grief, not on the social niceties of formal greetings."[1]

Similarly, mourners don't rise for guests, even for the *nasi* (a highly important person; in modern terms, *nasi* refers to a president), for whom others are commanded to rise (*Mo'ed Kattan* 27b and Ramah, *Shulchan Arukh, Yoreh Deah* 376:1).

A thought for mourners

5. If someone is not in touch with you during the week of shiva, try to adhere to the biblical law obligating one to judge others fairly (see *A Code of Jewish Ethics, Volume 1: You Shall Be Holy,* pages 70–94). I know of friendships that have been ruined because of a mourner's unwillingness to relinquish anger at someone who didn't visit.† In one case, a friend who was

*Except for the Sabbath, when the public laws of mourning are suspended and mourners are permitted to leave the house and go to synagogue.

†Sometimes mourners become enraged at people who don't visit or contact them, only to learn later that the person had not even been informed of the death.

traveling tried to call to explain that he was away, but the telephone line at the mourner's house was constantly busy. Then, on the last day of shiva, when he was planning to come, he was delayed and couldn't make it. The mourner was hurt, and made it clear that he didn't believe his friend had made much of an effort to call or to come, and a chill, which lasted a long time, fell over the friendship.

Obviously, the law mandating that we judge others fairly is not intended only for cases in which the offender is clearly not at fault. After suffering a death, how foolish it is to suffer the loss of a friendship also. In short, the friend's obligation is to make every effort to come; the mourner's obligation is to judge charitably those who don't.

Among the books detailing the laws of mourning and the responsibilities of mourners are The Jewish Way in Death and Mourning, *by Rabbi Maurice Lamm, and* Death and Bereavement: A Halakhic Guide, *by Rabbi Abner Weiss. The rest of this chapter, however, focuses on the obligation of relatives, neighbors, and friends to comfort mourners.*

Seudat Havra'ah *(the Meal of Consolation)*

6. Upon returning from the burial service at the cemetery, mourners are served a *Seudat Havra'ah.* At this meal, they are forbidden to partake of their own food, or prepare any food themselves; this obligation falls upon neighbors and friends (*Shulchan Arukh, Yoreh Deah* 378:1). Why is this so?

Most obviously, the Rabbis feared that in the immediate aftermath of burying a close relative, mourners might be too upset to eat, or even feel that it was inappropriate to do so ("My mother is lying in the ground, and I'm going to sit down and enjoy a meal?"). Therefore, if no food were put in front of them, they might not eat at all, and thus endanger their health.

Also, after losing a close relative, people often feel alone, even abandoned. At such a time, when a person might not even wish to go on living, Jewish law mandates that the community and friends reach out to the mourner and say, "We care about you," and provide the mourner with food (Jack Riemer).[2]

7. Bread, lentils, and eggs are three foods traditionally served at the *Seudat Havra'ah.* Some Jews offer fish and cheese at this meal, while the *Shulchan Arukh* speaks of others who serve meat and wine (*Yoreh Deah*

378:9); the last is in line with the verse, "Give strong drink to the mourner, and wine to the bitter in spirit" (Proverbs 31:6).* However, if served, wine must be consumed in small quantities (*Yoreh Deah* 378:8). In my experience, most mourners prefer a relatively simple meal, without meat or alcohol.

Paying a shiva visit

8. The obligation of *nichum aveilim,* comforting mourners, falls on all adult Jews. Children should be educated about this mitzvah and, provided they are mature enough to act appropriately, should be encouraged to accompany their parents.

9. It is particularly important to visit mourners who are receiving few visitors, perhaps because their primary residence is in another city, they have a small circle of friends, or the deceased was not well known.

Rabbi Aaron Levine records an incident in Israel some years ago in which a couple's only child died of polio. Because of the great fear of the disease's communicability, the mourning couple received no visitors, which added to their depression. When the Chazon Ish heard of the circumstance, he immediately called for a taxi and visited the couple.[3]

Shiva etiquette

10. Wait until the mourner speaks. According to the Talmud, "Reward comes to the one who remains silent in the house of mourning" (*Berachot* 6b). Many people say thoughtless and unintentionally hurtful things;† therefore, the Rabbis ruled that visitors should remain silent until the mourner initiates conversation. The preference for silence is derived from the behavior of Job's three friends. After they heard of the awful calamities that had

*In a perhaps hyperbolic passage, the Talmud comments that wine was created by God to bring comfort to mourners (*Sanhedrin* 70a).

†For example, "You have to get on with your life"; "You're lucky you had her for so long"; "You're young; there's plenty of time to have another child"; "Don't take it so hard"; "Be strong for the children" (Dr. Ron Wolfson, *A Time to Mourn, a Time to Comfort,* pages 203–204). My friend David Szonyi notes that even if these things happen to be true, such comments should not be made during the days immediately following the death, for they are too jarring and have the effect of trying to force the mourner to put a "cap" on legitimate feelings of grief.

befallen him, most notably, the death of his children and the loss of his health and wealth, Eliphaz, Bildad, and Zophar "met together to go and console and comfort him. When they saw him from a distance . . . they broke into loud weeping; each one tore his robe and threw dust into the air onto his head. They sat with him on the ground seven days and seven nights. None spoke a word to him, for they saw how very great was his suffering" (Job 2:11–13). What matters was that Job's friends were fully with him, not that they tried to comfort him at a time he felt anguish beyond words. Only after Job started to speak did they do so too (alas, they wound up saying terrible things; see paragraph 16).

Hence, the visitor's obligation is to wait for the mourner to speak: "Those who come to console a mourner are not allowed to speak until the mourner begins" (*Mo'ed Kattan* 28b and *Shulchan Arukh, Yoreh Deah* 376:1). Otherwise, you may start talking about the deceased just as the mourner needs respite from this subject. Alternatively, you may choose to speak about a trivial subject (I have been present at shiva houses where I have heard people discussing the baseball pennant race) at a time when what matters most to the mourner is to speak about his loss. By letting the mourner speak first, we enable the mourner to speak about whatever he or she most needs to focus on at that moment. As one rabbi summarizes the Jewish tradition on this subject: "If the mourner wants to talk, you listen. If the mourner wants to listen, you talk."[4]

Rabbi Jack Riemer was with Rabbi Abraham Joshua Heschel when they heard of the death of Rabbi Wolfe Kelman's sister, Toby Silverman. Rabbi Heschel insisted that they go to visit Rabbi Kelman and his other family members immediately: "We went to the airport, we flew to Boston, got into a cab, and went to the house. Heschel walked in, he hugged [the mourners], he sat silently for an hour. He didn't mumble a single cliché, 'How old was she?' What difference does it make? . . . 'I know how you feel.' You don't know how I feel. None of the clichés. He just sat there in silence for an hour. And then he got up, hugged them, and we left. I learned that you don't have to be glib. You just have to care."[5]

On the other hand, speaking, when it is appropriate, can be of great importance. During 1966–1967, Rabbi Joseph Soloveitchik (known in modern Orthodox circles as "the Rav") lost his mother, brother, and wife within the span of a few months. During the shiva for the Rav's wife, Tanya, Professor Saul Lieberman, the great talmudist of the Jewish Theological Seminary, went to visit him in Brookline, Massachusetts. Not surprisingly, the atmosphere at the shiva was very depressed, with Rabbi Soloveitchik sitting on the floor, and the visitors all quiet as well because of the tradition of not speaking until the mourner initiates conversation. When Rabbi Soloveitchik acknowledged Professor's Lieberman's arrival, Lieberman immediately engaged him in what turned into a vigorous discussion and debate on the applicability of the laws of mourning to the high priest. Rabbi Haskel Lookstein describes what ensued: "The discussion became extremely animated and was conducted in Yiddish and English interchangeably, with, of course, a lot of Hebrew thrown in as well. It required referencing certain books. Rabbi Aharon Lichtenstein, a son-in-law of the Rav, had to go up and down the stairs several times bringing down seforim *(books) that then were piled up on a coffee table in front of the Rav. The entire experience helped to draw the Rav from his state of great sadness and gave him a respite from his depressed feelings. It was a marvelous example of a combination of Rabbi Lieberman's key knowledge of Jewish law—including the fact that the only subject of halachic discussion [permitted to a mourner] . . . during this period were the laws of mourning—and Rabbi Lieberman's sensitivity and* chesed *(kindness) in trying to help Rabbi Soloveitchik emerge, if only temporarily, from his deep experience of mourning."*[6]

The mandate to wait until the mourner speaks needs to be applied flexibly. There are times when the mourner is so overcome with sorrow that he or she can't speak, and the visitor may have something to say that is important for the mourner to hear.

---

11. The obligation to be silent is not, of course, an obligation to be passive: "A warm embrace . . . an arm around the shoulder, an empathetic look, the sharing of tears together—these are the nonverbal messages to the bereaved that often say more than a thousand words" (Dr. Ron Wolfson).[7]

12. Before we enter a house of mourning, we should consider carefully what we wish to accomplish. Among our goals should be to

- assuage the mourner's loneliness and pain; therefore, think carefully before offering banal comments that can deepen the mourner's hurt;
- offer the mourner the chance to express what he is feeling;
- express our own memories and feelings about the deceased.

The last is very important since it is generally a great source of comfort to mourners when visitors share recollections about the person who died.

I have noticed that even humorous recollections can be deeply—sometimes particularly—appreciated at such a time.

---

*Even when we didn't know the deceased, we can still provide the mourners with opportunities to speak about their loss. We can ask a person who has lost their spouse, "How did you meet your wife?" or "What are some of your favorite memories of your husband?" I am providing specific examples because many of us become so tongue-tied when sitting with a mourner that we say nothing at all, or offer unhelpful clichés.**

Reverend Doug Manning, a Protestant minister who has written extensively about grief, tells of a woman he knew who lost a young child. Her despair was palpable and visitors, uncomfortable at her intense display of emotion, tried to calm her: "There, there now. Get ahold of yourself." "You can't carry on like this." "Come on now. Stop crying." With a sudden fire in her voice, the woman said to them: "Don't take my grief from me. I deserve it. I am going to have it."[8]

The expression "think before you speak" applies with particular force to anyone visiting mourners. We should not consider our words only in the seconds immediately before speaking, but even before arriving at the house.

The importance of avoiding platitudes is underscored by a recollection of Rabbi Harold Schulweis, who was visiting a woman from his congregation whose husband had died a year after their son's Bar Mitzvah. "She was surrounded by her family and friends, all of whom were desperately trying to make her feel better. I took her into the kitchen and said, 'This must be a terrible thing for you.' She cried with great relief and said, 'These people who are my friends and family are telling me, "It could have been worse . . . at least he saw the Bar Mitzvah . . ." Each time they try to comfort me like that, it's like salt in an open wound. At least you are allowing me to grieve.' [What this woman needed was] confirmation of her tragedy, the right to cry."[9]

Avoiding banalities applies as well to deaths that occur at advanced ages and are therefore regarded as less tragic. A rabbinic colleague told me that when a caller mentioned that her mother had recently died, and he expressed his sorrow, the woman responded in a rather casual, almost dismissive, manner, "Well, she

*It is probably a good idea for the mourning family to leave a few photo albums around the room, as these can help focus and direct conversations.

was ninety-four." But when my friend answered, "Yes, but it was your mother," the woman began weeping and acknowledged that she had responded as she did because people kept telling her that her mother had lived a long life, and that she should be grateful. In truth, though, the loss of her mother was a source of real pain and sorrow.

FOUR SPECIAL SITUATIONS

When the bereaved is experiencing guilt

13. Rare is the mourner who feels no sense of guilt toward the deceased. In intimate relations, people often wound each other, and when death occurs, the sense of guilt over our past behavior—even when it was not necessarily inappropriate or particularly wrong—can be overwhelming.

- What child cannot recall harsh words she said to a parent?*
- What parent cannot recall times when he dashed the hopes of a child?
- What spouse has not lashed out, on occasion, and blamed their spouse unfairly?†

Siblings, too, can often recall hurts inflicted on each other, sometimes decades earlier.

In addition, when someone dies, it is always possible to summon up recollections of lapses in care. "Did I do all that I could for Mother?" an adult child might ask herself. To which the answer must be "no" since none of us ever does *all* that we can for another. But I do know that when my father died, a friend's heartfelt comment, "You were a good son," meant a great deal to me.

---

*A friend of mine is particularly careful to conclude conversations with his parents with loving words. He told me that, while in college, he knew of a student who had a fight with his parents, and said angry, hurtful words. A few hours later, the boy's father was killed in an accident. Thinking about how the student must have felt, my friend resolved to always end conversations, even difficult ones, lovingly. Someday—and we don't know when—one such conversation will be the last words we speak to one another.

†A remarkable exception: At the funeral of his wife, Chaya Rivkah, Rabbi Shlomo Zalman Auerbach bade her farewell with the following declaration: "It is customary to request forgiveness from the deceased. However, I have nothing to ask your forgiveness for. During the course of our relationship, never did anything occur that would require either of us to ask the other's forgiveness. Each of us led our lives in accordance with the *Shulchan Arukh*" (see Hanoch Teller, *And from Jerusalem, His Word,* page 374). The fact that it is customary—as Rabbi Auerbach said—to ask the deceased's forgiveness suggests that even in loving relationships people hurt each other.

Among those who can help assuage excessive and unjustified feelings of survivor's guilt are doctors. A friend told me that his grandmother, who had cared for her ill husband for many years, was particularly comforted by the doctor, who assured her he couldn't remember seeing a patient so well looked after.

---

14. Guilt can generally be divided into two kinds, justified (or "real") and exaggerated (or "imagined").* In cases of exaggerated feelings, a friend should use reason and exercise compassion to help the mourner realize that she has no reason to torment herself (indeed, the supposed "victim" of her behavior would probably not want her to do so). Rabbi Aryeh Levine told of a case in which he went to speak with a woman whose father became ill with heart disease. The daughter, an only child, spent a great deal of time with her father until he pleaded with her to return to her own home, where her husband and children needed her. The woman would not hear of it, until finally the father said, "If you want to respect your father, you must do as I say. Go back now to your home." Once it became a matter of obeying the Fifth Commandment, the woman yielded and returned to her family.

Within days, the man suffered a heart attack and died. The distraught daughter blamed herself for abandoning her father. Convinced that she was responsible for his death, she became emotionally ill herself.

Reb Aryeh came to talk to her. In addition to expressing the belief that God alone determines the length of a person's life, he also employed reason to show her that she bore no responsibility for what had happened. "If you had remained with your father and he died, you would have been twice as stricken with grief. . . . You would have been sure that by refusing to leave him you caused him anguish—and that is what hastened your father's death." As Simcha Raz concludes: "[Reb Aryeh] went on talking in this vein, until the truth of his words hit home, and she was comforted."[10]

Of course, guilt is sometimes justified. When someone has inflicted real and undeserved hurt on the deceased (through commission or omission, such as in instances of neglect), the mourner—or whoever inflicted the pain—should be encouraged to do *teshuva,* repentance.† Thus, a man manipulated his late father's will to his advantage, at the expense of his brother. Later,

---

*A psychiatrist whom I know argues that much guilt is imagined and involves a confusion of regret and guilt: "It is often a delusion of grandeur on our part to imagine that our behavior effected an unfortunate outcome" (Dr. Isaac Herschkopf).

†Obviously, the repentance cannot be complete since the one who can grant forgiveness is dead.

when the brother died, the man experienced deep remorse over his behavior. The one thing he could and did do was to help his brother's son and daughter generously, and to make it clear that this was their due.

In instances when the damage is less tangible (for example, hurt feelings), mourners are encouraged to pray by the grave of the deceased and to ask forgiveness. Another possibility is to make charitable contributions in honor of the dead person.

Once death has occurred, repentance can never be complete, but it is always better—and often far better—than doing nothing.

An unpleasant, but potentially valuable, exercise: Think of various people close to you and imagine that, God forbid, they suddenly died. In addition to your sorrow, would you have reason to feel guilty over how you have treated them? If so, then figure out how you can compensate for past deeds and eliminate, or at least minimize, such hurtful or unfair behavior in the future. Act now while the person is still alive.

When a mourner is angry at the deceased

15. It is not uncommon that an immediate relative had a tense, angry, and sometimes unloving relationship with the deceased.* Without denying the validity of the person's feelings—if you feel they are justified—it is usually wise to encourage the person to observe some form of mourning.

Rabbi Harold Kushner recalls an instance when a woman had been so wounded by her father, who had deserted the family when she was a child, that she did not even wish to attend his funeral, let alone sit shiva or recite Kaddish. Yet Rabbi Kushner urged her to do so: "If you attend your father's funeral and regret doing so, you will feel bad about it for that day. If you don't attend his funeral and regret not having gone, you might well regret it for your whole life." Regarding saying Kaddish, Kushner urged her to say it, if not on a regular basis, then at least occasionally: "If you can't bring yourself to say Kaddish for your father because of the way he was and because of how he treated you, then say it for the father you never had but wish you did."

If it is appropriate, encourage the mourner to see that while the deceased's

*Anger is also sometimes the response to a premature death in which the deceased was somewhat culpable—for example, in the case of a smoker who died from cancer, a drunk driver killed in an accident, and almost always in the case of suicide.

behavior was hurtful and wrong, the behavior was probably not malicious. This is often (though not always) true, for example, in the case of children who felt hurt and unloved by parents.*

When a mourner is angry at God

16. "A person is not held responsible for what he [or she] says while in pain" (*Bava Bathra* 16b). The Talmud understands this statement as applying even when the mourner rails against God, which is not uncommon, particularly when death strikes someone who is young. It is our obligation as a visitor to be emotionally supportive of the mourner, and certainly not to respond sharply. Although we should feel free to express our own religious convictions, at times of great pain we should not condemn others and not assume that we are obligated to act as God's defender. That was the sin of Job's three friends. While Job was mourning the loss of his children and blaming God for his fate, Eliphaz said to him, "Think now, what innocent man ever perished?" (Job 4:7). Then Bildad commented: "If your sons sinned against Him, He dispatched them for their transgression" (8:4). Finally, Zophar told Job that God had punished him less than he had deserved (11:6). At the book's end, God makes it clear that He finds the condemnations of Job's friends to be inexcusable: "I am incensed at you and your two friends," God says to Eliphaz (42:7), and tells them that He will forgive them only if they first go and secure Job's forgiveness for their cruel words.

17. It is almost always inappropriate to try and explain why the deceased or the mourner has suffered. Such knowledge is not granted to human beings: "It is not within our ability to understand the prosperity [or peace] of the wicked or the sufferings of the righteous" (*The Ethics of the Fathers* 4:15).

18. An important—perhaps the most important—consolation the Jewish tradition offers mourners is its belief in an afterlife. Hence, the advice recorded in the Talmud: "Weep for the mourners and not for their loss, for [the deceased] has gone to eternal rest, but we [the mourners] are suffering" (*Mo'ed Kattan* 25b). The traditional Jewish belief is that the soul survives and remains aware of those left behind.

Many Jews are under the misconception that Judaism does not believe in

*For an example of how this exercise helped a hurt son cope with his anger at his dead father, see page 449.

an afterlife and are heartened to learn that it does.* Helping the mourner—if he is open to such a belief—to focus on the continuing existence of the soul of the one who died can help assuage his or her hurt and anger.

When a child dies

19. Professor Norman Linzer, of Yeshiva University's Wurzweiler School of Social Work, writes that "with the death of a husband or wife you lose your present; with the death of a parent, you lose your past; and with the death of a child, you lose your future."[11] So devastating a loss mandates particular care, and even preparation, on the part of visitors. It is not enough to monitor your words, but you must also consider in advance any behavior that may add to the mourners' pain. Many years after Rabbi Aaron Levine (an authority on the Jewish laws of mourning) and his wife lost their two-year-old son, Ephraim, he still recalled a woman with a small baby who paid them a shiva call: "I assume that she was unable to get a babysitter (or, at least, I shall so judge her favorably), so she brought her infant with her. Naturally, all were cooing and coddling over the new baby. I was able to restrain myself from asking her to please leave or at least to take the infant away. But I thought to myself: 'How inconsiderate can one be?' Here we were, my wife and I, just having lost a baby, and a woman was . . . displaying her own baby in front of us, to all around?' I'm sure the woman had no idea what hurt she was causing us. But it behooves all who go to a house of mourning to anticipate,

---

*I believe there is a connection between the Torah's nondiscussion of an afterlife and the fact that the Torah was revealed after the long Jewish sojourn in Egypt. The Egyptian society in which the ancient Israelites long resided was obsessed with death and afterlife, as reflected in the holiest Egyptian literary work, *The Book of the Dead.* The major achievement of many Pharaohs was the erection of pyramids, which were giant tombs. In contrast, the Torah focuses on this world, so much so that it forbids Judaism's *kohanim* (priests) from having contact with dead bodies (Leviticus 21:1; in Egypt, the priests helped prepare the body for interment). Thus, the Torah may well have been silent about afterlife out of its desire to ensure that Judaism not evolve in the direction of the Egyptian religion. Throughout history, religions that have assigned a major, and perhaps exaggerated, role to the afterlife often have permitted other religious and ethical values to become distorted. Thus, it was belief in an afterlife that motivated the Spanish Inquisition to torture innocent human beings; the inquisitors believed it was morally right to torture people for a few days in this world until they repudiated their supposed heresies and accepted Christ, and thereby save them from the eternal torments of hell. In our own times, the strong belief in afterlife among Islamist terrorists enables them to kill themselves while murdering innocent people—mainly non-Muslims—with whom they disagree. Thus, the nineteen Islamist terrorists who murdered three thousand people on September 11, 2001 were convinced that after crashing their planes into the Twin Towers and the Pentagon, they would immediately be granted heavenly reward. How much less evil might they—and, centuries earlier, the inquisitors—have done had they not believed in an afterlife.

if possible, all sensitivities and any situations that could cause discomfort to the mourners."[12]

The same Rabbi Levine once delivered a lecture at which he noted that it was all right to cry in front of mourners. But even so unobjectionable a statement, he soon learned, depends on circumstances. At the talk's conclusion, a woman told him that when she had been observing shiva for her child, another woman who had also recently lost a child visited. The woman was clearly still in the full throes of her own grief and began to cry uncontrollably. Noted the woman who spoke to Rabbi Levine: "I was deeply disturbed by her visit. I thought to myself: 'Is this what is going to happen to me a few months after shiva?' I don't think she should have come to visit me if she knew she was still in that state of mourning."[*][13]

---

20. There are several talmudic passages in which the Rabbis record statements of consolation upon the loss of a child offered by one rabbinic colleague to another. Many of those who spoke only succeeded in increasing the pain of the mourner. For example, when Rabbi Yochanan ben Zakkai's son died, his leading disciples came to comfort him. The first to speak was Rabbi Eliezer, who said: "Adam had a son who died, yet he allowed himself to be comforted. And how do we know that he allowed himself to be comforted? For it is said, 'And Adam knew his wife again' [and they had another son; Genesis 4:25]. You, too, let yourself be comforted."

Rabbi Yochanan responded with ill-concealed annoyance: "Is it not enough that I grieve over my own son, that you remind me of the grief of Adam?"

He responded in a similar manner when Rabbi Joshua asked him to be comforted as was Job over the loss of his children, Rabbi Yossi asked him to be comforted as was Aaron over the death of his two sons, and Rabbi Shimon mentioned how David was comforted when his son died.

When Elazar ben Arakh, perhaps his most brilliant disciple, entered, Rabbi Yochanan, who apparently felt that he was not ready to hear words of consolation, said to his servants, "Take my clothing and follow me to the bathhouse, for he is a great man, and I shall be unable to resist him."

---

*An infant or a baby should never be at a shiva, unless the mourner explicitly asked for them to be brought. At best, it destroys the appropriate moods of sobriety, and it always distracts both visitors and the bereaved from the important work at hand. Just as one would not bring an infant to a funeral, one should not bring an infant to a shiva visit.

However, before Rabbi Yochanan could depart, Rabbi Elazar sat down in front of him, and said: "I shall tell you a parable. To what may your situation be compared? To a man whom the king entrusted an object to be carefully guarded. Every day the man would weep and cry out, 'Woe is me! When shall I be freed of this trust and again be at peace?' You, too, Master. You had a son, he studied the Torah, the Prophets, the Holy Writings, he studied Mishnah, *halacha, aggada,* and he left this world without sin. Now that you have returned that which was entrusted to you, it is appropriate for you to be comforted."

Said Rabbi Yochanan to him: "Rabbi Elazar, my son, you have comforted me the way people ought to give comfort" (*The Fathers According to Rabbi Nathan* 14:6).

Although Rabbi Elazar's words comforted Rabbi Yochanan, who was himself on an unusually high spiritual level, one wonders if they would help most parents, few of whom will identify with the guardian who cried out daily, "When shall I be freed of this trust, and again be at peace?"

A woman who had lost a child confided to Rabbi Reuven Bulka that a well-meaning rabbi had told her after the death of her six-month-old daughter, "She died as a perfect soul, never having had the chance to sin." Bulka notes that the comment not only brought no consolation to the bereaved mother, it actually increased her pain: "True, the young girl had no opportunity to sin, but she also had no opportunity to do good, and that was the unaddressed, even ignored, lament, of the grieving family."*[14]

Does that mean that we cannot offer any meaningful consolation through words to parents who have lost a child?

My experience is that one can, but only if the person offering the consolation has him- or herself suffered a similar loss. Only when expressions of consolation come from fellow sufferers will the mourner, I believe, be able to feel that the consoler understands what he or she is feeling and is not uttering platitudes that they would never say if it were their own child who had died.

Rabbi Yisrael Ze'ev Gustman (d. 1991) served as the youngest member of the rabbinical court of Rabbi Chaim Ozer Grodzensky (see page 156) in Vilna, and later served as the rabbi in nearby Shnipishok. Rabbi Gustman survived the Holocaust by hiding. After the war, he came to Israel, where he headed a small

*Bulka concluded that "it takes more than good intentions to be an effective comforter or consoler. Presumptuous comments about the good side of a terrible tragedy are tricky at best, highly damaging at worst" (*Turning Grief into Gratitude,* page 103).

yeshiva in Jerusalem and, once a week, offered a public shiur *(class) in Talmud, which was attended by rabbis, professors, and even a Supreme Court justice. One regular participant was Dr. Robert J. (Yisrael) Aumann, an economics professor at Hebrew University.* In 1982, when Israel went to war in Lebanon, in an ultimately unsuccessful attempt to eliminate the terrorist PLO, Professor Aumann's son, Shlomo, a reserve army officer, was killed in battle. After attending the funeral, Rabbi Gustman paid a shiva visit to the slain soldier's family. He sat down next to Professor Aumann and, after the professor expressed gratitude to him for coming to the funeral and now to his house, said to him: "I am sure that you don't know this, but I had a son named Meir. He was a beautiful child. He was taken from my arms and murdered. I escaped. Later, I bartered my child's shoes so that we would have food, but I was never able to eat the food. I gave it away to others. My Meir is a* kadosh, *a holy one. He and all the six million who perished are holy." He then looked closely at the mourning father. "And I want to tell you what is now happening in the World of Truth, in* Gan Eden *(the Garden of Eden) in Heaven. My Meir is welcoming your Shlomo into the minyan, and is saying to him, "I died because I am a Jew, but I wasn't able to save anyone else. But you, Shlomo, died defending the Jewish people and the Land of Israel." And, Rabbi Gustman concluded: "My Meir is a* kadosh, *he is holy, but your Shlomo is a* shaliach tzibbur *[the representative of the community before God]† in this holy, heavenly minyan." The rabbi was quiet for a moment. "I never had the opportunity to sit shiva for my Meir. Let me sit here with you just a little longer."‡*

Professor Aumann replied: "I thought I could never be comforted, but Rebbe, you have comforted me."[15]

---

21. But what if you have, God willing, not suffered such a loss? Can you still be of assistance to the mourner? Rabbi Abraham Twerski who is also a psychiatrist, recalls an instance when he made a shiva call to a family that had lost a child: "When I entered, the room was full of family, but gradually everyone left, and the mother tearfully poured out her aching heart to me. Each time I visited, the same thing occurred. I listened, but there was nothing I could say. Several days later, the young woman's father called to thank

---

*In 2005, Professor Aumann was awarded the Nobel Prize in economics.

†*"Shaliach tzibbur"* usually refers to the person leading the prayer service.

‡In later years, when a student implored Rabbi Gustman to speak to others more often about his ghetto and war memories, and to tell the story about his dead son and the shoes, Rabbi Gustman responded: "I can't [talk about it], but I think about those shoes every day of my life. I see them every night before I go to sleep."

me for helping her. Helping her? I hadn't said a word. What happened was that everyone else in the family could not bear her crying, and they tried to divert her to something else. I was the only one who listened, and that was helpful. Do not minimize the importance of just being there and sharing the person's pain. There is a saying that 'a sorrow that is shared is halved.' I doubt that this is true. Sharing the pain does not reduce it by 50 percent. But there is nothing worse for the suffering person than to feel alone. Some people have told me that in such situations they stay away because they feel so awkward, not having any comforting words to say. That is a mistake. A person in grief feels worse when isolated. So just be there for someone. You don't have to say anything. The Sages prescribed the words, 'May *Hashem* [God] comfort you,' because only *Hashem* can provide consolation. All we can do is let the mourner know that we care."[16]

22. In addition to avoiding clumsy or unhelpful—and sometime counterproductive—words of consolation, avoid questions that are posed without any forethought on the questioner's part. As one mourner confided, "Please don't ask how I am doing. I lost my child, how do you think I am doing? But you can ask how I am coping."[17]

23. Jacob is the Bible's most prominent example of a parent who could not be consoled. When his other sons reported Joseph's disappearance to him and presented evidence indicating that he had been killed by a beast,* Jacob "rent his clothes, put sackcloth on his loins, and observed mourning for his son many days. All his sons and daughters sought to comfort him, but he refused to be comforted, saying: 'No, I will go down mourning to my son in Sheol.'† Thus, his father bewailed him" (Genesis 37:32–35).

Though we can all understand unending grief, particularly after the death of a child, the *Shulchan Arukh* law rules that a person "should not grieve too much for the dead, and whoever grieves excessively is really grieving for someone else.[18] The Torah has set limits for every stage of grief, and we may not add to them" (*Yoreh Deah* 394:1, based on *Mo'ed Kattan* 27b; the

*In actuality, his brothers hated Joseph and had sold him into Egyptian slavery. They then plotted to convince Jacob that Joseph was dead (see Genesis 37:25–35).

†Sheol is the biblical term that describes the place where the spirits of the dead are presumed to reside. Numbers 16:33 records that when the earth swallowed Korach, who led a revolt against Moses, he and his followers, "went down alive into Sheol." Psalms 9:18 suggests that Sheol is where the wicked go when they die, while Isaiah 38:10, citing the prayer of the righteous King Hezekiah (ca. 700 B.C.E.), merely suggests that it is where deceased people, both good and bad, are consigned.

chapter is titled "On Not Grieving Excessively"). Having said that, my experience is that Jewish law's limiting the period of mourning for a child to thirty days (as opposed to a full year for a parent) does not give most parents enough time to come to terms with their loss. Thus, I have known mourning parents who have recited Kaddish for a dead child for eleven months, instead of thirty days. I suspect that the limitation on mourning for children developed at a time when it was common for children to die of diseases (often at a very young age*), and mandating a full year of mourning for the death of a child would have required many parents to spend years in mourning. Today, when the death of a child is far less common, the period of mourning should perhaps be extended.

Even in the case of losing one's child, God forbid, there must be a cap on expressions of mourning, even if one cannot control what one is feeling. Thus, an incident occurred in the town of Dukor, Belarus, where my grandfather, Rabbi Nissen Telushkin, served as rabbi. A woman had lost one of her children and went into a perpetual state of mourning. When her other children would play and laugh, she would shout at them, "How can you laugh when your brother is dead?"† When my grandfather was asked by her family to speak to her, he tried to convey that such behavior would kill the spirit of her living children. Years later, when my father related the story, he didn't know whether my grandfather had succeeded.

In Hanoch Teller's biography of Rabbi Shlomo Zalman Auerbach, And from Jerusalem, His Word, *he records an incident in which a young widow with four children was consumed with the feeling that she must engage in some major act of spiritual self-improvement to lift up the soul of her dead husband. Rabbi Auerbach, understanding that the widow's house was probably turning into a suffocating environment for her children, told the woman that her desire to do something for the* illui neshama *(raising of the soul) of her late husband, "is surely a blessed and worthy desire." He then instructed her to "Go out and buy toys and games for the children. A lot of them! Then take the children out for walks and outings; this will be the very best* illui neshama *for your husband. Forget your mourning and concentrate on making the children rejoice and enjoy life."*[19]

*Not only in ancient times; many of us have heard of grandparents and great-grandparents who came from large families, but in which several of the children never reached adulthood.

†Today, this would probably be diagnosed as a form of clinical depression and be treated medically.

In Rabbi William Silverman and Dr. Kenneth Cinnamon's book When Mourning Comes, *the authors relate a moving fantasy about a parent's inconsolable grief:*

"The story is told of a man who had a little daughter, an only and beloved child. He lived for her. She was his life. When she became ill and the efforts of the most skilled physicians failed to cure her, he became like a man possessed, moving heaven and earth to bring about her recovery. All efforts proved unavailing, and the little girl died.

"The father's heart was broken. He was totally inconsolable. He became a bitter recluse, shutting himself away from his many friends and refusing every activity that might restore his poise and bring him back to a normal life.

"One night he had a dream. He was in heaven and was witnessing a giant pageant of all the little child angels. They were marching in an apparently endless line past a great white throne. Every white-robed angel tot carried a candle. He noticed that one child's candle was not lit. Then he saw that the child with the dark candle was his own little girl.

"Rushing to her, he took her in his arms, caressed her tenderly, and asked, 'How is it, darling, that your candle is not lit?'

"The child said, 'Father, they often relight it, but your tears always put it out.'

"Just then he awoke. From that hour on, he was no longer a recluse but began to mingle freely and lovingly with his former friends. No longer would his little darling's candle be extinguished by his tears."[20]

I present this story with—to use Kierkegaard's term—"fear and trembling." I certainly do not wish to add to the pain of anyone who has lost a child, but I only wish to offer examples conveying how some people have coped with the awful suffering of such a loss.

After shiva

24. If you see a mourner for the first time after shiva, but within thirty days of the death, you recite the traditional formula "May God comfort you among all those who mourn for Zion and Jerusalem." After thirty days, you should say simply, *"Titnachem,"* "May you find comfort." Once a year has passed, do not make reference to the death, unless appropriate. If you see a friend whom you have not seen in a long time, and a year or more has passed since the friend suffered a loss, it is usually fine to refer to what happened

("I am so sorry about your loss"), but not to dwell on it, unless the mourner clearly wishes to talk about it. As Rabbi Meir teaches: "A person who meets a mourner after a year and speaks [extensive] words of consolation to him then, to what can he be compared? To a physician who meets a person whose leg had been broken and healed, and says to him, 'Come to me, and let me break your leg again, and reset it, to convince you that my treatment is good" (*Mo'ed Kattan* 21b). Rabbi Meir was concerned that well-meaning attempts to do or say the right thing would cause mourners more pain than comfort.

25. As important as it is to visit mourners during the first week, it is equally vital to stay in touch afterward. Many people, though scrupulous about making shiva visits, are far less mindful during the following months. As one widower reported: "I felt so alone after the first few days following Marge's death. I had thought the enormous support of friends and sympathetic neighbors would never stop. I was so grateful. Suddenly, the phone stopped ringing. No one came to visit anymore and I didn't know what to do. I thought maybe I had done something wrong. Those next few months were the loneliest in my life. I'll never let a friend in grief drift that way." Dr. Leonard Zunin and Hilary Zunin, who cite this instance in their book *The Art of Condolence,* conclude: "The importance of continued intermittent contact over the next few months, whether via notes, invitations, phone calls, visits, or offers to help with practical matters, cannot be overemphasized."[21] In short, the benefits of staying in touch with the mourner after shiva cannot be overstated.

Rabbi Gerald Wolpe was eleven years old when his father died, and his mother, a widow at thirty-four, was consumed with earning a living. Wolpe recalls that "I missed [my father] every moment of the day and night, but I had to mask the tears and sorrow for my mother's sake. She was carrying her own burdens and I found I could not add to her grief by sharing my sense of loss."

The young boy's school day started at 8:30, but each morning he arose at 5:30 and walked to services at Boston's Temple Mishkan Tefila. An only child, the congregation accepted him as the appropriate person to recite Kaddish for his father, even though he was not yet Bar Mitzvah.

After a week of this grueling schedule, something quite unusual happened. Each morning, the synagogue's shamash *(sexton), Mr. Einstein, appeared at his front door just as the young Wolpe was leaving. Mr. Einstein explained: "Your home is on the way to the synagogue. I have to go this way and I thought it might be fun to have some company. That way, I don't have to walk alone."*

Over the eleven months Wolpe recited Kaddish, Mr. Einstein came every morning. Wolpe recalls how the two of them would trek together through snow and rain, and through the exquisite New England fall and stifling humidity of summer. Each day, Mr. Einstein related to the young boy stories about Jewish history, along with insights about questions of faith and particular prayers. He listened as the young Wolpe spoke of his grief. Wolpe would sit next to the older man at synagogue and "he moved into a void that was tearing at my heart and soul." For years afterward, even as Wolpe moved away from Boston to study, the two stayed in touched by phone and through letters.

Many years passed; in time, Wolpe was ordained at the Jewish Theological Seminary. "Mr. Einstein was in his nineties when I visited Boston with my wife and six-month-old son. I wanted him to see my baby so I phoned and asked him to come to the home he had passed so often. He agreed but said that it was impossible for him to walk, would I please come to get him by automobile. I realized that I had never known where he lived so I asked for directions and set out to meet him.

*"The journey was long and complicated. His home by car was fully twenty minutes away. I drove in tears as I realized what he had done. He had walked for an hour to my home so that I would not have to be alone each morning. My home was not on the path to the synagogue; it was completely out of his way. He had made me feel that I was helping him with companionship; the opposite was true. He knew my loneliness, and he did not want my day to begin without him. . . . By the simplest of gestures, the act of caring, he took a frightened child by the hand and he led him with confidence and with faith back into life."**

**Chicken Soup for the Jewish Soul* by Jack Canfield, Mark Victor Hansen, and Rabbi Dov Peretz Elkins, pages 122–124.

The Laws of Kindness

For it is kindness that I desire
and not sacrifice.

Hosea 6:6

10

PRACTICING KINDNESS

1. We generally think of kindness as a positive attribute ("She is such a kind, wonderful person"), but not as something that can be regulated and even legislated. But in the Jewish tradition, *gemilut chesed,* acts of kindness (the term is often translated as "acts of loving-kindness") are regarded as something in which all people must engage, whether they feel motivated to do so or not. Indeed, the Rabbis regarded performing acts of kindness as superior to the giving of charity in three ways (*Sukkah* 49b):

- Charity is done only with your money, but kindness can be performed both with your body and money (such as when you help an elderly person in need).

- Charity is given only to the poor, but kindness can be offered to poor and rich alike (for example, through hospitality).

- Charity is dispensed only to the living, while acts of kindness can be performed for both the living and the dead. The Rabbis cite arranging for the burial of a person who has died as among the most perfect acts of *gemilut chesed.* In Hebrew, this act is called *chesed shel emet* (true kindness), since it is done without expectation that the recipient will be able to repay the kindness (see chapter 8).

While rereading *The Diary of Anne Frank,* a fourth difference between charity and *gemilut chesed* occurred to me. Charity is performed when an opportunity presents itself, while kindness can be done at any time. As Anne Frank put it: "How lovely to think that no one need wait a moment before making the world better. We can start now slowly changing the world! . . . You can always, always, always give something, even if it is only kindness. Give, give again, don't lose courage. Keep it up and go on giving. No one has ever become poor from giving" (March 1944).

While the distinguishing feature of charity is generosity with money, a—

and in some ways *the*—distinguishing feature of *gemilut chesed* is generosity with time.

Kindness in the Bible and the Talmud

2. The Talmud teaches: "The Torah begins with an act of kindness, and ends with an act of kindness. It begins with an act of kindness, for it says, 'God made garments of skin for Adam and his wife and clothed them' (Genesis 3:21). And it ends with an act of kindness, for it says, 'He [God] buried him [Moses] in the valley' " (Deuteronomy 34:6; *Sotah* 14a).

Because imitating God is one of the Torah's 613 commandments (Deuteronomy 28:9; "walk in His ways"), the Rabbis carefully studied the Bible to find acts performed by God that human beings could emulate. Thus, in the evolution of Jewish law, the two acts cited above, providing clothing for those in need and arranging a burial, are regarded as among the great acts of kindness and charity that we can do for others.

3. The Prophets understand kindness as being one of God's central demands of human beings. Thus, while people usually associate religiosity with performance of ritual acts, the prophet Hosea teaches that God's priorities are different: "For it is kindness that I desire and not sacrifice" (Hosea 6:6). Hosea's lesson was hard for many Jews to absorb, and they continued to believe that offering sacrifices was the most important means to obtain God's forgiveness of sins. Indeed, in the first century, when the Jerusalem Temple was destroyed, many Jews feared that the path to repentance had been permanently blocked. Rabbi Yochanan ben Zakkai assured the Jews of his age and of all succeeding ages that this was not so: "Once as Rabbi Yochanan ben Zakkai was coming from Jerusalem, Rabbi Joshua followed him and beheld the Temple in ruins. 'Woe unto us!' Rabbi Joshua cried, 'that this, the place where the sins of Israel were atoned for, is laid waste.' 'My son,' Rabbi Yochanan said to him, 'be not grieved. We have another atonement as effective as this. And what is it? It is acts of loving-kindness, as it is said, "For it is kindness that I desire and not sacrifice" ' " (*The Fathers According to Rabbi Nathan* 4).

4. An entire book of the Bible, Ruth, repeatedly conveys the importance of kindness in daily behavior. The book highlights several acts of compassion and benevolence. When Machlon, Ruth's husband, dies, Ruth, a Moabite, is still a young woman. Yet she remains totally devoted to her grieving Israelite mother-in-law, Naomi, who, in addition to Machlon, has also lost her other son, and her husband as well. Although Ruth could have remained in Moab and remarried, she chooses to accompany the devastated Naomi back to Israel: "Where you go, I will go, where you lodge, I will lodge" (1:16).* Furthermore, Ruth is not the book's only exemplar of kindness. Boaz, a wealthy landowner who scrupulously observes the Torah laws allowing poor people to glean food from his fields (chapter 2), also makes sure that Ruth, who is living in poverty with Naomi, receives more than adequate portions of food and orders that none of his workers mistreat her.

The book of Ruth is so dominated by acts of kindness that the Rabbis note that in it there is no mention of ritual laws. They also recorded Rabbi Zeira's response to an inquiry as to why the book was included in the biblical canon: "To teach us how great is the reward of those who do deeds of kindness" (*Midrash Ruth Rabbah* 2:14).

5. In identifying God's three most important demands of human beings, the prophet Micah speaks of doing justice, walking humbly with God, and "loving kindness (*Micah* 6:8)." In depicting the ideal human being, God apparently wishes people not only to act with kindness, but also to love doing so.

Abraham Axelrod, a friend of Rabbi Aryeh Levine, explained Reb Aryeh's philosophy of life and commitment to goodness: "As he saw it, life's main purpose is to help others. If a few days went by and he found no opportunity to help someone with a bit of advice, a kind word, or simply with a little chat to make a person feel better, he began to wonder if he was perhaps superfluous in the world, and the Almighty had no further use for him on earth. And when people crossed his threshold from early in the morning till late at night to ask advice, guidance, and all kinds of personal help, Reb Aryeh felt they owed him nothing. On the contrary, he was greatly indebted to them."[1]

---

6. Kindness is one of the supports upon which the world is anchored: "The world stands on three pillars, Torah, work,† and acts of kindness" (*The Ethics of the Fathers* 1:2). Elsewhere, the Talmud teaches that performance of

*Naomi and Ruth's friendship is, along with that of David and Jonathan, *the* model of friendship in the Bible.

†The word *avodah,* which I have translated as "work," can, and more commonly is, translated as "worship of God" (that is, "working for God"). But it seems to me that the context of the statement, identifying the pillars necessary for the world to go on existing, makes more sense if

kind deeds is one of three traits that characterize Jews (*Yevamot* 79a). Given that we have all met unkind Jews, what the Rabbis seem to mean is that only when a Jew acts with kindness is he or she acting as a Jew should. Indeed, so basic a value is kindness that the Talmud states that we should question the religious identity of a person who claims to be Jewish but who acts unkindly (*Beizah* 32b): "Anyone who is not compassionate with people is certainly not a descendant of our forefather Abraham." The Talmud doesn't suggest that we question the Jewish origins of someone who violates Jewish ritual laws or even questions God's existence. But meanness, the Rabbis teach, places one outside the camp of the Jewish people.

7. The Talmud relates that Rabbi Joshua ben Levi once came upon the prophet Elijah at an entrance to a cave. When he asked Elijah when the Messiah would come, Elijah answered him, "Go and ask him yourself." Rabbi Joshua asked, "And where is he?" Elijah responded, "He is sitting at the gate of the city." When Rabbi Joshua asked how he would be able to identify him, Elijah answered, "He is sitting among the paupers afflicted with leprosy" (*Sanhedrin* 98a). A contemporary rabbi has commented on this passage: "That may not seem like much for a Messiah to be doing. But, apparently, in the eyes of God, it is a mighty thing indeed" (Rabbi Robert Kirschner).[2]

8. Another talmudic text teaches that the world will endure only as long as there are a minimum of thirty-six fully righteous people (*Sanhedrin* 97b and *Sukkah* 45b). In Hebrew, the letters *lamed* and *vav* have the numerical value of 36, and an unusually kind person is sometimes referred to as a *lamed-vavnik,* one of the thirty-six. What also characterizes *lamed-vavniks* is that they perform their acts of loving-kindness anonymously.

While there is no reason to keep all our kind acts anonymous, in A Code of Jewish Ethics, Volume 1: You Shall Be Holy, *I suggested that we "try to do some act of kindness on a routine basis that remains unknown to others. We should let it remain a secret between us, the recipient of our kindness (if it is an act that cannot be kept fully anonymous), and God" (page 225).*

---

translated as "work." I, therefore, understand "Torah" in this context as referring both to study of Torah and service of God (in the same way, when a Jewish baby is named, one of the blessings bestowed on the child is that he or she "enter into Torah," that is, a religious life in all ways).

How important is anonymity when performing acts of kindness?

Perhaps the most famous, if anonymous, tzaddik *in Jewish folklore is a wealthy man known as Joseph the Miser. There are several versions of the story about him, but all seem based on an actual figure who lived in Kraków, Poland. When poor people would come to his home and request assistance, he would act sympathetically and ask detailed questions so as to ascertain how much help the person needed. Then, the moment the questioning was finished, he would turn on the mendicant in fury: "Do you think I'm a fool? That I'll take the money I worked so hard to earn, and waste it on a good-for-nothing like you?" He would then chase the poor person from his house.*

*On his deathbed, the members of the Burial Society (*Chevra Kadisha*), figuring that this was the town's last opportunity to extract some charity from this tightwad, warned Joseph that if he didn't give them a large donation for the poor, they would leave his body unburied, an unthinkable indignity in Jewish life. But Joseph the Miser was unmoved. He cursed the members of the* Chevra Kadisha *and told them that he wouldn't give them a cent.*

Joseph died, and the infuriated Burial Society members, true to their word, refused to handle his body.

That Thursday, a poor man appeared at the rabbi's house. He was in dire need of money for the Sabbath so that he could buy food for his family. The rabbi gave the man a few rubles, blessed him, and asked him how he had been managing until now.

"The envelope," the man answered.

"What envelope?"

"Every Thursday morning, I would find an envelope under my door with just the amount of money I needed. I assume it came from the town charity fund, but this week they left nothing."

When the man left, the rabbi checked with the local charitable funds but nobody knew anything about an envelope.

A short time later, another poor man came by. He, too, had never solicited charity from the rabbi before, and he, too, explained about the envelope that used to be placed under his door on Thursday mornings.

When yet a third beggar came by with a similar story, the rabbi asked him when these envelopes had started arriving. They had begun a few days after the man had gone to Joseph the Miser's home, confided his needs, and been rudely ejected. As beggar after beggar showed up, each told the same story.

The rabbi hit his head in anguish, and summoned the members of the Burial Society. "We have committed a terrible sin," he told them. "Joseph the Miser *was the most generous man in this town. He simply wanted no public recognition for his acts of charity, that's why he pretended to be an ill-tempered miser." The rabbi arranged for Joseph to be given a distinguished burial, with many people, among them the poor, in attendance, and made provision that when he, the rabbi, died, he would be buried next to Joseph the Miser.**

Beautiful as this story is, it is still hard to understand why it was good for Joseph the Miser to act with such anonymity and nastiness that he caused himself to be despised.

Rabbi Israel Salanter is reputed to have said when he heard a certain man referred to as a "hidden tzaddik:*" "In this day and age, when there is much evil in the world, and people are in great need of models of goodness, why would a truly righteous person want to keep his acts of goodness hidden?"*

One finds a different take on anonymity in an autobiographical recollection of Rabbi Abraham Twerski. Twerski started his professional life as the assistant rabbi in his father's Chasidic synagogue in Milwaukee, Wisconsin. But then, in his twenties, and already married with children, he decided that he very much wanted to be a physician, and he enrolled in the medical school of Marquette University, a Catholic school. It was a financial struggle, and Twerski, in addition to taking out loans, received help from his father and from devoted members in his father's congregation. But after several years in the school, it became obvious that he still would have an additional $4,000 due in tuition and expenses, and he had exhausted all his resources. One day he called home and his wife told him that an article had appeared in the Chicago Sun-Times *that the well-known comedian Danny Thomas, a supporter of Marquette, had learned from a school official of Rabbi Twerski's plight and, on the spot, had announced, "Tell your rabbi he's got it." Twerski was not even aware of who Danny Thomas was but, needless to say, was overwhelmed by the generosity. Several days later, Danny Thomas called him to affirm that the money would soon be coming.*

Thomas also told him how unhappy he was about the publicity. Rabbi Twerski of course expressed his great gratitude. Several years later, Twerski had the opportunity to travel to Los Angeles and finally met Thomas. Again the actor expressed how unhappy he was about the publicity given his gift. Rabbi Twerski responded: "Mr. Thomas, every day the newspapers are filled with articles describing terrible events in the world, and terrible cruelties people inflict upon each other. Do you really think it's such a bad thing that an article

---

*As a final happy note, when the Burial Society went to Joseph's home, his body had suffered no deterioration; they also discovered a piece of paper in which Joseph bequeathed his entire estate for the support of the poor.

*appeared about how a well-known Lebanese Catholic actor helped a Chasidic rabbi finish medical school?"**

Twerski writes: "For the rest of Danny Thomas' life, we were in touch. I have no idea what Danny received spiritually from his generosity to strangers. I do know that I received a medical degree as well as confirmation of my belief and pride in humankind."

Years later, Rabbi Twerski finally had an opportunity to do something for Danny Thomas. The actor had come to Milwaukee to raise money for St. Jude Children's Research Hospital, which he had founded. At the dinner, Rabbi Twerski made a presentation announcing the pledges that he had helped solicit for this charity, which meant so much to Thomas. When Twerski spoke, he shared the story of what Danny Thomas had done for him: "I was embarrassed by my tearfulness and avoided looking out at the group. But finally, as I presented Danny with a gift, I had to look up and that's when I found many of those in the room weeping the same tears of gratitude and admiration for this great, kind man. I also gave him a beautiful volume of the Bible with a silver filigree cover inscribed with this verse from Micah: 'For what does the Lord God ask of you, but to do justice, love kindness, and walk humbly with your God.'"

All of this would not have happened had Mr. Thomas's initial wish, that his act of generosity remain anonymous, been fulfilled.

---

9. Look for opportunities to do favors for other people. Rabbi Avrohom Ehrman, author of *Journey to Virtue,* notes that shopping for a neighbor, offering someone a lift in your car, and helping a child (not necessarily your own) with homework "are included in the commandment to 'Love your neighbor as yourself.'"[3] Other suggestions—many of them compiled by Jack Doueck in *The Hesed Boomerang*—that will help make love of neighbor and the Golden Rule a part of our daily life include the following:

- Picking up trash from the sidewalk and putting it where it belongs.
- Giving up your seat on the train or bus to an elderly person or someone else who might need it.
- Helping someone walk across the street (a blind person, a senior citizen, a child, a person with a handicap).
- Allowing another driver to merge into your lane on the highway and doing so in a pleasant way.

---

*I heard this story from Rabbi Twerski, and while I am confident that I am accurately relating the spirit of the exchanges between him and Danny Thomas, the precise wording might be a bit different.

- Speaking with a homeless person on the street and really listening to him or her.
- Giving your old clothes directly to homeless people.
- Finding someone doing something good and praising him or her.
- Encouraging your children to donate their old toys that are still in good condition to children who might need and appreciate them.[4]
- At a social gathering, initiating a dialogue with someone who appears left out. Similarly, in a public setting, paying attention to the less popular individuals present rather than the popular ones who are already receiving more than their share of attention.

A final thought: Isaac Leib Peretz and the Rebbe of Nemirov

10. One of the great gems of Yiddish literature is the story Isaac Leib Peretz (1852–1915) tells about the Rebbe of Nemirov, but which is, in fact, based on a Chasidic tale told about Rabbi Moshe Leib of Sassov (1745–1807). Peretz's story centers on a Lithuanian Jew, a Litvak as such Jews were known, who is a *Mitnaged,* an opponent of Chasidism. The Litvaks, many of whom prided themselves on being disciples of the Vilna Gaon, saw themselves as religious rationalists, and viewed the Chasidic adoration of their rebbes as absurd. Hence, when this Litvak finds himself in the city of Nemirov during the days between Rosh Hashanah and Yom Kippur and sees that the local rebbe is not present at the morning prayer service, his curiosity is piqued. What sort of rabbi would not attend services during the Ten Days of Repentance?

The local Chasidim are untroubled by their rabbi's behavior. They assure the *Mitnaged* that during these days, when God is determining everyone's livelihood, peace, and health for the coming year, the rebbe spends the morning up in Heaven intervening directly on behalf of the members of his community.

The Litvak laughs, of course, and dismisses this as a ridiculous Chasidic fantasy. He decides to find out for himself what the rebbe really is doing each morning. Toward evening, he steals into the rebbe's room, slides under his bed and waits. That way, when the rebbe arises, he will watch and see where he goes.

During the night, the Litvak hears the rebbe groaning from his sorrow over the sufferings of his people. Finally, a few hours later, the rebbe arises. But he doesn't put on the typical garb of a rabbi. Instead, he goes to his closet and takes out a bundle of peasant clothes: linen trousers, high boots, a coat, a big felt hat, and a long wide leather belt studded with brass nails. From his coat pocket dangles a heavy peasant rope.

Finally, before leaving the house, he takes out an ax, puts it into his belt, and leaves the house. The mystified Litvak follows.

The rebbe walks down side streets, avoiding people, and finally reaches the outskirts of the town. He then goes into a wooded area. After thirty or forty steps, he stops by a small tree. He takes out the ax, and strikes the tree until it falls. Then he chops the tree into logs and the logs into sticks. He makes a bundle of the wood, and ties the bundle with the rope from his pocket. He puts the bundle on his back, tucks the ax back into this belt, and returns to the town.

He stops at a back street, at a small broken-down shack. He knocks on the window.

A frightened voice asks, "Who is there?" The Litvak recognizes it as the voice of a sick Jewish woman.

"I," answers the rebbe, in a voice very different from his own.

"Who is I?"

The rebbe answers in Russian, "Vassil."

"Who is Vassil, and what do you want?"

"I have wood to sell, very cheap," the rebbe says, his accent that of a peasant.

Without waiting for the woman to answer, he goes into the house. The Litvak looks within. The house is very poor, the furnishings broken. He can see the sick woman, wrapped in rags, and lying on a bed. "How can I buy? Where will a poor widow get money?"

"I'll lend it to you," answers the supposed Vassil. "It's only a few cents."

"But how will I ever pay you back?"

"Foolish one," says the rebbe reproachfully. "See, you are a poor, sick Jew, and I am ready to trust you with a little wood. And I am sure you'll pay. While you, you have such a great and mighty God, and you don't trust him for a few cents."

"And who will kindle the fire," said the widow. "Have I strength to get up?"

"I'll kindle the fire," answers the rebbe.

As the rebbe put the wood into the oven, he recites the first portion of the Penitential prayers.*

Then, as he puts the wood into the oven and the fire starts to burn brightly, he recites, now a bit more joyously, the second portion of the prayers. When the fire is set, he recites the third portion, and then he shuts the stove.

*The special *Selichot* prayers recited before and during the High Holiday period.

The Litvak who witnesses all this becomes a disciple of the rebbe.

And ever after, when he hears other disciples of the rebbe tell how the rebbe of Nemirov ascends to Heaven at the time of the Penitential prayers, he no longer laughs. He just adds quietly, "If not higher."*

11

GIVING ADVICE

1. The giving of advice is a tradition that goes back to the Bible. When the ancient Israelites asked the prophet Samuel to appoint a king for them, Samuel mustered all his powers of persuasion to dissuade them. He warned them that a king would end up drafting their sons to fight his wars and work his fields, while their daughters would be put to work as the king's cooks and bakers. A king would confiscate their lands and give it to his confederates, and eventually the people would "become his slaves" (I Samuel 8:17). The Israelites ignored Samuel's advice, and though a few of the later kings were just men and noble rulers, most went on to exploit their subjects in the manner Samuel had predicted, and which they would have been wise to guard against.

Whether people accept or reject it, good advice is often needed on the most important issues, including business and professional opportunities, the raising of children, and romantic issues as well. To convey to others good advice is therefore regarded an act of great kindness (see paragraph 4). But because advice can sometimes lead to detrimental results, the Rabbis cautioned us to avoid several pitfalls.

2. Make sure that your intention is pure and disinterested. This guideline is rooted in the Golden Rule's dictum to treat others as we would want to be treated. Rabbi Moshe Chayyim Luzatto, author of the *Mesillat Yesharim*

---

*Peretz's story is entitled "If Not Higher." In a popular Chasidic version of this story, the poor woman helped by the rebbe was an impoverished mother with an infant (Martin Buber, *Tales of the Hasidim, Book Two: The Later Masters,* pages 87–88).

(*The Path of the Just;* eighteenth century) explains: "The duty of the upright person is to give whatever counsel he would adopt for himself if he were similarly placed,* and to be mindful only of the good of the one who consults him, and to have no selfish purpose whatever" (chapter 11).

What should we do, therefore, if we have a personal interest in the decision made by the person seeking advice? Suppose someone consults us as to whether she should quit her job, and we know of a cousin or a dear friend in search of just that kind of job. Even if we believe that leaving the job is in the questioner's best interest, we must also tell her of our interest in the matter, particularly given the human tendency to rationalize. It is easy for many of us to convince ourselves that something is in somebody else's best interests when, in fact, it is in *our* interest that the person act in a certain way. In the situation described, we have the following similar, but subtly different, options:

- Tell her that we are not the right person to proffer advice and explain why ("I know somebody who is in need of work who is qualified for the job you are considering leaving. I'm afraid that my advice to you might be colored by this and not be exclusively in your best interests").

- Tell her of our interest in someone else getting the job, and why we still think it's within her interests to leave (if we indeed think that). But also emphasize that she should not rely exclusively on what we are saying because we cannot be fully objective.

In Dear Rabbi, Dear Doctor, *Abraham Twerski records a letter he received from a rabbi in the Midwest: "I have one congregant who is really a good person,*

*A friend notes that while Rabbi Luzatto's advice often applies, there are times when counseling another to act as you would can be very wrong. "What might be right for *me* is not necessarily right for the other person. A person whose advice is being solicited might think, 'What would I do if I were in his shoes?' But this is the wrong question to ask oneself. Better to ask yourself, 'What should I do if I were him and in such a predicament?' His needs, his desires, his strengths, his weaknesses are not the same as mine" (Dr. Isaac Herschkopf). Thus, Reb Aryeh Levine, who was known for his humility and his lifelong avoidance of public recognition, was once approached for advice by a man who held a prestigious government job, but knew that if he left it, he could definitely earn more money and perhaps find a job that would be more enjoyable. Reb Aryeh, responding to what he both knew and sensed about the man, advised him to remain where he was. He listed what he believed were several advantages in his present job, among them that "in this position, you enjoy esteem and honor." Reb Aryeh might have run from honor all his life, but he could also recognize that it had value, if not for himself, then for others (Simcha Raz, *A Tzaddik in Our Time,* page 182).

but he is a nudnik *[pest]. He imposes on me, day or night, without any regard for my need for rest or to be with my family. He will come to my home while we are at dinner, sit down at the table, and dominate the conversation, depriving me of precious time with my children. It is difficult for me to tell him that his behavior is unacceptable. He is a widower, semiretired. None of his children live here, and I feel sorry for him because I know he is lonely and that this is why he so frequently seeks my companionship. My problem is that he has consulted me about making* aliyah *[moving to Israel], and whether he should sell his home here. One daughter lives in Israel, and the other children live here. I cannot tell you how happy I would be if he moved to Israel. I would gladly pay for his ticket. But he is uncertain what to do and asks my advice. How can I advise him when I am so desirous of his leaving? I cannot really be objective as to whether this is best for him."*

Rabbi Twerski responded: "You really cannot advise him. The Talmud cites cases in which rabbis disqualified themselves as judges because of far less personal interest. If there are reasons why he should not *make* aliyah, *you are unable to see them. Your desire to be free of a* nudnik . . . *precludes you from being objective. You may tell him, 'Because of our relationship, I don't feel I can advise you properly. I think you should discuss this with someone who can be truly objective about the issues.' He has no idea how annoying he is to you, and may interpret the statement as meaning that because of your close relationship you don't want him to leave. Regardless, you should disqualify yourself on this question."*[1]

---

3. Make sure you are knowledgeable about matters on which you offer advice. To offer good counsel, it is not sufficient that your intentions are pure; you must also be quite sure that what you say is wise and helpful. Indeed, one of the sins to which Jews confess during the Yom Kippur service is "for the sin we committed . . . by offering bad advice." Unlike many other sins, such as cheating others or accepting bribes, this one is rarely committed with malicious intent. A particularly dangerous example is people who share strong prescription medications with friends, not realizing that while their symptoms may be similar, the causes could be totally different. Thus, the prescription pain reliever that might relieve one person's tension-based headache could turn his friend's throbbing headache into a hemorrhagic stroke.

Though there are professions—for example, psychiatry and the rabbinate—in which people are routinely consulted for advice, many professionals have not been adequately trained to offer it:* I have heard of rabbis who have advised an abused woman to return home, saying that he would talk to the husband and influence him to change his behavior. We now know that such interventions almost never succeed, and advice like this puts the abused spouse at grave risk.[2] I also know of a man who had trepidations about the character of a woman he would soon be marrying. Without considering the man's concerns, his rabbi assured him that premarital jitters are common and that it would be a terrible error to postpone or call off a marriage whose date had already been set. The wedding took place as scheduled, and within a matter of a month, the couple separated and, shortly thereafter, divorced. In short, if you're in the sort of position where people are going to be seeking your counsel, make sure you know enough before you offer it.

4. On the other hand, if you have insight about a practical or personal matter, share it. Rabbi Jonah Gerondi writes that giving advice is an act of kindness (*Gates of Repentance* 3:54). He understands that when people are in a predicament, it is an act of the greatest thoughtfulness to help them clarify their situation and to offer them advice on what to do.

This applies to small things as well. A friend who lives across the street from the United Nations—a major magnet for visitors to New York—always offers to help whenever he sees tourists trying to decipher a map.

The great wrong of self-serving advice

5. The Rabbis also root the prohibition against intentionally giving bad advice in another Torah law: "Do not place a stumbling block before the blind" (Leviticus 19:14). Jewish tradition understands this as not only outlawing playing a cruel trick on a blind person, but also as taking advantage of one who is "blind" to the matter at hand. Thus, anyone who takes advantage

*Rabbi Twerski notes that during his seven years of medical training, "not once . . . did I have a single lecture on some of the most common afflictions: spouse abuse, alcoholism, drug addiction, compulsive gambling, compulsive eating, bulimia, and other addictive disorders. In the several decades since I completed my training [Twerski attended medical school in the late 1950s and early 1960s], not enough has changed in the educational system, with the result that many professionals in various fields whose help is sought are simply not competent to provide it in these conditions, and the advice they give may be misleading and counterproductive. I have seen the tragic results of well-intended but very misleading advice."

of another's ignorance and gives that person inappropriate advice is regarded as having violated this biblical law.* A rabbinic commentary explains: "If a man seeks your advice, do not give him counsel that is wrong for him. Do not say to him, 'Leave early in the morning,' so that thugs might mug him. Do not say to him, 'Leave at noon,' so that he might faint from heat. Do not say to him, 'Sell your field and buy a donkey,' so that you may circumvent him, and take the field away from him" (*Sifra* Leviticus 19:14). As the first examples make clear, don't play cruel practical jokes on people, and, as the last example teaches, if you have a personal interest in the matter, you must disclose it.

My mother once received a phone call from a stockbroker with whom she was then dealing, aggressively pushing her to buy a certain stock. His enthusiasm was so pronounced that my mother, though normally a very cautious investor, bought the stock. It promptly proceeded to fall, and my mother later had reason to suspect that the company for which the broker worked needed to sell a large number of shares for one of their big clients and had encouraged their brokers to push the stock to clients.

---

6. Another biblical verse that is seemingly addressed only to those dealing with the blind—such as Leviticus 19:14—condemns by implication all those who offer people harmful advice: "Cursed be he who misleads the blind man on the road" (Deuteronomy 27:18). The figurative meaning of this verse is, indeed, frequently violated. For anybody who is lost and needs directions is, for all practical purposes, a "blind man on the road," yet many people who are not certain of the facts offer directions anyway.

In contrast, I came across a story which illustrates how a responsible person made sure a traveler did not get lost: "A man was taking a motorcycle ride along the Mississippi River when he came to a detour. He traveled the roads for what seemed like an eternity, and realized he was low on gas. When he stopped to check the map, a woman came out of her house and told him how to get back on the main route. He followed her directions until he got to a fork in the road she had not mentioned. On the left fork he saw a farmer walking back and forth across the road. So he went that way. 'Is this the way to Natchez?' he asked. 'Yes, it is,' the farmer answered. 'My neighbor up the road called and asked me to make sure you went the right way.'"[3]

---

*It applies as well to one who takes advantage of another's addiction or lack of self-control. Thus, for example, providing liquor to an alcoholic is a violation of this law.

When to offer bad advice

7. When we have good reason to believe that the person soliciting our advice will use our counsel to help him or her do something destructive, we are permitted—in fact obligated—to mislead the person (see *Mesillat Yesharim,* chapter 11). Rabbi Luzatto cites the verse in Psalms 18:27, "With the pure, act purely, with the perverse, act wily," which the Rabbis understand as meaning that we should act with guile to thwart those who intend to do wrong. Thus, the Bible tells the story of how a wise man intentionally offered an evil man bad advice, and thereby saved King David's kingship and life. This occurred when David's son, Absalom, launched a surprising and effective revolt against his father. After Absalom's initial attack, David and his troops fled, and Achitophel, Absalom's chief counsel, asked Absalom to let him set out immediately with twelve thousand troops: "I will come upon [David] when he is weary and disheartened, and I will throw him into a panic, and when all the troops with him flee, I will kill the king alone" (II Samuel 17:2). Absalom regarded Achitophel's advice as sound, but also summoned a second adviser, Chushai, who, unbeknownst to Absalom, was still loyal to David; the sole reason he had remained in Absalom's camp was so that he could function as a secret agent for David. When Chushai heard what Achitophel had suggested, he realized immediately that such an attack would succeed and therefore offered Absalom advice intended to thwart the attack. He told Absalom that although Achitophel was smart, "This time the advice that [he] has given is not good." Rather, he explained, David and his troops were experienced fighters who would immediately strike back at Absalom's forces, and deliver a quick blow against them. Therefore Absalom should not attack immediately with a relatively small force, but instead recruit a huge one "as numerous as the sands of the sea" from all Israel, with Absalom himself leading them in battle. Chushai spoke so convincingly that Absalom was persuaded (II Samuel 17:14).

In fact, of course, Achitophel's advice was sounder; had it been followed, Absalom's coup would have succeeded and David would have been killed. But Chushai's intention was to offer Absalom advice that would give David time to regroup and organize a large-scale military campaign. Indeed, when Chushai's advice was accepted, Achitophel immediately understood that this would lead to catastrophe for Absalom (and therefore for himself), and he went home and hanged himself (II Samuel 17:25). A few weeks later, Absalom and his forces failed in their attempt to defeat David, and Absalom himself was killed. All this came about because Chushai realized that when a bad person asks you for advice, your duty is to offer convincing, but bad, advice.

A last piece of advice on giving advice

8. Offer advice as a suggestion, not as a command. Rabbi Nathan, a close disciple of Rabbi Nachman of Bratslav (1772–1810), reported that Reb Nachman used to say: "One of the things I am very firm about is not giving advice in the form of orders." Rabbi Nathan explained Reb Nachman's technique when people solicited his guidance: "The Rebbe [never] gave advice . . . in the form of orders which had to be carried out exactly as he specified. His way was rather to offer guidance in the form of a good suggestion. The recipient was then free to follow it or not, as he chose. Certainly, the Rebbe wanted people to follow his advice, but he would never insist that everything should be precisely as he wished."* Reb Nachman explained to his disciple the rationale for his noncoercive approach: "I know that anything good in the world is never perfect. No matter what good there is . . . [some] bad [might] develop out of it because it is impossible for the good in this world to be perfect." For this reason, Reb Nachman refused to insist—as some other rabbis did—that people follow his advice exactly. He knew that there was a good chance that some bad, along with much good, might develop as a result, and didn't want the recipients of his advice to blame him.[4]

A minor, but illustrative, example: I was on an airplane recently when a woman sitting near me expressed considerable unhappiness that she had requested a window seat and been given an aisle instead. At that moment, I spotted one window seat a few rows in back of us, and advised her to take it before anyone

---

*Rabbi Saul Berman recalls an event in the early 1960s when the Student Struggle for Soviet Jewry was being organized. At the time, there was much rabbinic opposition in the Orthodox world to public demonstrations on behalf of Soviet Jewry. Many of the leading sages argued that such public action would antagonize the Soviet government and cause retribution against the already suffering and discriminated-against Russian-Jewish community. Student organizers went to discuss the matter with Rabbi Joseph Soloveitchik, hoping to receive his support. After hearing their arguments, he asked for time to deliberate. Some time later, he called the students in and, in Rabbi Berman's words, "told them that it [was] his considered opinion that public demonstrations would in fact be injurious to Soviet Jews and that he would not recommend engaging in such actions. The students were crestfallen. The Rav then added that this was not his *halachic* [binding legal] judgment, it was his considered political opinion and that the students should not view themselves as bound by his opinion—that they should simply take it into account as they gathered other opinions and moved towards a conclusion. After much deliberation, the students decided to go ahead with their plans for the Student Struggle for Soviet Jewry, and made history through their eventual impact on the freeing of Soviet Jewry." Some years later, Rabbi Soloveitchik told Rabbi Berman that he no longer opposed public demonstrations against the Soviet Union; indeed, he could not forgive the Israeli representative who had misled him on that matter and told him that such actions would be deleterious. At the time when he *else did (the plane doors had just closed, so I knew that no more passengers would be getting on and that no one had been assigned that seat). She thanked me and relinquished her aisle seat, which another passenger quickly occupied. A few minutes later, I heard her complaining to the stewardess: "My seat doesn't go back. I would never have given up my seat if I knew this seat didn't recline." Though trivial, this incident illustrated for me Reb Nachman's wisdom in realizing that even good commonsense advice can lead to unintended, unexpected, and disappointing results.*

Yet another reason not to offer advice in a definitive manner: it prevents or diminishes friction if your advice is not followed.

---

approached the Israeli representative, Israel had diplomatic relations with the Soviet Union, and Rabbi Soloveitchik assumed that the man had extensive knowledge on the matter and would give him an unbiased view as to the possible effects of demonstrations in the United States on Soviet policy toward Jews. The man had expressed opposition to such demonstrations, which influenced Rabbi Soloveitchik to tell the students that it was a bad idea. Years later, Soloveitchik realized that the man's advice was based not on the assumption that such demonstrations would hurt Soviet Jews, but on his fear that that it would damage the Soviet Union's relations with Israel. (Indeed, several years after Russia broke diplomatic relations with Israel—during the 1967 Six-Day War—Israel did begin to support public demonstrations on behalf of Soviet Jews.) In Rabbi Soloveitchik's view, the behavior of the Israeli representative violated the Jewish ethical norms on giving advice. The man's concern had been more with the interests of the State of Israel than with the interests of Soviet Jewry, on whose behalf his advice was being solicited. While Rabbi Soloveitchik "felt that such a stance was a legitimate one for Israel to take, it was not legitimate for them to have misled him as to their underlying motive" (Saul Berman, "The Approach of the Rav to *P'sak* and Public Policy," in Zev Eleff, editor, *Mentor of Generations*, pages 64–65).

Tzedaka: The Jewish Laws of Charity

Charity is equal in importance to all the other commandments combined.

Bava Bathra 9a

12

A PREEMINENT COMMAND

1. The Talmud teaches that "Charity is equal in importance to all the other commandments combined" (*Bava Bathra* 9a). And Maimonides, in summarizing the Jewish teachings on charity, concludes that "It is our duty to be more careful in the performance of charity than in the performance of any other positive commandment" ("Laws of Gifts to the Poor" 10:1). He adds that charitable giving is so fundamental to Jewish identity that "we have never seen nor heard of a Jewish community without a charity fund" (9:3).

Rabbi Chaim Ozer Grodzensky, the great rabbinical leader of pre–World War II Vilna, and author of Achiezer, *a classic set of responsa (answers by rabbinic scholars to questions on Jewish law), was asked late in life why he didn't devote more time to his writing. He answered: "When I was younger, I did think that the most important work for a person like me was to discover new [Torah] insights and to write them down in books. But now that I am older and more experienced, all that seems like child's play compared to the need to support widows, orphans, and Torah scholars. I used to think that my passport to the Garden of Eden [i.e., Heaven] was my magnum opus,* Achiezer. *Now I think my passport will be my ledger where I record my charity accounts."**

---

2. In Hebrew, the word for *charity* is *tzedaka.* But "charity" is not a fully accurate translation of *tzedaka.* "Charity" derives from the Latin *caritas* and suggests a donation made out of affection or love. In contrast, *tzedaka* derives from the word *tzedek,* which means "justice" (see, for example, Deuteronomy 16:20). Judaism regards someone who gives *tzedaka* as acting justly, and one who does not as acting unjustly. Thus, in communities ruled

*Cited in Rabbi Avrohom Feuer, *The Tzedakah Treasury,* page 313. Feuer's book, a very rich source of teachings on this aspect of Jewish life, contains material about the laws of charity and anecdotes relating how Jews have fulfilled this commandment.

according to Jewish law, as was common in the medieval world, communal leaders, believing that they had the right to stop people from acting unjustly, could and did require people to give *tzedaka,* just as governments compel citizens to pay taxes.*

British chief rabbi Sir Jonathan Sacks notes just how unusual the word tzedaka *is: "[It] combines into a single word two notions that are normally opposed to one another, namely charity and justice. Suppose, for example, that I give someone 100 pounds. Either he is entitled to it, or he is not. If he is, then my act is a form of justice. If he is not, it is an act of charity. In English, a gesture of charity cannot be an act of justice, nor can an act of justice be described as charity.* Tzedaka *is an unusual term because it means both."*†[1]

Dr. Elliot Dorff notes that the word caritas *creates the impression that "someone who provides money for charitable causes or engages in acts of charity is an unusually good person, going beyond the call of duty." In contrast,* tzedaka's *association with the word for justice "implies that caring for the poor is not an unusually good act [what philosophers call a 'supererogatory act'] but rather is simply what is expected of [us . . . in short] it is plain justice to help the poor, not an unusual display of love."*[2]

One contemporary Jewish thinker, Rabbi Irwin Kula, strenuously argues against what he regards as a false dichotomy between tzedaka *and charity, the former supposedly expressing justice and the latter love. Rather, as Kula explains, the claim made by* tzedaka *is that justice and love are intimately related: "You only love someone if it shows in your deeds. Therefore, if someone doesn't give charity, that, in and of itself, is proof they lack love. . . . Jews don't raise large*

*The Talmud records that Rava (fourth century C.E.) compelled his wealthy disciple Rabbi Nathan bar Ami to give 400 *zuzim,* a large sum, to charity (*Bava Bathra* 8b). Maimonides rules that if a person gives less than he is obligated, "[a Jewish] court may seize his property in his presence and take from him what is proper for him to give" ("Laws of Gifts to the Poor" 7:10). Such a law—giving to the court a power comparable to a government's right to tax—is no longer enforced in Jewish life.

†Rabbi Nachum Amsel notes that rooting the term for helping the needy in the word for justice underscores that "the Jew must then give *tzedaka* because it is the proper and right thing to do, not because he or she has a particular feeling for the recipient. One very practical difference would be the case of an insulting . . . foul-smelling beggar who demanded charity. It certainly would be hard to feel any love or compassion for such an individual. Nevertheless, Judaism obligates the Jew to give this person *tzedaka*" (*The Jewish Encyclopedia of Moral and Ethical Issues,* page 298).

amounts of money for charitable causes because they are motivated by justice, but rather because they love deeply. Splitting love and justice undermines both, particularly love, which, when real, is the ground for intense obligation. If there is no sense of obligation then quite simply there is no love, just some amorphous, flitting feelings."

—

The significance of charity in the Bible and Talmud

3. The Torah understands charity and justice as being the defining characteristics of Abraham, the first Jew, and his descendants: "For I [God] have singled him out, that he may command his children and his household after him to keep the way of God by doing what is charitable and right" (Genesis 18:19). It might be suspect genetics, but Maimonides states that not giving *tzedaka* constitutes such cruel and un-Jewish behavior that we should question the Jewishness of one who acts in this way ("Laws of Gifts to the Poor" 10:2).

—

*According to the book of Proverbs, one salient feature of the "woman of valor" (*aishet chayyil*) is that she "stretches out her hand to the poor; yes, she reaches her hands to the needy" (31:20).*

—

4. While charitable giving in today's world is associated with many causes, including donations to museums, orchestras, and universities, *tzedaka* in the Bible refers exclusively to help extended to the poor. The Torah ordains both a positive and negative command: When confronted by a person in need, "You shall open, yes, open, your hand to him" and not "harden your heart nor shut your hand against your needy brother" (Deuteronomy 15:7–8).

—

The Sefer HaChinnuch *understands the repetition in the biblical commandment—". . . open, yes, open"—as underscoring that we must give to a person in need even many times (commandment 479).*

—

The Midrash records that when Rabbi Joshua ben Levi went to Rome, he saw marble pillars covered with sheets, so they wouldn't crack from the heat, nor freeze from the cold. He also saw a poor person, with only a reed mat under him, *and another above him, as his sole protection against the elements (*Pesikta d'Rav Kahana 9*). Comments Barry Holtz: "It's a picture that makes one think of the urban poor today, sleeping over subway grates in the richest cities in the world."*[3]

Rabbi Herbert Weiner heard the late scholar Rabbi Abraham Chen comment on this passage: "And this is . . . the difference between Rome and Jerusalem. Not that Rome did not value human life nor that Jerusalem did not value marble pillars, but the order of priority, what is first and what is second, this makes all the difference."[4] *In short, marble pillars should be safeguarded and art museums should be supported, but treatment of the poor is more important.*

---

5. While it is wrong for anyone not to give charity (even those who are poor are instructed to give something; see page 245), the Bible particularly excoriates wealthy people who don't do so: "Woe to those who lie upon beds of ivory and stretch themselves upon their couches . . . who drink wine from bowls, and anoint themselves with the finest oils, but are not grieved at the ruin of Joseph" (i.e., the sufferings and poverty of their fellow Jews; Amos 6:1, 4, 6).

The Rabbis tell the story of a poor widow and her family who dwelt in the neighborhood of a wealthy farmer. When the woman's two young sons went to glean in the farmer's field, the farmer stopped them from taking any food (in violation of the biblical law that mandated that the poor be granted this privilege; *see page 210**). The whole time the sons were away, the famished mother said to herself: "When will my sons come back from the field? Perhaps I shall find that they have brought something to eat." Meanwhile, the sons said to themselves: "When shall we go back to our mother? Perhaps we shall discover that she has found something to eat."*

*Soon enough, "She found that they had nothing, and they found that she had nothing either. So they laid their heads on their mother's lap, and the three of them died in one day. Said the Holy One, blessed be He, 'Their very existence you [the rich who don't give what they should] take away from them. By your life, I shall make you, too, pay for this with your very existence" (*The Fathers According to Rabbi Nathan *38).*

---

6. The Bible also believes that a society's lack of charity makes it worthy of destruction. Thus, although there are few details in the Torah about the condemned city of Sodom (except for its extreme inhospitality to visitors; see Genesis 19:4–10), later biblical teachings interpret God's decision to destroy it as due in part to its lack of generosity: "She [Sodom] and her daughters had plenty of bread and untroubled tranquility; yet she did not support the poor and needy" (Ezekiel 16:49).

7. The Rabbis of the Talmud taught that "One who does charitable deeds is greater than one who brings sacrifices" (*Sukkah* 49b). Professor Jacob Neusner, a contemporary talmudic scholar, emphasizes the superiority of charity, an ethical act, over sacrifice, a ritual one: "Many people think that in the setting of the Jewish community, it is possible to distinguish secular from religious. Raising money is said to be secular. Praying or studying Jewish holy books (Torah) is religious. According to this view, raising money does not make one a 'better Jew' . . . while, for example, participating in a Passover Seder does. The sources in Judaism . . . prove that that distinction is wrong. *Tzedaka* is the highest expression of the holy way of living taught by Torah."[5]

Not giving charity as a crime against God

8. Because in Judaism God is seen as the One Who gives people wealth* and Who commands them to give a part of that wealth to the poor, refusing to give charity is regarded as a form of stealing. The thirteenth-century *Sefer Chasidim* imagines God as saying: "I gave you wealth so that you could distribute it [in part] to the poor, but you didn't do so . . . you kept all the money for yourself. Since you did not keep your part of the bargain, you will be punished as though you have robbed them . . ." (paragraph 415).

Don Isaac Abarbanel (fifteenth century), a Bible commentator and high official in the Spanish government, explained the Jewish attitude toward money and charity somewhat similarly: Since money is given to us by God, God has the right to tell us how to disburse it. For Abarbanel, the issue is not stealing, but that we should regard ourselves as God's agents, and thus as responsible for how we manage His money. Since God has made it known that He wants us to "invest" some of the money in tzedaka, *then, if we don't do so, God might choose to take the money from us and entrust it to someone else (commentary on Deuteronomy 15:7).*

A midrashic story tells of a poor man who was approached by the prophet Elijah, in disguise, who told him, "You have six good years [*coming to you*]. *When do*

*"Mine is the gold and the silver, says the Lord" (*Haggai* 2:8).

you wish them, now, or at the end of your life?" At first, the man thought Elijah was a sorcerer and ignored him. But when the prophet returned with the same question three more times, the man consulted with his wife—a virtuous and highly intelligent woman—and she instructed him to say, "Bring me the good years now." The man spoke to Elijah as his wife suggested; by the time he reached home, his children had found a buried treasure in the yard in front of their house. The wife said to her husband: "God has given us the means to last for six years, so let us engage in deeds of charity and loving-kindness during these years; perhaps God will continue then to give us more of His bounty." Every day, when the woman would give money and food to the poor she would tell her youngest son, "Record every item we dispense." And the boy did so.

At the end of the six years, Elijah returned and said to the man, "The time has come to take away what I gave you." The pious man replied, "When I took the money, I took it only with my wife's advice. Now that I am to return it, I will return it only with my wife's advice." He went to his wife and said, "The old man has come back to take away what is his." The wife replied, "Go tell him, 'If you find human beings more reliable than we are, give them what you left in trust for us.'"

And so the man answered. And God, who had sent Elijah, considered their words and the acts of charity they had performed, and continued to bless them with great wealth (Yalkut, *Ruth 607).*[6]

—

9. The Talmud teaches that "if a person averts his eyes to avoid giving charity, it is as if he committed idolatry" (*Ketubot* 68a). The Rabbis could have simply denounced such a person as hard-hearted, but why did they view him as an idolater? Because someone who flees from opportunities to give charity has turned silver and gold into his gods. That is why he refuses to part with them; like idols, they are too important to him.

Why tzedaka *is so important*

10. Jewish teachings regard poverty as perhaps the greatest affliction that can befall a person: "If all the suffering and pain in the world were gathered [on one side of a scale], and poverty was on the other side, poverty would outweigh them all" (*Exodus Rabbah* 31:14).* While this statement may

---

*One talmudic passage compares a poor person to a dead one (*Nedarim* 64b) while another declares that "poverty in a person's home is an affliction more severe than fifty plagues" (*Bava Bathra* 116a).

be hyperbolic (one suspects that most people would rather lose their money than their child or, for that matter, their limbs), the Rabbis recognized that an inability to provide oneself and one's family with basic needs constitutes a particularly terrible suffering.

Being dependent on the kindness of others for one's survival also causes great humiliation. During the Birkat HaMazon, *Grace after Meals, Jews pray daily that they not become dependent on the gifts or loans of others.*

---

11. While the Torah places great emphasis on helping the poor, it also teaches that there will "never cease to be needy ones in your land" (Deuteronomy 15:11). This verse should inhibit the more affluent from feeling that the problems of poverty are invariably the fault of those in need; rather, the Torah's words remind us that a certain degree of poverty is part of the human condition, an insight that should make us less judgmental of those who suffer from it.[7]

12. Poverty, particularly when it afflicts others, should never be viewed as a divine punishment. The Talmud describes such an attitude as quintessentially non-Jewish. As Rabbi Meir put it: "If a non-believer wants to criticize you, he might ask the following question: 'If your God loves the poor, why doesn't He sustain them?' " Indeed, this question was posed by Rufus, the brutal Roman general in Israel (second century C.E.) to Rabbi Akiva. When Akiva answered that God leaves the support of the poor in part to us, "in order that we be saved [by the charity we give] from the punishment of *Gehinnom* [hell]," Rufus responded that not only will our charity not save us in God's eyes, it will condemn us. He drew the following analogy: Suppose a king deprived a man with whom he was furious of food and drink, only to learn that someone came forward and fed the condemned man. Wouldn't the king be enraged at this person?

Indeed, there is a certain primitive but, from Judaism's perspective, immoral logic in equating suffering with the divine will. It is also convenient in that it frees the rest of us from trying to help the afflicted.

However, assuming that another person's suffering is God's will ends up turning human beings from God's partners in the task of *tikkun olam* (mending the world) into coldhearted spectators. Torment and catastrophe come to be seen as what God wants. If a person is drowning, don't help him; the fact that he is drowning means that God wants him to die. If a person has cancer, don't treat it. And if a person is poor, let him starve.

Human suffering does not call for judgment; it calls for action. When Rufus insisted that God must be angry at Jews for helping the poor and thereby thwarting His will, Akiva responded with a directive from Isaiah: ". . . share your bread with the hungry and take the wretched poor into your home" (Isaiah 58:7; the dialogue of Rufus and Rabbi Akiva is found in *Bava Bathra* 10a).

An old tale tells of a son walking with his father. The boy is distressed as they pass hungry beggars in the street, see people with crippling illnesses, and witness other scenes of suffering.

"This is terrible," the boy says to his father. "How can God allow this? Why doesn't He send help?"

"He did," the father answers. "He sent you." (Retold by Rabbi David Wolpe.)

How important are one's motives for giving tzedaka?

13. The Rabbis believed that the benefits rendered by charitable giving are so significant that a donor is fully credited by God even if her motives for giving are more for personal benefit than altruism. As the Talmud puts it: "If a person says, 'I am giving this coin to charity so that my [sick] child will live,' or 'so that I will make it into the World-to-Come,' he is completely righteous" (*Pesachim* 8a-b).*

Similarly, Rabbi Israel Baal Shem Tov, the eighteenth-century founder of Chasidism, noted why Judaism is more concerned with the act than with the motive: "Even though giving charity with an ulterior motive [such as becoming known as a philanthropist] is not as good as doing it with a pure motive [helping the poor without any thought of reward or recognition], it is still a good deed, since you sustain the poor no matter what your motive is."[8]

Dennis Prager presented the following hypothetical case to several thousand high school students: Two people, with precisely the same wealth, are approached by a person they know who is in desperate need of food and money for his family. The first person listens to the man's appeals, expresses great sympathy, and gives the

*But if we extend help to a poor person with an angry expression or with unkind words, we lose the merit of our good act (see page 171). That is because such an attitude hurts and humiliates the recipient, but our attempt to strike a bargain with God does not.

man $5. The second person is in a rush, but feeling obligated to tithe, gives him $100. Which was better, giving $5 from one's heart, or giving $100 because one's religion commands one to do so? Routinely, 70 to 90 percent of the teens answered that the person who gave $5 out of his heart had done the better thing.

This response suggests that most people care less about the good their money is doing than about how they feel giving it. When Prager asked the same students if they would vote the same if they were the needy person, they were taken aback; they had not considered that perspective. Prager explains: "Judaism would love you to give 10 percent of your income each year from your heart. It suspects, however, that in a large majority of cases, were we to wait for people's hearts to prompt them to give a tenth of their money away, we would be waiting a very long time. Therefore, Judaism says, 'Give 10 percent, and if your heart catches up, terrific.' In the meantime, good has been done."[9]

---

14. To encourage people to make donations, Jewish law permits making conditional vows to charity: "I will donate [state the amount] to charity if such-and-such happens." Rabbi Moses Isserles, the Ramah (sixteenth century), explains: "If a person says, 'If so-and-so, who is deathly ill, will be cured . . . I will donate such-and-such to charity,' but then the sick person dies, the person is not obliged to fulfill his vow because it was clearly conditional" (*Shulchan Arukh, Yoreh Deah* 220:15).

Normally, setting conditions for one's observance of a Jewish law is prohibited. Thus, it is forbidden to say, "I'll observe the Sabbath if I become rich" since Jews are obliged to observe the Sabbath whether they are poor or rich.* That Jewish law allows such conditional vows underscores how eager the Rabbis were to encourage charitable giving by any means necessary.

The first person to make a conditional vow of this kind was Jacob, Judaism's third patriarch: "Then Jacob took a vow, saying, 'If God will be with me, and guard me on this way that I am going . . . then this stone which I have set up as a pillar shall become a house of God, and whatever You [God] will give me, I shall give a tenth to You" (Genesis 28:20, 22).

---

*Therefore, we are permitted to set conditions only for that portion of charity that is over and above that which we are expected to give. For a discussion of the various views on how much charity one is obligated to give, see chapter 15.

15. Despite the Talmud's insistence that a self-interested motive for giving *tzedaka* does not negate its value, Rabban Yochanan ben Zakkai, a foremost talmudic sage, emphasized that the highest performance of the mitzvah involves giving with a pure intention. He once dreamed that two of his nephews were destined to lose 700 dinarim—a large amount of money—during the coming year. Throughout the year, he kept encouraging the men to give to charity, and they ended up donating a total of 683 dinarim. Then, just before the High Holidays, Roman authorities came to their place of business and confiscated 17 dinarim. The nephews were afraid that the authorities would return to take more, but Rabbi Yochanan told them that they need not be afraid; the 17 dinarim would be it. The nephews were puzzled about how their uncle knew the precise sum—they hadn't mentioned it—and Rabbi Yochanan told them about his dream. They asked why he hadn't told them about the dream earlier so that they could have given all 700 dinarim to charity. He answered, "I said to myself, 'It is better not to inform you so that you will perform the mitzvah of charity for its own sake' " (*Bava Bathra* 10a).*

Three rewards for giving charity

16. God's blessings. Perhaps because many people give less generously to charity than they should because they are afraid of diminishing their assets, the *Shulchan Arukh* reassures would-be donors that, "No person will become poor because of giving charity" (*Yoreh Deah* 247:2; see also Maimonides, "Gifts to the Poor" 10:2). In addition, the Torah promises that, in return for giving to the poor, "the Lord your God will bless you in all your efforts and in all your undertakings" (Deuteronomy 15:10).† The Talmud makes the even more explicit promise that you should "tithe so that you will become rich" (*Ta'anit* 9a).

Rabbi Tzvi Spitz asked the legal scholar Rabbi Yosef Shalom Elyashiv why, in light of such explicit biblical and talmudic assurances, there are many extremely charitable people who have not been blessed with material success.

---

*Apparently, Rabbi Yochanan believed that, for the sake of character development, it is better to give a somewhat smaller amount to charity (in this case, about 2 percent less) with the right intent than a larger amount with an ulterior motive (see ArtScroll commentary on *Bava Bathra* 10a, note 26). I imagine that had Rabbi Yochanan seen that his nephews were giving very small amounts to charity, he would have told them about the dream.

†The biblical and rabbinic belief that charitable giving is the right thing to do and will also be rewarded may be behind the rabbinic advice to give charity even during difficult times: "If a man sees that his livelihood is barely sufficient for him, he should still give *tzedaka* from it. How much more so when his livelihood is good" (*Gittin* 7a).

Rabbi Elyashiv responded: "There are many different types of wealth other than financial prosperity. Some people are rewarded with a great deal of pleasure from their children. Others experience an abundance of energy and robust health. All of these may be considered as a reward for having been highly charitable."[10]

17. Life itself. Perhaps the most important and immediate reward the Bible promises for charitable giving is life itself: "Charity saves from death" (Proverbs 10:2 and 11:4).* The Talmud understands this literally and offers several examples of people destined to die whose lives were spared because of their charitable acts. For example, the Talmud relates that Rabbi Akiva had a premonition† that his daughter would die on her wedding day, which caused him great anxiety, but about which he said nothing to her. On her wedding day, his daughter pulled a long sharp needle out of her dress and stuck it into a thin wall. The needle pierced the eye of a snake and killed it. Later, when she withdrew the needle from the wall, the snake's body fell to the floor. When she told her father what happened, Akiva, recognizing that the snake was the one destined to kill her, asked what kind act she had done that day. She answered that a poor man had knocked on the door, and since everyone else was involved in the wedding preparations, she had prepared food and served it to him. Rabbi Akiva who, until then, had apparently understood the verse, "Charity saves from death," metaphorically, now realized that it was meant literally. Even if one is destined to die, a charitable act can change one's fate (*Shabbat* 156b).

A similar story is related in Tractate *Bava Bathra* (11a). A man known as Benjamin ha-Tzaddik (the Righteous) served as the administrator of a communal charity, whose funds became exhausted during a famine. When a woman asked for aid, he swore that there was no money left. But after she said, "If you don't help me, a woman and her seven children will perish," Benjamin helped her with his own money. Some time later, he fell ill and was close to death. The angels in heaven said to God, "You, God, created Adam

---

*The idea that charity can save us from death or suffering is reinforced in the High Holidays liturgy. Perhaps the most famous line in the *U-ne-taneh Tokef* prayer is its conclusion, "And repentance, prayer, and charity can avert the evil decree" [alternatively, "avert the severity of the decree"]. This line is based on the talmudic teaching that charity, prayer, and changing one's behavior may cause God to cancel a bad decree (*Rosh Hashanah* 16b; the text also mentions a fourth activity, changing one's name).

†Based on predictions made to him by astrologers; many of the talmudic rabbis believed in astrology in the sense that the stars impel, but don't compel (see the discussion of this point in *A Code of Jewish Ethics, Volume 1: You Shall Be Holy,* page 29*n*).

singly to teach that preserving a single life is like saving a whole world. Are you going to let Benjamin the Righteous, who saved a woman and her seven sons, die after these few years he lived on earth?" Immediately, the Talmud concludes, Benjamin's verdict in heaven was rescinded, and twenty-two more years were added to his life.

Comments Danny Siegel: "This story simply states the principle: When nothing can be done, something can still be done. Even though his official responsibilities ended when the communal funds were exhausted, [Benjamin's] obligations as a Jew demanded some deliberate action."[11]

—

An alternative, but equally literal, reading of the verse "Charity saves from death," is suggested in the poignant short story "Charity," by Hugh Nissenson. Set in New York City's Lower East Side in 1912, the tale is narrated by a twelve-year-old boy whose father is a finisher of men's pants who works twelve hours a day and earns $7 a week, and whose mother supplements the income with another $3. The boy remembers, "I always went to bed hungry." Only on the Sabbath does the family eat well; the boy recalls how his mouth would water in anticipation of the Friday night meal.

On that night, his father, a religious Jew, would always bring home a guest even poorer than they. Often, the guest would remain for the entire Sabbath, and some would snore so loudly that the boy had trouble sleeping. Yet when he complained about this, his father would respond, "Remember, 'Charity saves from death.'"

One winter, the boy's mother contracted pneumonia. Soon, her coughing escalated, and she began to spit blood. Finally, one Friday afternoon, with her life at stake, she was hospitalized, and the boy was sent out to do the Sabbath shopping normally done by his mother. When he returned home, his father, as always, had invited a guest. At dinner, the man, Reb Rifkin, told them, "Would you believe it? Except for a little salted herring and a glass of tea, this is the only thing I've had in the mouth for six days." As always, the guest snored, but this time it didn't bother the young boy. Late that night, he spoke to his father, and told him, "I feel much better now."

"Do you?" the father asked. "Why?"

"Because Mama will get well."

"How can you be so sure?"

"You said so yourself."

"Did I?" the father answered. "When?"

"You said that charity saves from death."

"What's that got to do with Mama?"

"Everything."

He suddenly raised his voice. "Is that what you think a mitzvah *is? A bribe offered to the Almighty."*

"But you said so. You said that charity saves from death," I insisted. Rifkin, half-awakened, turned over and groaned.

"No, not Mama," my father said in a hoarse voice. "Him."[12]

---

18. Eternal life. The Talmud promises an eternal reward for acts of charity, particularly for those of unusual generosity. When Rabbi Yossi ben Kisma learned that Rabbi Chanina, while collecting charity, had mixed the funds collected with his own money, and had then decided to distribute all the money to charity (even though some of it was his own), he said, "I only wish that your portion [in the hereafter] would be my portion, and your lot would be my lot" (*Avodah Zarah* 18a). Elsewhere, the Talmud cites Rabbi Meir and Rabbi Akiva as teaching that charity will spare one from punishment in the next world (*Bava Bathra* 10a; see page 162).

In part to "remind" God of their charitable deeds, some medieval French Jews had the table at which they served food to the poor cut up when they died, with the wood used to erect their coffin. The author of the medieval Menorat Ha-Maor *calls this "a very distinguished custom" (see the book's chapter titled "Charity"). Rabbi Philip Birnbaum suggests that this custom was also meant to convey "that a man can take nothing with him except the good he has done."*[13]

The one time when a nonbelieving perspective is good

19. Even though Judaism, as a monotheistic faith, abhors atheism, when the nineteenth-century Chasidic rebbe Rabbi Moshe Leib of Sassov was asked, "If everything that God created is good, what good is there in the fact that He created human beings with the capacity to deny His existence?" he responded: "People whose faith in God is absolute might ignore a person in need of help, and think that God will take care of him. Instead, when you see someone needing help, think to yourself, 'maybe there is no God, and only I can help him.' "*

---

*As Rabbi Abraham Twerski concludes: "Have trust in God for yourself. When it comes to helping others, do not rely on your faith in God and His benevolence to free you from helping others" (*Living Each Day*, 77).

Giving charity as a privilege

20. When we have the opportunity to dispense charity, we should regard ourselves as fortunate, rather than burdened. Commenting on Psalms 23:6, "May only goodness and kindness pursue (*yir-de-funi*) me all the days of my life," the Chaffetz Chayyim pointed out that none of us lives in utter tranquillity. We are all pursued by some worrisome concerns, be they disease, bitter enemies, or bill collectors: "Fortunate is the person who discharges his 'pursuit quota' by suffering from those who pursue him for charity!"[14]

—

Byron Sherwin notes that in the Gospel of Mark (10:25), Jesus, in one of his most famous pronouncements, declares, "It is easier for a camel to go through the eye of a needle than for a rich man to enter the Kingdom of God." Rather than focus, as does this statement, on the potential punishment of the wealthy, Byron Sherwin argues that "the wealthy have an opportunity not granted to others. Heaven can be theirs, not by surrendering their wealth, but by using it as faithful stewards for the sake of God, and in fulfillment of the will of God that the indigent be cared for."*[15]

—

Two final thoughts

21. Rabbi Israel Salanter taught: "Most people are concerned with their own material well-being and their neighbor's soul. Better that they worry about their own soul and their neighbor's material well-being."†

---

*The context in which Jesus makes this statement (see Matthew 19:16–26) reflects a markedly different mind-set from that of the Rabbis of the Talmud. A young man had come to Jesus and told him that he had fulfilled the Ten Commandments and practiced the love of neighbor. He then asked, "What more do I need to do?" Jesus told him: "If you wish to be perfect, go and sell what you own and give the money to the poor. . . ." But when the young man heard these words, he was very sad, for he was a man of great wealth. After the young man had walked away, Jesus went on to make the statement concerning how hard, almost impossible, it is for wealthy people to save themselves in God's eyes. In contrast, the prevailing Jewish attitude is that a person, even if wealthy, should not give away more than 20 percent of his assets in one year lest he impoverish himself, and the rabbinic attitude, unlike that of Jesus, is that it is wrong to be poor if one can avoid it (see page 243). I also suspect that part of the reason the Rabbis never demanded that a person give away more than 20 percent of his or her wealth is so that people who have been generous don't feel guilty for having not done even more good. Thus, the Jewish attitude would seem to be: Give a significant percentage of your earnings to charity, and then feel free to spend the rest of your money as you wish.

†I have heard this said in Rabbi Salanter's name, but have been unable to track down the source. In Dov Katz's *Tenu'at Ha-Mussar* (*The Mussar Movement*), Volume 1, he cites a similar version of Rabbi Salanter's comment: "A person should be more concerned with spiritual than with material matters, but another person's material well-being is his own spiritual concern."

Nikolai Berdyaev (1874–1948), the Russian religious existentialist, expressed a similar thought in a more poignant manner: "The question of bread for myself is a material question, but the question of bread for my neighbor is a spiritual question."

---

22. Charity is an eternal possession. All our money and possessions can be lost or confiscated (such was the fate of German Jews in the 1930s, and many Jews in the Arab world after Israel's creation in 1948). When we give money to charity, however, we retain permanent possession of the good deed we performed; no one can ever take this from us. Therefore, paradoxically, the only money we possess forever is the money we give away.

When Don Isaac Abarbanel served as finance minister to the Spanish king, it is told that some members of the court, envious of his high standing, told the king that he was embezzling money from the royal treasury. The king asked Abarbanel to provide him with a full accounting of his assets. Some days later, Abarbanel gave the king a list that was much smaller than the king expected. "But this is only a small percentage of what I know you own," the king said.

Abarbanel answered: "When your majesty asked me for an accounting of my possessions, I knew it was because some of my enemies have been maligning me. If they succeed, then your Majesty will confiscate everything I have. These are hardly things I possess because I can lose them in just a moment. I, therefore, made a calculation of whatever money I have given to charity, because that can never be confiscated from me, and what I have given away is truly the only thing I can say that I own."[16]

This is a good thought to bear in mind when we have sustained, for example, a large loss in the stock market. The money lost is no longer ours and it is as if we had never possessed it, but the money we have given away to help others is still, so to speak, in our account and will never be lost.

13

HOW AND WHEN TO GIVE

1. "One should give charity with a warm and friendly expression, with happiness, and with a good heart, and one should mourn with the poor person in distress and speak words of consolation to him." Conversely, if one dispenses charity in an angry manner, one loses the merit of this mitzvah (*Shulchan Arukh, Yoreh Deah* 249:3).

Those who give charity angrily humiliate the recipient. Thus, for example, many people have had the experience of someone agreeing to do them a favor, but appearing to be so irritated they have said, "If that's how you feel about it, don't bother." However, those in need of *tzedaka* cannot afford to turn down *any* offer of help, and are forced to suffer embarrassment in these circumstances. The Talmud considers humiliating others to be a form of bloodshed (*Bava Mezia* 58b).

Maimonides views giving with a morose expression as the lowest of his eight levels of charity (see pages 187–191), yet it is still a positive act. It is only giving with an angry expression that is condemned ("Laws of Gifts to the Poor," 10:4).

---

2. If we are not able to give money, we should comfort the impoverished person with words. The Talmud teaches that if we encourage a poor person with kind words we are rewarded with eleven blessings, among them that God "will guide you at all times" and will spare you from serious depression so that even your "gloom shall be like noonday" (*Bava Bathra* 9b, based on Isaiah 58:10–12).

Focusing on the needs of the poor person to whom we are giving

3. The Torah commands us to give a poor person "sufficient for his needs" (Deuteronomy 15:8). Jewish law understands this to mean that we should try to provide precisely what that person lacks: "If he is hungry, he should be fed. If he needs clothes, he should be provided with clothes. If he has no household furniture or utensils, furniture and utensils should be

provided. . . . If he needs to be spoon-fed, then we must spoon-feed him" (*Shulchan Arukh, Yoreh Deah* 250:1).

—

Regarding this last, strangely specific, example, writer Danny Siegel recalls an incident related to him by a medical resident. A prominent physician was taking the resident and some medical students on morning rounds, offering insights at the bedside of each patient. They soon came to an older woman, whose complex ailments made it impossible for her family and friends to care for her. The woman was depressed and withdrawn, and refused to eat. To the students' astonishment, the professor stopped the rounds and spent twenty minutes spoon-feeding the woman. Siegel concludes: "[The woman] was capable of feeding herself, but she refused to do so. So, with deliberate and gentle care, the teacher taught a lesson in kindness. He did not do it as a demonstration to the students. No . . . he spoon-fed this old woman because this is what the demands of the hour were.[1]

—

The Talmud tells of an instance in which a man vowed not to marry a certain woman because she was unattractive. Rabbi Ishmael (late first–early second century) provided the woman, who was poor, with the makeup and clothing to make herself prettier; the man changed his mind, and Rabbi Ishmael declared his vow not binding. Though happy at the outcome, Rabbi Ishmael cried at how the harsh poverty encountered by the poor made them physically less attractive (see Mishnah Nedarim *9:10). I recall reading of a charity, Dress for Success, which has offices throughout the United States and which—among its other activities—provides attractive and professional attire to disadvantaged women so that they can make a more favorable impression on their potential employers. There are also charities that lend clean and beautiful wedding gowns to poor brides.*

—

Meyer Michael Greenberg was "known to the poor and homeless of New York City for a simple act of charity he performed for thirty years." Each year between Thanksgiving and Christmas, as autumn turned to winter, "and winter intensified the misery of those who had no shelter," Mr. Greenberg went to the Bowery, the Manhattan neighborhood in which many alcoholics and homeless people were found, and gave away pairs of gloves from a canvas bag slung over his shoulder. He became known to the residents of the Bowery as Gloves Greenberg, and when a man would ask him how much the gloves cost, Mr. Greenberg would answer, "A handshake." Although Greenberg knew that if he went to the missions in the area he could distribute hundreds of gloves in a few hours, he chose to give out the gloves one pair at a time: "I prefer to go looking for the people I want. The ones who avoid eye contact. It is not so much the gloves but telling people they count." On one occasion, he gave gloves to a man who had been his economics teacher decades earlier at Brooklyn College. On another occasion, Greenberg recalled: "I was handing out gloves in the Bowery, and I saw a man who had been a leading baritone at the Met when I was an extra, a spear carrier. He didn't recognize me, of course. The lead singers at the Met would never have associated with the likes of us. I wanted to say, 'You were so wonderful.'" But Greenberg chose to say nothing, as he feared he would embarrass the man.

Greenberg used to tell people that he carried with him the memory of cold mornings from his own childhood: "One winter, when I was eleven or twelve, I lost my gloves. I felt very guilty about it; don't ask me why. I never even asked for another pair. I don't think I ever had another pair until I went into the army. Ever since then, for me, being rich is being warm."

Mr. Greenberg started giving away gloves in the early 1960s, in honor of his father, who had recently died. He liked to quote words his father had told him: "Don't deprive yourself of the joy of giving."

Lawrence Van Gelder, the New York Times *reporter who wrote Mr. Greenberg's obituary (*New York Times, *June 21, 1995), reported that Russell Aaronson, the deceased's cousin, said that he intended to carry on Mr. Greenberg's charity.*

A friend shared with me the following: "Many years ago, I was shopping at a large department store, Alexander's, when I heard a familiar voice. It was one of my teachers from elementary school. This lady had been, by far, our best English teacher, but she had always been a bit strange. Apparently, now she had become stranger. She was arguing with the sales clerk that her credit card was valid though it had expired. The clerk could not reason with her and was about to call security.

"I surreptitiously gave the clerk my credit card and told her to add my teacher's items to my purchase. My former teacher hadn't recognized me two decades later and never realized that I had paid for her. It was a small way for me to thank her for all that she had taught me" (Dr. Isaac Herschkopf).

---

4. A second meaning of "sufficient for his needs": When dispensing charity, take into account the person's emotional, as well as physical, needs. For example, if a rich person becomes poor, the community should strive to maintain her at a higher level than someone who has always been poor. That is so because for such a person the descent into poverty causes greater suffering than it does for someone who has known nothing better. Basing himself on a talmudic text, Maimonides writes that if a rich person who formerly owned a horse becomes poor, we should provide him with a horse; the contemporary equivalent would be providing someone with a car. However, although the community is obligated to fulfill the person's needs, it is not obligated to restore her full wealth ("Laws of Gifts to the Poor 7:3," based on *Ketubot* 67b).

"If he [a rich person who has become poor] had been used to vessels of gold, we give him vessels of silver; if of silver, we give him vessels of copper" (Jerusalem Talmud, Peah *8:7); in other words, we support the person at a higher level than we do those who have been poor from birth, but at a lower level than the person is accustomed to.*

Danny Siegel has offered an insight into another talmudic teaching, one that I must admit had long bothered me. A man named Abba bar Ba gave money to his son Samuel to distribute to the poor. The son came across a poor man who used the money he received for meat and wine instead of more basic fare. Samuel told his father what he had witnessed, probably expecting his father to tell him to no longer waste charity money on such a man. Instead, his father said, "Give him more [than you have until now], for his soul is bitter [and he requires such luxuries to lift his spirits]" (Jerusalem Talmud, Peah *8:8; a similar story is related about Mar Ukva in* Ketubot *67b). Ever since I first read this story, my sympathies have been with the son, who clearly was upset by the poor man's rather presumptuous expectations. Siegel, however, understands the story within the context of the talmudic ruling regarding the formerly rich, and sees Abba bar Ba as teaching his son an important principle of* tzedaka*: "A person who was once well-to-do and who is now poor must be allowed to adjust gradually to his or her diminished economic status. The poor man . . . was evidently used to finer foods and wine, and Abba bar Ba is telling his son that he is suffering the trauma of poverty and must be allowed to reorient himself psychologically and physically at his own pace."*[2]

Rabbi Abraham Twerski, M.D., writes: "I recall after World War II, when some of the survivors of the Holocaust came to Israel (then Palestine), there were appeals to send clothing and whatever money one could spare for these people who had lost everything. Our congregation [in Milwaukee] undertook a campaign to gather used clothing and ship it to these people who had escaped the Holocaust with nothing but their lives. We once received a thank-you letter from one of the recipients, and it was written on personal stationery. I was appalled. Someone who has nothing and is in need of used clothing can afford to have personal stationery printed! I commented on this to my father, who told me that he recognized the name of this person, who was a member of a very wealthy family in pre-war Poland. 'You must understand,' he said, 'that for her, personalized stationery was taken for granted as an essential of life, along with bread and water. It was simply unthinkable not to have your own stationery. She did not consider this a luxury.'" [3]

In brief, the words "sufficient for his needs" remind us that we can't group all poor people into one undifferentiated category; rather, "each person is perceived as an individual with subjective, individualistic, idiosyncratic needs" (Byron Sherwin). [4]

Dr. Isaac Herschkopf expresses reservations about the fairness of this law: "Since money, or food, is finite, if the formerly wealthy are entitled to a larger portion simply because of their former wealth, it is inevitably at the expense of the other poor. If, for example, we have a thousand dollars to divide among ten people, each would receive a hundred. If, however, we say that the two formerly wealthy people in the group should receive more so as to make their decline more gradual, and we give them $150 each, then the remaining eight people will receive only $87.50 each. It doesn't seem fair to penalize the latter for the sake of the former."

For the reasons cited previously, I disagree with Dr. Herschkopf's objection, but it is important to consider the different responses people concerned with finding an ethical solution to a problem can reach. As regards Dr. Herschkopf's objection, perhaps the extra help allocated to the formerly wealthy should come through special gifts, over and above the donor's normal charitable contributions. Perhaps one solution is to solicit gifts from friends of the formerly wealthy person.

---

5. To fulfill the commandment of "sufficient for his needs" properly, we should think: "If I were to become poor, what activity or object of personal significance would I miss most?"[5] I know that I would find it particularly upsetting and dispiriting not to be able to purchase books I wanted. Another person might be especially pained at being unable to pay for her child's piano lessons. Try to ascertain a specific want and need of a poor person and fulfill it.

6. Be careful to help in a way that will not offend the recipient. When Rabbi Yannai saw a man give a poor person an unsolicited donation in public (instead of taking him aside and giving it to him in private) he said to him: "Better that you hadn't given at all than that you gave and embarrassed him" (*Chagigah* 5a). It is difficult enough for a proud person (and many, perhaps most, people are proud) to accept charity, so if we help someone, there is no reason for anyone else to know about it.

—

For instances when others should know, see page 193; as regards donating to beggars in public, see chapter 18.

—

7. If someone needs money, but would be ashamed to receive charity, then find a way to coax her into taking the money as a gift or, if that would also embarrass her, as a loan (*Ketubot* 67b).* The psychological advantage of a loan—particularly to someone who used to have money—is obvious: "A dole demeans by the very fact that the recipient is on a level subordinate to that of the donor but, in the case of the loan, both partners are deemed equal" (Byron Sherwin).[6] Such a loan should, of course, be interest-free.

—

While working on this chapter, I ran into an acquaintance who, I knew, had fallen upon hard times. We were at a supermarket and I offered to buy some food for him. At first he accepted, but then, embarrassed, he said he didn't need anything. A moment later, however, he said to me, "Okay, you can buy, but only on condition that this is a loan. I'll mark it down and pay you back."

—

I came across a story, I believe it was in the Sefer Chasidim,† *telling of the trouble caused by a man of good heart and intentions who did not take into account a recipient's feelings: Reuven asked Shimon to lend him some money and, without hesitation, Shimon agreed, but said, "I really give this to you as a gift."*

Reuven was so shamed that he never asked Shimon for a loan again. Clearly, in his case, it would have been better not to have given Reuven a gift of that kind.

—

*While today we think of charity primarily in terms of donations, the Bible—perhaps because it was written at a time when few people had large amounts of money that could be given away—primarily associates charity with interest-free loans (see, for example, Exodus 22:24).

†I have made several efforts, but I have not been able to locate the story.

An entry in the New York Times *Metropolitan Diary (December 30, 2002): "After church one recent weekend, four of us stopped for lunch at a neighborhood restaurant. As we were enjoying ourselves, the friend on my right and I noticed a man who had taken great care to make his tattered clothes look spiffy. He had finished his meal and was searching one pocket after another for enough dollar bills to pay for his lunch. He was becoming increasingly frantic as he seemed to realize that he did not have enough money to cover the check. My friend got up quietly as if going to the restroom, and in passing the man's table, leaned down, pretending to find a $10 bill on the floor. It was done so naturally that when my friend offered the bill to the distracted man, the man's whole body language changed.*

"He said, 'Thank you, thank you. I was sure I had that bill.' He was beaming. My friend smiled warmly and walked away.

*"I've been thinking of this ever since. My friend did a great kindness, not because of the $10 gift, but because the man was treated with gentleness, caring, and respect and not [made to feel that he was] given charity" (Alice Allen).**

---

8. Rabbis David Hartman and Tzvi Marx recommend that donors engage in "preventive *tzedaka*," and not just "crisis *tzedaka*," by not waiting until someone is impoverished before offering help. We should offer assistance to those who have fallen on hard times so that they can avoid total economic collapse. The biblical verse that mandates extending interest-free loans to the poor begins: "If your brother is in bad straits, and his means fail with him [that is, he loses the ability to support himself] . . . you shall strengthen him" (Leviticus 25:35). The Rabbis understand the command to "strengthen" another as meaning that we must offer help when someone is just beginning to stumble.

Rabbis Hartman and Marx note that "anticipating the needs of others and responding in a manner that forestalls total failure and helplessness . . . may lack the drama and glamour of crisis tzedaka, *yet because of this, it ranks as a high and refined level of* tzedaka."[7]

---

*For an incident in which Rabbi Aryeh Levine deduced how to help a student in need, without offending the boy's proud father, see *A Code of Jewish Ethics, Volume 1: You Shall Be Holy,* pages 52–53.

9. If you have lent someone money, and the person is now incapable of repaying it, try to avoid seeing her, so that she won't feel humiliated or live in fear that you will demand immediate repayment (see *Bava Mezia* 75b and *Sefer Chasidim* paragraph 327).

However, I believe that when the person is a friend, this teaching should be applied with flexibility. The borrower might feel more discomfited if she realizes that you are avoiding her. Perhaps it would be best to say, "Look, if you're not in a position to repay me now, I understand, and I trust that you will start to repay me when you're able to do so. Until then, don't worry about it."

If and when it becomes apparent that the person will not be able to repay you, forgive the loan, and consider the money part of your charitable giving (under United States tax law, this is not a permitted charitable deduction).

10. When a merchant sells something to a poor person below cost, he may regard the money he is losing as part of his charitable giving. Similarly, if a professional donates her services to the poor, this should be considered a form of charity and also count as part of one's giving. "However," notes Rabbi Avrohom Feuer, "one should be careful to differentiate between personal acts of kindness and professional services. Thus, if a doctor takes an hour off from his office hours to attend to the medical needs of an indigent, the monetary value of his 'billable' time is regarded as charity [though obviously not deductible for tax purposes]. But if he uses that hour to go grocery shopping for a poor family . . . this is a personal *chesed* (act of kindness) and no monetary value should be assigned to it."[8]

The Sefer Chasidim *lauds those who sell food to the poor at cost (forgoing any profit) or who donate it to them at a time of scarcity, when the poor are enduring additional hardships (paragraph 1049).*

---

11. Educators, social workers, youth leaders, and others working with children, some of whom live in poverty, should try to discern which are the most destitute, and what their primary needs are. Thus, Reb Aryeh Levine taught at Jerusalem's Etz Chayyim school at a time when many of the students came from financially deprived homes. Each morning, he watched the students carefully as they came to school. His son once asked him, "Why do you stand and look so closely at the students as they enter?"

Instead of answering, Reb Aryeh asked his son to accompany him the following morning and to join him in observing the students.

When his father asked him what he saw, the son answered that it was quickly apparent that some children were genuinely anxious to learn, while others seemed only to want to continue playing.

"Yet I look at different things altogether," said Reb Aryeh. "That child's trousers are torn. This one's shoes are quite tattered and worn. That boy over there is definitely hungry; how will he ever be able to learn?"

His son recalled how his father would often take money from his pocket so that a student could buy some food or take a bus home on a cold winter night, instead of having to walk.[9]

12. Commendable as it is to help a cause or a person in need, it is sometimes better not to donate all the money that is required. There are two reasons for this, both suggested in stories about prominent rabbinic leaders.

• Rabbi Yechezkel Landau of Prague (generally referred to by the name of his book, *Nodeh B'Yehuda;* eighteenth century), was asked for a large contribution to help a worthy cause, and donated almost all that was needed. When asked, "Since you've already given so much, why don't you complete the mitzvah, and give the whole sum?" he explained: "In *The Ethics of the Fathers* the Rabbis criticize a person who wishes to give himself, but does not wish others to give, as one who begrudges others (5:13). I want others, not just me, to share in this worthwhile cause."

In the second instance, the rabbi withheld the full amount not for the sake of other potential donors, but rather for the sake of the recipient.

• The Satmar Rebbe, Rabbi Yoel Teitelbaum (1887–1979), once gave a petitioner a little less than the sum he had asked for. Although the recipient was happy with the Rebbe's gift, after he left, the Rebbe's *gabbai* (assistant) asked him, "If you were prepared to give him such a large amount, why didn't you already give him all that he asked for?"

The rebbe answered: "Had I given this man all that he requested, I would actually have made him sad. He would have regretted not asking for more, thinking that I was ready to give him any amount that he wanted. By giving him a little less than he requested, I actually made him happier."[10]

This story illustrates the subjective element in charitable giving. Clearly, the rebbe tailored his gift to his understanding of the man making the request. Presumably, had the petitioner been the sort of person whose shame at soliciting charity caused him to understate his needs, the rebbe would have given the whole amount, and perhaps even more.

My friend Beverly Woznica, a longtime fund-raiser for Jewish causes, notes that "another reason those who can give the whole sum to a cause sometimes refrain from doing so is that giving by others will develop in these people a commitment to that particular cause."

---

13. An elevated form of *tzedaka* is to buy something that a poor person wishes to sell but that no one wants to purchase (*Sefer Chasidim,* paragraph 1035). Thus, the needy person profits and is not made to feel that he is the recipient of charity.

Journalist Arnold Fine recalls an incident from his Bronx childhood, when he and a friend went to the home of a poor woman who sold pretzels. The boys knocked on the door, but there was no answer. When they looked through the window, they saw the woman lying on the floor, apparently unconscious. The boys were not strong enough to break open the door, so they solicited the help of a passerby. The man broke open the door, and when they went inside, the house smelled of gas. The three of them opened all the windows and soon revived the woman. They discovered that the flame on her stove had been extinguished, but the gas had continued to seep out.

Within a few minutes, the woman recovered, but it was clear from the house's appearance that she lived in great poverty. The man noticed a very old book on a shelf, picked it up, and said to the woman: "Would you sell me this book? I'm a book dealer. I sell old books, and I would be more than happy to give you two hundred dollars for this book."

The woman didn't believe that the book could have any value. "In any case," she told the man, "let me give it to you. After all, you saved my life."

"Oh, no. That would not be fair," the man said. "You would be taking away my mitzvah.*" He then reached into his pocket and gave the woman two hundred dollars.*

Fine concludes: "We walked from the house together as the snow continued to fall. The man said he was late and ran ahead of us. We watched as he moved through the snow swiftly. When he reached the corner, he passed a garbage can, paused for a second, then threw the old book into the can and continued on his way. It was only then that we realized that he did not want the book, but wanted to do something for that little old woman without embarrassing her."[11]

Hunger: The ultimate charitable cause

14. Hunger, a perennial problem throughout history, has affected not only untold and nameless poor people (today, how many middle-class people personally know anyone who lacks sufficient food?), but also some of the greatest figures of Jewish history. Famine forced Abraham to leave Canaan for Egypt (Genesis 12:10) and Isaac to go to the kingdom of Abimelech (Genesis 26:1). It caused Joseph's brothers to go down to Egypt to find food. Hundreds of years later, hunger led Naomi and her family to flee Israel for Moab (Ruth 1:1–2). In later history, the Bible records famines during the reigns of King David (II Samuel 21:1) and Ahab (I Kings 18:1–2).[12]

Perhaps because hunger is an ongoing problem, the Bible warns us not to become accustomed and indifferent to the hunger pangs of others. We should realize, as noted, that "there will never cease to be needy ones in your land . . ." (Deuteronomy 15:11) and feel obligated to help provide them with food.

That a large number of people still starve to death is a terrible indictment of those of us who have the means to help feed the poor, but don't. In the first paragraph of the *Birkat HaMazon* (Grace after Meals), Jews praise God as One "who feeds the entire world (*hazan et ha-olam koolo*), with goodness, grace, loving-kindness, and compassion." Thus, this prayer assumes that despite periodic famines throughout the world, God has arranged human society so that nobody need starve. Although this strikes some people as naïve religious thinking, it is true. If human beings starve to death (and an estimated 7 to 11 million people do so each year),* that is because we do not equitably distribute what God has given us. In the words of Mahatma Gandhi: "There is enough for everybody's need, but not for everybody's greed."

My friend Sam Sutton, a philanthropist in the New York Jewish community, took some friends with him to Senegal to help address the issues of poverty and starvation. After witnessing the situation firsthand, Sutton and his group put in over $100,000 (beyond the charity they already were giving) to bring in pump and irrigation equipment developed in Israel for a group of villages. Each village had between two hundred and eight hundred residents. The equipment enabled them to grow vegetables year-round. This had a remarkable impact,

*See George McGovern, Bob Dole, and Donald Messer, *Ending Hunger Now,* pages 2 and 10. The figure of 11 million would translate into 30,000 deaths daily from starvation, or 1,250 people an hour. Brazilian president Luis Inácio Lula da Silva has said: "Hunger is actually the worst weapon of mass destruction. It claims millions of victims each year."

given that the area in which the villages were located had a five-month dry season during which no rain fell. The project was undertaken in conjunction with the American Jewish World Service.

After Sutton returned to New York, he learned that within his community, a prominent figure was criticizing him and his friends for disbursing significant amounts of money to people outside their community. Sutton met with the man and tried to convince him of the importance and rightness of what he and his friends had done. All his arguments fell on deaf ears, until he finally told the man: "The Jewish world rightly condemns those non-Jews who, during the Holocaust, could have helped save Jews and didn't. And we believe that when those people died they had to go before the Heavenly Court and give a* din ve-cheshbon *[a moral accounting] for their behavior. In addition to what we helped develop in Senegal, I also learned that for three dollars worth of salt pills a year, we can prevent young children from dying from dehydrating diarrhea. Someday, when I come before the Heavenly Court, I don't want to have to give a* din ve-cheshbon *for having known that I could have stopped many children from dying for three dollars a life and did nothing."*†

As regards the importance of giving to organizations which feed the hungry, see pages 219–220.

15. The horror of starvation is twofold: It causes many deaths, and it inflicts prolonged physical and emotional suffering on those who lack food. In speaking of the Babylonian's siege of sixth-century B.C.E. Jerusalem, the prophet Jeremiah (to whom Jewish tradition attributes authorship of

---

*Regarding the Jewish obligation to give to non-Jewish poor, see pages 200–201.

†The information about the pills came to Sutton from philosopher Peter Unger's 1996 book, *Living High and Letting Die:* "Each year millions of children die from easy to beat diseases, from malnutrition, and from bad drinking water. Among these children, about 3 million die from dehydrating diarrhea. As UNICEF has made clear to millions of us well-off American adults at one time or another, with a packet of oral rehydration salts that cost about 15 cents, a child can be saved from dying soon [most children might need as many as ten to twenty packets; hence the figure of $3 a child]. By sending checks earmarked for Oral Rehydration Therapy, or ORT, to the U.S. Committee for UNICEF, we Americans can help save many of these children. Here's the full mailing address: United States Commission for UNICEF, United Nations Children's Fund, 333 East 38th St., New York, NY 10016. Now, you can write that address on an envelope . . . and, in it, you can place a $100 check made out to the U.S. Committee for UNICEF along with a note that's easy to write: 'Where it will help the most, use the enclosed funds for ORT. . . .' If you'd contributed $100 to one of UNICEF's most efficient lifesaving programs a couple of months ago, this month there'd be thirty more children who, instead of dying painfully soon, would live reasonably long lives" (pages 3–4).

Lamentations), declares, "Better off were the slain by the sword than those slain by famine" (Lamentations 4:9). Starvation inflicts a slow and very painful death. Refraining from helping the starving is like standing by while someone is being tortured and doing nothing, even when you are in a position to stop the torture.

—

The literal meaning of the verse from Lamentations is different from the popular translation cited above: "Better were the slain by the sword than those slain by famine." The obvious and puzzling implication of this literal rendering is that somehow those who die quickly by the sword are "better" people than those who die from hunger.

The late Rabbi Israel Spira, a Hasidic rebbe and concentration camp survivor, claimed that it was only in the Nazi work camps that he came to understand the significance of this. Among the thousands of Jews imprisoned with him were young twin brothers, whose family had been among the rabbi's followers. The three helped one another whenever possible.

One day, when the inmates were taken to work, Rabbi Spira, along with one of the twins and a third man, was told to remain and clean the barracks. During the day, a Nazi guard shot the twin in one leg, ordered him to stand, and then shot him in the other leg. When the German officer again ordered the boy to stand and he couldn't, the officer shot him dead. Rabbi Spira and the other inmate were then made to carry his body to the pile of corpses that accumulated each day at the camp. While carrying the body, the rabbi shed tears; he later recalled that one thought filled his mind:

" 'How will I tell the other twin about his brother's death? How will I break the terrible news to one of two souls that were so close to each other?'

" 'Tell him that his brother is very sick,' the other Jew advised the rabbi.

"Evening came. The inmates returned to camp. 'Chaim'l, your brother is very sick, his life is in danger. It is quite possible that he is no longer alive,' said the rabbi . . . trying to avoid the boy's eyes.

"The brother began to cry. 'Woe unto me! What am I going to do now?'

"The rabbi tried to comfort the boy, but he refused to be comforted. 'Today was his turn to watch over the bread. I left all the bread with him, now I don't have a single piece of bread left.'

"The rabbi was shocked but continued his ruse, saying that the other twin had sent him Chaim'l's share. With a trembling hand, he took from under his coat a small piece of bread which was his ration for the day and gave it to the boy. Chaim'l glanced at the small piece of bread and said, 'It's missing a few grams. The piece I left with him was a much larger one.'

"'I was hungry and ate some of it. Tomorrow I will give you the rest of the bread,' replied the rabbi . . ."

"When Rabbi Israel Spira finished telling the story [to the author, Yaffa Eliach, in 1976, more than thirty years after the event] he said, 'Only on that day in Janowska did I understand the verse in the Scriptures, 'Better were the slain by the sword than those slain by famine.' "[*]

—

16. Because hunger pangs are so severe, when someone asks for food, we are obliged to help immediately. Even if we suspect that the person is lying about being hungry, we should give her food, or money to purchase food, since failing to do so may result in extreme suffering, even death.[†]

The Talmud rules that charitable funds should respond in the same way: "A poor man who asks for clothes should be investigated,[‡] but one who asks for food should not be investigated" (*Bava Bathra* 9a).[§]

17. If we invite poor people to our home, we should serve the meal quickly because they may be hungry, or simply looking forward to a better meal than they are accustomed to eating.

The special mitzvah of charity before holidays

18. It is particularly important to help the needy before holidays, so that they can fully share in the joy of these days (Deuteronomy 16:11–14). Not doing this is so callous that Maimonides writes: "[One who] eats and drinks with his family [on a holiday] without giving anything to eat and drink to the poor and the bitter in soul, his meal is not a rejoicing in a divine commandment, but a rejoicing in his own stomach. . . . Rejoicing of this kind is a disgrace to those who indulge in it" ("Laws of Holidays" 6:18).[¶]

---

[*] Yaffa Eliach, *Hasidic Tales of the Holocaust,* pages 153–155.

[†] Obviously, if we are *certain* that the person is lying, we are not required to give.

[‡] The Ritba (Rabbi Yom Tov ben Avraham), the Spanish Talmud commentator (thirteenth–fourteenth century), writes that if a person lacks clothing to protect him from the cold, his suffering should be regarded as immediate (as is the case with hunger) and he should be given clothes right away, without investigation. In addition, if the administrators of a charitable fund know the person to be honest, they should donate clothes without investigation.

[§] The Talmud also presents on the same page the opposing view of Rabbi Huna that we should check requests for food but not for clothing; however, this is a minority view, and the accepted opinion is the one cited above.

[¶] When Ezra and Nehemiah taught the ancient Jews the proper observance of Rosh Hashanah, they enjoined them to "send portions unto him for whom nothing is prepared" (Nehemiah 8:10).

Passover is the most expensive Jewish holiday to observe because it requires special foods and separate dishes, pots, and utensils. Jewish communities throughout the world have long organized Ma'ot Chittim *(funds for Passover) drives to help those in need celebrate the holiday. My grandfather, Rabbi Nissen Telushkin, of blessed memory, used to tell how, in the Russian shtetl of Dukor, where he served as rabbi, he and another man would go to every Jewish home in the town prior to Passover. Each house either gave or received; no one who was in a position to make a donation was allowed to be indifferent to the poor.*

In one of his books, Danny Siegel quotes a letter received some years ago by Project HOPE, a B'nai B'rith Passover food support program in Washington, D.C., for Jews in difficult circumstances. The letter reminds us that, despite the widely held image of American Jews as affluent, many poor Jews live in our communities. It also suggests the great good that even a small gift can do for others, both materially and psychologically:

> *Dear Gentlemen,*
>
> *A B'nai B'rith member just brought to my house a supply of Passover food. I wish I could express how excited my daughter and I were. Despite working a full-time job, inflation has hit me hard. This is the first year that I knew I would not be able to buy Passover food. . . . Now, we have gefilte fish, candy, egg kichel, and fruit, and two little bottles of wine. I shall join all the Jews in the world in four glasses of wine on Passover night.*
>
> *Everything you brought was what I needed. With the chicken I already have, we are all set. The social worker who put my name on your list said she was told your baskets weren't anything special this year. She was wrong. Everything in them was special.*
>
> *Because other Jews cared enough, my daughter (who, by the way, became Bat Mitzvah this year) and I will observe Passover. You have made us feel a part of a wonderful extended family. . . . Thank you very much.*

Rabbi Saul Berman offers an additional reason why the rabbinic leadership placed particular emphasis on helping the poor observe Passover: "The concern there was not simply to allow the family to fulfill ritual obligations, but equally significant, that even the poorest Jew should be able to participate fully in national celebrations. They wanted to assure that the poor continue their identification with the society as a whole, and not come to view themselves as outsiders."[13]

—

19. The Rabbis arranged the Jewish calendar to ensure that the holiday of Purim, during which it is mandatory to give gifts and money to the poor, never falls on the Sabbath, when the handling of money is forbidden. This is done so as not to disappoint the poor who eagerly anticipate the donations they hope to receive on this day (*Megillah* 4b; see Rashi's comment there). On this day, we should dispense charity to at least two people. So important is the fulfillment of this mitzvah that Maimonides rules: "It is better for people to spend more on gifts to the poor for Purim than to spend more for their own Purim meal, or for sending gifts *(mishloach manot)* to their friends, for there is no greater or more splendid joy than to bring happiness to the hearts of the poor, orphans, widows, and strangers. One who brings happiness to the hearts of these unfortunate people resembles the Divine Presence (*Shechina;* "Laws of *Megillah*" 2:17).

Despite this ruling, many Jews spend large amounts of money sending expensive baskets of fruit, drink, and sweets to their friends on the holiday. Pleasant as this custom is, we should also calculate how much we spend on these elaborate *mishloach manot*—which are almost always given to people who don't need food—and donate an equal or greater sum to poor people and organizations that support them.

20. Although one should not discuss business affairs on Shabbat, it is permitted to discuss pledges to charity and to announce a pledge on the Sabbath (see *Shulchan Arukh, Orach Chayyim* 306:6), and even on Yom Kippur.*

Paying charity pledges promptly

21. The Torah legislates: "When you make a vow to the Lord your God, you shall not be late in paying it . . . you must fulfill what has crossed your lips" (Deuteronomy 23:22, 24). Originally, these verses referred to a vow to bring a sacrifice. However, later Jewish law ruled that "donations to charity fall into the category of vows" (*Shulchan Arukh, Yoreh Deah* 257:3). Therefore, vows to donate to charity, particularly to help the poor, should be paid

---

*On giving money to poor people to buy food before and after Yom Kippur, see page 218.

immediately, as such aid can sometimes be a matter of life and death. Maimonides rules: "One who says I am undertaking to give [the following] to charity . . . is obligated to give it to the poor immediately" ("Laws of Gifts to the Poor" 8:1). If we are not intending to pay right away, we should specify at the time we make our pledge that it is our intention to pay over a specified period of time.

Maimonides' eight levels of charitable giving

22. In what is perhaps his most famous legal ruling, Maimonides notes that the highest level of *tzedaka* is giving a poor person a gift or loan, entering into a partnership with him, or giving him a job, "so that he will have no need to beg from other people" ("Laws of Gifts to the Poor" 10:7).* The highest goal of giving should be to reduce, one-by-one, the number of poor people.

On a macro level, Rabbi Moshe Feinstein similarly ruled that the highest level of *tzedaka* is to provide vocational and professional training to the poor since that will enable them eventually to earn their own livelihood.[14] Thus, this level of *tzedaka* implies that vocational training and job placement should rank, after providing food and immediate necessities for the hungry, as the foremost goals of both charitable giving and government aid to the needy.

Alex Haley, the well-known African-American writer and author of Roots *and* The Autobiography of Malcolm X, *tells of how an extraordinary act of charity—among the most remarkable I have ever heard—not only transformed the life of one man, but of an entire family as well. Haley's father, Simon, was born in 1892 in a small farming town, Savannah, Tennessee, the eighth child of his parents. All the children worked in the fields as soon as they were big enough, but Simon's mother cajoled her husband to "waste"† this child and let*

*Although people often assume that this was an innovative ruling, Maimonides based it on a talmudic teaching: "He who lends money [to a poor person] is greater than he who gives charity [Rashi suggests that it is because a poor person is not ashamed to borrow, and the loan, in accordance with Torah law, is interest free], and he who throws money into a common purse [to form a partnership with a poor person] is greater than either" (*Shabbat* 63a). A friend reports that the standard loan issued by Jewish loan societies to new immigrants in the East End of London a century ago was for five pounds, the amount needed to buy a sewing machine and set oneself up in business.

†To "waste" a child was an expression used among poor blacks, and it meant permitting a child to remain in school after the child was physically able to do farm work. Simon Haley's mother said to her husband, "Since we have eight children, wouldn't it be prestigious if we deliberately *wasted* one, and got him educated?"

him remain in school until eighth grade. For high school, he went to Jackson, Tennessee. To be able to pay for school, he worked as a waiter and a handyman, and during the winter would get up at 4 a.m. and go into prosperous white people's homes and make fires so that the residents could arise in comfort. He then enrolled in A&T College in Greensboro, North Carolina, a black college. His lack of money continually hindered him. On one occasion, he was called into a teacher's office and told that he'd failed a course, one that required a textbook that he'd been too poor to buy. He started to despair, wondering if he should give up and return to what seemed to be his destiny, sharecropping.

That summer he got a job as a sleeping car porter for the Pullman Company. One morning, at 2 a.m. he was summoned to a passenger berth of a white couple who were having trouble falling asleep. The couple wanted glasses of warm milk, which Simon Haley brought. The white man started to engage Haley in conversation (even though it was company policy that the black porters say nothing beyond "Yes, sir" and "No, ma'am"). But the man was interested, and even followed Haley back to the porter's cubicle, and learned his name, and about his life, the college he was attending, and even where he came from. When the train reached Pittsburgh, the white man gave Haley a $5 tip, an enormous tip in those days. Haley earned enough in tips that summer that he started to dream of what it might be like to have one semester that he could devote fully to studies, without being weighed down by an assortment of odd jobs; only then could he know what grades he could truly achieve.

On the first day of school, he was summoned to the college president's office. After establishing that Haley had indeed worked as a Pullman porter that summer, the president asked him, "Did you meet a certain man one night and bring him warm milk?"

"Yes, sir."

"Well, his name is Mr. R. S. M. Boyce, and he's a retired executive of the Curtis Publishing Company, which publishes The Saturday Evening Post. *He has donated five hundred dollars for your board, tuition, and books for the entire school year."*

This remarkable grant not only enabled Simon Haley to finish A&T, but to graduate first in his class. That, in turn, earned him a full scholarship to Cornell University in Ithaca, New York. While he studied for a master's degree at Cornell, his wife enrolled at the Ithaca Conservatory of Music. Alex Haley, their son, was born the following year.

As Alex Haley writes: "We children of Simon Haley often reflect on Mr. Boyce and his investment in a less fortunate human being. By the ripple effect of his generosity, we also benefited. Instead of being raised on a sharecrop farm, we grew up in a home with educated parents, shelves full of books, and with pride in ourselves. My brother George is chairman of the U.S. Postal Rate Commission, Julius is an architect, Lois a music teacher, and I'm a writer.

"Mr. R. S. M. Boyce dropped like a blessing into my father's life. What some may see as a chance encounter, I see as the working of a mysterious power for good.

"And I believe that each person blessed with success has an obligation to return part of that blessing. We must all live and act like the man on the train."[15]

—

23. Maimonides' eight levels of charity, in descending order, are:

- As noted, extending a loan or giving a job to a poor person so as to ensure that he will not need charity in the future.

—

Rabbi Chaim Soloveitchik is reported to have said of a certain man who gave substantial amounts to charity, "That man likes giving charity too much." What he meant was that the man seemed to enjoy the fact that other people were in need of his help. Better is the one who follows Maimonides' highest standard and helps people so that they will no longer need his, or anybody else's, charity.

—

- When the donor does not know to whom he is giving, and the recipient does not know who made the donation. This standard of anonymous giving is achieved when we make a donation to an organization that distributes help to the poor.

- When the donor knows who the recipient is, but the recipient does not know the identity of the donor.

—

The Talmud tells of Mar Ukba, a rabbinic scholar, who used to leave money at the door of a poor man. One day, the man wanted to see who his helper was and so, when Mar Ukba and his wife came to the door, he pushed it open and started to come out. The couple ran away as quickly as they could, even endangering themselves in the process, just so that the man should not see them (Ketubot *67b*).

—

A woman I know used to leave bags of groceries in front of the apartment of a neighbor who was in financial difficulty. She stopped doing so only when the neighbor got a job and her situation improved.

---

*The Jewish historian Yosef Hayim Yerushalmi relates that when he was completing his final year at the Jewish Theological Seminary rabbinical school, Professor Saul Lieberman asked him about his plans following graduation. Yerushalmi confided that he had wished to pursue graduate work in Jewish history at Columbia University, but that it was too late to apply for a fellowship. Lieberman told him that there were fellowships available through the American Academy for Jewish Research (AAJR) and that he was sure he could procure one for him. His only request was that the young man continue to attend his Talmud class at the seminary (the Jewish Theological Seminary is only six blocks from Columbia), a stipulation which Yerushalmi happily accepted. Over the coming years, Professor Yerushalmi went on to become a highly regarded historian, and later headed the Jewish history department at Columbia. A full two decades later, Yerushalmi learned that there had been no AAJR fellowship; Lieberman had provided the funds out of his own pocket.**[16]

- When the poor person knows who the giver is, but the donor does not know who the recipient is.

My mother, Helen Telushkin, of blessed memory, told me that when she was a young girl on New York City's Lower East Side, the noted philanthropist Jacob Schiff made bottles of milk available to poor people for a penny. By charging a penny—as opposed to giving away the milk for free—Schiff helped maintain the dignity of the poor.

- When one gives to someone in need before being asked.

*Rabbi Berel Wein tells a similar story: "My dear friend . . . Rabbi Alexander S. Gross, who founded the Hebrew Academy of Miami Beach, once showed me a letter that he kept in his wallet. That day was a particularly depressing day for both of us because of congregational, school, and community problems that all descended upon each of us in one fell swoop. Rabbi Gross took that letter out and gave it to me to read. It was a letter from a young student in junior high school, thanking Rabbi Gross for his education at the Hebrew Academy. The letter continued that since his parents . . . and the school's tuition committee could not agree on the matter of the tuition, he would now be forced to attend public school. But he wanted Rabbi Gross to know how much he appreciated what the Hebrew Academy had done for him. I said to Rabbi Gross: 'But he did graduate from the Hebrew Academy after all! How did that happen?' Rabbi Gross told me: 'It was simple. I paid for the balance of his tuition. This letter is my entrance ticket into the World to-Come.' " Wein went on to note that the young man subsequently became a leading figure in the Jewish community (*Tending the Vineyard,* pages 215–216).

If someone you know has lost a job, or a family is encountering unusual (e.g., medical) expenses, let that person know that you would like to help. By doing so before he asks, you not only spare him the embarrassment of requesting help, but also the anxiety of not knowing how he will cope. This level of tzedaka *is in line with the teaching of Isaiah who, speaking in God's Name, says, "And it will be before they call, I will answer" (Isaiah 65:24). We can emulate God in this regard by helping someone even before he or she asks.*

- When one donates to someone in need, but only after being asked.

- When one gives less than what someone needs, but does so in a pleasant way.

- When one makes a donation with a morose look on one's face (Maimonides, "Laws of Gifts to the Poor" 10:7–14; see paragraph 1 of this chapter).

24. As Maimonides notes, a particularly high level of *tzedaka* is making an interest-free loan to a person in need (see Exodus 22:24 and Deuteronomy 23:20–21). Throughout Jewish history, Jewish communities have set up Free Loan Societies (known as *Gemach,* from the Hebrew term *gemilut chesed,* "acts of kindness"), in which loans are given to help people cover basic needs (such as rent, food, school tuition), and larger sums are extended for broader purposes, such as to help a person start a small business. Such loans "spare the poor embarrassment" (Rashi's commentary on *Shabbat* 63a).

Charity and anonymity: The ambivalence of Jewish teachings

25. Jewish tradition offers a unique compliment for those who give anonymously: "One who gives charity secretly is greater than Moses" (*Bava Bathra* 9b).* However, the British writer, Chaim Bermant, has mordantly noted that this is a greatness to which few Jews aspire. Indeed, Jewish fund-raising institutions are known for bestowing publicity and public honors on donors who give substantial gifts.

---

*Another talmudic passage declares that God praises daily a rich person who tithes in secret (*Pesachim* 113a). And, as we have seen, Maimonides designated anonymous giving as the second highest of his eight levels of *tzedaka.*

Why has the Jewish community generally chosen to ignore the talmudic teaching that a person who gives anonymously is greater than Moses? For one thing, this aphorism is precisely that, an aphorism and, therefore, not legally binding. Second, although anonymous giving represents a high standard of philanthropy, the anonymity that is most important is that of the recipient (after all, it is humiliating to be exposed as being in need, but not to be "exposed" as a philanthropist).

Finally, and most important, Jewish law takes into account human nature.* Expecting people to give substantial gifts and receive no recognition for doing so represents a standard that most people won't meet. Thus, in Jewish communities around the world, thousands of buildings are named for their donors. Had these philanthropists been told that their gifts would be accepted only if offered anonymously, many would probably have contributed much less. Thus, despite the admirability of anonymous giving, Jewish communities have chosen to use methods that maximize charitable giving, recognizing that publicly acknowledging and honoring major donors leads to larger gifts.

Ramah (sixteenth century) codifies the right of a donor to have his gift publicly recognized: "One who dedicates a specific object to a charitable institution may inscribe his name on it so that it should be an eternal remembrance for him, and it is appropriate to do so" (*Shulchan Arukh, Yoreh Deah* 249:13).

My own views on this, I must admit, were somewhat moderated by a conversation I had many years ago, after a lecture in which I made a critical comment about rich people concerned that buildings be named for them. When my talk concluded, a wealthy man asked me, "Why do you write books?"

"To teach Judaism," I answered.

"But then, why don't you publish your books anonymously? It's because you want the gratification of having your name on the cover. I'm not going to write a book, so I want to be known for having done good by putting up a building for the Jewish community."

---

26. It is appropriate to inform others of the size of your gift if doing so will motivate them to increase their own donations. For example, if you are

*American law does as well, by permitting charitable donations to be tax deductible. If this deduction was eliminated, heads of charitable organizations fear that their fund-raising would be badly damaged.

soliciting a contribution from a person of similar means as yourself, letting her know how much you are giving may motivate her to give more than she would have otherwise. Similarly, announcing your gift in a public setting might prompt some people to pledge more than they had planned to.

However, if your gift is going to be less than other people might have expected, you should not do this. Doing so might lead others to give less, and so in this instance anonymous giving is crucial.

A friend told me that he had made a decision to donate a certain sum to an acquaintance who had lost his job. However, when another friend told him that she was planning to give twice what he had been intending to, he raised his gift to match hers.

---

27. As noted, it is normally crucial to safeguard the recipient's anonymity. Thus, if you donate money to a needy individual, you must keep his identity secret and not brag about how you helped so-and-so. However, there are times when it is worth speaking to select individuals who know the person and who will help more generously if they know the recipient's identity.

In some cases, and when dealing with donors of the highest character, their generosity will prevail whether or not they know the identity of the recipient. Thus, my grandfather, Rabbi Nissen Telushkin, was once raising money for a rabbinic scholar in need. He sent out an appeal to other rabbis for help and made sure to conceal all information that might betray the recipient's identity. Rabbi Eliezer Silver of Cincinnati, a noted scholar and communal leader, sent a signed check to my grandfather with the amount left blank. "Since you are the one most familiar with the circumstances and identity of the recipient," he wrote, "only you know the proper sum to fill in."

If one moves to a new city, when does one become obliged to give to the communal fund?

28. The Talmud (*Bava Bathra* 8a) rules that when a person moves to a new city, he or she assumes increasing charitable obligations over a period of one year.

- After you have lived in a city for thirty days, you are obliged to give to the *tamchui,* a communal pantry or soup kitchen to which people donate food for the hungry.

- After three months, you are obligated to give to the *kupah,* the charity box, which dispenses weekly allotments to the poor for basic needs.

- After six months, you are expected to donate to the *kesut* fund, clothing for the poor.

- After nine months, you should contribute toward expenses for burying the poor.

- After twelve months, you become obligated to support all other communal projects.

While terms such as *tamchui, kupah,* and *kesut* are unfamiliar to modern readers, the message of this talmudic ruling is clear. When moving to a new city, we should not regard ourselves as strangers and free of obligations, but must become involved in basic charitable giving within thirty days, and be fully integrated into communal giving within a year.

The array of charitable organizations that have long existed in the Jewish community bear testament to how seriously Jews have taken the mitzvah of tzedaka. *For example, among the few thousand Jews living in seventeenth-century Rome, seven charitable groups provided clothes, shoes, linens, and beds for the poor, two provided trousseaus for poor brides, another aided families struck by sudden death, and another was responsible for visiting the sick. A special society existed to collect charity for Jews in the land of Israel, and an additional eleven groups raised money for Jewish educational and religious institutions.*[17]

Choosing a worthy cause

29. Are we obliged to give to every good cause from which we receive a request? No, if only because doing so is both impractical and financially impossible. Many people receive ten or more charitable solicitations in the mail each week.* Even if we were to give relatively small sums to each, the total

*Such appeals often fall into the category of what people call "junk mail," but it seems offensive to refer to appeals to help those in need as "junk."

would add up and become very expensive. In addition, in today's world, if we send a check to one charitable organization, we are likely to find our name on the mailing lists of additional—sometimes many—organizations.

How then to decide which causes to support? Rabbi Avrohom Feuer quotes the advice offered by Rabbi Avrohom Pam: "After all is said and done, every person is drawn to certain individuals and institutions which for some reason seem to grab his heart. This is how it should be. A person must follow his heart in the service of God."[18]

In short, although Judaism teaches that God insists that we donate a part of our earnings to charity, He grants us the right to choose the causes to which we wish to give.*

—

In addition, as my friend Robert Mass suggests, giving to a charity to which we feel a particular connection elevates the mitzvah by making it heartfelt, so that we are giving with the right intention.

—

14

PRIORITIES IN GIVING

1. Rabbi Moshe Isserles, the Ramah, lays out in the *Shulchan Arukh* the basic priorities in dispensing charity. He emphasizes that our first duty is to take care of ourselves and our immediate family: "Sustaining oneself is every person's priority. No one is obliged to give charity until his basic economic needs are fulfilled." (However, we should not insist on an unrealistically high standard of living for ourselves before we are willing to help others.) Once our own needs are met, we should help others in this order:

*In the Talmud, this right is known as *tovat ha-na'ah* (the benefit of gratitude); thus, we have the right to give to the person or cause we want because we wish to earn that person's or cause's gratitude. *Pesachim* 46b notes that there are certain food donations the ancient Israelites were required to make to a priest (*kohen*), but that the donor had the right (the *tovat ha-na'ah*) to choose which priest to give it to (see also *Bekhorot* 27a).

- Our father and mother
- Our grown children (perhaps the reason parents precede grown children is because it is usually more difficult for aged parents to sustain themselves than young adults)
- Siblings
- Other relatives
- Neighbors
- The poor in our city
- The poor of another city (*Yoreh Deah* 251:3)*

We should, however, not exhaust our available money on the first priorities, but should keep some funds to help those to who are not relatives but who are in need.†

In addition, because of the importance Jewish tradition attaches to helping the Jewish community in Israel, the poor in Israel are to be helped along with the poor of our city, and the *Shulchan Arukh* rules that they take precedence over other poor (Ramah, *Yoreh Deah* 251:3). Such a priority would involve as well donating to organizations such as Jewish federations that designate a significant portion of the money raised to help those in need in Israel (as well as in other overseas countries and at home).

As regards Jews apportioning a significant percentage of their charitable

---

*Maimonides codifies an order of priorities when the communal fund has limited resources for feeding and clothing the poor. The order he suggests (in line with Mishnah *Horayot* 3:8) is morally problematic in our more egalitarian age: For example, priests *(kohanim)* take precedence over Levites, Levites over other Jews (Israelites), other Jews over *mamzerim* (children born of adulterous or incestuous unions), and *mamzerim* over converts. Why should the innocent child of an adulterous relationship be designated as a second-class citizen when it comes to receiving help? And, are we not supposed to treat a convert as equal to all other Jews? To be fair to the Mishnah and Maimonides, this applies only when all concerned parties are equal in wisdom, but if the *mamzer* [or the convert] is a scholar and the High Priest is not, the *mamzer* takes precedence (see "Gifts to the Poor" 8:18).

This last ruling, however, generates further difficulties. Is it just to discriminate against those who are less intelligent and/or knowledgeable but who may be in equal or greater need? At one time, Rabbi Judah thought such discrimination was appropriate but, through a surprising encounter with one of his students, came to realize that it wasn't; see *A Code of Jewish Ethics, Volume 1: You Shall Be Holy,* pages 63–64.

In truth, as my friend Rabbi Irwin Kula points out, we all have prejudices and hierarchies that help determine our priorities in charity (including government policies in extending aid), and in life in general. Thus, our welfare system privileges single mothers over families trying to stay intact, while, in an altogether different setting, universities privilege children of alumni. In Kula's view, "there are always hierarchies. The difference is that the Rabbis were more open and honest about acknowledging theirs."

†Otherwise, as Rabbi Michael Broyde argues, one who follows the Ramah's guidelines strictly might end up never giving charity to anyone outside of his or her family members.

giving to causes other than the poor (such as to support Jewish schools and communal institutions), Rabbi Michael Broyde argues that the parameters of charity have changed during this past century in societies such as the United States in which the government provides for the basic social welfare (food, shelter, and secular education) of its citizens. Thus, whereas charitable funds in the past needed to be directed to providing the poor with the necessities of life, a far greater percentage of charitable giving may now be directed to other causes.*

The Talmud assigns the following similar order of priorities in extending loans: If a poor man and a rich man need a loan (the rich person might be temporarily short of funds), the poor person takes precedence. If poor members of your family and other poor people in your city need a loan, your poor relatives take precedence. If the choice is between the poor of your city and the poor of another city, the poor of your own city take precedence (Bava Mezia *71a*).

---

2. Parents. Since they brought us into this world, raised, and supported us, and since the Fifth Commandment obliges us to "Honor your father and mother," we must make sure that our parents' fundamental needs are met. The *Sefer Chasidim* teaches that severe punishment will be exacted from anyone who helps support others, but does not provide for his needy parents and other close relatives (see paragraph 155).

Yet Jewish law asks us when possible to help our parents out of our general income, and not appropriate *tzedaka* money for this purpose; using money we are supposed to give to charity to support our parents is regarded as demeaning.[1]

An old Jewish joke tells of a very wealthy man who has never contributed to the United Jewish Appeal. A delegation goes to solicit him.

"We've been checking up on you, Goldstein," the leader of the group tells him. "We know that in addition to this mansion in Beverly Hills, you have a large estate in Palm Springs and a chalet in Switzerland. You drive a Rolls,

---

*My thinking on contemporary charitable priorities has been deeply impacted by Rabbi Michael Broyde's draft (but not yet published) paper "The Giving of Charity in Jewish Law: For What Purpose and Toward What Goal?" Obviously, despite government aid, in instances in which issues of hunger are involved, and where life is in any way threatened, this issue, along with redeeming captives (see chapter 20), should still have the highest priority.

your wife drives a Mercedes, and your business opened up eighteen new stores this year. We' re expecting you to give and to give big."

Goldstein is not fazed: "And in checking into my background, did you also find out about my mother who has been in a hospital for three months, requiring private nurses around the clock? It's not covered by insurance and do you have any idea how much that costs? And did you find out about my uncle who has been in a private mental sanitarium for twenty years? And do you have any idea how much that costs? And did you find out about my two sisters, each of whom is married to a man who can't hold down a job, and each of whom has two kids in private colleges? And do you have any idea how much that costs? . . . And if I don't give a penny to any of them, you think I'm going to help you?"

—

3. Siblings. After supporting needy parents and adult children, our next priority is to help our siblings in need. What counts here as well as our support is our attitude. Thus, the Chazon Ish wrote to a wealthy man who had a brother in difficult circumstances that not only should he extend help to his brother, but that he should do so joyfully, just as he would joyfully carry out other mitzvot, such as building a Sukkah or listening to the shofar: "An essential aspect of the mitzvah is the joy that we have merited to fulfill it."*[2]

This is in contrast to many people who help out needy relatives but do so with ill-disguised resentment.

—

My friend, David Szonyi, notes a number of questions that are not dealt with systematically in Jewish sources. For example, if your relative is ungrateful, do you have an obligation to continue to give him charity? And what if he squanders money?

A third example: If you have a very difficult relationship with a relative—a sibling, for example—are you still required to give? I have not found this question dealt with directly in any text, but I was moved by an incident recounted by Rabbi Michael Gold in his book God, Love, Sex, and Family. *Gold had a bitter fight with a younger brother and for a full year the two did not speak. During this time, he learned that his brother had lost his job and fallen behind on his mortgage payments; he was now in danger of losing his home. Gold immediately sent him a substantial check. At the time, he received no acknowledgment from his brother; they were still not on speaking terms. But later they did reestablish*

*This concept is known in Jewish writings as *simcha shel mitzvah,* the joy of performing a mitzvah. Obviously, in this case, the joy is not that his brother is in need, but that he himself is blessed with being in a position to help.

contact, and his brother even repaid the money. Still later, they reconciled and became very close.

"Why did I send him the money?" Gold asked himself. "I suppose it goes back to my childhood and the strong emphasis my parents put on being close to my brothers. I remember my father showing me a picture from Boys Town in Nebraska of an older sibling carrying a younger, with the caption, 'He ain't heavy, he's my brother.' My father told us that 'that's how I want you boys to be.' Perhaps by caring for my brother, I was fulfilling the commandment to honor my parents."[3]

—

Rabbi Paysach Krohn tells of an incident in which the Kapishnitzer rebbe, known for his acts of chesed *(kindness), came to the Manhattan office of one of his followers and told him that he needed money to help a family in dire straits. The man, who was a highly successful businessman, told the rebbe that he didn't need to come to the office, he could simply have made the request over the phone.*

The rebbe answered, "It is so important to me that I had to approach you personally."

"How much should I give?" the man asked.

"It's a personal decision for you to make," the rebbe answered.

"Can I write a check?"

"Of course."

"To whom?"

The rebbe said quietly. "Write the check to your brother."[4]

—

4. Other relatives. "A poor man who is one's relative has priority over all others" (Maimonides, "Laws of Gifts to the Poor" 7:13). Though this ruling seems straightforward, Maimonides does not specify how close the relative must be. Thus, for example, most people feel greater closeness, and more responsibility, to close friends than to third cousins. One assumes, therefore, that this law certainly applies to siblings, aunts, uncles, nephews and nieces, and first cousins and their children and in close-knit families even further (and, of course, one should not overlook friends, either).

—

A man once approached Reb Aryeh Levine with a large donation for the yeshiva the rabbi had created. Reb Aryeh, however, refused to accept the gift. "For you, it is forbidden to give any contribution," he told the man.

"Why?" the donor protested. "I am a man of means, you know."

Reb Aryeh answered: "You have family members whose situation is very *distressing. As long as you do not help them, I may not take your donation. The Bible teaches plainly, 'Do not hide yourself from your own flesh and blood' (Isaiah 58:7). And the Rabbis teach that the poor of your own city (in this case, your relatives) must come before other needy people when you give charity" (*Bava Mezia *71a).*

Reb Aryeh's words deeply impressed the man, and he started helping his relatives.[5]

The talmudic sage Rabbi Yossi Ha-Glili [from the Galilee] understood the biblical injunction to not hide from one's flesh and blood as even applying to one's former spouse. The Midrash relates that his wife used to humiliate him in the presence of his disciples. Although he was very unhappy in his marriage, Rabbi Yossi refrained from divorcing his wife because he could not afford to pay her divorce settlement (the money promised in the ketuba *in the event of divorce). Eventually, seeing his misery, one of his students gave him the money to secure the divorce, and Rabbi Yossi married a much kinder woman. Meanwhile, the divorced wife also remarried, but when her husband became blind and could no longer earn a living the couple were reduced to begging. When Rabbi Yossi heard of his ex-wife's difficult circumstances, he undertook to provide for the couple's housing and maintenance (see* Leviticus Rabbah *34:14).*

Rabbi Moshe Goldberger cites a story about an unnamed rebbe who believed in extending philanthropic aid even to distant relations. When one man spurned the rebbe's request for a contribution with the argument that the intended recipient was too distant a relative for him to feel any special connection or sense of obligation, the rebbe startled the man by asking him if he prayed daily. "Of course," the man answered. In that case, the rebbe told him, he should bear in mind that three times a day, in the Shmoneh Esray *prayer, observant Jews invoke the memory of their ancestors, Abraham, Isaac, and Jacob. "We ask God for help because of the merit of the Patriarchs," the rebbe said. "But aren't they too only distant relatives?"*[6]

Charity to non-Jews and non-Jewish causes

5. The *tzedaka* priorities listed above, such as donating to the poor of our city or to those of another city, do not specify the religion of those in need, but Jewish law legislates that charity is to be dispensed both to Jews

and non-Jews. Thus, the biblical verses that speak of helping the needy specify "the stranger [that is, the non-Israelite], the fatherless and the widow" (Deuteronomy 14:29; see also Deuteronomy 26:12). In line with this, the Talmud ruled that "We provide financial support to the Gentile poor along with the Jewish poor . . ." (*Gittin* 61a).* This ruling was issued at a time when the non-Jews amongst whom the Jews lived were usually idolaters with values antithetical and often hostile to Judaism. That Jews were instructed to help needy idolaters underscores the even greater applicability of this ruling in contemporary times, when non-Jews and Jews in societies such as the United States generally live together harmoniously.

Perhaps the most famous teaching in The Ethics of the Fathers *is Hillel's admonition: "If I am not for myself, who will be for me? But if I am only for myself, what am I?" (1:14). I have on occasion heard some individuals cite the first part of this statement to justify donating charity solely to Jewish causes: "After all," such people say, "if Jews don't support Jewish charitable needs, who will?" However, both clauses of Hillel's statement are equally valid, and just as it's wrong to ignore the needs of our own religious community, so, too, is it wrong to ignore the needs of the broader community.*

In addition, it is not always easy to determine what is Jewish charitable giving and what isn't. Thus, some charities are explicitly for Jewish causes, such as organizations to help provide the poor with food for Jewish holidays, or give funding to Jewish schools. Others are explicitly for non-Jewish causes, such as to aid poor people in Appalachia or to assist Native Americans. Still others are for Jews and non-Jews alike. Thus, it makes little sense to argue that supporting a Jewish school is a Jewish cause but funding medical research for a cure for cancer is a non-Jewish issue. Both are issues that affect the Jewish community and are causes Jews should support (though it is important to acknowledge that medical research institutes can approach non-Jews as well as Jews for donations, while Jewish schools, for all practical purposes, can approach only Jews for assistance).

Yet the question remains: What percentage of our giving should be donated to non-Jewish causes? While it's difficult to specify this (individuals in any case will make their own determination), I believe it is responsible for members of a religious or ethnic group to donate a high percentage of their charity to causes that serve their community because their community depends on its members

---

*Maimonides (twelfth century) ruled that it is forbidden to turn away a beggar, Jewish or Gentile, empty-handed ("Laws of Gifts to the Poor" 7:7).

for support. Thus, Jews in the United States comprise less than 2 percent of the American population, and if they don't support Jewish causes, who will?

*In addition, someone who gives most of his charity to his own religious or ethnic group is still, in effect, supporting charitable causes outside his community, as long as he also pays taxes. A middle-income taxpayer in the United States generally pays well over 25 percent of taxable income in federal and state taxes, a significant percentage of which is used to cover expenses that constitute a form of charity. That is because modern governments have taken over many of the functions once performed by charitable groups, such as welfare assistance and Medicaid for the poor. In the past, these expenses were met largely by synagogue and church groups. The fact that a significant percentage of our taxes is now used to support those in need should mitigate our feelings of guilt for giving a disproportionate percentage of our charity to our own religious, racial, or ethnic community.**

Still, it is wrong to give only to our own community, for doing so—in addition to violating laws from the Torah and the Talmud—is also damaging to our character. If we donate only to Jewish causes or to individual Jews in need, we may stop seeing everyone as being equally created in God's image, and therefore worthy of our help. After all, we are all members of one race, the human race.

—

Rabbi Moshe Feinstein was known to respond to charitable appeals from non-Jewish organizations that worked with handicapped and mentally ill people, both because he felt that such institutions deserved support, and out of a desire to show that religious Jews, and specifically rabbis, respected the work of these causes.[7]

—

The Talmud explains that we support non-Jewish poor, along with Jewish poor, mipnei darkei shalom, *"because of the ways of peace"* (Gittin *61a; in the context of the same discussion, the Talmud teaches that the entire Torah was given to foster peace in the world;* Gittin *59b). That such giving can indeed foster loving relationships between people of different religions is reflected in a story told about Rabbi Ezekiel Landau (see page 179), known in the Jewish world by the name of his important work of responsa,* Nodeh B'Yehuda.

Rabbi Landau once encountered a young Gentile boy crying bitterly. When

*Having said that, we must acknowledge that government programs still leave millions of people in the lurch. The growth of food pantries in the United States and the fact that tens of millions of Americans do not have health insurance bears testament to that. So while we can justify donating a high percentage of our charity within our community, we should also feel responsibility for helping to alleviate more suffering than we do.

he inquired about the reason, the boy told him that his stepfather was a baker who sent him out each morning to sell rolls in the street. That day, after he had sold his allotment of rolls, other boys had attacked him and taken the money. He knew that if he returned home empty-handed he would receive a severe beating from his stepfather. Rabbi Landau brought the boy back to his house and gave the grateful youngster the amount of money he had lost.*

Many years later, on the last night of Passover, someone knocked on Rabbi Landau's door; a non-Jewish man stood outside. "You don't remember me," he told Rabbi Landau, "but I am the boy you helped so many years ago. And now I've come to return the favor."

The story he told shocked and terrified the rabbi. The boy's stepfather, now one of the city's leading bakers, had concocted a terrible antisemitic scheme. Knowing that Passover ended, as do all Jewish holidays, at night, and that, on that night, Jews would go out and buy bread from Gentile bakers (since it is forbidden for Jews to prepare bread during the holiday), the stepfather had plotted with other bakers to poison the bread (he had no fear of killing non-Jews since they would buy their bread during the day).

After revealing the plot, the young man had but one request: "You must not make it known how you learned what I have told you; otherwise, my stepfather will have me killed." The man then left the rabbi's house.

Rabbi Landau was in a quandary. How could he make known to the Jews not to purchase the bread without endangering this young man?

The following morning, he sent messages to all the congregations in Prague, telling people that he would be speaking that morning in the main synagogue and that it was imperative that each family in the city send at least one member to be present. The rabbi's prestige was such that every family sent someone.

When he arose to speak he told the people: "Tonight, the Passover holiday is due to end. But I have just learned of a terrible misfortune. The calendars that were printed this year contain an error. They are all off by one day. In actuality, the holiday will not end tonight, but tomorrow night. Therefore, it is absolutely forbidden for any Jew to eat bread tonight."

The Jews were shocked that such an error had occurred, but once the rabbi had made his announcement, nobody thought of disregarding his edict. In the meantime, as nighttime approached, Rabbi Landau alerted a police official with whom he was on cordial terms, and the suspect bakeries were raided and the bakers caught.

---

*While the versions of the story that I have heard are consistent about the details of this incident, the one discrepancy I've come across is in the identity of the villain. In some versions, the villain is a stepmother instead of the stepfather.

Many Jews thought that it was Rabbi Landau's brilliance alone that had averted the tragedy. But, as the rabbi knew, it was all due to an act of charity and kindness he had performed long ago for a suffering young boy.

---

6. The Talmud teaches that in a town in which Jews and non-Jews reside, contributions should be solicited from both groups and distributed to both (Jerusalem Talmud, *Demai* 4:6). The most obvious implication is that for causes that help Jews and non-Jews alike (such as the aid extended in 2005 to victims of Hurricane Katrina in New Orleans and surrounding areas), Jewish charities should work in cooperation with non-Jewish charities. The broader implication is that cases of need transcend communal barriers.

Additional priorities

7. Generally, the needs of an impoverished woman should be met before those of an impoverished man. Thus, the Talmud rules that when funds are limited, a female orphan should be helped before a male since it is more embarrassing, and presumably more dangerous, for a woman to go begging door-to-door than it is for a man (*Ketubot* 67a).* Similarly, a poor woman should be given clothing before a poor man since it is assumed that women suffer more shame than men when they lack adequate or attractive clothing (see Mishnah *Horayot* 3:7, and Maimonides, "Gifts to the Poor" 8:15).†

Support for Jewish education

8. Judaism regards Jewish education as a paramount value: "The study of Torah equals in value all the other commandments" (*Peah* 1:1). The Rabbis understood that if Jews don't study Judaism, they will not live according to Jewish laws and values. Already two thousand years ago, the Rabbis of the Talmud established a universal school system‡ and insisted that the com-

---

*My friend David Szonyi demurs: "I'm not sure this really applies in contemporary American culture. A man might be more embarrassed than a woman to beg since men are raised to be more self-sufficient."

†The Rabbis also rule that when only limited funds are available to help arrange a marriage for a male or a female orphan, we should try to first arrange the marriage of the woman (*Ketubot* 67a–b). In the ancient world, no one was more vulnerable than an orphaned female, who had no natural protectors; hence, the Rabbis were particularly anxious to see her established in a family setting. However, Jewish law was also very concerned with marrying off young orphan males, so as to help them begin their own families.

‡Unfortunately, in our patriarchal past, compulsory schooling was provided only for boys, a situation that happily no longer prevails.

munity bear responsibility for providing education for poor children (see also Ramah, *Shulchan Arukh, Choshen Mishpat* 163:3). In the United States, the government extends no aid to private schools; Jewish schools, like all private schools, must raise their entire budget through tuition and charitable contributions. Therefore, donating money to Jewish educational institutions should be a charitable priority; it is particularly important because at many day schools, a third or more of the students are on scholarship.

In addition, today many Jews reach adulthood largely devoid of Jewish knowledge; therefore, contributions to support adult Jewish education are necessary and very important.

9. Aligned to the cause of Jewish education is support for the research and publication of vital Jewish books. In recent years, philanthropic contributions have enabled a new English translation and commentary on the Talmud (the ArtScroll Schottenstein edition), one of the most significant contributions to Jewish education of the past centuries to be made widely available. For over a hundred years, charitable contributions have enabled the Jewish Publication Society to publish important and accessible works of Jewish scholarship, including two translations of the Bible, into a contemporary and more readable English (regarding the generous philanthropic support that helped make possible the work on this code, see page xi).

Rabbi Avrohom Feuer reports that a wealthy philanthropist once approached Rabbi Yakov Kamenetzky with a dilemma. He had been asked to sponsor the publication of an important work of Jewish scholarship, but doing so would mean that he would have less money available to support the Jewish schools to which he normally donated. What should he do?

Reb Yakov referred him to the introduction to the important eighteenth-century Or Hachayyim *Torah commentary, in which the author thanked by name four patrons who generously funded the commentary's publication. The author spoke of them "as golden links in the chains upholding the Torah" and as "four royal kings of kindness." Reb Yakov then told the man: "Today, more than two hundred and fifty years since the* Or Hachayyim *was printed, it remains a source of wisdom and scholarship for the entire Jewish people. I have no doubt that these four sponsors supported many Torah institutions and that their names appeared on plaques and panels in many sacred locations. Sadly, those places are gone. . . . The only eternal memory that endures for all generations is the gratitude of the holy* Or Hachayyim *inscribed in the introduction to his great commentary. That is their sacred legacy for posterity." As Rabbi*

*Kamenetzky told the philanthropist, "Publishing a necessary Torah work is a public necessity (*tzorchai rabbim*)." And, in a personal blessing, the rabbi assured the man that by virtue of this good deed, he would be granted more money to support the study of the very books he helped publish.*[8]

15

HOW MUCH SHOULD WE GIVE?

Do the Torah and Talmud require us to give a set percentage to tzedaka*?*

1. Although Judaism has long been associated with the idea of tithing, there is no explicit verse in the Torah commanding us to donate a tenth of our annual earnings to charity. There are, however, several indications of 10 percent as an appropriate sum to designate for charitable giving. Most significantly, the Torah ordains that in the third and sixth years of every seven-year cycle one should set aside a tenth of one's crops for the landless tribe of Levi and for the stranger, the orphan, and the widow (Deuteronomy 14:28–29; see also Deuteronomy 26:12).*

In addition, as noted, Jacob, when fleeing for his life, makes a vow that if he returns safely to his father's home, he will set aside a tenth of his possessions to honor God (Genesis 28:20–22).[1]

Many centuries later, the Talmud takes for granted that it is a worthy act

---

*The *Etz Hayim* Torah commentary notes: "Presumably, the produce collected in each of these two years was expected to suffice for three or four years until the next collection. It seems unlikely that the poor were to be fed only two years out of seven" (page 1076). There was also an annual 10 percent levy of produce for the Levites, but that was to pay them for the work they did on behalf of the entire Israelite community. Such a levy, therefore, was more in the nature of a tax to support government activities and pay the people who performed them rather than a levy to support the poor.

to dispense a tenth or more of one's earnings to charity;* again, however, we find no specific laws mandating this percentage. Indeed, we find examples of talmudic sages who did not seem to have tithed their income. Thus, we learn that Rabbi Tarfon, a leading sage and a close colleague of Rabbi Akiva, was "very wealthy but did not give much charity to the poor" (*Kallah* 2). However, there is no indication in the text that Tarfon's giving only a small amount to charity put him in violation of any biblical or rabbinic law; his behavior was viewed as inappropriate but not illegal. Once, Rabbi Akiva came to him with a proposition: "Master, would you like me to purchase for you one or two towns?" Tarfon answered yes, and handed Akiva four thousand golden dinarim, a very large sum of money. Rabbi Akiva took the money and distributed it to needy students. "Some days later, Rabbi Tarfon met [Rabbi Akiva] and asked him, 'Where are the towns which you have purchased for me?' [Rabbi Akiva] took him by the hand, brought him to the school, and summoned a pupil who was holding the Book of Psalms." The student started reciting verses from the book, and eventually reached the verse, "That person who gives freely to the poor, his righteousness will stand him in good stead forever" [alternatively, "his righteousness endures forever"] (Psalms 112:9). Rabbi Akiva then exclaimed: "This [school and its needy students] is the town which I bought for you!" Rabbi Tarfon embraced Akiva and said to him, "My teacher, my superior—my teacher in wisdom, my superior in proper conduct." He then gave Akiva additional funds to give to the poor[2] (as compelling an anecdote as this is, I would not advise anyone to act as Akiva).

Rabbi Joseph Karo—in an unusually titled chapter, "How much is a person obliged to give and how should he give it?"—writes that a Jew should give a tenth for a standard fulfillment of the laws of charity, and 20 percent for an ideal fulfillment. One who gives less than 10 percent is, according to Rabbi Karo, regarded as giving with an "evil eye" (*Shulchan Arukh, Yoreh Deah,* 249:1).

Rabbi Meir, the Maharam of Rothenburg, Germany (thirteenth century), taught that tithing is neither biblically or rabbinically required, but is rather a minhag, *a custom (*Responsa *131). This is the dominant view of Jewish legal*

*The Sages, however, enacted a ruling that one should not give away more than 20 percent to charity (*Ketubot* 50a; see this chapter, paragraph 4). Rashi explains that the Rabbis were concerned that a person not impoverish himself to the point where he would need the support of others.

scholars: A minimum of 10 percent is the desirable amount to give, but there is no absolute biblical or rabbinic law requiring one to do so. However, the nineteenth-century legal authority and author of Pitchei Teshuvah, *Rabbi Avraham Tzvi Eisenstadt comments on the Maharam of Rothenburg's teaching that although the giving of 10 percent is a custom, it has become a binding custom and "should not be annulled except in a case of great need"* (Pitchei Teshuvah, Yoreh Deah *331:12*).

*Other rabbis argue that tithing is not a custom but was instituted as obligatory by the Rabbis of the Talmud.**

Finally, one of Judaism's greatest scholars, Rabbi Elijah of Vilna (eighteenth century), the Vilna Gaon, insisted that the Torah obligates Jews to give a minimum of 20, not 10, percent of their income to charity. In the Gaon's view, if one gives less, "then every minute of one's life one is transgressing several positive and negative commandments of the Torah, and one is considered as if one has rejected the whole of our holy Torah, heaven forbid." Fortunately for the souls of most modern Jews, the Gaon's is a decidedly minority view, and it is not clear which specific biblical commandments are being violated.

The story of Rabbis Akiva and Tarfon reminds us that the best way to motivate people to increase their giving is to make them feel good about what their donation has or can accomplish, rather than to make them feel guilty for not having done more. For example, bring someone who donates little or nothing to the hungry to a soup kitchen, and let him hand out food to the poor for an hour. The likelihood that this person will then increase his giving to the poor is great.

A story told about Rabbi Shneur Zalman of Liady (1745–1812), the founder of the Lubavitch Chasidic movement, reinforces this point. He visited a well-known miser, Mr. Solomon. Though exceedingly rich, Solomon never gave more than a small donation; it made no difference what the cause was. People were so incensed by Solomon's cheapness that they would throw his money back at him, along with some well-chosen curses. Nonetheless, when Rabbi Shneur Zalman

*See, for example Rabbi Yechiel Michel Epstein: "In truth, these allocations of one-fifth and one-tenth are not Torah obligations, but the Rabbis [of the Talmud] associated them with the verse (Genesis 28:22), 'And of all that You give me, I will set aside a tithe for You' " (*Arukh HaShulchan, Yoreh Deah* 249:2). Another example: Deuteronomy 14:22 rules, "You shall set aside every year a tenth part of all the yield of your sowing that is brought from the field"; in context, this does not seem to be an injunction to set aside a tithe each year for the poor. Nonetheless, the medieval *Tosafot* commentary on the Talmud (see *Ta'anit* 9a) cites the *Sifre,* which derives from this verse the obligation to set aside a tenth of one's income for charitable purposes.

needed five thousand rubles to ransom Jews being held captive, he insisted on including Solomon among the people to be solicited. Many tried to dissuade him, but Rabbi Shneur Zalman insisted on seeing Solomon. He even made a point of going to him first. He made one request of the two rabbis accompanying him; no matter what they saw or heard they were to remain silent. The rabbis heard Rabbi Shneur Zalman make a passionate appeal to Solomon. When he concluded, Solomon said, "A touching story indeed. Widows and orphans in captivity. When will all this suffering end? Here, Rabbi, take my humble donation." Predictably, he extended Rabbi Shneur Zalman a few coins. The rebbe appeared very pleased with the gift, and offered the man a warm smile. He even blessed him. "May God protect you always." Mr. Solomon seemed surprised and moved by the response. Before leaving, the rebbe wrote out a receipt to the man for his contribution, and shook his hand. "Thank you again, my friend," he said.

Outside, the two rabbis were incensed. "You should have thrown his donation back in his face!"

"Don't turn around and don't say a word," the rebbe said in a low voice as they started down the path to the front gate.

Suddenly, they heard the door opening behind them, and Solomon called out: "Rabbis, rabbis, please come back for a minute. I must speak to you."

They sat down once again in the man's plush living room. Solomon started to pace the floor, then turned to the rebbe. "Exactly how much money do you need to ransom these prisoners?"

"Five thousand rubles," the rebbe answered.

"Well, here is a thousand rubles," Solomon said, and handed the rebbe a thick stack of bills. Once again, the rebbe shook the man's hand, and warmly blessed him.

"This was a miracle," one of the rabbis whispered to the rebbe as they left the house. Once again, before they reached the front gate, they heard the front door opening. "Rabbis, please come in again, I need to speak to you."

This time Solomon said, "I have decided to give the entire sum needed for the ransom. Here it is, please count it to see that I have not made a mistake."

As they left the house for the third time one of the rabbis asked: "How did you get that notorious miser to give five thousand rubles?"

"That man is no miser," said Rabbi Shneur Zalman. "In his soul he was never a miser. But how could he desire to give if he never in his life experienced the joy of giving? Everyone to whom he gave his coins threw them back in his face."[3]

Additional laws on charitable giving

2. The absolute minimum that a person must give to charity each year is a third of a shekel. As Rabbi Assi teaches in the Talmud: "A person should never restrain himself from giving to charity at least one-third of a *shekel* each year" (*Bava Bathra* 9a). In accordance with this statement, the *Shulchan Arukh* rules that one who gives less than a third of a shekel has not fulfilled the mitzvah of *tzedaka* (*Yoreh Deah* 249:2).

It is hard to know precisely what a third of a shekel translates to in modern terms. It is definitely a small sum, thereby ensuring that almost all people at least fulfill this minimum requirement. Rabbi Avrohom Feuer estimates that it might be as little as $4 or $5 a year (this was in 1990; with inflation, the figure today might be double).[4]

3. Without designating a set percentage, the Torah legislated annual agricultural giving (in the ancient world, most Jews were farmers) to the poor. Thus, the Israelites were commanded not to collect all of their harvest each year, but to leave some for the poor to gather: "When you reap the harvest of your land, you shall not reap all the way to the edges of your field, or gather the gleanings of your harvest. You shall not pick your vineyard bare or gather the fallen fruit of your vineyard; you shall leave them for the poor and the stranger" (Leviticus 19:9–10; see also Leviticus 23:22 and Deuteronomy 24:19; a description of how this law was carried out in practice can be found in the book of Ruth, chapter 2).*

In addition, every seventh year was decreed a sabbatical year, during which the land was to lie fallow and the produce made available to the poor (Exodus 23:10–11). During that year, the land's owner had no greater claim to the food that grew than anyone else. During that year as well, loans that could not be repaid were abrogated, thereby enabling the poor to start fresh (Deuteronomy 15:1–10). In addition, it was—and is—always forbidden to charge interest on loans to those in need (Leviticus 25:35–37 and Exodus 22:24).†

---

*Though these agricultural laws of charity have not generally been observed in the Jewish community since the time of the Talmud, the *New York Times* reported several years ago the formation of a farming cooperative in Massachusetts, composed of Orthodox Jews, which was considering—in line with this biblical ordinance—inviting needy people to pick food from the corners of the field.

†In truth, according to the Torah, it is forbidden to charge interest on any loans. In the context of ancient Israel's agricultural society, people generally needed cash only for emergencies, and it was deemed wrong to charge interest at such a time. As the economies in which Jews lived and functioned became more urban and business oriented, money was increasingly viewed as a

There were further biblical provisions for the poor as well. Deuteronomy 16:9–14 ruled that prior to holidays, donations were to be made to the poor so that they could celebrate with the rest of the community (see pages 184–186).

Every fiftieth year was designated a Jubilee year and, at this time, all real estate holdings were returned to their original owner, thereby giving people, at least once in their lifetime, the chance to start anew (Leviticus 25:9–15).

Howard Jonas, the founder and chairman of IDT Corporation and a well-known philanthropist, claims that the biblical law of the Jubilee year turned him into an observant Jew: "At the age of seventeen, this one law literally made me . . . concede that the Bible was the work of Divine genius." What first struck Jonas about this law was its equity: "This meant that no matter how destitute or without hope a person might be, once every fifty years—at least once in the average lifetime—that person would have the means of production, the opportunity to rise to any level, placed back in his own hands." And what led Jonas to feel that the Jubilee law pointed to divine authorship of the Bible was that it served no one group's economic interests, but only the interests of justice: "Who, then, came up with the idea that for fifty years the wealthy could pile up as much wealth and power as they desired, but that at the end of fifty years they had to return any land they had acquired? Was it the wealthy? Obviously not. The poor, then? No way. Why wait fifty years if they had the power? [And] why only the farmland? Who, then, could possibly have come up with this [idea]?" Jonas found the biblical concern with justice to be consistent, and consistently unconcerned

---

commodity that could be rented out (that is, if I could charge you rent for using my land, why shouldn't I be able to charge you for using my money). In consequence, Jewish law developed a legal fiction, known as a *heter iska,* which permits a person to receive a set percentage for lending money; the lender is regarded as a business partner in the venture, though one who receives a guaranteed payment. But such permission is granted only for business loans. When lending to the poor for basic needs, it is absolutely forbidden to receive back more than one loaned. Unfortunately, throughout Jewish history many Jews disregarded these biblical provisions, and great evil and suffering ensued. The book of II Kings, chapter 4, records that a poor and desperate woman came to the prophet Elisha. She owed money to a lender, and could not repay it, and the man was now going to take her sons as slaves. Elisha performed a miracle for the woman and she was able to procure the money to repay her loan. But other people were not the recipients of such miracles, and we can assume that the enslavement of debtors continued to occur.

In biblical Hebrew, *neshech,* the word for interest paid on a loan, derives from the same root as *neshichah,* which means "bite." Rashi, in his commentary to Exodus 22:24, explains the etymological relationship of the two words: "*Neshech* means interest since it is like the bite *(neshicha)* of a snake which bites, making a small wound on one's foot, which one does not feel, but suddenly it blows up as far as one's head. So with interest—one does not feel it and it is not at first noticeable until the interest increases and causes one to lose much money" (I have followed the translation of Byron Sherwin, *Jewish Ethics for the Twenty-First Century,* page 134).

with class interests: "What about the law that prohibits judges from showing favoritism to either the rich or the poor? Which side, I ask you, pressed for that? . . . The priestly clan was a possible suspect [as the authors of the Torah's laws], since 'taxes' supporting them were institutionalized. But if this group 'wrote' the Bible, then why did they exclude themselves from the distribution of land . . . If the king 'wrote' the Bible, why would he forbid himself from having too many wives or horses (Deuteronomy 17:16–17)? Why would he agree to submit to the law in so many cases? Where was the Divine Right of kings? If neither the rich nor the poor were the beneficiaries, then who came up with all these laws, which were so just yet favored no one? Which tribal society more than 3,000 years ago would have ever come up on their own with a law that affords full legal protection and rights to any foreigner who wandered onto their territory? Foreigners at that time [and in many parts of the world even now] were subject to enslavement, robbing, raping, or killing. Who came up with the idea of respecting the rights of the sojourner and doing him or her no harm because you and your ancestors were sojourners in Egypt? Wouldn't exacting revenge on Egyptians and other foreigners have had a lot more appeal? . . . And then it hit me. The undeniable reality. The Bible really was God's revealed law. It was the source of all morality in the world. . . . [And] I decided then and there, while still a teenager, that I could no longer ignore it, and I became religiously observant."[5]

—

Even in a world in which few Jews are farmers and have the opportunity to practice the law of not harvesting the entirety of their field, these regulations still have an important lesson to teach. In the past, the lesson was "My field doesn't completely belong to me." In modern terms, when we get our paycheck, do we think, "Every penny of this is mine," or do we think, as the Torah wanted its adherents to think, "This doesn't fully belong to me" (Rabbi Irwin Kula).

—

An upper limit on giving

4. The Talmud rules that we should not give away more than 20 percent of our income to charity (*Ketubot* 50a). The Rabbis feared that by doing so we might impoverish ourselves to the point where we would end up dependent on other people's charity.* Although there are religious traditions in

*Maimonides writes: "This is not an act of saintliness *(chasidut),* but rather foolishness *(shtut).* Giving away all one's money causes that person to be in need of others" ("Laws of *Arakhin ve-Charamim*" 8:13), and Maimonides calls such a person a *chasid shoteh,* a pious fool (for more on this, see *A Code of Jewish Ethics, Volume 1: You Shall Be Holy,* page 136; in citing this teaching of Maimonides, I have followed the translation of Danny Siegel, *Giving Your Money Away,* page 55).

which poverty is viewed as spiritually desirable, Judaism, as noted, regards poverty as a curse and not a condition that one should voluntarily embrace.

However, there are instances when Jewish law permits giving away more than 20 percent of one's income or assets:

- when lives are at stake and money is necessary to save them;
- in one's will, when the money will be distributed after one's death;
- when one is so wealthy that distributing more than 20 percent of one's capital will not create *any* risk of impoverishment.

Some years ago, Professor Peter Singer, the Princeton philosopher and the most prominent secular ethicist in the contemporary world, wrote an article in The New York Times Magazine, *"The Singer Solution to World Poverty,"*[6] *arguing that the major ethical demand of our time is to feed the hungry and provide for the basic needs of the poor. Singer maintained that since the average American family could get by—at the time he wrote the article—on $30,000 a year, each family has a moral obligation to give any earnings above that amount to charities devoted to relieving world hunger. Thus, a family earning $100,000 a year should donate $70,000 a year to a charity such as Oxfam America. In Singer's view, to spend $100 on a restaurant meal in a world in which there are people who are starving is immoral and tantamount to standing by while someone is dying and doing nothing to help. A reader of the article asked me at the time: "As resistant as I am to Singer's thinking—I certainly don't want to give away so much of my income to charity—his logic seems compelling, doesn't it?"*

Moved as I was by Singer's passion to reduce suffering in the world, his article did not persuade me for several reasons. First, it seems to me that an ethical argument detailing human obligations must also take into account human nature. And this is precisely what Singer is ignoring. In effect, he's asking people, once their earnings exceed a certain level, to work full-time on behalf of strangers. But other than to practice the most extraordinary and unusual altruism, what would motivate a person to earn more than $30,000 since anything over that would, in effect, be "taxed" at 100 percent?

Since many people would rather relax than work, it seems to me that Singer's proposal would discourage human initiative. Wouldn't it be more sensible to take human nature into account and simply encourage people, particularly as they become more affluent, to give more of their income to charity, rather than to make a demand that almost everyone will ignore as being so far-fetched as to be ridiculous?

Second, once we accept Singer's premise that people are morally obligated to donate all excess income to the needy, there's almost no end to the demands we *can make of them. For example, Singer chooses to earn his living as a philosopher at Princeton. I have no idea what he's earning there, but let's guess it's $150,000 a year. Let's also say that if Professor Singer were to become a commodities broker, he could earn $400,000 a year. By his reasoning, it seems to me that he would be morally obligated to take whatever job paid the most, so that he would be in a position to help more people who might otherwise starve. After all, what moral right should we have to practice the profession we want if, by practicing another, more people's lives could be saved?*

Another objection to Singer's reasoning is suggested by radio talk show host and ethicist Dennis Prager. If Singer's thinking were to become widespread, the upshot would be a significant rise in unemployment. Clearly, a world in which people choose to live without frills so that they can donate their excess income to charity would be one in which, for example, no one would eat out except at "greasy spoons," no one would go to the opera or to theaters because tickets are so costly, and no one would buy expensive fountain pens. Certainly, no one would attend elite schools like Princeton, where tuition and expenses alone amount to almost $50,000 a year. It so happens that many people work in jobs creating items that are not essential for survival. In Singer's scenario, all such businesses would close down, the workers would be discharged (and might soon find themselves in need of charity), and all luxury items would eventually disappear from the face of the earth.

What would be the consequences of Singer's plan to cure world hunger? A world in which most people, deprived of material rewards for working harder, would work less (and therefore have less income to give away), a world in which people would be obligated to make career decisions based on pay and not personal desire, and all goods beyond life's basic necessities would be viewed as decadent and immoral.

World poverty and hunger are serious problems and require serious, but also feasible, solutions. In addition to encouraging efforts among the poor that could help remedy or mitigate their poverty (for example, providing job training that prepares people to earn decent wages, and arranging for loans—even if they can't be backed by collateral—for poor people to start small businesses), we should try to motivate those who have more than enough to give away more, but not all, of their excess income to charities that help the poor.

*A wise principle in Jewish law states "No ruling may be imposed on the public unless a majority of the people are able to abide by it" (*Horayot *3b). It strikes me as both more moral and helpful to the hungry and poor to make reasonable demands of people (such as those that insist on far higher levels of giving than is the norm) than it is to make utopian demands that will be* *ignored.* I have long been moved by the words of the great Christian theologian, C. S. Lewis, who wrote in* Mere Christianity: *"If our charities do not at all pinch or hamper us, I should say they are too small. There ought to be things we should like to do and cannot do because our charitable expenditures exclude them." Using this measure, it is likely that few of us are giving enough.*

—

5. Rabbi Moshe Feinstein suggested that people tithe not only their money, but their time as well. Thus, he suggested that advanced yeshiva students devote a tenth of their learning time to tutoring people with lesser knowledge. Based on this example, one might suggest that doctors devote a tenth of their practice to patients unable to pay, and lawyers do likewise. Again, though, such tithing, as I understand it, would be in the realm of custom, a highly commendable action, but not obligatory.

Does tithing apply to one's entire income?

6. No. The 10 percent levy applies to one's net, not gross, income. Thus, there is no reason to donate a tithe of the money paid in taxes since that money goes to the government and is not available to the person who earned it.† For example, if someone earns $100,000 and pays $25,000 in taxes, the tithe would be due on $75,000, not $100,000.

7. In summary, the dominant view is that while the Torah enjoins us to give charity, it does not lay down a specific percentage. Based on a number of biblical levies and talmudic suggestions, the custom developed in Jewish life that we should give between 10 and 20 percent of our income to charity. However, as noted (see page 208), this has become recognized as a binding custom.

---

*Though I critique Professor Singer's proposal, I want to acknowledge his role in prompting people to think about their charitable donations and whether they are giving enough.

†Rabbi Avrohom Feuer summarizes the thinking of Rabbi Moshe Feinstein (*Igrot Moshe, Yoreh Deah,* Volume 1, # 143) on this topic: "The amount a person pays as income tax is considered like money a person never earned in the first place; it is as if he was working and earning the money for the government" (*The Tzedakah Treasury,* page 133).

16

CHARITABLE PRACTICES AND CUSTOMS

Offer donations at vulnerable and dangerous times

1. The Talmud teaches that "people on their way to perform a mitzvah will not be harmed, either on the way there, or on the way back" (*Pesachim* 8b). Based on this text, a long-standing custom exists to give a sum of money to anyone embarking on a long trip, to be dispensed as charity upon arrival at her destination. The amount is generally modest—often only several dollars—and is usually donated to beggars. Such a gift is commonly called by the Hebrew/Yiddish term *shaliach mitzvah gelt* ("money for a messenger to perform a commandment").*

Widely practiced by traditional Jews, this custom is little known among nonobservant Jews, but it should be adopted. As well as acting as a shield to protect travelers, as the Talmud promises, it also elevates family and business trips. The traveler has to spend at least a few minutes thinking about how to distribute this money, and then spend time locating a person or cause to give it to. While this custom originally involved only giving money to Jewish travelers, spreading the word to non-Jews (both by telling them about it and giving them funds to disperse) would be a contribution of Jewish ethical practices to the world.

—

This custom can also be helpful to anyone whose fear of flying makes air travel a nerve-racking experience. Prior to a trip, people should promise to donate a specified sum of money upon their safe arrival and return. They can even make a variation of the commitment made by the Patriarch Jacob when his life was in peril: "If God will be with me, and protect me on this journey . . . [then I shall donate the following sum to such-and-such a charity upon my return"; see Genesis 28:20–22].

Several people who have undertaken this custom have told me that the

*A friend of mine notes that he always gives two bills, one for the destination to which the person is traveling, and the other for when the traveler returns, so that he or she has divine protection both on the way there *and* on the way home (generous as this custom is, the talmudic quote suggests that the divine protection does, in any case, apply in both directions).

*talmudic promise, and their stating and then fulfilling their pledge, has helped make travel less frightening for them.**

---

2. The *Shulchan Arukh* promises that "whoever is merciful to the poor, God will be merciful to him" (*Yoreh Deah* 247:3). Thus, it is customary for someone in need of mercy (such as one who is very ill) to increase her charitable giving. For example, if you are about to have an operation, you should make a charitable donation or several charitable donations before entering the hospital.

As noted, the Talmud teaches, "If a person says, 'I am giving this coin to charity so that my [sick] *child will recover . . . he is regarded as completely righteous"* (Pesachim *8a-b). The fact that a person believes that performing acts of charity will prompt God's mercy is itself a reflection of the donor's goodness; good people assume that God is good and therefore is moved by goodness.*

---

3. Help impoverished mourners. Jewish law ordains that a person observe seven days of mourning (shiva) upon the death of a parent, sibling, child, or spouse (see pages 116–117). During this week, the mourner is expected to stay at home and refrain from work. But someone in difficult financial circumstances is permitted to observe only three days of mourning and then work, but only in private and at home.† However, taking advantage of this leniency can be disheartening and humiliating. The Breuer's community in New York City's Washington Heights (composed of followers of the nineteenth-century German rabbi Samson Raphael Hirsch and his grandson, Rabbi Isaac Breuer) has addressed this problem compassionately: At the beginning of shiva, it provides several boxes to the family with a note explaining that they contain sufficient money to enable them to meet their expenses for the week. The mourners are instructed to use whatever they need, and simply return the boxes at the end of the week. The boxes are distributed to all mourning families, including the wealthy, so that no one feels ashamed or pressured to cut short the shiva.

*Obviously, those with an acute fear of flying should not rely exclusively on this custom, but should also consult a physician.

†The *Shulchan Arukh* actually directs a curse at a community that doesn't help someone in these circumstances (*Yoreh Deah* 380:2).

---

*This custom recalls an ancient tradition described in the Mishnah: "There was a secret chamber in the Temple in Jerusalem where pious people would leave money in secret, and those who had become poor would come and take it in secret" (*Shekalim *5:6). Indeed, the Breuer's community uses several boxes, so that even the administrators of the charitable funds, who check the boxes every few weeks, do not know which families took money and which didn't.*[1]

Giving when praying

4. According to the Talmud, Rabbi Elazar regularly gave a coin to charity before praying (*Bava Bathra* 10a). The *Shulchan Arukh* incorporates this suggestion, noting that "it is good to give charity before praying" (*Orach Chayyim* 92:10). Today, the collection is generally done while the service is taking place. Thus, during weekday services, a member of the congregation customarily circulates a charity box (on Shabbat, and most Jewish holidays, the handling of money, even for charitable purposes, is prohibited). Some people who are unfamiliar with this custom protest that solicitations are inappropriate during prayer services. But the Jewish view is that stopping prayers for a few seconds to dispense charity is pleasing to God. In short, before beseeching God for mercy, we should show it ourselves (see paragraph 2).*

5. The Talmud teaches (in the name of Mar Zutra) that "The merit of fasting is the charity dispensed" (*Berachot* 6b). Based on this statement, the sixteenth-century Rabbi Shlomo Elazar Eideles, the Maharsha, observed that a custom developed to give the money saved on food on a fast day to a charity that feeds the poor. For example, before Yom Kippur, you would calculate how much money your family spends on food each week, then divide the sum by seven and donate it to a charity that helps the hungry.

Doing so also serves to fulfill the words of the *Haftorah* (prophetic reading) chanted on Yom Kippur, "This is the fast I desire . . . to share one's bread with the hungry" (Isaiah 58:6–7); the Talmud also teaches that we should make sure that the poor have money to buy food to break the fast (*Sanhedrin* 35a).

---

*Giving during services also ensures that prayer doesn't become an escape from the world.

Giving on special occasions

6. It is a Jewish custom to throw a party, called a *chanukat ha-bayit* (dedication of a house), upon moving into a new home. Often, at such celebrations, the new owners affix a mezuzah on the doorposts of the house and the rooms. At a time when we celebrate our new dwelling, our thoughts should also turn to those who have no place to live, and it is good to make a generous donation to a cause that helps the homeless.

—

Rabbi Velvel Soloveitchik, the Brisker Rav, advised his son, Rabbi Raphael Soloveitchik, that the best type of chanukat ha-bayit *is to invite a poor person to share the first meal in your new home.*

—

7. Whenever you celebrate, make a point to give to others. In 1985, Leonard Fein, the American-Jewish writer, established Mazon: A Jewish response to hunger (*mazon* is a Hebrew word for food), and asked Jews to contribute to the organization a tax-deductible amount of 3 percent of the costs of private celebrations, such as Bar and Bat Mitzvahs, weddings, and any large parties.* Mazon, which is now based in Los Angeles, distributes this money to hunger relief projects and activities that help society's neediest members.

Another appropriate organization to direct such contributions toward is the New York–based American Jewish World Service, which concerns itself, in particular, with providing humanitarian assistance and emergency relief to disadvantaged people worldwide.[2]

—

Rabbi Abraham Twerski recalls that he was once invited to a wedding of some dear acquaintances. As much as he liked the young couple, he felt a bit uncomfortable because he knew the wedding was going to be very opulent and "I thought how wasteful it would . . . be when so many others are needy." Twerski wondered how he could really put his heart into the celebration. But all his misgivings ended when he learned that the couple had made preparations to donate the leftover food to an organization in Milwaukee that gave food to the needy. Then a nurse whom Rabbi Twerski knew suggested that the flowers be donated at the end of the evening to Mount Sinai Hospital, where the woman worked. It occurred to Rabbi Twerski that it would be a good idea to donate some of the

---

*Given that American Jews spend many hundreds of millions of dollars a year on such celebrations, this proposal has the capacity to raise tens of millions of dollars a year to help society's most impoverished members.

flowers to a local psychiatric hospital whose patients never received flowers. Twerski attended the wedding and danced and celebrated with great joy, and early in the morning thirty medical students from Marquette University arrived to pick up the flowers and distribute them: "A week later, I received a thank-you note from the newlyweds. They wrote that the fact that the flowers and food brought cheer to those less fortunate was a great way to start their new life, and a good omen for a happy marriage."

The whole incident put Twerski in mind of a teaching from Rabindranath Tagore (1861–1941), the Indian poet, writer, and 1913 winner of the Nobel Prize for literature: "Man discovers his own wealth when God comes to ask gifts of him."[3]

Giving to charity as a "fine" to improve one's character

8. The medieval text *Reisheet Chochmah (The Beginning of Wisdom)* suggests that those who wish to gain more control of their temper should decide on a sum of money that they will give each time they lose it without adequate cause (when they shouldn't have been angered at all or when their response was excessive). The sum should be large enough to have deterrent value and should serve as a kind of fine; thus, it should be over and above the amount you would otherwise give to charity.

Periodically count up the number of times you have lost your temper unfairly, then donate the designated amount to charity. Through this technique you will become a more patient and also a more charitable person.

For a further discussion of this technique, see *A Code of Jewish Ethics, Volume 1: You Shall Be Holy,* page 271.

Raising philanthropic children

9. Place a *pushka* (charity box) near where you keep your Shabbat candles, and put some money into the box before lighting the candles so that your final act before commencing Shabbat is giving charity. This custom is also a powerful way to convey to your children the importance of *tzedaka.* Indeed, since the lighting of the Shabbat candles is a joyful event, let your children be the ones who put the money in the box, so that they come to associate the giving of *tzedaka* with joy.

10. Starting at a young age, talk to your children about the causes to which you donate charity. Thus, your children will become aware early on of *tzedaka* as something important, and learn to think of themselves and their family as involved in it. When children turn Bar or Bat Mitzvah, they should be encouraged, as one of their first acts as Jewish adults, to donate 10 percent of the money they've received in gifts to charity. Discuss with them how they plan to spend the money, but let them make the final choice.

—

A friend suggests that parents leave the decision about the percentage to be donated to the Bar or Bat Mitzvah to decide. After all, they are now adults. Furthermore, letting them decide makes them feel that they are really giving the money—which they are—rather than merely following their parents' suggestion.

—

A final thought

11. Let the first check you write each year be to a charity. This should apply both to the religious new year (the first check we write after Rosh Hashanah) and the secular new year (January 1). This way you are guaranteed to start each year with an act of *chesed* (kindness). It is also a good custom to give *tzedaka* on the beginning of another new year—your birthday, and on your wedding anniversary as well.

17

SOLICITING AND MOTIVATING OTHERS TO GIVE

The great mitzvah of fund-raising

1. Many people who are themselves generous and willing to donate to good causes nonetheless find it difficult to ask others to do likewise.* Asking

*Some people are even willing to increase their own gifts just to avoid being pressured to solicit others.

others for a donation, even though the funds collected in no way benefit themselves, makes such people feel like *nudniks* (pests) or *schnorrers* (beggars).

The traditional Jewish attitude toward fund-raising is markedly different. The Rabbis (*Bava Bathra* 8b) point to a verse in the book of Daniel: "And those who make the many righteous [will shine] like the stars forever and ever" (12:3). "Those who make the many righteous," is understood as referring to charity collectors *(ga-ba-ai tzedaka),* whose great merit is that they persuade others to perform acts of charity.

One of the most successful fund-raisers I know, Beverly Woznica, who has long worked for Jewish federations, told me that she does not feel self-conscious when soliciting contributions. She sees herself as doing donors a favor by offering them the chance to do something very worthwhile. As another charitable fund-raiser once expressed it to me: "If a salesman trying to interest a wealthy person in buying a luxury car, a high end item of jewelry, or a yacht does not feel self-conscious—if he did, he would quickly be out of work—why should a tzedaka *solicitor trying to interest a person in helping to feed the poor, sustain a hospital, or expand a school feel so?"*

Rabbi Berel Wein, the writer and educator, was once visiting a childhood friend, and the two men stayed up late reminiscing. At midnight, Rabbi Wein announced that he was ready to go to sleep. His friend, a highly successful money manager, said, "All right, I've still got a few calls to make."

"Who are you going to call at midnight?" Rabbi Wein asked.

"You don't understand," the man replied. "I have some very important information to give a number of clients, absolutely great opportunities. I'll call them tonight, and when the market opens in the morning, they'll be ready. They'll appreciate the call. . . . They know I'll call them at three in the morning [if necessary] and tell them, 'Hey, we can make money tomorrow.' "

Rabbi Wein recalls his reaction: "I sat there and thought to myself, if I could be like him. If I really believed the speeches that I make, then I would call my congregants also at one o'clock in the morning and tell them, 'Look, I've got a great hachnassat kallah *[charity for brides] for you; it's available in the morning. There's a mitzvah over here, a Jew we can help. We can save him. At the opening bell we can save him for sure.' But I'm afraid I'll wake them up and they'll be angry, so I don't call after 9:30 or 10:00. I look at it as a burden, and the Lord looks at it as an opportunity."*[1]

Wein also likes to quote advice he was given by the late Rabbi Yosef Ka-

haneman, the founder of Israel's Ponovezh Yeshiva, and a masterful fund-raiser: "You should never feel embarrassed asking a Jew for money to support Torah, the Land of Israel, or the needy. You are not asking for yourself. You are giving the person a great opportunity to do infinite good with his wealth. Eventually, he will thank you for doing so."[2]

The appropriate mind-set for solicitors of tzedaka*—particularly when they are rejected—is reflected in an account of a man who accompanied a well-known rabbi to solicit a wealthy businessman. Not only did the businessman treat the rabbi in a brusque manner, but he also refused to contribute. When they left, the man expressed sympathy to the rabbi for the frustration this must have caused him, but the rabbi answered: "I don't feel discouraged, and neither should you. That man simply does not have the* zechut *(merit) to help our cause. That is his loss, not ours."*

When Letty Cottin Pogrebin, a contemporary writer and Jewish activist, solicits donations, she says to people: "Suppose you get hit by a truck and someone finds your checkbook. What would the check stubs reveal about your giving habits? How recently did you make your last contribution, and how generous was it relative to your means? Who were the beneficiaries of your giving, and why did you choose those causes?"[3]

In a similar manner, Rabbi Israel Stein has said: "We all write our autobiographies in our checkbooks, and leave a record for our children of the causes to which we gave."

---

2. The Talmud regards charitable soliciting so highly that it declares, "The one who causes others to give [charity] is greater than the one who actually gives" (*Bava Bathra* 9a). Maimonides included this teaching in his code of Jewish law ("Laws of Gifts to the Poor" 10:6). One reason, perhaps, is that by raising money from others, solicitors usually raise far more money than any one donor might provide. In addition, many people who donate to a charity might not have done so if someone hadn't motivated them.

Rabbi Hanoch Teller relates that Rabbi Yechezkel Abramsky, head of the London rabbinical court, once approached a wealthy businessman for a contribution to a yeshiva that was in dire straits. The businessman, a knowledgeable Jew, agreed to donate the entire sum needed, but with one caveat: Rabbi Abramsky would have to explain to him the logic of this rabbinic dictum and of Maimonides' ruling: "After all, why should [your] reward be greater than mine? It is I who am donating the money." Rabbi Abramsky replied: "When I knocked on your door, I was so nervous, I could hear my heart thump. You did not have to experience this fear. Overcoming this trepidation [the sense of terror in gathering up my courage to make an audacious request] is worth [even] more than the sum you are donating."[4]

Rabbi Eliyahu Lopian (1872–1970) noted additional reasons why someone who motivates others to give is regarded as even worthier than the giver:

a. *The one who gives receives praise, while the one who tries to influence others to give often receives abuse.*
b. *The one who gives, gives money, while the one who influences others to give, gives time—and time is life.*
c. *The one who gives gets merit for himself in the World-to-Come, while the one who influences others to give causes others to be rewarded as well.*[5]

Inspiring others to give

3. People usually give most generously when they feel empathy for the recipients of their charity. But because it is difficult for most wealthy and middle class people to feel true empathy—and not just sympathy and pity—for people who lack basic necessities, a solicitor for the poor must find imaginative ways to induce such a feeling. One master at doing this was Rabbi Elijah (Elya) Chaim Meisel (1821–1912) of Lodz. Once, during an exceptionally cold winter, he went to a rich citizen to ask for funds for firewood to heat the homes of the poor. The rabbi knocked, and the wealthy man came to the door in his evening jacket. Honored by the appearance of the distinguished rabbi, he invited him into the house. Rabbi Elya Chaim responded that since he would be staying just a minute there was no need to go inside. He then engaged the man in conversation, asking in great detail about each family member. Out of respect for the rabbi, the man answered all his questions, but by now his teeth were chattering. Still, the rabbi refused to enter. Finally, the man said, "Rabbi, why did you come here? What is it that you want?"

"I need money to buy wood for the poor. They are suffering greatly."

The shivering man promised to give a hundred rubles, a huge sum, whereupon the rabbi entered his house and sat down in the living room in front of a warm fireplace. The man brought the rabbi a glass of tea, and they sat and spoke. Finally, unable to restrain himself, the man said to Rabbi Elya Chaim: "Why didn't you just come in right away, and ask for the donation? You know that I wouldn't refuse you."

The rabbi answered: "Standing outside in the cold, you started to shiver, and when I told you how cold the poor were, you felt in your own bones the truth of my words. That's why you gave a hundred rubles. But had you and I sat together in comfortable chairs in front of a warm fireplace, drinking hot tea, and I had spoken to you of the sufferings of the poor, you wouldn't have felt it in the same way, and would have contented yourself with a ten-ruble contribution."

Rabbi Abraham Isaac Kook, the chief rabbi of Palestine (he died in 1935, before Israel was created), once solicited a wealthy donor specifically by calling attention to the man's wealth rather than to the recipients' needs. Thus, when Nathan Straus, one of the owners of Macy's, gave him a substantial donation for Ma'ot Chittim *(to help people buy food for Passover), he asked Rabbi Kook, "Is this enough?"*

Rabbi Kook responded with the story of a Russian landowner who lost his way on his very large estate, and ended up at the home of a Jew who lived on his neighbor's estate. The Jew was not prepared for such a guest, and served the man what he had available, which was bread and eggs. The landowner wanted to pay, but the Jew said no, it was his gift. But when the man insisted that he wished to pay, the Jew asked for a thousand rubles, an enormous sum. The landowner asked, "Are eggs so rare here?"

"No," the Jew answered, "but wealthy landowners like you are." Rabbi Kook turned to Mr. Straus. "I do not have the privilege of hosting such a special guest every day."

*Mr. Straus gave the rabbi a larger check.**

A story drawn from Jewish folklore shows the extent to which a rebbe—unfortunately unnamed—would go to ensure that his disciple developed empathy:

"A Chasid once came to his rebbe complaining of his bitter poverty, and pleading with the rebbe to give him a bracha *(blessing) for prosperity. The rebbe said, 'I will give you a* bracha, *provided that you follow my instructions to the letter.' The Chasid agreed he would do so.*

*Simcha Raz, *An Angel Among Men,* page 330. Straus was a highly generous man, and the *Encyclopedia Judaica* records that he donated two-thirds of his fortune to Palestine (Volume 15, page 430). His Hebrew name was Natan, and the Israeli city of Netanya was named after him.

"The rebbe gave the Chasid some money and said, 'You must do exactly as I say. With this money you are to buy the finest delicacies, take them home, and eat them in the presence of your wife and children. Under no circumstances may you give them even the tiniest morsel of your food. After you do this, come back to me.'

"The Chasid followed instructions, and his hungry children sat around the table, their mouths watering, looking longingly at the food their father was eating, which he would not share with them. Each bite of food he took was torture. How could he eat when his children were starving. It would have been easier for him to swallow rocks . . .

"When he returned, the rebbe said, 'You [found it so hard to] partake of the food when your children were starving. How will you be able to enjoy wealth when you know there are poor people who lack the basic necessities of life? But you asked for wealth, and wealth you shall have.

"The Chasid returned home and had phenomenal success. Whatever he bought, the price skyrocketed and he sold it at a huge profit. In time, he became wealthy. He built a hachnassat orchim *(hospitality house) for the homeless and a huge soup kitchen. He often slept in the [hospitality house] and shared the meals in the soup kitchen. He had learned to empathize."*[6]

Rabbi Abraham Twerski, who relates this story, concludes that it is impossible to fulfill Judaism's extensive interpersonal laws without empathy, which is why this particular trait "is unparalleled in refining a person's character."[7]

—

The ethics of soliciting

4. Every community is obligated to set up a charitable fund led by people who are trustworthy and well known (Maimonides, "Laws of Gifts to the Poor" 9:1). That such people must be trustworthy is self-evident, but why well known? Perhaps so as to make an impression on others, by conveying the message that it is a matter of prestige to sit on the board of a charitable fund.

—

*The Talmud rules that it is forbidden for a learned [and by implication any committed] Jew to live in a city without a charitable fund (*Sanhedrin *17b).*

—

5. Although solicitors must be drawn from people known to be scrupulously honest, they must also behave in a manner beyond reproach, so that

no one will have reason to question their integrity. For example, the Talmud rules that solicitors should visit in pairs and remain together the whole time. This regulation was put in place at a time when contributions were made in cash and a dishonest solicitor could easily hold on to some of the money he had collected (*Bava Bathra* 8b).

While contributions assessed by the community should be collected by two people (when the community leadership knows the amount to expect, there is less leeway for two solicitors to misappropriate funds), voluntary contributions should be collected by three people. In such cases, the Rabbis felt it appropriate to impose greater safeguards (Maimonides, "Law of Gifts to the Poor" 9:5).

---

6. If collectors for the *tamchui* (the fund that collects food to feed the hungry) find that they have extra food and no one to give it to (and the food might spoil), they should sell the food and hold the money for future use. However, they must sell it to others, not to themselves, lest they be suspected of buying the food at an artificially low price (see *Bava Bathra* 8b).

7. Because community needs can arise suddenly (such as through a hurricane or earthquake), officials are given discretion to divert charitable funds collected for one purpose to another. However, there is a dispute among Jewish authorities as to just how absolute this discretion is. Some rule, for example, that money donated to provide food for the poor no longer needed for that purpose may be diverted to other communal needs (see *Yoreh Deah* 256:4). However, another rabbi argues that it would constitute *gezel aniyim*, "stealing from the poor," to use such money for a general community project, as opposed to other needs of the poor. Other rabbinic scholars, among them *Tosafot* (see *Bava Bathra* 8b), and Ramban (Nachmanides), rule that since the donors always intended to rely on the discretion of the charity administrators, the funds may be used to meet any public need.[8] The *Shulchan Arukh* similarly rules that the charity administrators have the right to do with the money contributed "that which is good in the eyes of God and man" (*Yoreh Deah* 251:5). This view is the dominant one.

The above would seem to apply to money donated to general charitable funds, such as Jewish federations, whose donors expect funds to be used for a variety of Jewish communal needs. On the other hand, it seems only right that people who donate to charities with specific agendas, such as diabetes research, or to help the hearing-impaired, have the right to expect that the money will not be diverted to another, even if worthy, purpose.

—

8. Don't take advantage of those who are extremely generous. Thus, it is wrong to solicit a person who always gives more than he can afford,* or someone whose income has declined and who will, out of shame, give more than she should. The *Sefer Chasidim* rules that pressuring someone to donate more than he can afford is a form of robbery (paragraph 332), while the *Shulchan Arukh* threatens divine retribution for such behavior: "Any charitable trustee who shames people [by exerting unfair pressure on them to give] may count on God's punishment in the World-to-Come" (*Yoreh Deah* 248:7).

There is no perfect solution for knowing precisely how much pressure it is fair to exert. A friend of mine suggests that when distributing solicitation forms, one way to make sure that people do not feel undue pressure to contribute more than they feel comfortable giving is to print on the forms relatively modest donor levels; that way, everyone can feel themselves to be partners in the giving. Kind as this idea sounds, I know a synagogue, in great need, that did so, and found that many of its affluent members gave considerably less than they were capable of giving.

—

Rabbi Nisson Wolpin writes of a visit he paid to the home of Rabbi Michael Munk of Brooklyn, where he saw a striking antique silver pushka *(charity box). When he asked about it, Rabbi Munk explained that the heirloom had been in his family for almost two centuries and was originally given as a communal gift to his great-grandmother, who was known as "Chana Klapperpantofil" (Hannah with the noisy shoes). His great-grandmother had lived in a small town outside Danzig (today, part of Poland, but then in Prussia), with her husband, Rabbi Michael Leib Munk. Rebbetzin Munk used to go door-to-door almost daily, collecting money and food for those in need. It occurred to her that people might feel pressured to contribute because of her status in the community; perhaps, she feared, she was taking money from people who were not in a position to give it. So she bought a pair of heavy wooden clogs and wore them whenever she went collecting. The clogs made thumping noises and alerted people to her pres-*

*The Talmud tells of a man named Eleazar Ish Biratha who used to give so generously that collectors would hide when they saw him coming, lest he turn over to them all that he had. While such generosity might seem like a blessed trait, it might have been hard on Eleazar's daughter, whose dowry he gave away to provide for the marriage of an orphan boy to an orphan girl (*Ta'anit* 24a).

ence. Anyone who did not feel able to make a donation could pretend not to be at home when she knocked. On her seventieth birthday, the townspeople, grateful both for her fundraising and her sensitivity, presented her with the silver pushka *that her descendant displayed in his home almost two centuries later.*[9]

A humorous Chasidic folktale relates that Rabbi Levi Yitzchak of Berditchev (d. 1809), the renowned and saintly rebbe, used to collect his salary and then, even before he reached home, would give it all away to beggars and others in need. His wife, desperately in need of the money to support herself and their children, finally sued him for not supporting his family. The judge ordered that Rabbi Levi Yitzchak's salary was, from then on, to be handed directly to his wife. Levi Yitzchak was not only the defendant but, as the town rabbi, he was the judge as well.[10]

---

9. A solicitor should never lie and say that he is giving more than he is so as to influence the person being solicited to increase his contribution (see the Maharsha's comment on *Sukkah* 29b).

When too much money is collected

10. If a charitable campaign is launched for a specific purpose, and more money is collected than needed, the surplus should be used for a similar purpose. For example, if a synagogue launches a drive to help local poor people purchase food, and collects more than is necessary, the extra money should be given to similar charitable drives at other congregations or organizations (if no other congregations need the funds for food purchases, then the money should be applied to other needs of the poor).

However, if a collection is started for a specific person, the money, including the surplus, should go to the person for whom it has been collected, or to his or her heirs. Thus, if a man died penniless and funds were raised to pay for his funeral, any extra funds collected should be given to the dead man's survivors. In an instance where there are no immediate heirs, the money should be used toward the funeral needs of other indigents.

Some years ago, I received an e-mail from a friend describing the plight of a young married man with two children who was suffering from a virulent cancer. The letter noted that there was an experimental treatment costing $90,000 that could be performed on him, but it was not covered by insurance. Some weeks *after I contributed, I learned that, within a few weeks, the appeal had brought in about $300,000, far more than needed. Unfortunately, the procedure was unsuccessful and the man died. The collection's organizers consulted with rabbis, who ruled that the extra money should be given to the young widow for the maintenance of the children and herself. The rabbis reasoned that not only was this a just solution, but it was likely that the people who donated the funds would have wanted their money used in this way.*

—

A final thought: On taking money that might be tainted

11. While charitable administrators should not accept contributions from anyone who has acquired their money illegally, they should not be overly scrupulous in inquiring into the sources of money designated for charity. Doing so might cause the administrators, out of an exaggerated sense of honesty, to refrain from providing help to those whose need is immediate and definite.

Robert Mass, an attorney and a student of Jewish ethics, suggests that charitable organizations not accept contributions from convicted criminals, those under criminal indictment, and those who, by reputation, are involved in criminal enterprises; doing so undermines the ethical values the Jewish community is trying to instill.* Mass notes that after a person has admitted wrongdoing, taken his punishment, made restitution, and returned to the straight path, his *tzedaka* should be welcomed.

—

Shortly after Israel's creation in 1948, Rabbi Judah Leib Maimon, Israel's minister of religion, made a trip to the United States, accompanied by his secretary, Israel Friedman. At a meeting in Chicago, a man approached Mr. Friedman, and asked him if he knew Rabbi Aryeh Levine in Jerusalem.

"Certainly," Friedman answered, whereupon the man gave him a bank check for a thousand dollars, a very large sum in those days. When Friedman asked the man, "But from whom is it? Reb Aryeh will want to know," the donor answered, "What difference does it make?"

Upon their return to Jerusalem, Rabbi Maimon and Mr. Friedman presented the check to Reb Aryeh, and it turned out that to him it did make a big difference who the donor was. Indeed, he didn't want to accept the money, fearing that it had been acquired dishonestly. But when Tzvi Pesach Frank,

*In addition, it is a crime to accept money that the receiver believes is the proceeds of a crime.

Jerusalem's chief rabbi, was apprised of the situation, he said to Reb Aryeh, "Look here. I know how many families depend on your charitable gifts for their subsistence. Why should they suffer because you do not know who gave this money?"

Reb Aryeh cashed the check.[11]

The issue of charitable contributions of money acquired immorally or possibly illegally raises questions for which there does not seem to be a fully satisfactory answer. Some years ago, when I had an ethics advice column on beliefnet.com, I was asked about this. I responded that if you're collecting money for an organization that is helping people in need, you can end up hurting a lot of needy people if you become too picky about whose money you choose to accept. For example, consider one of America's premier philanthropists, Andrew Carnegie, a man who, a century ago, donated tens of millions of dollars (the equivalent in today's terms of a billion dollars or more) to build libraries and greatly expand universities. Yet Carnegie was also the owner of a steel company whose workers in Homestead, Pennsylvania, had a twelve-hour workday, seven days a week.

Do I regard such an employment policy as immoral? Yes, and it also violated a code most Americans regard as the pillar of ethics, the Ten Commandments, which requires an employer to give those who work for him—and even the animals who work—one day off a week (Exodus 20:10).

Should Carnegie's contributions have been rejected? No, because I believe it was in society's broader interests to allow him to do good. Otherwise, society would place itself in the self-destructive position of permitting a wealthy businessman to do many bad things (as long as he technically violated no law), while refusing to profit from his philanthropy.

What if the money is donated by someone who acquired it illegally?

Some years ago, a major Jewish institution received a $2 million donation from a man who, it was subsequently revealed, had acquired much of his wealth through insider trading (he had bribed employees of companies to reveal confidential information about upcoming mergers). The organization did not return the donation, arguing that it had already spent the money and that it would be difficult, if not impossible, to raise new funds to replace it.

However, it also refused to name its library for the imprisoned man (as it had earlier promised to do), an act with which I concurred. It would be incongruous, to say the least, to name a building for a man whose name had become a byword for stock-market deceit.

Thus, while in theory I believe that organizations should turn down ill-gotten gains, I find that I can't come up with a consistent principle as to what *they should do if they learn, only after the money has been spent, that the donor's wealth was procured, at least in part, illegally.**

—

One final, humorous, thought on this subject. In George Bernard Shaw's play, Major Barbara, *a Salvation Army leader, is accused of being open to accepting money from the devil himself. She answers, "Yes, I would, and I'd be happy to get it out of his hands and into mine."*[12]

—

18

ON GIVING TO BEGGARS AND OTHER POOR PEOPLE

Empathizing with beggars

1. Many of us regard beggars almost as a different category of human beings. For example, we sometimes hear people use the word "bum" interchangeably with "beggar." Yet as early as the sixteenth century, Rabbi Moses Isserles, the Ramah, reminded Jews that vis-à-vis God, we almost all act like beggars: "A person should bear in mind that just as he continually [literally "every hour"] seeks help for his livelihood from God, and as he begs God to listen to his pleading, so too should he listen to the pleadings of the poor" (*Shulchan Arukh, Yoreh Deah* 247:3).

—

The Ramah's teaching applies particularly to those of us who offer personal prayers to God for financial success. Over the years, some friends have confided to me that they frequently pray to God for their stocks to rise. Others have told me that before meeting with potential clients, they pray to God that they be suc-

*Obviously, if all the money was obtained illegally it would constitute stolen goods, and would all have to be returned.

cessful in "growing" their business. In short," begging" is not something unknown to us; it is an aspect of the relationship many of us have with God.

---

*Judaism's insistence that we empathize with, and help, beggars was long repudiated in much of the Western world, even among its most enlightened figures. Plato advocated that begging be outlawed: "No one is to go begging in the state. Anyone who attempts to do so . . . must be expelled from the market . . . and from the surrounding country [and be] conducted . . . across the border . . . so that the land may rid itself completely of such a creature" (*The Laws *11.90).*[1]

In 1572, at about the same time that the Ramah was urging Jews to listen to the pleadings of the poor, the British Parliament enacted a law ruling that all beggars were to be "grievously whipped and burned through the gristle of the right ear." Twenty-five years later, an Act of Parliament stated that someone caught begging was to "be stripped naked from the middle upwards, and openly whipped until his body be bloody."[2]

In eighteenth-century France, beggars were branded with the letter M, *standing for* mendicant, *and were subjected to public flogging and imprisonment under brutal conditions. Of 71,760 vagrants and beggars incarcerated in France prior to 1773, 13,899 died in prison. During this period, the government offered financial rewards for the arrest and prosecution of vagrants and beggars.*[3]

---

2. Rabbi Chiyya advised his wife: "When a poor person comes to the door, give him food so that the same may be done to your [i.e., our] children." She exclaimed, "You are cursing our children [by suggesting that they may become beggars]." But Rabbi Chiyya* replied: "There is a wheel which revolves in this world" (*Shabbat* 151b). The Ramah comments that there is a cyclical pattern of success and failure in the world, and eventually we, our children, or our grandchildren—even if prosperous now—may fall on hard times. If we are merciful to others, we will become worthy of mercy, which will be extended to us and our descendants (*Shulchan Arukh, Yoreh Deah* 247:3).

The decline from affluence to poverty has been the fate of many people not only in talmudic and medieval times, but also in our own age. During the 1930s, the generally highly educated and successful Jewish community of Germany was forced to flee from the Nazis. The novelist Lion Feuchtwanger wrote of "doctors

*Citing a teaching taught in the academy of Rabbi Ishmael.

and lawyers who now sold ties door to door" and of women with university educations who became cleaning ladies. Kate Frankenthal, a prominent physician in Germany, "was reduced to selling ice cream on the streets of New York, hiding her head when she recognized someone she had met at a lecture or medical conference."[4] Many Jews who fled the Arab world in the 1940s and 1950s experienced a similar fate, as did those who emigrated from the former Soviet Union in the 1970s, 1980s, and 1990s. Since many of these people had been financially comfortable, the enduring applicability of Rabbi Chiyya's words becomes apparent.

—

The special mitzvah of giving to beggars

3. Unlike other charitable giving, giving to beggars helps the recipient directly and immediately. The Talmud relates that Abba Chilkiah (first century C.E.) was a great *tzaddik* (saint), whose prayers the community would solicit when in need. Yet his wife's prayers were answered by God even more quickly than his because she stayed at home and so had the opportunity to give bread directly to beggars who came to the house (*Ta'anit* 23b).*

4. As noted (see page 184), we should respond affirmatively and immediately to anyone who says, "I'm hungry. Please give me food or money so that I can eat." Jewish law rules that a charitable organization confronted by such a plea should, likewise, waste no time investigating whether the person is telling the truth or deceiving others. Rather, money or food should be given to the supplicant at once (*Bava Bathra* 9a; see also Maimonides, "Laws of Gifts to the Poor," 7:6).

—

My mother, Helen Telushkin, would always give generously to beggars who said, "I'm hungry." She told me that when she was very hungry, such as on Yom Kippur, she found the pangs so hard to bear that it was impossible for her to ignore the pleas of anyone who claimed to need food.

—

*The Talmud, as Rashi explains, condemns those who build a gatehouse in such a way that homeowners cannot hear beggars calling for help from the street (*Bava Bathra* 7b; cited in Rabbi Dr. Warren Goldstein, *Defending the Human Spirit,* page 367). The Talmud also rules (*Shabbat* 63a–b) that one may not keep a fierce dog on one's property; Rashi explains that one reason is that beggars will be frightened to come to the house.

5. When eating at a restaurant, wrap up the uneaten portions of your meal, and give the food to a beggar whenever possible. If you are willing to do more, that is preferable. The Midrash records that Rabbi Tanchum would buy two portions of meat and of vegetables, "one for the poor, and one for himself" (Ecclesiastes *Rabbah* 7:30). While it is unrealistic to expect most people to do this regularly, why not do it occasionally? For example, ask a beggar what he would like to eat, and buy it for him.

6. Maimonides writes, "Whoever sees a poor person begging and averts his eyes and gives the poor person nothing, has violated a negative prohibition of the Torah, 'Do not harden your heart and shut your hand against your needy kinsman' " (Deuteronomy 15:7; "Laws of Gifts to the Poor" 7:2). It is acceptable, however, to give a beggar a small sum. As the Ramah suggests, "Give him something, if only a fig [that is, a small amount]" (*Shulchan Arukh, Yoreh Deah* 249:4). Rabbi Avrohom Feuer notes that, in modern terms, this would translate into giving, as a minimum, "the smallest coin that can buy some food item at the market."[5]

7. However, in large cities, where we may be confronted by several dozen beggars every day, it is permitted to give to some and not all of them.

The twentieth-century Rabbi Yaakov Yisrael Kanievsky, known as the Steipler, recalled that when he moved as a young man to the large city of Vilna, he asked Rabbi Chaim Ozer Grodzensky, "Since there are so many beggars outside the synagogue, am I obligated to give to each one?"

Rabbi Chaim Ozer told him: "When I lived in a small town before I came to Vilna, I was very scrupulous to greet every person I met in the street cheerfully. But since I came to Vilna, I stopped this practice, because in such a big city, it's impossible to greet everyone. The same applies to tzedaka. *In a big city, you simply cannot [afford to] give to everyone."*[6]

---

8. If you are a well-known individual whose behavior is scrutinized by others, be particularly careful to act generously toward those in need. The Talmud teaches that there was a poor supplicant whom Rabbi Pappa ignored. Another rabbi challenged him: "If you [whose behavior is monitored and observed by others] pay no attention to him, then no one will, and he may starve to death" (*Bava Bathra* 9a).

—

Rabbi Aaron Kotler, the founder and head of the Lakewood Yeshiva in Lakewood, New Jersey, once gave a donation twice to the same beggar, both as he entered and left the synagogue. Rabbi Kotler explained that he was concerned that someone might see him pass the supplicant and not give him anything and would assume that he had reason not to help this particular beggar.

—

9. The talmudic teaching "Poor non-Jews should be supported along with poor Jews" (*Gittin* 61a) mandates that Jews give to non-Jewish beggars as well as Jewish ones. This teaching is particularly relevant in large American cities, where beggars are overwhelmingly (but not exclusively) non-Jews.

—

A follower of the late Rabbi Shlomo Carlebach recalls a Friday night Shabbat dinner at the Carlebach synagogue in Manhattan, when Reb Shlomo brought over to her table a tall, pale young man in rumpled and dirty clothes, and told her, "Please give him as much food as he wants."

The man quickly consumed three large servings of the main course. "Finally, when he appeared satisfied, I looked at his blond hair and blue eyes, and blurted out rather impolitely, 'Are you Jewish?'

" 'No, ma'am,' he replied courteously. 'I'm a Christian from Texas.'

" 'So, how'd you end up at our shul dinner?' I asked.

"His eyes looked upward. 'I was sitting on a bench in Central Park late this afternoon, when your rabbi walked by. I had never met or seen him before, but he took one look at me, turned around, and walked right up to me. With the kindest eyes and sweetest smile, he asked ever so gently: "Brother, do you need a meal?" I started to cry and gratefully told him yes, I desperately did. He gave me the name and address of your synagogue, and told me to come over. He said there was good food and plenty of it. That's how I came to be here tonight. I really don't know what I would have done if your rabbi hadn't come by,' the blond Texan said slowly. 'I'll tell you honestly, this is the first meal I've eaten in three days.' When he walked right up to me and asked, 'Brother, do you need a meal?' I said to myself, "This man here is surely an angel from God" ' " (Yitta Halberstam Mandelbaum).[7]

Whenever we are tempted to walk past a person in need, we must remember that we too have the opportunity to be an "angel of God" in other people's lives.

—

Be generous with your words, not just your money

10. When giving to a beggar, do so in a kindly and gracious manner and, when appropriate, express sympathy for the poor person's plight.

The neighborhood in New York City where my family lives is filled with so many beggars that people often ignore them or put some money in their palms and immediately walk away. Such was the case one day when my wife, Dvorah, was walking with our daughter Naomi, then seven. Dvorah had put a coin in a beggar's hand, but after they had walked a few steps, Naomi said to her: "You didn't do a proper mitzvah."

"What should I have done?" Dvorah asked.

Naomi was prepared with the lesson she had learned at SAR (Salanter Akiva Riverdale Academy), her Jewish day school: "You didn't look the person in the face and say, 'God bless you.' Because when you give tzedaka, *you have to give with a full heart."*

My wife immediately returned and gave the beggar a dollar, looked him in the eye, and said, "God bless you!" Later, she told me, "When I looked him in the eye, I saw a human being, not a beggar."

---

11. In places where you encounter many beggars, the large majority of whom are non-Jews, it is appropriate on Shabbat to explain that Jews do not handle money on that day. In this way, the beggars will know that you are not refusing them personally, but only obeying a Jewish law.

Some people who live in areas where it is permissible to carry on the Sabbath have developed the custom of leaving their homes on Shabbat with small portions of food so that they can give something to beggars. I learned this idea from Emma Goldman, who was ten when she started carrying food from her house on the Sabbath to give to beggars who were hungry.*

---

12. If a beggar, particularly one you have come to know, wishes to speak with you for a few minutes, do so. Be generous with your time, not just with your money.

---

*Jewish law forbids carrying on the Sabbath outside of a private domain; that is, you may carry items inside a private residence, but cannot take them outside. However, the Rabbis created a legal device known as the *eruv,* by which large areas, if enclosed by a series of posts and wires are, in effect, converted to the status of a private domain, and carrying is permitted.

Rabbi Moshe Feinstein, the leading halachic expert of the last half of the twentieth century, was once rushing to an important meeting and had a car waiting for him. Still, as he approached the car, he stopped to speak with a beggar who wanted to share a thought with him. When the rabbi's students tried to wave the man away, Reb Moshe signaled them to stop. Finally, after spending a few minutes in conversation, he shook the beggar's hand, and stepped into the waiting car. When asked why he didn't just give the man a donation and explain that he had no time to talk, Reb Moshe answered: "You must understand that to that man, the conversation means more than money. My mitzvah of tzedaka *included showing him that I cared about what he thinks and that I am not too busy to speak with him."*[8]

Behavior to avoid

13. The Chaffetz Chayyim's son, Rabbi Aryeh Leib, noted that his father took particular care not to hurt the feelings of beggars, even when they said things that could have made him angry.

In other words, unless the beggar's behavior is extremely unpleasant and aggressive (perhaps even threatening), don't look for excuses to withhold assistance. And, try to avoid making hurtful comments, even when you are provoked.*

A man I know shouted at a beggar who kept pressing him for more money. After he read of the behavior of the Chaffetz Chayyim, he sought out the woman and, even though he didn't increase the size of his gift, he apologized to her for shouting.

---

14. Avoid the temptation to reprove beggars for not working: "[If a rich man says to a poor man], 'Why don't you go out and work at a job and get food to eat? . . . Look at those legs! Look at that belly! Look at that brawn!' the Holy One, blessed be He, will then say to the rich man: 'Is it not enough for you that you give him nothing of yours? Must you also begrudge what I gave him?' " (Leviticus *Rabbah* 34:7).

*It is also prudent to avoid speaking sharply to unpleasant beggars. In most cities today, there are beggars who are mentally disturbed, some of whom do not take the medications necessary to keep their illness in check. Thus, confrontations can sometimes lead to violence.

15. Do not look for excuses to avoid helping a beggar. The Chasidic rebbe Shmelke of Nicholsburg (d. 1778) taught: "When a poor man asks you for aid, do not use his faults as an excuse for not helping him. For then God will look for your offenses, and He is sure to find many of them."

In 1949, the New York Times, *which has been running an annual "Neediest Cases" fund-raising campaign since 1919, made the editorial decision to stop distinguishing between the "deserving" and the "undeserving" poor. As the paper explained: "What a bleak world it would be if we helped only those who were thoroughly blameless. A good many of us may make our own bad luck, and we suppose that some of the people represented in the Neediest Cases would not be in trouble now if they had managed their lives differently. It may even be appropriate once in a while, when help is asked, to recall Lord Chesterfield's words: 'Do not refuse your charity, even to those who have no merit but their misery.' "**

Julie Salamon, author of Rambam's Ladder, *cites a man she interviewed, Paolo Alavian, a successful immigrant to the United States who had long regarded beggars with contempt: "Now I realize that not everyone can make it. Now I see he may be young and look like he could work, but when you get close you see he has many problems—drugs, alcohol, disease, and bad habits."*[9] *Realizing that such behavior will always characterize some people might be behind the Bible's belief that "there will never cease to be needy ones in your land" (Deuteronomy 15:11).*

---

16. Rabbi Chayyim Halberstam (1793–1876), the Sanzer rebbe, taught: "Some people act as if they are exempt from giving charity to one hundred beggars in the event that one might be a fraud" (*Darkei Chayyim,* page 137).† In other words, it is wrong to use the fact that some of the people imploring you for money are cheats as a justification for not giving.

---

*Cited in Julie Salamon, *Rambam's Ladder,* pages 75–76. Salamon, in her discussion of this action by the *New York Times,* notes a conservative critique of this position: "The elite once held the poor to the same standards of behavior that it set for itself: moral character determined the strength of a person's claim for assistance. Those who worked and struggled and yet were overwhelmed by adversity deserved help; the idle and dissolute did not. Over time, though, elite opinion came to see the cause of poverty not in individual character and behavior but in vast, impersonal social and economic forces that supposedly determined individual fate. In response, need became the sole criterion for aid, with moral character all but irrelevant" (Heather MacDonald, *The Burden of Bad Ideas*).

†The Rebbe's comment brings to mind a teaching of the Christian theologian and writer C. S. Lewis: "It will not bother me in the hour of death to reflect that I have been 'had for a sucker' by any number of impostors, but it would be a torment to know that one had refused even one person in need."

---

*The anger prompted by unscrupulous beggars can easily become misdirected, as underscored in a story about the eminent nineteenth-century rabbi Yitzchak Elchanan Spektor: "A beggar once came to the city of Kovno and collected a large sum of money from the residents. The people of the town soon found out that he was an impostor; he really was a wealthy man. The city council wanted to make an ordinance prohibiting beggars from coming to Kovno to collect money. When Rabbi Spektor, the rabbi of Kovno, heard about the proposed ordinance, he came to speak before the council. He told them that although he sympathized with them, he had an objection to raise: 'Who deceived you, a needy person or a wealthy person? It was a wealthy person feigning poverty. If you want to make an ordinance, it should be to ban wealthy persons from collecting alms. But why make a ban against needy beggars?' "**

A contemporary Jewish writer, Rabbi Shmuley Boteach, argues that we should give even to beggars we have good reason to think will misuse the money. I am not sure I agree with Rabbi Boteach's conclusion, but I find his argument provocative and worthy of consideration. A number of years ago, Boteach writes, he was on vacation with his family in New Orleans and was approached by a homeless man carrying a brown paper bag in his left hand. Boteach could see a bottle inside the bag. "Hey, man," the beggar said. "Got some change?" Boteach reached into his pocket and gave the man a dollar. As he put it into the man's hand, he said to him, "Listen, please use it for something good." And the man said, "Oh, I will! I will!" And Boteach said to him, "No, seriously, you're way too smart to blow it on booze, you're way too smart to throw your life away. Try to get back on your feet. You know this isn't who you want to be. I can see that you have a gentle heart." And he said, "Thank you, man! Thank you! God bless you!" Boteach returned his blessing and rejoined his family.

His daughter immediately challenged him: "Why did you give him a dollar when you know he's going to spend it on liquor? You are only corrupting him. You know your words aren't going to help him at all."

Rabbi Boteach responded: "I didn't give him a dollar to buy him food or to buy him booze or anything like that. I gave him a dollar because when a man is reduced to asking, he has lost his dignity. None of us, God forbid, should be re-

---

*I came across this, and several other stories and teachings cited in this chapter, in Arthur Kurzweil's compelling and wide-ranging essay, "Brother, Can You Spare a Dime: The Treatment of Beggars According to Jewish Tradition," in Danny Siegel, *Gym Shoes and Irises: Personalized Tzedakah,* pages 103–117. Kurzweil himself found the above story in Irving Bunim, *Ethics from Sinai,* Volume 3, page 121.

duced to asking. There's a Jewish prayer, 'Please help us so that we never have to ask anyone for our daily bread.' I gave that man a dollar to show him that I wouldn't walk by him as if he didn't exist. . . . I wanted him to know that he wasn't invisible and I wanted to acknowledge him as a fellow human being. By giving him a dollar, I bought myself the chance to confer dignity on him. And when people feel dignified, they sometimes shape up their lives—they feel as if they have betrayed their own dignity."

"He's probably buying a drink right now," Boteach's daughter answered.

"It's possible," Boteach answered. "And I can't control that. But I did the best I could. . . . In taking the time to tell him he had value as a man, I was trying to inspire him to change. I spent less than a minute talking to that man, but who knows?"

Boteach was pleased during the coming days of the trip when his children used some of the money he gave them to give to beggars and accompanied their gifts with a request that they not spend the money on alcohol and that they make an effort to get off the streets.[10]

Rabbi Moshe Goldberger offers an alternative view: "The Torah does not say, 'Give money to all poor people.' Rather, the Torah instructs us to give tzedaka, *which means 'righteous charity giving.' Thus, if a drug addict asks for money, we should be careful not to give him cash, which would be enabling him in his wickedness. We may help him get drug rehabilitation instead."*[11] *Since few people are actually going to involve themselves in guiding someone to drug rehabilitation, in a case where one strongly suspects that the money will be used for drugs, one can simply give the person food instead of cash.*

---

17. Rabbi Elazar taught that we should be grateful for the deceivers among the poor because, were it not for them, we would be committing a grave sin every time we ignored the pleas of the poor (*Ketubot* 68a). Indeed, as Rashi suggests in his commentary on this passage, a great sin of such deceivers is that they cause people to distrust many who are in genuine need.

Two final thoughts

18. Rabbi Dr. Warren Goldstein, the chief rabbi of South Africa, reminds us that "beggars bring people into contact with poverty, which is important because an awareness of poverty creates a more compassionate society of people, who see the pain of those in need. When no begging is allowed, the rich are cut off from the poor, and society becomes more polarized and less compassionate."*[12]

The Israeli economist Meir Tamari, a leading expert on Jewish business ethics, notes that during the 1950s, even though religious kibbutzim in Israel (he lived on one) gave charity as they were supposed to and in accordance with Jewish law, "our children [who never saw beggars] had grown up completely unaware of the reality of poverty and suffering, an ignorance that has far-reaching effects on the moral and ethical development of a person."[13]

---

19. If a beggar calls out to you for help, it is wrong to keep walking and pretend that you have not heard her. As Rabbi Shlomo Carlebach taught: "If your ears are not open to the crying of the poor, then your ears are deaf, and you will not hear God calling either."

19

JUDAISM'S MESSAGE TO THE POOR

Responsibilities of the poor

1. Societies function best when we focus on our own responsibilities to others, and not others' responsibilities toward us.† For example, Jewish law mandates that a lender must not harass and humiliate the borrower if he is unable to repay the loan. On the other hand, it is equally emphatic in insisting that the borrower does all that he can to repay his debt. Problems develop when the lender focuses only on the borrower's responsibility to repay the loan, and the borrower focuses only on those laws forbidding the lender

*This is one of the moral dangers of living in a gated community.

†Dr. Isaac Herschkopf comments: "This is also the paradigm of marital therapy. I always tell each spouse not to focus on their partner's faults and how to improve them, but on their own."

from exacting excessive pressure to recover it. Both must honor their own responsibilities.

Similarly, Jewish law, as we have seen, obligates people with assets to help the poor. Yet it simultaneously insists that the poor do all they can to avoid becoming dependent on others.

The Rabbis encourage such behavior through a variety of teachings. They insist that all honest work is respectable and preferable to living on the dole: "Skin an animal's carcass in the marketplace, and earn a wage, and don't say, '[Support me] I am a priest, I am a great man, and such work is unbecoming to me'" (*Pesachim* 113a). The Talmud describes many great sages who earned their living through low-paying physical labor (among them were woodchoppers, water carriers, and blacksmiths), without asking to be supported by the community. As Maimonides summarizes the rabbinic attitude on this subject: "A person should always . . . endure in discomfort rather than become dependent on other people. . . . Even if he was a scholar and a dignitary and he became poor, he should engage in a craft [to support himself]—even a filthy craft, rather than become dependent on people" ("Laws of Gifts to the Poor" 10:18).*

The Talmud also advocates living simply so as to avoid becoming dependent on others: "Make your Sabbath like a weekday [eating plain rather than elaborate meals] and don't ask others for help" (*Pesachim* 113a). In ancient times, people generally ate only two meals, breakfast and dinner, but on the Sabbath, they ate three meals. Rabbi Akiva, however, recommended forgoing this third meal (known as *seuda shlishit*) rather than accepting charity to pay for it (Shabbat 118a).† As Maimonides later taught: "One should always restrain himself and submit to privation rather than be dependent on other people or cast himself upon public charity" ("Laws of Gifts to the Poor" 10:18).

---

*Maimonides' view was uncommon in that he expected religious scholars not only to refrain from accepting charity, but also to refrain from accepting payment even when they were performing religious work (see "Laws of Torah Study" 3:10, "for it is forbidden to derive benefit from the words of Torah in this world"). This strikes me as impractical and unfair. While one should not pursue rabbinical work to amass wealth, a person does have the right to be fairly compensated for his labors. In recent years, Rabbi Moshe Feinstein argued that a refusal to accept payment for rabbinical or teaching work—as Maimonides desired—would lead to people avoiding such jobs, and should be regarded as a ploy by the *yetzer hara* (the evil inclination) to deter people from studying Torah and working in the Jewish community (see *Igrot Moshe, Yoreh Deah,* 2:116).

†If, however, someone is already receiving charity, the charitable fund is instructed to give him enough so that he can have three meals on Shabbat (see Maimonides, "Laws of Shabbat" 30:9). Rabbi Akiva's statement is directed toward those who require charitable assistance only for the third meal; it is better to forgo this meal, Rabbi Akiva believes, than to start taking charity.

2. Don't become accustomed to an unsustainable or unrealistic standard of living. The Talmud tells of an incident in which Rabbi Nechemiah was approached by a man asking for food, who insisted that he generally dined on fatty meat and expensive wine. But since all that the rabbi had was lentils, the beggar consented to join the rabbi for this simple meal. Shortly, thereafter, the beggar died. Rabbi Nechemiah feared that his plain, unadorned diet had helped bring about the man's death, but the Talmud insisted that it was not the rabbi who was to blame: "Rather, the poor man caused his own death because he should not have pampered himself so much" (*Ketubot* 67b).*

Still, some Rabbis seemed to question this commonsense teaching. In support of their position, they cited the experience of Rava, who, like Rabbi Nechemiah, was also approached by a poor man asking for assistance. When Rava asked him what sort of food he generally ate, the man answered in a manner similar to the beggar who approached Rabbi Nechemiah: "Fatted chicken and aged wine." Rava replied, "But are you not concerned about imposing a burden on the community [who has to pay for your expensive tastes]?" The poor man responded, "Do I eat what is theirs? I eat what is God's."† Before Rava could respond to this seemingly self-centered, perhaps arrogant, argument, his sister, whom he had not seen in many years, suddenly arrived, bringing with her a gift of a fatted chicken and old wine. Rava understood his sister's arrival at that moment to be a divine omen in support of the beggar's attitude. He apologized to the man—"I said too much when I criticized you"—and invited him to share the meal (Ketubot *67b*).

---

3. Jewish law reserves high praise, and even the promise of divine reward, for poor people who do everything within their power to avoid taking charity: "One who needs charity and lives in deprivation, and postpones taking it so as not to trouble the community shall not die until he is in a position to provide for others" (*Yoreh Deah* 255:2, based on Mishnah *Peah* 8:9).

4. People are entitled to receive help from others only if they do what they can to help themselves first. Thus, Exodus 23:5 rules that "When you

*In addition, of course, lentils are decidedly healthier than fatty meat and wine.

†Psalm 145:15, on which the beggar was basing himself, suggests that we receive whatever food God intends for us: "The eyes of all look to You expectantly, and You give them their food when it is due."

see the donkey of your enemy lying under its burden and would refrain from raising it, you must nevertheless raise it with him." The obvious implication of the words "with him" is that the animal's owner must work with the passerby to help raise the animal. But, notes Rabbi Avrohom Feuer, "If the owner . . . refuses to do so because he expects the passerby to do it himself because it is a mitzvah, the passerby is excused . . ." (see Mishnah *Bava Mezia* 2:10). Basing himself on this Torah verse, Rabbi Ephraim of Luntshits (1550–1619), known as the Kli Yakar, the name of his Torah commentary, teaches that "we may derive an application of this idea to the poor among our people who impose themselves on the community by refusing to work though they are able. They cry that we do not supply them with their needs, but they are wrong. God did not command us to help them in those situations where they can help themselves."

In short, poor people should not refuse gainful employment they are capable of performing. Only if someone makes efforts to support himself and fails is the community and its members obliged to support him.

5. "Even a poor person who himself survives on charity should give charity" (*Gittin* 7b and *Shulchan Arukh, Yoreh Deah* 248:1). The Rabbis intuit that it is important for the self-image of the poor that they not see themselves just as victims, as "takers" and never "givers." That is why the Talmud asks even those supported by charitable funds to be occasional donors, although it is understood that their contributions will be small. Making such donations has the advantage of reminding the poor that there are those who are even poorer than they and whom they can help, just as they hope that well-off people will help them.

A young man I know, who lives in New York City, suffered severe injuries that left him partially paralyzed. He soon noticed that when he needed to enter a building, homeless beggars often rushed to open the door for him. He came to understand that it is important for people's self-respect to show, and to know, that they can help others.

The Talmud records that in the early days of their marriage, Rabbi Akiva and his wife were so poor that in the winter they slept in a straw storage shed, and he had to pick out straw from her hair. "If only I could afford it," he said to her, "I would adorn you with a golden Jerusalem" (a tiara). [Later] Elijah came to them in the guise of a mortal, and cried out at the door: "Give me some straw, for my wife is in labor and I have nothing for her to lie on." "See," Rabbi Akiva observed to his wife, "there is a man who lacks even straw" (Nedarim *50a*).

—

When accepting charity is obligatory

6. There is a subtle line that distinguishes pride from pridefulness. While the Rabbis esteem the first (praising someone who delays accepting charity for as long as is feasible; see paragraph 3), they criticize those whose excessive pride inhibits them from accepting the help necessary to survive: "He who needs to collect poor offerings [for survival] but doesn't, it is as if he shed [his own] blood" (Jerusalem Talmud, *Peah* 8:8).

There is nothing praiseworthy in refusing to accept help when we have no alternative and, as Maimonides puts it, "by [such] suffering [one] gains nothing but sin and guilt." He also specifies some of the indigent who are most in need of assistance, and the consequences of their not accepting it: "Whoever cannot survive without taking charity, such as an old, sick, or greatly suffering individual, but is too proud and refuses to accept charity is a shedder of blood and is held to account for his own soul . . ." ("Gifts to the Poor" 10:19; Maimonides' point is reiterated in the *Shulchan Arukh, Yoreh Deah* 255:2).

By implication, anyone who is in dire need must accept whatever help is necessary. It is as wrong for a person in need of psychiatric help, for example, to refuse it because of false pride or a sense of shame as it is for a person in need of charity to turn it down.

—

Rabbi Israel Salanter visited a town where many people were anguished and guilt-ridden over the death of a formerly wealthy man who had become impoverished, but who had not made known his need and had died of starvation. The townspeople berated themselves for not having realized the state into which the man had fallen. Rabbi Salanter consoled them: "That man did not die of hunger," he said. "He died of pride."

—

7. A poor person in need of assistance is obligated neither to sell his house* nor the tools of his trade to raise money; rather, he may keep them, and is still permitted to accept charitable aid (Mishnah *Peah* 8:8).

*Obviously, if he owns a house that has great value, he should sell it, buy a less expensive dwelling, and use the profit to help provide for his expenses.

When poverty is temporary

8. If a person runs out of money while on a trip, she is permitted to solicit help from a local Jewish community fund and is not obliged to repay the money since, at the time she received the funds, she was in genuine need (see Mishnah *Peah* 5:4).* Maimonides explains the rationale for this ruling: "To what can this be compared? To a poor person who has become wealthy, and who is not obligated to repay past assistance" ("The Laws of Gifts to the Poor" 9:15). The Talmud, however, records the view of Rabbi Chisda that those who aspire to piety and righteousness will pay back the money (*Chullin* 130b).

Temporary shortages by travelers were probably more common in the ancient world, where there were no traveler's checks, credit cards, or ATMs, and people had in their possession only cash, and perhaps jewels. Nonetheless, the underlying problem, a person finding himself—perhaps for an extended period—without sufficient funds still occurs. A doctor wrote me with the following dilemma:

"I have recently started a fellowship at a top medical center. While the fellowship is highly sought after, the pay is meager. When I complete the fellowship in five years, my salary could easily rise tenfold. However, in the meantime, because of my low salary, my family of three qualifies for food stamps. Given that our current low income is temporary and we're looking at a huge increase in the future, is it right/ethical for me to go on the dole at this time by taking food stamps? Does it make a difference that over the course of my life, I will almost certainly pay a lot more in taxes than I will receive in services?"

I noted that the doctor's circumstance is analogous to the situation described by the Talmud and Maimonides. Just as the fact that the traveler will soon have sufficient funds to support herself doesn't mean that she should refuse assistance now when she needs it, so the prospect that the doctor will make substantial amounts of money in five years doesn't mean that he should forgo assistance for his family, which now needs food. Therefore, if the doctor's salary is small enough to qualify for food stamps, I see no moral reason for him to refrain from taking them (were his income being supplemented by substantial savings or gifts from his or his spouse's family, that would constitute an exception).

In line, however, with Rabbi Chisda's advice—which I find compelling—I noted the following: "I believe that down the road you have a moral, though

---

*It seems to me that if a person runs out of funds because she took too little with her, she would be required to repay. I understand this ruling applying when someone takes a reasonable amount with them and encounters unexpected expenses.

not a legal, obligation to find a way to pay back the value of the food stamps you have received. Why?

"My reasoning is as follows: There is no requirement that you study on this special fellowship. You're already capable as a physician of working and earning enough money so that you need not receive government subsidies. It is only because you have made a personal decision to continue your studies (a decision, I suspect, motivated both by idealism—you want to acquire specialized knowledge that will enable you to help people—and by the desire to make more money in the future) that you have voluntarily put yourself in a deprived circumstance and therefore now need government assistance. This is what distinguishes you from other food-stamp recipients, the large majority of whom did not arrive at that state voluntarily.

"Therefore, I would suggest the following: Keep a basic tab of how much you receive over the coming year or years, and once you embark on your career, make donations in that amount to charitable organizations that provide food directly to people in need. Also, let this whole experience, which I assume from the tone of your letter, you find to be somewhat embarrassing, cause you to have greater compassion for those who are involuntarily poor, and make sure that when you do 'make it,' you treat a certain percentage of your patients who wouldn't otherwise be able to afford your services at very low rates or free of charge."

Regarding welfare cheats and those who pretend to suffer from handicaps and disabilities

9. It is a widespread perception that some of those who claim poverty are fakers and deceivers, and because of this many people ignore all who claim to be poor, including the truly needy. The Rabbis, therefore, felt tremendous anger toward such deceivers, for they provided others with an excuse not to help the truly needy (I have often heard people who ignore beggars say, "They're a bunch of fakers" or "They'll just use my money to buy drugs"). The Rabbis cursed deceivers with the wish that they suffer the dire fate from which they claimed to be suffering: "One who accepts charity but does not need it, in the end will not depart from this world until he truly needs it" (*Ketubot* 68a, reworking Mishnah *Peah* 8:9). Rabbi Akiva expressed this view even more graphically: "He that binds rags on his eyes or his loins and cries, 'Help the blind, help the afflicted,' shall in the end be speaking the truth' " (*The Fathers According to Rabbi Nathan,* chapter 3).

20

REDEEMING CAPTIVES

1. Although people often assume that *pidyon shevuyim* (redeeming captives) is an infrequent mitzvah, restricted, for example, to helping ransom kidnap victims, in the twentieth century alone captivity was the fate of:

- German Jews during the 1930s and 1940s;
- Jews throughout most of Europe during World War II;
- Jews in the Soviet Union who wished to lead committed Jewish lives from the 1920s until the late 1980s;
- Jews in Eastern Europe in the decades following World War II;
- Jews throughout much of the Arab world after Israel's creation in 1948;
- Jews in Ethiopia in the 1980s.

2. The Talmud speaks of redeeming captives as a *mitzvah rabbah,* a great commandment (*Bava Bathra* 8b). The first Jew to do so was Abraham. When he learned that his nephew Lot had been taken prisoner by soldiers who had attacked Sodom (where Lot lived), he mustered all those under his employment and leadership, some 318 people, and went in pursuit of the invaders. That night, Abraham and his troops defeated them in battle, and rescued Lot, along with the women and others who were being held (Genesis 14).

Rabbenu Bachya ben Asher, author of Kad HaKemach, *noted that because of the significance of this commandment, God referred to it in the first of the Ten Commandments, when He declared: "I am the Lord your God Who brought you out of the land of Egypt, the house of bondage" (Exodus 20:2). In Rabbenu Bachya's words, "God did not describe Himself as the One 'who created heaven and earth' because He wanted to mention the commandment to redeem captives—600,000 of them in this case—which is greater than the mighty wonder of Creation."*

---

3. Maimonides rules that "the ransoming of captives has precedence over the feeding and clothing of the poor. Indeed, there is no greater commandment than the ransoming of captives, for not only is the captive included in

the category of the hungry, the thirsty, and the naked, but his very life is in danger" ("Laws of Gifts to the Poor" 8:10).* Specifically because captives' lives are at stake, the *Shulchan Arukh* rules that not only is this a preeminent mitzvah, but that speed is a necessary component in its fulfillment: "Every moment one puts off redeeming captives, where it is possible to do so sooner, is like shedding blood" (*Yoreh Deah* 252:3).

In recent years, a classic example of one who properly fulfilled this mitzvah was Avital Sharansky, the Russian-Jewish activist who spent nine years traveling around the world orchestrating protests and political pressure on behalf of her husband, Anatoly (Natan), who had been imprisoned in the Soviet Union on a false accusation of treason; Sharansky was a committed Jew, whose real "crime" was that he wished to leave Russia for Israel. Shimon Peres—Israeli prime minister at the time of Sharansky's 1986 release—described Avital as a "lioness," who never stopped raising the issue of her husband's imprisonment with government leaders and with Jewish communities throughout the Western world.

---

4. Despite Jewish laws' extraordinary emphasis on the importance of this mitzvah, it is hard to rouse large numbers of people on behalf of those suffering in captivity, particularly when the suffering is occurring at a distance. During World War II, although American Jews knew that terrible things were happening to the Jews of Europe (they were not aware of the full scope of the Holocaust), relatively few of them pressured the U.S. government to take a stronger stance against the Nazi oppressors and to admit more Jewish refugees into the country. In addition, synagogues continued to organize Purim celebrations, people celebrated Bar Mitzvahs with parties, and life went on much as usual. It was perhaps to help motivate Jews to take this commonly ignored mitzvah seriously that Maimonides listed many biblical injunctions violated by those who turn their eyes away from the sufferings of captives:

- "You shall not harden your heart . . ." (Deuteronomy 15:7).
- "Do not stand by while your brother's blood is shed"(Leviticus 19:16).
- "Love your neighbor as yourself" (Leviticus 19:18). We can all imagine that if we were unfairly imprisoned, how much we would want people

---

*Both Maimonides and the *Shulchan Arukh* list the laws concerning redeeming captives within the sections involving the laws of charity.

to speak out, exert pressure, and offer money on our behalf; therefore, this verse obligates us to do the same for others.

- "Save those who are taken for death" (Proverbs 24:11).

—

The poignant significance of refraining from pleasurable activities while others are suffering is reflected in an incident Rabbi Berel Wein recalls about his grandfather, Rabbi Chaim Zvi Rubinstein, of Chicago. During the early 1940s, when Wein would visit his grandparents' house, he could always count on two topics being discussed; the fate of the Jews in Europe and whether the Rubinsteins' modest house would be painted in time for Passover. One year, the elderly, nonaffluent couple had finally managed to save the $250 necessary to have the interior of the house painted, and arrangements had been made for a painter to start the job. But one day in the early spring, Rabbi Rubinstein received a letter from the Vaad Hatzolah, *the Orthodox organization that was trying to save European Jews. The letter reported that the Nazis' anti-Jewish attacks were greatly expanding: Polish and Lithuanian Jews were being herded into work camps, and ghettos in Cracow and Warsaw were being walled in. The young Berel saw his grandfather's hands shake as he read the letter. After putting it down, his grandfather went over to the telephone, and called the painter: "Hello, this is Rabbi Rubinstein. Please don't come to our house. We're not going to paint our house this year. Yes, that's right, that's right. We don't want it painted. Don't you worry about the money, I'll take care of it . . . I'll take care of it." Mrs. Rubinstein was shocked at what she had overheard, but after her husband finished the call, he handed her the letter. After she read it, he said to his wife in Yiddish:* "Ken men machen shein a haus ven yidden in der velt hoben azoi fiil yesurim?" *("Can one make his house fancy when Jews are suffering so much?") When his grandmother expressed concern over the fee which the painter was counting on, her grandfather responded, "We will pay him his $250 as if he did the job, but we're not going to paint this house while Jews are suffering so much."*[1]

—

5. The high priority assigned to ransoming captives in Jewish law is so extraordinary as to make this mitzvah unique in Jewish life. In one characteristic ruling, Maimonides states that we should even take money collected for the building of a synagogue and use it to redeem captives: "Even though they brought the stones [to the building site], cut the beams and shaped them to size, and prepared everything for building, it should all be sold, [but] only for the sake of redeeming captives" ("Laws of Gifts to the Poor" 8:11; if, however, the synagogue has already been built, it should not be sold). The *Shulchan Arukh* rules that even if the money was collected not just for an ordinary synagogue, but to build the Beit HaMikdash, the Great Temple in Jerusalem, it should be used instead to redeem captives (*Yoreh Deah* 252:1).

When women come first

6. Women captives should be redeemed before male captives since, in addition to all their other suffering, women in captivity are subject to rape (see *Horayot* 3:7).*

Restriction on how much to pay to redeem captives

7. Given the high regard the Rabbis had for this commandment, one might have thought they would place no limitations on its fulfillment; rather, the community should pay whatever is necessary to free hostages. However, the high value that Jewish law and the Jewish community place on human life caused the Mishnah (*Gittin* 4:6) to prohibit "overpaying" for a captive: "One does not ransom captives for more than their value because of *tikkun olam*" [literally, "repairing the world"; in other words, as a general precaution]. The Talmud (*Gittin* 45a) offers two explanations for this:

- "So that they (the kidnappers) should not seize more captives." Thus, if it became known that Jews paid higher ransoms than other groups to free its members, kidnappers and brigands would target them. In Maimonides' words: "We do not redeem captives for more than their worth . . .† so that enemies will not pursue people to hold them captive" ("Laws of Gifts to the Poor" 8:12).
- "Because of the financial burden on the community"; that is, if we don't limit the size of the payments, the community might become impoverished.‡

---

*In instances in which male captives are also being raped, the Rabbis ruled that men should be ransomed first since they regarded homosexual rape as even more horrific than heterosexual rape (see *Horayot* 3:7; see also Maimonides, "Laws of Gifts to the Poor" 8:15).

†How can one establish the worth of a human being given that the Talmud also teaches that each life is of infinite value (Mishnah *Sanhedrin* 4:5)? The Rabbis devised a pragmatic formula, one that is unusable in the modern world; they evaluated the value of a life based on the prices paid for servants sold at a slave market (see Meiri on *Gittin* 45a).

‡Rabbi David Golinkin offers several examples drawn from Jewish history in which this Mishnaic ruling was ignored or circumvented. Thus, the records of the Cairo Genizah reveal that

---

*These differing explanations for why "overpaying" for a captive is forbidden have significant, and sometimes differing, legal implications. If overpayment is forbidden because it can lead to Jews being targeted by kidnappers, then it should always be forbidden. But if it is forbidden because it will impoverish the community, then it should be permitted for an individual willing to use his own resources. For example, the Talmud (*Gittin *45a) records the case of Levi ben Darga, who ransomed his daughter for thirteen thousand golden dinars, and the Sages did not stop him. This incident seems to support the conclusion that overpayment is forbidden because it can impoverish the community, although a later rabbi, Abaye, says that Levi ben Darga may have acted against the desire of the Sages. In any case, the restriction on not redeeming captives "for more than their worth" does not apply to oneself and one's spouse since husband and wife are considered as one (I would assume that most people think like Levi ben Darga, that it should also apply to one's children).*

---

*Rabbi Meir of Rothenburg, Germany (1215–1293), was taken hostage by Emperor Rudolf I in order to force Jews to pay discriminatory taxes that would have branded them as "serfs of the treasury" (*servi camerae*). When these taxes were first imposed, Rabbi Meir, along with thousands of other Jews, tried to flee Germany, but when a Jewish apostate informed on him, the rabbi was arrested.*

Because of Rabbi Meir's prominence and the esteem in which he was held, Germany's Jews offered to pay the Emperor twenty-three thousand pounds of silver, stipulating that it was a ransom they were paying, and not a tax. Rudolf I refused, hoping to use the Jews' devotion to Rabbi Meir to force them to agree to the tax and thereby accept their status as the Emperor's [fiscal] slaves. However, Rabbi Meir insisted that the Jews not pay any sum to redeem him and remained in prison until his death seven years later. Even then, the spiteful Rudolf I would*

---

although the normal price for a captive was 33⅓ dinars, Jews would pay as much as 100 dinars to ransom a person (Shlomo Dov Goitein, *A Mediterranean Society,* Volume 1, page 329). Several centuries later, Rabbi David ibn Zimra (Radbaz) of Egypt (fifteenth century) notes in his responsa (Volume 1, number 40) that Jews would sometimes pay well above the common rate to redeem captives. He justifies such "overpayment" with various arguments, such as that among the group of captives one might be a sage or the danger that if a captive, particularly a child, is not redeemed, he will be forced to convert. In the sixteenth century, Rabbi Shlomo Luria (in his talmudic commentary *Yam Shel Shlomo,* on *Gittin* 4:6) notes that the Jews of Turkey redeemed captives for excessive prices "since they are willing to overlook the financial burden on the community." Golinkin concludes that despite the clear Mishnah ruling, "in practice, many talmudic Sages and medieval rabbis found ways to circumvent this Mishnah by interpretation or by creating exceptions to the rule" (*Insight Israel: Second Series,* pages 187–188).

*Such status would have enabled the emperor to tax the Jews over and above the taxes they already were paying to local rulers (see *Encyclopaedia Judaica,* 1971 edition, Volume 11, page 1252).

not allow Rabbi Meir's body to be released for burial. Fourteen years later, in 1307, a member of the Jewish community, Alexander Wimpfen, ransomed Rabbi Meir's remains, and buried him in Worms, Germany.[2]

When dealing with terrorists

8. Despite the incident involving Levi ben Darga's daughter (see page 253), the view that overpayment is forbidden lest it lead to more Jews being endangered has generally influenced rabbinic responses to recent demands made by terrorists. Thus, most rabbis who have written on the subject oppose giving in to such demands, even if refusal to do so may lead to the hostages' deaths. As one modern rabbinic scholar concludes: "The few are to be placed in jeopardy for the sake of the many who would otherwise find themselves in the same position. Such a decision runs counter to all natural feelings of compassion, but experience has shown that this is the only way to defeat terrorism" (Louis Jacobs).[3] A contemporary Jewish scholar and ethicist, Professor Baruch Brody, similarly understands the talmudic prohibition of high ransoms to mean that at least some Rabbis were willing to allow "the current captives to die so that more will live in the future" (because more captives will not be seized).[4]

In recent rabbinic writings, overpayment to secure the release of hostages is understood not only as referring to monetary payment. Thus, contemporary terrorists often take hostages to secure the release of imprisoned terrorists. In one well-known instance, the Israeli government released some 1,150 convicted Palestinian terrorists in return for three captured Israeli soldiers. In an essay entitled "Ransoming Captives and Freeing Murderers," Rabbi Yehudah Levi commented: "Presumably, a POW ratio of a few hundred to one is excessive."*[5]

An opposing view

A strong dissent to the above arguments was registered in Israel by Rabbi Haim David Halevy, the Sephardic chief rabbi of Tel Aviv, and the author of

---

*While such an exchange will, of course, not impoverish the community economically, it nonetheless puts it at peril. Released terrorists are likely to return to terrorism. Thus, freeing murderers—particularly unrepentant murderers—is likely to lead to more murders. Rabbi Avraham Kilav notes the additional danger that "other terrorists will be emboldened by the knowledge that, if caught, they will soon be freed through an exchange" (Rabbi Avraham Kilav, "Releasing Terrorists," in *Crossroads: Halacha and the Modern World,* page 210).

Asei Lecha Rav, a multivolume set of legal responsa. Rabbi Halevy argued that it was right and appropriate for Israel to pay an exorbitant ransom for the return of soldiers. He acknowledged that earlier Jewish writings and responsa might well have forbidden such behavior. But, he argued, past legal precedents cannot necessarily serve as correct answers to new dilemmas since those responsa dealt with very different circumstances from the ones confronting Israel today. Thus, the earlier rulings forbidding such behavior were based on the Jewish community's dealings with bandits or gangs of bandits who kidnapped Jews and who would indeed respond to excessive payments by targeting Jews as future victims. Even then, Halevy noted, Jewish law would sometimes justify paying above "market rate" in unusual situations, such as in the case of children and sages, a precedent that could certainly apply to soldiers. In Halevy's view, a Jewish state confronted by warring enemies has to take into account issues that would never have been considered before, such as how its actions will affect soldiers' behavior. Knowing that their government will do anything to free them raises soldiers' morale and causes them to fight with greater courage and daring. However, if soldiers conclude that the government will not "overpay" to win their release, their main concern might well become not being captured, and this could have a catastrophic impact on how they fight (*Asei Lecha Rav,* Volume 7, question 53).[6]

Is it permitted to pay excessive ransom when it is a matter of life and death? Two views

9. Some rabbinical scholars maintain that when a captive's life is in danger or the captive is of special significance to the Jewish community, it is permissible to pay a ransom that would normally be regarded as excessive. In defense of this position, the medieval Talmud commentary *Tosafot* cites an incident involving Rabbi Joshua ben Chananiah in the years following the failed first-century Jewish revolt against Rome. At the war's end, many Jews were taken captive and, while visiting Rome, Rabbi Joshua heard talk about a child of exceptional abilities who was being held prisoner. Rabbi Joshua went and stood outside the prison near where the boy was held, and called out a verse from the Bible, to which the boy responded with an appropriate verse. The rabbi was deeply moved and impressed: "I am certain that this boy will be a great teacher in Israel. And I swear by the Temple service that I will not budge from here until I have redeemed him for whatever price they demand." The rabbi did indeed pay a hefty ransom and secured the boy's release, and he grew up to become the great sage, Rabbi Ishmael ben Elisha (*Gittin* 58a).

Tosafot comments that in instances when life is at risk or the captive has an exceptional intellect, the prohibition of paying an excessive ransom may be suspended (see the *Tosafot* commentary on *Gittin* 58a).*

Nachmanides (Ramban) argues that suspending this prohibition because of a threat to life is illogical since danger to life is inherent in every captivity. Because all instances of captivity can lead to death, *Tosafot*'s reasoning would end up justifying paying excessive ransom in almost every case. Therefore, Nachmanides rules that the prohibition against overpaying should apply even to instances when there is a clear and present danger to life (see his commentary on *Gittin* 45a).

It seems to me that Nachmanides' reasoning would serve to support the Israeli government's general refusal to give in to terrorists' demands (except, as noted, in some cases involving captured Israeli soldiers), even in instances when the terrorists are threatening to murder captives. The fear is that capitulation in such cases, though it might well save the captives' lives, will encourage terrorists to kidnap more victims. In the most famous instance, when Arab terrorists held Israeli prisoners in Entebbe, Uganda (in July 1976), and demanded that Israel release Arab terrorists from Israeli prisons, the Israelis pretended to negotiate with the terrorists, but then invaded the airport and rescued the hostages.†

---

*The *Shulchan Arukh* (*Yoreh Deah* 252:4) rules that in the case of a great scholar, or one who shows prospects of becoming a great scholar or leader *(adam gadol),* the community should redeem the person at any cost.

†Normally, we associate the "redeeming of captives" with ransom payments, but Israel's military action at Entebbe is reminiscent of Abraham's earlier act of *pidyon shevuyim* (see paragraph 2).

II

Jews and Non-Jews

Non-Jews and Jewish Law

The essence of neighborly love consists in loving all mankind, of whatever people and whatever tongue, by virtue of their identical humanity.

Rabbi Pinchas Eliyahu Hurwitz of Vilna (eighteenth century), *Sefer Ha-Brit*

21

BETWEEN JEWS AND NON-JEWS

Jewish law, non-Jews, and the impact of history

1. Summarizing Judaism's and Jewish law's attitude toward non-Jews would seem to be a straightforward matter: simply find and list the relevant verses and laws in the Bible, Talmud, and codes of Jewish law. However, one would soon find that these citations are sometimes contradictory and often misleading. They include profoundly moving verses and laws, such as the biblical command to love the stranger as yourself (see paragraph 6), alongside hostile teachings that would allow a Jew to take advantage of a business error made by a non-Jew.

These seeming contradictions occur because there is no one answer to the question "What is Judaism's attitude toward non-Jews?" any more than there is one answer to the question "What is America's attitude toward other countries?" The accurate, but complicated, response to that question is "friendly to some, hostile to others, and neutral to yet others." Indeed, it would be odd to expect America's attitude toward allies such as Canada and England to be the same as its attitude toward present-day Iran, whose government routinely organizes demonstrations at which protesters shout, "Death to America." Furthermore, Americans' attitudes toward even the same countries shift in response to differing historical circumstances. Anyone reading U.S. newspapers and magazines published between 1942 and 1945, while World War II was raging, would find tremendous hostility to Japan and Germany. Someone reading the same newspapers and magazines today finds far friendlier attitudes toward these two countries. In the same way, Judaism's and the Jewish people's attitudes toward the same religion may change, and for the same reason. The Crusaders Jews encountered in medieval Europe organized antisemitic attacks, during which Jews were offered the choice of conversion to Christianity or death. The Christians whom Jews encounter in the United States today are, by and large, friendly people who are happy to share the blessings of America with their Jewish neighbors. Common sense dictates that Jews, and Jewish law, would and should react differently to these two different types of non-Jews, even though both identify themselves as Christians.

Therefore, in dealing with Judaism's attitude toward non-Jews, we must take historical circumstances into account. This has not generally been the case with other subjects discussed in this book. The regulations concerning visiting the sick and comforting mourners, for example, were first laid down thousands of years ago and have remained essentially unchanged. However, laws concerning Judaism's attitude toward non-Jews are flexible because different attitudes and behavior by non-Jews toward Jews call forth different responses.

The value of all human life in the Bible

2. The Torah begins with the creation of the world and the story of Adam and Eve, the first two human beings. The couple are, of course, not Jews, since the Israelite religion did not come into existence until the time of Abraham, thousands of years later.

The most important thing the Bible tells us about Adam and Eve is that, unlike all the beings created before them, they were fashioned in the "image of God." (Genesis 1:26). This means three things:

- Human beings are like God in the sense that they know good from evil.
- Humans have the freedom (which animals do not) to choose good.
- Because people are created in God's image, all human life has special value.

Professor Michael Wyschogrod, a contemporary philosopher and an Orthodox Jew, believes that "the basic solidarity of Jews and Gentiles is rooted in the creation of man in the image of God, perhaps the single most powerful statement of the Hebrew Bible. This statement is made about Adam before [God's] election of Abraham. The Bible could have reserved this statement for Abraham and his descendants. But it did not do so. Instead, it made the statement about Adam and therefore about all of humanity, Jew and Gentile. . . ."

For more on the creation of human beings in God's image, and its significance for Jewish-Gentile relations, see pages 286–287.

3. From the Torah's teaching that God originally populated the world with only one person, Adam, the Rabbis of the Mishnah drew several conclusions, all of which apply to Jews and non-Jews alike.[1]

- *Human life has infinite value.* The Rabbis reasoned that if Adam had been killed, all humanity would have been destroyed; and if he were saved, the entire world would also be saved. Therefore, the Mishnah concludes that each human being is as valuable as the whole world: "Whoever destroys one life is considered by the Torah as if he destroyed an entire world, and whoever saves one life is considered by the Torah as if he saved an entire world" (Mishnah *Sanhedrin* 4:5).*

- *No one can claim to be better than another because of more distinguished ancestry.* "Only one person was originally created [for the sake of peace among human beings], so that a person should not say to his fellow, 'My father is greater than your father' " (Mishnah *Sanhedrin* 4:5). Because we are all descended from the same man, we are all related. It is significant that the rise of racist ideologies in nineteenth-century Europe was based on the repudiation of the biblical account of creation and the theory that races have separate origins without a common ancestor.

- *Each individual is unique.* Adam's singular creation "proclaims the greatness of the Holy One, praised be He. If a human being stamps several coins with the same die, they all look exactly the same. But the King of kings, the Holy One, praised be He, stamped all human beings with the die of the first man; and yet not one of them is identical with another" (Mishnah *Sanhedrin* 4:5).†

In many editions of the Mishnah, the rabbinic teaching cited above has been altered to read, "Whoever destroys one Jewish life is considered by the Torah as if he had destroyed an entire world, and whoever saves one Jewish life is considered by the Torah as if he had saved an entire world." In addition to being morally disturbing by suggesting that only Jewish lives have infinite value, this teaching

*The Jewish thinker who has most consistently taught the implications of this Mishnah (and translated it into the American idiom) with its emphasis on the infinite, and equal, value of all human life is Rabbi Irving (Yitz) Greenberg; see Shalom Freedman, *Living in the Image of God: Jewish Teachings to Perfect the World: Conversations with Rabbi Irving Greenberg,* chapter 2.

†Unfortunately, perhaps the best-known proofs of the distinctive "stamp" of every individual are primarily associated with criminologists, who have long known that each human being has distinctive fingerprints and now know that each also has distinctive genetic imprints.

makes no sense, since the proof of the infinite value of human life derives from Adam, who was not a Jew.

---

4. In the generations following Adam and Eve, the major biblical figure is Noah, whom the Torah describes as a righteous man (*tzaddik*) in a highly immoral world (Genesis 6:9–12). God resolves to flood the world, and to start over with Noah and his descendants. After the deluge, the Bible teaches that all humankind, Israelites and non-Israelites alike, are descended from Noah and his wife. One of their descendants is Abraham, the first patriarch of the Jewish people; Jews have long since spoken of themselves as the "children of Abraham."* Later Jewish legal sources refer to non-Jews as "children of Noah" (*b'nai noach*), a designation that is obviously complimentary, given the Torah's high regard for Noah.

Non-Israelite figures in the Torah

5. Because the Torah is the Jewish people's foundational and holiest document, many people assume that it favors Israelites, and that it portrays non-Israelites negatively. In fact, the Torah's depiction of Gentiles varies, as does its depiction of Israelites. Thus, two of Jacob's sons, Judah and Joseph, are shown to be heroic and virtuous, but two others, Levi and Shimon, are portrayed as men of violence who are denounced by their own father (Genesis 49:5–7). Moses is the greatest hero of the last four books of the Bible and of Jewish history, but Korach, a Levite from his tribe, is described as a power-hungry demagogue, and God arranges for him and 250 of his followers to be swallowed alive by the earth (Numbers 16). And, although the Israelites as a people are treasured as the children of the Patriarchs, God becomes so disgusted by their whining, ingratitude, and cowardice in the desert—even though they had seen the miracles God had performed in Egypt and during the Exodus—that He arranges for them all (except for Joshua and Caleb) to die before they have the opportunity to enter Canaan (Numbers 14:26–35).

The Bible also presents non-Israelites as both heroes and villains. As noted, the Torah describes Noah as a *tzaddik,* a righteous person, the only person in the Torah so designated. Melchizedek, the king of Salem and a contemporary of Abraham, is described as a priest of God Most High, and

*Though logically, Jews, like all human beings, can also be described as "children of Noah."

his blessing of Abraham is recorded in the biblical text (Genesis 14:18–19). In a later episode in Genesis, Tamar, Judah's Canaanite daughter-in-law, teaches her father-in-law a lesson in ethics,* and Judah is forced to acknowledge that "she is more righteous than I" (Genesis 38:26). Jethro, Moses' Midianite father-in-law and a member of the Kenite tribe, is characterized not only as a righteous person, but also a wise one. He is credited with teaching Moses how to delegate responsibility, and how to select able men to make decisions in minor disputes, thereby freeing the Israelite leader from the wearying task of adjudicating every conflict. The Bible makes it clear that the system of justice established in the desert is the legacy of Jethro (Exodus 18:13–26).† The biblical commentary known as the *Or HaChayyim* concludes concerning the episode with Jethro: "It seems to me that God wanted to show the Jews of that generation and all future generations that there are men of great understanding and intelligence among all the nations of the world" (see the commentary on Exodus 18:21).

Among the non-Israelite villains, the most despicable from the Bible's perspective are the fighters of the nomadic tribe of Amalek, who attack the Israelites in the desert when they are famished and weary; the Torah notes that they focused their attack on the most vulnerable Israelites, the stragglers (presumably meaning the weak and the sick). The Israelites are instructed to "remember what Amalek did to you . . . Therefore . . . you shall blot out the memory of Amalek from under heaven. Do not forget" (Deuteronomy 25:17–19).

Israel's animus for Amalek, prompted by this attack, was not one-sided, nor was Amalek's hatred for Israel limited to the generation of the Exodus. Centuries later, Haman, a descendant of Amalek's King Agag (Esther 3:1), tried to murder all the Jews in the Persian Empire. The Bible roots Amalek's evil in its lack of fear of God (Deuteronomy 25:18).‡

---

*This profoundly moving story does not lend itself to a brief summation; see Genesis 38.

†To this day, a Hebrew expression that is associated with Orthodox Jews is *Baruch Hashem* ("Blessed is the Lord"). Thus, when one asks an Orthodox Jew how he or she is doing, the person often will answer, *"Baruch Hashem"* (which is intended to convey that everything is as God wills). Yet few Jews realize that this expression, which comes from the Torah, is used there exclusively by non-Israelites. Perhaps its most well-known usage is by Jethro who, when he hears Moses tell about the miraculous escape of the Israelites from Egyptian slavery, comments: "*Baruch Hashem* who delivered you from the Egyptians and from Pharaoh . . ." (Exodus 18:10). Earlier in the Torah, Noah uses this expression as well (Genesis 9:26), as does Abraham's servant (assumed to be Eliezer; Genesis 24:27). In Genesis 14:20, the non-Israelite King Melchizedek uses a variant of this expression.

‡Regarding the relationship between the lack of fear of God and grossly immoral behavior, see *A Code of Jewish Ethics, Volume 1, You Shall Be Holy,* pages 487–491.

The most famous non-Israelite villain in the Torah is the unnamed Pharaoh of Egypt, who launches a campaign to drown all male Israelite infants at birth (Exodus 1:22). Yet the Bible does not want the Israelites to hate all Egyptians. Indeed, one of its commandments states, "You shall not abhor an Egyptian, for you were a stranger in his land" (Deuteronomy 23:8). As a reminder to Israelites not to let their antagonism toward Pharaoh escalate into dislike of all Egyptians, the Bible teaches that the infant Moses was saved by the daughter of the very Pharaoh who issued the order to kill the Hebrew babies. There is perhaps no stronger repudiation of racism in the Bible than this (see also paragraph 9); the man who tried to destroy the Israelites was thwarted in his plan by his own daughter. Pharaoh was evil, but his daughter was righteous.

Another non-Israelite villain in the Torah is the prophet Balaam, who is hired by Balak, Moab's king, to curse the Israelites in the hope that "perhaps I can thus defeat them, and drive them out of the land" (Numbers 22:6). The Bible depicts Balaam as having genuine prophetic ability and, like Moses, of being in personal contact with God. Though King Balak is willing to pay him well to curse the Israelites, Balaam, inspired by God, praises and blesses them instead: "How fair are your tents, O Jacob, Your dwellings, O Israel. . . . Blessed are they who bless you, accursed they who curse you" (Numbers 24:5, 9).

Why then is Balaam regarded as a villain? Because of an incident that happens a short time later. Perhaps to win back the favor of the highly irritated Balak, Balaam advises the Midianites to send out attractive women to seduce the Israelite men and lure them away from their attachment to God (see Numbers 31:16 and 25:1–3). Ever since, he has been regarded as an exemplar of someone blessed by God with great gifts, which he uses to oppose God's will instead of supporting it.

And, of course, the Torah expresses great antagonism toward the Canaanite nations, including a call to destroy their idolatrous temples, and either eject them from the land of Israel* or destroy them. People commonly assume that the Bible's position on idolatry is solely due to its theological error in positing many gods instead of one. But a close reading of the texts

*The Bible clearly wanted to preserve the highest standard of monotheistic religion in Israel in the same way that Muslims expect Islam to be observed more strictly in the holy city of Mecca, and Catholics expect Catholicism to be practiced more purely in the Vatican. In addition, the Bible warned that if the Canaanites remained in the land they would influence many Israelites to practice idolatry. They did indeed remain in the land and influenced the ancient Hebrews to follow them (see, for example, Judges 2:11–13; II Kings 21:6 records that King Manasseh, deeply influenced by local idolatry, even sacrificed one of his sons).

shows this to be false; the Bible's opposition was primarily directed against the immorality sanctioned by Canaanite idolatry. One looks in vain for passages in the Torah mocking the multiplicity of gods worshipped by the ancient Canaanites.* What one finds instead is abhorrence at Canaanite practices such as child sacrifice (Deuteronomy 12:31) and bestiality (see Leviticus 18:23–24), along with fear that, if the Canaanites remain in the land, "they [will] lead you into doing all the abhorrent things that they have done for their gods . . ." (Deuteronomy 20:18). When committed by non-Israelites, the theological error of idolatry, as opposed to its moral misbehavior, was not particularly troublesome to the Torah. Thus, Moses, in his farewell address, warns the Israelites against being lured into worshipping the sun, the moon, or the stars, but then says: "These the Lord your God allotted to other peoples everywhere under the heaven" (Deuteronomy 4:19).† The clear implication is that while Israel must worship God alone, the Lord was not troubled—at that point in time—by *other* nations worshipping His creations, such as the sun.‡ What God does not condone for Israelites and non-Israelites alike is immorality and cruelty.

The prophets reinforced the Torah's view of idolatry. While they, like the Torah, do not generally criticize the non-Israelite nations for worshipping other gods, they condemn them for acts of cruelty. Thus, the citizens of Edom might have been idolaters, but what really incensed the prophet Amos is that they pursued their adversaries with the sword "and repressed all pity"

---

*Passages ridiculing idolatrous beliefs do appear in later books of the Bible. For example, the psalmist mocks the passivity of the idolater's gods: "They have mouths, but cannot speak, eyes, but cannot see; they have ears, but cannot hear, noses, but cannot smell . . . Those who fashion them, all who trust in them, shall become like them" (Psalms 115:5–6,8). The most famous midrashic story about Abraham, one that is familiar to almost all Jews who have attended Jewish schools, makes fun of the passivity of the idols. Thus, the Midrash relates that Terach, Abraham's father, owned an idol store. One day, he left his son in charge. The young Abraham, already a believer in the One God, smashed all the idols but the largest, and then put an ax in the hands of the remaining idol. When his father returned, and saw the carnage in the store, he asked his son what had happened. Abraham explained that the largest idol had gotten into a fight with the smaller idols, and had picked up the ax and destroyed them. The outraged Terach yelled at his son, "Stop lying to me! You know that these idols can't walk or talk or move." Abraham responded with great logic: "If they can't protect themselves, then why do you pray to them to protect you?" (There are several versions of this Midrash; see, for example, Genesis *Rabbah* 38:13, and also Hayim Nahman Bialik and Yehoshua Hana Ravnitzky, *The Book of Legends* [a translation of *Sefer Aggadah*], pages 32–33). In this Midrash, the attack on idolatry, unlike that in the Torah, is on idolatry's foolishness, not its immorality.

†The prophet Micah comments in a similarly nonjudgmental fashion: "Though all peoples walk each in the name of its gods, we will walk in the name of the Lord our God forever and ever" (4:5).

‡The word for "sun" in Hebrew, *shemesh,* is related to the word *shamash* (to serve), implying that the sun, which others worship as a god, is simply a servant of God.

(Amos 1:11). Similarly the nearby state of Ammon is denounced for ripping "open the pregnant women of Gilead, in order to enlarge their own territory" (1:13). The same is true of Amos's critique of the ancient kingdoms of Damascus, Gaza, Tyre, and Moab (chapters 1 and 2).

In the case of the Israelites, the prophets denounce idolatry (along with immorality) and condemn it as a betrayal of God and a violation of the covenant between God and the Israelite people. God chose Israel to make known His existence to the world, and to make known that God's primary demand of human beings is ethical behavior (see Genesis 18:19). Indeed, in Amos's understanding, even chosenness, which many people assume correlates with an Israelite sense of superiority, does not entitle Israel to special rights, but rather special responsibilities: "You alone have I singled out of all the families of the earth. That is why I will call you to account for all your sins" (Amos 3:2).

The special status of the stranger (ger) *in the Torah*

6. Among the Torah's 613 commandments, three command love. Two are among the Bible's most famous laws: "And you shall love the Lord your God" (Deuteronomy 6:5) and "You shall love your neighbor as yourself" (Leviticus 19:18). The third is far less known: "The stranger [*ger;* that is, the non-Jew] who resides with you shall be as one of your citizens; you shall love him as yourself" (Leviticus 19:34). This commandment exhorts Jews to love non-Jews who live among them in peace.* Unlike the English word "stranger," which is etymologically related to "strange" and thus has a somewhat

*Later, during the time of the Talmud, *ger* came to mean, and still does, a convert to Judaism, and many Jews therefore assume that the loving legislation in the Torah concerning the *ger* refers to converts to Judaism. But the context in which the Bible commands the fair and loving treatment of a *ger*—often followed with the phrase "for you were strangers *(gerim)* in the land of Egypt" (see, for example, Leviticus 19:33–34)—makes it clear that the reference is to equitable treatment of non-Israelites residing among Israelites. Otherwise, the verse's only possible meaning would be, "and you shall love the convert for you were converts in the land of Egypt," which suggests that the Israelites in Egypt had embraced the idolatrous religion of their masters. Rather, what the Torah was telling the Israelites is, in effect: "Treat the stranger well, for you were strangers in Egypt, and understand how hard it is to be a stranger, because you know from your own experience how badly you were treated." This recurring biblical teaching, "for you were strangers in the land of Egypt" (see also Exodus 22:20, Exodus 23:9, Deuteronomy 10:19; see page 287) seems to serve as an early adumbration of Hillel's first-century B.C.E. summary of Judaism's essence: "What is hateful to you, do not do to your neighbor" (*Shabbat* 31a; see *A Code of Jewish Ethics, Volume 1: You Shall Be Holy,* pages 10–11).

pejorative connotation, *ger* derives from a root meaning "to dwell among," and has a positive connotation more suggestive of resident. In addition to commanding the Israelites to love the stranger, God later and explicitly identifies Himself as One who "loves the stranger" (*ve-ohev ger;* Deuteronomy 10:18): "Martin Buber . . . noted that there is no other case of a class or persons with whom God is identified as their lover."[2]

7. Biblical laws that mandate that strangers be treated justly are a characteristic and recurring feature of Torah legislation: "You shall not wrong a stranger or oppress him . . ." (Exodus 22:20), and later ". . . Hear out your fellow man and decide justly between any man and a fellow Israelite or a stranger" (Deuteronomy 1:16), and the previously cited, "The stranger who resides with you shall be as one of your citizens . . ." (Leviticus 19:34). Throughout history, strangers in societies all over the world often have been denied basic rights and discriminated against. In contrast, the Torah insists, "There shall be one law for you and for the stranger who lives among you" (Exodus 12:49, see also Numbers 15:15). To this day, this ancient biblical injunction represents the cornerstone of a just society.

The German-Jewish philosopher Hermann Cohen (1842–1918) believed that the biblical commandments protecting the stranger represented the beginning of a universal religious ethic: "The stranger was to be protected, although he was not a member of one's family, clan, religion, community, or people, simply because he was a human being. In the stranger, therefore, man discovered the idea of humanity."

God's love for all humankind

8. The Bible repeatedly emphasizes that God's love is for humanity, all of whom—particularly when they act righteously—are precious in His eyes. When the prophet Jonah is angered that God has chosen to forgive the penitent pagans of the city of Nineveh, Assyria (a historic enemy of Israel), the Lord mocks his exaggerated distress over the death of a plant to which he was attached, and responds: "You cared about the plant . . . which appeared overnight. . . . And should I not care about Nineveh, that great city, in which there are more than a hundred and twenty thousand persons who do not yet know their right hand from their left [that is, children] . . ." (4:10–11). The story of Nineveh is also significant because this non-Israelite city becomes a

model from which the people of Israel are expected to learn how to repent. To this day, the story of Nineveh's repentance is part of the Yom Kippur service.

9. In what may well have been the first explicit repudiation of racism in any literature, the prophet Amos tells the Israelites: " 'To me, O Israelites, you are just like the Ethiopians,' declares the Lord" (9:7). Given that racism has existed for thousands of years, it is probably not by chance that Amos compares Israel to Ethiopia. We can picture the crowds at the Israelite temple in Bethel murmuring among themselves: "Imagine comparing us to a group of Ethiopians, saying that God loves them as much as He loves us." But, of course, that is exactly what Amos is declaring: God loves all human beings equally since they are all created in His image.

10. The prophet Isaiah likewise makes clear God's love for all the people He has created. Prophesying a more peaceful world in the future, he declares: "In that day, there shall be a highway from Egypt to Assyria. . . . In that day, Israel shall be a third partner with Egypt and Assyria as a blessing on earth; for the Lord of Hosts will bless them, saying, 'Blessed be my people Egypt, my handiwork Assyria and my very own Israel' " (19:23–25).

Non-Jews in the Talmud and the codes of Jewish law

11. There are various rulings on non-Jews in the Talmud, including some that are discriminatory. However, even among the most hostile rabbinic figures, we find certain standards of behavior that are binding upon all Jews: It is always forbidden to steal from or deceive anyone, even an idolater (*Bava Kamma* 113b, *Chullin* 94a).*

Indeed, the Rabbis teach that "stealing from a non-Jew is worse than stealing from a Jew because of the profanation of God's name" (*Tosefta Bava Kamma* 10:15). When a Jew is found to have acted dishonestly toward another Jew, he brings contempt upon himself. But when a Jew acts dishonestly toward a non-Jew, he runs the risk of causing others to view Jews and Judaism with contempt; this makes such behavior even more reprehensible.

The following story, in its insistence that God punishes even adult children for their parents' sins, is troublesome, but also reflects the belief of at least one

*A Jew who acts dishonestly is regarded as "abhorrent to the Lord your God" (Deuteronomy 25:16). For example, a merchant who knows of a flaw in his merchandise must inform the would-be purchaser—Jew or non-Jew—of it (see Maimonides, "Laws of Sales" 18:1).

prominent medieval sage (the thirteenth-century Rabbi Judah the Chasid) that cheating a non-Jew is among the worst sins a Jew can commit: "Once there was a Jewish man whose children died shortly after they were married [but before they had children]. He sought the advice of a Torah sage, to whom he explained: 'I had a non-Jewish neighbor who died. Soon after, my children died, and the money I had given them was inherited by their wives and husbands. If Heaven judged that I was unworthy of having descendants, why didn't my children die before marriage, so that at least my wealth would not have gone to strangers?' He concluded: 'As long as the non-Jew was alive, everything was fine.'

"The Sage said: 'Perhaps your wealth was acquired dishonestly.'

"The man replied: 'I never wronged anyone—except that non-Jew, whom I used to deceive in business.'

"The Sage explained: 'When he died, his angel told him the truth, and the man cried out in anguish. The Holy One, blessed be He, takes up the cause of the oppressed, whether they are Jews or non-Jews'" (*Sefer Chasidim, *paragraph 661).*[3]

There are several ways to understand the punishing of the man's children. Perhaps Rabbi Judah believed that God punishes children for the sins of their parents.[†] *Alternatively, the children, who were now adults, might not have been completely innocent. Perhaps they knew of their father's wrongdoing, did nothing to stop it, and shared in the money he acquired dishonestly. If such reasoning seems unfair to the children, consider how most Jews feel about children of Germans and Poles who lived on property stolen by their parents from Jews during World War II, and who knowingly accepted such property when bequeathed to them by their parents.*

—

In a less extreme, but still dramatic, insistence that God will not permit Jews to bequeath money acquired dishonestly, Rabbi Moshe Rivkes (died ca. 1671), author of the Be'er HaGolah *commentary on the* Shulchan Arukh, *wrote: "I write this for future generations. I have seen many people become wealthy by causing non-Jews to err in business in order to gain profit thereby. However, they did not remain successful. In the end, all their wealth was lost [alternatively, confiscated by the government], and they had nothing to leave their descendants" (commentary on* Choshen Mishpat, *chapter 348).*

—

*Rabbi Judah believed, it seems, that after death every person is assigned an angel who advocates for him with God.

†Human beings are not allowed to do so since this violates the biblical law forbidding punishing children for the sins of parents or parents for the sins of children (Deuteronomy 24:16).

12. In addition to demanding that Jews avoid dishonest behavior toward Gentiles, Jewish law commands Jews to visit non-Jews who are ill and help in the burial of their dead just as they assist in the burial of Jews. Charity is also to be given to poor non-Jews, even to those whom the Talmud designates as idol worshippers (*Gittin* 61a). All this is done *mipnei darkei shalom* ("to promote peace"), for, the Talmud teaches, "the whole of the Torah is for promoting peace" (*Gittin* 59b). These laws are still in force and are even more applicable to contemporary Gentiles who, unlike the Jews' neighbors in the past, are generally law-abiding and civilized monotheists, not pagan idolaters.

13. However, this is not the whole picture. There are areas in which talmudic law allowed for discrimination against idolaters, although even here we find significant rabbinic figures who opposed such behavior. Generally, the permitted behavior can be characterized as "passive discrimination": One should not do anything to actively hurt an idolater, but one need not—and, in the opinion of some, should not—do anything to help him, either (in the same way that idolaters were not expected to help Jews). For example, Torah law rules that if an Israelite finds a lost object belonging to his "brother" he must seek out and return it to the owner. The word "brother" is understood by the Rabbis as referring to fellow Israelites. In such a case, the Torah insists, "you must not remain indifferent"; thus, unlike American law, for example, it is forbidden to walk by and ignore a lost object. Rather, "if your brother does not live near you, or you do not know who he is,* you shall bring it [the lost item] home and it shall remain with you until your brother claims it . . . so shall you do with anything that your brother loses and you find" (see Deuteronomy 22:1–3). The Talmud's dominant view, taught in the name of the rabbinic figure Rav, is that Jews are permitted to keep the lost objects of idolaters, since they do not fall into the category of "brother" (*Bava Kamma* 113b). In another text, Rav is cited as saying that it is actually forbidden for a Jew to return a lost object to an idolater (*Sanhedrin* 76b);† Maimonides, upholding Rav's teaching, comments that returning such an item "strengthens the hands of the wicked in the world" ("Laws of Robbery

---

*The statement "or you do not know who he is" proves that the word "brother" was meant figuratively and not literally.

†Rav's prejudice against idolaters was extreme. The Talmud records that he "would not cross a river on a ferry if there was a heathen passenger on board. He said, 'Maybe the time has come for this heathen to be punished for his sins, and I'll be caught along with him' " (*Shabbat* 32a). Contrast Rav's behavior with the strictly commonsensical attitude of Rabbi Yannai, recorded on the same page, who would not board a ferry without first checking to make sure it had no leaks.

and Lost Objects" 11:3). It should be noted that in the idolatrous societies in which Jews lived during the time of the Bible and the Talmud, non-Jews were not required to return lost objects to Jews. Even so, the Talmud records the view of Rabbi Pinchas ben Yair that "in a place where a desecration of God's name might result [which would probably be the case if the idolater knew that a Jew had found his possession], it is forbidden to keep a lost article" (*Bava Kamma* 113b).

Such views influenced later codifiers of Jewish law. Although ruling that Jews should keep lost objects of idolaters, Maimonides also teaches that a Jew who returns a lost object so as to sanctify God's name is to be praised ("Laws of Robbery and Lost Objects" 11:3).

Four centuries after Maimonides, Rabbi Moshe Rivkes (seventeenth century), author of the previously cited *Be'er HaGolah* commentary on the *Shulchan Arukh,* taught that Rav's permission to keep a Gentile's lost object was no longer applicable: "Rav made this remark with reference to actual idolaters . . . but not to non-Jews today who accept the Creator and whose moral code includes returning lost property" (see his commentary to *Choshen Mishpat* 266:1). In the early twentieth century, Rabbi Baruch Ha-Levi Epstein (1860–1941), author of the classic work *Torah Temimah,* wrote that since contemporary non-Jews observe the "Seven Laws of the Sons of Noah" (see page 405*n*), then, "without any doubt the law [regarding how to act towards them in monetary and other matters of justice] is identical in all respects to that which applies to a Jew" (commentary on Deuteronomy 22:3, note 22).

The Torah, which is revolutionary and uncompromising in its opposition to idolatry, sometimes took an evolutionary rather than revolutionary approach to ethical issues. For example, Torah law—in line with the ethical standards of the time at which it was revealed—permits polygamy, but in biblical narrative the polygamous relationships that are described in detail are miserably unhappy. Thus, when Sarah can't conceive, Abraham, at her suggestion, takes Hagar as a*

*While there is little the law can do to emotionally protect an unloved wife, the Bible does protect her offspring: "If a man has two wives, one loved and one hated, and both the loved and unloved have borne him sons, but the first-born is the son of the unloved one, when he wills his property to his sons, he may not treat as first-born the son of the loved one in disregard of the son of the unloved one who is older. Instead, he must accept the first-born, the son of the unloved one, and allot to him a double portion of all he possesses; since he is the first fruit of his vigor, the birthright is his due" (Deuteronomy 21:15–17). Despite permitting polygamy, the language used by the Torah in this ruling suggests that polygamous marriages are often unhappy: "If a man has two wives, one loved and one hated . . ." (Deuteronomy 21:15).

concubine. This generates terrible tension and, eventually, Sarah insists that Hagar and her son Ishmael be expelled (Genesis 21:10). Two generations later, Jacob loves Rachel and wishes to marry her. But Rachel's father, Laban, deceives him into first marrying Leah, Rachel's older sister, before allowing him to marry Rachel. Not surprisingly, Leah spends much of her married life feeling unloved (Genesis 29:31). Years later, the hatred felt by Jacob's other sons toward Rachel's son Joseph culminates in the brothers committing one of the worst crimes in the Bible, selling Joseph into slavery.*

Hundreds of years after this episode, a man named Elkanah takes two wives (one of whom, Hannah, eventually becomes the mother of the prophet Samuel). The Bible describes in painful detail the cruelty of the fertile but less loved Peninah toward the barren but deeply loved Hannah. Among other things, Peninah taunts Hannah with the claim that "the Lord had closed her womb" (see I Samuel 1:4–7).

Is it any wonder that despite the Bible's permission for men to take multiple wives, Jewish law, influenced both by the mores of later times and by these well-known biblical stories,† eventually outlawed polygamy?

Similarly, as noted, the Talmud, written during periods when Jews were the victims of oppression and discrimination, permitted Jews a lower level of morality in certain aspects of their relations with idolaters than with fellow Jews. Yet here, too, we find a narrative tradition in the Talmud and later Jewish literature that describes rabbis who insisted on practicing the highest standards of interpersonal behavior as heroes. And these narratives, several of which are cited in the following pages, increasingly came to represent the commonly accepted view of how Jews should behave.

For example, the Jerusalem Talmud relates the following story, which has the ring of folklore to it, to convey the notion that by practicing a high level of morality, Jews can bring pagans to an appreciation of Judaism and the Jewish God:

"Rabbi Samuel bar Sasartai [third century C.E.] went to Rome. The Empress lost a bracelet and he found it. A proclamation was issued throughout the land that if anyone returned it within thirty days, he would receive such-and-such a reward but if, after thirty days he did not do so, he would lose his head. After thirty days passed, he returned it.

---

*Eventually, Jacob ends up with four wives only one of whom, it would seem, he truly wished to marry.

†There are two additional indications of the Bible's preference for monogamy, both drawn from the opening chapters of Genesis. When God creates the world, he populates it with only two people, one of each sex. Later, the first reference in the Bible to marriage presupposes a state of monogamy: "Therefore shall a man leave his father and mother and cleave to his wife so that they become one flesh" (Genesis 2:24).

"She said to him: 'Were you not in the province?'

"He replied: 'Yes, I was here.'

"She said: 'But did you not hear the proclamation?'

" 'I heard it,' said he.

" 'What did it say?' she asked.

"He replied: 'If anyone returns it within thirty days, he will receive such-and-such a reward, but if he returns it after thirty days, he will lose his head.'

"She said: 'Why then did you not return it within the thirty days?'

"He said: 'Because I did not want you to say that I returned it out of fear of you, whereas, in fact, I returned it out of fear of the All-Merciful.'

"She said to him: 'Blessed is the God of the Jews'" (Jerusalem Talmud, Bava Mezia *2:5).*

It was unacceptable to Rabbi Samuel that one who feared God would keep another person's lost item.

---

14. The same page on which the Talmud records Rav's ruling that Jews may keep the lost items of idolaters (*Bava Kamma* 113b) also cites the teaching of Shmuel (second–third century C.E.), one of the most significant talmudic sages, that "the mistake of an idolater is permitted," meaning that a Jew is permitted to take advantage of a business error made by a heathen. For example, if an idolater miscalculated and overpaid for an item, a Jew is not required to return the overpayment, as long as the Jew in no way misled the idolater.*

Yet other significant rabbinic figures, whose views the Talmud also records, were never comfortable with taking advantage of anyone's mistake, including those of idolaters. Of Rabbi Shimon ben Shetach (first century B.C.E.), it is recorded that when his students bought him a donkey from a heathen, they found a very valuable jewel entangled in the skin [or perhaps in the harness] around its neck. When Rabbi Shimon insisted upon returning the item, declaring, "I bought only the donkey, not the jewel," they, in turn, argued with him that since the error was made by a heathen, he should keep the jewel. The rabbi rejected his students' reasoning: "What do you think, that Shimon ben Shetach is a barbarian?" He returned the jewel, and the

*The Rabbis' reasoning is that the money lost by the miscalculation is similar to the loss of any other object, and, as noted, the dominant view in the Talmud is that Jews are not required to return lost objects to idolaters.

seller, overwhelmed by the rabbi's honesty, proclaimed, "Blessed be the God of Shimon ben Shetach!"*

Unfortunately, in certain segments of the Jewish world, there are still Jews (one hopes they are few in number) who continue to teach that Jews are not required to correct business errors made by Gentiles. Some years ago, after I had delivered a lecture on Jewish ethics, a young man raised his hand and told me that he had decided to stop being religious a few years earlier when a rabbi at his yeshiva instructed the students that, according to Jewish law, if a non-Jew makes an error in a business dealing with a Jew, the Jew is not required to return the extra money. "Is that true?" the young man challenged me.

I responded with a question: "Did your rabbi also teach you that a Jew is permitted to eat pork on Yom Kippur?"

"Of course not," he responded.

"That, of course, is generally true. Yet if one is in danger of starving to death and pork is the only food available, then Jewish law would instruct one to eat it. But to say that a Jew may eat pork on Yom Kippur without specifying the very special circumstance in which such behavior is allowed is dishonest and misleading. Similarly, to say that a Jew is not required to correct a business error made by a non-Jew without explaining the relevant historical circumstance is equally misleading. As is clear, the Talmud's ruling was issued in a society in which non-Jewish governments and laws discriminated against Jews, and non-Jews were not required to correct business errors made by Jews. In those societies, the Rabbis made a pragmatic ruling that Jews were not required to practice a higher business morality toward non-Jews than non-Jews were required to practice toward Jews.† *It is one thing to say that rabbis such as Shmuel or Rav ruled that where non-Jews are permitted to be dishonest with Jews, Jews are permitted not to correct a business error made by a non-Jew. But it is an altogether different matter to imagine that rabbis such as Shmuel and Rav would have said, 'Even in a society in which Jews have equal rights, and in which non-Jews are expected and obligated to be fully honest in their business dealings with Jews, Jews don't have*

---

*There are two versions of this story—with slight variations—in rabbinic literature; see Jerusalem Talmud, *Bava Mezia* 2:5 and Deuteronomy *Rabbah* 3:3. No less significant than Rabbi Shimon's behavior is the rhetorical question he posed to his students: "What do you think, that Shimon ben Shetach is a barbarian?" Clearly, Rabbi Shimon believed that one who doesn't correct another's business error is acting not like a Jew, but a barbarian.

†Much as we could empathize with a black slave in nineteenth-century America who would not feel morally obliged, for example, to return a lost object to a white man.

to correct business errors made by non-Jews.' Such reasoning turns the Rabbis of the Talmud from pragmatists into dishonest, and rather vile, people."

Regarding other rulings in the Talmud directed against idolaters and other Gentiles, and their, in my view, unfortunate impact on Jewish law, see the discussion on Maimonides and non-Jews on pages 281–285.

A softening of hostile attitudes

15. Given the Torah's severe strictures against idolatry and idolaters, the Rabbis tried to limit the number of non-Jews to whom these laws applied. Thus, the Talmud understood the Torah's obligation to oppose idolatry actively as restricted to the Holy Land. However, "Gentiles who live outside of Israel are not regarded as idolaters [even if the religious rituals they practice are idolatrous]; rather, they are only carrying out customs learned from their ancestors" (*Chullin* 13b); that is, they are acting out of habit, not out of a true belief in and commitment to idolatry.

16. Even during tense, often hostile periods in Gentile-Jewish relations, the Rabbis welcomed wisdom from their non-Jewish neighbors. An oft-cited rabbinic aphorism teaches: "Wisdom from the Gentiles accept, but Torah from the Gentiles don't accept"* (Lamentations *Rabbah* 2:13; the latter might have been a response in part to the Christian claim that the New Testament had come to supersede the Torah).

The Rabbis were also willing to learn ethical and proper behavior from non-Jews. The Talmud relates the story of Dama ben Netina, "a worshipper of the stars in Ashkelon," who remains to this day a talmudic exemplar of the Fifth Commandment to honor one's parents. He was once about to conclude a sale to the Rabbis of valuable jewels for use in the High Priest's breastplate that would have yielded him a profit of 600,000 gold dinarim, a considerable fortune. Alas, the key to the place where the jewels were kept was beneath the headrest of his father, who was sleeping. Dama wouldn't wake his father—the story doesn't explain why the Rabbis were in such a rush that they couldn't wait for his father to awaken—and the delay caused

---

*Aware that partisans of one faith are often unwilling to acknowledge intelligence in those who are not coreligionists, the Talmud reminded Jews: "Anyone who speaks words of wisdom—even amongst the Gentiles—is considered a wise man" (*Megillah* 16a). Remarkably, the Talmud in this instance was referring to intimates of Haman, who had sought to destroy all Jews.

the sale to be canceled. Some time later, the Rabbis returned to Dama. This time, they urgently needed a red heifer, an extremely rare cow that he possessed and without which the Jews could not perform the rites of purification for those who had contact with a human corpse. Although Dama knew that the Rabbis would have been willing to pay him whatever price he asked, all that he requested was the amount of money he had lost earlier because he had not awakened his father (*Kiddushin* 31a). To the Rabbis, Dama, although an idolater, became a model for all Jews and for all time of how to honor one's parents. What is less frequently noted is that the story also esteems Dama for being a fair businessman who refused to take advantage of the purchasers' (the Rabbis') great need.

The rabbinic openness to learning proper behavior from Gentiles is also reflected in a talmudic discussion about two seemingly contradictory verses in the book of Ezekiel. In one, Ezekiel condemns the Jews for disobeying God's laws and for *"acting instead according to the rules of the nations around you"* (11:12; emphasis added). But elsewhere Ezekiel rebukes the Jews both for not obeying God's laws, *"nor have you observed the rules of the nations around you . . ."* (5:7; emphasis added). How is it, the Talmud wonders, that the prophet can condemn the Jews both for following and not following the laws of the nations around them? Rabbi Joshua ben Levi resolves the contradiction: The Jews are condemned for not emulating the good precepts and behavior of their neighbors, and also for following the immoral behavior of their neighbors (*Sanhedrin* 39b).*

Rabbi Dr. Aharon Lichtenstein was, until recently, the joint Rosh Yeshiva (director), along with Rabbi Yehuda Amital, of the Har Etzion yeshiva in Israel, one of the finest yeshivas in the world today. A son-in-law of the late Rabbi Joseph Baer Soloveitchik, Rabbi Lichtenstein also holds a Ph.D. in English literature from Harvard University, and is among the most forceful exponents in the Orthodox world of the need for Jews to enrich their own Jewish education with a solid grounding in non-Jewish wisdom. Rabbi Lichtenstein has observed: "Nor should we be deterred [from studying non-Jewish wisdom] by the illusion that we can find all we need within our own tradition. As [Matthew] Arnold insisted, one must seek 'the best that has been thought and said in the world,' and if, in

*Hundreds of year later, Bachya ibn Pakuda (eleventh century), in the introduction to his classic and widely studied *Duties of the Heart (Chovot HaLevavot),* refers to this teaching as a justification for citing the wisdom and practices of non-Jewish philosophers as teachings from which Jews can learn. In the words of Bachya, "[I have cited these words] to incline the souls of my readers to their ways and to draw their hearts' attention to the wisdom they had."

many areas, much of that best is of foreign origin, we shall expand our horizons rather than exclude it. . . . [Important Gentile thinkers have] their own wisdom, even of a moral and philosophic nature. Who can fail to be inspired by the ethical idealism of Plato, the passionate fervor of Augustine, or the visionary grandeur of Milton? Who can remain unenlightened by the lucidity of Aristotle, the profundity of Shakespeare . . . ? To deny that many fields have been better cultivated by non-Jewish rather than Jewish writers is to be stubbornly—and unnecessarily—chauvinistic. There is nothing in our medieval poetry to rival Dante . . . and we would do well to admit it. We have our own genius, and we have bent it to the noblest of pursuits, the development of Torah. But we cannot be expected to do everything."[4]

Non-Jews and the World-to-Come

17. Religions have often withheld from believers in other faiths the ultimate prize, salvation or life in the World-to-Come. For much of its history (though no longer), Catholicism taught that "there is no salvation outside the Church," and that a person had to accept Catholic teachings and observe the sacraments to be granted afterlife.* To this day, fundamentalist Protestants generally teach that a person who does not believe in Jesus' divinity will go to hell even if that individual leads an ethical life. In the talmudic literature, a minority view taught by Rabbi Eliezer declared that non-Jews are excluded from the World-to-Come. However, this view was rejected by Rabbi Joshua and by the Jewish tradition: ". . . the righteous among the nations of the world have a share in the World-to-Come" (*Tosefta Sanhedrin* 13:2).

---

*The Mishnah (*Sanhedrin *10:2) notes that the Gentile prophet Balaam (see paragraph 5) is one of those evil people who will have no share in the World-to-Come.*

---

*Characteristic of the earlier attitude was the teaching of Pope Boniface VIII (*Unum Sanctum,* 1302) that "we are compelled by faith to believe and hold that there is one holy, catholic, and apostolic Church, and we firmly believe in her and sincerely confess her, outside of whom there is neither salvation nor remission of sins." Pope Pius IX, in an address to an audience on December 9, 1854, qualified this teaching: "We must . . . recognize with certainty that those who are invincible in ignorance of the true religion are not guilty for this in the eyes of the Lord." In the 1960s, at Vatican Council II, the most liberal statement of the Catholic position on salvation for non-Catholics was issued: "Those who . . . do not know the Gospel of Christ or His Church, but who nonetheless seek God with a sincere heart and, moved by grace, try in their actions to do His will as they know it through the dictates of their conscience—these too may achieve eternal salvation" ("Dogmatic Constitution of the Church," number 16).

*But, as the Talmud points out, the fact that the Mishnah specifies Balaam's exclusion from the afterlife clearly implies that other non-Jews, as long as they are good people, will share in the next world (*Sanhedrin *105a).*

Rabbi Menachem Ha-Meiri and the end of discriminatory legislation

18. The French rabbi Menachem Meiri (1249–ca. 1310) issued a legal ruling intended to alter the status of non-Jews in Jewish law permanently. Meiri, who had extensive dealings with a number of tolerant Christian intellectuals in Provence, France (he notes that the writing of one of his major works, *A Treatise on Repentance,* was inspired by discussions with a Christian scholar),[5] ruled that all discriminatory legislation in the Talmud applied only to ancient pagans and idolaters who rejected the moral teachings of the Bible, and the belief in one God. However, he added, Jews are to act toward *umot ha-gedurot be-darchei ha-datot,* "nations restricted by the ways of religion" (unlike the pagan nations of antiquity), in the same way they are commanded to act toward fellow Jews.

Thus, Meiri's commentary on the talmudic tractate *Bava Kamma* 113b (the page on which the Talmud recorded the ruling that Jews do not have to return lost objects to idolaters) explains the rationale for the Talmud's ruling and then explains why it no longer applies: "[While] it is forbidden to rob even idolaters and persons undisciplined by religion . . . yet one is not obligated to take the trouble to restore their lost articles . . . since . . . restoring is an act of solidarity and we are not obligated to show solidarity with godless barbarians. . . . Still if he [that is, the idolater] is aware of the facts, we must restore it . . . and so too in any situation where not to restore would result in a dishonoring of God's name. Hence, you may infer that anyone belonging to a nation disciplined by religion, who worships God in any fashion—be it ever so different from our faith—is not in the above category. As regards these matters, he is entirely like a Jew—in respect to his lost articles or errors made [in a Jew's favor] or anything else, no distinction at all is made [between Jew and non-Jew]."[6]

Meiri's ruling effectively declares null and void all laws in the ethical sphere that discriminate against non-Jews (in nonethical spheres, traditional Jewish law continues to distinguish between Jews and non-Jews, for example, in not counting a non-Jew in the quorum [minyan] necessary to conduct a public prayer service). The worship of a multitude of deities with separate identities and competing, and sometimes unethical, wills having been largely eliminated from the world (perhaps Jewish monotheism's most far-reaching contribution to world civilization), Jews are now required to practice the same standards of morality toward non-Jews as toward co-religionists.*

Unfortunately, as was seen in the story cited on pages 275–276, some Jews continue to teach that the Talmud's discriminatory legislation is still applicable.† As a rule, people who offer such teachings have little, if any, contact with non-Jews. For them, non-Jews are an abstraction (in similar manner, I have heard of Jews in the past who visited small rural communities where they met non-Jews who thought Jews had horns). To insist, however, that in a society in which Jews are treated fairly, discrimination against non-Jews should be permitted, and even sanctioned by God, is a *chillul Hashem* (desecration of God's name).

With the increasing concentration of Jews outside of Israel in nondiscriminatory societies such as the United States, Canada, England, and Australia, the triumph of the Meiri's position, mandating total fairness toward non-Jews, has been assured.

As regards Jewish obligations to democratic societies in which they live, Dr. Abraham S. Abraham, a renowned legal scholar and a student of Rabbi Shlomo

---

*People sometimes note that Torah law permitted Israelites to charge interest on loans to non-Israelites, but not to fellow Israelites (Deuteronomy 23:20–21), and that despite Meiri's ruling, Jewish law still permitted them to do so. However, this is not an example of discriminatory legislation. The reasoning of Jewish law can be described as follows: Since non-Israelites charged interest on loans to Israelites, and to everybody else, and still do, Israelites were and are permitted to charge interest to non-Israelites. The regulation against charging interest to fellow Israelites was a special provision, a sort of family solidarity with our coreligionists (just as we can imagine a family patriarch or matriarch instructing his/her children and descendants not to charge interest on a loan made to a close relative, particularly if the loan is made to cover urgent, personal expenses).

†Rabbi Yechiel Yaakov Weinberg (see page 285) noted in a letter to a friend that there were rabbis who would teach their students the position of Meiri, but then inform them that his approach was only to be cited for apologetic purposes, but did not truly reflect Jewish teaching (see Marc Shapiro, *Between the Yeshiva World and Modern Orthodoxy,* page 183). In a book published in recent years in the United States, and geared largely toward the most traditional Jewish world, the author, a rabbi, offers Jews the following guidance: "If someone finds an object bearing identification marks, or money wrapped up, inside a store, and the store's customers are mostly Jewish, the finder must announce his find. If the customers are mostly non-Jewish, he may keep it" (the author does write elsewhere that articles belonging to non-Jews should be protected to ensure peaceful Jewish-Gentile relations). Can we imagine the reaction we Jews would feel if in a book written for Christians by a minister or priest, and geared toward explaining how to lead a proper Christian life, we came across a similar instruction? Would such a ruling raise or lower our opinion of Christianity?

Zalman Auerbach, reports that the rabbi told him: "Whenever the laws of the land do not differentiate between Jews and non-Jews, and between one ethnic group and another, the law of the land has the force of Torah law" (Abraham, Nishmat Avraham, *3:253).*

Maimonides, non-Jews, and the problem of fairness

Scholars of Maimonides (twelfth century), the most influential Jewish thinker since the time of the Talmud, often treat his writings and legal rulings as if he were a disembodied mind, without paying sufficient attention to the historical circumstances in which he lived. But to understand Maimonides' many problematic legal rulings concerning non-Jews without taking into account the horrific antisemitism to which he was subjected in his early years would be like a contemporary academic writing an intellectual biography of a Holocaust survivor without noting the person's Holocaust experiences.

Born in Cordova, Spain, in 1135, Maimonides lived during the period of the rise of the Almohades, a fanatical Berber Muslim dynasty that ruled Morocco and Spain in the twelfth and thirteenth centuries. In the early twelfth century, as historian Salo Baron explains, a Muslim jurist in Cordova claimed to have found a tradition "that Muhammad's original decree of toleration of Jews had been limited to a period of five hundred years from the *hegira* [Muhammad's flight from Mecca]." If, by that time, the Jewish Messiah had not arrived, the Jews were expected to give up their religion and convert to Islam. The time limit expired in 1107.[7] On the basis of this new doctrine, in 1146, Abd al-Mu'min, the builder of the Almohade Empire in North Africa and Spain, offered the Jews of Fez, then Morocco's capital, the choice of conversion to Islam or death. Almost all the Jews refused the offer, and many of them were murdered. Jews who did convert were put under constant surveillance, and those whose conversions seemed insincere (perhaps they were caught secretly practicing Jewish rituals) had their property confiscated and their wives given to Muslims.

Maimonides, the most famous victim of the Almohade persecution, fled with his family from Spain to Morocco, and finally to Egypt, where he was able to live openly as a Jew. But the terror of Almohade rule scarred the lives of all Jews unfortunate enough to come into contact with it. Professor Shlomo Dov Goitein, the foremost historian of Jewish life under Islam, summed up the Jewish century under the Almohades in one sentence: "All the horrors of the Spanish Inquisition were anticipated under Almohade rule."*[8]

In writing about non-Jews, Maimonides offered a very different approach than that offered by Meiri (see pages 279–280). While Meiri, in one fell swoop, wrote off all the discriminatory anti-Gentile legislation in the Talmud as directed only against idolaters,† and thus not applicable to the contemporary non-Jews amongst whom Jews lived, Maimonides often ruled that discriminatory laws were directed not only against idolaters but against non-Jews in general. Besides ruling, as noted, that it is permitted to keep the lost objects of non-Jews (see page 271),‡ he also allowed Jews to profit from business errors made by non-Jews, as long as the error was made solely by the non-Jew and the Jew did not intentionally mislead him. In the same chapter, he also ruled that a Jew, though not normally permitted to return a lost item to a non-Jew, was permitted to do so if he wished to "sanctify God's name" and cause non-Jews to believe that Jews are honest people (see "Laws of Robbery and Lost Objects" 11:3). What is somewhat problematic about this reasoning is that if a Jew's returning a lost object will cause Gentiles to conclude that Jews are honest, does that not mean that if Jews do not return lost items, Gentiles have the right to conclude that they are not honest?

---

*Prior to the rise of the Almohades, Jews and Christians living in the orbit of Islam were regarded as "people of the Book" (that is, the Bible) and, because they, too, were monotheists, Muslim authorities granted them a certain degree of toleration. True, they had to live as *Dhimmis*—in effect, second-class citizens with restricted rights—and were often subjected to public humiliation. For example, a century before Maimonides immigrated to Egypt, the Fatimid caliph Hakim ordered Christians to wear a cross with arms two feet long, while Jews had to wear five-pound balls around their neck, in "commemoration" of the golden calf their ancestors had worshipped in the desert (Exodus 32). In most Arab countries, *Dhimmis* were forbidden to ride on horses, for this was considered incompatible with their low status. They were permitted to ride donkeys, which were slower than horses, but could not use saddles, which made riding far less comfortable; it would be as if a contemporary ethnic group were forbidden to use automobiles, but allowed to ride bicycles. When following their dead at funerals, *Dhimmis* were not permitted to raise their voices, for this would annoy Muslims. But as long as they abided by such rules, they were permitted to practice their religion. The Jewish status as *Dhimmis* with a variety of restrictions persisted in the Arab-Muslim world into modern times.

†Meiri shifted the definition of idolatry from a primarily theological focus (one who rejects Judaism's monotheistic teachings) to a primarily ethical one. Thus, to Meiri the most compelling evidence for the idolatrous nature of the pagans in the time of the Talmud was their lack of moral constraints.

‡Maimonides ruled equally harshly against Jews whom he regarded as heretics (such as those who publicly desecrated the Sabbath or who ate unkosher food to show their contempt for God's laws), and forbade returning lost items to them ("Laws of Robbery and Lost Objects" 11:2).

More shockingly, Maimonides writes that a Jew who kills a non-Jew is not subject to execution by a Jewish court ("Laws of Murder" 2:11),* though a non-Jew who kills a Jew should be executed (I have no access to records of Almohade legislation, but suspect that a Muslim who killed a Jew was not executed, while a Jew who killed a Muslim was). Maimonides also rules that a non-Jew should be executed merely for striking a Jew ("The Laws of Injuries and Damages" 5:3), although elsewhere he writes that this law is not enforced ("Laws of Kings" 10:6; Maimonides might have been influenced by the very strict Muslim laws regarding a non-Muslim who hit a Muslim, no matter what the provocation).

While Jews are forbidden to kill idolaters with whom they are not in conflict, Maimonides rules that they should not save an idolater whose life is in danger, "for example, if such a person fell into the sea, one should not rescue him" ("Laws of Murder" 4:11). The obvious implication is that if a boat with Jewish sailors comes across a sinking boat with idolaters, the Jews should stand by and do nothing (this would not apply to non-Jews who are not idolaters).† It is, of course, possible that Maimonides would have ruled in such an instance that the Jews should save the drowning idolaters but for only one reason: If we don't save their drowning sailors and passengers, they won't save ours. As Rabbi Joseph Baer Soloveitchik remarked in a related, though somewhat different, instance: "From a moral standpoint [such a ruling] does not satisfy me."[9]

Few things are more revealing of Maimonides' anti-Gentile tendency than his codification of how non-Jews are to be treated when they are living under Jewish sovereignty and jurisdiction. In the concluding section of his code, in which he outlines the legal system that should characterize a state run according to Jewish law, he subjects non-Jews to extensive discriminatory

---

*Although the Hebrew term *Maimonides* used in this ruling is indeed the term for "idolater," most commentaries on Maimonides writings assume that he means that a Jew is not executed even for murdering a nonidolatrous Gentile. However, thousands of years before Maimonides, the Torah ruled—at a time when the Israelites had not yet come into existence—that "Whoever sheds the blood of man, by man shall his blood be shed; For in His image did God make man" (Genesis 9:6). Maimonides, in ruling that a Jew who kills a non-Jew should not be executed by a Jewish court (presumably the person will be punished by God), seems to contravene the spirit of the law in Genesis, which specifies, "by man shall his blood be shed." It should be noted, though, that writing at a time when slavery was still practiced, Maimonides does rule that "If a person kills either a Jew or a Canaanite slave, he should be executed" ("Laws of Murder" 2:10).

†See the story on page 289 of how, in 1977 a group of Israeli sailors saved a boatload of Vietnamese refugees who were at risk of drowning and brought them to Israel. Sailors of other countries, including East Germany, Norway, Japan, and Panama, had earlier ignored desperate appeals for help from the Vietnamese.

legislation, and often imposes a double standard in which they are to be treated much more harshly than Jews (the Torah, of course, repeatedly insisted upon one standard of justice for the Israelites and for the stranger who dwelled among them, but Maimonides believed that this applied only to non-Jews who had formally accepted upon themselves the Seven Laws of the Sons of Noah [see page 405*n*]). To be fair to Maimonides, he generally relied on rules concerning idolaters originally formulated in the Talmud.[10]

To cite a few examples:

• A non-Jew is subject to a death sentence for committing an abortion, although a Jew is not ("Laws of Kings" 9:4); the term *Maimonides* used throughout this chapter to refer to non-Jews is *ben noach,* "a son of Noah," a talmudic term that refers to all Gentiles.

• A non-Jew who kills a pursuer with murderous intentions when he could have saved the would-be victim by just wounding a limb is to be put to death ("Laws of Kings" 9:4), while a Jew who does the same thing has committed a serious sin, but is not subject to capital punishment ("Laws of Murder" 1:13).

• Non-Jews are subject to execution for any act of stealing, even if the stolen item has a value of less than a *prutah* (the smallest coin; "Laws of Kings" 9:9). In practical terms, this would mean that a non-Jew caught helping himself to some grapes at a supermarket would be judged guilty of a capital offense. In contrast, a Jew who stole an item valued at less than a *prutah* was subject to no punishment at all ("Law of Robbery and Lost Objects" 1:6; it was presumed that the victim would not be bothered by such a loss).

• Maimonides ruled that a non-Jew guilty of a capital crime could evade execution, and apparently all punishment, by converting to Judaism. To cite the instances mentioned by Maimonides, if a non-Jew cursed God, engaged in idolatry, committed adultery, or killed another, but then converted to Judaism, he was freed from punishment ("Laws of Kings" 10:4).* He does, however, rule that if the person the non-Jew had murdered was a Jew, or if the person with whom he committed adultery was a Jew, then he was still to be executed even after conversion.

---

*Obviously, such a ruling could lead to the worst kind of people, murderers, converting to Judaism to evade punishment.

The rationale for freeing the convert from execution is that now that the person has become a Jew, we insist upon a much more rigorous standard of evidence before executing him. For example, for a Jew to be executed, there must be two witnesses to his crime; for a non-Jew to be executed, only one witness is required. Lowering the standard of evidence required for convicting a non-Jew is again, of course, discriminatory ("Laws of Kings" 9:14).

The great twentieth-century rabbinic sage Rabbi Yechiel Yaakov Weinberg was deeply distressed by the body of anti-Gentile legislation in Jewish sources. He therefore endorsed all Jews accepting the position of Meiri, which effectively declared all previous anti-Gentile legislation no longer valid. Otherwise, as Rabbi Weinberg noted in an anguished letter to a friend,* how can we possibly expect non-Jews to regard us favorably? Indeed, it was in response to these types of hostile rulings that Rabbi Weinberg wrote in another letter: "The entire world hates us. We assume that this hatred is due to the wickedness of the nations, and no one stops to think that perhaps we also bear some guilt . . . Can the nations resign themselves to such a deprivation of rights?" [as is suggested in these previously cited rulings].[11]

Maimonides, the victim of Almohade fanaticism and violence, was understandably outraged at the mistreatment he and his fellow Jews had suffered. Similarly, I have met some Holocaust survivors (though by no means all) who spoke with great bitterness and mistrust of *all* non-Jews. But both the Almohades and Hitler are dead, and while contemporary groups such as Hezbollah do indeed want to murder Jews, the non-Jews among whom American Jews live today are overwhelmingly friendly, open, honest people, who deserve goodwill, fairness, and trust.

Maimonides is the guide to Jewish life in so many areas, and indeed, he is the figure I have quoted most often in this code. However, he cannot be the Jewish teacher today on the issue of Jewish-Gentile relations. He has been superseded by Menachem Meiri, and one can only imagine that this is what God, who created Jews and non-Jews alike in His image, would want.

---

*After citing examples of discriminatory legislation in Jewish sources, Weinberg writes: "God knows that I have written this with the blood of my heart, the blood of my soul" (cited in Marc Shapiro, *Between the Yeshiva World and Modern Orthodoxy,* page 182). In addition, Weinberg believed that a refusal to disavow discriminatory laws "disgrace[d] the Torah" (page 184).

In addition to making a profoundly negative impression on non-Jews, the existence of discriminatory legislation in Jewish law also makes the same impression on many Jews (see the anecdote cited on pages 275–276). Professor David Berger, a historian and an Orthodox Jew, notes: "This is the only area of halacha *[Jewish law] where I have been told by more than a handful of serious Orthodox Jews over the years that they really do not care what rabbinic authorities may say. They know what is right and wrong and are certain that a true understanding of the Torah would have to accord with so primal an instinct. We often point—with absolute justice—to the ethical teachings of the Torah as one of the arguments for believing in its divine origin. From this perspective, a set of laws so deeply in tension with our ethical sense can constitute a challenge to faith itself."*[12]

22

TWENTY-FIVE TEACHINGS, LAWS, AND PRINCIPLES

1. "And God created man in His image, in the image of God He created him; male and female He created them" (Genesis 1:27).*

Once we appreciate that all human beings are created in God's image, it is evident that a negative generalization about another religious or ethnic group, or displaying disrespect toward those who are not of our faith, is also an offense against God. Rabbi Moshe Cordovero, the sixteenth-century kabbalist, explains: "This may be likened to an expert goldsmith who fashions a vessel with great skill, but when he displays his work, one of the people begins to mock and scorn it. How angry that goldsmith will be; for by disparaging his handiwork, one disparages his wisdom. Similarly, it is evil in the sight of the Holy One, blessed be He, if any of His creatures is despised" (*The Palm Tree of Dvorah [Tomer Dvorah],* chapter 2). Therefore, it is wrong for

*For a further discussion of the implications of this verse in regard to Jewish-Gentile relations, see page 261.

Jews to use terms such as *shaygetz* or *shiksa* (meaning, literally, "an abomination") when referring to a non-Jewish man or woman. Although very few Jews are aware of just how ugly this word is, people should realize that if they are speaking in English and refer to another group in a foreign language, the word they use is probably not a term of endearment.*

2. ". . . and through you and your descendants shall all the families of the earth be blessed" (God speaking to Jacob; Genesis 28:14).

It is perhaps so obvious that it does not need to be said, but people will feel blessed by coming in contact with Jews only if their encounters with them are blessed, and not if they feel treated in any way unfairly (see paragraphs 6 and 17).

3. "You shall not wrong a stranger or oppress him, for you were strangers in the land of Egypt" (Exodus 22:20).

The Torah's rationale for this command is somewhat counterintuitive, since so many of us do not learn from our own suffering not to inflict suffering on others. The last people we would expect to abuse their children are those who themselves were abused as children, but, in fact, they are far more likely to do so than adults who were not abused. Similarly, historians have often explained the widespread German support for Nazism as a response, in part, to the severe terms the Allies imposed on the Germans at the end of World War I. In short, suffering is often not an ennobling teacher. But that is exactly what the Torah demands of the Israelites, and continues to demand of Jews today: Learn from the bad treatment you have experienced at the hands of others not to treat others in the same way.

4. "Do not stand by while your neighbor's blood is shed" (Leviticus 19:16).

The Torah makes it clear that its greatest heroes were concerned with all suffering, not just that of their own people. When Abraham learns that God intends to destroy the city of Sodom for its acts of cruelty, he argues with God not to do so if there are at least a few righteous people living there (Genesis 18:22–33). Later, when Moses sees the Midianite male shepherds mistreating

---

*The Hebrew word *goy,* which means "nation," is actually a neutral term, and originally had no pejorative connotations. In the Torah, for example, the Israelites themselves are referred to by this word: "And you shall be unto Me a kingdom of priests and a *goy kadosh*" (holy nation; Exodus 19:6). With the passage of time, *goy* came to refer to non-Jews exclusively, and in Hebrew the word does not have negative connotations. But if one is speaking in English, and suddenly interjects the word *goy*—instead of "non-Jew"—the effect is jarring and should be avoided.

Midianite female shepherds trying to water their flock, he stands up for the women and secures their rights (Exodus 2:16–17).

It is fitting, therefore, that Jews have played such a prominent role in leading the campaign to stop the genocide in Darfur. In addition to providing humanitarian aid to many of the displaced and traumatized people forced from their homes in Darfur and living in camps in Sudan and Chad, the American Jewish World Service (headed by Ruth Messinger), which founded the Save Darfur coalition in 2004, has used public education and political advocacy in the United States to try to end the crisis. In a statement issued at the time, the AJWS said: "As Jews, we have a particular moral responsibility to speak out and take action against genocide. We must respond and save as many lives as we can."

5. "The stranger who resides with you shall be to you as one of your citizens; you shall love him as yourself . . ." (Leviticus 19:34; see pages 267–268).

6. "Observe them [the laws of the Torah] carefully, for this will be proof of your wisdom and discernment to other peoples, who on hearing of all these laws will say, 'Surely this great nation is a wise and understanding people . . .' And what great nation has laws and rules so just as all this Teaching [Torah] that I [God] set before you this day" (Deuteronomy 4:6,8).*

Why would Israelites expect Gentiles to be impressed by their laws, no matter how just, if these laws exclude them from equal expectations of justice? How impressed would contemporary Jews be with a society that legislated humane values, but did not apply them to Jews?

7. "You shall not return a runaway slave to his master. . . . Let him stay with you anywhere he chooses in any one of your settlements, whatever suits him best; you shall not wrong him" (Deuteronomy 23:16–17).

The contemporary application of this verse—in a world in which slavery is formally outlawed (though there are, for example, many instances throughout the world of young women forced into prostitution)†—is that democracies should be generous in granting political asylum to those fleeing dictatorships and totalitarian regimes. The most immoral response in such

---

*This brings to mind Isaiah 49:6, which speaks of Israel as being an *or goyim,* "a light of nations," whose good acts will bless and light the world.

†Other forms of "slavery," though the term might not be formally used, exist as well, and the American Anti-Slavery Group (see iabolish.com) estimates that "today there are 27 million enslaved people around the world."

instances would be to "return a runaway slave to his master" (for more on this law, see page 47).

In June 1977, Menachem Begin's first official action as Israel's prime minister was to admit into the country sixty-six men, women, and children who had fled the Communist regime in Vietnam. The vessel on which these "boat people" had escaped had sprung a leak; the passengers had run out of food and were very low on water. Yet their desperate SOS signals had been ignored by passing ships from East Germany, Norway, Japan, and Panama. The captain and crew of a passing Israeli ship offered the passengers food and water and quickly brought them on board. Begin soon authorized their admission as permanent residents into Israel. At a meeting at the White House a month later, Begin explained to President Jimmy Carter: "We remembered, we never have forgotten, the boat with 900 people [the SS St. Louis*] having left Germany in the last weeks [editor's note: in actuality it was several months] before the Second World War . . . traveling from harbor to harbor, from country to country, crying out for refuge. They were refused. . . . Therefore, it was natural that my first act as prime minister was to give these people a haven in the land of Israel."*

---

8. "You shall not abuse a needy and destitute laborer, whether a fellow countryman [an Israelite] or a stranger [a non-Israelite]. . . . You must pay him his wages on the same day, before the sun sets, for he is needy and urgently depends on it; or else he will cry to the Lord against you and you will incur guilt" (Deuteronomy 24:14–15).

As the wording of this verse suggests, this law would apply with particular force to those who employ domestic help,* people who often require their wages for their daily needs and who have little or no savings.

Hayim Greenberg, the Labor Zionist philosopher and ideologue, described how the Communist Leon Trotsky, one of the top five officials to assume leadership, along with Lenin, of the Soviet government in Russia in 1917, bragged that his father was an atheist, and in no way bound by Jewish tradition.† *Trotsky also*

---

*If the person is employed on a full-time basis, then other mutually agreed upon arrangements can be made, such as payment once a week.

†His father, Trotsky noted, observed neither the Sabbath nor Jewish holidays, and often declared that he believed neither in *charoset* (the Passover food) nor in the existence of God (see Hayim Greenberg, *The Inner Eye*, Volume 2, page 238). It makes no sense to say that someone does not believe in a food; Trotsky obviously meant that his father (and Trotsky, too, for that matter) didn't believe in any of the Passover—and by implication, any Jewish—rituals.

recalled, this time without pride, how his father, who was quite wealthy, forced a poor peasant woman to come to him on foot twice, a distance of seven miles, to collect the one-ruble wage he owed her[1]*—exactly the kind of behavior that the Torah prohibits.*

Compare Trotsky's recollection of his father with one by the Chaffetz Chayyim's son of an incident related to him by workers at a printing press in Warsaw, who had prepared some of his father's books for publication. One worker told him how he had once seen the Chaffetz Chayyim running down a small side street just before Shabbat. "Since it was almost time to light candles, he wondered where the Chaffetz Chayyim was going at such a late hour. Afterward, he found out that one of the workers at the printing press left the shop before the Chaffetz Chayyim had paid him. The Chaffetz Chayyim found out his address and ran to his home to pay him before Shabbat so that he should not violate the prohibition against not paying wages on time."[2]

---

9. When the first Beit HaMikdash (the Great Temple) was dedicated in Jerusalem by King Solomon, he included the following request in his prayer to God: "Or if a foreigner who is not of Your people comes from a distant land . . . when he comes to pray in this House, oh, hear in Your heavenly abode and grant all that the foreigner asks You for. Thus, all the peoples of the earth will know Your Name and revere You as does Your people Israel . . ." (I Kings 8:41–43).

The Rabbis shared Solomon's concern with the issue of God and His relationship with the non-Israelite world. The Talmud records that during the holiday of Sukkot, sacrifices were brought to the Temple in Jerusalem on behalf of, and to bring atonement for, "the seventy nations of the world" (*Sukkah* 55b).

10. "And they shall beat their swords into plowshares and their spears into pruning hooks. Nation shall not lift up sword against nation, neither shall they learn war anymore" (Isaiah 2:4).

This particular teaching, which expresses Isaiah's vision of a world without war, may be the most famous verse from the Bible's prophetic books. Indeed, this verse adorns the Isaiah Wall across the street from the United Nations building in New York City, and thus is known to people of all faiths. But, given Judaism's strongly realistic, and nonutopian, orientation, the prophet Joel (most likely fifth century B.C.E.) noted that sometimes, such as when evil forces are in the ascendant, Isaiah's words need to be reversed: ". . . Prepare for battle, arouse the warriors. . . . Beat your plowshares into swords, and your pruning hooks into spears" (Joel 4:9–10).

11. "Seek the welfare of the city to which I [God] have exiled you and pray to the Lord on its behalf, for in its prosperity you shall prosper" (Jeremiah 29:7).

The Rabbis, who feared anarchy deeply, counseled the Jews: "Pray for the welfare of the government, for were it not for the fear of it, people would swallow each other alive" (*The Ethics of the Fathers* 3:2). Many people complain about police brutality and corruption—and such behavior should and must be protested—but the alternative should not be lax legal enforcement. How many people would want to remain in a city whose police department was on strike? If such a strike persisted, most citizens would choose to move to a city with a strong municipal government.

Jeremiah's concluding words, "for in its prosperity you shall prosper," aptly describe the Jewish historical experience. Jews have generally done well in prosperous societies where they have been allowed to be active participants in the economy and have been more likely to suffer antisemitism in economically struggling states. Thus, Hitler would have been a hater of Jews no matter what the state of the German economy, but he would have been unlikely to come to power if not for the depression then gripping Germany.

Jeremiah's command to "pray to the Lord on its behalf" is the basis for the Jewish tradition to offer prayers on behalf of the country in which they live during the Shabbat morning service.

---

12. "He [God] has told you, O man, what is good, and what the Lord requires of you: Only to do justice, and to love goodness, and to walk modestly with your God" (Micah 6:8).

The clear intent of the prophet's words is that this standard of behavior applies to dealings with Jews and non-Jews alike.

For more on the significance of this verse in Jewish life, see *A Code of Jewish Ethics, Volume 1: You Shall Be Holy,* pages 14 and 210–211.

13. "Whoever saves one life, it is as if he saved an entire world" (Mishnah *Sanhedrin* 4:5).

For more on this teaching, see page 262.

14. [Rabbi Chanina ben Dosa] used to say: "Anyone in whom one's fellow creatures takes pleasure, God takes pleasure. And anyone in whom one's fellow creatures do not take pleasure, God does not take pleasure" (*The Ethics of the Fathers* 3:10).

Rabbi Pinchas Eliyahu Hurwitz of Vilna (eighteenth century), author of *Sefer Ha-Brit,* teaches: "[The Mishnah uses the term] 'fellow creatures,' not the members of one's own nation, in order to include all mankind, whether from his people or from another people. . . . Our Rabbis have clearly stated that there is no difference in this regard between Jews and Gentiles" (II: 13:6).[3] Elsewhere in the same work, the author writes: "The essence of neighborly love consists in loving all mankind, of whatever people and whatever tongue, by virtue of their identical humanity" (II:13:1).[4]

15. Ben Zoma used to say: "Who is wise? One who learns from every person" (*The Ethics of the Fathers* 4:1).

As regards Judaism's insistence on acquiring wisdom from both Jews and non-Jews, see page 276.

16. "It was said of Rabbi Yochanan ben Zakkai that no man ever greeted him first, even a Gentile in the marketplace" (*Berachot* 17a).

A man who periodically chauffeured Rabbi Shlomo Carlebach recalled an occasion when, after a few minutes of warm conversation, Reb Shlomo asked if it was all right for him to just sit quietly and study the Talmud. Aware of how busy Rabbi Carlebach was, and how rare must be his opportunity for private study, the man assured him that he didn't mind at all and, throughout the long car trip, Reb Shlomo immersed himself in study, oblivious to his surroundings. "However, each time we pulled up to one of the many tollbooths we passed that day, he would snap out of his reverie, close the Talmud, look up at the tollbooth attendant, smile broadly, wave a greeting, and exchange a few words of friendship. No matter how ill-tempered or brusque the attendants appeared at the start, by the time Reb Shlomo had finished waving, smiling and joking, they were transformed. After we passed each booth, Reb Shlomo would return to his Talmud, closing it again as we approached the next tollbooth. Despite his complete immersion in the text, he didn't miss a single station or attendant."[5]

In similar manner, Rabbi Berel Wein reported that he was once driving with Rabbi Yakov Kamenetzky, a great rabbinical scholar. At one point, the two men had a long wait at a tollbooth, during which Rabbi Wein grew exasperated. When they finally arrived at the booth, Wein handed the collector the money and immediately drove off. The European-born Rabbi Kamenetzky remarked in his strongly accented English, "You didn't say, 'Tenk you.' "

17. "In an hour when an individual is brought before the heavenly court for judgment [the first question] the person is asked is: 'Did you conduct your business affairs honestly?' " (*Shabbat* 31a).

Rabbi Yom Tov Schwarz notes the importance of Jews being scrupulously honest in their commercial activities with non-Jews since this will help determine how Gentiles view them: "The Gentiles do not scrutinize us to see if we buy high quality *tefillin* (phylacteries) or a beautiful *etrog* (the citron fruit blessed on *Sukkot*), but rather whether we are truthful in our business dealings."[6]

18. "Whoever can influence the members of his household to stop sinning, but does not, is punished for the sins of the members of his household.* If he can influence the people of his city to stop sinning, but does not, he is punished for the sins of the people of his city. If he can stop the whole world from sinning, and does not, he is punished for the sins of the whole world" (*Shabbat* 54b).

Rashi (eleventh century), the classic commentator on the Talmud, presumes that "the whole world" (*be-kol ha-olam kulo*) refers only to the Jewish people and that the talmudic teaching applies specifically to a king of the Jews or a head of the Jewish nation (*nasi*) who can use his power—and exploit people's fear of him—to stop Jews from sinning. But the clear implication of this teaching suggests that if a Jew is in a position to influence non-Jews (a possibility that might have been unlikely both during the time of the Talmud and of Rashi), he or she must do so. Elie Wiesel, the well-known writer and Holocaust survivor, has repeatedly used his moral authority to try to stop the persecutions of many groups, and to make both Jews and non-Jews aware of the terrible evils being committed in different parts of the world that must be stopped.

---

*"If a Jew sees a non-Jew committing a sin and it is possible to deter him, he should do so. Thus did the Holy One, blessed be He, send the prophet Jonah to Nineveh to return [the inhabitants of the Assyrian city] to the proper path" (*Sefer Chasidim, *paragraph 1124).*

*The sinners themselves are obviously also punished, but the Talmud is underscoring that anyone who can prevent a sin and doesn't do so also bears responsibility.

*In more recent times, Rabbi Menachem Mendel Schneersohn, the Lubavitcher Rebbe, taught: "An integral component of the Jew's task is to bring it about that all people, not only Jews, acknowledge God as Creator and Ruler of the world. The world, we are told, 'was not created for chaos, but that it be inhabited' (Isaiah 45:18). A chaotic world results when there are no absolute criteria by which to live, when morals and ethics are based solely on man's understanding. Man is swayed by interests other than reason and justice; we have too recently seen the destruction that ensues when laws and philosophy are perverted to serve personal ends." (*Likutei Sichos, *11 Nissan 5743 [1983]).*[7]

In short, Jews have a vested interest, and a divinely ordained responsibility, to try to influence non-Jews with Godly values; as the twentieth-century experience of both Nazism and Communism shows, the values that might be chosen when God is rejected can be terrible for good people in general and for the Jews in particular.

---

19. "Whoever is not merciful to his fellow creature is certainly not of the descendants of our father Abraham" (*Beizah* 32b).

"Fellow creatures" refers to all human beings. That is probably why the Rabbis cite Abraham, whose concern for non-Israelites is demonstrated by two events described in the Torah. In the first, he sees three strangers traveling in the desert on a hot day, invites them into his tent, offers them a place to bathe and rest, and provides them with an elaborate meal (Genesis 18:1–8; see the discussion of this episode on pages 44–46). In the second, Abraham argues with God on behalf of the citizens of Sodom (see page 287).

20. "Whoever repudiates idolatry is called a Jew" (*Megillah* 13a).

Such a person is therefore entitled to the same help and protection we are expected to provide to Jews.

21. "The Jewish nation is distinguished by three characteristics; they are merciful, they are modest [alternatively, bashful], and they perform acts of loving-kindness" (*Yevamot* 79a).

For the significance of this teaching in Jewish life, see *A Code of Jewish Ethics, Volume 1: You Shall Be Holy,* chapters 20–22, and chapter 10 of this volume.

22. "The law of the state is law" (*Bava Kamma* 113a; this dictum is mentioned five times in the Talmud).

Jewish law obligates Jews to observe national or local laws as long as they are not immoral, do not require violation of Jewish law, and are not antisemitic, as was often the case in many societies in which Jews lived. In a society such as the United States, where Jews have equal rights, Jewish law obliges them to obey the laws of the state.

23. "Charity is equal in importance to all the other commandments combined" (*Bava Bathra* 9a).

As noted, Jewish law mandates giving charity to non-Jews and non-Jewish causes as well as to Jewish ones (see pages 200–201).

24. "Stealing from a non-Jew is worse than stealing from a Jew because of the profanation of God's name" (*Tosefta, Bava Kamma* 10:15).

In addition to profaning God's name, such behavior can also cause suffering to innocent Jews.* The fifteen-year-old Anne Frank, writing almost two thousand years after the *Tosefta,* offered this teaching in her diary: "What one Christian does is his own responsibility. What one Jew does is thrown back at all Jews" *(The Diary of a Young Girl).*

When people make ugly generalizations about other groups, are they acting unfairly? Of course. But unfortunately, many, perhaps most, people engage in a certain degree of negative stereotyping, particularly after having had an unpleasant experience with a member of another ethnic, racial, or religious group. Have you ever had a negative experience with a person of another group, and had the thought that, or made a comment such as "____ are lazy, or dishonest, or violent, or stupid"? If you have, then you can easily imagine how a non-Jew, deceived by a Jew, can come to hold prejudicial views against other Jews as well.

If you have never made such a generalization, you are to be commended. You are also a rare person.

25. "Jews must . . . not lie to a Jew or non-Jew, and not mislead anyone in any matter. . . . For if Jews cheat non-Jews, they will say, 'Look how God chose

---

*The *Sefer Chasidim* notes that a non-Jewish victim may avenge himself upon another Jew who had nothing to do with the Jew who cheated him; also, the rest of the local Jewish community may suffer in reprisal for the actions of a Jew who acts dishonestly toward non-Jews (paragraph 600).

for His people a nation of thieves and deceivers. . . .' Indeed, God dispersed us among the nations so that we could gather converts to Judaism, but if we behave deceitfully towards others, who will want to join us?"* (Rabbi Moshe of Coucy, thirteenth-century France, *Semag [The Big Book of Commandments],* 152b).

*For more on Jews' obligation to sanctify God's name in their daily behavior, see *A Code of Jewish Ethics, Volume 1: You Shall Be Holy,* pages 456–469. The subject of Judaism's openness to encouraging non-Jews to convert to Judaism will be discussed, God willing, in Volume 3 of this code.

III

The Animal World

Judaism's Attitude to Animals

The righteous man knows the needs of his animal.

Proverbs 12:10

23

DOMINION AND COMPASSION

Dominion

1. The opening chapter of the Bible describes God's creation of the world and of the creatures that inhabit it. Though everything in the world, both animate and inanimate, is created by God, it is human beings alone whom the Bible describes as created "in God's image." This biblical term indicates that human beings are Godlike in that they know good from evil and have the free will to choose between them. Unlike human beings, animals are not created in God's image and do not have free will; rather, they act on instinct, and not from moral choice. Thus, for example, we regard Nazi S.S. officers who tortured and murdered concentration camp inmates as evil. However, we do not regard the German shepherd dogs used by the S.S. to attack and terrify Jews and other inmates as evil. True, these dogs were trained to do cruel things, but they never made, and could not make, a free will decision to do so; indeed, had they been trained from an early age to attack the S.S. officers themselves, they would have done so.

Because they lack free will, the Bible regards animals as being on a lower plane than human beings; it also teaches that God gave human beings dominion over the animal world: "And God said, 'Let us make man in our image . . . They [humankind] shall rule the fish of the sea, the birds of the sky, the cattle, the whole earth, and all the creeping things that creep on earth" (Genesis 1:26). Two verses later, God reiterates this idea in His blessing to humankind: "Be fertile and increase, fill the earth and master it; and rule the fish of the sea, the birds of the sky, and all the living things that creep on earth" (Genesis 1:28).* These verses are viewed in the Jewish tradition as a

*In addition, and less frequently noted, God blessed the animal world as well, saying, for example, of the fish and birds: "Be fertile and increase, fill the waters in the seas, and let the birds increase on the earth" (Genesis 1:22).

warrant for human beings to use animals for labor (for example, on farms), to benefit from animals (such as through using wool shorn from sheep, and through *necessary* medical experiments conducted on animals; see pages 336–339), and to use animals for food (though permission to do so was only given later; see pages 331–332).

On the other hand, because animals are sentient creatures with emotions, and in many cases with strong familial feelings, they must be treated with compassion (see the rest of this chapter). Dominion, as an examination of biblical and other Jewish teachings reveals, does not mean that human beings may rule over animals without restraint.

Compassion for animals in the Torah

2. If asked whether the Torah has more legislation regarding the Sabbath or the treatment of animals, most Jews will assume the correct answer is the Sabbath, a central institution in Jewish life, and the subject of the Fourth Commandment. Yet there are far more statutes concerning animals than there are regarding the Sabbath; indeed, the compassionate treatment of animals is even included in the commandment ordaining the Sabbath (see paragraph 5).

3. Several biblical laws deal with the treatment of animals used for agricultural work. Deuteronomy 22:10 prohibits plowing one's field with an ox and a donkey harnessed together. Being of unequal size and strength, both animals, particularly the weaker one, will suffer; the donkey will experience strain, and the ox frustration. By implication, although the Torah speaks only of a donkey and ox, one should not yoke together any animals of significantly unequal strength.

4. Deuteronomy 25:4 forbids the muzzling of an ox while it is working in the field. Jewish law understands this prohibition as applying to any working animal, not just an ox (Maimonides, *Book of the Commandments,* negative commandment 219). It is cruel to muzzle an animal and thereby preclude it from eating of the food it is working with, seeing, smelling, and perhaps hungering for. It is also an act of ingratitude to the animal that is helping us harvest our crop.

In Rabbi Joseph Hertz's commentary on the Torah, he cites the shocking case of a wealthy—I believe nineteenth-century—Italian farmer who used to fasten iron muzzles on his workers so that "it might not occur to these poor peasants, working for starvation wages under the glowing sun of southern Italy, to satiate their burning thirst and their gnawing hunger with a few of the millions of grapes of the owner."[1] Nor was this a singular case. Rabbi Dr. Elijah Schochet notes that in ancient Carthage, mill workers were muzzled during their labors.[2] Three thousand years ago, the Torah forbade treating animals the way these employers treated human beings.

---

5. The Fourth Commandment (concerning the Sabbath), which regulates a day of rest for human beings, also applies to animals. On this day, "you shall not do any work, you, your son or daughter . . . or your cattle . . ." (Exodus 20:10). The Torah later returns to this theme, and places particular emphasis on the significance of both animals' and employees' rest on the Sabbath: "Six days shall you work, but on the seventh day shall you cease from labor, in order that your ox and donkey may rest, and that your servant and the stranger may be refreshed" (Exodus 23:12).

Rashi (eleventh century), commenting on this verse, emphasizes that providing proper rest for animals entails not confining them indoors, but rather allowing them to roam in the field and pluck and eat grass from the ground.

---

6. Although Jewish law permits eating animals and birds, the Torah specifically forbids taking away fledglings or eggs in the presence of the mother bird: "Let the mother go, and take only the young . . . (Deuteronomy 22:6–7). This is one of only three laws—along with honoring one's parents (Exodus 20:12), and acting honestly in business (Deuteronomy 25:15)—for which the Torah promises long life. Maimonides (*The Guide for the Perplexed* 3:48) notes that the "pain of the animals under such circumstances is very great" (one would hope that most people would simply forgo taking either the eggs or the young birds).*

A recent study reinforces Maimonides' explanation, reporting that "elephant calves, after seeing their mother slain, have been observed waking up in convul-

---

*Maimonides writes: "For in general, the eggs over which the bird has sat, and the young that need their mother, are not fit to be eaten. . . . In most cases [therefore], this will lead to people leaving everything alone, for what may be taken is, in most cases, not fit to be eaten."

*sions, crying."**[3] *Maimonides emphasizes that the law concerning the mother bird has implications that go beyond the compassionate treatment of animals: "If the law provides that such grief not be caused to cattle or birds, how much more careful must we be not to cause grief to our fellow man"* (The Guide for the Perplexed *3:48).*

The biblical commentator Kli Yakar suggests that there is a connection between the law regarding the mother bird and the law ordaining respect for parents: when children see parents act with compassion toward a mother bird, they will conclude that they must be kind to their own parents.†

---

7. Related to this law is a biblical prohibition against slaughtering an animal and its young on the same day (Leviticus 22:28), which Maimonides understands "as a precautionary measure in order to avoid slaughtering the young animal in front of its mother. For there is no difference between the pain of humans and the pain of other animals in this case, for the love of a mother and her compassion upon a child does not depend on the intellect, but rather upon the power of emotion, which is found with most animals, just as it is found in man" (*The Guide for the Perplexed* 3:48).‡

8. On three occasions, the Bible forbids the cooking of an animal in its mother's milk (Exodus 23:19; 34:26; and Deuteronomy 14:21). Jewish law derives from this repetition additional prohibitions, the most well known of which is a ban on eating milk and meat foods together. But the verse's most fundamental prohibition is its literal one, forbidding behavior that is heartless. Obviously, the mother animal will not be aware that her child is being cooked in the milk she produced, but such behavior results in a person taking perverse pleasure in the suffering of other creatures.§

---

*Human children who are separated from their parents often suffer from a disease called "Failure to Thrive."

†My wife, Dvorah Telushkin, draws another implication from this law. Seeing how great parental concern is for children, children must take care not to inflict gratuitous pain on parents, such as by not calling or staying in touch with them.

‡A friend of mine, a jogger, notes that the surest way to be attacked by an animal of any size is to threaten, or even approach, its young: "When, while running, I am inexplicably attacked by a bird, it means that I have inadvertently stumbled across its nesting ground."

§Nachmanides understands this prohibition as rooted in the Torah's desire to keep Jews from becoming a "cruel nation" (commentary on Deuteronomy 14:21). The same rationale applies to the previously cited regulation: "The essence of the prohibition is not in not killing the animal and its offspring [on one day] . . . but rather . . . the most important issue is so that we not become cruel" (commentary on Deuteronomy 22:6).

9. Though we may dislike someone, we are forbidden to take out our animosity on her animal. "When you see the donkey of your enemy lying under its burden, and would refrain from raising it, you must nevertheless raise it with him" (Exodus 23:5). In other words, you should not walk away from a suffering animal, just because, perhaps justifiably, you dislike its owner. Instead, you must work with your enemy to relieve the animal's load. Such cooperation may even bring about a reconciliation between you and the person you dislike (see *A Code of Jewish Ethics, Volume 1: You Shall Be Holy,* page 318).

10. The Torah rules that every seventh year the land is to lie fallow. During this year, the land's owners are forbidden to plant or harvest crops; all unseeded produce that grows is to be made available to both humans and animals: "But you may eat whatever the land will produce during its sabbatical year, you, your male and female servants . . . and your cattle and the beast in your land may eat all its yield" (Leviticus 25:6–7).

11. Concern with the feeding of animals is present in another Torah law. If one animal is attacked by another and killed, its flesh is forbidden for human consumption (since the animal has not been slaughtered in the ritually prescribed manner). Rather, the Israelites are instructed to give the dead animal's meat to dogs (Exodus 22:30).

12. While there is no explicit Torah law forbidding the causing of unnecessary pain to animals, the large variety of regulations ordaining the fair treatment of animals led the majority view in the Talmud to conclude that the prohibition of *tza'ar ba'alei chayyim* (prevention of cruelty to animals)* is a Torah prohibition (*Bava Mezia* 32b, and *Shabbat* 128b).† Thus, even when situations arise that are not covered by specific biblical legislation, the operative assumption is that causing unnecessary suffering to animals is prohibited.

The word "unnecessary" underscores that not all behavior that causes animals to suffer is forbidden. For example, the Bible permits the slaughtering of animals for human consumption, although Jewish law regulates the

---

*The term literally means "the suffering of living creatures."

†The Rabbis understood the law to help unload a burdened animal (Exodus 23:5) as mandating a general concern for the suffering of animals. Meiri, in his commentary on *Bava Mezia* 32b, argues that a general prohibition against causing unnecessary suffering to animals can be deduced from the previously cited law prohibiting the muzzling of an ox while it is working in the field (Deuteronomy 25:4; see paragraph 4). Maimonides and Judah the Chasid cite yet another basis; see footnote on page 307.

slaughter in an effort to try to minimize—though it is, of course, impossible to eliminate—the suffering. Similarly, animal suffering is permitted if there is a substantial human benefit to be attained (for example, if insights gained through medical experimentation on animals can lead to a cure for disease; see pages 336–338).

13. In *The Golden Rule,* Professor Jeffrey Wattles concludes that "golden rule thinking may . . . be characterized as recognizing moral implications in the fact that others are like oneself" (page 42). Obviously, this is the basis for applying the Golden Rule in our interactions with other human beings. But while biblical ethics presupposes a deep chasm in intelligence and free will between human beings and animals, there are also significant similarities (particularly in the physical sphere), and the Golden Rule should apply in those areas as well. Thus, animals hate pain, and therefore, as we have seen, the Torah prohibits unnecessary pain, such as that brought about by yoking a weaker animal to a stronger one. And animals, like humans, crave food, hence it is forbidden, as noted, to muzzle an animal working in the field, just as it is prohibited to prevent a laborer working in the field from eating (Deuteronomy 23:25–6).

A talmudic passage teaches: "Six things are said concerning human beings. In regard to three, they are like ministering angels, in regard to three others, like animals. Three like ministering angels: they have understanding like the ministering angels, they walk erect like ministering angels, they can use the sacred tongue like ministering angels. Three like animals: they eat and drink like animals, they procreate like animals, and they excrete like animals" (Chagigah *16a).*

---

14. In addition to biblical laws, several events depicted in the Torah underscore how important a person's treatment of animals is in assessing his character. When Abraham dispatches his servant (assumed to be Eliezer) to find a suitable wife for Abraham's son, Isaac, he gives him no explicit guidelines, other than that the woman should come from the area in which Abraham was raised.

Eliezer promptly departs for the city of Nahor with ten camels. He decides, perhaps along the way, that kindness—to both human beings and animals—is the most appropriate first criterion to look for in a spouse. As he arrives in Nahor at evening time, the time when women come out to draw water, he has his camels kneel down by the well outside the city, and prays to God: "Let the maiden to whom I say, 'Please lower your jar that I may drink,' and who replies, 'Drink, and I will also water your camels," let her be the one whom You have decreed for your servant Isaac" (Genesis 24:14).

Moments after offering his prayer, Rebecca comes to the well, offers Eliezer water, and then returns to the well again and again to draw water for all his camels. Eliezer promptly arranges with Rebecca and her family for her marriage to Isaac; she, about whom we know little other than her kindness to humans and to animals, soon becomes Judaism's second Matriarch.*

15. The only work done by Moses prior to becoming the Israelites' leader was as a shepherd for his father-in-law Jethro. The Rabbis did not regard Moses' vocation as coincidental; as a Midrash relates: "Once, while Moses was tending the flock of his father-in-law, Jethro, one young sheep ran away. Moses ran after him until the sheep reached a shady place, where he found a pool of water and began to drink. When Moses reached the sheep, he said: 'I did not know you ran away because you were thirsty. Now, you must be exhausted [from running].' Moses put the sheep on his shoulders and carried him [back to the herd]. God said, 'Because you tend the sheep belonging to human beings with such mercy, by your life I swear you shall be the shepherd of My sheep, Israel' " (Exodus *Rabbah* 2:2).

The Midrash similarly relates that King David first revealed his qualifications to lead by his behavior as a shepherd. He used to separate the sheep into three groups, allowing the youngest, and most helpless, to feed on the most tender grass, the older ones on fully grown grass, and the rams to feed on the stubble. Impressed by David's ability to feed each sheep according to its capacity, and to thereby ensure sustenance for the most vulnerable, God concluded that David should lead the people He regarded as His flock (Genesis Rabbah *2:2).*

The Bible sees a trustworthy shepherd as such a powerful image of decency and kindness that the most famous verse in Psalms recasts God in this role: "The Lord is my shepherd, I shall not want" (23:1).

---

16. One way in which Balaam, the prophet hired by Moab's King Balak to curse the Israelites, revealed his low character was through his cruelty to

*My friend Daniel Taub points out that in an even earlier biblical narrative, Noah, who is depicted as showing no particular compassion for his fellow humans who are about to perish in the flood, is required to spend an extended period learning how to be compassionate to animals.

his donkey. When an angel of God was sent to deter Balaam from setting out on his mission, the well-paid prophet couldn't discern the angel, but the donkey did, and refused to move forward. Highly irritated, Balaam started to beat the animal with a stick until God opened its mouth, and the donkey said to Balaam, "What have I done to you that you have beaten me three times?" (Numbers 22:27–28).

The prophet responded by brandishing his sword at the donkey; at that point, the angel of God spoke to Balaam in a manner similar to the prophet's donkey: "Why have you hit your donkey three times?" (Numbers 22:32).*

Ironically, the sword-brandishing Balaam was killed shortly thereafter by a sword (Numbers 31:8).

If animals could speak, one wonders how many mistreated creatures throughout history would voice the same complaint as Balaam's abused donkey?

In the popular American film Ghost, *a cat is, initially, the only character who can see a ghost. Rabbi Judah the Chasid (author of the thirteenth-century* Sefer Chasidim*) believed that such vision was granted to some animals: "When you ride an animal at night and it suddenly snorts loudly, stands still, and refuses to go on, this is an indication that it is seeing an evil spirit or demon. It is afraid of the demon and of what it might do to the rider. Don't beat the headstrong animal, and don't be ungrateful toward the faithful beast" (paragraph 668).*[4]

Compassion for animals in the later books of the Bible

17. When the prophet Nathan (circa 1000 B.C.E.) confronted and denounced King David over his seduction of Bathsheba, the wife of Uriah,† he chose to tell David a parable that suggests that animals were often held in great affection in ancient Israel. Nathan's story was about a rich man with large flocks who lived near a poor man. The poor man had only one small ewe. He took loving care of it, so that the lamb grew up together with his children, and would even be fed together with the family. When the rich man

*Both Maimonides (*The Guide for the Perplexed* 3:17) and Judah the Chasid (*Sefer Chasidim* #666) regard this biblical episode concerning Balaam and his donkey as the source for the biblical prohibition of cruelty to animals (see Rabbi J. David Bleich, "Animal Experimentation," in his book, *Contemporary Halakhic Problems,* Volume 3, pages 201–203).

†See *A Code of Jewish Ethics, Volume 1: You Shall Be Holy,* pages 390–391.

had a visitor who needed to be served an elegant meal, the man, loath to "waste" an animal from his own flock, took the poor man's lamb, slaughtered it, and fed it to his guest. "David flew into a rage against the man, and said to Nathan, 'As the Lord lives, the man who did this deserves to die' " (II Samuel 12:5). Of course, Jewish law never sanctioned the death sentence for the killing of an animal, but the intensity of David's response suggests that the love of family pets that characterizes tens of millions of Americans today might well have been known in ancient Israel as well.

18. When Jonah argued with God that the citizens of Nineveh had committed so much evil that they deserved to be destroyed rather than being granted the opportunity to repent, God justified His mercy not only by speaking of the many young—and presumably innocent—children in the city, but by also noting "the many beasts [that dwell there] as well" (Jonah 4:11). The implication is that surely they—the young children *and* the beasts—did not deserve to die, no matter how great the sins of the city's residents.

19. The Psalmist writes that God's compassion includes all His creatures: "Man and beast, You save, O Lord" (36:7). In another verse, recited by observant Jews three times daily, the Psalmist declares: "The Lord is good to all, and His mercy is upon all His works" (145:9).

The Jerusalem Talmud tells an apocryphal tale about Alexander the Great, the king of Macedon (fourth century B.C.E.*), who visited the mythical King Katzya to see how he dispensed justice among his people. The king's behavior was widely known to be merciful and fair. In one instance, when King Katzya found a way to resolve a dispute over a large sum of money by having both sides share it, Alexander laughed.*

King Katzya asked him: "Why did you laugh? Did I not judge well? Suppose such a case came before you, what would you have ruled?"

Alexander replied: "I would have put them both to death, and confiscated the treasure."

"Do you then love gold so much?" asked Katzya.

Immediately thereafter Katzya made a feast for Alexander and served him golden cutlets and golden poultry.

"I do not eat gold," Alexander exclaimed.

The king retorted: "If you do not eat gold, why do you love it so much?" He then asked him: "Does the sun shine in your country?"

"Certainly," Alexander answered.

"Does rain fall in your country?"

"Yes."

"In your land, is there some sort of small beast?"

"Yes," Alexander again replied.

". . . It is only for the sake of that small beast [that the sun still shines for you, and that the rain still comes down upon you]" (Jerusalem Talmud, Bava Mezia *2:5).*

---

20. The book of Proverbs notes that one characteristic feature of a righteous person (*tzaddik*) is that he "knows the needs of his animal" (12:10). In other words, an important characteristic of a righteous person is that he makes the effort to understand and meet an animal's needs and desires.

My son, Benjamin Telushkin, notes that one reason treatment of animals can be so good a gauge of character is because, unlike personal advantages that can accrue from many other activities, none accrues from being kind to animals. For example, if you tell people at a dinner table that you are a vegetarian, many will be impressed, and your statement will certainly make an impact. But making sure to feed your cat or dog before you eat any food yourself will earn you no praise, unless you boast about it. Also, other kind acts earn you gratitude. If you give to a beggar, you will usually receive at the very least a thank you, and often even a blessing. If you return a lost item to an owner, you will generally be the recipient of a heartfelt sense of gratitude, and much good will. In addition, the person who has benefited from your kind act may well tell others, and your reputation will be enhanced. But when you feed an animal, or care for an injured bird, you receive no thank you from the creature (there might or might not be some physical expression of gratitude), nor any recognition from the world. It is, one can argue, yet another form of chesed shel emet, *true kindness, which the Rabbis define as a kind act done without any expectation of payback or recognition.*

Compassion in the Talmud and Midrash

21. "Whoever has compassion for [God's] creatures is shown compassion from Heaven. Whoever does not have compassion for [God's] creatures is not shown compassion from Heaven" (*Shabbat* 151b). In short, if you want to be deemed worthy of God's compassion, make sure that God knows you to be compassionate, particularly in your treatment of those over whom you have power, be they employees (in the ancient world, this often meant servants), children, or animals.

22. Avoiding cruelty to animals is so basic a Jewish value that it is one of only seven commands that Jewish law considers also binding on non-Jews (see page 405*n* for an enumeration of the other six). Thus, the Rabbis rule that it is forbidden for anyone—Jew or non-Jew—to cut off flesh from a living animal and eat it. While human beings are granted the right to eat meat (Genesis 9:3), this does not give them the right inflict pain on animals needlessly.

Unfortunately, not only was this Jewish law prohibiting cruelty to animals ignored by many in the ancient world, but it has also been ignored in more modern times. Diane Ackerman notes in A Natural History of the Senses *that "Some of the strangest culinary habits arose in England during the eighteenth century, when bored city dwellers became fascinated by sadism. . . . The idea arose that torturing an animal made its meat healthier and better tasting and . . . people indulged in ghoulish preparations. . . . They tenderized pigs and calves by whipping them to death with knotted ropes; they hung poultry upside down and slowly bled them to death; they skinned living animals. Recipe openers from the era said such things as, 'Take a red cock that is not too old and beat him to death . . .'" The ancient Jewish prohibition against eating the flesh of a living animal was violated in England. Ackerman cites a grotesque recipe by a cook named Mizald for preparing and eating a goose while it is still alive. The recipe is so vile in its cruelty that I will not reprint it in full, but only cite its final sentence: "Take her [the goose] up and set her before your guests and she will cry out as you cut off any part from her and will be almost eaten up before she is dead; it is mighty pleasant to behold.**[5]

In a book published in London in 1776, Dissertation on the Duty of Mercy and Sin of Cruelty to Brute Animals, *Humphrey Primatt offers an accurate assessment of all those who behaved in the manner described in the previous paragraph: "If I know a man is cruel to his beast, I ask no more questions about him. He may be a noble man, or a rich man, or a polite man, or a sensible*

---

*The recipe even advises the cook to wet the head and heart of the roasting goose with a wet sponge so as to keep the bird alive for as long as possible. The Talmud records that a similarly sadistic technique was used by the Romans to prolong the agony of condemned prisoners burned at the stake (see pages 381–382 for a description of the death of the Jewish martyr Rabbi Chanina ben Teradyon).

man, or a learned man, or an orthodox man, or a church man, or anything else, it matters not; this I know, on the sacred word of a wise king, that being cruel to his beast, he is a wicked man" (page 208).*[6]

—

In a Wall Street Journal *article (October 26, 1998, page 1), entitled "Brains, Served Fresh and Raw," correspondent Peter Waldman reports that foreigners, in this case Taiwanese, visiting Indonesia are often willing to pay high sums for organs extracted from living exotic animals: "One captain of a big tuna trawler orders a dozen young crested black macaques—[monkeys and] an endangered species of primate—delivered to his boat, alive. The request is relayed . . . to the village of Bingaguminan, on the edge of Tangkoko Nature Preserve. Trappers there trek days in the jungle refuge to bag the rare animals. To take baby macaques alive, mothers are shot. Aboard the trawler, galley hands bind the monkeys' hands and feet. Then, using sharp bamboo sticks, the Taiwanese puncture the babies' soft skulls. As the convulsions ebb, brains are served raw. 'Prices have tripled for monkeys, but foreigners can't get enough,' says a dockside chef here."*

Comments Matthew Scully, author of Dominion: The Power of Man, the Suffering of Animals, and the Call to Mercy: *"There is really just one force on earth, save physical restraint, that could have stayed the captain's hand in this trawler scene. If we could have convinced him the monkey and its mother had rights, that wouldn't have done it. If we explained to him that this particular species of macaque is endangered, and may soon perish from the earth . . . no, that would not have satisfied him either. Only conscience, perhaps only the fear of God Almighty, could make such a man draw back."*[7]

—

In the United States today, there are trendy restaurants where it is "the craze" to eat lobsters alive.[8] *Meanwhile, in China, undercover agents of the Humane Society of the United States have filmed videos of dogs being tied down and skinned alive, their furs subsequently being exported to the West.*[9]

—

23. "It is forbidden for a man to eat until he has given food to his animals" (*Berachot* 40a). While a hungry human being who has food knows that he can eat within minutes, and therefore can generally bear his hunger with equanimity, a very hungry animal does not know until it is fed that it

*The "wise king" referred to is King Solomon, to whom tradition attributes the authorship of Proverbs, and specifically to the previously cited statement, "A righteous man knows the needs of his animal" (12:10).

will receive food; therefore, the animal's suffering in such an instance is greater than that of a human being. Today, of course, few Jews, aside from those who live on Israeli kibbutzim and moshavim, are farmers, so that the animals most Jews are likely to be responsible for are their pets. Feeding our pets before ourselves is not only good for them, it also teaches two important lessons to our children: Our obligation to be kind to all of God's creatures and the importance of delayed gratification. As my friend, Rabbi David Woznica, says: "It's very beautiful for a child to see his parents feeding the helpless before themselves." In addition, teaching a child to delay his own eating to feed an animal helps the child become accustomed to doing the right thing even when it might cause him or her a slightly uncomfortable delay.

This talmudic law applies, of course, even on fast days; *you* might be required to fast on Yom Kippur, but your animal is not, and you are therefore required to feed him.

Although animals have priority when it comes to eating, human beings come first when it comes to drinking. As the Sefer Chasidim *(thirteenth century) rules: "If both a man and an animal are thirsty, you should quench the man's thirst before giving water to the animal, and so it says, [Rebecca said to Eliezer], 'Drink, sir!' When he had finished drinking, she said, 'Let me draw water for your camels' (Genesis 24:46; see also 24:18, 19). We also read that Moses was told [by God]: 'Provide drink for the community and their beasts' (Numbers 20:8); first the community and only then the beasts. But when it comes to eating, animals take precedence . . . and so we read: 'I will provide grass in the fields for your cattle, and [then] you shall eat your fill' " (Deuteronomy 11:15). The* Sefer Chasidim *likewise notes that when Eliezer arrived at Rebecca's home, his animals were given straw, and only then was food set before him (see Genesis 24:32; paragraph 531).*[10]

A heartrending story from the Holocaust shows how seriously many observant Jews took the obligation to feed their animals early and properly. Rabbi Itzik Rosenzweig, an accomplished talmudic scholar, earned his living as a poultry farmer in Slovakia. On the day he and his family were deported to a Nazi death camp—along with hundreds of other Jews—their train was surrounded by jeering antisemitic neighbors, laughing and mocking them. Rosenzweig ignored the insults, but instead begged his tormentors, "Please, go to my house and give water and food to the chickens. They have had nothing to eat or drink all day." The crowd ignored him. In the far distance he spotted a Jew (Rabbi Moshe Yehudah

*Tziltz) who had not yet been deported. Rosenzweig yelled out to him, "Afflicting animals is forbidden by Torah law. Give the chickens food and water."**

---

24. A similar concern that animals be adequately fed is emphasized in a ruling in the Jerusalem Talmud: "A person is forbidden to acquire an animal or bird unless he [or she] can feed it properly" (Jerusalem Talmud, *Ketubot* 4:8).† By implication, we should not acquire a pet unless we also have the money, time, and commitment to take the animal to a veterinarian and to take care of its other needs.

When a new children's movie comes out about an adorable species—for example, 101 Dalmatians*—it leads to an upsurge of purchased, then abandoned, animals.*

One possibly broader implication of this talmudic law that we not acquire an animal unless we have adequate means to care for it is that a zoo should not acquire an animal unless it can adequately provide for its needs, such as not forcing a creature used to having space to roam to feel overly confined.

---

25. Rabbi Judah, the Mishnah's editor and the preeminent Jewish scholar of the early third century, was severely punished for lacking compassion for an animal, even though he did nothing explicitly forbidden by Jewish law. As the Rabbis explain: "The sufferings of Rabbi Judah came to him because of a certain event, and left him in the same way. What was the incident that led to his suffering? A calf was once being taken to be slaughtered. It [escaped and] ran to Rabbi Judah, where it hid its head under his coat, and cried [because it did not want to be slaughtered]. Rabbi Judah, however, [pushed the calf away, and] said, 'Go! For this you were created.' It was then said [in Heaven]: 'Since he does not show mercy, let suffering come upon him.' [For the next thirteen years, Rabbi Judah suffered from painful

---

*Retold in Dov Baer Weissmandl, *Min HaMeitzar (Out of the Depths),* page 32; see David Sears, *The Vision of Eden,* page 216. The late Jewish theologian Eliezer Berkovits concluded his book *Faith After the Holocaust* with the story of Rosenzweig: "Because of what man did to Itzik Rosenzweig, I have no faith in man; because of Itzik, in spite of it all, I have faith in the future of man" (pages 168–169).

†In recent years, Rabbi David Golinkin (Chair of the Rabbinical Assembly's Law Committee in Israel) has argued that the premeditated inadequate feeding of veal calves (see pages 320–322) violates this talmudic dictum as well (see "The Kashrut of Veal Raised in Factory Farms," in Golinkin, *Responsa in a Moment,* page 75).

ailments.] And his sufferings ended as a result of another event. One day, his maid was sweeping the house, and she came upon some young weasels. She was about to sweep them up, when Rabbi Judah stopped her. 'Let them be. It is written' [in Psalms 145:9]: "His mercy is upon all His works." It was then said [in Heaven], 'Since he [now] shows mercy, let us show mercy to him' [and he was immediately healed]; *Bava Mezia* 85a)."

One implication of this story is that suffering comes not only as punishment (certainly there were many many people far more deserving of punishment than Rabbi Judah), but to teach lessons that someone might not otherwise learn. Thus, the Talmud indicates elsewhere that compassion did not come easily to Rabbi Judah; this story suggests that his own suffering expanded his capacity to show mercy.*

People often express surprise and puzzlement at this story. Since Judaism permits the slaughtering of animals, why is Rabbi Judah's act regarded as so wrong, and so singularly uncompassionate?

Two possible reasons occur to me.

The animal was a young calf. To say to such a creature, "Go! For this you were created," is wrong. Perhaps, the Talmud is suggesting, animals are not created to be put to death at a young age (yet another reason to not eat veal; see pages 320–322). Rabbi David Aaron goes even further, arguing that the wrong committed by Rabbi Judah was that "he incorrectly said, 'For this you were created.' The Talmud is teaching us that, contrary to [Rabbi Judah's] declaration, animals [of all ages] were not created for human consumption."†

In addition, even though we live in a world in which animals are slaughtered, and most of us eat meat, there is still something heartless in pushing away a creature that has taken refuge with you, and hides itself under your coat.

The experience of Rabbi Judah is reinforced by the earlier cited Deuteronomy 22:6–7 (see page 302), which promises a direct reward from God for treating a mother bird with compassion. In other words, how we treat animals will help

---

**Bava Bathra* 8a describes an episode in which, during a famine, he regretted feeding people ignorant of Judaism.

†*Living a Joyous Life,* page 145. In other words, although Torah law permits the consumption of animals, Rabbi Judah had no right to conclude that this was the purpose for an animal's creation.

determine how God treats us. Thus, in this story, God inflicts suffering on Rabbi Judah when he does not show mercy to an animal, and God withdraws the suffering when he does.

---

26. A midrashic episode speaks of those who exploit animals as "wicked." Thus, the Rabbis describe a man who bought a sheaf of corn and held it in front of his donkey to goad the animal to move faster. Then, when the owner and donkey finally reached the master's home, he tied the sheaf high above the animal so that it could still not reach it. At this point, witnesses to the owner's action said to him: "You wicked man. The donkey has been running the whole way for the sake of this [sheaf], and now you refuse to give it to him" (see Exodus *Rabbah* 31:7).

This Midrash would seem to constitute an implicit condemnation of sports like greyhound racing, in which animals are forced to chase their "prey" around a course.

Compassion for animals in medieval and modern times

27. Maimonides (twelfth century), basing himself on a talmudic text, rules that if one encounters two animals, one lying down under its burden, and the other unburdened with the owner looking for someone to help him load it, one is obligated to first unload the burdened, and suffering, animal; only then may one load the other ("Laws of Murder" 13:13; see *Bava Mezia* 32b). Maimonides also believed that while it was necessary for human well-being to eat meat, the commandments concerning kosher slaughter were "introduced to bring about the easiest death in an easy manner. . . . In order that death should come about more easily, the condition was imposed that the knife should be sharp" (*The Guide for the Perplexed* 3:26; contrast Maimonides' twelfth-century concern to minimize the suffering of animals with the grotesque cruelties inflicted on animals being prepared for food in England many hundreds of year later; see page 310).

28. In *Sefer Chasidim,* several passages mandate the sympathetic and fair treatment of animals. Thus, it is permitted to use an animal for work, but one who puts too heavy a burden on it, or beats an animal that is having trouble walking, will be brought by God to judgment for having "caused sorrow to a living creature."* The author, Rabbi Judah the Chasid, similarly condemns in the same passage those who pull a cat's ears to make it scream and riders who cruelly hit horses (paragraph 44). Elsewhere, the author warns that one who hurts animals needlessly will be made to work like an animal in the Hereafter (paragraph 169). Rabbi Judah also condemns those who cut off the tail of an animal and then claim that such behavior causes no pain to the animal when "it is in fact causing a great deal of discomfort to the animal, because without a tail the creature cannot ward off insects" (paragraph 589).

An additional regulation in *Sefer Chasidim* limits the pain one can inflict even on an animal that is a pest: "When a dog that doesn't bite enters one's house, if a Jew wishes to chase the dog out he may do so with a small stick, but it is forbidden to pour boiling water on the animal, or to hit the dog with a heavy stick, or slam the door on it, or blind it. This is inconceivable!" (paragraph 670). While such behavior is inconceivable to most of us as well, the fact that the author describes such acts of cruelty (along with the passage cited earlier detailing evils done to animals in eighteenth-century England) suggests that many people either take no account of the pain suffered by animals, or actually enjoy inflicting it.

The behavior outlawed in the Sefer Chasidim *should serve to remind us of the importance of keeping our children from acting cruelly toward animals and even insects. Some years ago, when I was conducting an ethics advice column for Beliefnet.com I received the following letter: "My three-year-old and five-year-old take delight in squashing ants on the sidewalk. I've tried to tell them that it's bad to kill living things, but they've seen me swat bees and spiders in the house, so I feel hypocritical. How can I explain the difference to them?"*

I responded: "You are not a hypocrite. When you kill a bee in your home, there is a reason for you to do so; the insect is somewhat dangerous, and you have a right to protect yourself and your family.† *But when your children squash ants*

*The condemnation of those who overwork animals brings to mind the Torah's command to not treat employees in a ruthless manner (Leviticus 25:43).

†When you kill an insect such as a cockroach in your home, even if it does not pose an immediate danger, you are killing a trespasser (albeit, an unintentional one). Even so, my father, Shlomo Telushkin, tried to avoid killing insects, and would, when possible, maneuver them onto a piece of paper, which he would then deposit outside. Some great figures in the Jewish world have gone even further. Rabbi Chaim Vital, a disciple of the sixteenth-century Rabbi Isaac Luria (known as the Ari) recorded that "My master was careful never to kill any insect, even the smallest and least of them, such as fleas, lice, and flies—even if they were causing him pain" (*Sha'ar Ha-Mitzvot,* Noach; cited in Natan Slifkin, *Man and Beast,* page 53; this was a standard

on the sidewalk, there is no reason for them to do so; the ants pose no danger and aren't bothering them. You would, however, be a hypocrite if you went out into a forest to an area containing many bees just for the pleasure of killing them.

"I heard a story told about the late Rabbi Israel Spira, a Holocaust survivor, who had seen in his lifetime the worst of which human beings are capable, and who was exceedingly careful not to cause any needless suffering to human beings or animals. Once, when he saw one of his grandchildren purposely step on an ant, he said to him: 'Oh, how sad! The ants were marching joyfully to a wedding, and now you've killed the groom.'

"The young boy felt bad, and deeply regretted what he had done. By personalizing the insects, as the rabbi did, you may similarly motivate your two young children to feel more compassion for all living creatures and to change their behavior.

"But what if they don't? Is this an issue you should be concerned about? I believe you should, particularly if this behavior persists. It is sadistic to kill a living creature for pleasure; the fact that someone enjoys doing that—particularly as he gets older—is cause for concern. I know a woman who was dating a man who told her that, as a child, he used to cut insects in half just for fun. She married him, and when he became angry at her, he beat her. True, there may not always be a correlation, but if one of my daughters were dating someone who had spent time in his childhood killing insects for pleasure, I'd worry.

"Your children are now very young, so there's certainly no cause for you to panic. But this is an issue that must be addressed. Whatever a person's age, there is one thing human beings are not in need of, and that is to get more in touch with their sadistic inclinations."

Dr. Isaac Herschkopf notes that one of the childhood indicators of sadistic criminals in general, and of serial killers in particular, is cruelty to animals: "I have heard these demented murderers describe how they, as children, would stick firecrackers in salamander's mouths to watch them explode, throw live cats into incinerators, and tie dogs' or cats' tails together until they would rip each other apart to escape." Obviously, not all children who treat animals cruelly will end up as murderers, but Dr. Herschkopf's observation underscores why a child's cruelty to animals must be seriously addressed.

---

29. The *Sefer HaChinnuch* (thirteenth century), a widely studied work that teaches the 613 laws of the Torah and their rationales, explains that the

---

that the Ari accepted upon himself and should in no way be considered binding on others). However, when you kill an insect in the wild that poses no danger, you are the trespasser.

rules of ritual slaughter, such as the obligation to kill an animal at the neck and with a sharpened knife devoid of notches, was intended "so that we don't cause too much suffering to the animal, for though the Torah permitted man . . . to use animals for food, and for all his needs, it is forbidden to cause an animal needless pain" (451)* Later, the *Shulchan Arukh* (sixteenth century) codifies that if a *shochet* (ritual slaughterer) uses a knife that is not fully sharpened and with notches, and the cut, therefore, does not proceed smoothly, the meat is forbidden (*Yoreh Deah* 23:4). Similarly, the cut must be made at precisely the right spot on the animal's neck, neither too high nor too low, so that death comes instantaneously.

—

The Sefer HaChinnuch *also intuited that a person's treatment of animals will affect how he or she relates to human beings. Thus, if we treat animals sensitively, we will become more sensitive in our treatment of people (see 596).*†

—

30. Would that the biblical insight that animal suffering is real and must be curbed were so obvious as not to require further discussion. Unfortunately, that was not the case in the distant past nor throughout later history. No less an intellectual giant than René Descartes (1596–1650), the dominant figure in seventeenth-century Western philosophy, likened the screams and cries of hurt animals to the sounds of "broken machinery." Descartes insisted that animals do not experience suffering. This vile teaching had terrible consequences; when Descartes's followers dissected live animals, they disregarded the animals' cries as meaningless.

—

Rabbi Natan Slifkin, the leading contemporary rabbinic authority on the animal world, notes the absurd cruelty of Descartes's belief: "As is apparent to any observer, an animal reacts to pain with the same outward expressions as does a human."[11] Indeed, Descartes's statement brings to mind an observation made by George Orwell in an altogether different context: "You have to be an intellectual to believe something as stupid as that."

—

*Maimonides emphasized that the laws of kosher slaughter are intended to minimize animals' suffering: "Now, since the necessity to have good food requires that animals be killed, the aim was to kill them in the easiest manner, and it was forbidden to torment them through killing them in a reprehensible manner by piercing the lower part of their throat or by cutting off one of their limbs . . ." (*The Guide for the Perplexed* 3:48).

†Regarding people who seem more concerned with animal suffering than human, see pages 328–330.

31. One Chasidic master, Rabbi Zusya of Hanipol (d. 1800), was so pained by the sight of caged birds that he would purchase them from their owners and then set them free. He regarded this as a form of *pidyon shevuyim,* ransoming of captives, which is the highest form of charity when performed on behalf of human beings. Rabbi Zusya apparently felt that it was a moral imperative to spare animals, particularly birds, whose very nature demands freedom, the suffering of captivity.*

32. The nineteenth-century *Kitzur Shulchan Arukh,* a standard compendium of traditional Jewish law, commands Jews to intervene in situations that are causing animals distress. Thus, if we witness horses drawing a cart come to a rocky road or a steep hill, and are unable to climb the impasse on their own, it is our duty to assist. If we don't, the driver might strike the animals, and force them to exert themselves beyond their strength, and it is a mitzvah to prevent cruelty to animals (191:2).

33. Many Jews believe that Judaism has a particular animus against pigs, which is ironic, given that if we were pigs we would probably like Judaism (if we were cows or chickens, we likely wouldn't). Because of this belief, many people use "pig" as an insult, denouncing, for example, one who "eats like a pig," or calling a person a "pig" for acting in a greedy manner (even though there is no evidence with which I am familiar that pigs are more "greedy" than other animals, or than human beings, for that matter).

The late rabbi Avrohom Pam, the renowned head of Yeshiva Torah Vodaath, opposed denigrating creatures created by God. When a group of distinguished Orthodox rabbis issued a statement denouncing an attempt by

---

*Martin Buber also records this story about Rabbi Zusya, although in Buber's rendition, the rabbi's behavior was even more radical: "Once Rabbi Zusya traveled cross-country collecting money to ransom prisoners. He came to an inn at a time when the innkeeper was not at home. He went through the rooms . . . and in one saw a large cage with all kinds of birds. And Zusya saw that the caged creatures wanted to fly through the spaces of the world and be free birds again. He burned with pity for them and said to himself: 'Here you are, Zusya, walking your feet off to ransom prisoners. But what greater ransoming of prisoners can there be [at this moment] than to free these birds from their prison?' Then he opened the cage, and the birds flew out into freedom.

[When the innkeeper learned what Zusya had done, he shouted at him] 'You fool! How could you have the impudence to rob me of my birds and make worthless the good money I paid for them?' Zusya replied [he knew the innkeeper to be an observant Jew], 'You have often read and repeated these words in the psalms, "His tender mercies are over all his works" (145:9).' Then the innkeeper beat him until his hand grew tired and finally threw him out of the house. And Zusya went his way serenely" (Martin Buber, *Tales of the Hasidim,* Volume 1, page 245).

some secular Israelis to encourage bringing pig meat into Israel, the rabbi faulted the petition's wording (although he agreed with its goal): "The sentence about the importation of pigs is written in a way that could be seen as demeaning the pigs. Why should the pig be faulted for being a pig? The Almighty created him that way." Rabbi Pam added: "A statement from [such esteemed rabbis] must be extremely careful not to undermine the inherent dignity of all God's creatures. Let's reword it."[12]

Some people, I have discovered, find Rabbi Pam's concern about pigs to be humorous, almost silly: "Is he really worried about the demeaning of pigs?" I, however, am moved by his letter. It is a reminder that all creatures, including those that are not kosher, have been created by God, and that we have an innate responsibility to them.

Cruelty to animals in Jewish and contemporary life

34. While the thrust of biblical and talmudic legislation is to reduce animal suffering, certain practices among segments of the Jewish (and non-Jewish) community inflict cruel suffering on animals and should be forbidden. Two deal with food items that are widely regarded as kosher, but which I believe should be outlawed for Jewish and non-Jewish consumption alike: veal and foie gras.

Until a few years ago, the treatment of veal calves was horrific,* and in recent years there has been some, but clearly very insufficient, improvement in their treatment. A description of a visit in 2000 to a dairy farm yields the following portrait of the contemporary treatment of newborn calves. The calves are generally raised in semidarkness, in a bare wooden crate too narrow for them to turn around in. They are fed on diets very low in iron, so that the calf's flesh "instead of becoming the normal healthy red color of a 16-week-old calf on pasture, will retain the pale pink color and soft texture of 'prime veal.'" The calves are also denied hay or straw for bedding since the calf, out of its desire for roughage would eat it, and the iron it contains would change the color of the calf's flesh. The stall in which the calf is confined is

*As Richard Schwartz described in his 1988 book *Judaism and Vegetarianism:* "After being allowed to nurse for only one or two days, the veal calf is removed from its mother, with no consideration of its need for motherly nourishment, affection, and physical contact. The calf is locked in a small slotted stall without enough space to move around, stretch, or even lie down. To obtain the pale tender veal desired by consumers, the calf is purposely kept anemic by giving it a special high calorie, iron-free diet. The calf craves iron so much that it would lick the iron fittings on its stall and its own urine if permitted to do so; it is prevented from turning by having its head tethered to the stall. . . . The calf leaves its pen only when taken for slaughter" (page 28).

wooden for the same reason. If it had an iron fitting, the calf would lick it. For the same reason, the crate is too small to allow the calf to turn around. If it could, it would lick its own urine, "in order to satisfy his craving for iron."[13] The animals are often kept in darkness for twenty-three hours a day.[14] In two of the three farms in Israel in which veal calves are raised, the individual cages in which the animals are held "prevented the animals from having any contact with other calves, even preventing them from seeing another calf, causing unreasonable social isolation."[15]

If, as most rabbis assume, the prevention of [unnecessary] cruelty to animals is a Torah law,* then the treatment of veal calves violates both the letter and the spirit of the Torah. Yet veal is still widely eaten by Jews, and by Americans in general. Veal eaters say in their defense that the soft and tender veal tastes better than other meat.† Thus, they argue in effect that the cruelty inflicted on the calf should not be regarded as "unnecessary"; rather, it results in the tangible benefit of better tasting food. But is it logical to believe that the Torah, which concerned itself with not muzzling an animal working in the field, would be indifferent to the fate inflicted on veal calves? Thus, can veal eaters, once they become aware of how calves are treated, be confident that God will say to them, "Enjoy your meat. I really don't care how veal calves are treated during their lifetime, as long as they are slaughtered in the proper manner when they are killed"?

In theory, veal could be permitted if significant changes were made in how such calves were raised. A Rabbinical Assembly responsa reported that in Israel in 2002, a committee of members of the Ministry of Agriculture, with an official from the Veterinarian Services and a lawyer from an organization called Anonymous for Animals, recommended eight changes in how veal calves in Israel are raised. Among them:

- Increase the iron intake of veal calves to raise the level of hemoglobin in their blood.
- Limit their social isolation.
- Give the calves sufficient space to lie down, rest, stand, and lick and groom themselves.
- Let the calves' living quarters be lit throughout the daylight hours.

---

*Even those talmudic rabbis who don't believe it is a biblical law acknowledge that it is a rabbinic enactment.

†A friend, a physician, notes that many veal eaters delude themselves into thinking that since the meat is white, like chicken or turkey, it is healthier than red meat, which is laden with cholesterol, saturated fat, and calories. However, such is not the case.

- Have appropriate bedding available.
- Put no restrictions on their water intake.*

If these reforms were instituted, the treatment of veal calves would cease to be cruel and in violation of Jewish ethical and legal teachings concerning the treatment of animals (some veal lovers would probably complain that the resultant meat would not be as tender as that of calves confined and raised on an iron-free diet). Even so, it still seems unnecessarily cruel to slaughter animals in their youth (see paragraph 25).

But the mistreatment of veal calves is not something that we can simply attribute to those who refuse to declare such meat forbidden. If enough people stop eating veal until proper reforms are instituted, that mistreatment will stop. Either no more veal will be sold or all calves will be raised in more humane conditions. The answer is in our hands.†

---

*The late Rabbi Moshe Feinstein believed that the way veal calves were raised violated the biblical prohibition against cruelty to animals. As he explained, while human needs justify inflicting a certain amount of cruelty on animals, such cruelty can only be justified for substantial needs, not trivial ones: "Man is not permitted to do anything and everything that hurts animals, even if it is in order to profit from it; only something that is of genuine benefit to man, such as slaughtering animals for food . . . (*Igrot Moshe, Even HaEzer, *Volume 4, responsa 92).‡*

However, the violation of the laws of tza'ar ba'alei chayyim *(literally, "the suffering of living creatures") did not, in Rabbi Feinstein's view, render the veal meat forbidden for consumption.*§[16]

---

*Although these recommendations have not been implemented, the Ministry of Agriculture did subsequently instruct Israeli farms to provide sufficient water for veal calves.

†A short time after completing this chapter, and by coincidence, the Conservative movement's Rabbinical Assembly approved a responsa authored by Rabbi Pamela Barmash that declared: "In light of the wretched conditions in which veal calves are raised, it is forbidden to promote the continuation of poor conditions of raising animals by purchasing, selling, or consuming veal. We rule that only veal from animals raised under humane standards . . . can be sold, purchased, or consumed. Humane standards for the raising of veal calves include sufficient space for calves to lie down, stand up, turn around and groom themselves, proper nutrition in a mixed diet appropriate for young calves, with sufficient iron, dry clean bedding, and limited isolation of calves."

‡I am following the translation of Rabbi Feinstein's ruling found in Rabbi Natan Slifkin, *Man and Beast* (page 200). Slifkin's book is, in my view, the most important contemporary work on animals in Jewish law and thought (see the following paragraph for more material from this book).

§There are precedents in Jewish history for forbidding the eating of popular food items for reasons other than kashrut. Meir Tamari, the Israeli economist and one of the world's leading

35. In *Man and Beast,* Rabbi Natan Slifkin offers an extended discussion of foie gras, the fattened liver of geese and ducks. Aficionados of this delicacy speak of its meat as unusually tender and tasty. Unfortunately, the fattened livers do not come about naturally. The birds are force-fed until their livers grow as much as eight times their normal size. The geese are generally kept in tiny, crowded pens, and fed by means of a metal tube (attached to a pressurized pump) that is inserted into their throats, and through which a soft mush is squirted. In earlier times, the birds were restrained by the neck, as moistened balls of grain were shoved into their throats—and often pushed down with a stick—over a period of several weeks, until the birds' livers were greatly enlarged.

During earlier times, when Jews subsisted largely on a diet of noodles, cabbage, and potatoes, fattened goose liver was considered an important source of nutrients. Food writers Jane Ziegelman and Andrew Coe note that "the Jews regarded it as a health food and dutifully fed it to growing children, since they would benefit most from the additional calories."[17] Perhaps this explains why rabbis in the past were willing to overlook the obvious cruelty involved in force-feeding geese and ducks. But, as Rabbi Slifkin notes, "Today . . . there are no significant nutritional benefits from *foie gras* that are not already obtained from other sources, and it is a delicacy rather than a staple." And in recent years (Israeli Supreme Court ruling, August 2003), Israel, which was once the world's fourth-largest producer of foie gras, has outlawed its production on the grounds that it violated Israel's Cruelty to Animals Law. The justices cited the Jewish laws concerning *tza'ar ba'alei chayyim* (generally translated as "prevention of cruelty to animals") as a basis for their decision.

As is the case with veal, such cruelty continues to be permitted only because some people enjoy a certain taste. If we ask ourselves the question: "Is this what God would want us to do?" I believe the answer becomes obvious.

---

experts on Jewish business ethics, records a case in sixteenth-century Moravia in which local fishermen (in this instance, non-Jews) created a cartel and raised the price of fish greatly. The Jews in the area were distressed, as they considered fish a traditional and necessary part of the Sabbath diet (to this day, for example, for Jews from an eastern European background, gefilte fish is a Shabbat staple). That week, the *Tzemach Tzedek,* the leading legal authority of the time, pronounced all fish *treif* (unfit to eat), and therefore forbidden. Quite quickly, the cartel's price-fixing stopped, and fish was again permitted (*With All Your Possessions,* page 93). To prohibit—as rabbis such as the *Tzemach Tzedek* have done—certain food items because of overcharging, but not because of mistreatment of animals, leaves the unfortunate impression that monetary concerns matter more in Jewish law than cruel mistreatment of living creatures.

Even in the distant past, some rabbis seem to have regarded the force-feeding of geese and ducks as a grievous sin. In a talmudic passage written in the style of a folktale, Rabbah bar bar Channa relates that while traveling in the desert he saw certain birds whose feathers were falling out because of their excessive fat; he was clearly referring to ducks and/or geese that had artificially fattened livers. When the rabbi spoke to Rabbi Elazar of seeing these birds, Elazar responded: "Israel is going to be held to account because of them" (*Bava Bathra *73b). The Talmud commentator Rashbam† notes that fattening these birds violates the biblical strictures against causing unnecessary pain to animals. He even states that this cruelty might be responsible for delaying the coming of the Messiah, perhaps the strongest statement against cruelty to animals that I have seen in any Jewish source.*

---

36. While the treatment of animals has generally improved in modern times, in at least one regard there has been a major deterioration. Rabbi Aryeh Carmell writes that it "seems doubtful . . . whether the Torah would sanction 'factory farming,' in which animals are treated as machines, with apparent insensitivity to their natural needs and instincts."[18] Rabbi Carmell's comment applies to the way chickens are most commonly raised and treated today. A typical shed (490 feet long by 45 feet wide) holds thirty thousand or more chickens. Under the animal welfare guidelines of the National Chicken Council (a trade association for the U.S. chicken industry), chickens are supposed to be granted a living space of 96 square inches, just a little bit larger than the size of standard 8½ × 11 typing paper. While newborn and very young chickens might find this space sufficient, as the chickens "near market weight, they cover the floor [of the shed] completely; at first glance, it seems as if the shed is carpeted in white." In such an environment—the large majority of chickens being consumed in the United States are raised this way—chickens are unable to ever flap their wings, and less aggressive chickens cannot avoid dominant aggressive chickens. In the final days of their lives, when the chickens are at their largest, they have almost no room in which to move. Professor John Webster, of the University of Bristol's School

*The production of foie gras goes back to the ancient Egyptians, and an Egyptian statuette of a fattened goose, more than 4,500 years old, is exhibited at the Louvre in Paris (see Slifkin, *Man and Beast,* page 203, footnote 1).

†The standard commentator on the Talmud is Rashi, but there are certain sections of the Talmud for which we do not have his commentary, but rather that of his grandson, known as Rashbam.

of Veterinary Science, regards industrial chicken production (nearly 9 billion chickens are consumed in the United States every year) as "in both magnitude and severity the single most severe systematic example of man's inhumanity to another sentient animal."[19]

At the least, it seems morally compelling for consumers to purchase only chickens and eggs produced in free-range conditions. Such poultry and eggs are considerably more expensive, but the alternative makes us accomplices in the mistreatment of chickens who, like us, are creatures created by God. I am aware that one can point to cruelties taking place throughout the world against human beings and argue that such injustices must be corrected before we devote our limited time and resources to fighting injustice against animals. But the two issues are not mutually exclusive. Matthew Scully, author of *Dominion,* a balanced but passionate polemic on the need to treat animals mercifully, concedes that "there will always be enough injustice and human suffering in the world to make the wrongs done to animals seem small and secondary. [But] the answer is that justice is not a finite commodity, nor are kindness and love."[20]

*Is there such a thing as unkosher clothing?**

37. "If wearing furs provides for a legitimate human need, then man can use the fur. Therefore, if animal fur will indeed keep a person warmer than other materials, [this is] a legitimate need [and] animal fur would be permissible. However, if warmth can be equally provided from another material that [could be made without killing animals], then a Jew might be required to wear a coat of that other material. Similarly, if the only reason a person wears the fur coat is to 'show off' one's wealth, or to engage in a mere fashion statement, that would be considered a frivolous and not a legitimate need. It should be pointed out that even when furs are permitted, they may not be acquired from animals that were trapped and put through torturous pain. . . . Using trapped animals in this case would entail a violation of *tza'ar ba'alei chayyim,* unnecessarily causing pain to animals" (Rabbi Nachum Amsel).[21]

To this day, many animals whose skins are used in furs are trapped in

*In addition to the items discussed in paragraph 37, there is one form of clothing specifically prohibited in the Torah, a garment containing a mixture of linen and wool (Deuteronomy 22:11) and known as *shatnez.* No reason is offered in the Torah for this prohibition, and priests were enjoined to wear garments containing this mixture while performing their services (see Exodus 28:6, 15). The first-century historian Josephus suggests that the purpose of the law was so that the laity not wear the garments of the priests. Many people are not aware that traditional Jews regard this law as still binding.

steel leghold traps and suffer an average of fifteen hours of pain before they are clubbed to death by a trapper: "These traps are so painful to the animal that it often chews off its own leg in terror, limping off to die of infection, loss of blood, or starvation."[22]

In addition, the manufacture of fur clothing is possible only through killing large numbers of animals; a forty-inch-long coat requires the death of sixty minks, forty-two foxes, or forty raccoons.* At a time when coats can be made of high-quality synthetic fibers that do not require the painful and prolonged deaths of any animals, the question a person, particularly a religious one, must ask herself before buying such a coat is the same question we proposed asking before eating veal or foie gras: "Is this what God would want me to do?"

In a 1992 responsa, Rabbi David Halevi, the late Sephardic chief rabbi of Tel Aviv, responding to the cruelties of trapping, the practices prevalent in many fur farms, and reports of furs being obtained by beating animals to death with clubs, ruled that furs obtained through these means should be forbidden: "If the killing of animals for the obtainment of their furs were accomplished by a quick, easy death, that would be one thing; but in actuality this is not the case. . . . The animals are caught in . . . [traps] . . . that cause them great anguish until they are released and killed and stripped of their furs. This constitutes actual tza'ar ba'alei chayyim; *there can be no disagreement about it." After further elaborating on the cruelty of killing animals simply to procure their furs (particularly at a time when high-quality and equally warm synthetic furs are available), Rabbi Halevi concluded: "Therefore, one should refrain from wearing furs."*†

In 1999, there was an unsuccessful initiative in California to put labels on fur products describing how they were produced. The labels would have read: "Consumer Notice: This product is made with furs from animals that may have been

*In China, undercover agents for the Humane Society of the United States filmed videos of cats stuffed into little cages, huddled in terror, as one after another was noosed and hung inside the cage so as to avoid bleeding and other damage to the fur (see Scully, *Dominion,* page 121). This behavior brings to mind the words of the nineteenth-century British cardinal John Henry Newman: "There is something so very dreadful in tormenting those who have never harmed us, who cannot defend themselves, and who are utterly in our power."

†Rabbi Halevi's ruling is cited in David Sears, *The Vision of Eden: Animal Welfare and Vegetarianism in Jewish Law and Mysticism,* page 88. Sears acknowledges that Halevi's position is, at this stage, unusual among decisors of Jewish law.

killed by electrocution, gassing, neck-breaking, poisoning, clubbing, stomping, or drowning, and may have been trapped in steel leg-hold traps."[23]

—

To the oft-raised objection "But what can a few people not buying furs (or not eating veal or foie gras) accomplish?" one may cite the words attributed to the late anthropologist Margaret Mead: "Never doubt that a small group of thoughtful, committed citizens can change the world. In fact, it's the only thing that ever has."[24]

—

Jewish laws not compassionate to animals

38. While Jewish laws overwhelmingly mandate the sensitive treatment of animals, there are a few laws that fall into the category of what Rabbi Natan Slifkin terms "commandments of insensitivity to animals." Generally, these laws permit brutal treatment of animals in order to convey spiritual lessons to human beings. For example, the Torah rules that when the body of a homicide victim is found in the open country and the identity of the killer is unknown, the elders of the town nearest to the corpse are obliged to take a heifer to an overflowing wadi, and break its neck. After doing so, they make a declaration: "Our hands did not shed this blood, nor did our eyes see it done" (Deuteronomy 21:1–9). In this case, the heifer was sacrificed as a form of atonement, to underscore that the elders, although not guilty of murder, bore a certain measure of responsibility for not maintaining a safe environment in their city and its environs.

Rabbi Slifkin asks: "How can the same Torah that contains so many commandments teaching us sensitivity to animals, also contain commandments that involve such brutality? The answer is that this is the whole point. These procedures are supposed to be horrific in order to have the desired effect upon the people performing them. When a murder takes place and justice cannot be performed, then the calf having its neck brutally axed impresses upon the elders of the city that they were negligent in their leadership. The . . . slaughter of animal sacrifices impress upon us that we may be worthy of such a fate if we do not improve our ways. . . . These brutal rituals are the exceptions that prove the rule—that the Torah, in general, commands us to treat animals with great sensitivity."[25]

Do I find this explanation fully satisfying? No. Perhaps no explanation is adequate. But what is important to emphasize is that part of the reason these laws disturb us is because the Bible itself has sensitized us to high standards of respect for animal life. In large measure, it is only because of the biblical laws commanding us to let our animals rest on the Sabbath, not muzzle an animal working for us, and not slaughter an animal and its young on the same day (laws that are still observed, which is not the case, for example, with the law concerning the breaking of the heifer's neck) that the idea took root in the Western world that animals should be treated with compassion; that is why these laws bother us. But, as Princeton philosopher Walter Kaufmann wrote about the bloody wars waged by Joshua against the ancient Canaanites, "to find the [distinctive] spirit of the religion of the Old Testament in Joshua is like finding the distinctive genius of America in the men who slaughtered the Indians."*[26]

When animal activists go too far

39. While efforts to limit gratuitous animal suffering are noble, and usually indicative of good character, some people apparently love animals at the expense of human beings. This phenomenon is alluded to in a biblical verse that denounces those who "slaughter human beings and kiss calves" (Hosea 13:2).

A good character test as to whether someone's commitment to preventing animal suffering is admirable is whether the person cares more about the suffering of animals when both animals and human beings are being hurt. This sometimes seems to be the case with the leadership of PETA (People for the Ethical Treatment of Animals), the most well-known American organization dedicated to ending cruelty to animals. In early 2003, Palestinian terrorists sent a bomb-laden donkey to bomb an Israeli bus. While the donkey was walking toward the bus, the bombs exploded, killing the unfortunate donkey before it could kill the people for whom it was intended. Throughout the world, Jews and many others—though sorry for the donkey—were relieved that a great catastrophe, the murder of those on the bus, had been averted. The response of PETA was different: Ingrid Newkirk, the organization's long-term president, wrote a letter to Yasser Arafat, the chairman of the PLO

---

*There is also a rabbinic ruling I find painful. At the time of the funeral rites for a king, the Talmud permitted the severing of the tendons (and thereby the crippling) of the king's horse (*Avodah Zara* 11a). Rabbi J. David Bleich notes that "this practice is permitted despite its source in pagan rituals because it is intended as an act of homage to the deceased king" (see Bleich's *Contemporary Halakhic Problems,* Volume 3, page 218). I find the reasoning behind this ruling problematic. Why allow a cruel pagan custom to serve as a model for Jews as to how to honor a king? In addition, what does such behavior reflect about the character of a king who would want to have his memory honored by having a horse that had served him crippled? Does anybody believe that this is what David, Solomon, or Josiah would have wanted?

(Palestine Liberation Organization), and the force behind many of the anti-Israel terrorist attacks. Newkirk had but one request of Arafat: not that he stop engaging in terror against human beings or, for that matter, against both human beings and animals, but rather only that he "leave animals out of this conflict." PETA was so pleased with Newkirk's letter (which follows) that it posted it on the organization's website.

February 3, 2003

Yasser Arafat, President, Palestinian National Authority
Ramallah, West Bank

Your Excellency:

I am writing from an organization dedicated to fighting animal abuse around the world. We have received many calls and letters from people shocked at the bombing in Jerusalem on January 26 in which a donkey, laden with explosives, was intentionally blown up.

All nations behave abominably in many ways when they are fighting their enemies, and animals are always caught in the crossfire. The U.S. Army abandoned thousands of loyal service dogs in Vietnam. Al-Qaeda and the British government have both used animals in hideously cruel biological weaponry tests. We watched on television as stray cats in your own compound fled as best they could from the Israeli bulldozers.

Animals claim no nation. They are in perpetual involuntary servitude to all humankind, and although they pose no threat and own no weapons, human beings always win the undeclared war against them. For animals, there is no Geneva Convention and no peace treaty—just our mercy.

If you have the opportunity, will you please add to your burdens my request that you appeal to all those who listen to you to leave the animals out of this conflict?

We send you our sincere wishes of peace.

Very truly yours,

Ingrid Newkirk
President, PETA

Of course, there is nothing wrong in protesting the mistreatment of animals, as Newkirk did. Rabbi Slifkin writes: "The Torah even tells us not to disregard the life of a tree during a war" (see Deuteronomy 20:19). But to write to Arafat, whose followers repeatedly killed innocent people, and to speak only of not using a donkey, conveys the impression that the only thing that bothered Newkirk was the donkey's death, and not the intended murder of large numbers of Israelis.

Dennis Prager tells this story:

"It was mealtime on a flight somewhere over the United States. I noticed that both the middle-aged woman seated next to me and I had ordered special meals. I had a kosher meal, she a vegetarian one.

" 'Are you a vegetarian?' I asked the woman.

" 'Yes,' she responded.

" 'Why?'

" 'Because we have no right to kill animals. After all, who are we to claim that we are more valuable than animals?'

"I vividly recall my thoughts. When she said that we have no right to kill animals, I felt a certain sympathy for her and her position. After all, I thought, here I am eating a kosher meal, and I have always understood kashrut to be Judaism's compromise with vegetarianism.

"But when she delivered the second part of her explanation, I couldn't believe what I was hearing. In fact, I was so certain that she was engaging in hyperbole that I said, 'I certainly understand your opposition to killing animals, but you can't really mean what you said about people not being more valuable than animals. After all, if an animal and a person were both drowning, which would you save first?'

"I was sure I had posed a rhetorical question. So, when I received no response from the woman, I asked her if she had heard me. 'Yes,' she responded, 'I'm thinking.'

"That was a bombshell. I recall my reaction as if it had happened last week. She's 'thinking'? What on earth is there to think about?"

After this encounter, Prager started asking high school students throughout the United States, "If your dog and a person you didn't know were drowning, which would you try to save first?"

"In fifteen years of posing that question before students in secular schools, no more than a third of the group has ever voted to save the person." In religious schools, students overwhelmingly vote to save the person. Prager concludes that in societies in which people are not taught the religious notion that human beings, unlike animals, are created in God's image, the belief in the specialness and sanctity of human life is in danger of being—and often has been—lost. "What [persuasive and definitive] nonreligious reason could be offered for regarding people as more valuable than animals?[27]

24

VEGETARIANISM, ANIMAL RESEARCH AND EXPERIMENTS, AND HUNTING

Vegetarianism

1. A careful reading of the Bible suggests that God's ideal diet for human beings is vegetarian, not carnivorous. Adam and Eve, the first human beings, are commanded by God to limit their eating to vegetables and fruit: "See, I give you every seed-bearing plant that is upon all the earth, and every tree that has seed-bearing fruit; they shall be yours for food" (Genesis 1:29).* Generations later, after the sins of lawlessness and violence committed during the time of Noah (Genesis 6:11–13), followed by the devastating flood God wreaks on the world, God permits human beings to eat animals: "Every creature that lives shall be yours to eat . . ." (Genesis 9:3). The Bible never explains why God now permits the eating of animals. Perhaps He was concerned that a vegetarian diet would be too difficult nutritionally for most people to observe, or perhaps He felt that people would not observe it since meat eating is a strong desire.†

However, although human beings were now permitted to eat meat, they were still forbidden to consume blood, either by itself or with animal

*On the other hand, God does accept with favor the sacrificial gift offering of an animal by Abel, Adam and Eve's son (Genesis 4:4).

†The late Bible scholar Nechama Leibowitz—summarizing an argument offered by Rabbi Abraham Isaac Kook—explained that the permission to eat meat had less to do with nutrition than with humanity's propensity for violence: ". . . after the deluge, the descendants of Noah, that is, all mankind, were permitted to be carnivorous. Since the land had become filled with violence and man had given free rein to his worst instincts, man was no longer required to make the supreme moral exertions required to forgo the slaughter of animals. It was far more important that he should, at least, utilize what moral fiber he still possessed to refrain from killing his own kind and respecting the life of his neighbor." (*Studies in Bereshit/Genesis,* page 77). Thus, it should be viewed as no coincidence that immediately following the permission to eat meat is the law ordaining capital punishment for murderers: "Whoever sheds the blood of man by man shall his blood be shed" (Genesis 9:6). On the other hand, the fifteenth-century Spanish rabbi Joseph Albo argued that the slaughtering of animals was deleterious to man's character development: "In the killing of animals there is cruelty and aggression and the ingraining in men of the negative trait of spilling innocent blood . . ." (*Sefer Ha-Ikkarim* 3:15).

meat.* Professor Jacob Milgrom has noted that "none of Israel's neighbors possessed this absolute and universally binding blood prohibition."[1] Perhaps at the very moment the Bible was granting man the right to kill animals for food, it wished to ensure that this permission would not lead to widespread bloodletting and savagery. Indeed, based on this commandment, the laws regarding kosher slaughter ordain that after an animal is slaughtered, its blood must be fully drained. What eventually became a Jewish obsession with not eating *any* blood (for example, salting the meat so that every drop of blood is removed) helped to produce, I believe, a general Jewish abhorrence of bloodshed. Thus, Jews have committed fewer violent crimes than their non-Jewish neighbors in every society with which we are familiar.

Yet despite the Torah's permission to eat meat, when the prophets imagined what life would be like in the messianic age, they assumed that the creatures of the world would be herbivorous. Isaiah prophesies of a future age in which "the wolf shall dwell with the lamb, the leopard lie down with the kid . . . The cow and the bear shall graze, their young shall lie down together; and the lion, like the ox, shall eat straw" (11:6–7). To Isaiah, a messianic age in which some of God's creatures are killing others is inconceivable.

In short, in its depiction of two utopias, the Garden of Eden and the future Kingdom of God, the Bible assumes that both will be worlds in which animals do not kill and are not killed for food.

Dr. Isaac Herschkopf argues that instead of regarding meat eating as a strong and seemingly innate desire, it would be more accurate to compare it to drinking alcohol, smoking, or eating refined sugar. None of the desires that people have for these items are instinctual in the same way, for example, that sexual relations are desired. It is only after people are exposed to meat (or alcohol or cigarettes) that they start to desire it. Thus, a veggie burger tastes delicious to people unless they are used to eating turkey burgers, which, in turn, pale in comparison to beef burgers. Similarly, if we are hungry, we'll eat and enjoy an apple, unless an apple pie is sitting next to it.

---

2. Until the messianic age, the Torah assumed that meat eating, although permitted, should be an occasional act, to be carried out only "if your

*Few, if any, biblical laws are repeated as often as this one. First enunciated in Genesis 9:4, the prohibition is reiterated in Leviticus 3:17, 7:26–27; 17:10–12, 14; 19:26; Deuteronomy 12:16, 23; 15:23.

soul craves to eat meat" (Deuteronomy 12:20). The Talmud comments that this verse "teaches a rule of proper conduct, that a person should not eat meat unless he has a particular craving for it [and not as a regular regimen]" (*Chullin* 84a).

The same page of the Talmud also teaches that "a parent should not accustom his son to meat and wine." In commenting on the biblical passage about a wayward, rebellious son, the Talmud and later commentators regard a gluttonous consumption of meat and wine as an indicator of an adolescent's bad character (Mishnah *Sanhedrin* 8:2, *Sanhedrin* 70a, and Rashi on Deuteronomy 21:18).

3. The medieval Bible commentator Abarbanel found support for the ethical superiority of a nonmeat diet in the fact that this was the diet (*manna*) supplied by God to the Israelites in the desert. In the Torah, God refers to *manna* as "bread from the sky" (*lechem min ha-shamayim;* Exodus 16:4).* Abarbanel sees the *manna* diet as intended to teach Jews in all generations a lesson: "Meat is not an essential food, but is rather a matter of gluttony. . . . In addition, meat generates cruel blood in human beings. This is why you find that the predatory carnivorous beasts and birds are cruel. . . . But sheep and cattle, chickens, turtledoves, and doves, which live on the grass of the field, have no cruelty or wickedness . . ." (commentary on Exodus 16:4).

4. With the passage of time, however, most Jewish sources came to view meat eating as a positive thing, and built into the very structure of God's world: "The Holy One created animals that eat other animals so that man should not protest and say, 'How can it be that God permitted man to slaughter . . . animals and birds, and was not concerned with the pain of His creatures?' since he will see that God Himself created animals that eat animals" (*Sefer Chasidim* 589).

---

*In the desert, the recently freed Israelite slaves fear that they will die of starvation, and God promises Moses that He will rain down food for them. The following morning, dew falls on the camp, and when it lifts there remains "a fine and flaky substance, as fine as frost on the ground" (Exodus 16:4). The substance proves edible, and Moses informs the Israelites that this is the bread God has promised. From then on, the *manna* falls daily (a double portion rains down on Friday so that the Israelites do not have to gather *manna* on the Sabbath) until the Israelites enter Canaan and start to eat of the land's produce (Joshua 5:12). According to the Bible, the *manna* looked like coriander seeds, was white, and tasted like wafers in honey (Exodus 16:31). The Israelites prepared it in various ways, including boiling it and baking it into cakes.

—

To those Jews drawn to vegetarianism, the reasoning of the Sefer Chasidim *is not convincing. True, animals do eat animals but do we, as human beings, want to model our behavior on that of animals?**

—

5. Jewish culture has long linked meat eating with a mood of celebration. A well-known Jewish aphorism (based on *Pesachim* 109a) declares: "There is no joyful meal [on a festival] except with meat and wine." To this day, mention a holiday meal to most Jews, and what immediately comes to mind are foods such as chicken, chicken soup, and gefilte fish, along with wine and challah.

—

Some Jews assume that this aphorism mandates the eating of meat on the Sabbath and other holidays. In support of this position, they cite Maimonides' ruling that a person is obligated to rejoice during festivals along with his family and all those who are with him. "How is this done? He gives sweets and nuts to the children . . . and the adults eat meat and drink wine . . . and there is no joy except with meat and wine" (see "Laws of Holidays" 6:18).

I understand this statement differently. Maimonides' insistence on eating meat and drinking wine was presumably directed at the large majority of human beings for whom meat eating and wine drinking were luxuries. In effect, he was telling them: "Don't be parsimonious on the holidays; although meat and wine are expensive, don't scrimp. Spend the money so that you and your family enjoy yourselves." However, to imagine that Maimonides would insist that someone who experiences unhappiness at the thought of eating meat must do so makes as little sense as expecting that he would force a child who disliked sweets to eat them or that he would instruct an alcoholic to drink wine on a holiday. For such a person, drinking wine destroys, rather than enhances, the Sabbath or holiday's spirit.†

—

*Michael Pollan, author of *The Omnivore's Dilemma,* offers yet another argument against drawing conclusions from the behavior of meat-eating animals: "Humans don't need to kill other creatures in order to survive, carnivorous animals do" (page 310).

†On the other hand, there is one annual holiday meal during which the Bible mandates meat eating: The Passover feast, at which every Jewish family is instructed to consume the Paschal Lamb (Exodus 12:21–27). So basic was participation in the eating of this lamb that a Jew subjected himself to the punishment of *karet*—which involves the possibility of premature death at the hand of God—by refusing to participate in this ritual (Numbers 9:13). It is, therefore, clear that Judaism in the past did not sanction a complete vegetarian lifestyle. However, Jews have not sacrificed Paschal lambs since the destruction of the Second Temple (70 C.E.), and so the issue today is a moot one (also, see the following paragraph, which cites Rabbi Kook's belief that in messianic times all sacrifices will consist of vegetation, not animals). Therefore, there is now no meal at which a Jewish vegetarian is specifically enjoined to eat meat.

6. Although we find relatively little written in support of vegetarianism in medieval and early modern times,[2] in recent decades there has been increasing support in the Jewish community for a meat-free diet. The chief rabbi of Palestine, Abraham Isaac Kook, was a seminal figure in this movement. While Rabbi Kook himself was not a vegetarian,* he clearly believed the world, in its move toward messianic redemption, would and should evolve in this direction: "It is quite impossible to imagine that the Lord of all works, Who has compassion for all His creatures, Blessed be He, would enact an eternal law in his 'very good' [human beings] creation,† so that the human race can survive only by shedding blood, even if only the blood of animals."[3] In addition, although Rabbi Kook, like all Orthodox Jews, prayed daily for the rebuilding of the Jerusalem Temple, in which animal sacrifices would be offered to God, he also believed that in messianic times "the effect of knowledge [of God] will spread even to animals . . . and sacrifices in the Temple will consist of vegetation, and it will be pleasing to God as in days of old" (*Olat Re'iyah,* part 1, page 292).‡

One of Rabbi Kook's foremost disciples, David Cohen, the Nazir,§ became a vegetarian, and raised his son, Sha'ar Yashuv Cohen, the chief rabbi of Haifa, as a vegetarian.[4] A former Ashkenazic chief rabbi of Israel, Shlomo Goren, was also vegetarian, a decision he is reputed to have made after visiting a slaughterhouse. In the United States, Shraga Feivel Mendlowitz, the founder of the renowned

*The claim, often offered in religious Jewish vegetarian circles, that Rabbi Kook was a vegetarian is a myth. Rabbi Alfred Cohen reports that Rabbi Ben Zion Bokser, author of a book on Rabbi Kook, informed him that he had been in direct contact with Rabbi Tzvi Yehudah Kook, Rabbi Kook's son, and he had "categorically denied that his father had been a vegetarian" ("Vegetarianism from a Jewish Perspective," *Journal of Halacha and Contemporary Society* 1:2, Fall 1981, page 44, footnote 12).

†Genesis describes the day on which God created human beings as "very good" (1:31).

‡Rabbi Kook even applies to this new phenomenon (the nonslaughtering of animals) a verse in Isaiah, 'In all of my sacred mountain, nothing evil or vile shall be done, for the land shall be filled with devotion to the Lord" (11:9). Rabbi Alfred Cohen notes that the implication of Rabbi Kook's teaching "is that if there will be no animal sacrifice in the Temple, there will be no animal slaughter whatsoever" ("Vegetarianism from a Jewish Perspective," *Journal of Halacha and Contemporary Society* 1:2, Fall 1981, page 45). In *The Guide for the Perplexed,* Maimonides expresses the view that sacrifices represented a more primitive stage in human development and were commanded by God as a way to wean people away from the sacrifices offered to idols by having them directed to God instead. In Maimonides' words, such a procedure was necessary since man "according to his nature is not capable of abandoning suddenly all to which he was accustomed" (3:32).

§A Nazir is one who vows to consecrate himself to God, and to abstain from certain worldly pleasures, such as wine and all alcoholic drinks (see Numbers 6:1–21).

*Yeshiva Torah Vodaath in Brooklyn, stopped eating meat after the Holocaust on the grounds that "there has been enough killing in the world."**

Both the United States and England have long-standing organizations known as the Jewish Vegetarian Society.

The late Isaac Bashevis Singer, the Nobel Prize–winning Yiddish writer, and perhaps the most famous Jewish vegetarian in modern times, thought it inconceivable that there would ever be world peace as long as people hunted and slaughtered animals for food. When asked if he was a vegetarian for health reasons, Singer answered: "Yes. For the chickens' health." On another occasion, Singer said: "The man who eats meat upholds with every bite of meat or fish that might is right."

Animal research and experiments

7. Dr. Avraham Steinberg, author of the three-volume *Encyclopedia of Jewish Medical Ethics,* notes several important goals of medical experimentation on animals, among them:

- *Diagnosis:* helping to identify diseases, through the study of symptoms and the stages of illnesses
- *Treatment:* helping to treat diseases, by trying out new medications, technologies, and surgical techniques
- *Broadening understanding:* helping to understand the structure of organs and tissues and physiological processes
- *Teaching:* assisting in the teaching of students in medicine and biology[5]

Because human beings are given dominion over animals, Jewish law permits causing pain to animals if doing so brings gain to human beings. Thus, for example, the Ramah, the sixteenth-century codifier of Jewish law, states: "Whenever it is for the purpose of healing [human beings] . . . there is no prohibition against cruelty to animals" (*Shulchan Arukh, Even Ha-Ezer* 5:14).†

---

*Though ordained in Europe, Mendlowitz refused to use the title "rabbi," and insisted on being referred to as "Mr. Mendlowitz." In recognition of his groundbreakings work in Jewish education, Rabbi Moshe Feinstein remarked of Mendlowitz, "Were it not for him, there would be no Torah study . . . at all in America."

†Obviously, the only cruelty permitted is that which is necessary to help bring about the healing.

However, two major moral questions remain: How much pain is it permitted to cause animals, and how substantial must the gain to human beings be?

The following guiding principles represent the conclusion of the majority of Jewish thinkers who have written on this subject: Most significant, it is forbidden to inflict *gratuitous* pain on animals, such as repeating previously completed and competent, but painful, experiments. It would also seem to me forbidden to inflict pain where the gain is minimal.* However, Jewish law does permit causing pain to animals in instances in which the gain to human beings is substantial and necessary. This is the case with some, but not all, experiments conducted on animals, particularly those whose goal is to advance medical knowledge and treatment of disease.

Dr. Steinberg offers these guidelines on human diseases and the treatment of animals:

- "Whatever is needed to *cure* a sick patient, even one who is not dangerously ill, does not violate the law against cruelty to animals."

- "There is a need to mitigate the pain of the experimental animals as much as possible by analgesia and/or anesthesia, to provide proper facilities and adequate nutrition for the animals [and] to pay attention to possible complications due to the experiments." Furthermore, "the animal should be killed as rapidly and as painlessly as possible after the experiment."

- "It is preferable to use lower forms of animals wherever possible because the pain and suffering is greater among higher forms of animals with better developed nervous systems."

- "One should use the fewest animals possible consistent with the experimental needs."

- "Wherever alternatives, such as tissue culture or imaging techniques are available, they should be used. As these techniques improve, the need for animal experimentation may decrease." Steinberg cautions, however, that "for the foreseeable future, animal experiments will be necessary in those areas where no adequate alternatives exist."

---

*As the contemporary rabbinic scholar Rabbi J. David Bleich puts it: "The benefits must be practical in nature and not simply the satisfaction of intellectual curiosity" (*Judaism and Healing,* page 157).

- "Animal experiments should *not be done to reconfirm* well-known and well-documented findings." Steinberg acknowledges that "Many studies are repeated unnecessarily even after the findings have already been confirmed."

Dr. Steinberg regards the attempt by some animal-rights advocates to end all experiments involving animals as dangerous since "animal experimentation is absolutely essential for the advancement of knowledge to diagnose and cure disease." The stopping of such experiments "may lead to increased human suffering because new medical discoveries may be delayed or totally prevented."[6]

The cruelty of some experiments would seem to outweigh in significance gains in knowledge that might accrue. Dr. Peter Singer, a well-known animal rights advocate, reported in the early 1990s on experiments being conducted at the U.S. Armed Forces Radiobiology Research Institute in Bethesda, Maryland, in which rhesus monkeys were trained to run inside a large wheel. When the monkeys slowed down, they were given electric shocks. After being trained through this method to run for long periods, the monkeys were given lethal doses of radiation. Then, while they were sick and vomiting, they were forced to continue to run until they dropped. "This is supposed to provide information on the capacities of soldiers to continue to fight after a nuclear attack."

*In a different study, "three experimenters at Princeton University kept 256 young rats without food or water until they died." They wished to compare the energy levels of young rats under conditions of thirst and starvation with normal adult rats given food and water. "In a well-known series of experiments that went on for more than fifteen years, H. F. Harlow of the Primate Research Center, Madison, Wisconsin, reared monkeys under conditions of maternal deprivation and total isolation. He found that in this way he could reduce the monkeys to a state in which, when placed among normal monkeys, they sat huddled in a corner in a condition of persistent depression and fear." Concludes Singer: "In these cases, and many others like them, the benefits to humans are either non-existent or uncertain, while the losses to members of other species are certain and real."**

**Practical Ethics,* page 66. Singer notes that experimenters often justify their studies with the claim that they can lead to discoveries about human beings: "If this is so, the experimenter must agree that . . . animals are similar in crucial respects [to human beings]. For instance, if forcing a rat to choose between starving to death and crossing an electrified grid to obtain food tells us anything about the reactions of humans to stress, we must assume that the rat feels stress in

The fact that Jewish law justifies some animal experimentation does not mean that it justifies all, and, if the facts as Singer has described them are accurate, the realization that experiments of this sort have been conducted at renowned institutions should be a source of great sorrow, regret, and shame. This was surely not what the Bible intended when it gave human beings dominion over the animal world.

Hunting

8. Hunting, a popular sport in the United States and other Western societies,* is rarely practiced among Jews. I have never seen a statement in Jewish religious literature that speaks of hunting for sport in a positive manner. The traditional Jewish attitude is reflected in perhaps the most famous responsa of Rabbi Yechezkel Landau (ca. 1713–1793), commonly referred to by the title of his collection of responsa, *Nodeh B'Yehuda.* A wealthy Jewish businessman who had acquired a large country estate asked Rabbi Landau whether Jewish law would permit him to hunt the wild animals there for sport. In the context of a rather lengthy analysis of the issues, Rabbi Landau asked: "How can a Jew kill a living thing without any benefit to anyone and engage in hunting merely to satisfy the enjoyable use of his time? . . . For, according to the Talmud, it is permitted to slay wild animals only when they invade human settlements, but to pursue them in the woods, their own dwelling place, when they are not invading human habitations, there is no commandment to permit that. Such pursuits simply mean following the [wrongful] desires of one's heart."†

---

this kind of situation" (page 65). Does this rather obvious conclusion justify imposing such suffering on animals? I don't think so.

*The paragraph in the classic novel *To Kill a Mockingbird* (Harper Lee), in which the book's title is explained takes hunting as an American sport for granted. When Atticus Finch, the book's hero and a man of great kindness and gentility, gives his young son a rifle, he says to him: "I'd rather you shot at tin cans in the back yard, but I know you'll go after birds. Shoot all the blue jays you want, if you can hit 'em, but remember it's a sin to kill a mockingbird" (page 94). Finch considers it a sin because mockingbirds, he argues, in no way bother people; rather, they sing their hearts out and provide human beings with enjoyment.

†Gary Larson, author of the comic strip *The Far Side,* depicts a hunter shooting a bear from behind while the animal is quietly drinking water from a pond. In the next frame, the now-dead bear has been stuffed and is on display in the hunter's home, with his fangs and claws bared.

However, Rabbi Landau makes it clear that Jewish law permits the hunting of animals for valid financial reasons: "In the case of one who needs to do this and who derives his livelihood from hunting (for example, one who deals with furs and skins), we would not say that hunting is necessarily cruel, as we slaughter cattle and birds and fish for the needs of man. . . . But for one whose hunting has nothing to do with earning his livelihood, this is sheer cruelty" (responsa *Nodeh B'Yehuda* on *Yoreh Deah* 2:10).[7]

Even in such a case, however, the trapping of animals to secure their hides in the manner it is commonly done is forbidden by the laws outlawing cruelty to animals (see page 326 on furs).

Kirk Douglas, the great American actor, writes of the one—and only—wild game hunt he went on, in Kenya. "I was drunk with power as I softly pulled the trigger of my high-powered rifle and watched a leopard, a gazelle, an onyx, a zebra, and other defenseless animals fall to the ground. . . . The trophies I brought back were proudly mounted on the wall of my projection room. And then one day I realized how obscene it was and got rid of them. Later, I learned that as a Jew I had committed a sin. It is against my religion to hunt and kill wild animals, let alone eat them." Douglas now regards the hunt as "the most stupid thing I've ever done."[8]

Despite hunting's great popularity, there are no shortage of non-Jewish, as well as Jewish, opponents of hunting. I have found few more powerful expressions of opposition to this sport than the short poem by the British writer Walter de la Mare (1873–1956):

Hi! handsome hunting man
Fire your little gun.
Bang! Now the animal
Is dead and dumb and done.
Never to peep again, creep again, leap again,
Eat or sleep or drink again, Oh, what fun!

While Jews generally abhor hunting, they frequently indulge in fishing. What accounts for the willingness to dichotomize the two? Perhaps it is the fact that animals killed by hunting are always unkosher because they have not been ritually slaughtered. The killing of animals when done solely for recreation is regarded in Jewish sources, and by Jews in general, as bloodlust. Fish, however, as long as they have fins and scales, are kosher and may be eaten. In addition, as*

*There are no Jewish laws concerning the killing of fish, though the mandate against causing gratuitous pain to a living creature applies to fish as well.

Dr. Isaac Herschkopf notes, human beings identify less with fish than with animals because they occupy a different world (the water) than we do. In consequence, we are less able to interact with, and therefore identify, with them. The one "fish" human beings do often anthropomorphize, dolphins, are, in fact, mammals; they are not only the brightest of the ocean's creatures, but can also briefly leave the water and frolic with human beings, hence the greater concern for dolphins than other creatures who reside in the ocean.

—

9. In general, the aversion of Jews to hunting characterizes religious and nonreligious Jews alike. Almost a century ago, Walther Rathenau, the Jewish foreign minister during the early years of Germany's Weimar Republic, said: "When a Jew says he is going hunting to amuse himself, he lies." A century before Rathenau, Heinrich Heine articulated a psychological/moral reason for Jews' distaste for hunting: "My ancestors did not belong to the hunters so much as to the hunted, and the idea of attacking the descendants of those who were our comrades in misery goes against my grain."* In short, when Jews see a hunter pursuing an animal fleeing for its life, with whom are Jews more likely to identify, the hunter or the animal?

—

Other activities engaged in by some hunters—I emphasize "some"—likewise remind Jews of the sort of pitiless deceptions in which they can imagine the cruelest sort of antisemites engaging. Thus, Matthew Scully cites an advertisement from Outdoor Life, *the popular sportsman's magazine, for a bear-call device. The little instrument makes a noise that sounds like the frantic squawking of a terrified cub. When the adult bears hear this sound, they come running, only to be shot by armed hunters waiting in ambush. Scully asks: "What kind of dominion is that? What kind of person would use such a thing, drawing in animals by the sounds of their helpless young?"*[9]

—

10. Biblical and talmudic laws prohibit eating any animal not killed instantly and with a single stroke, in effect making hunting forbidden to Jews as a method of acquiring food. At most, biblical law does permit an Israelite to capture an animal (Leviticus 17:13) and then slaughter it. But to chase after an animal, often accompanied by pursuing dogs, is proscribed (*Avodah*

---

*A Jewish-born poet, Heine converted to Christianity early in life. Unlike many European Jewish apostates, Heine acknowledged that his conversion was done solely to evade antisemitism and remained sympathetic to the Jewish community.

Zarah 18b; see Rashi's commentary). In the words of Maimonides, "We should not kill animals . . . for the purpose of sport" (*The Guide for the Perplexed* 3:17). Also, we should remember that animals are often wounded but not killed by the hunter, and die a prolonged and agonizing death.

11. In the *Sefer HaChinnuch,* the author (whose identity is uncertain) condemns the indiscriminate killing of animals: "But to kill them [that is, animals] without any benefit involves wanton destruction and is called bloodshed. And even though it is not like the bloodshed of a person, due to the superiority of a human and the inferiority of an animal, it is still called bloodshed . . ." (commandment 186).

The Sefer HaChinnuch's *comment puts one in mind of the Greek poet Bion's (ca. 100* B.C.E.*) observation: "Though boys throw stones at frogs in sport, the frogs do not die in sport, but in earnest."*

---

12. Rabbi Tzvi Hirsch Kaidanover, author of *Kav HaYashar,* regarded hunting as gratuitous cruelty, and subject to divine retribution: "It is certain that those who shoot arrows . . . after birds and beasts for no purpose at all other than to learn archery, and kill animals for no reason, are destined to stand in judgment for it; for it is not the way of the compassionate *(rachmanim)* to commit evil to any creature for no reason."[10]

A final thought: The effect that the research and writing of this section had on me

---

For almost my entire life, I have been a confirmed and passionate meat eater. I used to like to have a steak once or twice a week, hamburgers, too, chicken on the Sabbath and maybe one night more during the week, and hot dogs by the dozen. Several times over the decades, during my teen years, in college, and on a few subsequent occasions, I would find myself feeling that it was wrong to kill a living creature merely to satisfy my taste buds (I knew that there were alternative ways to procure protein), and I would try to stop eating meat. I remember when I did so as a teenager, my grandfather, Rabbi Nissen Telushkin, a revered rabbinic sage, and a man whom I loved and admired deeply, was unimpressed with my effort. He noted that the Torah permitted meat eating, and did I really have to try to be more righteous and compassionate than the Torah? Furthermore, he told me something I already knew: Hitler was a vegetarian (in actuality, a sporadic one), so how could one regard vegetarianism as morally superior to a meat-based diet?

My efforts at vegetarianism never lasted more than a week, not because the antivegetarian arguments convinced me (though I did, and still do, venerate my grandfather), but because meats such as steaks and hot dogs were my favorite foods, and although my addiction to them was simply habit, and not physical, I found that I could not seem to give them up.

I concluded that although I believed a vegetarian lifestyle to be the Bible's ultimate goal, and a morally better way to live one's life, I would probably never have the willpower to do so. But then I spent two months researching these two chapters. And to my amazement, one day, looking at a chicken being prepared for our Friday night Shabbat dinner, I no longer wanted to eat it. Having learned, as has been described earlier, that most chickens spend their lives confined to an area about the size of a piece of typing paper, that their beaks are often cut off (because of the confined space in which chickens live, the beaks cause pain and injury between chickens), and that many chickens go through their lives never able to spread their wings, quite simply made me lose my appetite.

Why would I want to eat chicken and profit in some way from the infliction of so much pain and discomfort on sentient creatures? It's not that I believe that all creatures, human beings and animals alike, have the same value. I don't. But I am struck by the moral test regarding "dumb creatures" suggested by British philosopher Jeremy Bentham (1748–1832). The basis of our behavior toward animals must be "not can they reason, not can they talk, but can they suffer." As is clear to anyone who has witnessed an animal in pain, animals can most definitely suffer.*

I have long been impressed by the fact that the Torah and Jewish law wished to minimize the pain of animals being slaughtered, but it seemed wrong-minded to me to be concerned about minimizing the animal's pain during the moment of slaughter while permitting the mistreatment of animals during the months preceding the slaughter.†

And so I have stopped eating chicken and meat. Am I consistent? Not fully, since I still eat fish. I feared that if I gave up fish as well, my whole effort would fail. But still, maybe in the future! In any case, I'm impressed with the story Max Brod recounts in his biography of Franz Kafka. Viewing the fish at a Berlin aquarium, Kafka, who had become a complete vegetarian, said: "Now I can at last look at you in peace. I don't eat you anymore."

---

*For those members of our family who eat chicken, we now purchase free-range chickens.

†Of course, no rabbinic figure rules that it is permitted to mistreat animals. But by not declaring meat raised in factory-farming conditions such as veal forbidden to be eaten, such cruelties are allowed to continue.

IV

When Life Is at Stake

Matters of Life and Death

Do not stand by while your neighbor's blood is shed.

Leviticus 19:16

25

THE LAWS OF SELF-DEFENSE

1. Jewish teachings on self-defense are based on a ruling in Exodus (22:1–2): If someone is found tunneling into a residence—the implication being that the burglar is doing so at night—the residents have the right to take any steps necessary to stop the thief, including killing him (unless they have *clear* reason to believe that he poses no physical threat; see below).

Upon first reading, this law seems surprising since the Torah, unlike the codes of neighboring societies, did not execute thieves or those guilty of property offenses.* However, the Rabbis provided this rationale for permitting killing in this instance: Anyone who breaks into a house, particularly at night, is aware that he may encounter the occupants and that they likely will try to stop him. Thus, the thief has presumably concluded in advance: "If they confront me, I will have to kill them." Therefore, residents are advised to act on the basis of the rabbinic dictum "When one comes to kill you, kill him first" (*Yoma* 85b).

Though the Torah specifies the case of a burglar tunneling into a house, the Talmud makes it clear that the residents' right to kill in self-defense applies to any burglar who gains entry (e.g., by climbing down from the roof) and who seems to pose a mortal danger (*Sanhedrin* 72b). Such permission would also apply to anyone threatened by an armed assailant in the street.

However, if you have reason to believe that the burglar poses no physical danger, you are forbidden to kill him: "If it is as clear to you as the sun that this burglar is at peace with you (i.e., will not kill), do not kill him. But if it is not clear to

*The Bible scholar Moshe Greenberg notes that "both [ancient] Assyrian and Babylonian law know of offenses against property that entail the death sentence. In Babylonia, breaking and entering . . . and theft from another's possession are punished by death. Assyrian law punishes theft committed by a wife against her husband with death. In view of this, the leniency of biblical law in dealing with all types of property offenses is astonishing. No property offense is punishable with death" (Moshe Greenberg, "Some Postulates of Biblical Criminal Law," in Judah Goldin, editor, *The Jewish Expression*, page 27).

you that his intentions are peaceful toward you, then kill him" (Sanhedrin *72a; see also Maimonides, "Laws of Robbery," 9:10). The Talmud offers as an example the unusual case in which the burglar is the homeowner's father. The Rabbis reason that a father might steal from his son, but would never kill him.*

The Talmud also cites an alternative, if less accepted, view, that you have the right to kill a burglar only if you are certain *that he intends to kill you* (Sanhedrin *72a). This position seems less persuasive because it puts the homeowner's life at great risk; he might become aware of the burglar's intentions only when it is too late for him to resist.*

II Samuel describes a classic case of killing in self-defense. After a battle between two Jewish armies, Asahel of Judah started to pursue Abner, the commander of Israel's troops. Abner, a superior fighter, repeatedly pleaded with Asahel to desist: "Stop pursuing me or I'll have to strike you down. How will I look your brother Joab [the opposing commander] in the face?" But when Asahel refused to back off, Abner struck him in the belly and killed him (2:17–25).*

Some time later, Joab, pretending that he was summoning Abner to a peaceful meeting, stabbed him in the stomach and killed him; the Bible twice notes that this was done in retaliation for Abner's killing of Asahel (II Samuel 3:26–27, 30).

David, well aware that Abner had killed reluctantly and in self-defense, responded to this act by cursing Joab, his own general, and publicly mourning Abner's death. Years later, when David turned over the kingship to his son Solomon, he recalled Joab's brutal and unjustifiable killing of Abner, requesting Solomon to make sure that Joab did not die a peaceful death (I Kings 2:5–6; apparently, David, during his lifetime, had felt too dependent on Joab's military skills to act against him). This story establishes both that killing in self-defense is permissible and that it is an act of murder to retaliate against a person who has killed to protect himself.

The most succinct statement of the logic of killing in self-defense was offered by Tomáš Masaryk (1850–1937), the noted humanitarian and founding president of Czechoslovakia: "If I or my would-be killer has to die, is it not more moral that the one who seeks to kill the other die?"

---

*One army represented the tribe of Judah, loyal to David, the other represented the tribes of Israel loyal to Ish-Boshet, son of the recently deceased king, Saul.

2. If someone threatens your life, and is ordered (for example, through a judicial "restraining order") to desist from such behavior but does not do so, you have the right to regard your life as being at risk. As Rabbi Nachum Amsel explains: "Clear intent [to murder] would then have been established . . . as the person who is not really serious about murder would cease his pursuit or would disclaim evil intent following the warning. . . . Once the warning is issued and no change in behavior is demonstrated, the pursued victim can reasonably assume that the threat is legitimate, and may act accordingly,"[1] that is, by doing whatever is necessary to protect her life.

For example, if a restraining order is issued against a man for acting violently toward his wife, ex-wife, or girlfriend, and he still comes to her home, the woman has the right to take all necessary steps to protect her life. When she is at risk, she should, if possible, disable rather than kill the aggressor, although she may kill him if that is necessary to protect her own life. Again, the talmudic rule cited earlier (see pages 348–349), concerning the burglar who clearly poses no physical threat, applies here. Thus, if the woman has good reason to believe that she is not at risk, she has no right to kill.

---

3. Judaism does not believe in vigilante justice. On the personal level, if you can arrange for police to arrest someone who is plotting against you, that is what you should do. Permission to kill or harm such a person is granted only when the threat is imminent, and no proper authorities can forestall it.

4. On the basis of the biblical and talmudic laws of self-defense, Maimonides permits aborting a fetus that is endangering a pregnant woman's life. The fetus, Maimonides argues, is regarded as a *rodef,* a "pursuer" (admittedly, an unintentional one). Just as you are permitted to kill a "pursuer" who intends to kill you, so, too, is a woman allowed to abort a fetus that, if permitted to grow to term, will cause her death.

However, once the infant's head emerges from the birth canal, it is regarded as a fully autonomous being. At that point, even if the completion of its birth will cause the mother to die, one cannot harm it "because one life should not be sacrificed for another"* (see Maimonides, "Laws of Murder and Preservation of Life," 1:9, and Mishnah *Ohalot* 7:6).

*Until the fetus's head emerges, it is not regarded as a whole person, and has a lesser value than that of the mother. Once it emerges, the child is considered fully viable, and its life becomes equal in value to the mother's.

5. If, while fleeing for your life, you damage another's property (e.g., you crash a car into someone's house), the person suffering the damage should demand restitution from the person who was chasing you. But if she cannot recover payment, you are obligated to compensate her for the damage.

In a related, though slightly different, case, the *Shulchan Arukh* rules: "If a ruthless ruler forces a person to reveal the whereabouts of a friend's belongings . . . the person is exempt from repaying the loss, because it was an act done out of fear of being beaten or killed" (*Choshen Mishpat* 388:3). Apparently, Jewish law regards this act as more passive (because it was coerced), and therefore not subject to repayment, than damaging another's property while trying to save your life.

National threats

6. The teaching "When one comes to kill you, kill him first" applies on a national as well as a personal level. Just as an individual has the right to kill anyone trying to kill him, so, too, if enemies are trying to destroy your nation or people, you have the right to kill them. In the Bible, Esther helps bring about the hanging of Haman (Esther 7), though, at the time of his execution, Haman had not yet killed anyone, but had arranged for the execution of Esther's cousin Mordechai and the annihilation of the Persian Empire's Jews.

The clear upshot of Judaism's laws of self-defense is that a nation has the right to go to war, or to launch a preemptive war, against nations or terrorists who attack it,* or plot against it.

The Six-Day War, launched by Israel against Egypt and Syria on June 5, 1967, is a model of a preemptive war of self-defense. The two Arab countries had earlier concluded a secret agreement to combine their armies in a war against Israel. Then, on May 22, 1967, Egyptian president Nasser closed the Strait of Tiran to Israeli ships.† A few days later, Nasser proclaimed: "Our basic objective will be the destruction of Israel." Shortly thereafter, Hafez al-Assad, the Syrian defense

---

*Such was the case, for example, when Japan carried out a surprise attack against the United States at Pearl Harbor, Hawaii, on December 7, 1941, following which the United States immediately declared war against Japan, and when five Arab armies invaded the newly created State of Israel on May 15, 1948. Israel, which had desperately tried to forestall this conflict, went to war.

†Under international law, such an attempt at economic strangulation constitutes a *causus belli,* legal grounds to go to war, though Israel did not do so at that time. Instead, it tried to organize international pressure on Nasser to withdraw his prohibition of Israeli ships.

minister (and later president), declared, "I, as a military man, believe that the time has come to enter into a battle of annihilation [with Israel]." On May 31, Iraq's president, Abdel Rahman Aref, announced, "Our goal is clear—to wipe Israel off the map."

In response to these violations of international law and repeated threats of destruction, Israel launched a preemptive strike and, on the first day of the war, destroyed the entire Egyptian air force and most of Syria's planes.

French president Charles de Gaulle strongly criticized Israel for starting the war. But from the Jewish perspective, the war was started with the plotting, planning, and threats of Egypt and Syria against Israel.

—

Limits on self-defense

7. The right to kill in self-defense applies only to the person or people threatening your life. You are not permitted to kill an innocent party even if doing so will remove a mortal threat. In a seminal, oft-cited ruling (see *A Code of Jewish Ethics, Volume 1: You Shall Be Holy,* page 140), the Talmud recounts the case of a man who came to the fourth-century scholar Rava and told him that the governor of his town had ordered him to kill an innocent man; otherwise, he himself would be executed. What should he do? he asked. Rava told the man that it was forbidden for him to kill an innocent victim: "What reason do you see for assuming that your blood is redder [than that of your would-be] victim? Perhaps his blood is redder [than yours]?" (see *Sanhedrin* 74a, *Pesachim* 25b, and *Yoma* 82b).

—

It would seem to me, though I have not seen this discussed in the commentaries on this passage, that the man has the right to kill the governor making the threat since it is the governor, not the innocent victim, who is unjustly threatening his life.

—

8. Jewish tradition's dominant, but not exclusive, view is that we are forbidden to do anything to help bring about the death of an innocent person even when doing so will save many lives, including our own. The Jerusalem Talmud offers the following case. "A group of people are walking along a road when they are stopped by heathens, who say to them, 'Give us one of you and we will kill him. If not, we will kill all of you.' Let them all be killed, and let them not surrender one soul from Israel. But if the heathens single out one name, as was the case with Sheba ben Bichri, that person may be surrendered to them, so that the others may be saved. Rabbi Shimon ben Lakish [Resh Lakish] said: 'Only someone who is under a death sentence, the way Sheba ben Bichri was, may be turned over.'* But Rabbi Yochanan said, 'Even someone who is not under sentence of death . . . [but anyone whose name has been specified may be turned over]' " (*Terumot* 8:4).

According to Resh Lakish, the members of a group are obligated to sacrifice their lives if the person being demanded by the attacking force has not committed a crime deserving of death. However, if the person has, the group members have no obligation to sacrifice their lives.

Yet Rabbi Yochanan argues that it is permissible to accede to the attacking force's request, even if the person they are demanding is innocent. Rabbi Yochanan's reasoning is apparently that since the person specified will die in any case, whether alone or with the rest of the group, nothing is gained by resisting the command; all that will happen is that many people will lose their lives instead of just one.

Maimonides rules according to the view of Resh Lakish: Unless the person designated is guilty of a capital crime, members of the group should be willing to die rather than hand him over ("Laws of the Basic Principles of the Torah" 5:5).†

During the Russian civil war, a Jewish Communist fled to his hometown of Dukor, where my grandfather, Nissen Telushkin, was the rabbi. The local Jews all knew where the man was hiding, but the government officials did not. One afternoon, the police chief swooped down on the synagogue and arrested my grandfather, along with a group of men who were praying with him, and announced that they would shoot them all the next morning if they did not reveal the fugitive's hiding place. My grandfather ruled that since the man had not committed a capital crime, but would be shot if he was caught, it was forbidden to inform on him, even though all of their lives were endangered. Fortunately,

---

*In the tenth-century B.C.E., Sheba ben Bichri mounted a rebellion against King David. After the rebellion collapsed, he fled north and sought refuge in a small town. When David's troops surrounded the town, an unnamed woman, realizing that many people would be killed if the soldiers invaded, convinced the town's inhabitants to surrender Sheba (in actuality, they killed him; II Samuel 20:15–22). Because Sheba had engaged in an act of treason, the woman was regarded as having acted righteously; there was no reason to sacrifice her life and those of her townspeople to protect a traitor.

†Resh Lakish and Maimonides seemed to believe that handing over an innocent person to be killed is akin to murder, and in such a case one should allow oneself "to be killed rather than transgress" (*Pesachim* 25b).

*the police chief turned out to be corrupt and could be bribed to release the condemned men.**

During the Holocaust, under great pressure, many Judenräte, *organizations of Jewish leaders appointed by the Germans, turned over some Jews to the Nazis, with the intention of saving larger numbers. Unfortunately, since the Nazis' intention was to murder as many Jews as possible, the strategy of the* Judenräte *did not save many lives (and possibly as many, if not more, lives were lost because of their coerced cooperation with the Nazis). For example, the Nazi-appointed head of the Warsaw Ghetto, Adam Czerniakow, cooperated with the Nazis when they demanded the deportation of tens of thousands of Jews from the ghetto; he reasoned that he might thereby save the lives of hundreds of thousands of others. However, once the Nazis started demanding that he hand over large numbers of young children, Czerniakow, realizing the futility of such cooperation, and the evil in which he had involved himself and which he helped carry out, committed suicide.*

Dilemmas of warfare

9. Even during wartime, when we are permitted to kill enemy troops, we are forbidden to kill civilians or captured soldiers who pose no threat to life.[2] On the other hand, while a state should never *intentionally* seek to kill noncombatants, modern wars, fought with planes and bombs, inevitably do so. Furthermore, if one side resolves that it will never engage in any bombing mission that can possibly lead to the deaths of noncombatants, there would be no point in fighting; the country might as well surrender in advance, for its enemy will engage in such bombing. Therefore, what is forbidden is to intentionally target noncombatants.

Unfortunately, this dilemma exists on an ongoing basis in Israel, where terrorists, who target all Israelis, deliberately hide among the civilian population (many of whom support their actions). For example, terrorists sometimes build bomb factories in or near schools or hospitals. When Israel attacks the terrorists,

*Ironically, the man whose life they saved turned out to be an ideologue and an ingrate. When the Communists came to power, he attempted to close down my grandfather's synagogue. The fact that many people from that very synagogue had jeopardized their lives to save his was irrelevant to him. Fortunately, he was not successful. Others, aware of what my grandfather had done, permitted the synagogue to remain open.

it often unintentionally *kills civilians as well. While very regrettable, this also seems unavoidable, unless Israel were to give up the battle against terrorism altogether (itself an immoral position since a state is obligated to do what it must to protect its citizens' lives).*

During Israel's war against Hezbollah terrorists in the summer of 2006, the terrorists, who had initiated the conflict by kidnapping two Israeli soldiers and killing six others, fired thousands of missiles into Israeli cities from Lebanese villages, which killed many people. The Israelis, in trying to destroy the missile sites, often ended up badly damaging Lebanese villages and killing Lebanese who were not part of Hezbollah.

In such a case, who bears moral culpability for the deaths of those innocent Lebanese who were killed? Alan Dershowitz, the Harvard University professor of law, provides an illuminating parallel to American law: A bank robber who uses a teller as a shield and fires at police is guilty of murder if they accidentally kill the hostage in an effort to stop the robber from shooting, "The same should be true of terrorists who use civilians as shields from behind whom they fire their rockets. The terrorists must be held responsible for the deaths of the civilians, even if the direct physical cause of death was an Israeli rocket aimed at those targeting Israeli citizens."[3]

The moral cogency of Dershowitz's argument is borne out by the following, rarely noted, detail. When innocent Lebanese were killed, Israelis were sad, while Hezbollah members (as opposed to other Lebanese) were pleased, knowing that the deaths of the Lebanese would help their public relations cause and lead to increased hatred of Israel.

26

WHEN SOMEONE ELSE'S LIFE IS AT RISK

1. The biblical law "Do not stand by while your neighbor's blood is shed" (Leviticus 19:16) mandates that we intervene and extend help when another's life or well-being is at risk. As the Talmud teaches: "From where do we know that if one sees someone drowning in a river, or if one sees a wild beast attacking a person or bandits coming to attack him, that he is obligated to save the person? The Bible teaches, 'Do not stand idly by while your brother's blood is shed' " (*Sanhedrin* 73a).

However, Jewish law does not oblige us to sacrifice our life for another; intervention is required only when our actions will not put our own life at risk. Thus, in the case of a drowning person, if you can't swim, or if you can but the river's current is dangerously fast, you are obligated to do all that you can (i.e., extend a pole or summon help), but not to risk your own life (see *Sefer Chasidim,* paragraph 674).

In a case where a person is present who can, for example, save the imperiled swimmer, but who refuses to do so, you are obligated to offer money to try to induce him to do so (*Sanhedrin* 73a).*

The Talmud notes that the obligation to help also applies in a case where you witness a person being attacked by a wild animal. For example, if you can distract the animal without putting yourself at serious risk, you must do so.

In the case of muggers or gang members, if it is too dangerous to intervene, you must, at the very least, summon the police.

While this would seem self-evident, no such requirement exists under American law. In an infamous case in New York City during the 1960s, Kitty Genovese, a twenty-eight-year-old woman, was murdered over a forty-minute period within sight of at least thirty-eight witnesses (peering out from their apartment windows), none of whom summoned the police until after she was dead. Similarly, just a few days before my writing this, a disturbed vagrant pushed a woman onto the subway tracks in New York. She reported that twenty bystanders looked down at her, but made no effort to help, until one man stepped forward and pulled her up, seconds before a train entered the station. Under American law, both the witnesses to the Genovese murder and the bystanders at the train station committed no crime.

---

2. The Talmud teaches: "From where do we know that if someone pursues another [that is, an innocent person] to kill him that the pursued should be saved at the cost of the pursuer's life? The Bible teaches, 'Do not stand idly by while your brother's blood is shed' " (*Sanhedrin* 73a). In other

*The victim—if he has the means—is required to repay the person who laid out the money to help save him (Ramah, *Shulchan Arukh, Yoreh Deah* 252:12).

words, if we have great strength, fighting ability, or possess a weapon, we should use it to save an endangered person's life even if it means killing the pursuer.*

If the threat can be averted by injuring the assailant in the leg or arm, we should do so. Jewish law regards it as murder if one intentionally kills the assailant when harm to the pursued can easily be averted by disabling the pursuer (see *Sanhedrin* 74a and Maimonides, "Laws of Murder and Preservation of Life," 1:13).

However, if the pursuer seems intent on killing or seriously hurting his victim, and you are not sure that you can disable him, then you should stop the attacker by any means necessary, including killing. Your goal should be to use the minimum force necessary to prevent the criminal act. However, when the pursuer's intent cannot be ascertained, the primary goal, according to Jewish law, is to protect the pursued (see *Sefer HaChinnuch,* commandment 600).

Maimonides summarizes Jewish teachings on this sensitive and complex subject: "If it is possible to save the pursued by damaging one of the limbs of the pursuer (*rodef*), one should do so. Thus, if one can strike him with an arrow, a stone, or a sword, and cut off his hand or break his leg [or find another way to prevent him from achieving his objective] one should do so. If there is no way to be precise [in one's aim], and save the person being pursued without killing the pursuer, one should kill him, even though he has not yet killed his victim" ("Laws of Murder and Preservation of Life" 1:7).

Similarly, when police confront an assailant who has a weapon and is threatening them, they should try to preserve his life by disabling him. But they are not required to put their own lives at risk. In the words of an ancient biblical expression, damo b'rosho *("his blood is on his head"; see, for example, Joshua 2:19 and Ezekiel 33:4).*

---

3. To encourage people to help those whose lives are in danger, the Talmud exempts Good Samaritans from liability for damage caused while trying to save others: "If one chases after a pursuer in order to rescue the pursued, and breaks some utensils, whether of the pursuer, the pursued, or

*"When a person sees a pursuer pursuing a colleague to kill him . . . and he has the potential to save the pursued from the pursuer and does not do so . . . such a person violates two negative commandments, 'You must show him [in this case, the pursuer] no pity' (Deuteronomy 19:13), and 'Do not stand by while your brother's blood is shed' " (Maimonides, "Laws of Murder and Preservation of Life" 1:15).

of any other person, he is not liable for payment. This should not be so according to strict law,* but if you will not rule in this manner, no man will save his neighbor from a pursuer" (*Sanhedrin* 74a).

It takes great courage and goodness to intervene on behalf of a person who is being pursued. The last thing that is needed is to give people an additional reason to be afraid of intervening on behalf of others; hence, this Good Samaritan law, which removes liability for any damage one might unintentionally cause.

4. If you hear an individual or a group plotting to harm someone, the law of "Do not stand idly by . . ." obliges you to warn the intended victim (*Shulchan Aruch, Choshen Mishpat* 426:1). Thus, the Bible records that when Mordechai overheard two officers in King Ahasuerus's court plotting to assassinate him, he immediately spoke to his cousin Esther, the queen, to ensure that she told her husband about the threat to his life (Esther 2:21–23).

In addition to saving the victim's life, passing on such information can sometimes achieve other, unexpectedly positive, results. In May 1977, at a time when Israeli-Egyptian relations were hostile, General Yitzchak Chofi, director of the Mossad (Israel's CIA), uncovered information of a Libyan plot to hire Palestinian assassins to go to Cairo to murder Egyptian president Anwar Sadat. Israeli Prime Minister Menachem Begin arranged to have the information transmitted directly to Sadat, hoping that this "may warm the atmosphere between us." Chofi flew to Morocco to meet with Egypt's director of military intelligence and provided him with the names and addresses of the Palestinian plotters. The Egyptians acted on the information and found it completely accurate.

Historian Howard Sachar has noted that "Sadat was genuinely grateful." Whereas he had previously opposed all negotiations with Begin's government, Sadat now made it known that he was prepared to listen to serious Israeli proposals. His willingness to negotiate started a process that ultimately culminated in the Egyptian-Israeli peace treaty.[1]

While walking home one afternoon, my mother, Helen Telushkin, saw a group of teenage boys pointing to a house and heard them say that they would beat up the boy who would soon be coming out of it. My mother, acting as if she had not overheard what the boys were plotting (she did not want to be their victim),

*According to Jewish law, a person is always deemed responsible and liable for damage he has caused.

walked over to the house, knocked on the door, and, in a low voice, informed the woman who answered what she had heard.

---

5. If you are in a position to dissuade someone from harming another, you are required by the biblical law "Do not stand idly by . . ." to do so (see Maimonides, "Laws of Murder and Preservation of Life" 1:14). As a general rule, whenever you hear a person speak of another with great animosity, you should try to defuse the situation. If, after speaking to the person, you feel that the would-be victim is still at risk, you must inform him of what his enemy (or enemies) is saying.

The requirement to inform someone of threats to her safety trumps other considerations, including a professional's normally binding legal obligation to maintain confidentiality. In a widely publicized case in California in the late 1960s, Prosenjit Poddar confided to his therapist his intention to kill Tatiana Tarasoff, a woman who had rebuffed his romantic advances. The psychologist did not pass on the information to Tarasoff, whom Poddar subsequently did murder.

The woman's family sued the psychologist and the state of California. which employed him (the psychologist was working at a state university), for concealing this information, and won. The majority of the appellate court judges ruled that even privileged information should be transmitted when an innocent person's life is in danger. In short, the would-be victim's right to life and to be spared physical harm supersedes the would-be killer's right to confidentiality.

Dr. Moshe Halevi Spero, a psychotherapist and scholar of Jewish law, summarizes the Jewish position on this issue: "The prohibitions against disclosing professional secrets, and against breaching professional oaths to maintain absolute secrecy, are waived in circumstances involving even the possibility of sakanot nefashot*" (danger to life).*[2]

Dr. Isaac Herschkopf, a professor at NYU medical school, notes: "When I teach this case, I make the point that if Poddar had stated his intention to kill himself rather than Tarasoff, everyone would have agreed that any intervention was not only permissible, but indeed mandatory to prevent it. Why should Tarasoff's life be less precious than Poddar's? Quite the contrary; given that, from Judaism's perspective, Poddar was the rodef, *the pursuer, it was, if anything, even more mandatory."*

---

6. When a clear evil such as spousal abuse seems imminent, or is happening and we cannot stop it, we should either contact the police (if the danger is immediate), or urge the victim to separate from the abuser (a recommendation of therapy in the absence of separation is unrealistic since it rarely helps if the abuse already is taking place). When the danger seems great, urge the victim to obtain permanent or temporary protection through a restraining order, move to a shelter for battered women or other safe location, or have a relative or friend move into her home.

—

Many, but unfortunately not all, Jewish sources are strict about spousal abuse. If a man abuses his wife, "he should be excommunicated, and let him be forced by Gentile [authorities] to give her a writ of divorce" (Beit Yosef, commentary to the* Arba'ah Turim, Even Ha-Ezer *154:15).*

—

I have used the female pronoun ("her") when writing about the victims of spousal abuse because the large majority of victims are women. This, however, is not always the case; spousal abuse can and does occur in both directions.

—

7. The same applies in instances of child abuse, for a young victim is usually even more vulnerable than an abused spouse. Unfortunately, many people don't intervene even when they have strong reason to suspect such abuse among their neighbors or relatives. In addition, in the Orthodox world, a long-standing reluctance exists about informing non-Jewish authorities of crimes committed by fellow Jews. The regulations prohibiting informing arose in societies in which Jews were subjected to unfair treatment before non-Jewish courts (comparable to the mistreatment of African-Americans in American courts in the nineteenth and much of the twentieth century). In such societies, to inform on a fellow Jew was regarded, often justifiably, as an evil act. However, this reasoning does not apply to democratic societies in which Jews have equal rights. Certainly, in cases involving a Jew who is committing a violent crime, no hesitation about involving Gentile authorities should apply, nor should it have applied in the past.†

If you have *good* and strong reasons to suspect that a child is being abused, your primary concern must be the young person's well-being (by

*The *Beit Yosef* is a commentary written by Rabbi Joseph Karo, the author of the *Shulchan Arukh.*

†Rabbi Moses Isserles (Ramah), the preeminent legal authority for sixteenth-century European Jews, wrote: "A person who attacks others should be punished. If the Jewish authorities do not have the power to punish him, he must be punished by civil authorities" (*Shulchan Aruch, Choshen Mishpat* 388:7).

having the proper authorities make a thorough investigation), while issues of "informing" and potentially defaming another's reputation become secondary.

—

A persuasive ad from the Family Violence Prevention Fund underscores the importance of speaking up if you hear the cries of someone being abused: "If the noise coming from next door were loud music, you'd do something about it."

—

8. The biblical verse that forbids people from mistreating a servant reads, "He [i.e., the master] shall not rule over him ruthlessly *in your sight*" (Leviticus 25:53; emphasis added). The implication of "in your sight," suggests that if you see someone mistreating another—even in a situation that is not life-threatening—you should intervene. Yet most people don't. Certainly, throughout history, people commonly saw masters mistreating slaves and, despite this verse, said nothing. Today, people often remain silent when they see peers (to whom they are free to speak their mind) shouting at, mistreating, or otherwise acting "ruthlessly" toward people over whom they have power. If this happens "in your sight," then you should not regard your presence as a coincidence. Rather, you should presume that God has placed you in this situation for a reason. Uncomfortable though it may be, speak up and try to save the oppressed from the hands of the oppressor.

—

A friend related the following: "Many years ago, I was sitting in synagogue while visiting a friend in New Jersey. The man sitting directly in front of me kept on slapping his son every time the boy wasn't praying. I kept on trying to look the other way and ignore the silent tears rolling down the boy's cheek. I almost made it. It was during one of the last prayers in the service, the Aleynu, *that he noticed the boy daydreaming. He raised his hand for what appeared to be the biggest slap of all. Without thinking, I grabbed his arm. He looked at me in amazement. I tried unsuccessfully to mollify him, before he took a swing at me. We then got into a bare-knuckle brawl, and both of us got bloodied, he worse than me. I didn't regret that, or hitting him; I was, however, concerned about the embarrassment I had caused my host, who prayed in that synagogue every week, and the awkwardness he would now have with his neighbor. When I apologized to my host, he confided to me that he had been wanting to punch this guy for years. A few days later, he told me that he derived great* nachas *(pleasure) from seeing the father with a black eye for a change."*

While I fully empathize with my friend's behavior, and fear that I probably would have lacked the courage to act as he did, I only hope that the boy did not suffer even more later when he was alone with his father. On the other hand, it was probably good for the boy to see how disgraceful and evil other people found the father's behavior; that alone could help him realize that he was a victim, and undeserving of such treatment.

---

9. Someone who has information that can be helpful to a person on trial is obligated to come forward, whether or not he has been subpoenaed. To withhold testimony that can help save someone from undeserved punishment is likewise seen as standing idly by while your neighbor's blood [or reputation] is shed (*Sifra* on Leviticus 19:16). In monetary cases, Maimonides applies this verse to one who withholds evidence that can prevent his fellow's money from being lost, but who does not come forward to testify (*Book of the Commandments,* negative commandment 297).

Jewish law mandates providing judges with all testimony that is relevant. As Maimonides rules elsewhere in his Book of the Commandments: *". . . we are commanded to give the court whatever evidence we have, whether it will badly damage the person on trial, or will save his life or his money" (Positive Commandment 178).*

Contemporary, and more common, applications of the law of "Do not stand idly by . . ."

10. Most talmudic examples that deal with stopping pursuers—for example, preventing someone from murdering his victim or saving a drowning person—concern events that occur rarely, if ever, in most of our lives. However, there are other ways in which we can fulfill the biblical command; for example, by demonstrating and exerting political pressure on behalf of those who are being persecuted. A model of this was the U.S.-based Soviet Jewry movement of the 1960s–80s in which demonstrations were repeatedly held on behalf of Jews being persecuted and often imprisoned in the USSR for attempting to lead more actively Jewish lives, teaching Hebrew, or trying to emigrate.* The protests directed against the Soviet Union were widely

*While the people being persecuted were not executed (in one instance, in Leningrad in 1970, two Jews were sentenced to death, but worldwide protests caused the government to rescind the sentence), they were frequently subjected to incarceration in very harsh circumstances in which their lives were at peril.

understood as fulfilling the command "Do not stand idly by while your brother's blood is shed."

I believe this law implies a general obligation to not be indifferent to those being persecuted, and also, by extension, to provide help to the families of the persecuted. Although there are times when we won't be able to stop another's blood from being shed (for example, when radical Islamist "suicide bombers" carry out attacks), we can, and should, offer financial and emotional support to those victims who have been wounded, but not killed, and to their families.

---

11. It seems to me that this command mandates making our organs available to those whose lives can be saved by them. Thus, when there is no issue of endangerment, such as when we arrange to have organs donated after our death, I believe that we are *obligated* to do so. In addition, because one body can provide several organs, such an act may save not one, but many lives. Therefore, for example, we should arrange—through joining organizations such as the Halachic Organ Donor Society—that, in case of death, we want our organs to be made available. This is particularly important in the case of those who die in an accident and whose family members might not be aware of their desire (in addition, the organs of those who die suddenly, rather than after a long illness, are often the most viable); we should also make it known to our family that we wish this to be done.

Rabbi Moshe Feinstein ruled that it is also a mitzvah for relatives of the deceased to consent to donate a dead person's organs to a patient in need.[3]

When Jonathan "J.J." Greenberg, a dynamic, influential, and highly beloved Jewish communal worker, was killed in an accident in Israel in September, 2002, his parents, my dear friends Rabbi Yitz and Blu Greenberg, arranged for his organs to be donated. "We knew instantly that this is what J.J. would want," his mother said. His lungs, his kidneys, his liver, and a cornea were quickly transplanted to five patients, including Abed El-Salam Kaluti, a fifty-one-year-old Palestinian from Jerusalem. When asked what J.J. would have felt about giving his liver to an Arab, his brother, David Greenberg, said, "He would have been proud that in the Jewish state you can save lives without any political considerations." After the transplants, his parents stayed in touch with the recipients.*[4]

---

*Greenberg, the executive director of the New York–based Jewish Life Network, also helped develop the Birthright Israel program, and the Partnership for Excellence in Jewish Education.

Such cases are not singular. In April 2003, Lyric Benson, a promising young actress, was murdered by a jealous ex-boyfriend. Her parents arranged for her organs and tissues to be donated. Her heart went to a sixty-two-year-old married man with two children, her kidneys to a twenty-five-year-old man and a sixty-two-year-old woman, her liver was implanted in a fourteen-year-old boy, and a lung went to a twenty-four-year-old college student. In addition, others received bone and tissue donations.

I write about these cases with great specificity both because these two people, whose lives were cut tragically short, should have their names associated with these wonderful lifesaving activities, and also because I have found that many people think of postmortem organ donations as benefiting one person, and don't realize how many lives can be saved and/or greatly benefited from just one donor.

—

As regards the donating of organs by living donors, see paragraph 16.

Taking care not to endanger another

12. It is forbidden to put another person's life or well-being needlessly at risk. Thus, we may not keep a vicious dog or an unstable ladder in our home. If we do and they cause injury, guilt rests on our head.* Therefore, if we possess a broken or hazardous object, we should fix it or get rid of it.

—

*Rabbi Pinchas ben Yair would not enter Rabbi Judah's home because the rabbi kept dangerous mules on his estate: "The Angel of Death is in this man's house, and I should accept his hospitality?" (*Chullin *7b). Today, such an attitude should prompt us to avoid attending parties at which drinking a great deal of liquor (or using prohibited drugs, which is, of course, also illegal) is encouraged, so that departing guests are at risk of being killed, or killing others, in driving accidents.*

—

Self-sacrifice and its limits

13. The Talmud presents the following hypothetical case: "Two men are traveling together [in the desert], and one has a pitcher of water. If they share

*"From where do we learn that a person may not keep a bad dog in his house nor place a shaking ladder in his house? From the biblical verse (Deuteronomy 22:8), "You shall not bring blood [guilt] on your house" (*Ketubot* 41b).

the water, both will die, but if only one drinks, he can reach civilization [and survive]. Ben Petura taught, 'It is better that both should drink and die, rather than one of them look on while his comrade dies.' But Rabbi Akiva came and taught, [The verse in the Torah] 'that your brother may live with you' (Leviticus 25:36) means [only if you both can survive must you share the water, but in cases of conflict] your life takes precedence over his' " (*Bava Mezia* 62a).

While the Talmud never formally rules as to which of these two opinions is binding, Rabbi Akiva's preeminence in Jewish law and thought has guaranteed that his view has been widely accepted by Jewish scholars. Akiva's insistence that we are not *obligated* to sacrifice our life in an attempt to save someone else seems compelling for two reasons:

- Jewish law could not legislate that A be *required* to give the water to B, for if that were the case, then B would be required to give the water back to A, and on and on, until two emaciated bodies would be discovered in the desert alongside a bottle of water.

- Akiva's explanation that "your life takes precedence" also makes intuitive sense. Otherwise, the biblical and rabbinic ethic would presume that your responsibility to your neighbor is greater than to yourself, and that your neighbor's obligation to you is greater than to himself.

The legal scholar Aaron Kirschenbaum understands Akiva as actually forbidding A to give the water to B since this would be "tantamount to declaring his companion's blood . . . redder than his own, a declaration which Jewish law is not prepared to endorse."[5] *But Professor Kirschenbaum, I believe, has overstated the implication of Akiva's conclusion. Rabbi Louis Jacobs emphasizes that while Jewish law does not* demand *self-sacrifice, it does not* forbid *it: "My contention is that if circumstances are such that the man with the water believes his neighbor's life to be of greater value [editor's note: for example, perhaps many people are dependent upon him], Judaism would not frown upon his sacrifice . . . but look upon it as an act of special piety."*[6]

*Jacobs also cites a ruling by Rabbi Judah the Chasid (thirteenth century) that seems very relevant to this discussion: "If a scholar and an unlearned man are sitting together and a heathen wishes to kill one of them, it is a mitzvah for the unlearned man to say to them, 'Kill me and spare my neighbor' " (*Sefer Chasidim, *paragraph 698). However, this passage, specifically because it was written by a scholar, has long made me uncomfortable because it seems self-serving; it would have been more convincing had it been written by a nonscholar.*

When we are not required to intervene

14. Jewish law does not require someone to intervene when the risk to his life is substantial. Professor Aaron Kirschenbaum explains: "The whole purpose of the obligation 'You shall not stand by while your neighbor's blood is shed' is the preservation of life. If its fulfillment can be accomplished only by the sacrifice of the life [of the would-be rescuer], then its purpose has been undermined and frustrated. Under such circumstances, the obligation falls away."*[7]

In addition, Jewish law does not *require* us to intervene (though it encourages us to do so) even when the danger to our life is not great (e.g., at the scene of a fire, where we can pull a person out of a room that is not yet engulfed in flames) but views it as a saintly act (*midat chasidut*) to do so (Aaron Kirschenbaum).†

In our own time, there are many instances of people who put their lives at great risk during the Holocaust, when the risk to others was definite and immediate. Although Jewish law would not demand *that people act in this manner, we regard those who do as great saints. To cite two examples related to me by Dr. Isaac Herschkopf:*

"My aunt, Saba Wainapel, was an inmate, but also the chief nurse at the inmate infirmary in Auschwitz and at other camps where she and my uncle were incarcerated. She once received an order to prepare a list of all the patients

---

*But while there is no obligation to intervene, it is still viewed as an act of heroism, and worthy of great praise. Thus, Louis Jacobs cites several instances from the Bible in which people put their lives in great danger to save others:

- Abraham risked his life to save his captured nephew Lot, although Abraham was in no way endangered by the forces who had taken Lot prisoner (Genesis 14:14–16).
- Moses saw an Egyptian overseer mercilessly beating a Jewish slave and, at the risk of his life, attacked and killed the man (Exodus 2:11–12).
- David risked his life by undertaking to fight Goliath, the seemingly invincible Philistine enemy of the Israelites (see I Samuel 17:20–54).

As Jacobs concludes: "In all these passages, there is implicit the thought that it is a natural thing for men, at times, to consider others even at the risk of their own safety."

†"The Bystander's Duty to Rescue," page 522. The Jerusalem Talmud requires a person to put himself in *some* danger if the danger to the other party is great; however, this ruling is not accepted as binding by most legal scholars. The Jerusalem Talmud tells of an incident in which Rabbi Imi was caught by a band of robbers. One rabbi, upon hearing the news, concluded that Rabbi Imi's situation was hopeless, and said, "Let us prepare some shrouds for [him]." But Resh Lakish, a man of considerable personal courage, said, "[To the contrary], up to the point at which I am killed, I myself can kill. I will go, and through strength, will deliver him to safety!" Resh Lakish met with the robbers and succeeded in negotiating Rabbi Imi's release (*Terumot,* near end of chapter 8).

who had been in the infirmary for over a week. She knew exactly what it meant; they would all be summarily executed. When she tried to ignore the demand, it was repeated with a cocked gun at her head. My aunt sat down and wrote the list. The first name on it was her own. The other names were all the nursing personnel who worked under her. She didn't put a single patient's name on the list.

"When the Nazi officer came with his soldiers to take away the people on the list and immediately realized what she had done, he stared at her. She knew she was about to be killed to set an example. Instead, the officer laughed and left.

"Her husband, my uncle, Dr. David Wainapel, was the physician in charge of the Jewish infirmary at Auschwitz and at other camps in which he and my aunt were inmates. At one time, the camp was overwhelmed by a typhus epidemic. The disease quickly killed innumerable inmates, and my uncle, lacking antibiotics, was helpless to fight it.

"Gambling with his life, he asked to meet the infamous Dr. Josef Mengele. Even asking for such a meeting could have prompted the officer to whom he spoke to shoot him for insolence. Actually meeting with Mengele was even more dangerous, since he was a sadist who was known to murder impulsively.

"My uncle informed Mengele that without penicillin the entire Jewish population would be dead within weeks. Mengele laughed: 'Why should I fight the bacillus that is doing my work for me?' My uncle softly responded, 'Because it is a very stupid bacillus.' Mengele reddened and, with an angry wave of his hand, dismissed my uncle.

*"Within hours, my uncle received the penicillin. Mengele, an extraordinarily evil yet highly intelligent man, understood my uncle's reference to the bacillus not being able to distinguish Jew from Aryan."**

---

15. Some individuals, such as firefighters, police officers, and soldiers, are expected to assume significant risks that others are asked to take only voluntarily. However, when the danger is very great, Jewish law does not require all professionals to assume it, either; they have to volunteer to do so. Thus, for example, the 1976 Israeli rescue operation at Entebbe, Uganda (to save passengers threatened with death by pro-Palestinian terrorists), was composed of soldiers who had volunteered for the mission.

16. Jewish law does not mandate that living persons donate organs—for example, if a sick person needs a kidney to live, and your kidney would be appropriate for the ill person. However, Rabbi Ovadiah Yosef, Israel's former

*For more such examples, see pages 34–37.

Sephardic chief rabbi and a well-known scholar of Jewish law, rules that making such a donation is a "great mitzvah," particularly given that the danger in donating a kidney has become relatively small (but it is not nonexistent).*[8] In short, the less the danger the more we are encouraged to donate the organ. However, as long as there is some danger to the owner, most legal scholars do not *require* a person to donate an organ.

—

Dr. Avraham Steinberg's comprehensive Encyclopedia of Medical Ethics *cites a case in which twin brothers were approached to donate a kidney for their sister: "One brother was married and his wife opposed the donation. The unmarried brother was concerned about not being able to find a mate if he gave up a kidney. [The rabbinic scholar who was consulted, J. Zilberstein] ruled that it is preferable for the married brother to donate a kidney, provided that he is able to carry on normal marital life after the donation. In that case, the wife's objection is overruled for the sake of saving a life."*[9]

A physician who lectures on ethics and with whom I discussed this ruling questioned its fairness: "Why are the feelings of the single brother's future *wife more important than the feelings of the married brother's* current *wife? Isn't* shalom bayit *[peace in the home] as important as a potential marriage?"*

—

A final thought

17. A well-known passage in the Mishnah (*Sanhedrin* 4:5) teaches that before a witness testified in a capital case, the judges delivered a formal admonition warning him against committing perjury, and thereby bringing about the death of an innocent person. They noted that after Cain murdered Abel, God called out to him, "The bloods of your brother cries out to me from the ground" (Genesis 4:10). The Rabbis explained that the unusual word "bloods" (instead of "blood") implies that not only the blood of the victim cries out, but also that of his or her never-to-be-born descendants. Thus, for example, murderers bear moral responsibility for the deaths of all those people who would have descended from the victim. Conversely, "When you

*There is also the danger that in the future, your remaining kidney could fail, and you would no longer have a spare. For this reason, I believe that anyone who has donated a kidney should be pushed to the top of the waiting list of those to be given organs if, at some future time, he or she is in need of one.

save your brother's life, you are regarded as if you saved his life and the lives of his descendants" (Rashi, *Bava Bathra* 11a).

—

At the conclusion of Schindler's List*—the film that tells the story of how Oskar Schindler saved over eleven hundred Jews during the Holocaust—the movie notes that fifty years later, the descendants of those saved by Schindler numbered over six thousand. In Jewish terms, therefore, Schindler is credited with not only saving these eleven hundred people, but their descendants as well.*

—

A friend told me the following: "Many years ago, I had the great privilege of saving a teenage girl's life. We were all at my children's school, and I saw her suddenly turning blue and choking on a piece of meat. I ran over and, as her knees buckled, I managed to perform a Heimlich maneuver and save her. Years later I saw the woman, now married, and she and her husband insisted on introducing me to their newborn baby. We all had tears in our eyes" (Dr. Isaac Herschkopf).

—

27

WHEN OBSERVING JEWISH LAW THREATENS LIFE

1. Jewish tradition understands the verse, "You shall keep My laws and My rules, *and you shall live by them . . .*" (Leviticus 18:5; emphasis added) as meaning that Torah laws are binding only if observing them will not lead to our death (*Yoma* 85b; on the three exceptions to this rule, see paragraph 2). For example, observing the Sabbath, one of the Ten Commandments, is a cornerstone of biblical law. Nonetheless, when a situation arises in which adhering to Shabbat laws will put someone's life at risk—for example, if a person has a life-threatening ailment and needs to be driven to a hospital (normally, Jewish law prohibits driving on the Sabbath)—these laws are suspended so that the sick person's needs can be met. As the Talmud rules: "The saving of life supersedes the Sabbath" (*Shabbat* 132a).

Other rabbis base their permission to violate the Sabbath in cases where life is in danger (pikuach nefesh) *on different rationales, for example: "Violate one Sabbath on his [i.e., the sick person's] account, so that he may live to observe many Sabbaths"* (Yoma *85b). However, as life affirming as this sounds, it would not justify violating Sabbath laws in two instances in which these laws should be violated:*

• *To prolong the life of a patient so near death that she will not survive to the next Sabbath. Jewish law obliges a doctor to do all that he can to prolong the life of even a nonviable patient.* Rabbi Menachem Meiri (thirteenth century) explains the importance of doing so: "Perhaps the person will repent during that hour and atone for the sins he committed during his life."*

• *To save the life of a non-Jew. If the justification for violating the Sabbath laws is so that the ill person "may live to observe many Sabbaths," we would have no rationale to save the life of a person who, even if he survives, will not observe the Sabbath. The same problem applies to Rashi's rationale for why saving of life supersedes the Sabbath: "The reason for this decision is that a Jewish soul is dearer to God than the commandments. God says, 'Let the commandment be nullified so that the person can live'" (commentary on* Yoma *82b). But all human beings are created in God's image and so are precious to God. Therefore, the saving of any human life—Jewish or non-Jewish—supersedes the Sabbath.*

---

2. Even when life is at stake, we may not violate the prohibitions against:

• Murder. It is forbidden to kill an innocent person to save a life; for example, to avoid being killed yourself (see page 352) or to procure an organ for someone in need (see below).

• Idol worship. The Talmud prohibits engaging in idolatry, even if doing so will save your life. It is not fully clear, however, when this law applies. Rabbi Ishmael rules that if one is told "Engage in idol worship so that you will not be killed," one *should* comply with the demand as long as the act is not done in the presence of ten or more adult Jews, a minyan

*See ArtScroll commentary on *Yoma* 85b, note 11, which cites the *Be'ur Halacha* on *Shulchan Arukh* (*Orach Chayyim* 329:4).

(*Sanhedrin* 74a). Other rabbis command a Jew to martyr him- or herself even if no minyan is present, in fact, even if the only other person present is the idolater issuing the threat.

Rabbi Ishmael's reasoning strikes me as more compelling: Why would God prefer that a good person die when no irrevocable evil will ensue (as would be the case if one killed an innocent person to save one's life)? Surely the world will not be a better place if the good person is martyred while the idolater who murdered him continues to live; indeed, it seems to me that the world will become a worse place.

• Certain types of illicit sexual behavior, such as engaging in incest (*Yoma* 82a).

In recent years, it has become increasingly common for severely ill Americans and other Westerners to go to China to obtain organs from the bodies of prisoners who have been executed. This seems immoral for four reasons:

*1. Although Jewish law believes that capital punishment sometimes is justified (e.g., in cases of premeditated murder where the guilt of the defendant has been established beyond a reasonable doubt), China, in addition to executing people for murder, also, on occasion, executes people for lesser crimes, such as robbery and fraud.**

2. Because of the lack of due process and the haste with which Chinese prisoners are arrested, tried, and executed, many of those condemned may well be innocent.

3. These organs usually come from people who did not consent to their donation or whose consent was coerced.

4. By allowing such transplants to occur, Americans and others encourage China's authoritarian/totalitarian regime—which profits from the selling of the organs—to execute ever more prisoners.

Undoubtedly, among those executed in China are people who have committed horrific crimes for which they may well deserve to die. But there are others who are innocent, or who committed crimes for which the death sentence is so

*A recent newspaper article reported: "Liaoning Provincial Higher People's Court in China turned down an appeal from Wang Zhendong, who was convicted of fraud and sentenced to death. His offense: As head of Yingkou Donghua Trading Group Company, he promised returns of 60 percent for those who bought his ant-breeding kits" (*Metro New York,* February 6, 2008, page 8).

unfair a punishment as to constitute an act of murder itself. To profit from such deaths is morally reprehensible.

Perhaps this practice could be curbed if Western governments were to outlaw such organ transplants. More important, and as an alternative to people going to China to procure organs, we must influence more Americans to arrange to have their organs donated. This would solve the dilemma of an insufficient supply of organs for those in need (see page 363). In short, it seems wrong, even when life is at stake, to use the organ of a Chinese prisoner, particularly if that person was executed for a lesser crime than murder.

---

3. The Yom Kippur fast is another oft-discussed situation in which the imperative to violate Jewish law to preserve life and health sometimes applies. Someone who suffers from a life-threatening ailment, and whose condition would be adversely affected by refraining from food and liquids for an entire day, is required to eat. So concerned is Jewish law that life not be endangered needlessly that the Rabbis rule that if a doctor insists that a patient eat on Yom Kippur and the patient refuses, we listen to the doctor.* However, if a doctor says that the patient need not eat, but the sick person insists, "I need to eat," we listen to the patient (this applies as well to a pregnant woman who, aware of the significance of the Yom Kippur fast, insists that she needs food; she is fed until her desire is satisfied; see Maimonides, "Laws of *Shivitat Asor*" 2:9).† The Talmud roots this ruling in a biblical verse (Proverbs 14:10), "The heart knows the bitterness of its soul" (that is, there are

*We assume that the patient's decision to fast, even when her life is at stake, is prompted by a form of delirium (*Yoma* 83a), or that she is obsessive about rituals in a self-destructive manner. Rabbi Harold Kushner writes of making a condolence call to a couple whose nineteen-year-old daughter had died suddenly. When Kushner came to the house, the father told him that the previous Yom Kippur, he and his wife had, for the first time, broken the fast and eaten, the implication being that God had now punished them for this violation by taking away their child (*When Bad Things Happen to Good People,* page 8). While eating on Yom Kippur is indeed a serious sin in Jewish law, it is obviously wrong to assume that God killed the child as punishment. Still, fear of God's wrath might motivate a sick person to insist that he will take no food on Yom Kippur even when he should.

Alternately, a patient might feel terrible about breaking what many regard as one of Judaism's most fundamental prohibitions, but this, too, involves faulty reasoning. Eating on Yom Kippur is prohibited only to those who are healthy, while the commandment to seriously ill people is to eat. Thus, a person who is supposed to eat on Yom Kippur, but doesn't, commits as much a violation of Jewish law as the person who is supposed to fast, but doesn't. As Rabbi Israel Salanter taught: "A sick person who is very ill is exempt from all the commandments except one, 'And you shall be very careful with your lives' " (Deuteronomy 4:15).

†My friend Dana Kurzweil notes that this is an example of patients' rights almost two thousand years before this concept was known.

times when the sick person knows her needs better than the physician; see *Yoma* 83a).

—

The great Eastern European talmudist Rabbi Chaim Soloveitchik was known to be lenient about allowing sick people to eat on Yom Kippur. When challenged about this, he answered, "I'm not lenient about allowing sick people to eat on Yom Kippur. I'm just very strict in cases of pikuach nefesh *(where life is in danger)." Regarding how such people are fed, Reb Chaim "disagreed with the legal view that on the Day of Atonement one feeds a sick person who is in danger small amounts of food at a time, each amount less than the forbidden measure of food for that day. Rather, he instructed those who were taking care of an individual to serve him a regular meal, just as they would on other days" (Rabbi Joseph B Soloveitchik).*[1]

An observant physician I know suggests that those with chronic conditions who know that they will have to eat on Yom Kippur (such as type 1 diabetics) prepare food that is nutritious in advance, but not necessarily the most tasty. For example, one should not use condiments such as ketchup and mayonnaise to add flavor, and, if one needs water, one should drink tepid tap water rather than water chilled in the refrigerator. In this way, even while eating, a person can maintain cognizance that it is still a special and holy day.

—

When Rabbi Yaakov Kamenetzky was a young, newly appointed rabbi in Tzitevian, Lithuania, he ordered a diabetic congregant not to fast on Yom Kippur. But the man could not countenance the idea of breaking Judaism's most sacred fast and refused to follow the rabbi's ruling. His health quickly declined, and he died. Rabbi Kamenetzky refused to eulogize the man at the funeral for, as one of his biographers explained, "[Reb Yaakov] felt it was necessary to demonstrate that the Torah's command to preserve one's health is not to be taken lightly, and that fasting when there is a danger to one's life is false piety" (Yonason Rosenblum).[2]

—

Dr. Falk Schlessinger was one of Rabbi Kook's physicians during the last days of the rabbi's life (1935). Shortly before the fast day of Tisha Be'Av, *Rabbi Kook, aware of how ill he was, told the doctor, "My* yetzer ha-ra *(evil inclination), tells me to fast, while my* yetzer ha-tov *(good inclination) tells me not to."*[3]

—

4. The Talmud posits the general principle that "in matters of uncertainty involving life, we rule leniently" (*safek nefashot le-hakel; Yoma* 83a,

Shabbat 129a; see also *Shulchan Arukh, Orach Chayyim* 618:1). When it comes to financial or other disputes, Jewish law rules that we follow the majority opinion of the adjudicating judges. However, in questions involving endangerment of life, we follow the lenient opinion, even if it is the minority view (*Yoma* 83a).* For example, if a majority of physicians say that a patient is healthy enough to fast on Yom Kippur, but a minority hold that fasting will endanger the patient's life, we follow the minority opinion.

Rabbi Joseph B. Soloveitchik writes: "Even if there is only a doubtful possibility that a person's life is in danger, one renders a lenient decision; and as long as one is able to discover some possible danger to life, one may use the doubt to render a lenient decision" (Halakhic Man, *pages 34–35*).†

---

5. Elsewhere, the Talmud holds: "Regulations concerning danger [to life] are more stringent than ritual prohibitions" (*chamira sakanta mi-isura; Chullin* 10a). In ritual areas, talmudic law relies on probability. For example, say there are ten meat stores in a marketplace, nine of which are kosher, and one finds a package of meat in the general vicinity and it is impossible to ascertain from which store it came, or to whom the meat belongs. The Talmud rules that one is permitted to eat the meat, on the probability that it is kosher (*Chullin* 95a; today, in our more affluent age, observant Jews would avoid eating the meat). Yet if there are ten cups of wine, one of which contains poison, it is forbidden to drink from any of them. Rabbi Louis Jacobs explains: "In the matter of religious law . . . the law allows reliance on the probability principle. . . . But in the case of the cups of wine, the probability principle cannot be relied upon since . . . if the cup imbibed contains poison, it will kill."[4]

"The Sanzer Rav, Rabbi Chayyim Halberstam, was once ill on Passover and his doctor told him that it was forbidden for him to eat the Marror, *the bitter herb, because it would be dangerous to his health. At the Passover seder, Rav Chayyim*

*In this regard, Jewish law's approach is consistent with contemporary society's view of danger. Thus, if a new medication is found to be safe the large majority of the time, but dangerous in a small percentage of cases, it is not allowed on the market.

†Rabbi Moshe Feinstein, writing on the issue of violating the Sabbath in an instance in which the chances of saving the person are slim, argues that "just as on a weekday, we would do anything in our power to save a life, even when the chances of success are not definite, so, too, the Sabbath laws do not stand in the way of even a doubtful rescue" (see *Igrot Moshe, Yoreh Deah,* 2:146).

took a large piece of Marror *and made a blessing: 'Blessed are You Who sanctified us with his commandments and commanded us to guard our health,' and immediately returned the* Marror *to the table."*[5]

—

6. Whenever there is danger to life, Jewish law insists that we act without hesitation to try to preserve life. For example, in discussing an instance in which someone is buried under debris on the Sabbath, the Talmud teaches, "The more eagerly one sets to work at [removing the debris], the more praiseworthy one is." In addition, we should not waste time obtaining permission from religious authorities (*Yoma* 84b). Maimonides rules in a similar manner: "It is forbidden to hesitate before transgressing the Sabbath laws on behalf of a person who is dangerously ill" ("Laws of the Sabbath" 2:3).

7. If a sick person refuses to violate a Jewish law that is injurious to his health, we are permitted to coerce him to do so; for example, to pressure someone who refuses to drive in a car on the Sabbath to get to a hospital or to a doctor. Rabbi David ben Zimra (the Radbaz; sixteenth century), in responding to a query about a "very pious" patient who refused to have Jewish laws desecrated for his sake, wrote: "This [patient] is a pious fool,* and he is punishable for so acting. Generally speaking, I do not see any piety in such behavior, but rather the deliberate destruction of a soul. The patient must therefore be fed against his will, or forced to do whatever else the physicians say to do. Otherwise, it is tantamount to shedding blood" (*Responsa of Radbaz,* Volume 4, number 1139).

8. If there is reason to believe that fasting will lower people's resistance during an epidemic, it is permitted, even for those who are not yet ill, to eat on Yom Kippur. In 1848, Rabbi Israel Salanter, responding to a raging cholera epidemic in Vilna, posted notices in the city's synagogues on the eve of Yom Kippur urging Jews not to fast "on this holy and awesome day" since doing so would lower their resistance. There are two accounts of what transpired. According to one, Rabbi Salanter, "apprehensive that on account of the dread of the day he would not be obeyed, ascended the *bima* [the platform where the Torah Ark is located] of the Great Synagogue at the end of the morning service, took out wine and cake, recited the *kiddush* and ate in the presence of the entire congregation." According to another, Rabbi

---

*On the notion of a "pious fool" in Jewish law, see *A Code of Jewish Ethics, Volume 1: You Shall Be Holy,* page 136.

Salanter only announced that all who felt weak should eat and that they need not consult with a physician before so doing. Indeed, he had earlier arranged to have food prepared in side rooms adjoining each synagogue's sanctuary.[6]

9. Psychological terror also constitutes a form of *pikuach nefesh,* endangerment of life. For example, if a young child has locked himself in a room, and is very frightened, "one may break the door [an act normally forbidden on the Sabbath] and take the child out" (*Yoma* 84b).

10. In instances when there is an obligation to violate the Sabbath or other laws, Maimonides rules that these acts "should not be performed by Gentiles, children, or servants. . . . Rather, they should be performed by Israel's great and wise figures." Having prominent people publicly violate Shabbat to save lives clearly demonstrates that the ordinances of the Torah are intended to increase "mercy, kindness and peace [in the world]" ("Laws of the Sabbath" 2:3; see also *Yoma* 84b).

---

*A modern instance of Jews acting on this directive is the New York–based Hatzolah organization, which is composed of religious Jews who drive ambulances and extend emergency medical care every day of the year, even though the organization could hire non-Jews to staff its ambulances on the Sabbath and Jewish holidays.**

One Shabbat, Rabbi Kook's mother was very ill, and the doctor examining her needed more light than the electric bulb near her bed provided. He asked Rabbi Kook's attendant to bring over a kerosene lamp—an act normally forbidden on the Sabbath—and hold it near the woman's face. The attendant, aware that the Sabbath laws were suspended because of the woman's grave illness, started to bring over the lamp. But Rabbi Kook stepped over and insisted that he do so. "For you," he explained to his attendant, "this act involves only one mitzvah,

*Rabbi Moshe Feinstein ruled that not only are Jews permitted to drive the Hatzolah ambulances on Shabbat and Jewish holidays to save lives, they are also permitted to drive home when returning from a rescue mission, even though no life is then at risk (*Igrot Moshe, Orach Chayyim* 4:80). Rabbi Feinstein's reasoning was that if such permission were not granted, people would be reluctant to undertake the mission in the first place, and eventually sick people would die as a result (see the discussion of Rabbi Feinstein's ruling in Rabbi Chaim Jachter, *Gray Matter,* pages 29–31).

saving a . . . life. For me, however, it is a double mitzvah, saving a . . . life, and honoring one's parents."[7]

---

11. The Talmud delineates the parameters of permitted Sabbath violations with a poignant example: "We may desecrate the Shabbat for a day-old infant if he is still alive, but if he has already died, we may not do so, even for someone as great as David, King of Israel" (*Shabbat* 151b). In other words, when life can be saved or even just extended, all rituals are ignored. Otherwise, the Shabbat laws apply.

My mother, Helen Telushkin, of blessed memory, died on the Sabbath at her home in Brooklyn. In accordance with Jewish law, her body was not moved from the room where she died, and my sister, my wife, our children, and I sat with her body. Simultaneously, neighbors sat outside the door to her room, reciting Tehillim *(Psalms). Only after the Sabbath ended did we call the undertaker. Soon, thereafter, the* Chevra Kadisha *(the Jewish burial society) came to prepare her body for burial.*[*]

---

12. Permission to violate Jewish law applies to *all* threats to life, not just medical and psychological ones. In an incident in the city of Brisk during World War I, Russian officials arrested five Jews shortly before Yom Kippur. Rabbi Chaim Soloveitchik learned that the men could be ransomed for five thousand rubles; otherwise, they would probably be killed.[†] When the rabbi failed to raise the necessary funds before the holiday's onset, he dispatched messengers to all the Brisk synagogues to inform congregants that they could not begin *Kol Nidrei* (the opening prayer of Yom Kippur) until they received word from him to do so. He then went from congregation to congregation with his assistant, to collect money. He even accompanied some wealthy people home, well after the holiday had begun, to collect the sums he had assessed them. By late at night, all the money had been collected, and emissaries were dispatched to all the synagogues to permit the prayers to begin.[8] Reb Chaim, meanwhile, went and paid the ransom.

---

*For more on the *Chevra Kadisha* and on our obligations to the dead, see chapter 8.

†In Rabbi Joseph Soloveitchik's telling of this story, he did not delineate what crime the arrested Jews were accused of, but it was clear to his grandfather, Rabbi Chaim Soloveitchik, that they were certainly not guilty of a capital offense, and perhaps of no criminal offense at all.

13. While most discussions of this issue focus on permission to violate ritual laws when life is at stake, ethical laws—with certain exceptions (such as not committing murder; see page 352)—may also be violated. For example, a person is permitted to steal money or food to preserve his or her life. The Talmud records that when Rabbi Judah was seized with *bulmos,* a life-threatening disease whose symptoms include ravenous hunger, he took bread from a shepherd without permission (*Yoma* 83b).

In such cases, the *Shulchan Arukh* rules that we are permitted to save our lives, but *only* if we intend to pay for what we have taken (*Choshen Mishpat* 359:4; see also 380:3). A person lacking money should still first worry about saving his life and then later try to pay off the debt.

——

However, Rashi argues that it is forbidden to save yourself with another's money [or property], the implication being that this applies even if you intend to repay the money (see last line of Rashi's commentary on Bava Kamma *60b). Rashi here expresses an uncharacteristically minority—and rejected—viewpoint.*

——

As regards permission to lie to save a life, see *A Code of Jewish Ethics, Volume 1: You Shall Be Holy,* pages 424–428.

National threats

14. When a Jewish community is under siege, all Jews are commanded to take up arms in its defense, and if the attack occurs on the Sabbath soldiers should go to battle immediately, and not delay until the Sabbath is over (Maimonides, *Mishneh Torah,* "Laws of the Sabbath" 2:23). Such, of course, was the case in October 1973 when the Egyptian and Syrian armies attacked Israel on Yom Kippur, and the army was immediately mobilized throughout the country.

——

In the second century B.C.E., *there was a group of pious Jews, known as Chasidim, who refused to fight on the Sabbath, even when attacked. They were wiped out by the troops of the Syrian monarch Antiochus, "men, women and children, up to a thousand in all." Immediately thereafter, Mattathias, the founder of the Maccabees, ruled: "If we all do as our brothers have done, if we refuse to fight the Gentiles for our lives as well as for our laws and customs, then they will soon wipe us off the face of the earth." The book of Maccabees concludes: "That day they decided that, if anyone came to fight against them on the Sab-*

bath, they would fight back, rather than die as their brothers . . . had done" (see I Maccabees 2:3–41).

While the book of Maccabees makes it seem as if Mattathias's ruling permitting Jewish soldiers to fight on the Sabbath was innovative, my father, Shlomo Telushkin, found it hard to believe that this was so: "More than eight hundred years earlier, King David had fought many wars. If his opponents knew that he and his troops wouldn't fight on the Sabbath, wouldn't they have always attacked them then?" It is therefore more likely that the Chasidim, who refused to fight in self-defense, were trying to impose a new, unintentionally suicidal, standard in Jewish life.

---

15. Jewish law also allows soldiers to violate Jewish laws in wartime when their health—and, by extension, their lives—may be compromised if they don't. "When the vanguard of the army conquers a foreign land, and settles in it, it is permitted for them to eat unkosher meat, pork and similar food, if they are hungry and can find only these forbidden foods" (Maimonides, "Laws of Kings," 8:1; see *Chullin* 17a). Based on this example, Jews in concentration camps—and others who are involuntarily without access to kosher food for an extended period—clearly are permitted to eat whatever is available. However, a Jew should not voluntarily place himself in this situation, such as by going to live in a place where he or she will lack access to kosher food.

28

WHEN ILLNESS AND PAIN MAKE LIFE INTOLERABLE

1. Judaism regards life as of immeasurable value. In the most famous formulation of this belief, a passage in the Mishnah teaches: "Whoever saves a single life, it is as if he saved an entire world" (*Sanhedrin* 4:5). The Rabbis based this teaching on the fact that God created humankind with only one person, Adam (Genesis 2:5–7). Had he been killed, all humanity would have been destroyed; and, if he were saved, all humanity would survive. Because

God deemed it worth creating the world for the sake of one person,* Judaism reasons that each person's life, like Adam's, is of infinite value.†

What are the implications of this teaching for daily behavior, particularly in situations involving great emotional and/or physical suffering? For example:

- Do the Bible and Talmud take intense suffering into account in deciding whether or not a life is worth living? Or do Jewish sources assume that life, even of low quality, should always be preserved?

- Does Jewish law require Jewish doctors to do everything in their power to prolong the life of someone in chronic pain and suffering from a terminal illness?

Quality of Life

Preferring death to a life of torment and degradation

2. The Talmud records a first-century mass suicide by four hundred young Jewish men and women who were being transported by ship to Roman brothels; in the words of the Talmud, "they sensed what they were wanted for." One question obsessed them: "If we drown ourselves in the sea, will we enter the World-to-Come?" Basing himself on a biblical verse, "I [God] will retrieve from the depths of the sea" (Psalms 68:23), the eldest among them taught that God would bring to salvation all those who drown in the sea; thereupon, the women, and then the men, drowned themselves.

These Jews did not kill themselves because they expected the Romans to kill them; rather, they knew that the Romans hoped to keep them alive as

---

*In Hebrew, the word for "person" is *ben adam,* "child of Adam."

†Among the implications of the teaching that every human life possesses immeasurable value are:

- One who murders another human being has committed the ultimate crime; murdering twenty more people increases the crime's magnitude, but not its severity.
- No ideology can justify killing innocent people; as my friend Daniel Taub puts it: "There can be no 'greater good' that justifies destroying a life of infinite value."
- Both individuals (through contributions to appropriate organizations and needy individuals) and governments are responsible for ensuring that all who are hungry are given enough food to survive. As Rabbi Irwin Kula asks: "What does it mean to say that every human being is infinitely valuable when people die for a lack of a dollar's worth of food a day?"

female and male prostitutes. To avoid such a fate, they committed suicide, and the Talmud writes of their act with approval (*Gittin* 57b).

While Saul was fighting against the Philistine army, Philistine archers wounded him. The Israelite king pleaded with his arms-bearer: "Draw your sword and stab me, lest the uncircumcised men come and stab me and make sport of me." The arms-bearer, in awe of a king who had been anointed at God's command, refused to slay him, so Saul fell on his own sword and died. A short time later, the Philistines cut off his head and impaled his body, along with those of three of his sons, in a public square (I Samuel 31). Rabbi David Kimchi (the Radak), an early thirteenth-century Bible commentator, wrote: "Saul did not sin in killing himself . . . because he knew that in the end he was bound to die in that war. . . . It was therefore better for him to take his own life, rather than have the [Philistines] make sport with him" (commentary on I Samuel 31:4).

Despite the example offered in this story, throughout history Jews have not generally chosen to escape protracted torment and anguish through suicide, certainly not in large numbers. It has often been noted that, during the Holocaust, relatively few Jews in concentration camps committed suicide, although it was possible for an inmate to run into an electrified fence and die quickly. It is likely that many inmates held out hope that the Germans would eventually be defeated and they would be liberated, which in fact happened. A friend of mine, a child of two Holocaust survivors, notes that "had the Jewish inmates committed suicide, my children and I would not be alive today."*

Hastening death to avoid excruciating pain

3. Rabbi Chanina ben Teradyon (second century) was one of the Ten [rabbinic] Martyrs who were executed by the Romans after the failure of the Bar Kochba revolt (135 C.E.). His offense consisted of continuing to teach Torah in public even after the Romans had decreed it to be a capital crime. In a horrible reprisal, the Romans built a bonfire, and wrapped Rabbi Chanina's body in the Torah scroll from which he had been teaching when he was arrested. Out of a sadistic desire to prolong the rabbi's suffering, the Romans put tufts of wool soaked in water over his heart, and then set both the wool and the parchment on fire. When his students urged him to open his mouth

*The most famous exception to the above statement is the mass suicide at Masada (73 C.E.), which was also done to avoid enslavement and forced prostitution.

wide so that the fire would enter and he would die quickly, Rabbi Chanina refused, saying, "It is better that He [God] who gave my soul should take it, and let no person harm himself."

As the fire continued to rage and Rabbi Chanina's sufferings intensified, the Roman executioner, awed by the rabbi's faith, said to him, "Rabbi, if I increase the flame and remove the tufts of wool from over your heart, will you bring me into the World-to-Come?" Rabbi Chanina answered him, "Yes." "Swear to me," the executioner insisted, and Rabbi Chanina swore that he would do so. Immediately, the executioner removed the tufts of wool and then increased the fire. Rabbi Chanina quickly succumbed. The executioner himself then jumped into the fire, and a heavenly voice announced: "Rabbi Chanina ben Teradyon and the executioner are both invited to enter the World to Come" (*Avodah Zarah* 18a).

Dr. Fred Rosner, a leading Orthodox medical ethicist, deduces from this narrative that, while it is permitted to remove impediments to death (i.e., the tufts of wool) so as to allow nature to take its course, Rabbi Chanina's refusal to open his mouth means that it is forbidden to directly hasten one's own death.[1]

"But does the story teach that?" challenges Hebrew Union College professor Leonard Kravitz, noting that one can understand this episode quite differently. Thus, when Rabbi Chanina was first subjected to the pain of the fire, he resisted his students' suggestion that he open his mouth and hasten his death. But when his suffering grew ever more excruciating, Chanina acceded to the executioner's suggestion that he bring about death more quickly.[2] In addition, Kravitz argues, one cannot maintain that all that the executioner did was remove an impediment to death (the tufts of wool) since he also increased the fire's magnitude.*

Ultimately, there does seem to be little difference between Rabbi Chanina opening his mouth and hastening his death, and his promising a reward to the executioner for bringing about his death more quickly.†

Rabbi Moshe Tendler acknowledges that the Talmud's positive assessment of the executioner's "increasing the flame presents a serious challenge to the unanimity

*For more on Kravitz's dissenting views on euthanasia, see pages 396–398.

†In a sense, this story is parallel to—though with an opposite conclusion—the earlier-cited story of King Saul and his arms-bearer. There, Saul pleaded with the arms-bearer to kill him quickly, so as to avoid suffering an even worse fate at the hands of the Philistines. The arms-bearer refused, and Saul killed himself. Here, Rabbi Chanina does not take action to end his own life directly, but relies on the executioner to do so.

of halachic opinion that active euthanasia is never condoned." Tendler hypothesizes that the executioner originally had placed the wet wads of wool and had lowered the flame as his own special act of cruelty; he had not been ordered to do so by the government: "Burning at the stake had a formal protocol which was not followed by the cruel executioner. Restoring the flame to its original intensity was not an act of hastening death but merely the removal of the extra measure of cruel torture introduced by the executioner."[3]

However, in addition to this theory being speculative, a close reading of the text does not leave one with the feeling that the executioner was a more sadistic character than the other representatives of the Roman government; if anything, he seems better. What strikes me as more plausible is that Rabbi Chanina was at first determined not to do anything to hasten his death, but, as his situation became more and more acute, with death inevitable, he finally concluded that it would be best to die as quickly as possible.

An analogy can be drawn with those individuals who jumped out of the high floors in the Twin Towers on 9/11. At first, when the people inside the towers started to feel the fire's heat, they tried to escape or to find some way to hang on for as long as possible. But when the fire started to create an unbearable heat, and both escape and rescue seemed impossible, some people chose to leap to certain death if only to put an end to their suffering.

---

4. The maid who hastened the death of Rabbi Judah. "On the day that Rabbi Judah was dying, the Rabbis declared a public fast and offered prayers that God have mercy [and spare him]. . . . Rabbi Judah's maid went up to the roof of his house and offered this prayer: 'The angels in heaven desire Rabbi Judah to join them, and the mortals on earth desire him to remain with them. May it be the will of God that the mortals overpower the angels.' However, when she saw how much Rabbi Judah was suffering,* she offered a second prayer: 'May it be the will of God that the angels overpower the mortals [and let the rabbi die].'' As the Rabbis continued their incessant prayers, she took a jar and threw it down from the roof. [It made a great noise] and for a moment the [startled] Rabbis ceased praying, and the soul of Rabbi Judah departed" (*Ketubot* 104a).

On the one hand, one can argue that no specific act hastening Rabbi Judah's death occurred here. Rather, the maid's act removed an impediment

*Literally, how often he had to go the bathroom, each time painfully taking off his tefillin and putting them on again.

(the Rabbis' continuous prayers) and the cessation of prayer enabled Rabbi Judah's soul to depart.

Alternatively, one can, like the Talmud, regard the maid's behavior as intended to bring about Rabbi Judah's death quickly. The maid apparently shared the Rabbis' belief that prayers could keep Judah alive, although they might not reduce or eliminate his agony. To Rabbi Judah's colleagues, simply keeping him alive was sufficient (perhaps they still held out hope that he would recover), a belief with which the maid concurred until she witnessed the extent of his agony. At that point, she not only prayed for his death, but also tried to hasten it by startling the Rabbis and interrupting their prayers.

In one regard, her action was more radical than that of Rabbi Chanina's executioner, who intensified the fire only after Chanina made it clear that he wanted to die quickly.* Here, it was the maid on her own who reached the conclusion that it was preferable for Judah to die; the rabbi himself had said nothing to her. Yet the Talmud does not condemn the maid for her behavior, and she is assumed to have acted mercifully and appropriately.

Preferring death to inconsolable loneliness

5. "[Resh Lakish, the dear friend and learning partner of Rabbi Yochanan, died, and Rabbi Yochanan was plunged into deep grief.] The Rabbis said: 'Who shall go and take his mind away from his grief? Let Rabbi Eleazar ben Pedat go, for his scholarship is brilliant.'

"Rabbi Eleazar went and sat before Rabbi Yochanan. Every time Rabbi Yochanan uttered an opinion, he said, 'There is a *baraita* [a rabbinic source] which supports your opinion.'

"Said Rabbi Yochanan: 'You are supposed to be like the son of Lakish. Whenever I stated an opinion, the son of Lakish used to raise twenty-four objections, to which I was compelled to give twenty-four answers, and as a result the subject became clear. You, however, say, " 'There is a *baraita* which supports you.' Do I not know myself that I have spoken well?"

"He continued to tear his garments and weep, saying, 'Where are you, son of Lakish?' Eventually, he lost his reason, so the Rabbis prayed for God to 'have mercy on him' and he died (*Bava Mezia* 84a)."†

---

*It was far less radical in that the maid left it in God's hands as to whether He would choose to let Rabbi Judah die more quickly, whereas the executioner took concrete steps to hasten Rabbi Chanina's death.

†The expression "have mercy on him" is a rabbinic euphemism; what the Rabbis were praying for is that God take pity on him by ending his life. A friend, Rabbi Israel Stein, has told me that when he makes the *mi-sheh-beirakh* prayer for one who is in great pain, and for whom there is

Here, in a case involving intractable depression followed by permanent mental illness and a loss of reason, the Rabbis take the position adopted by Rabbi Judah's maid and pray for the rabbi's death.

---

*In line with the above text, a fourteenth-century talmudic commentator Rabbi Nissim Gerondi (the Ran), ruled that it is sometimes appropriate to pray for a patient's death. Commenting on a talmudic passage in which Rabbi Akiva reproves those of his students who had not visited a fellow student who was ill (*Nedarim *40a; see page 63), the Ran understands Rabbi Akiva's words as meaning that those who visit the sick should do more than simply attend to his physical needs: "You could have prayed for his recovery. If you had found him in such a state that he was in great pain and without hope of recovery, you could have prayed for his quick death."[4] Dr. Fred Rosner, the contemporary medical ethicist, reinforces this point: "There are times . . . when it is appropriate to pray for the death of a suffering patient in intractable physical pain or with severe psychological or mental pain."[5]*

Rabbi Chaim Palachi, a nineteenth-century Turkish scholar, ruled that even when it is permitted to pray for a patient's demise, such prayers should not be offered by those involved in the person's care, particularly family members whose prayers might have a taint of self-interest. For example, a close relative might be motivated by the desire to be relieved of a time-consuming and emotional burden, and/or the financial cost of continuing medical care.[6]

As regards the applicability of the story of Rabbi Yochanan in the contemporary world, Dr. Isaac Herschkopf notes that "today, depression is rarely intractable," and can often be treated by a combination of therapy and medication. As a last resort, "shock therapy almost always alleviates the intensity of the sorrow." Herschkopf believes that modern techniques might have been successful in treating Rabbi Yochanan's condition before it deteriorated—as the Talmud suggests—into seemingly irreversible mental illness.

---

6. A talmudic story, apparently legendary in character, tells of Choni, a first century B.C.E. rabbinic leader who saw a man planting a carob tree. He asked the man why he was doing so since carob trees do not bear fruit for seventy years. The man replied, "I found a world containing fully grown

---

no rational (as opposed to miraculous) hope for recovery, he prays for the person to get well by dying and thereby entering *olam haba* (afterlife). In Rabbi Stein's words, "sometimes death comes as a friend."

carob trees, and just as my ancestors planted those trees for me, so too, will I plant them for my children." Almost immediately, Choni was overcome with drowsiness and fell asleep. Rocks rose to cover him and he became hidden from sight. He slept for seventy years, and when he awoke, he saw a person who looked like the same man picking fruits from a carob tree. Choni asked the man, "Are you the man who planted this tree?" The man answered, "No, I am his grandson." Choni soon realized that he had slept for seventy years. Wherever he went and told people who he was—he had been a well-known rabbi—they looked at him as if he were mad. At the study house, he heard a rabbi saying, "These teachings are as clear to us as they were during the time of Choni." Choni called out, "I am Choni," but the people present did not believe him and did not accord him the respect he was used to receiving. At this point, the Talmud records, "Choni became anguished, prayed for heavenly mercy, and died." A later sage, Rava, commented: "This is an example of the popular adage, "Either friends or death" (*Ta'anit* 23a).

From the Talmud's perspective, death was preferable to a life in which Choni would neither have friends nor be accepted as a teacher.

Again, it is important to emphasize that Choni did not actively kill himself. Rather, the Talmud records, God so loved Choni that He would grant his personal prayers, even when they seemed audacious.* Therefore, in praying to God for a merciful end, Choni had reason to hope that he would soon die.

Well-known as this story is, a religious friend of mine expresses extreme disagreement both with Choni's behavior and the Talmud's rather sympathetic portrayal of his desire to die: "Choni's behavior was incredibly short-sighted. Why couldn't he make new friends and earn new respect? This was a poor reason to pray for death." Also, my friend argued, given that the Talmud gives no indication that Choni's mind was impaired, there was no reason for him to assume that his productive life was over: "Rabbi Moshe Feinstein issued important rulings on Jewish

*The Talmud records that during a drought, the people begged Choni to pray for rain. He did so, but rain didn't fall. Choni then drew a circle around himself, and said to God: "Master of the Universe, your children have turned their faces to me because I am like a member of the household before You. I swear by Your great name that I shall not move from here until You have mercy on Your children [and send rain]." First, some rain fell as a trickle, then as a torrent. On both occasions, Choni told God, "Not such rains did I request." Finally, rain fell in a moderate manner. The leading rabbi of the age, Shimon ben Shetach, sent Choni a message: "Were you not Choni, I would have pronounced a ban of excommunication upon you [for being disrespectful toward God]. But what can I do to you? For you misbehave towards God by boldly demanding rain and yet He fulfills your wish, like a son who misbehaves towards his father by boldly demanding whatever he desires and yet his father fulfills his wish" (*Ta'anit* 19a).

*law in his eighties, the same age at which Verdi was still composing operas. Pablo Casals was still undertaking world tours and performing concerts at eighty-eight, an age at which Michelangelo was still sculpting."**

—

Preferring death to a life without pleasure

7. The Midrash relates a story about a very old woman who complained to Rabbi Yossi ben Halafta (second century) that because of her great age and, presumably, her diminished strength, she had no appetite and little desire to live. When Rabbi Yossi asked her by what merit she had lived so long, the woman answered, "I go to synagogue services every morning, and I allow nothing to interfere with this." Rabbi Yossi advised the woman to absent herself from the synagogue for three consecutive days. She did so and died (*Yalkut Shimoni Ekev* 871).

In this instance, there is no indication that the woman was suffering from pain or terminal illness. Yet she had lost her zest for life and wanted to die. One might have thought that the rabbi would have scolded her for such an attitude, and said something along the lines of "God has blessed you with a long life, so how can you treat it as a curse? You should continue to go to daily services to extol your Creator and search out what mission God still has for you in this world." Instead, he suggests how to provoke heaven into ending her life.

Rabbi Dr. Moshe Tendler, a biologist and medical ethicist, sees a practical implication to this story: "The Midrash . . . clearly teaches that mental anguish [editor's note: if it will continue unabated] is to be viewed as an unacceptable quality of life. If one may pray for the life of no quality to end, certainly no one is obligated to initiate heroic measures to prolong it."†[7]

—

David Szonyi, a therapist, argues that "in contemporary terms, this is a troubling story. It seems as if the woman was depressed, and today such a woman might *(not necessarily* would*) be helped by an antidepressant, and/or therapy,*

*Michelangelo was deep into his eighties and still hard at work when he made the declaration "I regret that I have not done enough for the salvation of my soul, and that I die just as I am beginning to learn the alphabet of my profession" (see Desmond Morris, *The Book of Ages,* page 88).

†Normally, we do not derive laws from midrashic texts, but the talmudic commentary *Tosafot* notes that it is permitted to derive a law from a Midrash as long as it does not oppose a legal source (*Berachot* 48a; see Fred Rosner, *Biomedical Ethics,* page 230).

and/or more social contact." Szonyi asks: "Is it really a proper role for a rabbi, even a sage, to advise an old woman on how to end her life?"

Euthanasia

8. The assumption of traditional Jewish medical ethics is that euthanasia—"the act of putting to death painlessly a person suffering from an incurable and painful disease or condition"[8]—is, in the words of Lord Immanuel Jakobovits, the late chief rabbi of England, "plain murder."[9] Along the same lines, Rabbi Moshe Feinstein wrote: "It is absolutely forbidden to do anything or to provide any drug that will shorten a patient's life for even a moment. To do so would be an act of murder" (*Igrot Moshe, Choshen Mishpat* 2:73). A similar view is conveyed in the writings of Rabbi J. David Bleich: "Any positive act designed to hasten the death of the patient is equated with murder in Jewish law, even if death is hastened by only a matter of moments. No matter how laudable the intention of the person performing an act of mercy killing may be, the deed constitutes an act of homicide."[10]

Menachem Elon, a former justice of the Israeli Supreme Court and a renowned scholar of Jewish law, regards the prohibition against euthanasia as a cornerstone of Jewish morality: "Even if the whole world were to decide that active euthanasia is permitted, a country that professes to be founded upon Jewish and democratic values should rule according to the Jewish principle that . . . active euthanasia is murder."*

The absolute opposition to euthanasia has generally been adopted across the spectrum of Jewish denominations. Professor Louis Ginzberg, the late great Talmud scholar of the Conservative movement, wrote that "from the point of view of Jewish law, saving from pain is no excuse, neither for homicide nor suicide, and that, further, in evaluating human life, its duration is of no moment."[11] And Rabbi Israel Bettan, writing for the Reform movement in 1950, a short while after a committee of two thousand physicians in New York drafted a bill for presentation to the New York legislature to legalize euthanasia, noted: "The Jewish ideal of the sanctity of human life and the

---

*Justice Elon emphasizes that Jewish law permits passive euthanasia: "One may, and indeed should, ease suffering through passive euthanasia, or as it is called in Jewish sources, 'removal of impediments' [to death]" (Menachem Elon, "Israel as a Jewish and Democratic State," in Naftali Rothenberg and Eliezer Schweid, eds., *Jewish Identity in Modern Israel,* page 164; for more on removal of impediments to death and objection to the term "passive euthanasia," see pages 391–392).

supreme value of the individual soul would suffer incalculable harm if, contrary to the moral law, men were at liberty to determine the conditions under which they might put an end to their own lives and the lives of other men."[12]

9. The above conclusions are consistent with two key passages, Mishnah *Shabbat* 23:5 and *Shabbat* 151b. The Mishnah rules that it is forbidden to close the eyes of a dying person. The Talmud comments on this passage that it is "like touching the dying flame of a candle, and thereby extinguishing it"; one who does so is regarded as "a shedder of blood" (*shofaikh damim,* see also, Maimonides, "Laws of Mourning" 4:5).

The tractate Semachot *expands upon the point raised in this talmudic text, teaching that a* goses *(a person in a dying condition whom it is presumed will soon be dead), is regarded as a living person in all respects. Rabbi Meir taught that he "can be compared to a flickering flame. As soon as a person touches it, it becomes extinguished. So too, whoever closes the eyes of a dying man is considered to have taken his life'" (see chapter 1:1–4).*

When I was writing an ethics advice column for beliefnet.com, the most painful query I received dealt with euthanasia. A fifty-seven-year-old man's mother had recently died after a prolonged decline into Alzheimer's. "By the end, she was reduced to an animal state. It was the worst horror I had ever witnessed in my life. My father is eighty-three years old, and in good physical health. He has begged me to promise him that I will take his life rather than let him descend into Alzheimer's. He is an extraordinary man who stood by my mother until the very end. . . . This is not a theoretical problem. Although I am not a physician, I can see in my father some of the same early warning signals I noted in my mother. His short-term memory is starting to erode. He has trouble reading. Yet his body is remarkably healthy; I am sure it will outlive his mind. I have not made the promise he wishes. I am repulsed by the idea of taking any life, let alone my dad's. . . . On the other hand, I would want the same for myself. If I could not do it myself, I would want someone to terminate my life before what makes me who I am is obliterated. What do I tell my father? I cannot imagine letting him go through what my mother suffered, or rather, what all of those who loved her suffered . . . but I cannot imagine being the agent of his death. Time is running out. On top of everything else, I am afraid that my refusal to make this promise might lead him to take his own life prematurely. What should I do?"

I responded: "Your father wants you to do for him what he couldn't do for his wife, your mother. And why couldn't he kill your mother? Probably for the same reason that you believe you won't be able to put him to death. You are repulsed by the idea of taking any life, let alone your father's.

"Needless to say, the situation you describe is awful. And throughout history, I am sure that there have been parents who have made such requests of their children, and some children (I would guess very few) who have complied. But, as you note, you 'cannot imagine being the agent of his death.' The guilt you might feel would be something you would have to live with for the rest of your life. And as much as you emphasize the horror of the last years of your mother's life, you do not mention that you walk around now consumed by guilt for not having ended her life. Also, if you follow your father's request, you will be committing a crime, and not a minor one either. Therefore, you will have to keep the manner of your father's death a secret, which is not always easy to do. Further, if what you did became known, many people will be skeptical of your motives. For example, did you choose to end your father's life while there was still some money left in his estate, money that you would then inherit? I am not saying that this would be a factor in your making the decision to end your father's life, but such speculation would do great damage to your name; in addition, you might well incur criminal prosecution.

*"I do believe that you should validate whatever aspects of your father's wishes that you can. Modern medicine sometimes pressures patients and their families to take many measures to prolong life, even when the life that is being prolonged will be one without dignity or pleasure. I see no reason to subject a person to such a prolongation of life particularly when the person has expressly stated, as has your father, that he does not want his life prolonged. Also, I would suggest that while your father still has his wits about him, he execute a living will outlining precisely the sort of procedures he does not want done. For example, 'If I should be in an incurable or irreversible mental or physical condition with no reasonable expectation of recovery, I direct my attending physician to withhold treatment that serves only to prolong my dying.'**

"A parent must understand that to lay upon his children the burden of

---

*As regards the issue of "withdrawing treatments" that serve, in effect, to prolong dying, most non-Orthodox rabbis permit doing so, while most Orthodox rabbis hold that withdrawing treatments maintaining a person's life is prohibited. The Orthodox thus generally distinguish between *withholding* treatments that have not yet begun (which can sometimes be permitted) and *withdrawing* treatments that are in place (which is prohibited). Because of issues such as these (many people put instructions into living wills to "withdraw treatments" when there is no hope for recovery), Rabbi J. David Bleich opposes living wills, arguing that "Judaism denies man the right to make judgments with regard to quality of life. . . . Nor, in the final analysis does the desire of the patient to have, or not have, his life prolonged play a role in the halachic obligation to initiate or maintain life-sustaining procedures" (*Judaism and Healing*, page 139).

killing them when the parent's life no longer seems worth living is simply an unfair demand. What you can and should tell your father is, 'Dad, you're the one who gave me life, and you can't ask me to take away yours. But let me tell you what I can do for you. Because I love you, I will be here for you throughout your illness, and treat you with the love and compassion you have shown me. Also, I promise that I will not allow any procedures to be performed on you, or any medications administered to you, except those that will relieve pain. I will not allow your life to be artificially extended.'

"Your situation is so difficult and so sad that I hope I have not said anything that will make it sadder or harder. All I can offer in addition to advice is my heartfelt prayer that God shows your father mercy."

Removing impediments to death

10. Removing impediments to death involves removing treatments that prolong the dying of a terminal, suffering patient while doing nothing to actively bring about the patient's death. An important precedent for permitting such behavior is the ruling of the Ramah (sixteenth century), based on a passage in *Sefer Chasidim* (paragraph 723): "If there is anything which causes a hindrance to the departure of the soul, such as the presence near the patient's house of a knocking noise, such as wood chopping, or if there is salt on the patient's tongue, and these things hinder the soul's departure,* it is permissible to remove them because no act is involved, only the removal of the impediment [to the dying process]" (*Shulchan Arukh, Yoreh Deah* 339:1). In the well-chosen words of Doctors Tendler and Rosner, "to prolong life is a *mitzvah,* to prolong dying is not."[13] Or, as Rabbi Moshe Feinstein wrote: "If physicians have no way to cure a dying patient or ease his burden, but they do have the ability to prolong the dying process, they should not intervene" (*Igrot Moshe, Choshen Mishpat* 2:74; see paragraph 11 in this chapter).

Some people refer to this behavior as "passive euthanasia," but Dr. Kenneth Prager, professor of clinical medicine and director of clinical ethics at Columbia University Medical Center, and an observant Jew, argues that "the term euthanasia is so provocative that many ethicists recoil from using it."

---

*Presumably, salt on a person's tongue creates an uncomfortable and unpleasant sensation and revives the person; a loud unpleasant noise does so as well.

—

In the context of a responsa dealing with a case in which a terminally ill and suffering patient acquires a second illness for which there is a cure (for example, pneumonia), Rabbi Feinstein rules that it is permitted for the patient to make it known that he does not wish to treat the second illness. He relies in part on the previously discussed case of Rabbi Chanina ben Teradyon (see pages 381–382): "Whereas Rabbi Chanina ben Teradyon would not open his mouth to hasten his death, we may infer that if his mouth had been open, he would not have been required to close it in order to prolong the dying process. From this, we further infer that a patient does not have the obligation to prolong a life of pain" (Igrot Moshe, Choshen Mishpat *2:74*).[14]

—

In contrast, Rabbi Eliezer Waldenberg, a legal scholar, argues that a patient's life must be prolonged at all costs, despite what the patient wants: "Even if the patient himself cries out, 'Let me be and do not give me any aid, death is preferable,' everything possible must be done on behalf of the patient" (Tzitz Eliezer, *volume 9, number 47, section 5). Yet Rabbi Waldenberg's ruling seems to fly in the face of the earlier-cited Midrash about the very old woman who confided to Rabbi Yossi that she was tired of life and wished to die (see page 387). Similarly, if Rabbi Waldenberg had been present at Rabbi Chanina's execution, one wonders if he would have felt compelled to cry out to the executioner, "Don't listen to Rabbi Chanina, and don't do anything to hasten his death."*

—

Does Jewish law require doctors to do all within their power to prolong the life of a patient in chronic pain and suffering from a terminal illness?

11. In a seminal ruling specifically addressed to physicians, Rabbi Moshe Feinstein wrote: "If a patient is terminally ill and in intractable pain, so that there is no hope of his surviving in a condition free of pain, but it is possible, through medical or technological methods, to prolong his life, then it is improper to do so. Rather, the patient should be made as comfortable as possible and left without any further intervention" (*Igrot Moshe, Choshen Mishpat* 2:73).*[15] On the other hand, if medicines can be found to make the

*In the context of this responsa, Rabbi Feinstein goes on to make the statement previously cited that *actively* hastening the patient's death *by even a moment* is "murder" (see page 388).

patient comfortable, "so that he will not be in pain, [then] efforts should be made to prevent the patient from dying." Thus, for Rabbi Feinstein, the key concern regarding terminal patients, particularly those who can live for only a few more months, is the absence of "intractable pain."

An appeal to expand the category of patients who should not be treated

Dr. Kenneth Prager, an observant Jew, argues that even in instances in which pain can be contained, there are still reasons why it might be wrong to prolong a terminal patient's life. He feels, therefore, that Rabbi Feinstein's ruling "does not address the ever-increasing number of patient's in Intensive Care Units on life support with no hope of leaving the hospital alive who are being kept alive by ventilators, dialysis machines, pressors (potent medications to maintain their failing blood pressure), potent antibiotics, and even artificial pumps that assist a failing heart. These patients are nearly always prevented from feeling pain by the administration of narcotics that render them unconscious. They cannot communicate with their families. Patients may be kept in this condition for literally weeks or even months during which time they develop horribly large and deep ulcers of their skin, disfiguring bloating of their entire body, and undergo repeated skin punctures for IVs and catheters. My experience with the Orthodox rabbinate is that they have been loath to allow withdrawal of life support in these situations even though the intensive care is clearly prolonging the misery of the dying process. These treatments, in my view, also violate the dignity of patients because of the disfigurement and breakdown of their bodies, sometimes with actual putrefaction of their tissues. I have even had rabbis who were loath to withhold attempts at resuscitation in these patients, thereby subjecting these poor people to the degradation of chest compression, rib fractures, and electric shocks in an attempt to prolong the dying process for an even longer period. I believe that such efforts are in direct contradiction to those *posekim* (decisors of Jewish law) who have declared that if a physician cannot help a patient, but can only cause prolonged suffering, these physicians do not have permission to treat the patient. *Verapo yerapeh* ("and heal shall he heal") the biblical expression from which the Talmud derives *reshut* (permission) for doctors to practice medicine (see Exodus 21:19 and *Bava Kamma* 85a) only pertains when the physician can help the patient. However, 'permission' to be a doctor ceases once the doctor can no longer help the patient. For too many rabbis, the sanctity of life has become an end in itself and they feel that efforts should be made to prolong the lives of patients at all costs, as long as the patients are not suffering, regardless of the breakdown of their bodies."*[16]

12. Jewish law favors pressuring, but not coercing, a patient to accept even painful treatments as long as "the medical consensus holds that the treatment will benefit him and may lead to a cure" (Rabbi Moshe Feinstein, *Igrot Moshe, Choshen Mishpat* 2:73). However, when such a consensus is lacking, pressure should not be exerted to administer a drug if the patient refuses treatment. Thus, in cases of terminal illness, the patient should be told the truth both about his prognosis and potential suffering, and then asked if he wishes to receive medication. If he refuses, one need not administer it, because when one cannot cure the illness, there is no reason to prolong a life filled with suffering. But even in such cases, artificial hydration and nutrition administered through feeding tubes must be provided. However, if the patient is mentally competent and refuses to eat, no forced feeding is permitted; the patient should, though, periodically be informed that food and drink are available.[17]

13. It would seem that only when doctors believe that there is better than a 50 percent chance that a treatment will arrest or reverse the disease's process is the patient obligated, according to Jewish law, to accept treatment (Rabbi Moshe Feinstein, *Igrot Moshe, Choshen Mishpat* 2:74). If the chances of a cure are under 50 percent, it would seem then that the patient may make the decision.

The treatment of pain

14. The primary responsibility of a physician who is treating a patient with a terminal and painful illness is to treat the pain: "All reputable commentators on the halachic perspectives on terminal care concur that analgesics and narcotics may be given to relieve pain and suffering even if these increase the danger of depressing respiration and of predisposing the patient

---

*In Prager's view, "the ancient notion of a *goses* (a legal term referring to a patient so sick that it is presumed he will be dead within 72 hours) is a very useful one. But unfortunately the definition of this term has been muddied in the halachic mind because of the sophisticated technology that can keep virtually everyone, no matter how sick, alive for a while, without, however, healing the patient. We need a new invigorated definition of the term *goses* by the rabbinate to accommodate the realities of changing medical technology."

to contracting pneumonia" (Dr. Fred Rosner).[18] Thus, while it is forbidden, for example, to purposely overdose and kill a patient in pain with morphine, it is permitted to give a sufficient dose to relieve the suffering even if doing so increases the likelihood of the patient's demise.

15. As opposed to the law in most American states, Jewish law would permit the use of marijuana to alleviate the nausea that is a common side effect of some forms of chemotherapy (popularly referred to as "medical marijuana"). Rabbi J. David Bleich notes that this permission extends to the use of even more serious and illegal drugs: "There is no halachic objection [for example] to the use of heroin in the control of pain in terminal patients. The danger of addiction in such circumstances is, of course, hardly a significant consideration." Bleich concludes that "Jewish teachings would enthusiastically endorse legislation legalizing the use—with adequate accompanying safeguards—of those substances in the treatment of terminal patients."[19]

Conflicting views on legalization of medical marijuana

The tragic experience of Peter McWilliams, a well-known author who died in 2000, exemplified to me the cruelty of categorically prohibiting "medical marijuana." McWilliams, who suffered from both cancer and AIDS, needed marijuana to control the extreme nausea caused by his medical treatments. Unable to procure the illegal drug, he started growing marijuana plants to be used solely for medicinal purposes. At his trial, the judge did not permit him or his lawyer to explain to the jury that he suffered from AIDS and cancer, and that he needed the marijuana to control nausea and vomiting. McWilliams was convicted. At the time of his death, he was waiting for a ruling from Judge George King as to how long a sentence he should serve, and whether he would be allowed to serve out his sentence at home or would be sentenced to prison. William F. Buckley, the conservative columnist and a friend of McWilliams's, wrote shortly after his death: "What was he doing when he died? Vomiting. The vomiting hit him while in his bathtub, and he choked to death. Was there nothing he might have done to still the impulse to vomit? Yes, he could have taken marijuana, but the judge's bail terms forbade him to do so, and he submitted to weekly urine tests to confirm that he was living up to the terms of his bail. . . . Is it being said, in plain language, that the judge's obstinacy resulted in killing McWilliams? Yes." Reflecting on the fifty-year-old McWilliams's wry, humorous, and affectionate nature, Buckley concluded: "Imagine such a spirit ending its life at 50, just because they wouldn't let him have a toke. We have to console ourselves with the comment of the two prosecutors. They said they were 'saddened' by Peter McWilliams's death. Many of us are—by his death, and by the causes of it."[20]

While I agree with Buckley's comment, Dr. Isaac Herschkopf, a psychiatrist and a member of the board of IADAF (International Anti-Drug Abuse Foundation), believes that the above anecdote, poignant as it is, oversimplifies the conundrum of whether medical marijuana should be legalized: "In many cases, there are anti-emetics available by prescription that are more effective than cannabis, the active ingredient in marijuana." Even when such medications are offered as an alternative, Herschkopf argues, they are frequently refused because the patients who insist on marijuana don't want injections and pills; they want to smoke marijuana and "get high." In addition, "whenever and wherever marijuana laws have been lessened, the inevitable result has been a critical rise in both its usage and the usage of more virulent drugs, such as cocaine and heroin, for which marijuana serves as a 'gateway.' Medical marijuana, like euthanasia, is a very slippery slope that can have catastrophic consequences."*

——

Postscript: A dissenting view on euthanasia

As noted, the opposition to euthanasia among religiously committed Jews is very strong, and cuts across denominational lines. This chapter reflects that view, and I am nervous about any tampering with Judaism's long-standing opposition to "mercy killing." However, I believe it worthwhile to include—because the challenge is so thoughtful and based on the very sources cited in this chapter—a dissenting opinion of Rabbi Leonard Kravitz, professor of Midrash at the Hebrew Union College (Reform) in New York. Rabbi Kravitz argues that—unlike the opinions expressed until now—the talmudic rabbis were quite open to ending a life when the quality of life was greatly diminished.

Thus, by promising his executioner entry into the World-to-Come if he would remove the wet wads and increase the flames, Rabbi Chanina encouraged the executioner to kill him quickly. As noted, the Talmud concludes this incident by noting that a heavenly voice immediately announced that both Rabbi Chanina and his executioner were invited into the World-to-Come, a

*Herschkopf argues that those who espouse the legalization of marijuana will often privately acknowledge that they are using "medical marijuana" as the best way to get "their foot in the door" to promote the full legalization of marijuana.

clear endorsement of the executioner's act of euthanasia. As Kravitz understands this passage, the story's implication is that when death is definite, the pain unbearable, and the suffering person wants to die, one may help him (as did the executioner) to do so.

Similarly, Kravitz argues that Rabbi Judah's maid's behavior was clearly a form of euthanasia, and not passive euthanasia either. Rather, she took action to bring about Rabbi Judah's death; even more remarkably, she did so without consulting Rabbi Judah, but just based on her own heartfelt sense of right, and it is clear from the passage that the Talmud regards her as a righteous figure. (In contrast, Dr. Kenneth Prager argues that this case—halting the prayers of the Rabbis that were keeping Rabbi Judah alive—constitutes, at most, the removal of an impediment.)

Kravitz also argues that the story of Rabbi Yossi giving an old woman advice on how to hasten her death offers us "an example of the acceptance of euthanasia; and note that euthanasia was requested in this instance not because of the suffering caused by pain, but because of the distress caused by the physical resultants of old age." (Once again, Prager argues that this constitutes removing an impediment, the woman's daily prayers, and has nothing to do with euthanasia.)

He also cites the passage from the *Shulchan Arukh* in which the Ramah permits removing impediments to death, for example, putting one's hands into a patient's mouth to remove salt (see page 391). Certainly, Kravitz argues, such behavior cannot be regarded as passive; it involves activity, and Jewish law permits it.[21] (Prager argues that this case also does not constitute euthanasia, but rather is again similar to removing an impediment, like taking someone off a ventilator.)

In Kravitz's view, a key passage that should influence the Jewish attitude to euthanasia is the talmudic discussion on how capital punishment should be administered. Interestingly, the Rabbis cite the verse "Love your neighbor as yourself" as even applying to someone sentenced to death. They conclude that it is the court's obligation to ensure that the prisoner suffer as little as possible; rather, his punishment should be a *mitah yaffa,* "a good death" (see *Ketubot* 37b).* Rashi understands *mitah yaffa* as meaning "a quick death."[22] By implication, Kravitz argues, if society owes a quick and easy death to those who have committed capital crimes, then it certainly owes the same to innocent people who are suffering and who wish to be relieved of their agony.

**Euthanasia* is a Greek word meaning a "good death."

Despite the clear and strong opposition to euthanasia in the Jewish tradition—almost all writers on the subject categorize it as a form of murder—Rabbi Kravitz has articulated a rarely heard challenge to this argument, insisting that Jewish law's opposition to euthanasia is not as absolute as is commonly depicted.

V

Justice and Tolerance

Two Cardinal Virtues

For I have singled him [Abraham] out that he may instruct his children and posterity to keep the way of the Lord by doing what is just and right.

Genesis 18:17, 19

29

"JUSTICE, JUSTICE, YOU SHALL PURSUE"

1. Biblical commandments are to be observed whenever the opportunity presents itself. Thus, when an elderly person walks by, we are expected to rise (Leviticus 19:32), but we are not required to go in search of old people to show respect. However, the commandment to practice justice is different: "Justice, justice, you shall pursue" (Deuteronomy 16:20) ordains the Torah. "Pursue" suggests that not only are we obligated to act justly when we can, but we must also seek ways to ensure that justice prevails (such as if we hear of someone who has been unjustly treated and are—or might be—in a position to help).

Sometimes (but not often), the demands of justice may even trump those of law. Professor Alan Dershowitz of Harvard University Law School recalls that when he was about fifteen years old, his grandfather confided in him: "You have to understand that our family is not without its blemishes." The young Dershowitz was puzzled, given that he had always thought of his grandfather and his family as wonderful, honest people. His grandfather explained: "In the late 1930s and the early 1940s [when there were severe limits on immigration into the United States], I filed false affidavits . . . about people I wanted to bring into America, to save them from the Holocaust. I went around and invented synagogues. I wrote letters with affidavits saying that this synagogue, which was just a basement somewhere, needed a rabbi, needed a cantor, needed a secretary, it needed everybody!" In the end, his grandfather succeeded in bringing into the United States thirty to forty people who otherwise would have perished in Europe: "cantors who couldn't sing, secretaries who couldn't organize, rabbis who weren't rabbis. But they were Jews, and they needed to be saved." Years later, at a lecture at Harvard in which he discussed his grandfather's behavior, Dershowitz concluded: "To me, my grandfather's action personified the Torah's teaching of 'Justice, justice, you shall pursue.' It doesn't say, justice you shall simply apply, but tirdof, *you must chase after justice."*[1]

---

2. The Chasidic rebbe, Ya'akov Yitzchak of Pzhysha (known as the "holy Yehudi"; 1766–1814) was asked, "Why in the verse, 'Justice, justice you shall pursue' is the word 'justice' repeated?" The rebbe answered that the repetition is meant to convey that not only must the ends we pursue be just, but so too must the means we employ to achieve those ends.*[2] This teaching is a corrective to many people's instinct to regard all means as justified when pursuing an end they regard as right.

While moral theorists have long debated the subject of means and ends, my experience is that the use of cruel means to achieve an end is often—again, not always—an indication that the end itself is immoral. In The Education of Lev Kopelev, *the memoir of a Russian Communist who later became a dissident, Kopelev recalled that along "with the rest of my generation, I firmly believed that the ends justified the means. Our great goal was the universal triumph of communism, and for the sake of that goal everything was permissible—to lie, to steal, to destroy hundreds of thousands and even millions of people, all those who were hindering our work or who could hinder it, everyone who stood in the way."† Kopelev recalls how party members were instructed to "throw your bourgeois humanitarianism out of the window."‡[3]*

The mere fact that the Communist revolution demanded that its adherents "throw your bourgeois humanitarianism out of the window" should have indicated to all Communists that the means they were being asked to employ would inevitably become part of the end. Thus, in 1956, when Nikita Khrushchev, the Soviet premier, publicly acknowledged the innumerable murders and other

---

*Martin Buber understands the rebbe's response as meaning: "The use of unrighteousness as a means to a righteous end makes the end itself unrighteous" (*Ten Rungs: Hasidic Sayings,* page 7).

†Lenin had earlier written: "We say that our morality is entirely subordinated to the interests of the class struggle of the proletariat . . . We repudiate all morality derived from non-human [ed. note: that is, God] and non-class concepts." When we reread these words, it becomes clear that they are simply Lenin's way of saying that the end ("the interests of the class struggle") justifies all means. Lenin's moral philosophy was, in turn, fully consistent with that of Karl Marx, who insisted in *Das Kapital* that "Right can never be higher than the economic structure of society . . ." And what is the upshot of such theories? Professor Wilfred Cantwell Smith concluded: "For Marxism, there is no reason (literally no reason; our universe, the movement posits, is the kind of universe where there cannot conceivably be any reason) for not killing or torturing or exploiting a human person if his liquidation or torture or slave labor will advance the [class struggle and] historical process."

‡While serving with the Red Army during World War II, Kopelev criticized Red Army atrocities against the German civilian population. He was arrested in 1945 and sentenced to a ten-year-term in the Gulag Archipelago for fostering "bourgeois humanism" and "compassion towards the enemy."

crimes committed by his predecessor Josef Stalin, Communists throughout the world claimed to be shocked, and some even left the party. But because Stalin's—and before him, Lenin's—evils had long been apparent in the means they used to gain and consolidate power, it should have come as no surprise that the society they established was as vicious as the means by which they established it.*

---

3. The particular biblical concern with justice is underscored in two early passages in the Torah, both involving Abraham. At one point, when God decides to destroy the evil city of Sodom, He shares this information in advance with Abraham. Reasoning aloud, God asks Himself, "Should I hide from Abraham what I am about to do . . . ? For I have singled him out that he may instruct his children and posterity to keep the way of the Lord by doing what is just and right" (Genesis 18:17, 19). In this verse, justice is equated with keeping "the way of the Lord."

When God shares with Abraham His intentions to destroy Sodom, and its equally evil neighbor, Gomorrah, Abraham responds by arguing with God, insisting that it is wrong to destroy a city composed of evildoers if righteous people also live there. In fact, Abraham challenges God in the name of the very justice that God intends him and his descendants to practice: "Shall not the judge of all the earth act with justice?" (Genesis 18:25).†

Eventually, God establishes to Abraham's satisfaction that there are fewer than ten righteous people within the city (for whom God sends angels to lead out) and that no one else living there is worthy of being saved.‡ Still, Abraham's question, in insisting that God, no less than human beings, is bound by the demands of just behavior, establishes the unique biblical emphasis on this virtue. Even in late medieval England, a king's unjust behavior went unchallenged on the grounds of the "divine right of kings," which was widely understood as meaning that the monarch, who was seen as serving by

---

*The sense of shock and disappointment was not universal. In China, under the leadership of Mao Zedong, himself a mass murderer, giant photographs of Stalin continued to be displayed (I saw one on a visit to Tiananmen Square in 1978) and his leadership lauded.

†Moses and Aaron confront God as well with a challenge in the name of justice. When many Israelites refuse to take sides between Moses and the rebel Korach, God, disgusted by the Israelites' behavior, says to Moses and Aaron, "Separate yourselves from this community, and I shall annihilate them in an instant." The two leaders challenge God, "Shall one man sin, and You be wrathful with the whole community?" (Numbers 16:20–22). God relents, and restricts His punishment to Korach and his followers.

‡Had there been ten or more righteous people there, Abraham would have gone on arguing to save the whole city, evil people included. With a core of good people, there is reason to hope that the evil people will also be affected.

the grace of God, had the right to do whatever he wanted. Abraham (and the Hebrew Bible's theology) was quite different. For Abraham, justice is a value to which "the King of kings" Himself is bound.

Legal justice

4. A functioning and equitable legal system is so basic to a moral society that the establishment of courts of law is the one positive demand Jewish law makes of non-Jewish societies (*Sanhedrin* 56a-b).* The implication is that Judaism opposes anarchy: Why else would it require that all societies have a mechanism for enforcing laws? In *The Ethics of the Fathers,* Rabbi Chanina teaches: "Pray for the welfare of the government,† for without fear of governmental authorities, people would swallow each other alive" (3:2).

Justice in the Torah: The basic verses

Even though many of the laws below relate to judicial procedures, they are not relevant only to judges and lawyers. Indeed, laws ordaining that we judge people fairly, stay far away from falsehood, and not be intimidated by others are applicable, on a daily basis, to all our lives.

5. The most all-encompassing command to judges is "In justice shall you judge your fellow man" (Leviticus 19:15). In addition to establishing the basic principle that justice must prevail in the courtroom, the Talmud (*Shevuot* 30a) derives several legal procedures from this verse:

- A court should not allow one litigant to speak as long as he wishes, and then instruct the other, "Keep your words brief."
- A court should not permit one litigant to sit, while letting the other stand; both should either be standing or sitting (see also Maimonides, "Laws of Sanhedrin" 21:3).

Maimonides also notes that judges must take care not to treat one litigant in a kindly manner and the other harshly ("Laws of Sanhedrin" 21:1, based on *Tosefta Sanhedrin* 6:2).

---

*The Rabbis teach that God requires non-Jews to observe the "Seven Laws of the Sons of Noah" *(Sheva mitzvot b'nai Noach),* presumed to date from the time of that most righteous Gentile, Noah. Six laws are negative: not to deny or blaspheme God, and not to murder, steal, eat a limb from a living animal, or engage in forbidden sexual acts (such as incest and bestiality). The final statute is to set up courts to ensure obedience to the other six laws (*Sanhedrin* 56a–b).

†To this day, such a prayer is offered during the Sabbath morning service.

As these examples demonstrate, a fundamental component of justice is a level playing field, the equal treatment of both litigants.

For more on how the commandment to judge others fairly applies to our interactions with others, see *A Code of Jewish Ethics, Volume 1: You Shall Be Holy,* pages 70–94.

6. Justice must apply to all people equally:

- "You shall have one law for stranger and citizen alike" (Leviticus 24:22).
- "You and the stranger shall be alike before the Lord . . . The same rule shall apply to you and to the stranger who resides among you" (Numbers 15:15–16).
- ". . . decide justly between any man and a fellow Israelite or a stranger" (Deuteronomy 1:16).

The Rabbis of the Talmud later formalized the principle of equality: "The Torah taught, 'you shall have one law for stranger and citizen alike,' [which means] that the law must treat you all equally" (*Ketubot* 33a).

These verses also imply that when legislation is passed, it should apply to everyone, and not be specifically directed against an individual. Thus, Maimonides rules that any law promulgated by a king—a tax law, for example—is valid as long as it applies to all residents. But if it is aimed against one person (or even a small group of people), it is deemed robbery ("Laws of Robbery and Lost Objects" 5:14).

In ancient Babylon (today's Iraq), which was governed by the Code of Hammurabi, the law was not intended to treat all people equally. Different penalties were imposed, depending on whether the injured party was a member of the aristocracy or a commoner. For example, if a man struck and killed an aristocrat's daughter, the courts "shall put his daughter to death" (law 210). But if the woman who was killed was a commoner's daughter, the perpetrator had to pay one-half mina of silver. Torah law differed from this Babylonian statute in two ways. First, under biblical law, the only party punished for a crime was the one who committed it; thus, if a man killed another man's daughter, the punishment was inflicted on the killer, not on his daughter (for more on this, see page 416). Second, the punishment was the same whether the victim was an aristocrat or a commoner.[4]

---

7. The law "Stay far away from falsehood" (Exodus 23:7) serves as the basis for many regulations regarding judicial behavior. For example:

- A judge who suspects that the witnesses are lying, but cannot prove it, should not reason to himself, "Since the witnesses have given testimony [which I don't believe but cannot disprove], I will decide the case on the basis of their testimony, and let the guilt be on their heads." If he believes that witnesses are lying, he should keep questioning them (in Jewish courts, it is the judges who examine the witnesses) in an effort to disprove their testimony,* or recuse himself;† the judge is forbidden to pronounce a judgment that in his heart he believes is false. To do so, the Talmud teaches, violates the commandment, "Stay far away from falsehood" (*Shevuot* 30b–31a, Maimonides, "Laws of the Sanhedrin" 24:3).

- A judge is forbidden to speak about a case with one litigant if the other is not present (*Shevuot* 31a). Rashi explains that a person who has the opportunity to explain his case in the absence of his opponent will not be embarrassed to lie. Even if the litigant is not lying intentionally, his version of the case will undoubtedly favor himself, and the judge—in the absence of the second party challenging the first one's version—might become biased in the first litigant's favor.

———

When I was an adolescent, I used to read the column "Can This Marriage Be Saved?" in the Ladies' Home Journal, *a magazine to which my mother subscribed. The column always had the same format. First, a husband or wife would explain why he or she was unhappy in their marriage, then the other spouse would present his or her side. Finally, a marriage counselor would suggest how the couple could improve their relationship. After reading the first spouse's recounting of the marriage's problems, I invariably felt complete sympathy for him or her, and couldn't imagine how the other spouse could respond to the accusations and complaints that had been made. But frequently, after reading the second spouse's account, I ended up siding with him or her. How often, then, would I have been misled had I read only*

*The Talmud extols "a judge who renders an absolutely truthful judgment" (*Bava Bathra* 8b), which *Tosafot,* the medieval commentary, understands as referring to a judge who, when he feels that there is something misleading about the case as it has been presented in the courtroom, endeavors to search out the truth himself.

†A friend argues that "at first blush, recusal makes no sense. Indeed, it contradicts 'Justice, justice, you shall pursue.' Basically, the judge is seeing injustice and walking away from it. My suspicion is that the recusal is being utilized as a procrastinating maneuver. It is not unlike physicians who are unable to deal with a medical crisis who deliberately put a patient into a coma to buy time until they can devise a solution to the problem."

one spouse's version of events, or had the other spouse not been given the opportunity to know what had been said, and been able to offer his or her version.

Dr. Isaac Herschkopf recounts that when practicing marital therapy, "when the first party speaks, it takes all my resolve not to glare accusingly at their spouse. Invariably, I think to myself that the matter is open and shut. There is nothing that the other spouse can say that would justify his or her behavior. Then, when the spouse responds and levels his or her own accusations, my sympathies often shift 180 degrees. When the back-and-forth accusations are done, I'm back to where I started. I always remind myself that my client is neither the wife nor the husband, but the marriage itself.

Similarly, the judge must continually remind himself that his client is neither party, but justice itself."

• The Rabbis also apply the verse "Stay far away from falsehood" to a case in which there are two litigants, one dressed in rags, the other in elegant attire worth a hundred *manehs* (a huge amount of money). The Rabbis feared that the court would be more sympathetically disposed toward the well-dressed litigant. To ensure that the court stay "far away from falsehood," the Talmud insisted that the well-dressed litigant either provide appropriate clothing to his opponent or dress down himself (*Shevuot* 31a).*

This rabbinic insight applies to all of us. When a man is dressed in very poor clothing, it is not uncommon to hear people refer to him as a "bum." In addition, most of us will be more inclined to accept a smartly dressed person's version of an event over the word of a poorly dressed one.

• Based on this verse, the Rabbis rule that if a student is watching his teacher judge a case and sees that his teacher is about to rule incorrectly (either by not recognizing evidence that would absolve a poor person or that would convict a wealthy one), he is required to speak up (*Shevuot* 31a).

The two examples the Rabbis offer both deal with the possibility of the judge ruling unfairly against a poor person, although the verse "Stay far away

*Rashi comments that making sure that the poor litigant has appropriate clothing is necessary so that the person not remain subdued or present his case without confidence, out of fear that the court will not believe what he says about his better-dressed opponent.

from falsehood" would equally demand that a student speak up if his teacher is wrongly favoring the poor litigant. The Maharsha (1555–1631), a noted talmudic commentator, argues that the Rabbis presented these examples because a student is more likely to be afraid of speaking out against a wealthy, and presumably powerful, litigant than against a poor one. Other commentators suggest that a student seeing his teacher wrongly favoring a wealthy litigant might remain silent, fearing that pointing out the teacher's error will greatly embarrass the teacher since it will seem as though he is favoring the rich man because he is rich, a gross violation of Jewish law.[5] *In either case—and in light of Jewish laws' very great concern with not humiliating someone in public—I believe that it would probably be best if the student signaled the teacher and offered his argument in private, thereby giving the teacher both an opportunity to save face and to think about his ruling, and perhaps requestion the litigants before impulsively making the wrong decision.**

—

• Finally, keeping ourselves far away from falsehood demands a standard of complete intellectual honesty. The Talmud rules that a judge should not defend his opinion if he is not confident it is correct, merely out of the desire to avoid the embarrassment of retracting it (*Shevuot* 30b). Many people defend their mistakes, even after they have good reason to believe that a position they took was incorrect. A judge's refusal to reconsider his view in the light of new evidence or arguments is a particularly grave matter. For while the initial error can be regarded as unintentional, a judge who constructs misleading and perhaps false arguments to avoid making a retraction commits an offense that is now intentional and premeditated.

—

One of the most famous instances of judges and government officials refusing to reverse an obviously unjust conviction was the Dreyfus case in late nineteenth- and early twentieth-century France. Because of antisemitism, Alfred Dreyfus was falsely accused by French army officials of having spied for Germany, convicted by a military court (1894), and sentenced to

---

*The Maharsha suggests a formulaic and noninsulting way in which the student should offer his objection: "My teacher, have you not taught us . . ." This type of statement minimizes both the teacher/judge's embarrassment, and the likelihood that he will react defensively and try to dismiss the student's objection.

life imprisonment on Devil's Island. As increasing proof of his innocence emerged, along with evidence that the army prosecutors had lied (by this time it was clear that the guilty party was a Colonel Esterhazy), the French government was finally forced to order a new trial—but arranged to have Dreyfus convicted again. Only after increasing public pressure was exerted did the government relent and pardon, and later exonerate, Dreyfus. The cause of justice was ultimately articulated in France not by a judge but by the novelist, Émile Zola. Convinced of Dreyfus's innocence, Zola published a dramatic newspaper article headlined "J'accuse" ("I accuse") in which he wrote: "I do not want my country to remain in lies and injustice. One day, France will thank me for having helped to save its honor."

—

8. "Stay far away from falsehood" has another implication, one that is relevant to modern-day courts in which cross-examinations are not conducted by disinterested judges, but by partisan lawyers. Professor Michael Broyde, a leading academic and rabbinic scholar of Jewish law, notes that this verse means that when a lawyer questions a witness whose testimony is detrimental to his client but whom the lawyer believes is telling the truth, he or she "is forbidden to undermine the credibility of the witness . . . in order to cast false doubt on the truthfulness of the testimony."*[6] In contrast, Monroe Freedman, a well-known and outspoken defender of the American adversary system, maintains that proper representation of one's client "often requires an affirmative answer" to the question: "Should you examine a prosecution witness whom you know to be accurate and truthful in order to make the witness appear to be mistaken or lying?"[7]

—

Seymour Wishman, a criminal defense lawyer, recalls a difficult defense he had to mount on behalf of a client accused of raping a nurse. Although Wishman

*In addition to violating the biblical verse, this also violates the Talmud's serious strictures against embarrassing a person in public for no valid reason (*Sotah* 10b and *Bava Mezia* 58b; trying to protect one's client from the effects of damaging, but truthful, testimony does not justify humiliating an innocent person, particularly in public). A friend of mine who read this passage and who is himself a lawyer expressed some hesitancy about instructing lawyers not to try to undermine a witnesses' credibility, even in instances in which the lawyer believes the witness to be offering truthful testimony. It is, my friend argued, "part of the rules of the game [for a lawyer to do so], and he may be doing his own client a disservice when, because of his own scruples, he fails to use a tactic that might help his client's case. At the very least, it would seem to me that the lawyer should let the client know about his position on these issues before taking the case." Of course, Professor Broyde's point is that refraining from trying to discredit a truthful witness does not simply reflect the lawyer's "own scruples," but the position of Jewish law.

had no reason to assume that the nurse had fabricated the charge, he was pleased to learn that the examining police physician had neglected to mention the presence of any physical evidence that force had been used against the woman. The lack of such evidence (which might well have resulted, as Wishman acknowledges, from the examining physician's negligence) enabled the lawyer to pursue a highly aggressive and reputation-damaging cross-examination of the nurse.

Wishman: *"Isn't it a fact that after you met the defendant at a bar, you asked him if he wanted to have a good time?"*

Witness: *"No! That's a lie!"*

Wishman: *"Isn't it true that you took him and his three friends back to your apartment and had that good time?"*

Witness: *"No!"*

Wishman: *"And after you had that good time, didn't you ask for money?"*

Witness: *"No such way!"*

Wishman: *"Isn't it a fact that the only reason you made a complaint was because you were furious for not getting paid?"*

Witness: *"No! No! That's a lie!"*

Wishman: *"You claim to have been raped and sodomized. As a nurse, you surely have an idea of the effect of such an assault on a woman's body. Are you aware . . . that the police doctors found no evidence of force or trauma?"*

Witness: *"I don't know what the doctors found."*[8]

Wishman was proud after the trial when the presiding judge congratulated him for dealing with the woman "brilliantly." But he acknowledges that he was considerably less proud when he accidentally encountered the nurse some months later at her workplace. As soon as she recognized him, she began shouting, "That's the son-of-a-bitch that did it to me!" Of course, what the woman was referring to was not the alleged rape, but the verbal "rape" to which the lawyer had subjected her in the courtroom, in essence accusing her of being a prostitute who had made a false charge of rape because she hadn't been paid.*

Wishman subsequently acknowledged that the justification criminal defense lawyers often offer for such brutal behavior, "I was only doing my job," increasingly has come to sound to him like the defense offered by many Nazis after World War II.[9] *One can only imagine how lawyers who conduct such*

*Unless the judge truly thought that the nurse had fabricated a charge of rape because she had not been paid, one wonders what this statement reveals about his commitment to the pursuit of justice.

*cross-examinations would feel if their wife or daughter were raped and then exposed to such a cross-examination.**

In Deborah Tannen's book The Argument Culture, *she cites an example of brutal and malicious questioning of a witness by a defense lawyer. In this case, the defendant, a Holocaust denier, was accused of violating Canadian laws prohibiting hate speech. Among the prosecution witnesses at the trial were concentration camp survivors. The defense lawyer asked them whether they had seen their parents gassed to death. Obviously they hadn't, since they were survivors, and the only people who witnessed other people being gassed were those who were with them in the gas chambers. When the witnesses acknowledged that they had not seen their parents murdered, the defense lawyer suggested that for all they knew their parents were alive, but simply didn't want to see them again.*[10]

—

9. "You shall not fear [or be intimidated by] any man, for judgment is God's" (Deuteronomy 1:17):

• Based on this verse, the Talmud rules that prior to hearing a case, a judge may tell the litigants who seek him out, "I don't want to take your case." A judge is also permitted to do so if he knows that one of the litigants is a harsh person whom the judge fears will harass him if he rules against him. However, once a judge has heard the litigants present their arguments and has reached a conclusion as to who is the guilty party, he cannot withdraw and say, "I don't want to get involved in your dispute, for [to do so would violate the command of the Torah] . . . 'You shall not fear any man' " (*Sanhedrin* 6b).

In his *Book of the Commandments,* Maimonides writes of this law: "By this prohibition, a judge is forbidden to be deterred by fear of a vicious and wicked evildoer from giving a just judgment against him. It is the judge's duty to render judgment without any thought of the injury the evildoer might cause him" (negative commandment 276). The standard imposed by Maimonides requires great courage,† but one who lacks such courage should not become a judge.

• The Rabbis also apply this verse (along with the previously cited, "Stay far away from falsehood") to a case in which a disciple sees his

*Obviously, such would not be the case if Wishman had reason to believe that the nurse really had been motivated by the desire for payment. But his description of the event indicates that he had no reason to believe that, which is why such questioning might well put a lawyer in violation of the verse "Stay far away from falsehood."

†Maimonides writes that the obligation of the judge to rule justly applies even if he fears that the litigant might murder his child or burn down his property.

master about to pronounce a wrongful judgment. Rabbi Joshua ben Korcha rules that the student must point out to the teacher the error he is about to make (*Sanhedrin* 6b). Being in conformity with the wording of the Torah's prohibition, "You shall not fear any man," Rabbi Joshua's ruling suggests that all of us must protest an injustice even if the person perpetrating it is our mentor or simply more powerful than we are.* Rabbi Chanina understands the Torah's words as meaning: "Do not hold back your words because of anyone" (*Sanhedrin* 6b).

10. "Do not favor the poor nor show deference to the rich" (Leviticus 19:15). "You shall neither side with mighty to do wrong . . . nor shall you show deference to a poor man in his dispute" (Exodus 23:2–3). The many Jewish laws commanding the compassionate treatment of the poor (see, for example, chapters 12, 13, and 18), are applicable outside, but not inside, the courtroom. In a judicial setting, there must be one standard of justice for poor and rich alike. Thus, a judge should not reason to himself: "Since this man is poor and both I and this rich man are obliged to support him, I shall decide the case in his favor so that he will receive support in a clean [and nonembarrassing] manner" (*Sifra* on Leviticus 19:15).

The Talmud holds up King David as a model of someone who showed both justice and charity. In the courtroom, he judged strictly on the basis of law, acquitting the innocent and condemning the guilty. But after pronouncing a ruling in which he sentenced a poor man to pay damages, he would help the man out of his own pocket, thereby fulfilling the demands of both justice and kindness, justice to the injured party by ensuring that he received what was due him, and kindness to the poor man by enabling him to pay his debt (*Sanhedrin* 6b).†

In Volume 1 of this code, I related the story of New York Mayor Fiorello La Guardia, who was presiding at the police court during the Depression when a poor man was brought in for having stolen a loaf of bread. The man acknowledged

---

*Although laypeople, unlike judges (see preceding footnote), are not obligated to put their lives at risk to right an injustice, many people are unwilling to assume any risk at all. Such passivity enables injustice to triumph.

†This talmudic teaching is offered in explanation of the biblical verse: "[King] David administered justice and kindness to all his people" (II Samuel 8:15). Louis Jacobs summarizes the talmudic approach to this issue: "If the judge wishes to help a poor man, he should not do it by deciding unjustly in his favor. If justice so demands, the judge must decide against the poor man and then compensate him out of his own pocket" (Louis Jacobs, *A Tree of Life,* pages 178–179). In short, if a judge wants to give charity, let him do so out of his own pocket, but he should not pervert the law so as to force someone else to pay.

that the charge was true but said in his defense that his family was starving. La Guardia said, "I've got to punish you. The law makes no exceptions. I can do nothing but sentence you to a fine of ten dollars." The mayor reached into his own pocket, paid the fine himself, and then declared, "I'm going to fine everybody in this courtroom fifty cents for living in a town where a man has to steal bread in order to eat." The bailiff collected the fine, and gave the man $47.50.[11] *Compare this story about La Guardia and the Talmud's recounting of King David's behavior with Victor Hugo's classic novel,* Les Misérables, *in which the Frenchman Jean Valjean steals bread for his hungry family, and ends up serving nineteen years in prison.**

---

11. "But if other damages ensue, the penalty shall be life for life [in an instance in which a person has been murdered, and] an eye for an eye . . ." (Exodus 21:23–24). ". . . eye for eye, tooth for tooth, the injury he inflicted on another shall be inflicted on him" (Leviticus 24:20).

As one of the Torah's most famous laws, "an eye for an eye" is often cited by critics of "Old Testament morality" as reflecting a barbaric standard of behavior. In the New Testament, Jesus is cited as teaching, "You have learnt how it was said, 'An eye for an eye and a tooth for a tooth.' But I say this to you: offer the wicked man no resistance. On the contrary, if anyone hits you on the right cheek, offer him the other as well" (Matthew 5:38–39).

Although "an eye for an eye" does mandate punishing a person who maims another (Jewish law did not enforce this verse literally; see next paragraph), what is infrequently noted is that it limits the retribution which can be taken. For example, "an eye for an eye" forbids taking two eyes for an eye, even though people who avenge themselves on another often exact a far worse vengeance than the suffering that was inflicted upon them.

Although one can, I believe, make a moral argument as to why people who *intentionally*—as opposed to accidentally—blind another deserve to lose their own right to go on seeing, Jewish law has always ruled that courts should not blind those who deprive others of their sight;† rather, offenders must make financial compensation—the sum to be determined by the court—to their victims. The Rabbis believed that punishment be commensurate with the crime, but not exceed it: "Now if you assume that actual retaliation is intended, it could sometimes happen that both life and eye would be

---

**A Code of Jewish Ethics, Volume 1: You Shall Be Holy,* page 415, offers a painful example of how court systems in many societies, and throughout history, have often favored the rich, even in instances in which they have clearly been in the wrong.

†I am basing this on the earliest legal records we possess.

taken [in payment for the eye], as, for instance, if the offender died as he was being blinded" (*Bava Kamma* 84a). Thus, even though the language of the biblical verse seems definitive, the Rabbis understood it as meaning that on moral grounds, someone who intentionally blinds another *deserves* to lose his sight. But the court exacts only financial compensation, lest it commit the greater injustice of killing the offender while blinding him.

"An eye for an eye," therefore, establishes two biblical principles of justice: Evil must be punished,* but punishment must be proportionate to, and not exceed, the offense.

12. Another instance of "an eye for an eye" legislation in the Torah concerns the law of *aid zomeim* (false witness), which ordains that in criminal cases, we punish a false witness with the same punishment he intended to have inflicted on the party against whom he testified; in the Torah's words, "You shall do to him as he schemed to do to his fellow" (Deuteronomy 19:19).† In modern terms, if witnesses testify falsely that A has committed a crime for which he could be incarcerated for ten years, the false witnesses themselves should be subject to a prison term of equal length.

I know of no legal system, including Israel's, that enforces such a law, though it seems eminently fair. For example, American law justly imposes severe punishment on a man who rapes a woman. But if a woman maliciously lodges a false charge of rape against a man (and testifies falsely), it seems just that she be sentenced to the same punishment she wished to have him suffer.

In the biblical book of Esther, Haman goes to King Ahasuerus to present a false charge against Mordechai, whom he wishes to have hanged on a gallows that he has already erected (5:14 and 6:4). But before Haman can carry out this plan, his plot against the Jews is exposed, and Ahasuerus orders Haman to be hanged on the very gallows he had prepared for Mordechai (7:9). This fate fulfills the

*This is the opposite of Jesus' teaching to "offer the wicked man no resistance." Oddly enough, while Jesus would seem to be forgiving of one who maliciously blinds another, he seems, at least according to another New Testament passage, quite unforgiving of those who refuse to accept him as their teacher: "But the one who disowns me in the presence of men, I will disown in the presence of my Father in heaven" (Matthew 10:33). Thus, while advocating that those who maim others should not be punished (a standard that has had no impact on legislation in Christian societies), Jesus rejects people who reject him, an attitude suspiciously similar to "an eye for an eye."

†The Talmud narrowly restricted the instances in which this law applied to cases in which new witnesses disqualified the false witnesses by noting that they were not present at the scene of the crime ("How could you have testified about X when you were with us at that time?"). I am following here the more straightforward meaning of the biblical verse.

punishment decreed in the biblical verse for false witnesses, "do to him as he schemed to do to his fellow."

---

13. "Parents shall not be put to death for children, nor children be put to death for parents; a person shall be put to death only for his own crime" (Deuteronomy 24:16; see also Ezekiel 18:20).

Biblical law limits punishment to the perpetrator, exempting his family members. An example occurs in book II of Kings: When King Joash (835–796 B.C.E.) was assassinated (12:21–22), his son, Amaziah, succeeded him, and had his father's two assassins executed. The Bible states that Amaziah "did not put to death the children of the assassins, in accordance with what is written in the Book of the Teaching of Moses . . ." (see 14:5–6). Professor Daniel Friedmann, a contemporary Israeli legal scholar, notes that the fact that the Bible records this detail "as proof of Amaziah's righteousness* shows that in those days [such behavior] was not a matter of course, and it was perhaps expected that the entire family would be executed. Amaziah's moderation was an important step toward abolition of collective responsibility and in the direction of personal accountability."[12]

Although this law might seem obvious and even unnecessary to modern readers, it was an innovative ruling when introduced by the Torah. The Babylonian Code of Hammurabi (several centuries earlier than the Torah) ruled that if a builder erected a house for a client and the house collapsed and killed the homeowner's daughter, then the builder's daughter was to be executed (law 229; see page 406 for another similar instance from Hammurabi's code). This ruling stemmed from the belief that children are not autonomous beings but the possessions of their parents, and it is therefore just to kill a child for an offense committed by a parent (since the builder deprived the homeowner of his daughter, the law retaliates against the builder by depriving him of his daughter).

Even in modern times, totalitarian and authoritarian regimes have frequently violated this law. In the early years of the Soviet regime, Leon Trotsky helped institute the policy of liquidating kulaks (peasants who owned small tracts of land) and had their children defined as "declassed persons," that is, people denied rights because of their bourgeois origins. Later, under Stalin, countless numbers (we have no fully accurate statistics but it was in the millions) of kulaks and their children were murdered.†

---

*II Kings 14:3 reports that King Amaziah "did what was pleasing to the Lord . . ."

†Hayim Greenberg, the American Labor Zionist philosopher, noted the cruel irony in Trotsky's persecution of the children of kulaks, given that Trotsky himself was the son of a wealthy

---

*In 1840, when a large number of Jews in Syria were falsely accused of having killed a Catholic monk to use his blood in a religious ritual (an event known as the Damascus Blood Libel), the Syrian authorities also seized sixty Jewish children in order to coerce their parents to confess, yet another instance of punishing innocent children, this time for the noncrimes of their parents.**

---

14. While few, if any, today would justify a court punishing children for their parents' crimes, in daily life many people—maybe even we ourselves—do discriminate against and ostracize people for the sins of their parents. For example, children of a parent who has been involved in scandalous behavior often report that other children are forbidden by their parents to play with them. Jeremiah prophesied of a better world in which this would no longer occur: "In those days, they shall no longer say, 'Parents have eaten sour grapes, and children's teeth are blunted . . . whosoever eats sour grapes, his teeth [and his teeth alone] shall be blunted" (Jeremiah 31:29–30).

15. Is it ever just to regard family members as responsible for the sins of another family member? Yes, but only if the family members do nothing to stop their relative, and perhaps even profit from that person's wrongdoing. In such a case, the relatives share in the culpability, certainly morally, even if not legally. The Talmud teaches: "In a family where there is a tax collector [this was written during a period when Judaea was under Roman rule, and tax collectors extorted funds], all are [regarded as] tax collectors; a robber, all are robbers, because they protect him [and do not protest his deeds]" (*Shevuot* 39a).† The Talmud presumes that family members of tax collectors know the source of their family income, and if—once they reach maturity—they continue to live off stolen funds, they are morally culpable. Obviously, if they truly don't know the source of the ill-gotten gains, they are not guilty.

And what about parents? Should they ever be held responsible for the

---

landowner (Trotsky's father owned some 650 acres of land, whereas many of the kulaks he killed did not own even a twentieth as much land): "[Nonetheless] he caused the murder of so many Kulak children that he could not himself know the exact amount" (*The Inner Eye,* Volume 2, pages 238–239).

*After months of international pressure the surviving prisoners were released (two had died under torture, and seven others remained permanently disabled). The children were freed as well (see *Encyclopaedia Judaica* 5:1249–1252).

†In similar manner, the Torah imposes a death sentence on one who offers his child as a sacrifice to Molech, and then says: "And if the people of the land should shut their eyes to that man when he gives of his offspring to Molech . . . I Myself will set My face against that man and his kin . . ." (see Leviticus 20:2–5).

crimes and misdeeds of their children?* This issue, which would seem to hinge on the parents' ability to affect their children's behavior, is a source of controversy in contemporary Israel. On occasion, after a terrorist attack has been carried out (between September 2000 and 2006 alone, over eleven hundred Israelis were murdered in such attacks), the Israeli army locates the terrorist's home and blows it up (after first evacuating the people inside). Gordon Zacks, a contemporary American-Jewish political activist and philanthropist was visiting defense minister Moshe Dayan in the early 1970s during the time when this policy was implemented. Dayan informed Zacks that he had been asked to meet with a group of Palestinian elders, and invited him to come to the meeting. Zacks recalls: "We entered a sprawling tent stitched together from countless goatskins. All the elders sat in a large circle. After the pleasantries and the coffee, the conversation began in earnest. 'In the Bible,' the senior elder said solemnly, 'it is written: To visit the sins of the father upon the children is unfair. How then can you possibly justify visiting the sins of the son upon the parents of the child [by blowing up the homes in which the terrorists lived and which are generally the parents' homes as well]? We think this practice is unfair and un-Jewish, and it should cease immediately.' Dayan looked them straight in the eye and said: 'Gentlemen, let me be perfectly clear. I do not see your daughters whoring in Tel Aviv. If you can control the behavior of your daughters, you certainly can control the behavior of your sons.† There will be no change in policy. I hold *you* accountable for assuring that terrorism stops.' " Zacks concludes: "Dead silence. That was the end of the meeting. The elders knew that Dayan understood their culture and that he was right—there were no Arab prostitutes in Tel Aviv . . . The policy on terrorism articulated by Dayan remains in force to this day."

But has it been effective? This is hard to gauge. Certainly, it has not ended anti-Israel terrorism, but it is impossible to know how many parents have exerted successful pressure on their children not to become terrorists and thereby bring about the possible destruction of the family home.

---

*Jewish law assumes that parents bear moral responsibility for the behavior of their minor children. That is why when the child becomes Bar Mitzvah and assumes adult responsibilities, the parents recite an unusual blessing: "Praised be He who has released me from the responsibility for this one's misdeeds" (*Shulchan Arukh, Orakh Chayyim* 225:2). Jews thank God that their children have reached the age at which they are accountable for their own actions, a powerful illustration of how Judaism celebrates responsibility and free will.

†My friend David Szonyi argues that Dayan's reasoning seems flawed because "sons are more difficult to control than daughters, particularly in a traditional, patriarchal society."

---

*In at least three instances in the Bible, the Torah law of not punishing children for parents' sins seems to have been ignored; they are all jarring to read. First, when the Israelites conquered the city of Jericho, Joshua forbade them on pain of death from taking booty. However, a man named Achan violated the divine edict and stole a variety of items, including a costly garment, and large amounts of silver and gold, all of which he hid in his tent. God became enraged not only against the thief, but also against the whole Israelite community: "Israel has sinned . . . they have taken some of the devoted things" (Joshua 7:11). When Joshua, acting at God's behest, investigated the robbery he discovered that Achan was the thief, whereupon Achan, along with his family (who presumably knew what he had hidden in their tent), were executed. "Then the Lord turned from His burning anger"(7:24–26).**

Second, II Samuel 21:6 records that King David handed over seven descendants of King Saul to be killed by the Gibeonites as retaliation for the serious harm done years earlier to the Gibeonites by Saul. This episode is particularly disturbing as there is no indication that these descendants shared in Saul's guilt in any way (strangely, the Bible never records the precise nature of Saul's offense, other than to say that he bore "bloodguilt . . . for he put some Gibeonites to death"; 21:1).

Third, there is the Torah law of mamzerut *(Deuteronomy 23:3). While the biblical text never defines the word* mamzer, *Jewish law understands it as referring to a child of an adulterous or incestuous union (see the ruling of Rabbi Joshua in Mishnah Yevamot 4:13, and* Shulchan Arukh, Even Ha-Ezer *4:13). Such a child (*mamzer *is generally translated as "bastard"†) along with his or her descendants are forbidden for all time to marry other Israelites except for those who are either* mamzerim *or converts.‡*

While this law does not of course literally *violate the provision in Deuteronomy that prohibits executing children for the crimes of their parents, a prohibition that cuts someone off from almost all possibilities of marriage is very severe.*

---

*While Torah law never punished stealing with death, the exception in this case was presumably due to Achan's having violated a direct command from God. While the wording of the text indicates that Achan's family was killed with him, Rashi argues that they were taken to witness the execution, but were not themselves killed.

†I use the word "bastard" hesitantly, since in common American usage, it often refers to a child born to an unmarried woman (with the relaxation of sexual standards in recent decades, the term is now used infrequently, except as a curse). Under Jewish law, no legal stigma or disabilities attach to a child born to an unmarried woman.

‡Such a marriage would be very disadvantageous for a convert since, as noted, any children resulting from this union would continue to bear the stigma of *mamzerut* (*Kiddushin* 67a).

It has sometimes been explained that the rationale for this law is that people who are about to sin sexually are often overtaken with lust. Understanding how difficult it might be for people in such a circumstance to observe the Seventh Commandment's prohibition of adultery, the Torah decreed the law of mamzerut, *in effect warning the couple: "If you want one another so badly, that's your sin, but know that any child you conceive will be cursed till the day of its death." This, the Torah hoped, would give would-be adulterers the strength to resist temptation, in the same way, for example, that any couple would resist having relations if they knew that the child that would result from their love-making would be born deformed (see Maimonides,* The Guide for the Perplexed *3:49).*

Because the Rabbis felt that the child of an adulterous union was an innocent victim of the parents' sin, they became very creative in devising legal fictions to free a child from the taint of mamzerut, *even when it seemed very apparent that the child had resulted from an act of adultery. The Talmud (*Yevamot *80b) cites Rabbi Tosfa'ah's ruling that if a man has been away from home for a full year and yet his wife gives birth, we assume that the woman had a very long pregnancy. Maimonides does not dispute this ruling, but notes that a fetus never remains inside the mother for more than a year ("Laws of Forbidden Intercourse" 15:19).* The Ramah (Rabbi Moshe Isserles) rules in the* Shulchan Arukh *that if a man is away for up to twelve months, we assume that the baby is his (*Even Ha-Ezer *4:14). Of course, both Maimonides, a physician, and the Ramah—and, I presume, Rabbi Tosfa'ah—knew that human pregnancies do not last twelve months; they simply did not want to impose the stigma and status of* mamzer *on an innocent child.*†

*Professor Michael Berger notes that the twelve-month rule requires the acquiescence of the husband since if he denies that the baby is his, he is believed.

†On the other hand, there were rabbis who were unwilling to consider all possible ways to free someone from the taint of *mamzerut* and thus inflicted terrible suffering on people who had committed no sin. In one of the most painful and harsh rulings I have ever seen by a rabbinic decisor, Rabbi Ishmael ben Abraham Isaac ha-Kohen of Modena (1723–1811) ruled that it was permitted to have the word *mamzer* tattooed on the forehead of such a child so that people would know that he is a *mamzer* and not allow him to marry their daughter (*Zera Emet,* 3: 111; cited in Louis Jacobs, *A Tree of Life,* page 265; despite this ruling, and presumably basing itself on other rulings issued by the rabbi, the *Encyclopaedia Judaica* [9:83] describes Rabbi Ishmael as "generally moderate . . . and alive to the needs of the time"). Even though Jewish law prohibits tattoos, the rabbi ruled that it was preferable to violate the rabbinic law forbidding one to hire a Gentile to make a tattoo than to run the risk of the *mamzer* marrying a non-*mamzer,* thereby violating a Torah law. For other rabbis it was not enough that the *mamzer* suffered greatly from his illegitimate status, they also set out to prove that he deserved his fate. Thus, the normally fair-minded *Sefer HaChinnuch* states: "The very conception of the *mamzer* is exceedingly evil, having been brought about in impurity and abominable thoughts . . . and there is no doubt that the nature of the [evil] father is hidden in the son. Consequently, God, in His kindness, has kept the descendants of the holy people away from him [the *mamzer*] just as He has separated us and kept us far away from every evil thing" (commandment 560).

Even when a mamzer *has already married into a family, the Ramah rules: "If one who is unfit has become mixed in a particular family, and the matter is not publicly known, then once he has become mixed, he is mixed, and one who knows of the disqualification is not permitted to disclose it and must leave the family in the presumption of being untainted, since all families in which there has been an admixture will become pure in the future" (Ramah,* Shulchan Arukh, Even Ha-Ezer *2:5). In similar manner, the Talmud cites Rabbi Yochanan's statement: "I swear by the Sanctuary that it is in our power [to reveal which families in the Land of Israel are genealogically tainted]. But what can I do? For behold, great people of our generation are mixed in with them" (*Kiddushin *71a).*

I am convinced that these searches for leniency arose from discomfort with declaring an innocent child to be a mamzer. *The Torah forbids punishing a child for the sins of the parents and if the Rabbis had to declare that a woman was pregnant for a full twelve months to avoid doing so, Rabbis Tosfa'ah, Maimonides, and Moshe Isserles had no compunction about making such a declaration.*

When necessary, rabbinic scholars employed a variety of additional techniques and arguments to avoid imposing the status of mamzer *on a child. For example, in the case of a woman who was suspected,* with good reason, *of having been unfaithful to her husband, the Talmud ruled that we assume the child to whom she gave birth is legitimate because "the majority of acts of intercourse are ascribed to the husband" (*Sotah *27a, Maimonides "Laws of Forbidden Intercourse" 15:20 and* Shulchan Arukh, Even Ha-Ezer *4:15). Thus, even if the woman committed adultery, there is no reason to assume that the child resulted from one of her acts of infidelity.**

Talmudic insights on justice

16. The preeminence of justice. "Any judge who renders a judgment that is absolutely true, even if he sits in judgment for only one hour [that is, a short while], is considered by Scripture as if he became partner with God in the act of [the world's] creation" (*Shabbat* 10a). Elsewhere, the Talmud states: "Any judge who renders a judgment that is absolutely true, causes the Divine Presence to dwell in Israel" (*Sanhedrin* 7a). Because God endowed human beings with free will, He chooses not to intervene every time an injustice is

*At the time of the Talmud and during the medieval period, there was no way to determine paternity scientifically.

perpetrated. If God were to do so, so that people knew that He would stop them from doing evil, or would punish them for doing so, people would act better, but they would no longer be human beings with free will, but automatons. So the price we pay for free will is that in this world injustice often triumphs, at least temporarily. However, although God may often refrain from explicit action, He does wish righteousness to triumph. God therefore relies on human beings to act as His partners in helping to bring about justice. Therefore, when a judge judges justly he becomes a partner with God in helping to fulfill God's hopes for this world.

—

The Rabbis describe the evil city of Sodom (Genesis 19) as filled with dishonest judges. They tell a story about Eliezer, Abraham's righteous servant, who, while visiting Sodom, was beaten severely; his assailant even drew blood. Yet when he brought the man into court, the judge ordered Eliezer to pay his attacker for having bled him (bleeding sometimes was performed as a medical procedure on sick patients). In a rare Midrash with a humorous ending, the Rabbis report that the infuriated Eliezer picked up a stone, threw it at the judge, and opened a big wound. He then said to the judge: "Now, go and pay the fee you owe me for bleeding you to the man who attacked me."[13]

—

*The Talmud teaches: "Because of delays in pronouncing judgment, perverting judgment, corrupting judgment [through carelessness] . . . war and plundering and plague and famine come" (*Shabbat *33a). Rashi explains the difference between these three types of judicial transgressions:*

- *"Delays in pronouncing judgment" occur when judges have reached a conclusion, but delay handing down their ruling. In addition to being unfair to the litigant awaiting vindication or victory, at a certain point justice delayed becomes justice denied and can make the citizenry cynical about the judicial process.*

- *"Perverting judgment," the worst kind of judicial misconduct, occurs when a judge intentionally hands down an unjust ruling. Such cases occur frequently in totalitarian societies when judges impose punishments that have been predetermined by the government. For example, Anatoly (Natan) Sharansky was convicted in 1978 on the basis of fabricated evidence of having committed treason against the Soviet Union. After making a statement in the court in which he reiterated his desire to go and live in Israel, and after delivering messages both to his wife, Avital, and the Jewish people, he* *concluded, "And I turn to you, the court, who were required to confirm a predetermined sentence: to you I have nothing to say."**

• *"Corrupting judgment [through carelessness]" occurs when the judges don't take the necessary time to analyze a case properly and instead arrive at a poorly thought-out and incorrect ruling.*†

---

17. All cases should be treated with equal seriousness. The Talmud cites Resh Lakish's directive to judges: "A case involving one *prutah* (a small coin) should be as precious to you as a case involving a hundred *manehs*" (a large sum; *Sanhedrin* 8a). Many, perhaps most, judges are pleased, and feel somewhat honored, to adjudicate a case involving large sums of money‡ and/or prominent litigants, rather than a small case involving people of no renown and limited means. But just as we are to assume that God is as concerned with dispensing justice to "little" people as He is to famous ones, so are judges expected to treat all cases with equal seriousness.

---

*The Talmud notes a practical upshot to Resh Lakish's teaching: "It tells the judge to assign priority to whichever case comes first" (*Sanhedrin *8a).*

---

18. Don't rush to conclusions. *The Ethics of the Fathers* cautions sages, judges, and, by implication, all of us: "Be deliberate in judgment" (1:1); in other words, consider matters carefully before reaching a conclusion. Another teaching in *The Ethics of the Fathers* advises judges to "interrogate the witnesses extensively" (1:9). While dishonest testimony might at first appear to be convincing and even irrefutable, careful attention to the precise details of the witnesses' testimony might lead the judges to detect inconsistencies, inaccuracies, or indications of perjury. But if we jump to quick conclusions (many of us have an exaggerated belief in the accuracy of our first

---

*In addition to the wrongs perpetrated within the Soviet judicial system, the Communist government not infrequently labeled dissidents as insane and involuntarily committed them to mental asylums. In addition to being a corruption of justice, such behavior also effectively destroyed the Soviet mental health system by turning hospitals into prisons and psychiatrists into prison guards.

†I have relied on the explanation of this passage offered in the ArtScroll translation and commentary on *Shabbat* 33a, footnote 7.

‡In addition, judges were not paid a regular salary, but were remunerated from the sum involved in the case; when that sum was small, there was no way for the judge to receive fair compensation for his time. Nonetheless, he was prohibited from delaying judging such a case.

impressions), or accept testimony without searching examination, we are apt to reach a wrong conclusion—not every time, but often.

---

*The Rabbis held that the proper attitude in the courtroom is skepticism, even mistrust: "When the litigants stand before you, consider them both as guilty." However, to avoid justices turning into cynics, once the trial ends and the parties have accepted the verdict, judges are instructed to regard both litigants favorably: ". . . but when they are dismissed from you consider them both as innocent, provided they have accepted the judgment" (*The Ethics of the Fathers *1:8).*

This teaching applies to all of us, not only to judges. The late Rabbi Avrohom Pam, a veteran educator, recalled an episode in which a young child was punished "when an item was found in his knapsack which a fellow classmate had been missing. The apparent culprit insisted that he had not stolen the item and that he had no idea how it had gotten into his knapsack. The teacher refused to believe him and punished him by having him wear a sign which read, 'I am a thief.' A long time passed before another boy came along and admitted that he had stolen the item. He had wanted to return it but was too ashamed to admit his guilt, so he stuffed the item into the other boy's knapsack."*

Michoel Rothschild and Rabbi Shimon Finkelman have commented on this episode: "If this could happen in a case where the evidence seemed so convincing, how careful must we be not to take action based on reports without first investigating the matter."[14]

On interrogating witnesses extensively

In eighteenth-century Vilna, two witnesses came forward with allegations of sexual impropriety against the daughter of one of the city's leading citizens, allegations intended to force the woman's husband to divorce her. The witnesses' testimony was so clear-cut that the Beit Din *(Jewish court) of Vilna was inclined to accept it as true. However, the Vilna Gaon—perhaps because he knew the woman—suspected that the accusations were false. He requested the judges of the* Beit Din *to question the witnesses yet again, this time in his presence. The Gaon*

*Even if the boy had been guilty, such a public humiliation strikes me as cruel and unlikely to transform the culprit's behavior. Furthermore, once the teacher learned that he had made a false accusation, was he willing to wear a sign saying "I am a fool" or "I slandered and humiliated an innocent person"?

listened as the court examined the men closely, and asked them to review their testimony several times. The details they provided were indeed precise, and there were no discernible discrepancies between their accounts. Nonetheless, when the questioning was finished, the Gaon pronounced his verdict: "These men are false witnesses."

*The court was stunned, and the witnesses turned pale, as the Gaon explained how he came to his conclusion: "When the Mishnah (*Sotah *5:4) discusses the questioning of witnesses, it states that the judges question the first witness alone, and then bring in the second witness and examine him. The goal of the judges, the Mishnah explains, is to determine 'whether their words are found to be in agreement.' But why doesn't the Mishnah simply say, 'if their words are in agreement?' rather than, 'if their words are* found *to be in agreement' "?*

The Gaon explained: "Had the Mishnah said, 'if their words are in agreement,' we might have thought that each witness's testimony had to be identical to the other's. But such is not the case, even when two witnesses are describing the same event. People have their own recollections, and their own styles of speaking about and reporting what they saw." The Gaon explained that what convinced him the witnesses were liars was that they gave identical accounts of the so-called events they were describing; every minor detail corresponded with the other's testimony, and the language they used was virtually the same. "By employing the expression, 'found to be in agreement,' the Mishnah intended to convey that the testimony has to be in agreement, but not that every detail has to match perfectly. That they did match so precisely, and that the wording of their testimony was virtually identical to the other's testimony, and identical each time they reviewed their account, made it clear that this testimony was rehearsed between the two of them, and false."*

The witnesses' confidence was shaken by the Gaon's penetrating and forceful analysis, and they confessed their plot.†

---

19. Compromise is the preferred solution. The prophet Zachariah teaches: ". . . render truth and peaceful judgment in your gates" (8:16). The Talmud considers whether there can truly be such a thing as a "peaceful judgment":"For where there is [strict] judgment, there is no peace, and where

---

*Thus, if you and a friend write down recollections of an event you both witnessed, your recollections will likely agree in general, but you will not both recall the exact same details.

†I have relied on the account of this event in Betzalel Landau, *The Vilna Gaon,* pages 72–73. No record exists of the precise words spoken by the Gaon, so the comments here attributed to the Gaon are based on the arguments he raised to discredit the witnesses.

there is peace, there is no [strict] judgment. What then is the judgment . . . which has within it elements of peace? Let us say that it is compromise" (*Sanhedrin* 6b).*

In the rabbinic worldview, compromise, in which both sides relinquish some of their claims (so that neither fully prevails) is the preferred resolution. Rabbi Irwin Kula argues that the reason for this preference for compromise is the rabbinic intuition that, far more often than not, neither side is 100 percent correct. Therefore, because there is almost always at least a partial truth on each side, compromise is not just the most pragmatic solution, it is also the most just. In addition, compromise is the one solution that most easily enables the two litigants to remain on friendly, or at least nonhostile, terms.† Thus, prior to bringing suit, or even in the early stages of a trial, a judge should encourage the litigants to talk through their dispute carefully and try to resolve it between themselves, rather than turn it into a court case.

A small synagogue had been bequeathed a house by an elderly man. However, the man's three children were extremely upset by their father's bequest. One of the sons contacted the will's executor and made it known that he regarded what had happened as a travesty of justice and that he and his brothers felt strongly that they should have inherited the house.

The president knew that the deceased man's children had deeply hurt him by rarely coming to see him, or even speaking with him on the phone. Yet he dreaded the prospect of becoming involved in a lawsuit. He also feared that the children would bad-mouth the synagogue and its officers, and tell people that he had swayed their father to make the bequest.

He asked my advice as to what I thought Jewish law and ethics would advise him to do. He confided that he was tempted to simply allow the children to have the house. Then, he added: "But I would feel disloyal to this man. He made it very clear to me that it was his wish that the synagogue, which brought him much comfort in his old age, profit by his gift."

Thinking of the talmudic passage cited earlier, I suggested: "Compromise. Tell the lawyer to offer the children 50 percent of the value of the house, with

---

*In another passage, the repetition of the word "justice" in the verse "Justice, justice you shall pursue" is explained as follows: the first usage of the word is intended to extol the general pursuit of justice; the second underscores that compromise is the preferred type of justice (*Sanhedrin* 32b).

†If neither litigant gets all that he wants, both parties feel that the other side has also suffered. Most people can tolerate not getting everything they want, but they can't tolerate their adversary getting everything that he or she desires.

the stipulation that they draft a letter in which they acknowledge the generosity of the synagogue in light of the bequest contained in the father's will." This letter would remain confidential, unless they spoke ill of the synagogue or its officers in the community, in which case the letter would be released.

My reasoning was both moral and pragmatic. Moral, because although Jewish law recognizes the legal *right of a parent to disinherit a child, it generally opposes parents availing themselves of this right. In the words of the Mishnah, "the spirit of the Sages are not pleased with him" (Mishnah* Bava Bathra *8:5). Therefore, while the father's wish to donate to the synagogue should be honored, it seemed reasonable to leave his children with something. Pragmatic, because I felt that it was in the temple's interest to not get into a bitter conflict since such conflicts tend to cause lingering feuds, malicious gossip, and hurt to both sides.*

Dr. Isaac Herschkopf, a psychiatrist, notes that compromise is usually the best solution in cases of marital dispute. For example: the wife insists on living near her family on Long Island, while the husband is equally insistent that they live near his family in New Jersey. "The solution? Live in Manhattan, more or less equidistant from both. When the couple complain, 'But in that instance, neither of us is happy,' I respond, 'Precisely.'"

When compromise is forbidden

20. "Rabbi Shimon ben Menasia [instructed judges]: 'When people come before you for judgment, before you have heard their case, or even afterward, if you have not yet made up your mind as to who is in the right, you are allowed to recommend that the litigants compromise and reach a settlement. But if you have already heard their case and have made up your mind as to which party is in the right, you are not permitted to tell them to work out a compromise, for it says [in the Bible], 'Before a dispute flares up, drop it' (Proverbs 17:14), which means, before the dispute has come out into the open [and has been brought into court], you can withdraw from it, and propose a settlement. But after the case has been brought into court [and you, the judge, have made a determination as to which party is in the right] you cannot drop it anymore [and propose a compromise]" (*Sanhedrin* 6b).*

---

*See the translation of Avraham Yaakov Finkel to Rabbi Yaakov ibn Chaviv, *Ein Yaakov,* page 596. The same page of the Talmud (*Sanhedrin* 6b) cites the opposing view of Rabbi Judah, speaking in the name of Rav, that as long as the judge has not announced his ruling (this announcement constituting the formal reaching of a verdict), a compromise may still be mediated.

In short, once the case is clear, strict justice, not compromise, must prevail in court. In such an instance, the Rabbis declare, "Let the law [that is, strict justice] cut through the mountain" (*Sanhedrin* 6b; see also Maimonides, "Laws of the Sanhedrin" 22:4).

21. Avoid judging a case in which you have positive or negative feelings toward one of the litigants.* "A person should not act as a judge for someone he loves or for someone he hates. For no one can find fault with someone he loves or find merit for someone he hates" (*Ketubot* 105b). Also, because highly charged emotions can easily lead to distortions of justice, the Rabbis rule that two judges who hate each other must not sit together on the bench (*Sanhedrin* 29a; Jewish courts generally were composed of three judges in minor cases, and twenty-three, or even seventy-one, in major cases). The Rabbis understood that in such situations, at least one of the judges will probably be guided less by truth than by the desire to dispute the other and prove him wrong (see also Maimonides, "Laws of the Sanhedrin" 23:7).

Yigal Allon, commander of the prestate Palmach fighting force, and who later occupied several high positions in the Israeli government, often clashed with Israeli defense minister Moshe Dayan, including several strong disagreements before and during the 1967 Six-Day War. Allon complained that because of the ill will between them, "I came to understand that whatever I proposed, Dayan would propose the opposite."[15]

My friend Daniel Taub, a lawyer, suggests that a judge consider recusing himself in a case in which he so venerates another of the judges (perhaps a former teacher) that he would find it hard to rule differently from him.

---

22. Anyone who has relevant information about a case is required to come forward. Under American law, a person who is served with a judicial subpoena to appear in court is required to do so; a subpoenaed witness's failure to testify can result in the person being held in contempt of court and jailed. However, a person who has relevant testimony to offer but who has

*Today, we take it for granted that a judge should recuse himself when he knows one of the litigants. But throughout history, and certainly at the time the Talmud was compiled, most Jews lived in small communities in which judges knew the people whose cases they were adjudicating. It would have been unrealistic to ask them to withdraw from all cases in which they knew one or both litigants.

not been subpoenaed (perhaps neither of the parties in the litigation is even aware of what the person knows), has no obligation to appear in court, even if he knows that his testimony is relevant and might determine the case's outcome. In contrast, a talmudic passage teaches that there are three people whom God hates, one being someone who knows of evidence that will help another, but does not present it (*Pesachim* 113b).

Although not offering relevant testimony is worthy of divine condemnation, the Rabbis conclude that it is not an actionable offense. Thus, Rabbi Joshua rules that if A can give evidence in court that will save B from financial loss but fails to do so, B cannot recover financial restitution from A. In the Talmud's words, "[A person who refuses to offer testimony] is exempt by the laws of man, but liable by the laws of Heaven (*patur me'dinei adam, ve-chayyav be'dinei shamayim;* see *Bava Kamma* 55b).* Rabbi Louis Jacobs explains: "A's failure to testify is an offense of omission and the law can only enforce compensation . . . for an offense of commission."[16] Concerning cases in which one party has acted wrongly but the courts cannot compel payment, the *Tosefta* comments: "[Such a person] is not liable to pay by law, but Heaven will not forgive him until he does pay compensation" (*Tosefta Shevuot* 3:2).

This Jewish legal teaching has considerable relevance outside the courtroom. For example, if you have information that will exonerate someone who is rumored to have done some wrong or whose good name is otherwise being besmirched, and you remain silent, you yourself have done a great wrong.† If you do not offer your information to those whose views can be affected by it, you have put yourself into the unenviable status of being one of those whom the Talmud says are hated by God.

The Sefer HaChinnuch, *a commentary on the 613 commandments, draws a distinction between civil cases, "involving goods and possessions, and capital cases. . . . In civil cases, a man is not duty-bound to testify about them of his own accord, but only if a party to the dispute or a litigant summons him. But in capital cases, or with testimony concerning other [serious] prohibitions in the Torah . . . for instance . . . in regard to testimony about a physical attack, where one struck his fellow, in all such cases a man is duty-bound to come of his own accord and*

---

*Such people are also in the category of those who stand by while their neighbor's blood is shed (see page 362).

†Quite possibly, the victim of the false charges has not come to you because she is not aware of the information you possess. But what is most relevant is not what she does or does not know, but what you know and what you do with that knowledge.

give his testimony before the court, in order to eradicate the evil . . ." (commandment 122).[17] *In Maimonides'* Book of the Commandments, *likewise a listing of and commentary on the 613 commandments, he, unlike the* Sefer HaChinnuch, *condemns as a sinner one who withholds testimony even in a financial matter, and thereby allows another's money to be lost (negative commandment 297).*

---

23. In serious criminal cases, confessions are not accepted as evidence. The Talmud teaches: "No man may call himself an evildoer" (that is, in legal terms, a man cannot incriminate himself; *Sanhedrin* 9b).

Among the most unusual features of talmudic law is its insistence that in capital and other serious criminal cases, confessions are not accepted (though in monetary cases they are).* Maimonides offers a psychological explanation for this ruling: ". . . the court shall not put a man to death . . . on his own confession . . . for it is possible that he was confused in mind when he made the confession. Perhaps he was one of those who are in misery, bitter in soul, who long for death . . . Perhaps this man thus comes and confesses to a crime which he did not commit" ("Laws of Sanhedrin" 18:6).†

The disallowing of confessions in criminal cases had far-reaching implications in the past, most significantly that Jewish law-enforcement officials (unlike those in many of the societies surrounding the Jews) never tortured people suspected of crimes. In both Roman and Catholic jurisprudence, for example, confessions were regarded as the best, most reliable evidence of guilt (many people still think they are). This belief is precisely what led both these societies to sanction torturing suspects so as to secure confessions.‡

In addition to being inhumane, torture causes people to admit to almost anything, just to stop the torment. For example, after a highly publicized incident in Egypt several years ago in which a tortured man offered a false confession, a *New York Times* editorial noted: "Centuries of experience show that

*The rationale is that since all souls belong to God (see Ezekiel 18:4), a person is not permitted to confess and thereby possibly forfeit his life (in the same way, Jewish law forbids suicide). However, a person is permitted to do what he wants with his property and money; hence, confessions of responsibility in financial matters are permitted.

†Law-enforcement personnel report that, in the aftermath of sensational murders that have received extensive media attention, police are often approached by emotionally disturbed individuals making false confessions.

‡A contemporaneous description of Roman "justice" during the second century C.E.: "He [the governor] ordered that glowing iron balls should be applied under his [the accused's] armpits. He ordered that reeds should be sharpened and driven [under] the nails of his hands" (cited in Saul Lieberman, "Roman Legal Institutions in Early Rabbinics and in the *Acta Martyum,*" in *Jewish Quarterly Review,* July 1944, page 17). Equally horrific tortures to procure confessions characterized the treatment of suspected heretics by the Spanish Inquisition.

people will tell their tormentors what they want to hear, whether it's confessing to witchcraft in Salem, admitting to counterrevolutionary tendencies in Soviet Russia, or concocting stories about Iraq and Al-Qaeda."[18]

Particularly in totalitarian societies, which lack normal moral constraints, people confess for reasons other than simple fear of physical torture. Nikolai Bukharin, a Soviet leader who fell afoul of Stalin, admitted to acts he had never done, hoping that doing so would spare his wife and newborn son from being murdered by the Soviet tyrant.*[19]

Even in societies such as the United States, in which physically coerced confessions have no legal validity, the desire of police to secure confessions has led to many cases in which police officers have used immoral, and often counterproductive, means to reach their goals. A famous case occurred in Escondido, California, in 1998 after twelve-year-old Stephanie Crowe was found stabbed to death in her bedroom. Neighbors had called 911 the preceding evening to report the presence of a vagrant in the neighborhood acting strangely. But the local police, working in conjunction with the FBI's Behavioral Analysis Unit, quickly concluded that the murder was an inside job. They brought in the dead girl's fourteen-year-old brother, Michael, and questioned him uninterruptedly for three hours and then, later, for six hours (the parents were unaware he had been taken in for questioning). Having convinced themselves, despite the absence of physical evidence, that Michael was the killer, the detectives concluded that all forms of verbal trickery were justified to secure a confession. They therefore told the young man a series of lies, among them that:

- when Stephanie had been found, she had strands of his hair in her hands;
- her blood had been found in his room;
- her blood had been found all over his clothes.

The fourteen-year-old boy, who repeatedly denied stabbing his sister, was, of course, shocked by this "incontrovertible" evidence that apparently pointed to his guilt. The detectives then offered Michael an explanation as to

*Bukharin's wife, Anna Larina, was not executed, but the government did separate her from her son and she spent many years in prison, labor camps, and exile. It is infrequently commented upon that the last words of many Communist party leaders executed by Stalin's forces in the 1930s were "Long live Stalin." The historian Adam Ulam notes that this otherwise inexplicable praise of victims for their executioner "can be explained on human grounds; they hoped to purchase immunity or relative immunity for their families." Ulam notes that centuries earlier, in Tudor England, "people dispatched to the scaffold delivered little speeches just before their execution in praise of Elizabeth or Henry VIII for the same kind of reason" (see G. R. Urban, *Stalinism: Its Impact on Russia and the World,* pages 102–103).

why he might not recall what he had done: There might be "two Michaels," they suggested, a good and a bad one; the "bad Michael" had committed the crime and concealed knowledge of it from the "good Michael." Shortly thereafter, Michael Crowe confessed to having killed his sister in a fit of jealous rage.*

The young man was saved from a long jail term only when, on the eve of the trial, Stephanie Crowe's blood was discovered on the sweatshirt worn by the vagrant, Richard Tuite, who, it turned out was, indeed, the murderer.[20]

While it would be pleasant to report that cases such as the above (which could not happen under talmudic law) are the rarest of aberrations, it has become increasingly evident that police investigators often tell egregious lies to suspects in an attempt to influence them to confess (for example, telling suspects that their fingerprints have been found on a weapon used in a crime, even when this is not so). Police officers who make such claims presumably believe that the people whom they are questioning are guilty, so that tricking them into confessing achieves a moral end, the capturing of a felon. However, false claims, particularly when directed against youthful defendants and people of low intelligence, often induce innocent people to conclude, as did Michael Crowe, that they must have committed a crime and then blanked out (it rarely occurs to an innocent person that a police investigator would lie to him, certainly about so important a matter). The use of these techniques helps account for the disconcerting statistic that 15 percent to 25 percent of prisoners later found to be *definitely* innocent had earlier confessed to crimes they had not committed.†[21]

It is difficult to know what practical conclusions to draw from such data. Common sense dictates that the prohibition of confessions in cases of

---

*The detectives also procured confessions from two of Michael's friends, one of whom admitted involvement in the crime after a similar type of questioning, and following two interrogations that lasted a total of twenty-two hours.

†A study by Steven Drizin and Richard Leo of 125 cases in which prisoners confessed and were later exonerated revealed that 40 of them were minors at the time of their confession, and 28 were mentally retarded. However, a surprising 57 were otherwise competent adults. Eighty percent of those confessing had been grilled by police for more than six hours straight, 50 percent for more than twelve hours; some of the other false confessions had been elicited after up to two days of almost nonstop questioning (see Carol Tavris and Eliot Aronson, *Mistakes Were Made [But Not by Me]*, page 147). Furthermore, "A 2002 study from Northwestern University showed that 59% of all miscarriages of justice in homicide investigations in Illinois . . . involved false confessions" (*Time*, December 12, 2005, page 46). Some states, including Minnesota, Illinois, and Maine, now require police to videotape all interrogations and confessions of suspects in capital cases. It is, in part, because of the sort of questioning techniques employed by many police departments that even an innocent person should not submit to a police interrogation without an attorney present.

serious crimes would lead to far fewer being solved, and likely to a dramatic rise in violent crime. Therefore, to prohibit the admissibility of confessions at this time seems undesirable. Even Jewish law might sanction such a measure. As Rabbi Norman Lamm, a careful student of this subject, has written: "The government, however, and the *Sanhedrin* as a temporary [emergency] measure, may accept self-incriminating testimony from a defendant so as to 'improve society according to the needs of the hour.' "* Nonetheless, "the ideal law is that which disqualifies confessions to a crime as a matter of principle."[22] While the inability of prosecutors to secure convictions of many violent criminals if confession were disallowed might well constitute a crisis, the false confession rates of 15 percent to 25 percent can hardly be dismissed as insignificant.

30

THE RIGHT OF OTHERS TO THINK DIFFERENTLY

1. Tolerance is among the most difficult of virtues. The Hebrew word for it, *sovlanut,* derives from *sevel,* to suffer.† In other words, we have to endure a certain amount of discomfort and sometimes even suffering, to tolerate views with which we disagree.‡

Savlanut, a related Hebrew word, means "patience," suggesting that one aspect of tolerance is patience with those who hold views we believe to be wrong.

2. Practicing tolerance is also difficult because its benefits are not necessarily obvious (as is the case with such virtues as justice and fairness). In

*See also Maimonides, "Laws of Kings" 3:10, on the right of a king to make a major change in a law if an emergency demands doing so.

†In English, the word "tolerance" is related to "tolerate."

‡Rabbi Aharon Lichtenstein relates tolerance to the possession of power. Thus, "to tolerate is to suffer the pressure of what is . . . by my lights, thoroughly erroneous, and to refrain, nonetheless, from the exercise of power to coerce its devotees to cease and desist" ("The Parameters of Tolerance," in Moshe Sokol, ed., *Tolerance, Dissent, and Democracy,* page 140).

fact, one might well question why tolerance should be regarded as a virtue at all. For if we feel certain that a view is wrong, and perhaps even harmful, shouldn't we strive to suppress it? What is good about permitting people to spread misguided or harmful ideas or advocate behavior we believe to be wrong?

The Reasons Tolerance Is Necessary

People have the right to think differently

3. The basis of tolerance is the acknowledgment that other people have the right to think about the world differently from the way we do. Rather than regarding such differences as irritating and unfortunate, a talmudic passage suggests that they are natural: "Rabbi Meir used to say, 'In three things people are different one from the other: in voice, appearance, and opinions' " (*Sanhedrin* 38a). Thus, just as it doesn't bother us if our neighbor's voice or appearance differs from ours (indeed, it would be extremely boring if everybody looked and sounded exactly alike), so it should not bother us if our neighbor's views differs from ours as well (Rabbi Menachem Mendel of Kotzk).*

One upshot of Rabbi Meir's teaching is that parents should not try to make all their children alike or copies of themselves. Rather, as Proverbs teaches, "Raise a child according to his *way" (22:6; emphasis added). Observe your child carefully, and support her interests and enthusiasms in order to develop her potential. If your daughter is artistic, don't impose upon her your long-cherished dream that she become a doctor, or make her feel that she is disappointing you by pursuing a path that differs from what you want. Children, too, are entitled to their own "opinions" about the kind of life they wish to lead.*

---

4. While the sight of a large crowd causes many people to have dismissive thoughts (e.g., "a mindless mob"), the Talmud commands us to recite a blessing, "Blessed is the Wise One who knows secrets" (that is, everyone's in-

---

**Emet ve-Emunah.* The talmudic passage itself narrowly restricts the meaning of Rabbi Meir's aphorism, saying that if people all thought alike, they would hide their valuables in the same place, and this would be a great boon to thieves.

nermost thoughts; *Berachot* 58a). This implies that we should remember that each person in the crowd has a different way of understanding the world, and "we bless God for having created such diverse minds"(Reuven Kimelman).[1]

A Midrash expresses a similar thought: "Just as the faces of people [in a large crowd] are not like each other, so their minds are not the same; rather, each has his own way of thinking" (Numbers Rabbah *21:2).*

Different people have different needs

5. When it comes to ethical behavior, such as laws against harming others, we need a uniformly binding code of conduct. But in many other areas of life, uniformity is unnecessary and can cause pointless, and sometimes great, misery. For example, some people's longings for spirituality are satisfied through a lengthy prayer service with a great deal of singing; others prefer a shorter service, with a focus on study. There is no reason to believe that one approach is better than the other, although many people look down upon those whose spiritual longings differ from their own.

Similarly, because we are all different, it is wise to offer a variety of approaches to people in need: *When it comes to human emotions, one size definitely does not fit all.* Psychologist David Pelcovitz relates how Israel's educators have learned to take into account people's diverse styles of coping with tragedy: "I was in Jerusalem shortly after a suicide bombing and was asked to join an Israeli psychologist in meeting with a group of adolescents who had just lost a beloved teacher in the bombing. The school set up five rooms for the adolescents. One room was set aside for writing condolence letters to the family of their teacher, other rooms were designated for a discussion group (led by the psychologist), music, art, and saying *Tehillim* (Psalms). The teens chose the room that best matched their style and seemed to find solace in finding an opportunity to deal with their grief in a manner that uniquely suited their styles." Pelcovitz concludes: "There is no one correct way to deal with upsetting situations."[2]

Thus, tolerance emanates in part from the realization that people have different needs, and that as long as meeting their needs does not cause suffering to others, they should be free to act as they wish, rather than being made to feel inferior.

Truth is multifaceted

6. While Jewish law generally tries to reach uniformity on basic legal and ritual issues (e.g., all followers of Jewish law agree that pork and shellfish are not kosher), the Talmud supports the validity of divergent views in non-legal areas. For example, in a dispute between Rabbis Evyatar and Yonatan concerning each man's understanding of a biblical passage about an incident with a "concubine" (described in Judges 19), the Rabbis conclude that "These and these are the words of the living God" (*Gittin* 6b). In other words, not only does each of the Rabbis have the right to understand the passage differently, but each one's view may well be legitimate. Thus, tolerance is not rooted simply in acting amicably toward those whom we believe to be wrong, but also in recognizing that there might be some truth in positions with which we disagree; indeed, they may well be "the words of the living God."

7. Elsewhere, the Talmud teaches that intellectual growth depends on exposing oneself to a variety of viewpoints: "One who studies Torah from only one teacher will never achieve great success" (*Avodah Zara* 19a).* We therefore need to expose ourselves even to views with which we disagree. Otherwise, we will end up with a one-sided and incomplete understanding of a subject, or of the world.

8. As these texts suggest, on many of life's most important issues, there is no one truth. Rabbi Aryeh Kaplan has suggested that perhaps that is why God gave humankind the Torah, which can be interpreted in so many different ways ("maybe [God] wanted a certain amount of variety and interchange"), as opposed to the *Shulchan Aruch,* the sixteenth-century code of Jewish law, which lends itself to less interpretation.[3] The Rabbis taught that there are seventy faces (*shivim panim*) to the Torah, an expression meant to convey that there are dozens of *legitimate* ways to interpret it.

9. The Talmud frequently records views that the majority of the Rabbis rejected. The Mishnah explains that this was done so that later generations or different courts could rely on these views if changed conditions led them to reach a different conclusion from earlier sages: "Why do they record the opinion of a single person among the many, when the law [*halacha*] must be according to the opinion of the many? So that if a court prefers the opinion

---

*Literally, "will never see a sign of blessing [in his studies]."

of the single person, it may rely on him" (Mishnah *Eduyot* 1:5).* The Rabbis understood that the best decision for one generation might turn out not to be the best for a later one and thus wanted all students of the law to be aware of the views that were rejected.

—

To cite a well-known example of this principle drawn from American law: In 1896, in Plessy v. Ferguson, *the Supreme Court ruled 7–1 that "separate but equal" facilities (in this case, referring to separate railroad cars for whites and blacks) were constitutional. At the time of this ruling, the one dissenting justice, John Marshall Harlan, recorded his view that the constitution was intended to be "color-blind" and that it recognized "no superior, dominant, ruling class of citizens. In respect of civil rights, all citizens are equal before the law." Following this decision, legislation based on the doctrine of "separate but equal," and promoting racial segregation expanded steadily throughout the American South. Then, almost sixty years later, in 1954, in* Brown v. Board of Education, Plessy v. Ferguson *was overturned, and the justices (this time ruling in a case involving segregated public schools) concluded that "separate educational facilities [were inherently] unequal." Justice Harlan's insistence that the constitution was color-blind, though rejected in his own day, was embraced by a 9–0 verdict of the court.*

—

While members of the Sanhedrin were obligated to abide by the court's rulings, a member who was in disagreement was permitted to teach his dissenting views, both in private and in public, and to criticize the court's decisions, as long as he continued to obey the court's ruling and counseled others to do the same (see Mishnah Sanhedrin *11:2).*

—

The intellectual advantages gained by being tolerant

10. The one other instance in which the Talmud uses the expression "These and these are the words of the living God" (*Eruvin* 13b) is in its description of the *Bat Kol* (heavenly voice) that applied these words to the more than 300 legal disputes between the Schools of Hillel *(Beit Hillel)* and

*Another reason to list minority positions is so that people in later generations who would argue on behalf of such views would realize that the earlier Rabbis had already considered and rejected them; see Mishnah *Eduyot* 1:6.

of Shammai *(Beit Shammai).* In this case, however, the *Bat Kol* goes on to declare that Jews should follow the rulings of Hillel and his disciples.*

The Talmud explains why: "Because they [the School of Hillel] were kindly and humble, and because they studied their own rulings and those of the School of Shammai, and even mentioned the teachings of the School of Shammai before their own" (*Eruvin* 13b). Apparently, Hillel and his disciples' greater humility and tolerance made them not only ethically worthy of being chosen over their opponents, but also more likely than the School of Shammai to reach accurate conclusions.[4]

Why? Shammai and his followers apparently were so certain they possessed the *whole* truth that, the above text suggests, they did not bother to study their opponents' views in depth. In contrast, the School of Hillel's tolerance led it to study Shammai's views as alternatives to be carefully considered. Consequently, the members of the School of Hillel were repeatedly forced to defend, refine, and deepen their own views. The Talmud records instances in which Hillel's disciples, after studying the opposing positions, reconsidered and changed their views (see, for example, Mishnah *Eduyot* 1:12–13).†

In short, tolerant people are not only more likely to be "kind and humble," but are also more likely to reach accurate conclusions.

---

*Two differing traditions exist in the Talmud concerning the personal relations between the Schools of Hillel and Shammai. One teaches that members of the two groups married one another and "treated each other with affection and kinship" (*Yevamot *14b). But another describes an incident in which disciples of Shammai ambushed and killed many of Hillel's disciples, so that they could outvote them and institute the law according to their interpretation. The Talmud calls to this "triumph" of the School of Shammai (a ruling that was later overturned) "as grievous for Israel as the day on which the Golden Calf was made" (Jerusalem Talmud,* Shabbat *1:4;* Shabbat *17a).*

---

*If the rulings of both sides were valid expressions of God's will, why did Jewish law find it necessary to choose one set of rulings over another? Because when it comes to law, anarchy results when there is no uniformity on basic legal requirements. For example, a century after the incident of the heavenly voice, two leading rabbis, Gamliel and Joshua, had a dispute over the day on which Yom Kippur would fall that year. As president of the Sanhedrin, Rabbi Gamliel had supreme authority, and he compelled Rabbi Joshua *not to* observe Yom Kippur on the day on which Joshua thought it fell (Mishnah *Rosh Hashanah* 2:8–9). Gamliel feared that, otherwise, followers of each rabbi would start to observe two different calendars, and the Jewish community would split apart.

†There is only one instance (in the context of a highly technical legal dispute) in which Shammai's disciples acknowledged the validity of the position offered by Hillel's followers (see Mishna *Terumot* 5:4).

Obviously, these accounts do not necessarily negate each other; they might simply be describing events that happened at different times. However, the disturbing account from the Jerusalem Talmud reminds us of intolerant individuals' unhealthy potential to turn violent.

Another talmudic passage reinforces the view that challenges to authority can lead to more, not less, truth. After the death of his study partner Resh Lakish (see *pages 384–385**), Rabbi Yochanan lamented: "With Resh Lakish, whenever I would say something, he would pose twenty-four difficulties [i.e., challenges] to me, and I would give him twenty-four solutions and as a result the subject became clear"* (Bava Mezia *84a*).

Serious challenges, as long as they are not just offered to be provocative, should be treated with respect since they deepen understanding and lead to a fuller appreciation of the truth.

Uniform thinking can produce errors

11. The Talmud rules that if the seventy-one members of the Sanhedrin (Jewish High Court) unanimously believe a defendant in a capital case is guilty, not only is the death sentence not carried out, but the defendant, it would seem, is released: "Rabbi Kahana said: 'A Sanhedrin, all of whose members felt that he was guilty [must] acquit him. What is the reason? We have learned that [where the vote is to convict] the judgment [in capital cases] must be delayed overnight [to give the judges the opportunity] to search for a defense [for the accused], but these judges [having voted unanimously to convict] will no longer consider any basis for acquittal" (*Sanhedrin* 17a).* In other words, the Rabbis feared that in so one-sided an

*Regarding the logic of disregarding a unanimous verdict, Aaron Schreiber, a professor of law and a Jewish legal scholar, writes: ". . . part of the 'due process' accorded to a criminal defendant in Jewish law was that after the deliberations of the court and before any judgment was reached, the judges were required to spend the night together in pairs, searching for a possible defense for the criminal defendant (see Mishnah *Sanhedrin* 5:5). Here, since the judges of the Sanhedrin unanimously felt that the defendant was guilty, they would no longer search for a possible defense in his behalf. Accordingly, he was deprived of the 'due process' requirement. He could not therefore be convicted and had to be acquitted. This rule would reflect the extreme lengths to which Jewish law would go to accord a criminal defendant 'due process.' " Schreiber compares the release of a criminal who is guilty to "the 'Miranda' and 'Poisoned Fruit' doctrines in the United States, which prevent the imposition of sanctions upon defendants who clearly appear to be guilty of crimes, where the police have engaged in acts that violate the defendants' constitutional rights" (*Jewish Law and Decision-Making,* pages 270–271).

environment, one in which no member of the court seemed to be seeking out alternative evidence or exonerating circumstances, the truth may become distorted. In modern times, only authoritarian and totalitarian governments seek uniformity and unanimity. Thus, leaders in Communist, Fascist, and other dictatorships often proclaim election majorities of 99 percent and higher.

Tolerance toward other religions

12. Dennis Prager suggests that one of the most important days in the life of a religious person is when he meets a member of a different religion, or of a different denomination within his own religion, who is both a good and intelligent person. After such an encounter, one can no longer dismiss the other group's followers as being of low intelligence or character, the way intolerant people often do.

Those who spend time only with those who are of like mind often regard other groups with contempt. But to dismiss out-of-hand views that differ from, or challenge, our own is wrong. In a remarkable statement of tolerance dating from 1598, Rabbi Judah Lowe, the Maharal of Prague (ca. 1520–1609), taught that it is worthwhile to listen and respond even to alternative religious viewpoints, as long as the person expressing them is not malicious or coercive: "If a person does not intend to goad, only to convey his faith, even if his words are opposed to your own faith and your own religion, you should not say to him: 'Do not speak and keep your words to yourself. . . .' On the contrary, let him speak as much as he wants . . . Reason requires that nothing be hindered, that no mouth be closed, and that religious dispute be open for everybody. . . . This is the only way by which men can reach ultimate truth. Any proponent who wants to overcome his opponent and demonstrate his own correctness would very much want his opponent to confront him to his utmost . . ." (*Be'er Ha-Golah, *2: 424–426).†*

---

*Coercion occurred when Jewish communities in pre-modern Europe were forced to come to the synagogue and listen to Christian clergy's proselytizing speeches. For example, Pope Gregory XIII (1572–1585) ordered missionizing sermons to be delivered in synagogues every Sabbath and on Jewish holidays. Lest Rome's Jews stay away from services to avoid these sermons, he further decreed that a minimum of one hundred Jewish men and fifty Jewish women, all over the age of twelve, be in attendance when sermons were delivered. The Church even established a special school to train preachers for this work. A half-century later, in 1630, Austrian Emperor Ferdinand II similarly ordered the Jews of Vienna to attend such sermons, and mandated that any Jew who was observed talking or sleeping during the sermon be punished (Ben Zion Bokser, *Jews, Judaism, and the State of Israel,* pages 125–126).

†The medieval Christian-Jewish debates in which Jews were forced to participate were pointless, in addition to being cruel, because the Jews generally feared to present their most powerful

*Yet I believe that it is unwise, in general, for Jewish groups to engage in interfaith dialogue on issues of theology; for example, to take part in a formal, public discussion in which Christian participants explain why they believe Jesus to have been God's son and the Messiah, and then Jews explain why they don't. When done on a group level, there's little to be gained by such a discussion, and a good chance that bad feelings will ensue. However, if I understand the Maharal correctly, he does think it both acceptable and worthwhile for individuals to speak of their deepest beliefs one-on-one (obviously it must be done respectfully, and without one party's agenda being to convince the other person that his religious beliefs are wrong, and that he must convert). Conversations between individuals are less likely to harden into annoyance and antagonism than are group discussions. Indeed, personal conversations on issues of faith (and sometimes struggles with faith) can sometimes lead to mutual respect and affection. I came across a story Rabbi Walter Wurzberger told of visiting Rabbi Soloveitchik in the hospital. As he walked in, a doctor was thanking the Rav over and over. When Wurzberger asked Rabbi Soloveitchik what had happened (normally one hears patients thanking the doctor, not the reverse), the Rav answered that the doctor was a Catholic man who was having issues of religious doubt, and the Rav was able to supply him with thoughts about faith and God that the doctor found helpful and reassuring. That is why he was thanking him.***

As opposed to formal forums on theological issues, interfaith cooperation and dialogue on matters of social justice are definitely worthwhile. It is beneficial for each side to consider the other's perspective on what their religious tradition believes are the best ways to address problems of racial injustice, confronting oppressive foreign governments, and helping poor people to improve their lot.

---

13. Many religious Jews believe that Judaism's monotheistic faith, which is based upon God's revelations to the Patriarchs and to Moses, is the only true expression of God's will, and that other religions are therefore wrong. In

---

arguments as these provoked wrath, and sometimes attacks, against them. Also, only when we overcome our opponent's best arguments do we feel confidence in our own position. One strongly suspects that the most important reason authoritarian rulers do not allow their opponents freedom of speech is because of fear that they won't be able to respond to their critics in a convincing manner. Indeed, one feature communist, fascist, and all other totalitarian regimes share is that they jail and otherwise muzzle those who express opposing viewpoints.

*This incident is particularly interesting because of Rabbi Soloveitchik's well-known opposition to interfaith dialogue on matters of faith; this story would seem consistent with the Maharal's view, allowing for one-on-one discussions of spiritual matters between people of different faiths. I am thankful to Dr. Joel Wolowelsky, who helped me track down this story.

recent years, the United Kingdom's chief rabbi, Sir Jonathan Sacks, has argued forcefully against this view: "Judaism is a particularist monotheism. It believes in one God but not in one religion, one culture, one truth. The God of Abraham is the God of all mankind, but the faith of Abraham is not the faith of all mankind."[5]

In Rabbi Sacks's striking formulation: "God is God of all humanity, but no single faith should be the faith of all humanity. . . . God no more wants all faiths and cultures to be the same than a loving parent wants his or her children to be the same."[6]

The dangers and evils that ensue when people are convinced that they possess the whole truth was noted by Isaiah Berlin (1909–1997), the political scientist and philosopher: "Few things have done more harm than the belief on the part of individuals and groups (or tribes or states or nations or churches) that he or she or they are in sole *possession of the truth. . . . It is a terrible and dangerous arrogance to believe that you alone are right . . . and that others cannot be right if they disagree. This makes one certain that there is one goal and only one for one's nation or church or the whole of humanity, and that it is worth any amount of suffering (particularly on the part of other people) if only the goal is attained."*[7]

In similar manner, Jacob Bronowski, author of The Ascent of Man, *declared in the television series based on his book: "We have to cure ourselves of the itch for absolute knowledge and power . . . In the end, the words [we all need to hear] were said by Oliver Cromwell: 'I beseech you . . . Think it possible you may be mistaken.'"*

---

14. The same tolerant approach should apply in the political realm. Ideologues on the left and right often demonize each other, seeing their opponents not only as wrong and foolish, but also as possessing evil intentions—an ugly aspect of American political life.

In an effort to defuse this sort of intolerance, during election campaigns I like to ask partisans of each candidate: "Can you think of at least one reason someone would vote for the candidate you oppose that doesn't reflect badly on either the person's character or intelligence?" I'm constantly amazed and saddened at how rarely people can think of a single intelligent and/or nonselfish reason someone would vote for the other side. Their inability to do so means that many politi-

cally passionate people end up regarding about half of the populace as either of inferior intelligence or character.

Tolerance and intolerance within the Jewish world

15. While antisemitic writers have long claimed that Jews are united in an international conspiracy to control the world's economies and governments,[8] anyone familiar with Jewish life from within knows that Jews are hardly united. As is the case with many groups, Jewish communal life is filled with tension, intolerance, and often mutual contempt. Unfortunately, this has often been the case between Orthodox and non-Orthodox religious denominations. Rabbi Irving (Yitz) Greenberg has cautioned: "I don't care what denomination in Judaism you belong to, as long as you're ashamed of it." Since each denomination is committed to *tikkun olam,* repairing the world, each movement can hardly claim that this perfection has not been achieved only because of the other movements' misguided teachings or behavior. Intolerant people have a tendency to look for, and exaggerate, their opponents' faults, while minimizing their own.

Rabbi Abraham Twerski, a psychiatrist and a Chasid, recalls: "I was once traveling on a bus, dressed in my customary garb, wearing a broad black hat and a [long] black coat. A man approached me and said, 'I think it's shameful that your appearance is so different. There is no need for Jews in America to be so conspicuous, with long beards and black hats.'

" 'I'm sorry, mister,' I said to the man. 'I'm not Jewish. I'm Amish, and this is how we dress.'

"The man became apologetic. 'Oh, I'm terribly sorry, sir,' he said. 'I did not mean to offend you. I think you should be proud of preserving your traditions.'

" 'Well, well,' I said. 'If I am Amish, then my beard and black hat don't bother you, and I should be proud of my traditions. But if I am Jewish, then I must be ashamed of my Jewishness? What is wrong with you that you can respect others, but have no self-respect?' "[9]

In 1938, in the days following the Nazi national pogrom known as Kristallnacht, the Reform congregation in Providence, Rhode Island, conducted a special service to which it invited recently arrived Jewish refugees from Europe. Many of *the refugee Jews came to the synagogue wearing hats or* kippot, *which violated the Reform congregation's practice of men remaining bareheaded in temple.* A prominent member of the congregation insisted that the refugees remove their head-covering, and kept pressing the rabbi, William Braude, who was also a renowned rabbinical scholar, "Did you give permission to these people to wear hats?" Rabbi Braude was so upset by the man's mean-spirited intolerance that he felt too intimidated to tell him to let these poor refugees from Nazism alone, and to permit them to keep their heads covered.*[10]

—

Some years ago, an Orthodox rabbinic organization put out advertisements before the High Holidays urging Jews to remain at home rather than attend a Reform or Conservative service. Ironically, when a prominent American Baptist leader said that God does not hear the prayers of Jews because they are not offered through Jesus, Jews of all denominations were understandably outraged.† But should not all Jews be equally upset by advertisements such as those of the rabbinic organization? And if we shouldn't be (some would argue that those who took out the ad honestly felt they had to warn people away from what they regard as sinful behavior), then what right do we have to be annoyed at men like the Baptist leader who obviously felt that he was also trying to warn people away from wrongful behavior?

—

A friend, a Reform rabbi in Jerusalem, attended an Orthodox synagogue to recite Kaddish for his recently deceased father (his Reform congregation does not have daily services). He was recognized by members of the Orthodox congregation, one of whom stood up and announced that it was forbidden to answer "Amen" to his Kaddish since, as a Reform rabbi, my friend was a heretic and responsible for other people acting sinfully.[11] *Obviously, refusing to answer "Amen" when a Reform rabbi offers a prayer to God only further alienates Jews of different religious beliefs from each other.‡*

—

*Today, in most Reform congregations men cover their heads, but in the past, particularly in temples that followed the tradition known as Classical Reform, they were bareheaded.

†It is infrequently noted that the Reverend Bailey Smith, the Baptist leader who made this statement, went on to say that he would defend with his life the right of Jews to offer such prayers.

‡My friend found another Orthodox synagogue in which the members did answer his Kaddish. While he was grateful to them for doing so, he noted that nobody there spoke to him during the eleven months he was reciting Kaddish.

Sources of intolerance within Judaism

16. The Torah regarded idolatry with abhorrence: Idolatry led people to sacrifice their children and to deny not only the universal God but also His universally binding morality. Furthermore, given that within the context of ancient idolatrous societies, it would have been difficult, if not impossible, to establish monotheism,* the Torah's absolute prohibition of, and contempt for, idolatry becomes understandable.

However, even aside from its unbending opposition to idolatry, there is a strong streak of intolerance in Judaism. Oddly, it is epitomized in the thinking and writing of Moses Maimonides, medieval Judaism's premier rabbinic scholar, philosopher, and intellectual. Relying in part on certain talmudic precedents, Maimonides outlined societal norms that he thought should be instituted in a state run according to Jewish law. For example, he ruled that Jews who deny a tenet of Judaism, such as that the entire Torah is the revealed will of God, or who eat unkosher food to show their contempt for God and Judaism (and not simply because they like it), deserve to die:† "If it is within one's power to kill them with a sword in public view, then kill them. If that is not possible, one should devise schemes that can bring about their deaths." He then offered the following guidance as an example of how to act toward a heretic: If you see such a person fall into a well, and there is a ladder in the well, you should remove the ladder, and even lie to the would-be victim, "I must hurry to take my son down from the roof. I shall return the ladder to you soon" ("Laws of Murder and Preservation of Life" 4:10). Maimonides' rationale for killing such people, or for indirectly causing their deaths, is that they alienate Jews from God ("Laws of Idolatry" 10:1).‡

Maimonides intended his code to serve as the legal code of a future Jewish state, but had the modern state of Israel chosen a political and legal

---

*Once, however, monotheism was established as a widespread belief, rabbinic intolerance for idolaters declined. Thus, in a famous talmudic ruling, the Rabbis declared that contemporary idolaters outside the land of Israel should not be viewed as evil; rather, "they are only carrying out *customs* learned from their ancestors" (*Chullin* 13b; emphasis added).

†Even though eating unkosher food was never a capital offense in Jewish law.

‡Maimonides himself, or rather his writings, subsequently became the victim of terrible intolerance from fellow Jews. Less than three decades after his death, three leading rabbis in France, arguing that there were heretical teachings in Maimonides' books, denounced his writings to the Dominicans, who headed the French Inquisition. The Inquisitors were happy to intervene and burn some of Maimonides' writings. They also used this incident as an excuse to start looking into other Jewish books. Eight years later, when the Dominicans started burning the Talmud, one of the rabbis involved, Jonah Gerondi (author of the classic work, *Gates of Repentance*), concluded that God was punishing him and French Jewry for their unjust condemnation of Maimonides. He resolved to travel to Maimonides' grave in Tiberias, Israel, to beg forgiveness.

system based on his directives, Israel would today be a highly repressive society. Hence, while Maimonides' views are cited in this book more than those of any other Jewish scholar, and he has been among the greatest influences on my own understanding of Jewish law, it seems to me that his code *alone* cannot function as a fully sufficient ethical and legal code for contemporary Jews.*

In the twentieth century, sages such as Rabbi Abraham Isaac Kook, and the Chazon Ish, one of the preeminent figures of right-wing Orthodoxy, ruled that we no longer apply the laws concerning heresy to any Jews, even those who deny Judaism's most basic beliefs; not only should we not harm such people, but if the situation presents itself, we should help them. The Chazon Ish wrote that we live today in "a time of God's concealment," that is, when divine providence is more obscured than it was in the ancient past "when miracles were commonplace," and God's existence was apparent to all. Therefore, he ruled that it is wrong to regard non-believers today as acting with the same "maliciousness and lawlessness" as the heretics of old (see his book, Chazon Ish, Yoreh Deah, *chapter 2).*

The moral danger of intolerance

17. The belief that we possess the whole truth can cause us to act inappropriately and sometimes cruelly. Intolerance emanates from the belief that one's position is so right, and one's opponent's so wrong, that it would be catastrophic to respect the opposing viewpoint and those who hold it. This attitude can be likened to the *deserved* contempt with which mainstream doctors regard faith-healing sects that will not, for example, permit diabetic members to take insulin injections, but insist that they try to heal themselves through prayer alone.† While this is abhorrent, such instances are rare, although those involved in disputes often claim that they are fighting for a matter of life-and-death, or of absolute right and wrong. Thus, throughout Jewish history, leaders have often argued that the positions advocated by their adversaries are so dangerous that they must be suppressed. However, later assessments by both Jewish scholars and the general community have

---

*Maimonides' proposed treatment of non-Jews living in a Jewish state is equally problematic (see pages 281–285).

†In some cases, when members of certain religious sects have done this, the diabetics have drifted into irreversible comas and died.

rarely supported these claims. Rabbi Elijah, the Vilna Gaon (1720–1797), was probably the greatest Jewish religious scholar since Moses Maimonides (twelfth century), and the recognized spiritual leader of his age.* During the Gaon's lifetime, the Chasidic movement was begun by Rabbi Israel Ba'al Shem Tov (1698–1760). The Gaon believed that the Chasidic leadership was composed of ignoramuses who were not committed to the proper observance of Jewish law. So certain was he of this that when the Chasidic leaders Rabbis Menachem Mendel of Vitebsk and Shneur Zalman of Liady tried to meet with him to demonstrate that the new movement did not conflict with traditional Judaism, the Gaon refused to see them. Furthermore, he issued bans of excommunication, ruling that it was forbidden for other Jews to do business with, marry, maintain social relations with, or even assist at the burial of Chasidim. At one point, the Gaon declared: "If it were within my power, I would do to the Chasidim what Elijah the Prophet did to the priests of Ba'al." In other words, he would kill the Chasidim, as Elijah led the Jews to kill 450 idolatrous priests of Baal (see I Kings 18:40).[12]

Because of the Gaon's preeminence, his words deeply influenced his followers, who persecuted the Chasidim. Shortly after the Gaon's death, an anti-Chasidic rabbi made a false accusation of treason to the Russian government against Rabbi Shneur Zalman of Liady, the founder of the Lubavitch movement, that almost led to the rabbi's execution.

Yet, two hundred years later, how do Jews view the Vilna Gaon and the Chasidim? Almost all knowledgeable Jews regard the Gaon as a great intellectual and spiritual figure, and simultaneously view the rise of Chasidism, and its rabbinic figures such as the Ba'al Shem Tov, as a very important spiritual development in Jewish life. Of course, the Vilna Gaon would have been horrified by this. Ironically, had this great but intolerant man been granted the power to deal with the situation, he would today be regarded as a brilliant man who nevertheless brought about the deaths of innocent people. Sometimes, the greatest blessing for intolerant people is to be denied the power that they desire.

When intolerance is a virtue; a rare, but important, exception

18. On both moral and rational grounds, it makes little sense to tolerate those who, if they gain power, will deny freedom to those with whom they disagree. Thus, it seems morally wrong to grant democratic rights to those

---

*In popular Hebrew parlance, the term *gaon* means "genius." Thus, he was called "the genius of Vilna."

whose intention is to utilize democracy's tolerance to overthrow it.* That was Hitler's tactic: to come to power through democratic elections and then to destroy democracy. Nor did he and his followers make any effort to deny that this was their goal. As Joseph Goebbels, the future Nazi minister of propaganda, wrote in 1928: "We become members of the Reichstag [the German parliament] in order to paralyze the Weimar . . . with its own assistance. If democracy is so stupid as to give us free tickets and per diem† for this blockade, that is its own affair. . . . We do not come as friends nor even as neutrals, we come as enemies. As the wolf bursts into the flock, so we come." Seven years later, after the Nazis had come to power and ended democracy, Goebbels acknowledged yet again that this had always been their intention: "We National Socialists never asserted that we represented a democratic point of view, but we declared openly that we used democratic methods only in order to gain power, and that, after assuming power, we would deny to adversaries without any consideration the means which were granted to us in the times of opposition." Similar tactics—using free elections in an attempt to destroy the democratic process—have been tried by Communist parties, and by certain Islamist groups today.

Granting democratic rights to those who intend to use these rights to destroy democracy makes as little sense as allowing someone who announces that he intends to commit a crime to acquire a weapon.

The Talmud records that in the first century of the Common Era, a man named Bar Kamtza slandered the Jews of Israel to officials in the Roman government, telling them that the Jews were fomenting rebellion. Upon hearing of Bar Kamtza's behavior, the Rabbis wished to execute him before his accusations could cause any further harm, but Rabbi Zechariah ben Avkulas ruled that Bar Kamtza had, as of yet, committed no capital offense, and it would therefore be wrong to kill him. Bar Kamtza continued his slanders, and the results were catastrophic. Rabbi Yochanan later commented: "The tolerance displayed by Rabbi Zechariah ben Avkulas [in refusing to allow the traitorous Bar Kamtza to be

*On pragmatic, as opposed to moral, grounds, it might make sense not to outlaw Communist or Fascist groups in countries such as the United States, where they pose no threat of achieving political power. Withholding rights from such groups might prompt some people to regard them as martyrs and, therefore, extend them support. On the other hand, in a country such as Germany in which the people did vote the Nazis into power, it would make sense to outlaw even small groups—and even if they are currently nonviolent—that intend to destroy democracy.

†Daily expenses.

put to death] destroyed our Temple, burned down our Sanctuary, and [caused us to be] exiled from our land" (Gittin *56a*).

In 1984, the Israeli Supreme Court upheld the decision of the Central Elections Commission to disqualify the Kach Party from participating in the Israeli election because it was committed to expelling Arabs from Israel and greatly limiting Arab rights. Simultaneously, the court upheld the exclusion from the election of an Arab party that supported Arab terrorism against Jews.[13]

Final thoughts: Two antidotes to intolerance

19. Disagree with people but don't impugn their motives. A contemporary Talmud scholar, Professor Reuven Kimelman, summarizes the authoritarian and potentially violent mind-set of the religiously (and politically) intolerant: "Two opposing sides cannot both be in possession of the truth. If I have the truth, then what you have is false. If I am right, then you are wrong. And, since falsehood has no rights, I, in service of the truth, am duty-bound to work for your conversion or, failing that, your destruction."

The hatred such thinking promotes can be prevented only "as long as both parties entertain the possibility of the other acting for the sake of Heaven."[14] Therefore, even when you disagree with someone, unless you know for a fact that the other person's motives are malicious and/or self-serving, don't impugn your opponent's motives.

This mode of thinking is also helpful in cases involving forgiveness of someone who has hurt us but has not sought our forgiveness. My friend Rabbi Leonid Feldman suggests that we try to focus on the other person's intentions, which are usually more benign than their actions. For example, I know a man who felt misunderstood and cruelly mistreated by his father. Prior to his father's death, the two men had a perfunctory reconciliation, but the son's anger at his father remained fierce. When he conducted this exercise, he was able to realize that although his father had hurt him, his father had never thought, "What can I do to really hurt my son and destroy his emotional well-being?" True, he had been a bad father, but it was not out of a desire to be a bad father. This realization finally enabled the man's anger at, and demonization of, his father to subside.

---

20. Judge people by their behavior far more than by their beliefs. Rabbi Harold Kushner has noted that "There are people whose theologies I do not share, but I consider their religions to be 'true' when I see the way they live their faith."[15] In other words, while not accepting as true basic tenets of another belief system, Kushner nonetheless recognizes that these faiths have the capacity to inspire their adherents to live lives of kindness, integrity, and holiness. For example, Jews obviously do not believe the claims Christianity makes for Jesus (e.g., that he was the son of God and perfect). But they can still appreciate that such beliefs, among others, motivate many of the people who hold these beliefs to lead righteous lives. Similarly, Orthodox Jews find Reform Judaism's willingness to overturn, suspend, or regard as optional many biblical and talmudic laws as profoundly wrong, while Reform Jews regard Orthodox insistence that Torah laws cannot be abrogated and that talmudic legislation is still obligatory as wrong as well. But once one meets those who hold these beliefs and who are leading day-to-day lives of goodness, can one dismiss such people as altogether lacking in value because one dislikes their theology? There is, it would seem, more than one way to lead a moral life, and this can sometimes be done even by those who possess theological beliefs we regard as wrong. We can feel passionately about our own religious tradition without regarding with contempt and disdain those who live by another set of beliefs but who lead lives of goodness.*

---

*Kushner's notion of assessing others on the basis of their behavior, not theology, corresponds in some respects to the Meiri's (thirteenth century) willingness to suspend all anti-Gentile legislation in the Talmud on the grounds that such legislation was directed against idolaters, and he judged idolatry primarily on the basis of the immoral behavior it sanctioned: "It has already been stated that these things [anti-Gentile legislation] were said concerning periods when there existed nations of idolaters, and they were contaminated in their deeds and tainted in their dispositions . . . but other 'nations that are restricted by the ways of religion,' which are free from such blemishes of character . . . are without doubt exempt from this prohibition [that is, from anti-Gentile legislation]." (Meiri commentary on *Avodah Zarah,* page 53.)

NOTES

CHAPTER 1. THE MAJOR PRINCIPLE OF THE TORAH

1. Rembert's study, published in the May 1983 issue of the *Journal of Moral Education,* is cited in Wattles, *Golden Rule,* 120. The statement from Wattles is on the same page.
2. Twerski and Schwartz, *Positive Parenting,* 171.
3. I have followed the translation of Siegel, *Family Reunion,* 33.
4. Unfortunately—at least from my perspective—Maimonides believed this commandment to be applicable only to fellow Jews and, on one occasion, seems to limit its applicability only to those Jews who are themselves religiously observant. Thus, in explicating love of neighbor, he writes: "Whatever you would like other people to do for you, you should do for your comrade in the Torah and commandments" (see "Laws of Mourning" 14:1). It is possible, however, that the words "your comrade in the Torah and commandments" is just a formulaic expression meaning "fellow Jews." Thus, the Talmud rules that the law of "Love your neighbor" applies even to a person who has committed a capital crime and imposes upon society the obligation to execute the prisoner in a quick manner (*Sanhedrin* 52a and *Ketubot* 37b; see page 397). On the basis of this ruling, the nineteenth-century talmudic commentator Maharam Shick concludes that if love of neighbor applies even to a wicked person deserving execution, then it obviously applies to all Jews, both observant and nonobservant. The one explicit exception in Maimonides is one who tries to seduce others to idolatry; Maimonides rules that it is forbidden to love such a person ("Laws of Idolatry" 5:4). Regarding Maimonides' restriction of love your neighbor to fellow Jews, some Jewish thinkers believed this to be the Torah's position, others didn't. For example, two of the great Torah commentators of the nineteenth century, Rabbi Jacob Zvi Mecklenburg (author of *Haketav Ve'Hakabbalah*) and Meir Loeb Malbim (referred to as "the Malbim"), both believed this verse to apply to Jew and non-Jew alike. In the words of the Malbim, the verse's meaning is, "Love every man as yourself," while Rabbi Mecklenburg, in commenting on this verse, writes that his neighbor *(re'ehu)* "is every human being." In any case, Leviticus 19:34, with its command "you shall love the stranger as yourself," means that the laws concerning love of neighbor apply to non-Jews who live among Jews in peace (see pages 267–268).
5. Siegel, *Family Reunion,* 34.

6. Cited in Leibowitz, *Studies in Vayikra (Leviticus),* 196.
7. Harvey, "Love," in Cohen and Mendes-Flohr, eds., *Contemporary Jewish Religious Thought,* 559.
8. Ibid.
9. Wattles, *Golden Rule,* 98–99. The citations are from Nash's book, *Golden Rule in Business.*
10. Leibowitz, *Studies in Vayikra (Leviticus),* 195.
11. Oz, *Tale of Love and Darkness,* 132–135.
12. Finkelman, *Rav Pam,* 145–146.

CHAPTER 2. HOW TO FULFILL THIS COMMANDMENT

1. Weiss, *Insights,* vol. 1, 48.
2. Cited in ibid., 48.
3. Dessler, *Strive for Truth* (a translation of the Hebrew *Michtav Me-Eliyahu*), vol. 1, 126–127.
4. Ibid., 130–131.
5. Carmell, *Masterplan: Judaism: Its Program, Meanings, Goals,* 118–119.
6. Pliskin, *Love Your Neighbor,* 302.
7. Ibid., 303.
8. See Rigler, *Lights from Jerusalem,* 49–50. In citing examples from Rigler's book, I have sometimes made minor alterations in how the characters phrased their compliments.
9. Mandelbaum, *Holy Brother,* 160–161.
10. These points were suggested to me by Dr. Isaac Herschkopf.
11. Cited in Pliskin, *Love Your Neighbor,* 304.
12. Nathan of Nemirov, *Rabbi Nachman's Teachings,* translated by Rabbi Aryeh Kaplan, 46 (based on *Sichos Ha-Ran* 43).
13. See Telushkin, *Biblical Literacy,* 209–212.
14. See Block and Drucker, *Rescuers,* 42–47.
15. Kushner, *Invisible Lines of Connection,* 81–82.
16. Shatz, "As Thyself," in Schachter, *Reverence, Righteousness, and Rahamanut,* 251–275.
17. Buber, *Tales of the Hasidim: Book Two, The Later Masters,* 86.
18. Twerski, *Do Unto Others,* 30.
19. Cited in Goffman, *Stigma,* 118.
20. Levine, *To Comfort the Bereaved,* 154.
21. Pliskin, *Love Your Neighbor,* 312.

CHAPTER 3. BEING A GOOD HOST

1. Pliskin, *Love Your Neighbor,* 69.
2. Artson, *It's a Mitzvah,* 201.
3. Wein, *Second Thoughts,* 25–26.
4. Israel, *Kosher Pig,* 61.
5. Bulka, *Turning Grief into Gratitude,* 124–125.
6. I believe I came across this directive in *Derech Eretz Rabbah* or *Derech Eretz Zuttah,* but I can't find the source for it.
7. Israel, *Kosher Pig,* 59.
8. Ibid., 61–62.

CHAPTER 4. THE DUTIES OF A GUEST

1. Goldberg, *Mussar Anthology,* 21; Telushkin, *Book of Jewish Values,* 228–229.
2. Cited in Bialik and Ravnitzky, *Book of Legends,* 681.

CHAPTER 5. PROVIDING MORE THAN JUST COMPANY

1. Although Maimonides' language suggests that he understands the commandment ordaining love of neighbor as applying only to fellow Jews, twice in his code he specifies that Jews should visit non-Jewish sick as well ("Laws of Mourning" 14:12; "Laws of Kings" 10:12).
2. Raz, *Tzaddik in Our Time,* 134–135.
3. Pliskin, *Love Your Neighbor,* 58.
4. Rosner, *Biomedical Ethics and Jewish Law,* 88.
5. Ibid., 55.
6. Schachter with Nestlebaum, *Loving Kindness: Daily Lessons in the Power of Giving,* 318, 319.
7. Ibid., 315.
8. Cited in Levine, *How to Perform the Great Mitzvah of Bikur Cholim,* 31–32; the statement came in personal correspondence from Rabbi Twerski to Rabbi Levine.
9. Twerski, *Do Unto Others,* 16–18.

CHAPTER 6. THREE OBLIGATIONS

1. See Abraham, *Nishmat Avraham,* Vol. 2, *Yoreh Deah,* 256–257.
2. Cited in Epstein, *Visiting the Sick,* 3.
3. Glatt, *Visiting the Sick,* 37.
4. Ibid., 37–38.
5. The Talmud teaches that on the Sabbath, the wording of the prayer recited in the presence of the patient should be altered: *"Shabbat he m'leez'ok ve're'fuah krovah la'voh"* ("The Sabbath prevents us from crying out for your recovery, but recovery will come soon"; *Shabbat* 12a).
6. See Artson's discussion of the mitzvah of visiting the sick in *It's a Mitzvah,* 62–73.
7. Schur, *Illness and Crisis,* 26.
8. Schachter, *Loving Kindness,* 314–315.
9. Ozarowski, "*Bikur Cholim:* A Paradigm for Pastoral Caring," in Friedman, *Jewish Pastoral Care,* 61.
10. See translation from *Orchot Chaim* in Abrahams, *Hebrew Ethical Wills,* 40.
11. Rabbi Mordechai Kamenetzky, "It's All About the *Choleh*" [the sick person], in Glatt, *Visiting the Sick,* 59.
12. Cited in Klagsbrun, *Voices of Wisdom,* 222.
13. Finkelman, *Reb Moshe,* 180.
14. Raz, *Tzaddik in Our Time,* 135.

CHAPTER 7. ETIQUETTE FOR VISITING THE SICK

1. Steinberg, *Encyclopedia of Jewish Medical Ethics,* vol. 3, 1121.
2. Artson, *It's a Mitzvah,* 67.
3. Ozarowski, "*Bikur Cholim:* A Paradigm for Pastoral Caring," in Friedman, *Jewish Pastoral Care,* 67
4. Teller, *And from Jerusalem, His Word,* 318–320.
5. See Wolfson, *Time to Mourn, a Time to Comfort,* 39.

6. Levine, *How to Perform the Great Mitzvah of Bikur Cholim,* 39.
7. Artson, *It's a Mitzvah,* 66.
8. Shofnos and Zwebner, *Healing Visit,* 71.
9. Kurzman, *Ben-Gurion,* 399–402.
10. I have followed the translation of Glatt, *Visiting the Sick,* 159.
11. Bleich, *Judaism and Healing,* 46.
12. See the discussion of Rabbi Feinstein's view on fulfilling the mitzvah of *bikur cholim* by telephone in Glatt, *Visiting the Sick,* 65, 67–68.
13. Bleich, *Judaism and Healing,* 27–33.
14. Teller, *Sunset,* 135.
15. Raz, *Tzaddik in Our Time,* 140–141.

CHAPTER 8. OBLIGATIONS TO THE DEAD

1. Greenberg, foreword to Berman, *Dignity Beyond Death,* 13.
2. Weiss, *Death and Bereavement,* 53.
3. Both Osgood's and Rabbi Lamm's statements are cited in Berman, *Dignity Beyond Death,* 150.
4. Singer, *In My Father's Court.* This episode appears in the chapter entitled "A Gruesome Question."
5. Epstein, *Tahara Manual of Practices,* 147.
6. Weiss, *Death and Bereavement,* 76.
7. Rabinowicz, *Guide to Life,* 15–19, has a helpful and surprisingly comprehensive—though brief—discussion of the Jewish attitude toward cremation.
8. Spitz, "Why Bury?" in Riemer, *Jewish Insights on Death and Mourning,* 125–126.
9. Tendler, *Responsa of Rav Moshe Feinstein,* 50.
10. Lamm, *Jewish Way in Death and Mourning,* 12.
11. Berman, *Dignity Beyond Death,* 31.
12. Ibid., 32.
13. Ibid., 141.
14. Ibid., 143.
15. Lamm, *Jewish Way of Death and Mourning,* 7.
16. I have based these observations concerning the *kittel* on an unpublished Yom Kippur sermon, "What the Best Dressed Jew Would Wear," which Rabbi Riemer sent me.
17. Roth, *Patrimony,* cited in Riemer, *Jewish Insights on Death and Mourning,* 127–128.
18. Berman, *Dignity Beyond Death,* 167–168.
19. Told in Eliach, *Hasidic Tales of the Holocaust,* 217–218.
20. Szold to Peretz, September 16, 1916, in Lowenthal, *Henrietta Szold,* 92–93.

CHAPTER 9. CARING FOR THE BEREAVED

1. Wolfson, *Time to Mourn, a Time to Comfort,* 206.
2. Jack Riemer, cited in ibid., 178.
3. Levine, *To Comfort the Bereaved,* 65.
4. Jack Riemer, cited in Wolfson, *Time to Mourn, a Time to Comfort,* 202.
5. Ibid.
6. Schochet and Spiro, *Saul Lieberman,* 234.
7. Wolfson, *Time to Mourn, a Time to Comfort,* 200.
8. Manning, *Don't Take My Grief Away,* 61–62.

9. Rabbi Harold Schulweis, cited in Wolfson, *Time to Mourn, a Time to Comfort,* 199.
10. Raz, *Tzaddik in Our Time,* 174.
11. Linzer, *Understanding Bereavement and Grief,* cited in Telushkin, *Jewish Wisdom,* (New York: Yeshiva University Press, 1977), 256.
12. Levine, *To Comfort the Bereaved,* 140.
13. Ibid.
14. Bulka, *Turning Grief into Gratitude,* 103.
15. Rabbi Ari Kahn, "The Rabbi and the Professor," distributed by aish.com.
16. Twerski, *Dear Rabbi, Dear Doctor,* 30–31.
17. Cited in Bulka, *Turning Grief into Gratitude,* 108.
18. The ArtScroll translation and commentary understands this talmudic passage as being more in the nature of a curse than of a psychological observation and renders it as follows: "Anyone who grieves over his dead to excess will ultimately weep for another dead." The commentary explains this teaching (in line with a statement of Rashi) as meaning that "whoever chooses to wallow in grief will be paid with further grief."
19. Teller, *And from Jerusalem, His Word,* 369.
20. Silverman and Cinnamon, *When Mourning Comes,* 18.
21. Zunin and Zunin, *Art of Condolence,* 176. The preceding statement from the widower is found on the same page.

CHAPTER 10. PRACTICING KINDNESS

1. See Raz, *Tzaddik in Our Time,* 199.
2. Kirchner's comment is cited in Vorspan and Saperstein, *Tough Choices,* 237.
3. Ehrman, *Journey to Virtue,* 8.
4. Doueck, *Hesed Boomerang,* 30–31, 116–117.

CHAPTER 11. GIVING ADVICE

1. Twerski, *Dear Rabbi, Dear Doctor,* 13–14.
2. See, for example, Russ, Webber, and Ledley, *Shalom Bayit.*
3. May, *Story File,* 98.
4. Nathan of Breslov, *Tzaddik,* 361.

CHAPTER 12. A PREEMINENT COMMAND

1. Sacks, *Dignity of Difference,* 113.
2. Dorff, *Way into Tikkun Olam (Repairing the World),* 107–108.
3. Holtz, *Finding Our Way,* 165.
4. Cited in Weiner, *9½ Mystics,* 239–240.
5. Neusner, *Tzedakah,* 2.
6. I have followed in the main, with some changes and shortening, the story as related in Bialik and Ravnitzky, *Book of Legends,* 678.
7. In addition, this verse helps explain why Jewish giving has historically focused more on the problem of the "individual poor rather than with trying to solve the problem of poverty" (Sherwin and Cohen, *How to Be a Jew,* 214). Elsewhere, Sherwin notes that "when discussing economic justice, many contemporary Christian ethicists call for the imminent realization of full employment and an end to poverty. Jewish ethicists perceive this view as a messianic hope rather than a realistic confrontation with the problems presently besetting us in our 'messy' [as opposed

to messianic] world. An example of the messianic approach characteristic of a great deal of Christian ethics is the 1986 'U.S. Catholic Bishops' Pastoral Letter on the Economy.' In that document, the eradication of poverty and the attainment of full employment are considered realizable goals, rather than desirable hopes. Nowhere does this document quote the biblical assumption that 'there will never cease to be needy ones in your land.' " (*Jewish Ethics for the Twenty-First Century,* 131).

8. Cited in Tamari, *Al Chet,* 43.
9. Cited in Telushkin, *Jewish Literacy,* 512–513.
10. Feuer, *Tzedakah Treasury,* 164.
11. Siegel, *Tzedakah,* 10.
12. Hugh Nissenson, "Charity," in *In the Reign of Peace,* 51–63.
13. Birnbaum, *Encyclopedia of Jewish Concepts,* 522.
14. Cited in Feuer, *Tzedakah Treasury,* 80.
15. Sherwin, *Jewish Ethics for the Twenty-First Century,* 150.
16. Twerski, *Do Unto Others,* 26–27.

CHAPTER 13. HOW AND WHEN TO GIVE

1. Siegel, *Gym Shoes and Irises,* 118.
2. Siegel, *Tzedakah,* 9.
3. Twerski, *Lights Along the Way,* 189.
4. Sherwin, *In Partnership with God,* 107.
5. See *Dynamics of Tzedakah,* 26.
6. Sherwin, *Jewish Ethics for the Twenty-First Century,* 146.
7. Hartman and Marx, "Charity," in Cohen and Mendes-Flohr, eds., *Contemporary Jewish Religious Thought,* 48.
8. Feuer, *Tzedakah Treasury,* 145.
9. Raz, *Tzaddik in Our Time,* 319; see also 317–318.
10. Feuer, *Tzedekah Treasury,* 173.
11. Canfield, Hansen, and Elkins, *Chicken Soup for the Jewish Soul,* 29–33.
12. Schwartz, *Judaism and Global Survival,* 75.
13. Berman, "Poverty," in Linzer, *Judaism and Mental Health,* 68.
14. See Domb, *Ma'aser Kesafim,* Hebrew section of book, 25.
15. Haley, "Man on the Train," in Covey and Hatch, *Everyday Greatness,* 25–28.
16. Schochet and Spiro, *Saul Lieberman,* 184.
17. Abrahams, *Jewish Life in the Middle Ages,* 325ff.
18. Feuer, *Tzedakah Treasury,* 36–37.

CHAPTER 14. PRIORITIES IN GIVING

1. See the discussion of this point in Domb, *Ma'aser Kesafim,* 100.
2. See Pliskin, *Growth Through Torah,* 410–411.
3. Gold, *God, Love, Sex, and Family,* 54–56.
4. Krohn, *Around the Maggid's Table,* 92.
5. Ibid., p. 111.
6. Goldstein, *Priorities in Tzedaka,* 67.
7. Cited in Finkelman, *Reb Moshe,* 175.
8. Cited in Feuer, *Tzedakah Treasury,* 390–391.

CHAPTER 15. HOW MUCH SHOULD WE GIVE?

1. There is one earlier mention of tithing in the Bible, although it is not related to charity. When Abraham learned that his nephew Lot had been taken captive, he went out with the more than three hundred members of his staff to rescue Lot and his property. After Abraham's victory, the local monarchs and the priest Melchizedek greeted and blessed him for the assistance he provided, and Abraham, in turn, gave Melchizedek a tenth of everything he had captured (Genesis 14:20).
2. I have generally followed the translation of Neusner, *Tzedakah,* 104–105.
3. Retold by Rabbi Tuvia Bolton, "The Rusty Penny." See chabad.org.
4. Feuer, *Tzedakah Treasury,* 122, 435.
5. Jonas, *I'm Not the Boss, I Just Work Here,* 32–40.
6. Singer, "The Singer Solution to World Poverty," *The New York Times Magazine,* September 5, 1999.

CHAPTER 16. CHARITABLE PRACTICES AND CUSTOMS

1. Feuer, *Tzedakah Treasury,* 189–190.
2. See the discussion of these two groups in Bush and Dekro, *Jews, Money and Social Responsibility,* 140.
3. Twerski, *Do Unto Others,* 37–39.

CHAPTER 17. SOLICITING AND MOTIVATING OTHERS TO GIVE

1. Weiss, *Vintage Wein,* 94–95.
2. Wein, *Tending the Vineyard,* 106.
3. Pogrebin, "Women and Philanthropy," in Bush and Dekro, *Jews, Money and Social Responsibility,* 172.
4. Teller, *Sunset,* 273.
5. Cited in Krohn, *Around the Maggid's Table,* 170–171.
6. Twerski, *Simcha,* 193–194.
7. Ibid., 194.
8. See ArtScroll commentary on *Bava Bathra* 8b, note 21.
9. *Jewish Observer,* March 1999, cited in Feuer, *Tzedakah Treasury,* 360–361.
10. Told in Sherwin, *In Partnership with God,* 111.
11. Raz, *Tzaddik in Our Time,* 110.
12. I'm indebted to Rabbi Harold Kushner for this reference.

CHAPTER 18. ON GIVING TO BEGGARS AND OTHER POOR PEOPLE

1. Cited in Goldstein, *Defending the Human Spirit,* 339.
2. Cited in Robert Teir, "Maintaining Safety and Civility in Public Spaces: A Constitutional Approach to Aggressive Begging." *Louisiana Law Review* 54 (1993): 295.
3. See Olwen Hufton, *The Poor of Eighteenth-Century France: 1750–1789* (Oxford: Oxford University Press, 1974), 225–226, cited in Goldstein, *Defending the Human Spirit,* 341.
4. See Anderson, *Hitler's Exiles,* 5–6.
5. Feuer, *Tzedakah Treasury,* 371.
6. Ibid.
7. Mandelbaum, *Holy Brother,* 83–84.

8. Finkelman, *Reb Moshe,* 176.
9. Salamon, *Rambam's Ladder,* 14.
10. Boteach, *10 Conversations You Need to Have with Your Children,* 90–93.
11. Goldberger, *Priorities in Tzedaka,* 47.
12. Goldstein, *Defending the Human Spirit,* 370.
13. Tamari, *With All Your Possessions,* 256.

CHAPTER 20. REDEEMING CAPTIVES

1. Weiss, *Vintage Wein,* 213–216.
2. See *Encyclopaedia Judaica,* vol. 11, 1251–1252.
3. Jacobs, *What Does Judaism Say About?,* 167. The Talmud (*Gittin* 45a) also raises the problem that payment of extravagant ransoms will be overly burdensome to the community.
4. Dr. Baruch Brody, "Jewish Reflections on Life and Death Decision Making," in Pellegrino and Faden, *Jewish and Catholic Bioethics,* 22.
5. Levi, *Facing Current Challenges,* 340.
6. For a further discussion of Rabbi Halevy's ruling, see Angel and Angel, *Rabbi Haim David Halevy,* 109–111.

CHAPTER 21. BETWEEN JEWS AND NON-JEWS

1. Rabbi Saul Berman offers an alternative rendering of this Mishnaic teaching; instead of translating the text as speaking of the creation of "one person," one should speak of "one couple," Adam and Eve. If they had been destroyed, all of humanity would likewise have been destroyed. While I am not convinced that Rabbi Berman's rendering is literally what the Mishnah meant, his point is well taken. Only a couple, and not a single individual, have the capacity to reproduce and to keep the world inhabited.
2. Ernst Simon, "The Neighbor Whom We Shall Love," in Fox, *Modern Jewish Ethics,* 33.
3. I have followed, with slight variations, the translation of Sears, *Compassion for Humanity in the Jewish Tradition,* 48.
4. Lichtenstein, "A Consideration of Synthesis from a Torah Point of View," *Gesher* 1 (1963; 10–11; cited in Schachter, *Judaism's Encounter with Other Cultures,* xv–xvi.
5. Katz, *Exclusiveness and Tolerance,* 124, citing the *Chibbur Ha-Teshuva,* 2.
6. I have followed the translation of Greenberg, *Studies in the Bible and Jewish Thought,* 386–387.
7. Baron, *Social and Religious History of the Jews,* vol. 3, 124.
8. Goitein, *Jews and Arabs,* 80.
9. Cited in Shapiro, *Between the Yeshiva World and Modern Orthodoxy,* 182–183 ft. 47. Shapiro cites a recollection of Professor Gerald Blidstein, a student of Rabbi Soloveitchik, in which he asked the Rav (as he was known to his students) about how he ruled in instances in which saving a non-Jew's life would entail violating the Sabbath. Rabbi Soloveitchik answered: "I have been in Boston many years and I always rule that one saves the lives of Gentiles because if we don't permit this, they won't treat our sick ones." Dr. Blidstein then asked the Rav if this purely pragmatic reason satisfied him from a moral standpoint, and Rabbi Soloveitchik answered: "No, from a moral standpoint it does not satisfy me."

10. But not always. See, for example, a virulently anti-Gentile ruling in "Laws of Forbidden Sexual Relations" 12:10, a ruling that seems to have been innovative with Maimonides.
11. From Rabbi Weinberg's letter to his friend Professor Samuel Atlas, translated and quoted in Shapiro, "Scholars and Friends," in *Torah U-Madda Journal,* vol. 7, 112.
12. Berger, "Jews, Gentiles, and the Modern Egalitarian Ethos," in Stern, *Formulating Responses in an Egalitarian Age,* 89.

CHAPTER 22. TWENTY-FIVE TEACHINGS, LAWS, AND PRINCIPLES

1. Greenberg, "Leon Trotsky," in *Inner Eye,* vol. 2, 238.
2. See Pliskin, *Love Your Neighbor,* 423.
3. Cited in Sears, *Compassion for Humanity in the Jewish Tradition,* 2.
4. Cited in Greenberg, *Studies in the Bible and Jewish Thought,* 388.
5. Mandelbaum, *Holy Brother,* 27–28.
6. Schwarz, *Eyes to See,* 253.
7. Cited in Sears, *Compassion for Humanity in the Jewish Tradition,* 96–97.

CHAPTER 23. DOMINION AND COMPASSION

1. Hertz, *Pentateuch and Haftorahs,* 854.
2. Schochet, *Animal Life in Jewish Tradition,* 315 ft. 112.
3. Scully, *Dominion,* 8.
4. I have followed the translation of Finkel, *Sefer Chasidim,* 274.
5. Ackerman, *Natural History of the Senses,* 147.
6. The Primatt quote is cited in Schochet, *Animal Life in Jewish Tradition,* 59.
7. Scully, *Dominion,* 10.
8. Ibid., 134.
9. Ibid., 12.
10. I have relied mainly, but not exclusively, on Finkel's translation of large portions of *Sefer Chasidim,* 271.
11. Slifkin, *Man and Beast,* 110.
12. Cited in Sears, *Vision of Eden,* 223–224.
13. Singer and Mason, *Ethics of What We Eat,* 58–59.
14. Artson, *It's a Mitzvah,* 213–214.
15. Rabbi Pamela Barmash, unpublished 2007 responsa on "Veal Calves" for the Rabbinical Assembly Committee on Jewish Law and Standards.
16. See the discussion of Rabbi Feinstein's responsa in Schwartz and Flug, "Veal: The Other White Meat?" in *Journal of Halacha and Contemporary Society* (Spring 2003): 8.
17. Ziegelman and Coe, "A Goose for all Seasons," *Moment,* June 2001.
18. Carmell, *Masterplan,* 69.
19. Singer and Mason, *Ethics of What We Eat,* 23, 24.
20. Scully, *Dominion,* xii.
21. Amsel, *Jewish Encyclopedia of Moral and Ethical Issues,* 11.
22. Artson, *It's a Mitzvah,* 204–205.
23. Scully, *Dominion,* 109.
24. I say that the words are attributed to Margaret Mead because Keyes, *Quote Verifier* (85), notes that no one has actually been able to find these words in her writings,

or in citations from her speeches; yet, in many collections of quotations, she is cited as the author of these words.

25. Slifkin, *Man and Beast,* 150.
26. Kaufmann, *Faith of a Heretic,* 193, 260–261.
27. Prager, *Think a Second Time,* 77–78.

CHAPTER 24. VEGETARIANISM, ANIMAL RESEARCH AND EXPERIMENTS, AND HUNTING

1. Milgrom, "The Biblical Diet Laws as an Ethical System," *Interpretation,* July 1963.
2. A description of support for vegetarianism among some traditional Bible commentators is found in Yael Shemesh, "Vegetarian Ideology in Talmudic Literature and Traditional Biblical Exegesis," *Journal of the Review of Rabbinic Judaism* 9 (2006): 141–166. Several of the citations in this section derive from sources culled by Professor Shemesh, who is both a religiously observant Jew and a longtime vegan. Though Shemesh finds several statements of support for vegetarianism in medieval Jewish Bible commentators, the article starts with the statement: "Let me make it plain at the outset that Judaism is not a vegetarian religion" (141).
3. Rabbi A. I. Kook, *The Vision of Vegetarianism and Peace from a Torah Perspective* (Hebrew), collected and edited by Rabbi Kook's famous disciple, Rabbi David Cohen, (also known as "the Nazir"), 8.
4. In a meeting with the Lubavitcher Rebbe, Rabbi She'ar Yashuv Cohen informed the Rebbe that he had never eaten meat in his life; see Sears, *Vision of Eden,* 177.
5. Steinberg, *Encyclopedia of Jewish Medical Ethics,* vol. 1, 259–260.
6. Ibid., 258–272.
7. See translation in Freehof, *Treasury of Responsa,* 216–219.
8. Douglas, *Climbing the Mountain,* 57–58.
9. Scully, *Dominion,* 103.
10. Kaidanover, *Kav HaYashar,* cited in Slifkin, *Man and Beast,* 183.

CHAPTER 25. THE LAWS OF SELF-DEFENSE

1. Amsel, *Jewish Encyclopedia of Morals and Ethics,* 254–255; based on Maimonides, "Laws Concerning Murder" 1:7.
2. See Goren, *Meshiv Milchamah* 1:14, cited in Zemer, *Evolving Halakhah,* 221.
3. Dershowitz, "Arithmetic of Pain," *Wall Street Journal,* July 19, 2006.

CHAPTER 26. WHEN SOMEONE ELSE'S LIFE IS AT RISK

1. See Sachar, *History of Israel,* vol. II, *From the Aftermath of the Yom Kippur War,* 46–47.
2. Spero, "Halakhic Definitions of Confidentiality in the Psychotherapeutic Encounter: Theory and Practice," *Tradition,* Winter 1982, 308.
3. Feinstein, *Igrot Moshe, Yoreh Deah,* vol. 2, responsa 174.
4. See Uri Dan and Andy Soltis, "A Lifesaver in Death," *New York Post,* October 21, 2002.
5. Kirschenbaum, "The Bystander's Duty to Rescue," in Golding, ed., *Jewish Law and Legal Theory,* 521.
6. Jacobs, letter in the *Jewish Chronicle* 12/1/61, 24.
7. Kirschenbaum, "The Bystander's Duty to Rescue," in Golding, *Jewish Law and Legal Theory,* 532 ft. 11.

8. See Rabbi Ovadiah Yosef, "A Responsa Permitting Kidney Transplants" (Hebrew), *Dinei Yisrael* 7: 25–43.
9. Steinberg, *Encyclopedia of Medical Ethics,* vol. 3, 1095.

CHAPTER 27. WHEN OBSERVING JEWISH LAW THREATENS LIFE

1. Soloveitchik, *Halakhic Man,* 34.
2. Rosenblum, *Reb Yaakov,* 104.
3. Raz, *Angel Among Men,* 450.
4. Jacobs, *Religion and the Individual,* 16.
5. Weiss, *Insights,* vol. 2, 33–34.
6. See the discussion of this incident in Etkes, *Rabbi Israel Salanter and the Mussar Movement,* 170–172.
7. Raz, *Angel Among Men,* 442–443.
8. Pliskin, *Love Your Neighbor,* 49, citing Rabbi Shlomo Yosef Zevin, *Ishim ve-Shitot,* 65.

CHAPTER 28. WHEN ILLNESS AND PAIN MAKE LIFE INTOLERABLE

1. Rosner, *Biomedical Ethics and Jewish Law,* 229.
2. Kravitz, "Some Reflections on Jewish Tradition and the End-of-Life Patient," in Hurwitz, Picard, Steinberg, and Sklarz, *Jewish Ethics and the Care of End-of-Life Patients,* 81–82.
3. See Tendler and Rosner, "Quality and Sanctity of Life in the Talmud and Midrash," in Tendler, *Responsa of Rav Moshe Feinstein,* vol. 1, *Care of the Critically Ill,* 142.
4. See the discussion of this point in Tendler, "Pain: Halakha and Hashkafah," in Carmy, *Jewish Perspectives on Suffering,* 76.
5. Rosner, "Quality and Sanctity of Life," in *Biomedical Ethics and Jewish Law,* 230.
6. Kravitz, "Some Reflections on Jewish Tradition and the End-of-Life Patient," 123.
7. Tendler, *op. cit.,* 75–76.
8. *The Random House College Dictionary, Revised Edition* (1988), 456.
9. Jakobovits, *Jewish Medical Ethics,* 123.
10. See, for example, Bleich, "Treatment of the Terminally Ill," in Hurwitz, Picard, Steinberg, and Sklarz, *Jewish Ethics and the Care of End-of-Life Patients,* 59.
11. Golinkin, *Responsa of Rabbi Louis Ginzberg,* 172–174. Ginzberg's responsa to a question posed by a Dr. Sol Ginsburg is dated January 8, 1936.
12. Bettan, "Euthanasia," in Walter Jacob, ed., *American Reform Responsa* (New York, CCAR, 1999), 263.
13. Tendler and Rosner, "Quality and Sanctity of Life in the Talmud and Midrash," in Tendler, *Responsa of Rav Moshe Feinstein,* vol. 1, *Care of the Critically Ill,* 146.
14. Ibid., 57.
15. Ibid., 40. The book contains translations of the most important rulings of Rabbi Feinstein on this subject.
16. Private communication from Dr. Prager in response to a draft of this chapter that I sent him.
17. See Rosner's discussion of Rabbi Feinstein's ruling in Rosner, *Biomedical Ethics and Jewish Law,* 226.
18. Ibid., 227.

19. Bleich, "Treatment of the Terminally Ill," in Hurwitz, Picard, Steinberg and Sklarz, *Jewish Ethics and the Care of End-of-Life Patients,* 66.
20. The citation is from Buckley's nationally syndicated column of June 24, 2000.
21. Kravitz, "Some Reflections on Jewish Tradition and the End-of-Life Patient," 86.
22. Ibid., 78.

CHAPTER 29. "JUSTICE, JUSTICE, YOU SHALL PURSUE"

1. The Dershowitz quote is an extract from a speech he gave at Harvard University at a Day of Dedication and Celebration of Jewish Life at Harvard, April 6, 2003.
2. See Buber, *Ten Rungs: Hasidic Sayings,* 7.
3. Cited in Conquest, *Harvest of Sorrow,* 233.
4. Kaufmann, *Faith of a Heretic,* 179–182.
5. See the discussion of this point in the ArtScroll commentary on *Shevuot* 31a note 4.
6. Broyde, *Pursuit of Justice and Jewish Law,* 74.
7. Freedman, *Lawyers' Ethics in an Adversary System,* viii, cited in Tannen, *Argument Culture* (Indianapolis, In: Bobbs-Merrill, 1975), 302 ft. 137.
8. Wishman, *Confessions of a Criminal Lawyer.* The cross-examination of the complainant in the rape case and Wishman's pangs of guilt over his courtroom behavior are found on 3–18.
9. Ibid., 151.
10. Tannen, *Argument Culture,* 143.
11. Fadiman and Bernard, *Bartlett's Book of Anecdotes,* 329.
12. Friedmann, *To Kill and Take Possession,* 132.
13. *Sanhedrin* 109b; see also Bialik and Ravnitzky, *Book of Legends,* 36.
14. See Rothschild and Finkelman, *Chofetz Chaim: Daily Companion,* 134–135.
15. Quoted in Segev, *1967: Israel, the War, and the Year that Transformed the Middle East,* 391.
16. Jacobs, *Tree of Life,* 183.
17. Rabbi Aaron ha-Levi of Barcelona, *The Book of [Mitzvah] Education,* vol. 2, trans. Charles Wengrov, 27.
18. *New York Times* editorial, December 10, 2005, cited in Tavris and Aronson, *Mistakes Were Made (but Not by Me),* 273 ft. 17.
19. Bullock, *Hitler and Stalin,* 501.
20. Tavris and Aronson, *Mistakes Were Made (but Not by Me),* 133–135, 147.
21. Ibid., 141.
22. Lamm, "Self-Incrimination in Law and Psychology," in Lamm, *Faith and Doubt,* 282.

CHAPTER 30. THE RIGHT OF OTHERS TO THINK DIFFERENTLY

1. See Kimelman, "Judaism and Pluralism," *Modern Judaism,* May 1987, 147.
2. Pelcovitz, *Keeping Faith in the Face of Terror,* 2.
3. See Rabbi Aryeh Kaplan's discussion of this point in Cope-Yossef, "Reflections on a Living Torah: Rabbi Aryeh Kaplan," in Elper and Handelman, *Torah of the Mothers,* 44–45.
4. This is despite the fact that one talmudic passage (*Yevamot* 14a) claims that Shammai's followers had greater analytic abilities than did Hillel's disciples.
5. Sacks, *Dignity of Difference,* 53.
6. Ibid., 55, 56.

7. Cited in ibid., 63. This 1981 text is not found in Berlin's essays, but in notes he had prepared for a friend who had solicited his help in preparing a lecture. Berlin was to go abroad the following day, and these hurried notes, Sacks explains, "convey as well as anything he wrote his lifelong opposition to intolerance and what he believed to be its source."
8. According to antisemites, the document proving this conspiracy is *The Protocols of the Elders of Zion,* a late-nineteenth-century forgery by the Russian secret police. *The Protocols* were translated by Henry Ford's *Dearborn Independent* in the early 1920s (additional, false material was added), and the Nazis distributed millions of copies during the 1930s. As of the early twenty-first century, the *Protocols* remain a perennial bestseller in the Arab world.
9. Twerski, *Generation to Generation,* 92.
10. Magonet, *Returning,* 28.
11. The man who made this announcement might have been relying in part on a decision of Rabbi Moshe Feinstein, who ruled that non-Orthodox rabbis attending a service at an Orthodox synagogue should not be given *aliyot,* called to the Torah. In Rabbi Feinstein's view, since these rabbis do not accept the traditional understanding of divine revelation (precisely that which is asserted in the blessing recited when one is called to the Torah) the blessing for them is a mere verbal formula and it is forbidden to answer "Amen" (*Igrot Moshe, Orach Chayyim,* vol. 3, 21).
12. See the discussion of the Gaon's animus to the Chasidim in Schochet, *Hasidic Movement and the Gaon of Vilna,* 8–10.
13. Ravitzky, "The Question of Tolerance in the Jewish Tradition," in Yaakov Elman and Jeffrey Gurock, *Hazon Nahun,* 359.
14. Kimelman notes that the intellectual flaw in concluding that your view is absolutely right is that it "seeks to absolutize a particular configuration of the tradition into universal validity" ("Judaism and Pluralism," *Modern Judaism,* May 1987, 32, 35).
15. Kushner, *Lord Is My Shepherd,* 83.

BIBLIOGRAPHY

A NOTE ON CITATIONS FROM JUDAISM'S CLASSIC TEXTS

When citing statements from the Hebrew Bible, the *Tanakh,* I have generally relied upon the translation of the Jewish Publication Society (Philadelphia, 1985), a scholarly yet highly readable rendering of the Bible into contemporary English. On occasion, however, I have translated the verses myself, or used other translations that seemed to me preferable for a specific verse.

There are three English translations of the Mishnah, and the one on which I have relied most is Jacob Neusner's *The Mishnah* (New Haven, Conn.: Yale University Press, 1988). There is an older and still valuable translation of the Mishnah by Herbert Danby (Oxford: Clarendon Press, 1933). In addition, I have also frequently consulted Pinchas Kehati's excellent Hebrew commentary on the entire Mishnah, *Mishnayot Mevuarot* (Jerusalem: Heichal Shlomo, 1977), which has been translated into English as well (Jerusalem: Department for Torah Education and Culture in the Diaspora of the World Zionist Organization, 1988).

In quoting from the Talmud, I have for the most part relied on the ArtScroll translation, one of the great works of modern Jewish literature. ArtScroll, which is based in Brooklyn, New York, has in recent years completed a translation into English of the entire Babylonian Talmud,* along with extensive explanatory notes. The ArtScroll edition is a line-by-line translation, and anyone who has Hebrew skills can utilize this translation to learn the Talmud's basic vocabulary and methodology. I have also consulted the highly accurate and literal translation of the Soncino Press (London, 1935), and the extraordinary Hebrew translation and commentary of Rabbi

*When people speak of studying the Talmud, they almost always mean the Babylonian Talmud, and not the shorter and earlier Jerusalem Talmud. In any case, ArtScroll has now started publishing a translation and commentary on the Jerusalem Talmud as well.

Adin Steinsaltz on almost all of the Talmud. In addition, Random House has brought out many volumes of Steinsaltz's Talmud into English, in a very readable translation (under titles such as *The Talmud, The Steinsaltz Edition, Volume 1: Bava Mezia Part I*). Although I have repeatedly consulted these works, I have also translated many of the cited texts myself.

Yale University Press has published Judah Goldin's translation of *The Fathers According to Rabbi Nathan* (1955).

The citations from the Midrash *Rabbah* have primarily followed the Soncino translation (London, 1983: ten volumes), although I have checked all translations against the original and have often made some alterations. The *Mekhilta* has been translated and published in three volumes by the Jewish Publication Society (Philadelphia, 1933).

Yale University Press has published a multivolume translation of Moses Maimonides' *Mishneh Torah* under the title *The Code of Maimonides.* In recent years, Rabbi Eliyahu Touger has been bringing out a very readable translation of Maimonides' *Mishneh Torah,* with the Hebrew and English on facing pages (the set is not yet complete). In addition, Rabbi Touger provides extensive notes on Maimonides' text and also cites the talmudic and other sources for Maimonides' rulings (the work is published by the New York–based Moznaim Publishing Corporation). I have also relied on the Hebrew language edition of the *Mishneh Torah* by the Mossad HaRov Kook publishing house (Jerusalem), which contains the wide-ranging commentary of Rabbi Shmuel Tanchum Rubenstein.

The sixteenth-century code of Jewish law, Rabbi Joseph Karo's *Shulchan Arukh,* has, with the exception of a few small sections and the first volume *(Orach Chayyim),* not been translated into English. The *Mishnah Berurah,* the Chaffetz Chayyim's comprehensive work on the laws of *Orach Chayyim,* the first volume of the *Shulchan Arukh,* has in recent years appeared in a multi-volume English translation, which also contains a translation of the *Orach Chayyim*'s text (Feldheim).

The other Hebrew works that are cited are listed, along with the other books I consulted, in the following bibliography.

Aaron, David. *Living a Joyous Life: The True Spirit of Jewish Practice.* Boston: Trumpeter, 2007.

Aaron Ha-Levi of Barcelona, Rabbi. *Sefer ha-Hinnuch (The Book of [Mitzvah] Education).* Translated and annotated by Charles Wengrov. 5 vols. Nanuet, N.Y.: Feldheim, 1984.

Abraham, Abraham, S.M.D. *Nishmat Avraham: Medical Halachah for Doctors, Nurses, Health-Care Personnel and Patients.* vol. 2. *Yoreh Deah.* Brooklyn: ArtScroll/Mesorah, 2003.

Abraham, Israel. ed. *Hebrew Ethical Wills.* Philadelphia: Jewish Publication Society, 2006.

Abrahams, Israel, *Jewish Life in the Middle Ages.* New York: Atheneum, 1969.

Abramowitz, Leah. *Tales of Nehama: Impressions of the Life and Teaching of Nehama Leibowitz.* Jerusalem: Gefen Books, 2003.

Ackerman, Diane. *A Natural History of the Senses.* New York: Random House, 1991.

Amsel, Nachum. *The Jewish Encyclopedia of Moral and Ethical Issues.* Northvale, N.J.: Aronson, 1994.

Anderson, Mark, ed., *Hitler's Exiles: Personal Stories of the Flight from Nazi Germany to America.* New York: New Press, 2000.

Angel, Marc, and Hayyim Angel. *Rabbi Haim David Halevy: Gentle Scholar and Courageous Thinker.* Jerusalem: Urim Publications, 2006.

Anonymous. *Orchot Tzaddikim (The Ways of the Tzaddikim).* Translated by Rabbi Shraga Silverstein. Nanuet, N.Y.: Feldheim, 1995.

Ariel, Yaakov Aryeh, and Libby Lazewnik. *Voice of Truth: The Life and Eloquence of Rabbi Sholom Schwadron, the Unforgettable Maggid of Jerusalem.* Brooklyn: Mesorah, 2000.

Artson, Rabbi Bradley Sharvit. *It's a Mitzvah: Step-by-Step to Jewish Living.* West Orange, N.J.: Behrman House, 1995.

Auchincloss, Louis. *The Rector of Justin.* Boston: Houghton Mifflin, 1964.

Bachya ibn Paquda. *Duties of the Heart (Torat Chovot HaLevavot).* Translated by Daniel Haberman. 2 vols. Nanuet, N.Y.: Feldheim, 1996.

Baron, Salo. *A Social and Religious History of the Jews,* vol. III. Philadelphia: Jewish Publication Society, 1957.

Bellow, Saul. *Seize the Day.* New York: Penguin Classics, 2003.

Berger, David. "Jews, Gentiles, and the Modern Egalitarian Ethos: Some Tentative Thoughts," in *Formulating Responses in an Egalitarian Age,* Marc Stern, ed., 83–108. New York: Rowman and Littlefield, 2005.

Berkovits, Eliezer. *Faith After the Holocaust.* New York: Ktav, 1973.

Berman, Rochel. *Dignity Beyond Death: The Jewish Preparation for Burial.* Jerusalem: Urim, 2005.

Bialik, Hayim Nahman, and Yehoshua Hana Ravnitzky. *The Book of Legends: Legends from the Talmud and Midrash.* Translated from the Hebrew *Sefer Ha-Aggadah* by William Braude. New York: Schocken Books, 1992.

Bierman, Michael, ed. *Memories of a Giant: Eulogies in Memory of Rabbi Joseph B. Soloveitchik.* Jerusalem: Urim, 2003.

Birnbaum, Philip. *Encyclopedia of Jewish Concepts.* New York: Hebrew Publishing, 1979.

Bleich, Rabbi J. David. *Contemporary Halakhic Problems,* vol. 3. New York: Ktav/Yeshiva University Press, 1989.

———. *Judaism and Healing: Halakhic Perspectives.* New York: Ktav, 1981.

Bloch, Abraham. *A Book of Jewish Ethical Concepts: Biblical and Postbiblical.* New York: Ktav Publishing House, 1984.

Block, Gay, and Malka Drucker. *Rescuers: Portraits of Moral Courage During the Holocaust.* New York: Holmes and Meier, 1992.

Bokser, Ben Zion. *Jews, Judaism, and the State of Israel.* New York: Herzl Press, 1973.

Boteach, Shmuley. *10 Conversations You Need to Have with Your Children.* New York: Regan Books/HarperCollins, 2006.

Broyde, Rabbi Michael J. "The Practice of Law According to the Halacha." *Journal of Halacha and Contemporary Society* 20 (Fall 1990): 5–45; in particular, pages 21–22.

———. *The Pursuit of Justice and Jewish Law.* New York: Yeshiva University Press, 1996.

Buber, Martin. *Tales of the Hasidim,* Book One: *The Early Masters,* and Book Two: *The Later Masters.* New York: Schocken, 1975.

———. *Ten Rungs: Hasidic Sayings.* New York: Schocken, 1973.

Bulka, Rabbi Reuven. *Best Kept Secrets of Judaism.* Nanuet, N.Y.: Feldheim, 2002.

———. *Turning Grief into Gratitude.* Ottawa: Paper Spider, 2007.

Bullock, Alan. *Hitler and Stalin: Parallel Lives.* New York: Alfred A. Knopf, 1993.

Bunim, Irving. *Ethics from Sinai: An Eclectic, Wide-Ranging Commentary on Pirke Aboth.* 3 vols. New York: Feldheim, 1966.

Bush, Lawrence, and Jeffrey Dekro. *Jews, Money and Social Responsibility: Developing a "Torah of Money" for the Contemporary Life.* Philadelphia: Shefa Fund, 1993.

Canfield, Jack, Mark Victor Hansen, and Rabbi Dov Peretz Elkins. *Chicken Soup for the Jewish Soul.* Deerfield Beach, Fla.: Health Communications, 2001.

Carmell, Aryeh. *Masterplan: Judaism: Its Program, Meanings, Goals.* Nanuet, N.Y.: Feldheim, 1991.

Carmy, Shalom, ed. *Jewish Perspectives on the Experience of Suffering.* Northvale, N.J.: Jason Aronson, 1999.

Chaffetz Chayyim. *Ahavat Chesed: The Love of Kindness as Required by God.* Spring Valley, N.Y.: Feldheim, 1967.

———. *Choffetz Chayyim: A Daily Companion,* arranged for daily study by Rabbi Yehudah Zev Segal. Brooklyn: ArtScroll/Mesorah, 1999.

———. *Choffetz Chayyim: A Lesson a Day: The Concepts and Laws of Proper Speech Arranged for Daily Study.* Compiled by Rabbi Shimon Finkelman and Rabbi Yitzchak Berkowitz. Brooklyn: ArtScroll/Mesorah, 1995.

———. *Lessons in Truth: Daily Studies in Honesty and Fundamentals of Jewish Faith.* Translation and commentary by Rabbi Shimon Finkelman. Brooklyn: ArtScroll/Mesorah, 2001.

———. *Middos: The Measure of Man* (Compiled anonymously, this book is an anthology of the Choffetz Chayyim's philosophical and ethical insights, translated by Raphael Blumberg). Jerusalem: n.p., 1987.

———. *Sefer Chaffetz Chayyim* (Hebrew). Jerusalem: Mercaz Hasefer, 1998.

Chaim Volozhiner. *Ruach Chaim: Rav Chaim Volozhiner's Classic Commentary on Pirkei Avos.* Translated by Chanoch Levi. Southfield, Mich., and Nanuet, N.Y.: Targum Press and Feldheim, 2002.

Cohen, Rabbi Alfred. "Vegetarianism from a Jewish Perspective." *Journal of Halacha and Contemporary Society* 1, no. 2 (Fall 1981).

Cohen, Arthur, and Paul Mendes-Flohr, eds. *Contemporary Jewish Religious Thought.* New York: Free Press, 1988.

Complete ArtScroll Siddur. Translated with commentary by Rabbi Nosson Scherman. Brooklyn: ArtScroll/Mesorah, 1984.

Conquest, Robert. *The Harvest of Sorrow: Soviet Collectivization and the Terror-Famine.* New York: Oxford University Press, 1987.

Cordovero, Rabbi Moshe. *The Palm Tree of Devorah.* Southfield, Mich.: Targum Press, 1994.

Dessler, Eliyahu. *Strive for Truth.* Nanuet, New York: Feldheim, 2004.

Douglas, Kirk. *Climbing the Mountain.* New York: Simon & Schuster, 1997.

Domb, Cyril, ed. *Ma'aser Kesafim: Giving a Tenth to Charity.* New York: Feldheim, 1980.

Dorff, Elliot. *The Way into Tikkun Olam (Repairing the World).* Woodstock, Vt.: Jewish Lights, 2005.

Dostoevsky, Fyodor. *The Brothers Karamazov.* New York: Farrar, Straus and Giroux, 2002.

Doueck, Jack. *The Hesed Boomerang: How Acts of Kindness Can Enrich Our Lives.* Deal, N.J.: Yagdiyl Torah Publications, 1998.

Ehrman, Rabbi Avrohom. *Journey to Virtue: The Laws of Interpersonal Relationships in Business, Home, and Society.* Brooklyn: ArtScroll/Mesorah, 2002.

Eleff, Zev, ed. *Mentor of Generations: Reflections of Rabbi Joseph B. Soloveitchik.* Hoboken, N.J.: Ktav, 2008.

Eliach, Yaffa. *Hasidic Tales of the Holocaust.* New York: Oxford University Press, 1982.

Elman, Yaakov, and Jeffrey Gurock. *Hazon Nahum: Studies in Jewish Law, Thought, and History Presented to Dr. Norman Lamm on the Occasion of his Seventieth Birthday.* New York: Yeshiva University Press, 1997.

Elper, Ora Wiskind, and Susan Handelman, eds. *Torah of the Mothers: Contemporary Jewish Women Read Classical Jewish Texts.* Jerusalem: Urim, 2006.

Epstein, Rabbi Mosha. *Tahara Manual of Practices.* 3rd ed. Bridgeport, Conn.: n.p., 2005.

Epstein, Sharon Selib. *Visiting the Sick: The Mitzvah of Bikur Cholim.* Northvale, N.J.: Jason Aronson, 1999.

Etkes, Immanuel. *Rabbi Israel Salanter and the Mussar Movement: Seeking the Torah of Truth.* Philadelphia: Jewish Publication Society, 1993.

Fadiman, Clifton, and Andre Bernard. *Bartlett's Book of Anecdotes.* Boston: Little, Brown, 2000.

Feldman, Daniel Z. *The Right and the Good: Halakhah and Human Relations.* Northvale, N.J.: Jason Aronson Inc. 1999.

Feuer, Rabbi Avrohom Chaim. *The Tzedakah Treasury: An Anthology of Torah Teachings on the Mitzvah of Charity.* Brooklyn: ArtScroll/Mesorah, 2000.

———. *Iggeres Haramban/A Letter for the Ages: The Ramban's Ethical Letter with an Anthology of Contemporary Rabbinic Expositions.* Brooklyn: ArtScroll/Mesorah, 1989.

Finkel, Avraham Yaakov. *Sefer Chasidim.* Northvale, N.J.: Aronson, 1997.

Finkelman, Rabbi Shimon. *The Chazon Ish: The Life and Ideals of Rabbi Avraham Yeshayah Karelitz.* Brooklyn: ArtScroll/Mesorah, 1989.

———. *Rav Pam: The Life and Ideals of Rabbi Avrohom Yaakov HaKohen Pam.* Brooklyn: ArtScroll/Mesorah, 2003.

———. *Reb Moshe: The Life and Ideals of HaGaon Rabbi Moshe Feinstein.* Brooklyn: ArtScroll/Mesorah, 1986.

Foner, Eric, and John Garraty, eds. *The Reader's Companion to American History.* Boston: Houghton Mifflin, 1991.

Fox, Marvin, ed. *Modern Jewish Ethics: Theory and Practice.* Columbus: Ohio State University Press, 1975.

Frank, Anne. *Anne Frank: The Diary of a Young Girl.* New York: Bantam, 1993.

Freedman, Shalom. *Living in the Image of God: Jewish Teachings to Perfect the World: Conversations with Rabbi Irving Greenberg.* Northvale, N.J.: Aronson, 1998.

Freehof, Solomon. *A Treasury of Responsa.* Philadelphia: Jewish Publication Society, 1963.

Friedman, Rabbi Doyle, ed. *Jewish Pastoral Care.* Woodstock, Vt.: Jewish Lights, 2005.

Friedmann, Daniel. *To Kill and Take Possession: Law, Morality, and Society in Biblical Stories.* Peabody, Mass.: Hendrickson, 2002.

Gerondi, Rabbi Jonah. *The Gates of Repentance (Sha'arei Teshuvah).* Translated by Shraga Silverstein. Nanuet, N.Y.: Feldheim, 1967.

Glatt, Rabbi Aaron, M.D. *Visiting the Sick: A Halachic and Medical Guide—with Down-to-Earth Advice.* Brooklyn: ArtScroll/Mesorah, 2006.

Glover, Jonathan. *Humanity: A Moral History of the Twentieth Century.* New Haven, Conn.: Yale University Press, 2000.

Goffman, Erving. *Stigma: Notes on the Management of Spoiled Identity.* New York: Touchstone, 1986.

Goitein, S. D. *Jews and Arabs: Their Contacts Through the Ages.* New York: Schocken, 1964.

———. *A Mediterranean Society.* Calif.: University of California Press, 2000.

Gold, Michael. *God, Love, Sex, and Family.* Northvale, N.J.: Aronson, 1998.

Goldberg, Hillel, ed. *Musar Anthology.* Harwich Lithograph, 1972.

Goldberger, Rabbi Moshe. *Priorities in Tzedaka: Higher Forms of Giving.* Brooklyn: Distributed by Judaica Press, 2007.

Goldin, Judah, ed. *The Jewish Expression.* New Haven, Conn.: Yale University Press, 1976.

Golding, Martin, ed. *Jewish Law and Legal Theory.* New York: New York University Press Reference Collection, 1993.

Goldstein, Dr. Warren, Chief Rabbi of South Africa. *Defending the Human Spirit: Jewish Law's Vision for a Moral Society.* Nanuet, N.Y.: Feldheim, 2006.

Golinkin, David. "*Pidyon Shvuyim:* The Redemption of Captives." In *Insight Israel: Second Series,* Jerusalem: Institute of Applied Halakhah, 2006, 183–192.

———. *Responsa in a Moment.* Jerusalem: Institute of Applied Halakhah at the Schechter Institute of Jewish Studies, 2000.

———. ed. *The Responsa of Professor Louis Ginzberg.* New York and Jerusalem: The Jewish Theological Seminary of America, 1996.

Greenberg, Hayim. *The Inner Eye.* 2 vols. New York: Jewish Frontier Association, 1953, 1964.

Greenberg, Moshe. *Studies in the Bible and Jewish Thought.* Philadelphia: Jewish Publication Society, 1995.

Halberstam, Joshua. *Everyday Ethics: Inspired Solutions to Real-Life Dilemmas.* New York: Penguin, 1994.

Haley, Alex. "The Man on the Train." In *Everyday Greatness,* by Stephen Covey and David Hatch. Nashville: Rutledge Hill Press, 2006.

Harvey, Steven. "Love." In *Contemporary Jewish Religious Thought,* edited by Arthur Cohen and Paul Mendes-Flohr. New York: Free Press, 1988.

Herschkopf, Isaac Steven, M.D. *Hello Darkness, My Old Friend: Embracing Anger to Heal Your Life.* Available at www.XLibris.com, 2003.

Hertz, Rabbi Joseph. *The Pentateuch and Haftorahs.* London: Soncino Press, 1960.

Himelstein, Shmuel. *Words of Wisdom, Words of Wit.* Brooklyn: ArtScroll/Mesorah Publications, 1993.

Holtz, Barry. *Finding Our Way: Jewish Texts and the Lives We Lead Today.* New York: Schocken, 1990.

Hurwitz, Peter Joel, Jacques Picard, Avraham Steinberg, and Benjamin Sklarz. *Jewish Ethics and the Care of End-of-Life Patients.* Hoboken, N.J.: Ktav, 2006.

Israel, Richard. *The Kosher Pig and Other Curiosities of Modern Jewish Life.* Los Angeles: Alef Design Group, 1993.

Jachter, Rabbi Chaim, with Rabbi Ezra Frazer. *Gray Matter: Discourses in the Complex Halachic Issues of Today.* Brooklyn: Yashar Books, 2006.

Jacobs. Rabbi Louis. *Ask the Rabbi.* London: Vallentine Mitchell, 1999.

———. *Jewish Values.* London: Vallentine Mitchell, 1960.

———. *Religion and the Individual: A Jewish Perspective.* Cambridge, England: Cambridge University Press, 1992.

———. *A Tree of Life.* London: The Littman Library of Jewish Civilization, 2000.

———. *What Does Judaism Say About?* New York: Quadrangle, 1973.

Jakobovits, Immanuel. *Jewish Medical Ethics.* New York: Bloch Publishing, 1959.

Jonas, Howard. *I'm Not the Boss, I Just Work Here.* Baltimore: Leviathan Press, 2004.

Judah Ha-Chasid. *Sefer Chasidim.* Jerusalem: Mosad Ha-Rav Kook, 1969.

———. *Sefer Chasidim: The Book of the Pious.* Condensed, translated, and annotated by Avraham Yaakov Finkel. Northvale, N.J.: Aronson, 1997.

Judah Lowe ben Bezalel (Maharal) of Prague. *Sefer Be'er Ha-Golah.* Edited by David Hartman, Jerusalem: Machon Yerushalayim, 2002.

Katz, Dov. *T'nuat Ha-Mussar (The Mussar Movement).* 5 vols. Tel Aviv: n.p., 1945–1952.

Katz, Jacob. *Exclusiveness and Tolerance.* New York: Schocken, 1962.

Kaufmann, Walter. *The Faith of a Heretic.* New York: Anchor Books, 1963.

———. *Religions in Four Dimensions: Existential, Aesthetic, Historical, Comparative.* New York: Reader's Digest Press, 1976.

Keyes, Ralph. *The Quote Verifier: Who Said What, Where, or When.* New York: St. Martin's Press, 2006.

Kilav, Rabbi A. Y. Halevi. "Releasing Terrorists." In *Crossroads: Halacha and the Modern World,* 201–210. Gush Etzion, Israel: Zomet, 1987.

Kirschenbaum, Aaron. *Equity in Jewish Law.* 2 vols: Hoboken, N.J.: Ktav, 1991.

Klagsbrun, Francine. *Voices of Wisdom: Jewish Ideals and Ethics for Everyday Living.* New York: Pantheon, 1980.

Kook, Rabbi Abraham Isaac. *The Vision of Vegetarianism and Peace from a Torah Perspective.* Collected and edited by David Hakohen. Jerusalem: n.p., 1983.

Kramer, Chaim. *Crossing the Narrow Bridge: A Practical Guide to Rebbe Nachman's Teachings.* Edited by Moshe Mykoff. Jerusalem: Breslov Research Institute, 1989.

Krohn, Rabbi Paysach. *Around the Maggid's Table.* Brooklyn: Mesorah, 1989.

Kurzman, Dan. *Ben-Gurion: Prophet of Fire.* New York: Simon & Schuster, 1983.

Kushner, Harold. *The Lord Is My Shepherd.* New York: Alfred A. Knopf, 2004.

———. *When All You've Ever Wanted Isn't Enough.* New York: Pocket Books, 1987.

———. *When Bad Things Happen to Good People.* New York: Schocken, 1981.

Kushner, Lawrence. *Invisible Lines of Connection: Sacred Stories of the Ordinary.* Woodstock, Vt.: Jewish Lights, 1996.

Lamm, Maurice. *The Jewish Way in Death and Mourning.* New York: Jonathan David Publishers, 1969.

Lamm, Norman. *Faith and Doubt.* Hoboken, N.J.: 2007.

———. *Seventy Faces: Articles of Faith.* Vol. 2. Hoboken, N.J.: Ktav, 2002.

Landau, Betzalel. *The Vilna Gaon.* Brooklyn: Mesorah Publications, 1994.

Lee, Harper. *To Kill a Mockingbird.* New York: Grand Central Publishing, 1989.

Leibowitz, Nechama. *Studies in Bereshit (Genesis).* Jerusalem: World Zionist Organization, Department for Torah Education and Culture in the Diaspora, 1981.

———. *Studies in Vayikra (Leviticus).* Jerusalem: World Zionist Organization, Department for Torah Education and Culture in the Diaspora, 1980.

Levi, Yehudah. *Facing Current Challenges: Essays on Judaism.* Brooklyn: Hemed Books, 1998.

Levine, Rabbi Aaron. *How to Perform the Great Mitzvah of Bikur Cholim, Visiting the Sick.* Willowdale, Ont.: Zichron Meir Publications, 1987.

———. *To Comfort the Bereaved: A Guide for Mourners and Those Who Visit Them.* Northvale, N.J.: Jason Aronson, 1996.

Lichtenstein, Aharon. "The Parameters of Tolerance." In *Tolerance, Dissent, and Democracy: Philosophical, Historical, and Halakhic Parameters,* edited by Moshe Sokol. Northvale, N.J.: Aronson, 2002.

Lin Yutang, ed. and trans. *The Wisdom of Confucius.* New York: Modern Library, 1938.

Locke, John. *An Essay Concerning Human Understanding.* New York: Routledge, 2000.

Lookstein, Rabbi Dr. Haskel. "Our Rebbe: A Sermon of Tribute to Rabbi J. B. Soloveitchik." *Memories of a Giant: Eulogies in Memory of Rabbi Joseph B. Soloveitchik,* edited by Michael Bierman, pp. 236–247. Jerusalem: Urim, 2003.

Lowenthal, Marvin. *Henrietta Szold: Life and Letters.* New York: Viking, 1942.

Luzatto, Rabbi Moshe Chayyim. *The Path of the Just (Mesillat Yesharim).* Translation by Shraga Silverstein. Nanuet, N.Y.: Feldheim, 1966.

Magonet, Jonathan. *Returning: Exercises in Repentance.* New York: Bloch, 1997.

Maimonides, Moses. *The Guide of the Perplexed.* Translated with introduction by Shlomo Pines. Chicago: University of Chicago Press, 1963.

Mandelbaum, Yitta Halberstam. *Holy Brother: Inspiring Stories and Enchanted Tales about Rabbi Shlomo Carlebach.* Northvale, N.J.: Jason Aronson, 1997.

Manning, Doug. *Don't Take My Grief Away: What to Do When You Lose a Loved One.* New York: HarperOne, 1984.

May, Steve. *The Story File.* Peabody, N.J.: Hendrickson, 2000.

Morris, Desmond. *The Book of Ages: The Ever-Changing Life Cycles of Man Revealed by the Famous (and Infamous) Throughout History.* New York: Viking, 1983.

Nathan of Breslov. *Tzaddik: A Portrait of Rabbi Nachman.* Translated by Avraham Greenbaum. Jerusalem: Breslov Research Institute, 1987.

Neusner, Jacob. *Tzedakah: Can Jewish Philanthropy Buy Jewish Survival?* New York: UAHC Press, 1997.

Nissenson, Hugh. *In the Reign of Peace.* London: Secker and Warburg, 1972.

Oshry, Rabbi Ephraim. *Responsa from the Holocaust.* New York: Judaica Press, 1983.

Oz, Amos. *A Tale of Love and Darkness.* Translated by Nicholas de Lange. New York: Harvest Books, 2005.

Ozarowski, Rabbi Joseph. "*Bikur Cholim:* A Paradigm for Pastoral Caring." In *Jewish Pastoral Care; A Practical Handbook,* edited by Rabbi Dayle Friedman. 2nd ed. Woodstock, Vt.: Jewish Lights, 2005.

Papo, Rabbi Eliezer. *Pele Yoetz Hashalem* (Hebrew). Jerusalem: n.p., 1986.

Pellegrino, Edmund, and Alan Faden, eds. *Jewish and Catholic Bioethics: An Ecumenical Dialogue.* Washington D.C.: Georgetown University Press, 2001.

Pliskin, Zelig. *Growth Through Torah.* Brooklyn: Benei Yakov Publications, 1988.

———. *Love Your Neighbor: You and Your Fellow Man in Light of the Torah.* Brooklyn:. Aish HaTorah Publications, 1977.

Pollan, Michael. *The Omnivore's Dilemma: A Natural History of Four Meals.* New York: Penguin, 2006.

Prager, Dennis. *Think a Second Time.* New York: Regan Books/HarperCollins, 1995.

Prager, Dennis, and Joseph Telushkin. *The Nine Questions People Ask About Judaism.* New York: Simon & Schuster, 1981.

———. *Why the Jews: The Reason for Antisemitism.* New York: Simon & Schuster, 1983.

Rabinowicz, Rabbi Tzvi. *A Guide to Life: Jewish Laws and Customs of Mourning.* Northvale, N.J.: Jason Aronson, 1989.

Rakeffet-Rothkoff, Aaron. *The Rav: The World of Rabbi Joseph B. Soloveitchik.* 2 vols. Jersey City, N.J.: Ktav, 1999.

Raz, Simcha. *An Angel Among Men: Rav Avraham Yitzchak HaKohen Kook.* Jerusalem: Kol Mevaser, 2003.

———. *A Tzaddik in Our Time: The Life of Rabbi Aryeh Levin.* Translated from the Hebrew, revised and expanded by Charles Wengrov. Jerusalem: Feldheim, 1976.

Reines, Chaim. "The Self and Others in Rabbinic Ethics." In *Contemporary Jewish Ethics,* edited by Menachem Marc Kellner, 162–174. New York: Sanhedrin Press, 1978.

Riemer, Jack, ed. *Jewish Insights on Death and Mourning.* New York: Schocken Books, 1995.

———. "What the Best Dressed Jew Would Wear." Unpublished sermon, sent to the author.

Rigler, Sara Levinsky. *Lights from Jerusalem.* Brooklyn: Mesorah, 2007.

Rosenblum, Yonason, *Rav Dessler, The Life and Impact of Rabbi Eliyahu Eliezer Dessler, the Michtav M'Eliyahu.* Brooklyn: ArtScroll/Mesorah, 2000.

———. *Reb Yaakov: The Life and Times of HaGaon Rabbi Yaakov Kamenetsky.* Based on the research of Rabbi Noson Kamenetsky. Brooklyn: ArtScroll/Mesorah, 1993.

Rosner, Fred, M.D. *Biomedical Ethics and Jewish Law.* Hoboken, N.J.: Ktav, 2001.

———. *Contemporary Biomedical Issues and Jewish Law.* Jersey City, N.J.: Ktav, 2007.

Rothenberg, Naftali, and Eliezer Schweid, eds. *Jewish Identity in Modern Israel.* Jerusalem: Urim, 2002.

Russ, Ian, Sally Webber, and Ellen Ledley. *Shalom Bayit: A Jewish Response to Child Abuse and Domestic Violence.* Panorama City, Calif.: Shalom Bayit Committee, 1993.

Sachar, Howard Morley. *A History of Israel, Vol. II: From the Aftermath of the Yom Kippur War.* New York: Oxford University Press, 1987.

Saks, Jeffrey and Susan Handelman, eds. *Wisdom from All My Teachers: Challenges and Initiatives in Contemporary Torah Education.* Jerusalem: Urim, 2003.

Sacks, Jonathan. *The Dignity of Difference: How to Avoid the Clash of Civilizations.* London: Continuum, 2002.

Salamon, Julie. *Rambam's Ladder: A Meditation on Charity and Why It Is Necessary to Give.* New York: Workman, 2003.

Schachter, Rabbi Fishel, with Chana Nestlebaum. *Loving Kindness: Daily Lessons in the Power of Giving.* Brooklyn: ArtScroll/Mesorah, 2003.

Schachter, Jacob, ed. *Judaism's Encounter with Other Cultures: Rejection or Integration?* Northvale, N.J.: Aronson, 1997.

———. *Reverence, Righteousness, and Rahamanut.* Northvale, N.J.: Aronson, 1992.

Schochet, Elijah. *Animal Life in Jewish Tradition: Attitudes and Relationships.* New York: Ktav, 1984.

———. *The Hasidic Movement and the Gaon of Vilna.* Northvale, N.J.: Aronson, 1994.

Schochet, Elijah, and Solomon Spiro. *Saul Lieberman: The Man and His Works.* New York: Jewish Theological Seminary, 2005.

Schreiber, Aaron. *Jewish Law and Decision-Making.* Philadelphia: Temple University Press, 1979.

Schur, Rabbi Tsvi. *Illness and Crisis: Coping the Jewish Way.* New York: National Council of Synagogue Youth, 1987.

Schwartz, Richard, Ph.D. *Judaism and Global Survival.* New York: Lantern Books, 2002.

———. *Judaism and Vegetarianism.* Marblehead, Mass.: Micah, 1988.

Schwarz, Rabbi Yom Tov. *Eyes to See: Recovering Ethical Torah Principles Lost in the Holocaust.* Jerusalem: Urim, 2004.

Scully, Matthew. *Dominion: The Power of Man, the Suffering of Animals, and the Call to Mercy.* New York: St. Martin's Press, 2002.

Sears, David. *Compassion for Humanity in the Jewish Tradition.* Northvale, N.J.: Aronson, 1998.

———. *The Vision of Eden: Animal Welfare and Vegetarianism in Jewish Law and Mysticism.* Spring Valley, N.Y.: Orot, 2003.

Segev, Tom. *1967: Israel, the War, and the Year that Transformed the Middle East.* New York: Metropolitan Books, 2007.

Shapiro, Marc. *Between the Yeshiva World and Modern Orthodoxy. The Life and Works of Rabbi Jehiel Jacob Weinberg, 1884–1966.* London: Littman Library of Jewish Civilization, 1999.

———. "Scholars and Friends: Rabbi Jehiel Jacob Weinberg and Professor Samuel Atlas." In *The Torah u-Madda Journal,* vol. 7. New York: Yeshiva University, 1997.

Shatz, David. "As Thyself: The Limits of Altruism in Jewish Thought." In *Reverence, Righteousness, and Rahamanut,* edited by Jacob Schachter, 251–275. Northvale, N.J.: Aronson, 1992.

Sherwin, Byron. *In Partnership with God: Contemporary Jewish Law and Ethics.* Syracuse: Syracuse University Press, 1990.

———. *Jewish Ethics for the Twenty-First Century.* Syracuse: Syracuse University Press, 1999.

Sherwin, Byron, and Seymour Cohen. *How to Be a Jew: Ethical Teachings of Judaism.* Northvale, N.J.: Jason Aronson, 1992.

Shofnos, Chana, and Bat Tova Zwebner. *The Healing Visit: Insights into the Mitzvah of Bikur Cholim.* Southfield, Mich.: Targum Press, 1989.

Siegel, Danny. *Gym Shoes and Irises: Personalized Tzedakah.* Spring Valley, N.Y.: Town House Press, 1982.

———. *Tzedakah: Jewish Giving, a Privilege.* New York: United Synagogue of Conservative Judaism, n.d.

Silverman, William, and Kenneth Cinnamon. *When Mourning Comes: A Book of Comfort for the Grieving.* Northvale, N.J.: Jason Aronson, 1994.

Simon, Ernst. "The Neighbor Whom We Shall Love," in *Modern Jewish Ethics: Theory and Practice,* edited by Marvin Fox. Columbus: Ohio State University Press, 1975.

Singer, Isaac Bashevis. *In My Father's Court.* New York: Farrar, Straus and Giroux, 1991.

Singer, Peter. *Animal Liberation.* New York: Avon, 1990.

———. *Practical Ethics,* 2nd edition. Cambridge, England: Cambridge University Press, 1993.

Singer, Peter, and Jim Mason. *The Ethics of What We Eat: Why Our Food Choices Matter.* Emmaus, Pa.: Rodale Press, 2006.

Slifkin, Rabbi Natan. *Man and Beast: Our Relationships with Animals in Jewish Law and Thought.* Brooklyn: Zoo Torah, distributed by Yashar Books, 2006.

Sokol, Moshe, ed. *Tolerance, Dissent, and Democracy: Philosophical, Historical, and Halakhic Parameters.* Northvale, N.J.: Jason Aronson, 2002.

Soloveitchik, Rabbi Dr. Joseph B. *Halakhic Man.* Translated by Dr. Lawrence Kaplan. Philadelphia: Jewish Publication Society, 1984.

Spero, Shubert. *Morality, Halakha and the Jewish Tradition.* New York: Ktav, 1983.

Steinberg, Avraham, M.D. *Encyclopedia of Jewish Medical Ethics.* 3 vols. Nanuet, N.Y.: Feldheim, 2003.

Stern, Marc. ed. *Formulating Responses in an Egalitarian Age.* New York: Rowman and Littlefield, 2005.

Tamari, Meir. *Al Chet: Sins in the Marketplace.* Northvale, N.J.: Jason Aronson, 1996.

———. *The Challenge of Wealth: A Jewish Perspective on Earning and Spending.* Northvale, N.J.: Jason Aronson, 1995.

———. *With All Your Possessions: Jewish Ethics and Economic Life.* New York: Free Press, 1987.

Tannen, Deborah. *The Argument Culture: Stopping America's War of Words.* New York: Ballantine, 1998.

Taub, Rabbi Shimon. *The Laws of Tzedakah and Maaser: A Comprehensive Guide.* Brooklyn: ArtScroll/Mesorah, 2001.

Tavris, Carol, and Elliot Aronson. *Mistakes Were Made (but Not by Me): Why We Justify Foolish Beliefs, Bad Decisions, and Hurtful Acts.* Orlando, Fla.: Harcourt, 2007.

Teller, Hanoch. *And from Jerusalem, His Word: Stories and Insights of Rabbi Shlomo Zalman Auerbach.* New York: New York City Publishing, 1995.

———. *Sunset.* New York: New York City Publishing, 1987.

Telushkin, Joseph. *Biblical Literacy: The Most Important People, Events, and Ideas of the Hebrew Bible.* New York: William Morrow, 1996.

———. *The Book of Jewish Values: A Day-by-Day Guide to Ethical Living.* New York: Bell Tower, 2000.

———. *A Code of Jewish Ethics, Volume 1: You Shall Be Holy.* New York: Bell Tower, 2006.

———. *Jewish Literacy: The Most Important Things to Know About the Jewish Religion, Its People, and Its History.* New York: William Morrow, 1991, 2001, 2008.

Tendler, Rabbi Dr. Moshe, "Pain, Halakha, and Hashkofah." In *Jewish Perspectives on the Experience of Suffering,* edited by Shalom Carmy. Northvale, N.J.: Jason Aronson, 1999.

———. *Responsa of Rav Moshe Feinstein: Care of the Critically Ill.* Translated and annotated. Hoboken, N.J.: Ktav, 1996.

Twerski, Rabbi Abraham J., M.D. *Angels Don't Leave Footprints: Discovering What's Right with Yourself.* Brooklyn: Shaar Press, 2001.

———. *Dear Rabbi, Dear Doctor.* Brooklyn: Shaar Press, 2005.

———. *Do Unto Others: How Good Deeds Can Change Your Life.* Kansas City: Andrews McMeel, 1997.

———. *Lights Along the Way.* Brooklyn: Mesorah Publications, 1995.

———. *Generation to Generation.* Brooklyn: Traditional Press, 1986.

———. *Simcha: It's Not Just Happiness.* Brooklyn: Shaar Press, 2006.

———. *Living Each Day.* Brooklyn: ArtScroll/Mesorah Publications, 1988.

Twerski, Rabbi Abraham J., M.D. and Ursula Schwartz, Ph.D. *Positive Parenting: Developing Your Child's Potential.* Brooklyn: ArtScroll/Mesorah, 1996.

Urban, G. R., ed. *Stalinism: Its Impact on Russia and the World.* Cambridge, Mass.: Harvard University Press, 1986

Vorspan, Albert, and David Saperstein: *Tough Choices: Jewish Perspectives on Societal Justice.* New York: UAHC Press, 1992.

Wattles, Jeffrey. *The Golden Rule.* New York: Oxford University Press, 1996.

Wein, Berel. *Living Jewish: Values, Practices, and Traditions* Brooklyn: Shaar Press, 2002.

———. *Second Thoughts: A Collection of Musings and Observations.* Brooklyn: Mesorah, 1997.

———. *Tending the Vineyard.* Brooklyn: Shaar Press, 2007.

Weiner, Herbert. *9½ Mystics: The Kabbala Today.* New York: Holt, Rinehart and Winston, 1969.

Weiss, Rabbi Abner, Ph.D. *Death and Bereavement: A Halakhic Guide.* Brooklyn: Mesorah/Orthodox Union, 1991.

Weiss, James David. *Vintage Wein.* Brooklyn: Shaar Press, 1992.

Weiss, Rabbi Saul. *Insights: A Talmudic Treasury.* 2 vols. Jerusalem: Feldheim, 1990, 1996.

Wishman, Seymour. *Confessions of a Criminal Lawyer.* New York: Viking Penguin, 1982.

Wolfson, Dr. Ron. *A Time to Mourn, a Time to Comfort.* Woodstock, Vt.: Jewish Lights Publishing, 1996.

Wolpin, Rabbi Nisson, ed. *The Ethical Imperative: Torah Perspectives on Ethics and Values.* Brooklyn: ArtScroll, 2000.

Yalkut Shimoni (Hebrew). New York: Title Publishing Company, 1944.

Zaitchik, Chaim Ephraim. *Sparks of Mussar.* Nanuet, N.Y.: Feldheim, 1985.

Zemer, Rabbi Dr. Moshe. *Evolving Halakhah: A Progressive Approach to Traditional Jewish Law.* Woodstock, Vt.: Jewish Lights, 2003.

Zunin, Leonard, M.D., and Hilary Stanton Zunin. *The Art of Condolence: What to Write, What to Say, What to Do at a Time of Loss.* New York: Harper, 1992.

INDEX

About the Author

Rabbi Joseph Telushkin, spiritual leader and scholar, is the author of the acclaimed *A Code of Jewish Ethics, Volume 1; The Book of Jewish Values;* and also *Jewish Literacy,* the most widely read book on Judaism of the past two decades. Another of his books, *Words That Hurt, Words That Heal,* was the motivating force behind the 1996 Senate Resolution 151, sponsored by Senators Joseph Lieberman and Connie Mack, to establish a "National Speak No Evil Day" throughout the United States. Rabbi Telushkin is a senior associate of CLAL, the National Jewish Center for Learning and Leadership; the rabbi of the Los Angeles–based Synagogue for the Performing Arts; and a board member of the Jewish Book Council. He lives with his family in New York City and lectures regularly throughout the United States.

Visit www.acodeofjewishethics.com to download study guides of key ethical issues raised in *A Code of Jewish Ethics.*

A Note on the Type

The text of this book was set in Meno, an old-style font designed by Richard Lipton for Font Bureau in 1994. A native New Yorker who began his career as a calligrapher, sign painter, and graphic designer, Lipton worked for Bitstream in the 1980s where he designed Arrus, and, with Jacqueline Sakwa, Cataneo.

Meno is distinguished by its Roman characters based on French baroque forms from the late sixteenth century and italics based on Dirk Voskens's work in seventeenth-century Amsterdam. The Meno family is comprised of fifteen fonts, including three weights of roman and italic, along with titling, small caps, and swash styles.